Advanced dBASE III PLUS™ Programming and Techniques

Miriam Liskin

Osborne **McGraw-Hill**
Berkeley, California

Osborne **McGraw-Hill**
2600 Tenth Street
Berkeley, California 94710
U.S.A.

For information on translations and book distributors outside of the U.S.A., write to Osborne **McGraw-Hill** at the above address.

A complete list of trademarks appears on page 873.

ASHTON-TATE
20101 Hamilton Avenue
Torrance, California 90502
(213) 329-8000

Advanced dBASE III PLUS™ Programming and Techniques

15 16 17 DOC/DOC 9 9 8 7 6 5 4 3 2

ISBN 0-07-881249-6

CONTENTS

ACKNOWLEDGMENTS

I would like to thank some of the people who contributed directly or indirectly to the publication of this book by providing exactly the kind of help I needed at some of the crucial turning points in my life:

My parents, Philip Liskin and Florence Mindell, my first and best teachers, who led me to believe very early in life that I could be and do anything I set my mind to.

The "Kirsch Lab Encounter Group," for all the good times. And thanks, Becky, for suggesting that there might be a computer career in my future.

Cliff Krouse, who helped me get my foot in the door by giving me my first job in the microcomputer industry, "taught me everything he knew," and introduced me to the joys of data base management.

Stan Politi, editor and publisher of *Computer Currents,* who launched my writing career. And thanks to the entire staff, past and present, of the best little computer newspaper around—Lynne Verbeek, Anne Skjelbred, Metece Riccio, Pam Ivie, Eve Levine, Lynne Candelario, Bill Bevis, Kris Warrenburg, Nancy Humphrey, Carol Warner, and Ken Margolis—for a congenial place to work, outstanding gourmet lunches, remembering my birthday, and for inspiring, appreciating, and debugging all those dBASE programs.

Linda Allen, literary agent, who had faith and worked hard for me back in the days when there was no objective evidence that anything would ever come of it.

Denise Penrose, technical editor for the dBASE III edition of this book, who taught me a great deal about writing a book and kept me on track with marginal notes like "How did I get this far and suddenly feel so lost?"

Cindy Hudson, editor-in-chief of Osborne/McGraw-Hill, who supported this project from the start.

My coworkers, students, and clients of the past five years, who consistently challenged me to come up with better programming solutions and clearer explanations. I hope there are at least a few new tricks in here for each of you.

INTRODUCTION

This book is a comprehensive guide to the design and implementation of a dBASE III PLUS data base application. dBASE III PLUS may be used in two distinctly different ways: by typing commands at the dot prompt (or, to a more limited extent, through the built-in ASSIST menus) or by writing programs in the dBASE III PLUS language. This book will help you make the most of both modes of operation. It addresses the needs of four categories of dBASE III PLUS users:

- People who want to learn to utilize more of the power and sophistication of the built-in dBASE III PLUS commands and functions from the dot prompt.
- People who are comfortable working at the dot prompt and want to learn the dBASE III PLUS language as a first programming language.
- People who have written programs in other higher-level languages (or one of the versions of dBASE) but have little or no experience with system design.
- People who have designed systems and written programs in other languages and who want to learn how best to utilize the dBASE III PLUS built-in commands and functions and the strong points of its programming language.

No previous programming experience, either with dBASE III PLUS or any other language, is necessary. This book does assume a basic familiarity with using dBASE III PLUS at command level (at the dot prompt) to work with simple filing systems involving one data base, although many of the more difficult concepts and advanced commands will be reviewed. To use this book effectively, you should already understand

- How to create a data base file with character, numeric, logical, date, and memo fields.
- How to modify the structure of an existing data base.
- How to add, view, edit, and delete individual records and groups of records.
- How to use the full-screen cursor movement and editing commands.
- How to navigate through the pull-down menus used by the ASSIST system and the report, label, query, view, and screen editors.
- How to build an index for a data base.
- How to use indexes to control the order in which records are displayed or printed and how to retrieve individual records rapidly.
- How to design and print columnar reports with subtotals.
- How to design and print labels.
- How to specify selection criteria for records to be displayed on the screen or printed on reports or labels.

Unlike many textbooks on programming, this book is not organized on the basis of specific commands, programming structures, or algorithms. The dBASE III PLUS language is used primarily as a development tool for creating vertical applications where comparable packaged software is either nonexistent or very expensive, inflexible, or both. Most people buy dBASE III PLUS because they need software that is custom designed to the requirements of their type of business, profession, or nonprofit organization or to the requirements of their particular organization. This book is therefore structured to follow the process of designing, implementing, testing, refining, and maintaining a typical business application.

Many small data base applications are handled adequately by using the built-in dBASE III PLUS commands and functions at the dot prompt. For more complex needs or less knowledgeable operators you can use the dBASE III PLUS programming language to create a specialized turnkey system. Because the programming language can take advantage of all the same file management capabilities as those accessible from the dot prompt, the development process generally takes far less time than that required if the same programs were written in another higher-level language like Pascal or COBOL. No matter what language you use, however, learning to analyze a manual system, work out specifications for the computer-based replacement, design a security system, and implement a scheme for allowing multiple users to update the same files in a local area network environment is much more difficult than simply learning the syntax of a new programming language. This is true not only for novices, but also for more experienced programmers who have never had sole responsibility for the design of a complete data base application.

In many ways, learning to use dBASE III PLUS to its fullest capacity parallels the development of an application: from working at command level you will graduate to writing simple batch-type programs made up of exactly the same commands, and then you will gradually progress to writing longer and more complex programs. For readers who have no experience with other higher-level languages, this approach eases the transition to learning dBASE III PLUS programming. If you have programmed in other languages, you will recognize the basic programming structures and concepts in the dBASE III PLUS language. This book presents the best ways to make use of the unique features offered by dBASE III PLUS: the built-in file management capabilities that free you from the burden of trying to write a faster sort or index search routine or the tedium of writing procedures to dissect a data base record into its component fields. Instead, you can concentrate on fulfilling the functional requirements of your application.

This book uses as a case study a sample accounts receivable system for an imaginary company called National Widgets. You may want to build this system on your own computer as you read; or if you are currently working on a dBASE III PLUS system, you may prefer to parallel the development process with your own application. You will find that you are the most relaxed and receptive to new ideas if you have a specific project to which you can relate the concepts in this book but are not under deadline to complete the project.

The best way to learn any programming language is by experimentation. You will get the most out of this book if you take an active, exploratory approach to the learning process. Whenever you find yourself wondering, "Why did she do it this way instead of that?" or "What would happen if I tried something slightly different?" go ahead and try it. There is almost always more than one correct way to accomplish any goal. If, in certain contexts, one method has strong advantages, they will be pointed out; but you should feel free to vary the techniques presented or substitute others that seem more appropriate to your situation.

This book is not intended to be a substitute for the dBASE III PLUS manuals. While it covers a broad range of programming commands and techniques, not every dBASE III PLUS command or function is discussed in detail, and some do not appear in any of the sample programs. In some cases, this reflects the varying utility and general applicability of the commands themselves, while in others, more subjective factors—the author's personal preferences and style—are responsible. Any dBASE III PLUS user can benefit greatly by periodically skimming through the reference sections of the Ashton-Tate documentation. You may find that commands or options that did not stick in your mind the first time you read the manual because you had no immediate use for them will later suggest easy solutions to new programming problems or better ways to accomplish certain objectives.

The programs in this book attain a level of sophistication applicable to real-world data base problems. As the development of the National Widgets system progresses, it may seem that the programs are being tailored increasingly to the requirements of this imaginary business. Try not to lose sight of the basic principles illustrated by the specific exercises—in particular, the way the data base files are related to one another, the programming strategies, and the way the programs interact with the user. For example, Chapter 18 presents a program to print the National Widgets Customer Reference List, complete with financial transactions. The same program structure could also be used to print a donor list with gift transactions for a nonprofit organization, a patient list with a history of all office visits for a doctor's office, or an inventory report listing all stocked items with shipping and receiving transactions. The National Widgets programs and procedures are presented as models that may be adapted, expanded, and combined in different ways to suit the unique requirements of your own data base systems.

The programs and sample data bases in this book are available on disk for $10 by writing to

Miriam Liskin
P.O. Box 2219
Berkeley, CA 94702

Please specify which version of dBASE III you are using.

I

PLANNING THE SYSTEM

Part I covers the design and prototyping phase of application development. After introducing the imaginary company National Widgets, Inc., which is used as a detailed case study throughout the book, Part I presents a systematic method (and applies it to this company) for analyzing data entry, storage, and reporting requirements and setting up the necessary data base structures and indexes. A general strategy will be outlined and specific methods described for entering realistic test data and working out as many procedures as possible at command level.

If you have no prior experience with system design, you should study carefully the way that the users' description of their needs is translated into the file structures and command level procedures. Readers who understand the principles of systems analysis but who have not used dBASE III PLUS extensively should focus on the way the files are structured and related to one another and on the process of modeling the application at command level.

If your applications are simple, Part I will help you use dBASE III PLUS at the dot prompt to its fullest capacity and push the built-in report and label generators to their limits. But this command level testing phase is an excellent way to begin the development of any dBASE III system, even when you are sure at the outset that additional programming will be required. Working at the dot prompt is a fast and efficient way to clarify the relationships among the data files; ensure that the file structures are correct and complete; and define the weekly, monthly, and annual processing cycles.

1

DEFINING YOUR NEEDS

The first step in setting up a dBASE III PLUS application is to define what the system must accomplish. If the computer will replace an existing "paper" system, a detailed description of the manual procedures, accompanied by a set of samples of the various paper forms and reports, is the logical starting point for outlining the functions of the new software. The users will almost always want to add new capabilities not included in the current manual system, and this "wish list" will also become an important part of the system specifications. In other cases, no manual system exists, and the dBASE III PLUS application must assume responsibility for a new set of information management tasks. This situation may arise when a business branches out in a new direction, an organization decides to begin in-house processing of information formerly maintained by an outside service bureau, or the managers hope to use the computer to produce analytical reports that were too difficult or time-consuming to produce by hand.

To define your needs, specify in as much detail as possible:

- *The input to the system*—the information that will be entered into the computer.
- *The system's processing functions*—the calculations the computer must carry out and the ways information will be transferred among the data base files.
- *The output of the system*—the ways in which the data will be displayed on the screen and printed on paper.

This chapter outlines a systematic method for gathering the information you need to design a dBASE III PLUS data base system. If you have designed and implemented applications in another higher-level language, many of the concepts presented here will be familiar to you. If you have worked with dBASE III PLUS at command level (typing dBASE III PLUS commands at the dot prompt) or through the ASSIST menu system, you already have some understanding of how the built-in commands can be used to accomplish the three fundamental processes just summarized. If you have never written a program before, or if you have no formal training in systems analysis, you should study carefully the methods described in this chapter, but don't feel that you are starting off at a disadvantage. You will find that common sense and the ability to think logically are greater assets during the planning stages than prior programming experience.

This chapter introduces the imaginary company that will be used as a case study throughout this book. Readers who are new to programming and system design may want to follow this example closely as a tutorial. If you are already involved in designing a dBASE III PLUS application for your organization, you might instead choose to apply the general principles observed in the case study to your own application.

STUDY THE EXISTING MANUAL SYSTEM

Before you can begin building a dBASE III PLUS application, you must make a thorough study of the manual system that the programs will augment or replace. If no manual system exists, you will have no choice but to proceed directly to a description of the proposed new software. You should recognize, however, that without the concrete examples provided by a paper system, you will need to spend more time and energy to formulate the overall goals for the system and then to define the particulars.

In the course of your investigation, you must interview everyone in the organization who is or will be involved in the normal cycle of processing. Each person will have a set of personal aims and priorities, as well as a unique perspective on the flow of information within the organization, and each one can provide valuable insight into how the new system might improve on existing procedures.

If you, the prospective programmer, are affiliated with the company, you will have the advantage of familiarity, but you must also learn to take a step back and adopt the vantage point of an outsider. Depending on your position in the organizational hierarchy, you may be accustomed to dealing only with the big picture and long-range plan, or you may be more intimately familiar with the day-to-day procedures. Although you will have to ask fewer questions than an outside consultant, it may seem awkward to be interrogating your co-workers. An in-house programmer may also have more difficulty spotting those instances in which the transition to a computerized system would be made easier by altering the work flow or redefining job responsibilities.

An independent consultant naturally brings a more objective perspective to the project and is less likely to regard existing procedures as sacrosanct, but an outsider must spend more time becoming familiar with the organization, its structure and personnel, and the specialized vocabulary of the business or profession. You may also have to work to gain the confidence of the staff. Any feelings of anxiety or hostility surrounding the acquisition of the computer will to a certain degree extend to you, the programmer. In this atmosphere, it can be difficult to foster the spirit of active cooperation and participation that will help you to elicit the information you need.

Describe the Work Flow And Schedule

During the first phase of the system development, you must describe in detail the present and projected work flow and processing schedule. This analysis need not—in fact, should not—be couched in technical jargon. Whether or not you are an experienced programmer, at this stage you should think solely in terms of how information is entered, updated, transformed, and printed in the course of a normal processing cycle. You will also find that conducting your preliminary discussions in ordinary conversational English helps you to communicate better with the users and clarify your own understanding of the existing procedures.

For each operation or task in the manual system, your conversations with the staff must provide the answers to these crucial questions:

- What specific items of information are involved?
- How big is each item?
- How many of each item are there?

- What mathematical calculations are carried out?
- What transfers of information are involved?
- How often is the operation performed?
- How long does it take to carry out each task?

These general queries may take the form of specific questions such as

- What information do you keep on your customers besides name and address?
- What is the highest price you charge for any item?
- How many customers do you have now?
- How many orders per month do you anticipate two years from now?
- How is the sales tax calculated?
- How are the order totals posted to the customer ledger cards?
- How often do you type invoices?
- How much time does it take to type a set of mailing labels?

The Work Flow at National Widgets This book will use as a case study a dBASE III PLUS system that keeps track of customer information and accounts receivable data for an imaginary company called National Widgets, Inc. This firm, located in Berkeley, California, is a mail-order supplier of accessory products for microcomputers. National Widgets has been in business for three years and had about $600,000 in gross sales last year. The company is managed by the owner and employs four other people full-time: a bookkeeper, two clerk-typists who also answer the telephones, and one person who handles shipping and receiving.

National Widgets has a microcomputer that is currently used for word processing, spreadsheet analysis, and managing prospect mailing lists with dBASE III PLUS. In the past year the number of customers and the volume of orders have grown to the point that the manual accounts receivable and order processing system is becoming unwieldy, and the owner now hopes to begin using the computer for accounting and inventory management as well. Because the owner could not find an inexpensive, off-the-shelf accounting package that could produce the desired inventory reports and integrate mailing list management functions with the accounts receivable system, the company hired a consultant to customize a system with dBASE III PLUS. Accounts receivable was chosen as the first application to be implemented for two reasons. First, the staff is already comfortable using dBASE III PLUS to work with name-and-address lists, so the customer data base will seem relatively familiar and unintimidating. Second, the owner and bookkeeper have both placed a high priority on improving the company's cash flow by exercising a tighter control over the accounts receivable.

The consultant spent a full day with the employees of National Widgets, interviewing them, watching them at work, and collecting a set of samples from the manual system. These observations yielded the following description of the present operation of the manual accounts receivable system.

National Widgets has about 350 regular customers who account for about one-third of its monthly volume of 500 orders. At the current rate of growth, both the number of customers and the number of orders are expected to double in the next two years. The bookkeeper maintains the customer records on 8 1/2-by-11-inch *ledger cards,* which are stored in alphabetical order in a vertical file. Because many first-time customers never place another order, a ledger card is prepared for a new customer only if the company representative who calls mentions that the company has ordered from National Widgets in the past or asks for a credit application.

Almost all of the orders from regular customers are placed by telephone and are transcribed onto *standard order forms* by the clerk who answers the phone. A typical order contains from three to eight different items, totaling about $100. Of the orders from first-time or occasional customers, more than half come in by phone and are shipped C.O.D. The remainder are sent in with a check attached to an order form clipped from one of National Widgets' ads in local newspapers and magazines. Some of these people never order again, while others eventually become regular customers. In the current manual system, there is no easy way for the clerk to determine whether someone has previously placed an order, unless the customer specifically mentions it, asks for credit terms, or is already familiar to the clerk.

Every afternoon, the day's orders are typed on *three-part invoices* by the bookkeeper, who looks up the prices in the current price list and calculates any applicable volume discounts. For prepaid orders the invoice is marked PAID, and the customer's check is paperclipped to the office copy of the invoice. Currently, there is no formal procedure for processing back-orders. If an item is temporarily out of stock, the entire order is held for a period of time, usually no more than a week. If the item still has not come in, the original invoice is amended by hand and the remainder of the order is shipped to the customer, who is contacted by telephone to see whether or not a new order should be written for the missing item. The bookkeeper calculates the shipping charges and, for customers in California, the sales tax (at the 6 1/2 percent rate for Bay Area counties). Payment terms are net 30 days for all regular customers. The bookkeeper sends one copy of the invoice back to the warehouse, where the clerk uses it to pull the items ordered and then sends it along with the shipment as a packing slip.

The bookkeeper updates the *customer ledger cards* at least once a week to reflect the latest batch of invoices and payments. Ledger cards are made up for new customers, and any changes in address, staff contact, or telephone number for regular customers are noted. In the last six months, the bookkeeper has noticed a number of ledger cards for customers who have had no activity for over a year, but no formal guidelines govern when an inactive customer should be removed from the file.

After the ledger cards are updated, the invoice totals are transcribed onto a worksheet (formerly on paper, but currently maintained using a spreadsheet program) in the form of a *monthly invoice register*, with columns for invoice number, date, subtotal, discount, sales tax, shipping charges, and net invoice amount. The checks are separated from the invoices and the amounts entered onto *bank deposit slips*. Finally, a clerk mails the second copy of the invoice to the customer and files the third copy in a filing cabinet in numerical sequence.

At the end of the month, the bookkeeper goes through the ledger cards and types *monthly statements* for all customers who have one or more past-due invoices (usually about 75 to 100 customers). The monthly statement includes all outstanding invoices and any payments that have been applied to these invoices, as well as all activity for the current month.

National Widgets sends two *mailings* per year to all of its regular customers: a new price list in the spring and, in the fall, an announcement of Christmas specials and year-end sale items. For these mailings a clerk types the customers' addresses on pressure-sensitive mailing labels. These are transferred to folded and stapled flyers, which are sorted by hand into ZIP code order. Early in December, Christmas cards are sent to all regular customers. For this mailing, which is not sorted by ZIP, the addresses are read from the ledger cards and typed directly onto envelopes.

At various times during the year, selective mailings (typically consisting of new product announcements or special sale notices) are sent to specific groups of customers based on the type of computer equipment they own or the products they order frequently. Since the customer ledger cards do not contain any record of what types of products a customer orders, the clerk who types the labels for these mailings is guided by his or her personal recollections of each customer. If no one remembers a particular customer, the clerk must pull some invoices from the file to decide whether or not the company should be included in a mailing.

Every three months the bookkeeper prepares the *quarterly sales tax report* from the monthly invoice registers, and at the end of the year, she compiles an *accounting summary* to be used by the accountant to prepare the annual financial statements. Total sales, discounts, tax, and payments are taken from the invoice registers, total receivables are added up from the customer ledger cards, and cost of goods is calculated from the inventory control records.

Study Samples From The Manual System

As you question each staff member about his or her job, collect a set of the documents that make up the manual system. A study of these paper forms will enable you to extract a detailed list of all the items of information that must go into the data bases if the dBASE III PLUS system is to duplicate the existing procedures. The samples you collect should contain matching data—for example, an invoice, a statement for the same customer, and a copy of the ledger card as it looked at the time the statement was typed—so that you can trace the flow of information through the system.

The Samples From National Widgets The set of samples from the National Widgets manual system is relatively small: a customer ledger card (illustrated in Figure 1-1), an order form, a price list, an invoice (Figure 1-2), a statement, mailing labels, a monthly invoice register (Figure 1-3), a bank deposit slip, a quarterly sales tax report, and an annual accounting summary. The elements of the manual system and their functions are summarized in Figure 1-4.

Lewis and Associates
408 Grand Avenue
Oakland, CA 94610

839-5014
Accts. Payable: Joan Mills

Date		Invoices	Payments	Balance
12/2 85	Invoice #2158	102 15		102 15
1/10 86	Check #321		102 15	-0-
4/11	Invoice 4012	74 62		74 62
5/2	Invoice 4468	65 20		139 82
5/9	Check #408		74 62	65 20
6/9	Check #441		65 20	-0-
9/19	Invoice 6736	124 84		124 84
11/3	Check #563		124 84	-0-
2/10 87	Invoice 7958	138 50		138 50

Figure 1-1. A customer ledger card

INVOICE

NATIONAL WIDGETS, INC.
843 PARKER ST.
BERKELEY, CA 94710
(415) 549-1847

INVOICE NO: 7958

DATE: 2/11/87

SOLD TO: Lewis and Associates
408 Grand Avenue
Oakland, CA 94610

TERMS: NET 30

ITEM	QTY	DESCRIPTION	PRICE	SUBTOTAL	DISCOUNT	AMOUNT
DISK 101-42	2	FLOPPY DISKS, 10 EA	34.00	68.00	3.12	68.00
RIBBON 270-10	6	NEC CLOTH RIBBON	5.20	31.20		28.08
PRTWHL 321-11	1	NEC PRINT WHEEL	12.50	12.50		12.50
PRTWHL 321-11	1	NEC PRINT WHEEL	15.00	15.00		15.00
		SUBTOTAL				123.58
		SHIPPING				6.90
		TAX				8.02
		TOTAL				138.50

Figure 1-2. An invoice

National Widgets, Inc.

Invoice Register - December 1987

Invoice #	Date	Customer	Subtotal	Discount	Tax	Shipping	Net Am't.
2156	12/2	ABC Plumbing	76.32		4.58	4.00	84.90
2157	12/2	John Anderson	239.01	10.40	14.86	8.20	251.67
2158	12/2	Lewis & Assoc.	103.44	10.34	6.05	3.00	102.15
2159	12/2	Carol Klein, M.D.	56.80		3.69	2.40	62.89
2160	12/3	MTK Industries	152.10		9.89	7.00	168.99

Figure 1-3. A monthly invoice register

Customer ledger cards	Record of customer name, address, phone number, contact name, invoices, payments, and running balance
Order forms	Customer name and address and items ordered
Invoices	Three-part form: packing slip, customer billing copy, and office file copy
Monthly invoice register	Spreadsheet listing all invoices with monthly totals for orders, discounts, sales tax, and shipping charges
Bank deposit slips	Checks and cash payments received from customers
Monthly statements	Billing summary listing all outstanding invoices and all current month transactions, printed for customers who have a balance due
Mailings to customers	Mailing labels or envelopes printed for all customers or selectively based on equipment owned or products ordered
Quarterly sales tax report	Summary of California sales tax due
Annual accounting summary	Summary of total sales, discounts, sales tax, cash receipts, accounts receivable, and cost of goods, used by accountant for preparing financial statements

Figure 1-4. The elements of the manual system

DESCRIBE NEW OPERATIONS AND REPORTS

Once you have a clear picture of the existing systems and procedures, the next step is to obtain a list of all of the desired new functions for the system in order of priority, including information not currently being tracked, additional calculations, and, most important, new reports and printed forms. In practice, it is often difficult to separate this step from the study of the existing system. Especially if the staff members express a high level of optimism and enthusiasm for the computer, their descriptions of their current job responsibilities will often be interspersed with items from their own personal "wish lists" for the new data base system. In the early planning stages, encouraging the users to mention anything that comes to mind will broaden your perspective, although low-priority operations that are difficult to program or slow to execute may be dropped from consideration later.

As you scrutinize the manual system to determine the details of how the company does its work, keep in mind the reasons for computerizing these functions in the first place—the anticipated improvements in efficiency and the addition of useful functions that are not currently being done by hand. It is a common expectation that a computer can do any job faster and with less expenditure of time, but this is not always the case. It usually takes about the same amount of time to enter data into the computer as it does to write or type it on a paper form. If you must then print the information, using the computer may actually take longer than using paper forms. You can expect to realize the greatest gains by computerizing

- When you can enter information once and then print it out in several different formats or sorted orders.
- When the computer takes over calculations that are tedious to perform by hand.
- When using the computer enables anyone in the office to perform tasks that otherwise would require special expertise.
- When the computer's reporting capabilities provide more timely access to management information.
- When the computer's ability to easily cross-reference information enables you to produce reports that would be far too time-consuming to consider doing manually.

Although most people emphasize new information that they want the system to track, the reports to be printed will actually prove most useful in pinning down the structures of the data base files. Of course, all the items of information that appear on a report must be present in the data base. In addition, the data base must also include any fields needed to specify the sort order or selection criteria for any report. Studying the report samples will also highlight items of information that have been requested but that do not appear on any reports; these should be carefully reconsidered to evaluate whether they belong in the data base at all.

For each new report, you must solicit answers to the same crucial questions that you answered for existing reports:

- How often will the report be printed?
- Who will use the report?
- What specific items of information should be included?
- For a columnar report, in what order should the columns be printed?
- For a full-page report, where on the page should each item be placed?
- In what order should the data records be printed?
- What calculations must be done within each record?
- What subtotals, totals, and statistics are required?
- What criteria will determine the records to appear on the report?

Sometimes the easiest way to obtain this information without phrasing your questions in technical terms is to ask for a rough sketch of a typical page of each new report, including some representative data.

The New National Widgets System

The new National Widgets data base system must assume the functions of the present system and reproduce all of the existing reports. The system will initially be installed on the company's single-user microcomputer, but the owner hopes to purchase two additional computers before the end of the year, as well as the hardware and software needed to connect the three micros in a local area network. At this time, the data base system will be expanded to include multi-user capabilities.

The conversion to computerized operation offers one immediate advantage: it will eliminate duplicate entries. In the manual system, for example, after invoices are typed the same information must be entered on the customer ledger cards and copied to the monthly invoice register, a process that is time-consuming, tedious, and prone to error.

Since the owner and the bookkeeper wish to exert tighter control over the company's accounts receivable, the new system must print an *aging report* in alphabetical order by customer name. For each customer the report should list all open invoices, with the unpaid balance broken down into the standard aging categories: current, 0-30 days, 30-60 days, 60-90 days, and 90+ days. This aging information, which was considered too time-consuming to calculate by hand, should also be printed on the computer-generated *monthly statements.*

The owner also hopes that the new system will help to provide more timely accounting information, as well as a way to monitor the company's product line, stocking policies, and pricing structure. In addition to the invoice register, a *cash receipts listing* of bank deposits must be printed, for either a daily total or a monthly summary. A *monthly posting summary* must be printed, listing all invoices, discounts, shipping charges, sales tax, and payments. To help identify the company's most profitable product lines and better plan production and stocking quantities, order data must be retained for up to a year, and the system must produce an *order summary report* that summarizes all items ordered by inventory category, for either the current month or any period within the current fiscal year.

The mailing functions must be expanded to include the production of personalized letters instead of, or in addition to, mailing labels. The company would also like the system to help identify the equipment a customer owns and the types of products he or she buys repeatedly. Maintaining this information would make the production of selective mailings faster and less dependent on the personal recollections of the typists. It would also allow the company to compile a *customer profile* that includes statistics on the number and dollar value of orders for customers, grouped by either the equipment they own or the products they order.

In the manual system the only resource the clerks can use to check whether a customer is already on file or to look up a balance is the single set of ledger cards on the bookkeeper's desk. It would be desirable to give the clerks who take phone orders more immediate access to the customer data, but with the new data base system running on a single-user computer, looking up a customer on-screen may not be more convenient than the manual equivalent of pulling the ledger card from the file. In fact, if the system is already in use by someone else or is printing a lengthy report, it could be considerably less convenient. The system must therefore print a customer reference list on paper or on continuous form *index* or *Rolodex* cards for the clerks to keep at their desks. Finally, some provision must be made for archiving customers and deleting those who have not placed an order in the past year (or any other arbitrary period of time).

The new functions to be carried out by the National Widgets data base system are summarized in Figure 1-5.

Additional customer data	Type of equipment owned and products ordered, for targeting selective mailings
Customer deletion	Drop from active file all customers who have not placed an order for over one year
Index cards	Record of customer name, address, phone number, contact name, and type of equipment
Personalized letters	Printed for all customers or selectively based on equipment owned or products ordered
Customer profile	Summary of number and dollar value of orders, based on equipment owned or products ordered
Aging report	Summary of each customer's open invoices, grouped into standard aging categories and subtotaled
Monthly statements	Existing format, with aging information added
Cash receipts listing	Summary of cash received in one day or one month
Monthly posting summary	Summary of total sales, discounts, sales tax, cash receipts, accounts receivable, and cost of goods, used by accountant for preparing financial statements
Order summary	Summary of orders by inventory category

Figure 1-5. Additional requirements for the computerized system

OUTLINE OPERATIONS AND TIME SCHEDULE

Once you have obtained a description of the manual procedures that must be duplicated by the new data base system, and the desired additions and enhancements, you are ready to outline the functional components of the new system and establish a time schedule for performing each operation. If you have a background in programming, you may want to draw a flow diagram, but your analysis need not be constrained by such a formal structure. Instead of, or in addition to, a flow diagram, make an outline of the system that lists all of the data entry, file maintenance, and reporting functions.

Working from the report samples and descriptions furnished by the company's staff, you could easily overlook those data base functions that have no direct counterparts in the manual system. For example, the basic customer data entry and update procedures—entering new customers, changing customer information, looking up customer data, and deleting customers—have a readily identifiable *analog* (equivalent) in the manual system: namely, updating the customer ledger cards. However, entering order information may be lumped together with typing invoices, especially in the mind of the clerk or bookkeeper who processes orders received in the mail, whereas in the computer system, *entering* order data is a completely separate operation from *printing* invoices.

The data base system must also generate a set of reports that do not exist in the same form in the manual system. For each data base file, you must provide a *reference list* (a complete listing) of all of the fields in all of the records. The reason for printing these lists is twofold. First, they will often prove to be the fastest way of looking up information in the data bases. Second, during the testing and debugging stages of system development, the reference lists provide your best guide to exactly what information is in the data bases. If the user wants to find out whether a customer is already on file or make a quick check on an outstanding balance, it is easier to look at the Customer Reference List than to call up the record on the screen, especially if someone else is already using the computer for another task. If, for example, you find that certain items are not showing up on the invoices, you can determine by printing the Order File Reference List whether the problem lies in the invoice-printing program or whether the data is missing from the files, in which case either the order entry program or the operator may be at fault.

Your final system outline will serve several purposes. It is your most compact, concise overview of the system, as well as a checklist to ensure that you do not overlook anything as you write the programs. Fleshed out with some narrative description, it can also serve as the backbone for a proposal describing the work to be performed and, as the project nears completion, become the core of the end-user documentation.

The Outline of the National Widgets Accounts Receivable System

Figure 1-6 presents the final outline of the National Widgets accounts receivable system that will be used as the case study.

A. Customer information

1. Update individual customer information (add, inquire, change, delete)
   - Manual analog: Update customer ledger cards
   - Quantity: 500 customers, 10-15 new per month
   - Frequency: Every day
2. Archive and delete inactive customers
   - Manual analog: Remove ledger cards for inactive customers from the file
   - Frequency: Once a year
3. Zero customer year-to-date totals
   - Manual analog: None
   - Frequency: Once a year or on demand
4. Customer lists
   - Manual analog: Customer ledger cards

   a) Customer Reference List
   - Contents: All customer fields, all financial transactions
   - Frequency: On demand
   - Order: Alphabetical
   - Selections: All customers, new customers since a specified date, or customers with no activity since a specified date

---

Figure 1-6. Outline of National Widgets accounts receivable system

b) Rolodex or index cards

Contents: All customer fields
Frequency: On demand
Order: Alphabetical
Selections: All customers, one customer at a time, or new customers since a specified date

5. Customer profiles

Manual analog: None
Contents: Year-to-date and total dollars or number of orders
Frequency: On demand
Order: By type of equipment or product category
Selections: By type of equipment or product category

6. Mailings to customers

Manual analog: Labels typed by clerks, no personalized letters currently produced

a) Print mailing labels for all customers

Quantity: 500 customers (anticipated 1000)
Frequency: Twice a year
Order: By ZIP code

b) Print mailing labels for selected customers

Quantity: 50-200 per run
Frequency: 5-6 times a year
Order: By ZIP code
Selections: By product class, type of computer equipment, last order date, total orders

c) Print personalized letters for selected customers

Quantity: 50-200 per run
Frequency: 5-6 times a year
Order: By ZIP code
Selections: By product class, type of computer equipment, last order date, total orders

d) Print envelopes for Christmas cards

Quantity: 500 customers
Frequency: Once a year
Order: Alphabetical

Figure 1-6. Outline of National Widgets accounts receivable system *(continued)*

B. Order processing

1. Update order information
(add, inquire, change, delete)
Manual analog: Order forms
Quantity: 500 orders per month
Frequency: Every day
2. Print Order Reference List
Manual analog: None
Contents: All order fields
Frequency: On demand
Order: Alphabetical by customer, then by invoice number, or else by invoice number
Selections: All current orders, all orders in historical file, or one customer at a time
3. Print orders for warehouse
Manual analog: Copy of typed invoice
Quantity: 500 orders per month
Frequency: Every day
4. Print invoices
Manual analog: Typed invoice
Quantity: 500 orders per month
Frequency: 3-4 times a week
5. Post invoice information to customer file
Manual analog: Update customer ledger cards
Frequency: After printing each batch of invoices
6. Update Order History File
Manual analog: Invoices, filed in chronological order
Frequency: After printing each batch of invoices
7. Purge and reinitialize Order History File
Manual analog: Move old invoices to storage site
Frequency: Once a year

C. Financial transactions

1. Update transaction (invoice and payment) information
(add, inquire, change, delete)
Manual analog: Update customer ledger cards
Quantity: 500 orders and 500 payments per month
Frequency: Every day

Figure 1-6. Outline of National Widgets accounts receivable system (*continued*)

2. Print Transaction Reference List

Manual analog:	None
Contents:	All invoice and payment fields
Frequency:	Once a month or on demand
Order:	Alphabetical by customer, then by invoice number
Selections:	All current transactions, all transactions in historical file, or one customer at a time

3. Print Invoice Register

Manual analog:	Invoice Register spreadsheet
Contents:	All invoice fields
Frequency:	Once a month
Order:	By invoice number
Selections:	Specified range of invoice numbers

4. Print Cash Receipts Listing

Manual analog:	Bank deposit slips
Contents:	All payment fields
Frequency:	On demand
Order:	Chronologically by payment date
Selections:	Specified range of payment dates

5. Print Aging report

Manual analog:	None
Contents:	All invoice and payment fields
Frequency:	Once a month
Order:	Alphabetical by customer, then by invoice number
Selections:	All unpaid invoices

6. Print monthly statements

Manual analog:	Typed statements
Contents:	Customer name and address, all unpaid invoices, all invoices and payments from current month
Frequency:	Once a month
Order:	Alphabetical
Selections:	All customers with past-due balance

7. Order Summary

Manual analog:	None
Contents:	All order fields
Frequency:	3 times a year
Order:	By inventory category, then by part number
Selections:	All items, by category, or by type of equipment

Figure 1-6. Outline of National Widgets accounts receivable system (*continued*)

8. Accounting Summaries

Manual analog:	Annual accounting summary
Contents:	Total sales, discounts, sales tax, cash receipts, accounts receivable, cost of goods
Frequency:	Monthly
Selections:	Transactions for one month or entire year

9. Update Transaction History File

Manual analog:	None
Frequency:	Once a month

Purge and reinitialize Transaction History File

Manual analog:	None
Frequency:	Once a year

Figure 1-6. Outline of National Widgets accounts receivable system (*continued*)

2

ESTABLISHING THE DATA FILES

Once you have summarized all of the components of the application in a functional outline, the temptation will be very strong to immediately turn on the computer and begin creating the data bases. But while dBASE III PLUS allows you to make virtually any changes to the structure of a file without losing data that has already been entered, you will find that a little advance planning on paper can save you a great deal of time later on. With small sample files the mechanics of lengthening, shortening, or adding fields may take only a few minutes, yet these changes can have far-reaching effects throughout the system. The more report forms, format files, and programs you have already written for displaying or updating information in the data bases, the more time you will have to spend redesigning screen and report layouts and rewriting programs to accommodate the new file structures. And if you overlook a necessary change to a file update program, you risk losing crucial information from the data base.

If you have been working with dBASE III PLUS, you already know how to CREATE a data base file. But you also need to know how to decide what information belongs in each of the files in a complete data base system. This chapter outlines a strategy for laying out the file structures so that they support the relationships that must exist among the files. Readers who are unfamiliar with this aspect of the system design process should study this discussion carefully. If you are following along with the National Widgets case study as a tutorial, you can CREATE the data bases described in this chapter and build the required indexes. If you are working on another application, you may want to apply the same methods to set up your own files.

PLANNING THE DATA BASE STRUCTURES

The first step in planning the file structures is to identify all of the individual items of information to be maintained by the system and group them into one or more data base files. The design of the file structures will be guided by the overall goals for any dBASE III PLUS system:

- To carry out all of the required operations and produce all of the requested reports.
- To make efficient use of disk space.
- To optimize the performance of the system from the operator's point of view.
- To maximize the accuracy of the information in the data base.
- To facilitate maintaining, modifying, and expanding the system.

Each data base file will contain a group of related items of information that belong together logically and share a single format. Since dBASE III PLUS allows you to work with up to ten data bases at one time, you can omit from a file any field that can easily be looked up in another. For example, in the sample system an invoice record need not contain the customer's full name and address, since these can be read from the Customer File. However, unless you are very short on disk space, you should occasionally include certain fields that are not strictly necessary. If the Customer File includes fields for total invoices and total payments, you don't really need a separate field for the balance, which can be calculated by subtracting the payments from the invoices. (The invoice and payment totals themselves can be computed by totaling the invoice records contained in a second data base.) But adding these "extra" fields to the Customer File allows you to perform the (relatively slow) accumulation of the totals only once, after which you have instant access to the numbers.

In most cases, a file structure should not contain multiple sets of identical fields. For example, with 128 fields at your disposal, there is room in the Customer File for invoice data. However, a particular customer might have no invoices, or 1, or 50. If you were to allocate five sets of fields in the Customer File to store the invoice number, date, amount, and payment information, you would be wasting disk space if most customers had fewer than five orders at any given time, and you would have to create duplicate customer records for those who had more. This type of "one-to-many" relationship generally calls for two separate data base files, although in cases where the relationship would be better described as "one-to-a-few," wasting some disk space might be preferable to making the system more complex by adding another file.

Laying Out the Files

One good way to lay out your data bases is to start with a blank sheet of paper for each file. Working from the system outline, your notes, and the samples gathered from the manual system, write down all of the fields you'll need. The standard dBASE III PLUS notation—the field name, field type, length, and, for numeric fields, number of decimal places—is a convenient shorthand to use for this list. You might also want to add a brief description of the contents of any fields that do not have an immediately obvious purpose. On the same set of worksheets, make a note of the indexes you will need for each file. Looking at these lists spread out side by side will help you make your first versions of the file structures as complete as possible and ensure that where the same field is present in more than one file, the name, type, and length are consistent.

Begin with the files you understand the best and write down all the fields you are sure will be required before proceeding to the more problematic items on the list. While you are sketching out the file structures, do not be concerned with the order of the fields—simply add each item to the appropriate worksheet as it occurs to you. You can number the fields later or simply insert each new field in its proper place as you CREATE the structure. The preliminary worksheet for the National Widgets Customer File is illustrated in Figure 2-1.

Using Indexes

Indexes play a central role in any data base system. Building an index allows you to process a file in a sequence other than the order in which the records were entered, without having to physically rearrange (i.e.,

CUSTOMER FILE

ACCOUNT NUMBER *	C	~~8~~ 10	
COMPANY	C	25	
ADDRESS	C	25	
~~CITY/STATE/ZIP~~	~~C~~	~~35~~	
AREA CODE	~~N~~ C	3	
PHONE	C	8	
CONTACT NAME	C	25	
FIRST ORDER DATE	Date		
LAST ORDER DATE	Date		
YTD INVOICES	N	10	2
YTD PAYMENTS	N	10	2
TOTAL INVOICES	N	10	2
TOTAL PAYMENTS	N	10	2
BALANCE	N	10	2
COMMENTS	Memo		
EQUIPMENT	C	25	
CITY	C	20	
STATE	C	2	
ZIP *	C	5	

* INDEX KEYS

Figure 2-1. The Customer File design worksheet

sort) the file. You will use indexes throughout the system to control the order in which records are displayed on the screen, printed on reports, or copied to a text file for use with an external word processor. Indexes offer several important advantages over sorting:

- Building an index is often faster than sorting a file.
- Since an index contains only the fields(s) on which it is based and pointers to the corresponding data records, maintaining several indexes that access a file in several different orders takes much less disk space than several sorted copies of the file.

- Up to seven indexes may be opened together with a data base and automatically updated to reflect all new entries and changes (which would otherwise necessitate re-sorting the file).

Indexing also allows you to use the SEEK or FIND command to retrieve any record in a file in a matter of seconds, if you know the contents of the field or fields upon which the index is based (the *index key*). Each data base file should therefore have one index that is based on the field or combination of fields that uniquely identify any record in the file. For an inventory file the logical choice for this key is the part number; for a customer file, the account number.

The logical relationships among the data bases that make up the system are defined by the fields they have in common, and the most effective ways to work with two files together depend on indexing one or both data bases on the common field(s). For example, in the sample system, indexing the Customer File and the Transaction File on the customer account number allows you to open both files together and, for any record in one file, find the matching record(s) in the other. Chapter 4 will illustrate how to use these indexes to search the Customer File for a particular record and then display (or print) the name and address together with all the customer's invoice records from the Transaction File. Working from the Transaction File, you could find the matching record in the Customer File to post an invoice total.

Since a customer may have more than one invoice, the Transaction File might contain many records with a given account number. But in the Customer File the account number field is used as a unique identifier for each customer so that you can easily retrieve exactly the customer you want and, more important, determine which transactions belong to a particular customer. In general, whenever you have a "one-to-many" relationship between two files, the contents of the common field must be unique in the file with one record in order to guarantee that a SEEK command will always retrieve the correct record.

File and Field Name Conventions

Before you begin creating files, give some consideration to file and field naming conventions. Within the constraints imposed by dBASE III PLUS and MS-DOS, you should strive for readability and consistency. Choose names for your files and fields that clearly suggest their contents.

With dBASE III PLUS you can take certain liberties with file names and extensions, but it is rarely to your advantage to do so. Using nonstandard file names will usually make it more confusing to work with your data bases at command level and more difficult for other programmers to modify and maintain the system. For example, file names longer than eight characters are permitted in a USE command, but both the MS-DOS DIR (directory) command and the dBASE III PLUS equivalent only recognize the first eight characters of the file name. And although dBASE III PLUS and MS-DOS permit punctuation within file names, using punctuation is not recommended, primarily because other software (notably some communications programs and disk format conversion utilities) may not be able to handle these characters.

You may deviate from the standard extensions (.DBF for data bases, .PRG for programs, and so on), with the proviso that you must always specify an extension if it differs from the default. For example, dBASE III PLUS can maintain a list of the disk files that make up an application in a *data CATALOG* (to be discussed more fully in Chapters 3 and 4). A CATALOG is stored in the form of an ordinary data base file, but it is given the extension .CAT so that it does not show up in the list of data base files displayed by the dBASE III PLUS DIR command.

Using a common prefix for all of the files in a particular system makes it easy to see at a glance which files belong together. With only eight characters at your disposal, you should set aside no more than three for the prefix. For the system in this book, NW will represent National Widgets. This prefix allows all of the files in the accounts receivable system to be displayed, copied, or backed up from a hard disk to floppy disks with a single command—DIR NW*.*, COPY NW*.*, or BACKUP NW*.*—no matter what other files (for example, the dBASE III PLUS program itself, a word processor, or other unrelated data bases) are present in the same subdirectory.

A good convention for naming index files is to combine the names of the data base and the field(s) upon which the index is based. In the sample accounts receivable system, index file names will begin with the standard prefix NW, followed by the first letter or two of the data file name (C for Customer or TH for Transaction History). The remaining characters will be taken from the field the index is based on (or most important fields, in a compound index). Thus, the index for the Customer File that accesses the file in account number order will be called NWCACCT.NDX, and the Inventory File index that is based on CATEGORY+PARTNUMBER is named NWICATPT.NDX. Figure 2-2 shows how index names in the National Widgets system are devised. A complete listing of all index files created in the National Widgets system appears in Figure 26-5.

Field names in dBASE III PLUS may be up to ten characters in length. One embedded "punctuation mark"—the underscore (_)—is permitted, but it will not be used in this book. If you name your fields strategically, you will not need to use the underscore for added readability, and you will avoid the inconvenience of slowing down to type a shifted character that is so far from the center of the main typewriter keyboard. Field names that approximate common English words are easier to type, pronounce, and remember, and they make the programs you write easier for any dBASE III PLUS programmer to understand. If a field appears in more than one data base, the same field name should be used throughout the system. When you have more than one data base open, fields are referred to by a combination of the file name (or alias) and field name. For example, NWCUST—>ACCOUNT means "the National Widget Customer File's ACCOUNT field." (This expression may be read aloud as "NWCUST ACCOUNT" or "the NWCUST file ACCOUNT field.") Because of this nomenclature, duplicating field names need not cause any confusion;

	Standard Prefix Name	**Data File**	**Field(s) on Which the Index is Based**	**File Name Extension**
NWCACCT.NDX	NW	C	ACCT	.NDX
	National Widgets	Customer File	ACCOUNT Number Field	Index
	(An index based on the ACCOUNT filed from the NW Customer file)			
NWICATPT.NDX	NW	I	CATPT	.NDX
	National Widgets	Inventory File	CATEGORY +PARTNUMBER	Index
	(An index based on the CATEGORY + PARTNUMBER fields from the NW Inventory File)			

Figure 2-2. Naming indexes

rather, using the same name emphasizes the relationship between the files by highlighting the data they have in common.

As you set up the data bases, you can document your work by printing a copy of each file structure with

```
LIST STRUCTURE TO PRINT
```

Begin each file on a new sheet of paper, so that when you make the inevitable changes in one structure, you need not reprint any of the other pages. Make sure that you have opened all of the indexes associated with each file so you can add the index names and keys to your printed documentation with

```
DISPLAY STATUS TO PRINT
```

You can open the indexes in the USE command that opens the data base with

USE *data base file* INDEX *index file list*

Or, if the data base is already open, you can open the indexes with

SET INDEX TO *index file list*

Note that LIST STRUCTURE is used so that if there are too many fields to fit on the screen at once, the printed listing is not disrupted by a "Press any key to continue..." message. For the indexes, DISPLAY STATUS was chosen instead so that dBASE III PLUS would pause after the first screen of the status display; pressing the ESC key at this point enables you to bypass printing the status of all of the SET options and the function key assignments.

THE NATIONAL WIDGETS SYSTEM FILES

The National Widgets system requires four different file structures:

- The Customer File
- The Inventory File

- The Transaction File for invoice and payment data
- The Order File for the individual items on each invoice.

The system will also maintain up to a year's worth of historical data in two files, which have structures identical to the Order and Transaction files:

- The Transaction History File
- The Order History File.

If you are creating the National Widgets case study, you can use Figures 2-3, 2-4, 2-5, and 2-7 as a guide to CREATE the four basic data base structures. The two history files may be generated from the Transaction and Order files with

USE *data base file*
COPY STRUCTURE TO *new data base file*

Next build the necessary indexes for the (still empty) files with

INDEX ON *index key* TO *index file*

The Customer File

The Customer File, NWCUST.DBF, will contain the basic name and address information for National Widgets' regular customers, as well as fields that summarize the customers' financial transactions and a memo field for variable-length comments. The first version of the Customer File structure is shown in Figure 2-3.

The ACCOUNT field serves as the unique identifier for each customer. Although you may be accustomed to seeing numeric account codes, this field will *not* be a number. Instead, it is a character field that contains an abbreviation for the customer's company name or, for an individual, the last name. (Using this scheme, you might enter NATIONALWI into the ACCOUNT field for National Widgets, or perhaps NATWIDGET if there were other customers whose names began with "National.") This convention for assigning account codes enables anyone who knows a customer's company name to remember—or guess—the account number. Because upper- and lowercase letters are not equivalent, data should be entered

```
. USE NWCUST INDEX NWCACCT, NWCZIP

. LIST STRUCTURE TO PRINT

Structure for database: C:NWCUST.dbf
Number of data records:        0
Date of last update   : 03/13/86
Field  Field Name  Type       Width    Dec
    1  ACCOUNT     Character     10
    2  COMPANY     Character     25
    3  ADDRESS     Character     25
    4  CITY        Character     20
    5  STATE       Character      2
    6  ZIP         Character      5
    7  AREACODE    Character      3
    8  TELEPHONE   Character      8
    9  CONTACT     Character     25
   10  EQUIPMENT   Character     25
   11  FIRSTORDER  Date           8
   12  LASTORDER   Date           8
   13  YTDINV      Numeric       10      2
   14  YTDPMT      Numeric       10      2
   15  TOTINV      Numeric       10      2
   16  TOTPMT      Numeric       10      2
   17  BALANCE     Numeric       10      2
   18  COMMENTS    Memo          10
** Total **                     225


. DISPLAY STATUS TO PRINT

Currently Selected Database:
Select area:  1, Database in Use: C:NWCUST.dbf    Alias: NWCUST
    Master index file:  C:NWCACCT.ndx  Key: account
           Index file:  C:NWCZIP.ndx  Key: ZIP
           Memo file:   C:NWCUST.dbt

File search path:
Default disk drive: C:
Print destination:  PRN:
Margin =      0
Current work area =    1

Press any key to continue...

*** INTERRUPTED ***
```

Figure 2-3. The Customer File

into this field in all uppercase or all lowercase; and to help ensure consistency, no spaces or punctuation marks should be used.

FIRSTORDER and LASTORDER are the dates of the customer's first and last (most recent) orders, respectively. Using the date arithmetic capabilities of dBASE III PLUS, you can use these fields to determine how long a company has been a customer of National Widgets, or to purge the Customer File based on the amount of time elapsed since the last order. The next four fields store the customer's year-to-date invoices and payments and total cumulative invoices and payments. Although the balance is a derived quantity (calculated as TOTINV − TOTPMT), the BALANCE field is included in the structure to provide immediate access to this important number.

The Customer File needs two indexes. The first, based on the ACCOUNT field, will be used to retrieve customer data for on-screen editing and transaction posting. Because the ACCOUNT field contains the first part of the company name, this index also allows for printing customer lists in alphabetical order. For bulk mailings the Customer File will be indexed by ZIP.

The Inventory File

The system this book will develop for National Widgets does not encompass any inventory management functions, so the first version of the Inventory File structure contains only the fields required by the accounts receivable system. Because it is so easy to modify a dBASE III PLUS file structure, there is no need to include at the outset fields that will play no part in the application being implemented. The Inventory File structure is shown in Figure 2-4.

The CATEGORY field contains a code representing the general type of product (for example, DISK for floppy disks or COVER for dust covers); the combination of this field with the part number uniquely identifies each stocked item. The part numbers used by National Widgets consist of three numbers followed by a dash and two more numbers (for example, 101-43), so PARTNUMBER must be a character field to accommodate the required punctuation. If an item is used only with a particular type of hardware (for example, a ribbon for an Epson printer), the EQUIPMENT field will contain a code representing the manufacturer of the equipment.

The Inventory File is indexed by the unique combination of CATEGORY and PARTNUMBER for retrieving records and printing price lists and stock status lists. By using this index, you may look up the item description, cost, and price in the Inventory File when they are required to be printed on invoices and other accounting reports.

```
. USE NWINVENT INDEX NWICATPT

. LIST STRUCTURE TO PRINT

Structure for database: C:NWINVENT.dbf
Number of data records:       0
Date of last update   : 03/13/86
Field  Field Name  Type       Width    Dec
    1  CATEGORY    Character      6
    2  PARTNUMBER  Character      6
    3  DESCRIP     Character     25
    4  EQUIPMENT   Character      6
    5  VENDOR      Character     10
    6  COST        Numeric        7      2
    7  PRICE       Numeric        7      2
** Total **                      68

. DISPLAY STATUS TO PRINT

Currently Selected Database:
Select area:  1, Database in Use: C:NWINVENT.dbf   Alias: NWINVENT
    Master index file:  C:NWICATPT.ndx  Key: CATEGORY+PARTNUMBER

File search path:
Default disk drive: C:
Print destination:  PRN:
Margin =      0
Current work area =    1

Press any key to continue...

*** INTERRUPTED ***
```

Figure 2-4. The Inventory File

The Transaction Files

The Transaction File contains the invoice and payment information required by the accounting system, with the invoice detail lines stored separately in the Order File. The Transaction File contains one record for each invoice transaction, linked to the Customer File by the ACCOUNT field and to the Order File by the INVOICE field. The structure of the Transaction File is shown in Figure 2-5. Up to a year's worth of transactions will be maintained in a Transaction History File, illustrated in Figure 2-6.

The Transaction File keeps track of the dollar amounts that must be printed on the invoice register and summarized for the accounting reports: the retail value of the merchandise ordered, any applicable discount and shipping charges, the sales tax, and the net invoice amount. The SUBTOTAL and DISCOUNT fields will be totaled from the individual line items in the Order File, and the tax is to be calculated as TAXRATE * (SUBTOTAL − DISCOUNT) / 100. (Dividing by 100 is necessary because the tax rate will be entered as a percent—for example, 6.50 rather than 0.065.) The NETAMOUNT field can also be calculated by the

```
. USE NWTXN INDEX NWTACCT, NWTINVC

. LIST STRUCTURE TO PRINT

Structure for database: C:NWTXN.dbf
Number of data records:        0
Date of last update   : 03/13/86
Field  Field Name  Type       Width    Dec
    1  ACCOUNT     Character     10
    2  INVDATE     Date           8
    3  INVOICE     Character      5
    4  SUBTOTAL    Numeric        7      2
    5  DISCOUNT    Numeric        7      2
    6  TAXRATE     Numeric        5      2
    7  TAX         Numeric        6      2
    8  SHIPPING    Numeric        6      2
    9  INVAMOUNT   Numeric        7      2
   10  PMTDATE     Date           8
   11  PMTAMOUNT   Numeric        7      2
   12  REFERENCE   Character     15
   13  INVPOSTED   Logical        1
   14  PMTPOSTED   Logical        1
** Total **                      94

. DISPLAY STATUS TO PRINT

Currently Selected Database:
Select area:  1, Database in Use: C:NWTXN.dbf   Alias: NWTXN
    Master index file:  C:NWTACCT.ndx  Key: ACCOUNT+INVOICE
           Index file:  C:NWTINVC.ndx  Key: INVOICE

File search path:
Default disk drive: C:
Print destination:  PRN:
Margin =      0
Current work area =    1

Press any key to continue...

*** INTERRUPTED ***
```

Figure 2-5. The Transaction File

```
. USE NWTXNHST INDEX NWTHACCT, NWTHINVC

. LIST STRUCTURE TO PRINT

Structure for database: C:NWTXNHST.dbf
Number of data records:        Ø
Date of last update   : Ø3/13/86
Field  Field Name  Type       Width    Dec
    1  ACCOUNT     Character     1Ø
    2  INVDATE     Date           8
    3  INVOICE     Character      5
    4  SUBTOTAL    Numeric        7      2
    5  DISCOUNT    Numeric        7      2
    6  TAXRATE     Numeric        5      2
    7  TAX         Numeric        6      2
    8  SHIPPING    Numeric        6      2
    9  INVAMOUNT   Numeric        7      2
   1Ø  PMTDATE     Date           8
   11  PMTAMOUNT   Numeric        7      2
   12  REFERENCE   Character     15
   13  INVPOSTED   Logical        1
   14  PMTPOSTED   Logical        1
** Total **                      94

. DISPLAY STATUS TO PRINT

Currently Selected Database:
Select area:  1, Database in Use: C:NWTXNHST.dbf   Alias: NWTXNHST
    Master index file:  C:NWTHACCT.ndx  Key: ACCOUNT+INVOICE
           Index file:  C:NWTHINVC.ndx  Key: INVOICE

File search path:
Default disk drive: C:
Print destination:  PRN:
Margin =      Ø
Current work area =    1

Press any key to continue...

*** INTERRUPTED ***
```

Figure 2-6. The Transaction History File

system, using the formula SUBTOTAL − DISCOUNT + SHIPPING + TAX. Although they are derived fields, TAX and NETAMOUNT are included in the structure so that they are always available for quick on-screen inquiry.

The PMTDATE and PMTAMOUNT fields keep track of payments applied to the invoice, and the REFERENCE field allows for a check number or other payment reference. Placing the invoice and payment data in one record makes it easy to determine whether an invoice has been paid, and thereby to decide which invoices should appear on the Aging report and which may be archived and removed from the active Transaction File at the end of the month. INVPOSTED and PMTPOSTED are logical fields that keep track of which transactions have already updated the Customer File totals, so that no transaction is posted twice.

In order to link the transactions with the matching customer records, the Transaction File must be indexed by ACCOUNT. By adding the INVOICE field to the index key, you can display or print each customer's set of transactions in order by invoice number (which corresponds to chronological order). Making the invoice "number" a character field makes it simple to concatenate this field with the ACCOUNT field to build the index.

The Transaction File will also be indexed by INVOICE alone, to print the Invoice Register and to establish the link between an invoice record and the matching line items in the Order File. Remember that when dBASE III PLUS "alphabetizes" character fields containing numbers, it proceeds from left to right, character by character. Just as any word beginning with A comes before any word beginning with B, regardless of the second letter, the numbers 10 and 100 will "alphabetize" before 2. Alphabetical order corresponds to true numerical order only if the full five digits are always entered. If you want to avoid the awkwardness of entering leading zeroes (as in 00001), simply begin a new numbering sequence with 10000 as the first invoice number.

The Order Files

The Order File contains the individual invoice line items. This data base is linked to each of the other three by a common field. The INVOICE field allows you to match up a set of order records with the corresponding invoice record in the Transaction File. To enable you to examine all of the items a particular customer has ordered over a period of time, the Order File also contains an ACCOUNT field to identify the customer. Finally, the combination of CATEGORY and PARTNUMBER will be used to look up the item description and selling price in the Inventory File. The structure of the Order File is shown in Figure 2-7. The Order History File, illustrated in Figure 2-8, will maintain order detail for up to a year.

The SUBTOTAL field is calculated by multiplying PRICE, which is derived from the Inventory File, by QUANTITY, which is entered by the operator. In the same way that the TAX is calculated in the Transaction

```
. USE NWORDER INDEX NWOACCT, NWOINVC

. LIST STRUCTURE TO PRINT

Structure for database: C:NWORDER.dbf
Number of data records:        0
Date of last update   : 03/12/86
Field  Field Name  Type       Width    Dec
    1  ACCOUNT     Character     10
    2  INVOICE     Character      5
    3  CATEGORY    Character      6
    4  PARTNUMBER  Character      6
    5  EQUIPMENT   Character      6
    6  QUANTITY    Numeric        4
    7  PRICE       Numeric        7      2
    8  SUBTOTAL    Numeric        7      2
    9  DISCRATE    Numeric        5      2
   10  DISCOUNT    Numeric        7      2
   11  INVAMOUNT   Numeric        7      2
** Total **                      71

. DISPLAY STATUS TO PRINT

Currently Selected Database:
Select area:  1, Database in Use: C:NWORDER.dbf   Alias: NWORDER
    Master index file:  C:NWOACCT.ndx  Key: ACCOUNT+INVOICE
           Index file:  C:NWOINVC.ndx  Key: INVOICE

File search path:
Default disk drive: C:
Print destination:  PRN:
Margin =      0
Current work area =    1

Press any key to continue...

*** INTERRUPTED ***
```

Figure 2-7. The Order File

File, the DISCOUNT is computed as DISCRATE * SUBTOTAL / 100 (dividing by 100 is necessary because the discount rate is entered as a percent, rather than as a fraction). INVAMOUNT, the dollar amount to be printed on the invoice, is therefore equal to SUBTOTAL – DISCOUNT.

The Order File is indexed by INVOICE in order to link the order data with the matching invoice records in the Transaction File to print invoices and post transactions. The index based on the combination of ACCOUNT and INVOICE allows you to associate a customer with all of the items he or she has ever ordered and to list them chronologically.

```
. USE NWORDHST INDEX NWOHACCT, NWOHINVC

. LIST STRUCTURE TO PRINT

Structure for database: C:NWORDHST.dbf
Number of data records:         0
Date of last update    : 03/12/86
Field  Field Name  Type       Width    Dec
    1  ACCOUNT     Character     10
    2  INVOICE     Character      5
    3  CATEGORY    Character      6
    4  PARTNUMBER  Character      6
    5  EQUIPMENT   Character      6
    6  QUANTITY    Numeric        4
    7  PRICE       Numeric        7      2
    8  SUBTOTAL    Numeric        7      2
    9  DISCRATE    Numeric        5      2
   10  DISCOUNT    Numeric        7      2
   11  INVAMOUNT   Numeric        7      2
** Total **                      71

. DISPLAY STATUS TO PRINT

Currently Selected Database:
Select area:  1, Database in Use: C:NWORDHST.dbf    Alias: NWORDHST
    Master index file:  C:NWOHACCT.ndx  Key: ACCOUNT+INVOICE
           Index file:  C:NWOHINVC.ndx  Key: INVOICE

File search path:
Default disk drive: C:
Print destination:  PRN:
Margin =      0
Current work area =    1

Press any key to continue...

*** INTERRUPTED ***
```

Figure 2-8. The Order History File

ESTIMATING FILE SIZES

Once you have established the file structures, you can make a rough estimate of the size of the data bases by multiplying the record length by the number of records you expect to use. Since this is only an approximate calculation, it will not take into account the extra space in a DBF file occupied by the "header" that stores the structure of the file. (A more precise calculation that does account for the size of the file header is presented in the file backup program written in Chapter 23.) If a data base contains memo fields, the text of the memos is contained in a separate file in which space is allocated as needed in 512K chunks. You should estimate the number of records that will actually contain memo text and the average length of this text in 512K blocks.

The calculations for the National Widgets system are illustrated in Figure 2-9. Even without taking the size of the indexes or program files into account, this rough calculation rules out running the system on 360K floppy disks. Without the historical files the application could run on 1.2M floppies, but this means sacrificing some of the analytical reports—one of the primary motivations for computerizing in the first place. However, a 10M hard disk will easily accommodate a year's worth of data.

Estimating the size of an index file is less precise, but at the very least, each index entry requires 8 bytes plus the length of the index key, and there will be at least one entry for each record in the data base. For the purpose of estimating disk space requirements, multiply this number by 1.5 to obtain the average size of the index.

A typical system will require between 100K and 300K for program files, with perhaps 50K more for report and label forms and memory

Customers:	250 customers * 225 bytes	=	78,750
Memo text:	350 customers * 0.5 * 512 bytes	=	89,600
Inventory Items:	2000 items * 68 bytes	=	136,000
Transactions:			
Per Month:	500 invoices/month * 92 bytes	=	46,000
Per Year:		=	552,000
Order Line Items:			
Per Month:	500 invoices/month * 5 items/invoice * 71 bytes	=	177,500
Per Year:		=	2,130,000
Total:			
Per Month:	78,750 + 89,600 + 136,00 + 46,000 + 177,500	=	527,850
Per Year:	527,850 + 552,000 + 2,130,000	=	3,209,350

Figure 2-9. Estimating the file sizes

variable files. If you must copy data to a text file for input to another program (as we will in this system to print letters with an external word processor), you must also make sure that you have enough disk space for the text file. You can estimate this space as the combined length of the relevant fields multiplied by the number of records to be copied. For the National Widgets mailings, we will copy only the customer name and address fields, which together total 102 bytes, from all of the customer records, resulting in a text file approximately 102 * 350 = 35,700 bytes in size.

3

TESTING WITH SAMPLE DATA

Once you have created a preliminary set of file structures, the next system development phase consists of working out as many procedures as possible at command level. In this testing phase, you must enter some sample data into the files and then use the dBASE III PLUS built-in commands to simulate the ways in which the system must perform calculations, display and print information from one or more data bases, and move data among the files.

A system outline that details all of the functional capabilities of the data base system (see Figure 1-6 for an example) makes an excellent framework for the command level testing phase. The outline serves as a checklist to help ensure that you do not overlook any essential operations, and you can refer to the numbered items in the outline when you make notes on the successes and failures of your experiments and the strengths and limitations of working at the dot prompt.

Even if you know in advance that additional programming will be necessary or desirable, this command level testing is essential to the system design. Working through a full processing cycle at the dot prompt is the most effective way to

- Confirm that the file structures will accommodate the required data.
- Fine-tune the relationships among the data files.
- Outline the data entry sequence and startup procedures for implementing the full system.

- Guarantee that you will be able to carry out all the necessary tasks.
- Determine the capabilities and limitations of the dBASE III PLUS built-in commands.

This chapter outlines the general strategy for testing a system at command level and introduces some of the methods that are described more fully in Chapters 4 and 5. If you have worked with dBASE III PLUS at command level, you already have some understanding of how to use the built-in APPEND, EDIT, DELETE, CHANGE, and BROWSE commands to perform the basic file maintenance operations—entering, editing, viewing, and deleting records. You should know how to retrieve a particular record by number or by using FIND or SEEK to perform a fast search on an indexed data base. Using the report and label generators, you should be able to print data in a variety of formats.

The next two chapters illustrate many of these techniques in detail with the files from the National Widgets system. You will also explore the more difficult concepts involved in defining the startup procedures for the final system and working with two data bases together to display or print information from matching records or to move data between the files. If you have little or no prior experience with system design, you should pay close attention to these issues and be careful not to lose sight of the general principles underlying the specific examples. Readers who are following the National Widgets case study as a tutorial may want to make some notes on the approach discussed in this chapter. If you are designing your own application, the basic methodology may be applied to your data base.

TESTING METHODS AND STRATEGY

The first step in testing an application is to use the APPEND command to enter some representative data into each of the files, following the same sequence that will be used to start up the full system. The test data must come from the real application, rather than the imagination of the programmer, and the data chosen should cover the full range of possibilities that the system must eventually handle. When you invent your own sample data, especially if you are an outsider unfamiliar with the intricacies of an organization's work flow, you will be tempted to make the data conform to the initial file structures and tentative command sequences instead of presenting every challenge that the full system must meet. Using real data also allows you to more easily check the accuracy of your calculations and file update procedures by comparing the results with the manual system.

Entering the test data will pinpoint any obvious problems with the file structures: overlooked items, fields that are never filled in, inappropriate choices for data type, fields that are too long or too short, and matching fields in two files whose lengths or types differ. You will also uncover any difficulties associated with gleaning the required information from the existing manual system and interpreting the input materials, and you should be able to arrive at a rough estimate of how long the initial data entry will take. Any special preparations, such as assigning new part numbers, defining category codes, or calculating beginning balances, will be brought to your attention early, helping to ensure that these preliminaries are completed by the time the programs are ready.

Another major goal during the early stages of command level testing is to outline the sequence of steps that will be used to start up the final system. *Data entry must begin with the files that depend least on information contained in other data bases.* In the National Widgets system, the Inventory File is the logical place to begin, since it contains no fields that are derived from other files or that must be validated by lookups in other files. This file will be used to look up item prices and descriptions for printing invoices, so it must exist before data can be entered into the Order File.

Before you can delineate the initial data entry sequence, the designers and users of the system must make some important decisions: How much historical data will be maintained? At what point in the processing cycle will the conversion from the manual system take place? *The answers to these questions will enable you to outline for the operators the order in which the files must be set up, which fields must be filled in initially, and what values must go into these fields.* For example, National Widgets will begin using the computer for its accounts receivable in March 1987. Although no history from previous years will be maintained, all transaction activity from the current year (1987) must be entered into the system. The first entries into the Customer, Order, and Transaction files must therefore accurately reflect each customer's status as of January 1, 1987, including all data for invoices that were open (unpaid) at this time. This scenario typifies the way in which most "accounting" data bases are implemented.

In Chapter 4 we will begin setting up the National Widgets sample files by entering 50 frequently ordered items, drawn from five to ten different categories, into the Inventory File. Next we will enter 25 customers, among them some who have a high volume of activity, some with only an occasional order, one who has not placed an order in over a year, some who pay quickly, and a few who usually maintain a high balance. Anyone who places an order will be entered into the Customer File, since the computer makes it easy to purge inactive customers later on.

Because the LASTORDER date field, as well as the YTDINV, YTDPMT, TOTINV, and TOTPMT fields, will be updated automatically as transactions are posted, you must be especially careful with these entries. We are starting at the beginning of a year, so the two year-to-date fields may be left blank (zero). TOTINV and TOTPMT should reflect only invoices that have been fully paid on or before December 31, 1986, since data for invoices that were open on January 1 must be entered into the Order File, from which Transaction File records will be generated and posted to the Customer File. This posting process will also update the LASTORDER field, so you must enter this field yourself only for those customers who have had no orders in 1987 and had no unpaid invoices on January 1.

Next we will enter into the Order File all of the line items for those invoices that remained open at the end of 1986. These orders will then be summarized into Transaction File entries (the details of this process are described in Chapter 4) and the invoice data posted to the total fields in the Customer File. Customer balances can be calculated, and finally, the year-to-date fields zeroed out. This sequence of steps defines the flow of data through the system, as well as establishing the customer balances and matching transaction detail as of the January 1, 1987, startup date.

In the sample system, the order data for the 25 test customers necessarily includes items that are not among the 50 sample inventory records, and when you test your own systems with small sample files, similar situations will arise. For testing purposes you may fill in the missing data manually, but this example should serve as a reminder that your finished system must cope with such contingencies as missing inventory items or customer records.

Using the test data, you can work out, or at least approximate, the remaining data input, processing, and output functions that make up the standard processing cycle. These experiments should further clarify the relationships among the data files and uncover any missing fields or indexes that are necessary to support these linkages. In an accounting system, reports are generally printed monthly, quarterly, or annually, and special closing procedures are run at the end of the month and at the end of the year. In an application that is not so closely tied to the calendar, your definition of a cycle may be quite different, but *your command level procedures should simulate as closely as possible the way in which the final system will perform calculations, move data among the files, and display the results.*

As you will see in Chapter 4, many of the processing functions depend on the linkage of data files through indexes based on common fields. This linkage is established with the SET RELATION command. Computations within a record, such as calculating the extended price, discount, and tax on an order, can be accomplished with the REPLACE command, and data from multiple records can be summarized into another file with TOTAL. The UPDATE command allows you to transfer data from one file into the appropriate fields in another—for example, to post invoice and payment totals to the Customer File. Files may be combined with APPEND and records purged en masse with DELETE and ZAP.

During your trials with these commands, you will undoubtedly make mistakes, use inappropriate commands, and perform operations in the wrong sequence. Incorporating frequent LIST or DISPLAY commands will help you measure the success of your efforts, provided that you examine these lists carefully and, if necessary, recheck your calculations by hand. You can minimize the frustration of having to reenter the same data many times by backing up *all* of your data files (and, to further speed up disaster recovery, the indexes as well) before you apply any potentially destructive commands like REPLACE, DELETE, or UPDATE to an entire data base.

Many of the printed formats that make up the output of the system can be handled adequately by the standard dBASE III PLUS report and label generators. Even in cases where stringent formatting requirements or complex calculations demand special programming, producing a rough facsimile of the report allows the users to approve the basic page layout and report contents and will help you confirm that you have provided adequately for the data in your file structures. Where it is clearly impossible to produce a particular printed format—for example, in the sample system, an invoice—without programming, you should at least open all of the files involved and display the relevant fields to prove that the required data is in fact available to you.

These experiments should help you realize your final goal for the command level testing phase: determining both the capabilities and the limitations of working at the dot prompt. These insights should guide you in deciding how much custom programming the system requires. Typically you will find some operations and reports that are impossible to produce without programming, some functions for which the dBASE III PLUS intrinsic commands are perfectly adequate, and many procedures that could be improved in some way by substituting a program for the equivalent sequence of built-in commands.

If you have not written programs before, you will find that the command level procedures you develop will clarify the interactions among the files and serve as models for the programs you later learn to write. But this kind of experimentation can be equally instructive for people who have worked extensively with other programming languages, such as BASIC, that do not provide any simple data file manipulation capabilities. Without having fully explored the use of dBASE III PLUS at the dot prompt, an experienced programmer is likely to write programs that represent no real improvement over the built-in commands or to design elaborate systems of internal pointers when they are unnecessary—in such situations, the ability of dBASE III PLUS to relate files based on common fields and indexes would be simpler, faster, and more conducive to preserving the integrity of the data.

DOCUMENTING YOUR WORK SESSION

Because you will undoubtedly try out many alternatives before you settle on the best methods, you should use all of the tools at your disposal to document your work. Changes in the file structures and indexes, as well as the startup sequence for data entry, may be noted on the file structure listings you have printed for reference (see Figures 2-2 through 2-7). In addition, keep a running list of any problems you encounter as well as the advantages and difficulties of working at command level. Utility programs like Spotlight or SideKick can be particularly helpful during this period. You can use the pop-up calculator to verify a computation, and you may find the electronic "notepad" handier than scribbling comments on paper, especially since you can import a portion of the image displayed on the screen into your note file to illustrate a point.

The dBASE III PLUS program itself provides a number of ways to keep a record of your work at command level. Most variations of the LIST and DISPLAY commands allow you to add the phrase TO PRINT to send the output to the printer as well as to the terminal. If you like, you can log all or part of your work session on paper by using SET PRINT ON and SET PRINT OFF (or the equivalent CTRL-P or CTRL-PRTSC toggles) to turn the printer on and off. When PRINT is ON, all sequential output—that is, any text sent line by line to the screen—is also sent to the printer. This includes all the commands you type, responses and status messages from dBASE III PLUS (such as the new position of the record pointer after a SKIP command or the display of the number of records APPENDed or INDEXed), and output from LIST and DISPLAY commands. However, none of your activity in the dBASE III PLUS full-screen edit modes (such as APPEND, EDIT, BROWSE, and CREATE) will be printed.

If you need to preserve a copy of a full-screen display, or if you prefer to be more selective about what commands you record on paper, you can make use of the ability of the IBM PC and compatible systems to print an exact image of the screen by pressing SHIFT-PRTSC ("print screen"). Screen prints are especially useful for documenting the need to enlarge a field to accommodate a long entry; retaining a record of your final, successful version of a complex REPLACE or UPDATE command; or preserving a screen that illustrates the correct sequence in which a lengthy series of commands must be carried out.

You can also log your work session to a text file on disk called an *ALTERNATE file.* The ALTERNATE file is opened with

SET ALTERNATE TO *file name*

The ALTERNATE file is given the extension .TXT unless you explicitly override this default. To begin sending output to the text file, use SET ALTERNATE ON; and to suspend recording, use SET ALTERNATE OFF. You can SET ALTERNATE ON or OFF as many times as you like during a work session, and when you are finished, you can close the file with CLOSE ALTERNATE. This command is in every way equivalent to SET PRINT ON/OFF, except that console output is routed to a disk file instead of to the printer. Like the printed log, the ALTERNATE file records only sequential output, not full-screen displays. You can edit the resulting text file with your word processor to obtain a concise record and an attractively formatted printout of the productive parts of your work session.

If you have worked with dBASE III PLUS at command level, you know that the program maintains a *HISTORY* of the most recent commands you have typed. Any of the commands in HISTORY may be retrieved, edited if necessary, and resubmitted, enabling you to correct typing or syntax errors or repeat a previous command or a variation of a previous command without having to retype it. To access commands in HISTORY, use the UP ARROW and DOWN ARROW keys to browse backward or forward through the command list. When the desired command is displayed on the screen, you can use the standard full-screen cursor movement keys to edit or add to the command, and then press RETURN to execute it.

By default, dBASE III PLUS retains 20 commands in HISTORY, but you can increase this number, up to a limit of 16,000, with

SET HISTORY TO *number of commands*

You can display the entire command list with LIST HISTORY or DISPLAY HISTORY at any time. You can route the command list to a text file as well as to the screen; to do this, open an ALTERNATE file before issuing the LIST HISTORY command and close it immediately afterward so that the resulting text file contains only your commands. Coupled with strategic use of SHIFT-PRTSC to document the output of certain commands, the command history file can provide the most concise record of the commands used during a work session. Later on, as will be described in Chapter 7, sections of the text file can be extracted to create short dBASE III PLUS programs.

dBASE III PLUS also provides the means to maintain a list of all the disk files that comprise an application, in the form of a data base file called a CATALOG. This file contains one record for each file, with fields for the path name, file name, type (for example, "dbf," "ndx," or "fmt"), alias (for DBF files only), title (an 80-character description of the file), and a numerical code used to designate files that must be opened and used together (for example, a data base and its associated indexes and format file). You create a new CATALOG or open an existing CATALOG with

SET CATALOG TO *catalog name*

and close it with SET CATALOG TO.

With a CATALOG open, whenever you issue a command that opens or creates files, dBASE III PLUS checks the CATALOG, and if the specified files are not already present, adds the files to the CATALOG data base. By default, dBASE III PLUS also prompts you to enter a TITLE for each file, but you can disable this query with SET TITLE OFF. You can update or edit the CATALOG yourself, like any other data base file, with APPEND, EDIT, and DELETE, but you should never change its structure (if you do, dBASE III PLUS can no longer recognize the file as a CATALOG). Remember, however, that since a CATALOG has the extension .CAT rather than the default .DBF, you must specify the full file name and extension in the USE command that opens the file.

By allowing dBASE III PLUS to build a CATALOG of the files in your application, you will obtain not only a record of all of the files you have created and used, but also a record of which indexes, format files, and query files belong with which data bases, and, through the TITLE field, a description of the purpose or function of each file. As described earlier, you can and should strive to accomplish these same objectives with a consistent file naming scheme. Nevertheless, using a CATALOG during the development process will enable you to maintain a complete, accurate, and detailed description of the disk files that make up your application and the relationships among them, in a form that facilitates printing the file list as part of your system documentation.

4

DEVELOPING COMMAND LEVEL PROCEDURES

As outlined in Chapter 3, the first step in developing a dBASE III PLUS application is to enter some representative sample data into all of the files and work out as many procedures as possible at the dot prompt. Command level testing enables you to refine your file structures, establish the relationships among the data bases, and determine the limits of what you can accomplish without programming. This chapter will demonstrate the strategies and methods described in Chapter 3, using examples drawn from the National Widgets system case study. We will begin by entering some sample data first into the Inventory and Customer files and then into the Order File; this data will be used to illustrate several types of file update procedures. Throughout this chapter the system outline developed in Chapter 1 (see Figure 1-6) will be used as a checklist for the functional requirements of the system. Although we will not cover every item on this list in detail, a range of techniques will be presented for modeling many functions of the National Widgets system—and your own data base applications—at command level.

DATA BASE ENTRY PROCEDURES

The Inventory File will be established first in the National Widgets system since it does not depend on information in any of the other data bases. (*Note:* Although this file is needed to look up prices and item descriptions, the accounts receivable system does not include any inventory management functions per se, and the Inventory File does not appear in the system outline.) Initially, we will enter 50 items, selected from seven product categories, and print the file for reference with LIST TO PRINT. The sample Inventory File is shown in Figure 4-1. If you are creating the case study yourself, you can use the APPEND command to enter these 50 records into your Inventory File.

The Inventory File is opened with the CATEGORY + PARTNUMBER index:

```
USE NWINVENT INDEX NWICATPT
```

Working at command level you can use the DISPLAY, EDIT, CHANGE, and BROWSE commands for viewing and updating existing entries. Records may be deleted or recalled either with CTRL-U from one of the full-screen edit modes or with the DELETE and RECALL commands from the dot prompt. If you are paralleling this development process with your own application, you may find that you are ready to begin command level testing before the users have completed the task of assigning such codes as the Inventory CATEGORY's or VENDOR I.D.'s in the sample system. In that case, you can define your own codes, keeping them as close as possible to the formats that will be used in the final system.

Initializing the Customer File (Section A, Item 1 in the system outline) is not so straightforward. As shown in Chapter 3, the TOTINV and TOTPMT fields should reflect all invoices that were fully paid at the end of 1986, while the year-to-date fields (YTDINV and YTDPMT) and the BALANCE (which will be calculated) may be left blank. For those customers who placed their first order in 1987, all five of these fields will be zero. In a company whose manual system is rudimentary (or nonexistent), arriving at the correct values for fields like TOTINV and TOTPMT may not be a simple matter of referring to the running balance column on a ledger card. The testing phase is the ideal time for this to come to light, so that the decision can be made either to allot more time and personnel to the job or to abandon the task entirely and begin accumulating historical totals from the present on.

FIRSTORDER is a required entry for all customers except those who are new in 1987 (for these customers, the field will be filled in from the invoice date of their first order). The LASTORDER date need not be entered for any customers who have placed an order in 1987 or had an

```
. USE NWINVENT INDEX NWICATPT

. LIST TO PRINT

Record#  CATEGORY PARTNUMBER DESCRIP                     EQUIPMENT VENDOR        COST   PRICE
     48  ACCESS   508-13     Polaroid Glare Screen       IBM       DESKTOP      16.30   24.95
     49  ACCESS   508-14     Polaroid Glare Screen       COMPAQ    DESKTOP      14.40   21.95
     46  ACCESS   533-12     Plexiglas Printer Stand               DESKTOP      24.50   39.95
     47  ACCESS   541-15     Terminal Swivel Mount                 DESKTOP      68.00   92.50
     50  ACCESS   541-22     Non-magnetic Copy Stand               DESKTOP      21.00   32.50
     40  COVER    540-10     Dust cover, Apple II        APPLE     COVERSLTD    16.50   24.95
     42  COVER    540-11     Dust cover, Macintosh       APPLE     COVERSLTD    17.00   26.50
     41  COVER    540-12     Dust cover, IBM PC, XT      IBM       COVERSLTD    18.50   29.95
      5  DISK     101-40     5-1/4" SSDD 10 Sector                 TRUEDATA     19.00   28.00
      6  DISK     101-41     5-1/4" SSDD 16 Sector                 TRUEDATA     19.00   28.00
      1  DISK     101-42     5-1/4" SSDD Soft Sector               TRUEDATA     19.00   28.00
      8  DISK     101-43     5-1/4" DSDD 10 Sector                 TRUEDATA     21.00   31.50
      7  DISK     101-44     5-1/4" DSDD 16 Sector                 TRUEDATA     21.00   31.50
      9  DISK     101-45     5-1/4" DSDD Soft Sector               TRUEDATA     21.00   31.50
     10  DISK     101-60     5-1/4" SSDD 10 Sector                 DISKUS       23.50   38.00
     11  DISK     101-61     5-1/4" SSDD 16 Sector                 DISKUS       23.50   38.00
     12  DISK     101-62     5-1/4" SSDD Soft Sector               DISKUS       22.80   38.00
     13  DISK     101-63     5-1/4" DSDD 10 Sector                 DISKUS       29.40   48.00
     14  DISK     101-64     5-1/4" DSDD 16 Sector                 DISKUS       29.40   48.00
     15  DISK     101-65     5-1/4" DSDD Soft Sector               DISKUS       28.75   48.00
     34  FORMS    803-20     14-1/2 x 11" Green bar                USPAPER      28.50   45.25
     35  FORMS    803-21     14-1/2 x 11" White                    USPAPER      24.00   42.50
     37  FORMS    803-31     9-1/2 x 11" Green bar                 USPAPER      25.00   37.50
     36  FORMS    803-32     9-1/2 x 11" White                     USPAPER      24.50   37.50
     38  FORMS    820-20     3-1/2 x 1" Labels, 1-up               USPAPER      14.50   21.95
     39  FORMS    820-23     3-1/2 x 1" Labels, 4-up               USPAPER      39.50   64.95
      3  PRTWHL   321-11     NEC Courier 10              NEC       DAISYCO       8.45   12.50
     16  PRTWHL   321-15     NEC Prestige Elite 12       NEC       DAISYCO       8.45   12.50
      4  PRTWHL   321-18     NEC Emperor P.S.            NEC       DAISYCO       9.60   15.00
     17  PRTWHL   341-51     Qume Courier 10             QUME      DAISYCO       4.80    7.95
     19  PRTWHL   341-52     Qume Courier 12             QUME      DAISYCO       4.80    7.95
     18  PRTWHL   341-54     Qume Prestige Elite 12      QUME      DAISYCO       4.80    7.95
     20  PRTWHL   361-10     Diablo Courier 10           DIABLO    DAISYCO       5.20    8.75
     21  PRTWHL   361-15     Diablo Manifold 10          DIABLO    DAISYCO       5.20    8.75
     22  PRTWHL   361-18     Diablo Courier Legal 10A    DIABLO    DAISYCO       5.20    8.75
     32  RIBBON   240-30     Okidata 80, 81, 82, 83      OKI       MBSRIBBON     2.75    4.25
     33  RIBBON   240-31     Okidata 84                  OKI       MBSRIBBON     3.00    4.95
     30  RIBBON   240-50     Epson MX/FX80               EPSON     MBSRIBBON     5.20    9.45
     31  RIBBON   240-51     Epson MX/FX100              EPSON     MBSRIBBON     9.75   14.95
      2  RIBBON   270-10     NEC 7700 Cloth Ribbon       NEC77     MBSRIBBON     4.20    6.95
     23  RIBBON   270-11     NEC 7700 Multistrike        NEC77     MBSRIBBON     4.20    6.95
     25  RIBBON   270-12     NEC 3500 Cloth              NEC35     MBSRIBBON     7.20   12.95
     24  RIBBON   270-13     NEC 3500 Multistrike        NEC35     MBSRIBBON     7.80   13.50
     26  RIBBON   270-50     Diablo Hytype II Cloth      DIABLO    MBSRIBBON     4.50    6.95
     27  RIBBON   270-51     Diablo Hytype II Multi      DIABLO    MBSRIBBON     4.75    7.25
     28  RIBBON   270-53     Diablo 620 Multistrike      DIABLO    MBSRIBBON     6.50    9.50
     29  RIBBON   270-72     Qume Multistrike            QUME      MBSRIBBON     3.50    5.95
     43  STOR     481-10     5-1/4" Disk Case, Blue                DISKSTORE     1.15    2.85
     44  STOR     481-20     Locking Disk Storage Tray             DISKSTORE    12.50   19.95
     45  STOR     481-30     Oak Disk Storage Case                 DISKSTORE    29.75   44.95
```

Figure 4-1. The Inventory File

unpaid invoice left over from 1986, since it will be updated automatically when invoices are posted. This field presents less of a problem than the cumulative total fields described previously—placing an unnecessary entry into the LASTORDER field that will later be overwritten is less risky than including an invoice amount in TOTINV that will be added in again by the system. In the sample data base, we will enter the last 1986 order date into the LASTORDER field and allow this date to be replaced by any subsequent invoices posted. If you are working on your own application, scrutinize your manual samples carefully to uncover any similar situations that must be taken into account during the initial data entry.

If you are creating the National Widgets system yourself as an example, you will find the data for the 25 sample customers listed in Figure 4-2. As you enter this information or the test data from your manual system into your own data base files, you will see that maintaining a file with APPEND and EDIT is most efficient if you have designed the structure so that the fields that are most frequently updated by the operator are at the beginning of the structure and calculated fields come last. This way, you can press PGDN (once if all the fields fit on one screen or several times for a data base with more fields) to save each record and begin a new one after you have made your last required field entry, instead of having to bypass a great many fields with DOWN ARROW or RETURN. If you know that you or other users of the system will in fact work extensively with the files at command level, you might rearrange some fields at this point. If you plan to create custom data entry screens through format files or programs (as we will in the National Widgets system), the order of the fields is immaterial.

Whenever you intend to add records to a data base or edit the index key fields, make sure to open the file with all of the associated indexes, so that they are updated to reflect the new entries and changes. If you open more than one index, the *master index* (the one named first in the USE command) controls the order in which the records are displayed or printed, and it is the only index that may be used as the basis of a FIND or SEEK command. The first index should therefore be the one that will allow you most easily to call up a particular record to be viewed, edited, deleted, or recalled. In the National Widgets system, the Customer File will be opened with both the account number and ZIP code indexes. Since customer data will be retrieved by customers' unique account codes, the account number index should be named first in the USE command:

```
USE NWCUST INDEX NWCACCT, NWCZIP
```

If more than one index is open, you can designate a new master index or temporarily disable all of the indexes and view the data base in sequential order with the SET ORDER command. The syntax of this command is

SET ORDER TO *index file number*

The *index file number* corresponds to the order in which the indexes were specified in the USE command that opened the data base. For example, with the National Widgets Customer File opened as described previously, you could switch to using the ZIP code index as the master index with

```
SET ORDER TO 2
```

To view the Customer File in the order the records were entered, as if no indexes were open, you would use

```
SET ORDER TO Ø
```

Since this command does not actually open or close the index files, it works much faster than opening a new set of indexes with SET INDEX TO *index file list* or closing and then reopening the data base with a new USE command.

Whether you are following along with this example or working with your own files, you will probably not have to make any real changes immediately after entering the first batch of test data, but you should make sure that you can FIND or SEEK any record by its unique index key in order to DISPLAY or EDIT the record. You should also delete at least one record to verify that deletions are handled properly in the file update and reporting procedures we will develop.

There is a subtle difference between FIND, which has been retained from dBASE II, and SEEK, which was first introduced in dBASE III. Both commands perform a fast search on an index file, but while FIND assumes that its object is a literal character string, SEEK accepts any legitimate dBASE III PLUS expression. Thus, if you use FIND at command level, you need not surround your search string with quotes. In the Customer File, for example, you could use FIND to search for a particular customer by account number:

```
USE NWCUST INDEX NWCACCT
FIND LEWIS
```

The corresponding SEEK command would be

```
SEEK "LEWIS"
```

```
. USE NWCUST INDEX NWCACCT, NWCZIP

. LIST TO PRINT

Record#  ACCOUNT    COMPANY                     ADDRESS                         CITY                    STATE ZIP   AREACODE TELEPHONE
CONTACT                   EQUIPMENT                  FIRSTORDER LASTORDER     YTDINV        YTDPMT      TOTINV      TOTPMT
BALANCE COMMENTS
      2  ABCPLUMB   ABC Plumbing                1850 University Avenue     Berkeley                 CA    94703 415         861-4543
Ed Williams               Kaypro 10, Epson FX-100    12/02/85    12/11/86           0.00          0.00  796.41      796.41
0.00 Memo
      3  ANDERSON                               3420 19th Street           San Francisco            CA    94114 415         563-8961
John Anderson             Apple IIe                  08/08/85    12/01/86           0.00          0.00  279.52      279.52
0.00 Memo
     19  ARONOFF                                601 First Street           Benicia                  CA    94510 707         745-1813
Gina Aronoff              Apple IIc, Imagewriter     10/09/86    12/15/86           0.00          0.00  232.50      232.50
0.00 Memo
     21  CHIPCITY   Chip City Electronics       288 Lorton                 Burlingame               CA    94010 415         348-6801
Fred Larson               Osborne Exec, Epson MX-80   /  /        /  /              0.00          0.00    0.00        0.00
0.00 Memo
     18  DELTADESGN Delta Design                2405 Sycamore Drive        Antioch                  CA    94509 415         754-7373
Andrea Bennett            Macintosh, Imagewriter     09/15/86    09/15/86           0.00          0.00  138.15      138.15
0.00 Memo
     14  ELLISMFG   Ellis Manufacturing         3091 Park Boulevard        Palo Alto                CA    94306 415         494-1421
Barbara Goddard           IBM PC, Okidata 84         10/18/85    11/17/86           0.00          0.00  669.00      669.00
0.00 Memo
     12  FLOORPLAN  Floor Plan Carpet Center    1482 Lowrie Avenue         South San Francisco      CA    94080 415         871-3204
Louise Robbins            NorthStar Advantage        11/20/86    11/20/86           0.00          0.00  184.18      184.18
0.00 Memo
      9  GREENTHUMB Green Thumb Landscaping     1240 Hearst                Berkeley                 CA    94702 415         549-8901
Celia Lopez               Kaypro 4, Okidata 92       08/15/86    12/19/86           0.00          0.00  347.73      347.73
0.00 Memo
     10  HOMEMOVIES Home Movies Video Rentals   2982 College Avenue        Berkeley                 CA    94705 415         843-1148
Mark Vogel                Columbia, NEC 2010         09/12/86    09/12/86           0.00          0.00  248.15      248.15
0.00 Memo
     17  HRINSURANC H & R Insurance             1225 Van Ness Avenue       San Francisco            CA    94109 415         398-1441
Jill Henley               DEC Rainbow                07/12/85    10/27/86           0.00          0.00  538.43      538.43
0.00 Memo
     15  IMAGEMAKER The Image Makers            1900 Powell St, Suite 832  Emeryville               CA    94608 415         653-1250
Lisa Burns                IBM PC, NEC 7710           11/12/86    11/12/86           0.00          0.00  389.50      389.50
0.00 Memo
     25  JENSEN     Arthur Jensen, MD           450 Sutter St, Suite 1418  San Francisco            CA    94108 415         397-8260
Lucy George               Compaq Deskpro, Brother    03/26/85    12/18/86           0.00          0.00  608.42      608.42
0.00 Memo
     13  JOHNSON    J. Thomas Johnson, CPA      50 California, Suite 1032  San Francisco            CA    94111 415         433-6488
                          IBM XT, Epson MX-100       06/27/86    12/05/86           0.00          0.00  168.42      168.42
```

```
Carolyn Sumner
0.00 Memo
      8  KELLY       Kelly and Sons Furniture  14800 Bancroft Avenue     San Leandro          CA      94578 415       357-7482
Richard Kelly              Eagle PC, TI 820           / /        / /             0.00      0.00      0.00        0.00
0.00 Memo
      4  KLEIN       Carol Klein, M.D.         3204 Telegraph Avenue     Oakland              CA      94609 415       891-2204
Judy Barnes                IBM PC, Diablo 630        10/14/85   12/29/86         0.00      0.00      693.73      693.73
0.00 Memo
      1  LEWIS       Lewis and Associates      408 Grand Avenue          Oakland              CA      94610 415       839-5014
Joan Mills                 Corona PC, NEC 3510       10/14/85   09/19/86         0.00      0.00      366.81      366.81
0.00 Memo
      5  MTK         M.T.K. Industries         1430  61st Street         Emeryville           CA      94608 415       655-7200
Leslie Cohen               IBM XT, Epson FX-100      06/24/85   12/11/86         0.00      0.00     1042.85     1042.85
0.00 Memo
      7 *PHOENIX     Phoenix Construction      3214 Pacheco Blvd.        Martinez             CA      94553 415       939-8610
Vector 3005, TI820         04/28/86   07/07/86    0.00          0.00      249.57       249.57    0.00 Memo
     24  QUICKPRINT Quick Print, Inc.          2532 Milvia               Berkeley             CA      94704 415       865-3091
Sarah Bernstein            Corona PC, Okidata 92     05/17/85   09/23/85         0.00      0.00      358.73      358.73
0.00 Memo
      6  RAPIDTYPE   RapidType Secretarial Svc 2457 Union Street         San Francisco        CA      94123 415       861-4048
Kathy McDonald             Xerox 820, Diablo 620      / /        / /             0.00      0.00      0.00        0.00
0.00 Memo
     11  SHAPEUP     Shape Up Fitness Center   2832 MacDonald Avenue     Richmond             CA      94804 415       236-7687
Jeanne Lee                 Apple II, Okidata 83      02/14/86   11/12/86         0.00      0.00      435.42      435.42
0.00 Memo
     22  WESTJAN     Western Janitorial Svc.   3640 Mt. Diablo Blvd.     Lafayette            CA      94549 415       283-7150
Gail Armstrong             Kaypro 10, Epson MX-100    / /        / /             0.00      0.00      0.00        0.00
0.00 Memo
     16  WHITNEY     Financial Planning Svcs.  1800 Peralta, Suite 18    Fremont              CA      94536 415       791-7474
James Whitney              Eagle PC, Daisywriter      / /        / /             0.00      0.00      0.00        0.00
0.00 Memo
     23  WORKFORCE   Work Force Temporary Svc. 2900 Laguna St., Suite 10 San Francisco        CA      94123 415       563-3492
Hal Moffett                Vector 5005               10/02/86   10/02/86         0.00      0.00      158.13      158.13
0.00 Memo
     20  YORKPUMP    York Pump, Inc.           632 Charcot Avenue        San Jose             CA      95131 408       946-9975
Sharon Fern                Compupro                   / /        / /             0.00      0.00      0.00        0.00
0.00 Memo
```

Figure 4-2. The Customer File

If the object of the FIND command is a memory variable rather than a literal string (a more likely occurrence within a program than in command level work), you must use a macro:

```
FIND &MACCOUNT
```

This forces dBASE III PLUS to search for *the value of the variable MACCOUNT*, not the literal character string M-A-C-C-O-U-N-T. For the same reason, to search a compound index for an expression consisting of several fields or memory variables, you must first combine them into a single character variable:

```
USE NWTXN INDEX NWTACCT
STORE MACCOUNT + MINVOICE TO MKEY
FIND &MKEY
```

SEEK, which accepts any expression as its object, is more convenient in this context:

```
USE NWTXN INDEX NWTACCT
SEEK MACCOUNT + MINVOICE
```

The sample Customer File is listed in Figure 4-2. The number of fields makes this listing harder to read than the Inventory File printout. We will shortly use the dBASE III PLUS report generator to create a more aesthetically pleasing report, but the crude LIST serves the immediate purpose of documenting the test data and giving you a handy reference to the contents of the file.

Note that the COMMENTS field is displayed simply as "Memo". Unless you explicitly name a memo field in a LIST command, dBASE III PLUS assumes that you do not want to see the actual contents of the field or even know which records have text entered in the memo field. You must use a second LIST command (illustrated in Figure 4-3) to display the memo text. This completes the initial documentation for the Customer File.

FILE UPDATE PROCEDURES

Entering order and payment data requires more complicated operations than simply APPENDing records to the files. Not all of the fields will be entered by the operator; some are derived from other data bases and

```
. USE NWCUST INDEX NWCACCT, NWCZIP

. LIST ACCOUNT,COMMENTS

Record#  ACCOUNT     COMMENTS
      2  ABCPLUMB
      3  ANDERSON
     19  ARONOFF
     21  CHIPCITY    This guy likes to talk.  Appreciates good advice,
                     but will take up a lot of your time on the phone
                     if you go along with it.

     18  DELTADESGN  Referred by Chris Johnson.

     14  ELLISMFG    Don't accept any orders unless accompanied by
                     prepayment.  These people have always been slow to
                     pay, and have been avoiding phone calls regarding
                     seriously past due balance which is now in
                     collections.


     12  FLOORPLAN
      9  GREENTHUMB
     10  HOMEMOVIES  Owner is a friend of Jim's, so they get a 10%
                     discount on all orders.  However, they take a long
                     time to pay.

     17  HRINSURANC
     15  IMAGEMAKER
     25  JENSEN
     13  JOHNSON
      8  KELLY
      4  KLEIN       Referred by Dr. James Reynolds.


      1  LEWIS
      5  MTK         Interested in receiving additional information on
                     computer furniture, ergonomic workstations, glare
                     screens, etc.

      7 *PHOENIX
     24  QUICKPRINT  Send information on printer stands when new flyer
                     is ready.

                     This is a small printer who is looking for jobs
                     printing custom letterhead or forms for us or for
                     our customers.

      6  RAPIDTYPE   This company is a word processing and secretarial
                     service.  They are looking for one vendor to
                     provide a high volume of supplies.  Quick delivery
                     and varied product line more important than lowest
                     prices, but would like volume discounts.


     11  SHAPEUP
     22  WESTJAN
     16  WHITNEY
     23  WORKFORCE
     20  YORKPUMP
```

Figure 4-3. The Customer File memo text

some are calculated. Working out these update procedures requires an understanding of how to use more than one file at a time, what functional relationships exist among the data bases, how these relationships may be established, and the ways in which information may be transferred among the files. The linkages among the National Widgets system files are illustrated schematically in Figure 4-4, which includes the files, the indexes, and the common fields that serve to define the relationships. For the sake

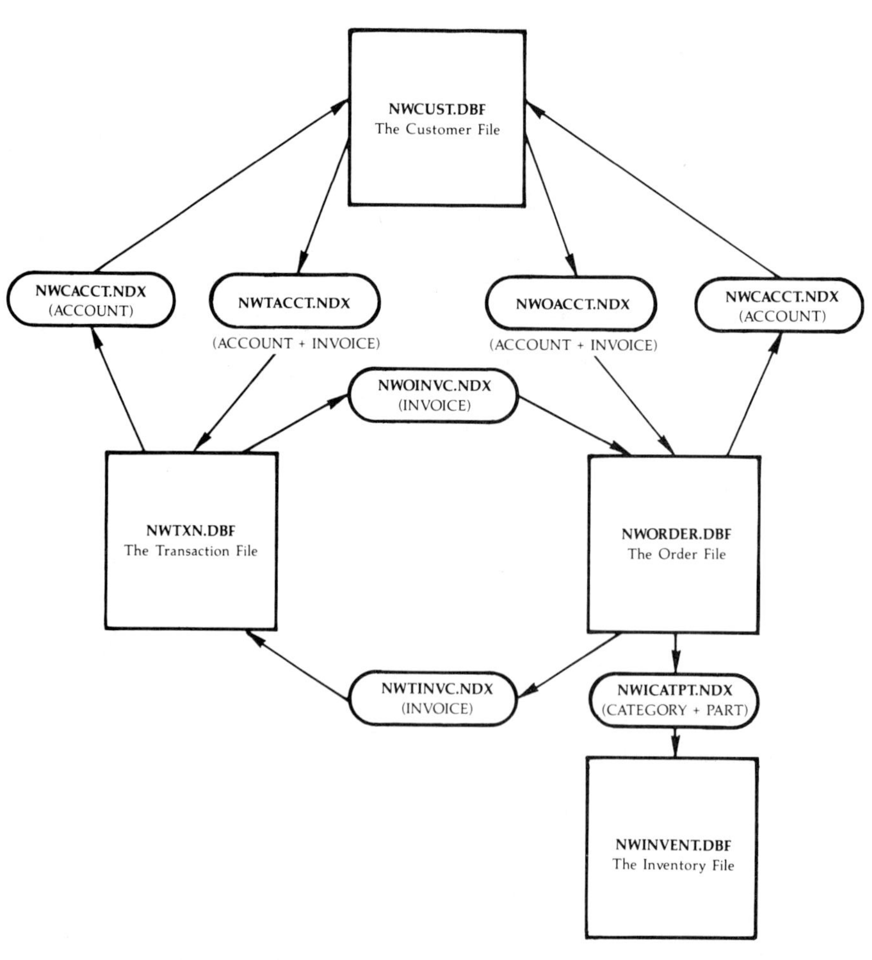

Figure 4-4. The relationships among the data base files

of clarity and simplicity, the two history files, NWTXNHST.DBF and NWORDHST.DBF, have been omitted, since they are linked to the Customer and Inventory files in the same way as NWTXN.DBF and NWORDER.DBF, respectively.

Several general types of file updates will be used in the National Widgets system:

- Performing calculations within the records of one file
- Updating fields in one file from data in another file
- Creating a new file by summarizing data in another file
- Combining two files
- Deleting records in a batch.

Calculations within a record, for all or some of the records in a data base, will be carried out with the REPLACE command. You can thus avoid having to enter or update any fields that can be computed by the system. The update procedures involving multiple files depend on the relationships based on common fields that were built into the structures and the indexes we have created. In many cases, the SET RELATION command provides a convenient way to establish these linkages, allowing you to print or display data from two files together and extending the power of REPLACE to use fields from two files in a calculation. The TOTAL command will be used to create a new data base by summarizing data in another file, and the UPDATE command will be used to transfer data between individual fields in two files. APPEND FROM will be used to combine two files, and ZAP and DELETE will purge all or selected records from a data base.

Performing Calculations Within a File

The REPLACE command allows you to overwrite the current contents of a field with a new value, which you may specify as an expression consisting of any combination of other fields, constants, memory variables, and functions. For example, the customer BALANCE may be calculated with

```
USE NWCUST
REPLACE ALL BALANCE WITH TOTINV - TOTPMT
```

Since the REPLACE command does not add new records to the file or change any index key fields, the Customer File was opened with no indexes. (If the file had already been opened with one or more indexes, you could have used SET ORDER TO 0 to view the file in sequential order.) Processing the file sequentially is somewhat faster, because with an index open dBASE III PLUS must read two files rather than one—the data base and the index. Further slowing the process, more disk access time will be required to retrieve each record, because records that are close together in indexed order may be physically far apart on the disk.

Accessing Multiple Files

dBASE III PLUS permits you to open up to ten data base files at one time, in ten separate *work areas* that may be referred to by number (1 through 10) or letter (A through J, effectively ruling out the use of these single letters as possible file names). You need not open your first file in area 1 (A), the second in area 2 (B), and so on. If you prefer to always associate each data base with a particular work area, you might in a given situation open three files in areas 2, 7, and 10, although in general there is little reason to do this.

You switch from one work area to another with the SELECT command. dBASE III PLUS maintains ten separate record pointers, so that when you SELECT one work area, the program "remembers" its place in all other open files, giving you simultaneous access to one record from each of up to ten data bases.

Once a work area contains an open data base, it may also be SELECTed by the file's *alias*. An alias is an alternate name for a data base that you assign in the USE command that opens the file:

```
SELECT 3
USE NWCUST INDEX NWCACCT, NWCZIP ALIAS CUSTOMER
```

When you do specify an alias, the file name (in this example, NWCUST) is assigned automatically. If you used the above commands to open the Customer File in work area 3, you could thereafter SELECT this file with any of these three commands:

```
SELECT 3
```

or

```
SELECT C
```

or

```
SELECT CUSTOMER
```

The alias is the most convenient of the three, since you—or another person reading your programs—do not need to remember which data base was placed in which work area. Fields in all files except the one in the current work area are referred to by a combination of file alias and field name—for example, CUSTOMER—>CONTACT for the CONTACT field in the NWCUST.DBF file that was opened with the alias CUSTOMER. This expression is usually pronounced "customer contact" or "customer file contact field."

Ten files may seem generous enough for most purposes, but there is a more meaningful limit: MS-DOS allows an application program to open only 15 disk files of any type at once. Disk files include data base files, indexes, programs, format files, report and label form files, procedure files, memory variable files, alternate files, and if a data base contains memo fields, the separate file used to store the memo text. Recall that if you have activated a CATALOG file with the SET CATALOG command, dBASE III PLUS opens the CATALOG data base in work area 10, and it too counts as an open file.

When you work with more than one data base, it is important to remember not only how to open files, but also how to close them properly. The USE command (with no data base name specified) closes only the file in the selected work area. CLOSE DATABASES closes all data bases in all work areas except the CATALOG file, if any, that is open in work area 10, and CLOSE ALL closes all data base and CATALOG files. Both CLOSE commands also select work area 1.

Linking Two Files With SET RELATION

Both at command level and in dBASE III PLUS programs, you can use the SET RELATION command to link two files based on a common key field or combination of fields. You can thus display or print data from both files together, use fields from both records in calculations, or transfer information between the matching records in the two files. The sample system will make extensive use of SET RELATION. For example, this command will link the Transaction File to the Customer File by the ACCOUNT field to print the full company name on the Invoice Register, and it will find in the Inventory File the PRICE to be entered into an Order File record based on a match on the CATEGORY and PARTNUMBER fields.

SET RELATION is most useful when each record in one file matches one and only one record in another. In order to find this unique record, you must index the second file on the field or fields that will be used to match up the two files. To link two data bases with SET RELATION, you must open each file in one of the ten work areas. The syntax for the command is

SET RELATION TO *common field(s)* INTO *file alias*

Once the RELATION is SET, any commands that move the record pointer in the first file also automatically position the second file to the matching record—or the first matching record if there is more than one. If there is no match, the record pointer will be positioned at the end-of-file, and all of the fields in this "record" will appear to be blank. *You may SET only one RELATION at a time from any given work area.* You can cancel the linkage between two files with

SET RELATION TO

or

SET RELATION

For example, for each record in the National Widgets Order File, there is one Inventory File record with the same CATEGORY and PARTNUMBER. In order to link these two files with SET RELATION, you must index the Inventory File by the common fields—CATEGORY + PARTNUMBER. We have already created this index, which is named NWICATPT.NDX, in Chapter 2. Both files must be open in any two of the ten dBASE III PLUS work areas, and the Order File must be selected:

```
SELECT 1
USE NWINVENT INDEX NWICATPT
SELECT 2
USE NWORDER
SET RELATION TO CATEGORY + PARTNUMBER INTO NWINVENT
```

Whenever the dBASE III PLUS record pointer moves in the NWORDER.DBF file, the NWINVENT.DBF file is automatically positioned to the record with the same combination of CATEGORY + PARTNUMBER. You can prove this with a LIST command that includes the common fields from both files:

```
SELECT NWORDER
LIST CATEGORY, PARTNUMBER, NWINVENT->CATEGORY, NWINVENT->PARTNUMBER
```

If SET RELATION still seems mysterious, recall that you can get the same results *for a single record* using the SEEK command, as illustrated in Figure 4-5. In this command sequence the Inventory File is opened in work area 1 and the Order File in work area 2. The Order File is then positioned to a record chosen at random—Record 5. Next, the Inventory File is selected and a SEEK command is used to find the record that matches the CATEGORY and PARTNUMBER from Record 5 in the Order File. (Recall that when you SELECT the Inventory File, the record pointer in the Order File does not move.) Once the data bases are positioned at matching records, as verified by the two DISPLAY commands, you can access any fields from the Inventory File when the Order File is selected (and vice versa).

For *each record you process* in the NWORDER file, SET RELATION causes dBASE III PLUS to do "behind the scenes" exactly what SEEK does. This is a tremendous advantage when working at the dot prompt because it

```
. SELECT 1
. USE NWINVENT INDEX NWICATPT
. SELECT 2
. USE NWORDER
. GOTO RECORD 5
. DISPLAY
      5  ELLISMFG    06981 DISK    101-65            1    0.00     0.00  0.00
0.00    0.00
. SELECT NWINVENT
. SEEK NWORDER->CATEGORY+NWORDER->PARTNUMBER
. DISPLAY
     15  DISK    101-65 5-1/4" DSDD Soft Sector           DISKUS        28.75
48.00
. SELECT NWORDER
. DISPLAY CATEGORY, PARTNUMBER, NWINVENT->PARTNUMBER, NWINVENT->DESCRIP,
NWINVENT->PRICE
      5  DISK    101-65 101-65 5-1/4" DSDD Soft Sector     48.00
```

Figure 4-5. The relationship between the Order and Inventory files

makes data from more than one data base accessible to commands, such as LIST, DISPLAY, REPORT, LABEL, and REPLACE, that process large groups of records or entire data bases.

We will make use of this relationship as we continue to initialize the National Widgets system data base files. The next step is to enter the line items from the 1986 invoices that were still open on January 1, 1987, into the Order File. If you are creating the National Widgets example yourself, you can use APPEND to enter the Order File data from the listing in Figure 4-6. Only the ACCOUNT, INVOICE, CATEGORY, PARTNUMBER, and QUANTITY must be entered. The SET RELATION command described previously enables the EQUIPMENT and PRICE fields to be filled in from the matching Inventory File records and the SUBTOTAL, DISCOUNT, and INVAMOUNT to be calculated.

The linkage between the Order and Inventory files allows the Inventory File data to be used for any purpose, not just for display. Thus, you can read the PRICE and EQUIPMENT fields into the Order File:

```
SELECT 1
USE NWINVENT INDEX NWICATPT
SELECT 2
USE NWORDER
SET RELATION TO CATEGORY + PARTNUMBER INTO NWINVENT
REPLACE ALL EQUIPMENT WITH NWINVENT->EQUIPMENT, PRICE WITH NWINVENT->PRICE
```

Note that once again, because we are not performing any calculations that affect the fields on which NWORDER is indexed (INVOICE and ACCOUNT), this file is opened without indexes for faster processing. If you open the data bases in a different order, or if one or more of the files are already open, be sure to SELECT the Order File before you type the REPLACE command.

If dBASE III PLUS fails to find a matching record in the Inventory File for a particular order, the EQUIPMENT and PRICE fields will be filled in with blanks. Since the sample Inventory File contains only 50 records, it should be no surprise to you when this happens, but it should serve as a reminder that *your own systems must provide some kind of test to apprise the operator when data that is essential to a file update procedure is missing*. The sample system also needs a way to change the PRICE field in individual orders if they differ for any reason (a special sale, perhaps) from the standard values read in from the Inventory File. If you are experimenting with the National Widgets Order File, you can use EDIT or BROWSE for this purpose.

The remaining calculations can be carried out completely within the Order File. The first time you try any new calculations, it is prudent to

```
. USE NWORDER INDEX NWOACCT, NWOINVC

. LIST

Record#  ACCOUNT    INVOICE CATEGORY PARTNUMBER EQUIPMENT QUANTITY  PRICE SUBTOTAL DISCRATE DISCOUNT INVAMOUNT
      1  ABCPLUMB   07302   DISK     101-45                      2   0.00     0.00     0.00     0.00      0.00
      2  ABCPLUMB   07302   FORMS    803-20                      1   0.00     0.00     0.00     0.00      0.00
      3  ABCPLUMB   07302   RIBBON   240-51                      2   0.00     0.00     0.00     0.00      0.00
      4  ELLISMFG   06981   FORMS    820-20                      1   0.00     0.00     0.00     0.00      0.00
      5  ELLISMFG   06981   DISK     101-65                      1   0.00     0.00     0.00     0.00      0.00
      6  ELLISMFG   06981   STOR     481-20                      1   0.00     0.00     0.00     0.00      0.00
      7  FLOORPLAN  07055   ACCESS   541-22                      1   0.00     0.00     0.00     0.00      0.00
      8  FLOORPLAN  07055   FORMS    803-32                      2   0.00     0.00     0.00     0.00      0.00
      9  FLOORPLAN  07055   DISK     101-63                      1   0.00     0.00     0.00     0.00      0.00
     10  FLOORPLAN  07055   COVER    540-13                      1   0.00     0.00     0.00     0.00      0.00
     11  GREENTHUMB 07418   ACCESS   533-12                      1   0.00     0.00     0.00     0.00      0.00
     12  GREENTHUMB 07418   FORMS    803-32                      2   0.00     0.00     0.00     0.00      0.00
     13  GREENTHUMB 07418   STOR     481-30                      1   0.00     0.00    10.00     0.00      0.00
     14  GREENTHUMB 07418   RIBBON   240-30                      3   0.00     0.00     0.00     0.00      0.00
     15  JENSEN     07401   DISK     101-45                      2   0.00     0.00    10.00     0.00      0.00
     16  JENSEN     07401   STOR     481-10                      2   0.00     0.00     0.00     0.00      0.00
     17  JOHNSON    07223   ACCESS   541-15                      1   0.00     0.00     0.00     0.00      0.00
     18  KLEIN      07538   FORMS    803-21                      1   0.00     0.00     0.00     0.00      0.00
     19  KLEIN      07538   PRTWHL   361-10                      1   0.00     0.00     0.00     0.00      0.00
     20  KLEIN      07538   PRTWHL   361-12                      1   0.00     0.00     0.00     0.00      0.00
     21  KLEIN      07538   RIBBON   270-51                      6   0.00     0.00    15.00     0.00      0.00
     22  YORKPUMP   07039   DISK     102-10                      2   0.00     0.00     0.00     0.00      0.00
```

Figure 4-6. The Order File

REPLACE one item at a time, with LIST commands in between to confirm that you have achieved the desired results:

```
REPLACE ALL SUBTOTAL WITH PRICE * QUANTITY
LIST ACCOUNT, INVOICE, PRICE, QUANTITY, SUBTOTAL
REPLACE ALL DISCOUNT WITH DISCRATE * SUBTOTAL / 100
LIST ACCOUNT, INVOICE, DISCRATE, SUBTOTAL, DISCOUNT
REPLACE ALL INVAMOUNT WITH SUBTOTAL - DISCOUNT
LIST ACCOUNT, INVOICE, SUBTOTAL, DISCOUNT, INVAMOUNT
```

If you are confident that there are no missing inventory items and that you will not need to adjust any prices, you may combine all of these steps into a single REPLACE command:

```
REPLACE ALL EQUIPMENT WITH NWINVENT->DESCRIP, PRICE WITH NWINVENT->PRICE,
  SUBTOTAL WITH PRICE * QUANTITY, DISCOUNT WITH DISCRATE * SUBTOTAL / 100,
  INVAMOUNT WITH SUBTOTAL - DISCOUNT
```

This command works because the individual calculations are carried out in the order they are listed, so that by the time the SUBTOTAL field is required to compute the DISCOUNT, it has already been calculated from the QUANTITY and the PRICE, which has already been read in from the Inventory File.

Creating Summary Files With TOTAL

The TOTAL command may be used to summarize data in one file into totals that are written into another data base. This command works much like printing a report with one level of subtotals, using the "summary-only" option to suppress the individual records and print only the subtotals and grand totals. The difference is that instead of printing the subtotals on paper, TOTAL *creates a new data base with the same structure as the original,* and each subtotal line becomes a record in this file. Just as if you were printing a report, the data base that generates the subtotals must be indexed or sorted on the field(s) that determine where the subtotal breaks occur, so that each set of records to be subtotaled is read together in a group.

In the National Widgets system, the TOTAL command will be used to summarize the Order File data by invoice number to create Transaction File records. Because TOTAL cannot add records to an existing file, the TOTAL command will write its output to a temporary data base. This file will simply be appended to the Transaction File and then thrown away; so it is given a name, NWORDTMP.DBF, which emphasizes the temporary nature of its existence. Since APPEND matches up fields in the two files by name, the fields that must be transferred—in this case, ACCOUNT, INVOICE, SUBTOTAL, and DISCOUNT—have been given the same names in both NWORDER.DBF and NWTXN.DBF. This is the command sequence:

```
USE NWORDER INDEX NWOINVC
TOTAL ON INVOICE TO NWORDTMP
USE NWTXN INDEX NWTACCT, NWTINVC
APPEND FROM NWORDTMP
DELETE FILE NWORDTMP.DBF
```

Although it only makes sense to total numeric fields, the TOTAL command processes every field in the structure, replacing character and date fields in the summary file with their counterparts in the original data base. The temporary file, NWORDTMP.DBF, generated by the TOTAL command, is listed in Figure 4-7. If you examine this file, you will see that the data in the character and date fields came from the first record in each subtotal group in NWORDER.DBF. Later, you can use MODIFY STRUCTURE to delete the unwanted fields from the summary file or APPEND the file to another data base with the desired structure, as we have done.

For this first batch of orders, which came from 1986, the order line item detail has now served its purpose—to generate the open invoice transactions carried forward into 1987—and the Order File may be emptied with the ZAP command to prepare for the entry of 1987 orders:

```
USE NWORDER INDEX NWOACCT, NOWINVC
ZAP
```

The ZAP command is equivalent to

```
DELETE ALL
PACK
```

ZAP was used instead because it executes much faster. This command can empty a large file in a matter of seconds, because it does *not* DELETE all of the records one after the other and then PACK and REINDEX the file. Instead, the internal record count is reset to 0, and the file (now considered empty by dBASE III PLUS) is reindexed.

For all subsequent batches of orders, the Order File must not be emptied out until invoices have been printed and the records in the current

```
. USE NWORDTMP

. LIST

Record#  ACCOUNT    INVOICE CATEGORY PARTNUMBER EQUIPMENT QUANTITY  PRICE SUBTOTAL DISCRATE DISCOUNT INVAMOUNT
      1  ABCPLUMB   Ø73Ø2   DISK     1Ø1-45                     5   91.7Ø   138.15     Ø.ØØ     Ø.ØØ    138.15
      2  ELLISMFG   Ø6981   FORMS    82Ø-2Ø                     3   89.9Ø    89.9Ø     Ø.ØØ     Ø.ØØ     89.9Ø
      3  FLOORPLAN  Ø7Ø55   ACCESS   541-22                     5  147.95   185.45     Ø.ØØ     Ø.ØØ    185.45
      4  GREENTHUMB Ø7418   ACCESS   533-12                     7  126.65   172.65    1Ø.ØØ     4.5Ø    168.15
      5  JENSEN     Ø74Ø1   DISK     1Ø1-45                     4   34.35    68.7Ø    1Ø.ØØ     6.3Ø     62.4Ø
      6  JOHNSON    Ø7223   ACCESS   541-15                     1   92.5Ø    92.5Ø     Ø.ØØ     Ø.ØØ     92.5Ø
      7  KLEIN      Ø7538   FORMS    8Ø3-21                     9   67.25   1Ø3.5Ø    15.ØØ     6.53     96.97
      8  YORKPUMP   Ø7Ø39   DISK     1Ø2-1Ø                     2   62.ØØ   124.ØØ     Ø.ØØ     Ø.ØØ    124.ØØ
```

Figure 4-7. The totaled orders

Order File have been appended to the Order History File. We will use this command sequence in the National Widgets system to generate invoice entries in the Transaction File and update the Order History File for all orders entered in 1987:

```
USE NWORDER INDEX NWOINVC
TOTAL ON INVOICE TO NWORDTMP
USE NWTXN INDEX NWTACCT, NWTINVC
APPEND FROM NWORDTMP
DELETE FILE NWORDTMP.DBF
USE NWORDHST INDEX NWOHACCT, NWOHINVC
APPEND FROM NWORDER
USE NWORDER INDEX NWOACCT, NWOINVC
ZAP
```

The invoice printing step, which cannot be carried out without programming, was omitted from this command sequence. If you are creating the case study system, you can test these commands with some sample Order File data of your own invention. These file update procedures complete the command level simulation of Section C, Item 1 (Update order information) and Section C, Item 6 (Update Order History File) from the system outline.

While the Transaction File records are initially created by the TOTAL command, the operator must fill in all the fields that are not derived from the Order File (INVDATE, TAXRATE, and SHIPPING) before the system can calculate TAX and INVAMOUNT with a REPLACE command. One way to find the new records into which data must be entered manually is to use a LOCATE command to search for the first record with a blank invoice date:

```
LOCATE FOR INVDATE = CTOD("        ")
```

If the Transaction File is large, there is a faster way to find the first new record than LOCATE, which begins at the top of the file and checks every record. You can determine how many records are created by the TOTAL command by reviewing the status message displayed as the command runs or by looking at the number of records in the resulting summary file. For example, the Order File might contain 45 records after entry of a typical batch of orders, and the TOTAL command might display the following:

```
45 Record(s) totaled
12 records generated
```

To find these 12 new entries in the Transaction File after APPENDing the contents of NWORDTMP.DBF, you could open the Transaction File, use GOTO BOTTOM to position the record pointer to the last record, and then SKIP −12 to arrive at the first newly appended record. Note the record number—suppose, for example, it is Record 121—because you will need it again shortly.

After filling in the INVDATE, TAXRATE, and SHIPPING fields, you can perform the remaining calculations for the new records only:

```
GOTO RECORD 121
REPLACE REST TAX WITH (SUBTOTAL - DISCOUNT) * TAX / 100, INVAMOUNT WITH
  SUBTOTAL - DISCOUNT + TAX + SHIPPING
```

The scope, REST, specifies that the REPLACE command should begin at the current position of the record pointer—the first "new" Transaction record—and process the rest of the records to the end of the file.

In the sample system, prepaid orders may be handled by entering the payment into the invoice record at the same time as the INVDATE, TAXRATE, and SHIPPING fields. For later payments you can use the index that accesses the Transaction File by invoice number, NWTINVC.NDX, to FIND or SEEK any record by invoice number, and then use the EDIT command to enter the payment fields. For example:

```
FIND 02158
EDIT
```

If the fields to be filled in are at the end of the structure, as they are in the sample Transaction File, you will have to skip through the preceding fields with RETURN or DOWN ARROW to reach the items of interest. You could instead use the CHANGE command, which allows you to name the specific fields to be edited and the order in which they are displayed on the screen:

```
CHANGE FIELDS PMTDATE, PMTAMOUNT, REFERENCE, ACCOUNT, INVDATE, INVOICE
```

In this command, the ACCOUNT, INVDATE, and INVOICE fields are included for reference, to confirm that you are updating the right record. If you prefer to view more than one record at a time, you can use BROWSE, which also allows you to update selected fields:

```
BROWSE FIELDS PMTDATE, PMTAMOUNT, REFERENCE, ACCOUNT, INVDATE, INVOICE
```

If the Transaction File is too large to find the record you want by paging through the records, you may SEEK a particular record without exiting from the BROWSE screen. To invoke this or the other special BROWSE options, press CTRL-HOME. You may select SEEK, and dBASE III PLUS will prompt you to enter the index key and then carry out the search.

You can avoid having to retype the field list repeatedly by using the SET FIELDS command to restrict the fields that are displayed and accessed by EDIT, BROWSE, LIST, and many other commands. The syntax of the command is

SET FIELDS TO *field list*

Successive SET FIELDS commands add fields to the list. You can return to displaying all fields with SET FIELDS TO ALL, or you can temporarily cancel the field list with SET FIELDS OFF and then place the list back in effect with SET FIELDS ON. You could thus use the following command to access only the desired fields from the Transaction File to add payment data:

```
SET FIELDS TO PMTDATE, PMTAMOUNT, REFERENCE, ACCOUNT, INVDATE, INVOICE
```

Although the field names in this command were typed in the same order as in the preceding CHANGE and BROWSE examples, you cannot use SET FIELDS to change the order in which the fields are presented for display or editing—the fields are always displayed by dBASE III PLUS in the same order as in the file structure.

With these command level procedures, we have satisfied the requirements of Section C, Item 1 (Update invoice and payment information) in the National Widgets system outline.

Transferring Data Between Files With UPDATE

The UPDATE command allows you to change the values of fields in one file based on data contained in another. The file to be updated and the file that will provide the data must be open in two different work areas, with the file to be updated in the selected work area. The two files must share a common field. The most efficient way to use this command is to index the file to be updated on the common field and read the file that provides the data in sequential order. To do this, you use the RANDOM keyword to tell dBASE III PLUS that this file is in random order with respect to the common field. For each record in this file, dBASE III PLUS uses an internal SEEK to find the matching record in the file to be updated, just as it does when you use SET RELATION to link two files.

The general format for the UPDATE command is

UPDATE ON *common field* FROM *file* RANDOM REPLACE *field* WITH *expression*

You may REPLACE more than one field with a single UPDATE command, subject only to the limitation that the command line may not exceed the 254-character maximum length.

UPDATE will be used in the National Widgets sample system to post invoice and payment data from the Transaction File to the Customer File year-to-date and total fields. The file to be updated—the Customer File—and the file that will provide the data—the Transaction File—are matched up by the contents of the ACCOUNT field. Because there is no way to make the UPDATE command process only some of the records in the Transaction File, the "new" (previously unposted) records must be copied to a temporary file, which will be used for the UPDATE. The logical field INVPOSTED can be used to identify these unposted transactions:

```
USE NWTXN
COPY TO NWTEMP FOR .NOT. INVPOSTED
```

Or, if you were sure that only the latest batch of new Transaction File entries remained unposted, you could use a GOTO command to locate the first new record, as in the command sequence that calculated the TAX and INVAMOUNT fields:

```
USE NWTXN
GOTO RECORD 121
COPY REST TO NWTEMP
```

The rest of the UPDATE sequence is written as follows:

```
SELECT 1
USE NWTEMP
SELECT 2
USE NWCUST INDEX NWCACCT
UPDATE ON ACCOUNT FROM NWTEMP RANDOM REPLACE LASTORDER WITH NWTEMP->INVDATE,
  YTDINV WITH YTDINV + NWTEMP->INVAMOUNT, TOTINV WITH TOTINV +
  NWTEMP->INVAMOUNT, BALANCE WITH BALANCE + NWTEMP->INVAMOUNT
```

This command updates the file in the current work area (the Customer File) with information from NWTEMP.DBF, based on a match on the ACCOUNT field. The contents of the LASTORDER date field are replaced by the invoice date field, INVDATE, from the Transaction File; the invoice amount field from the Transaction File, INVAMOUNT, is added into the current contents of the Customer File year-to-date invoices, total invoices, and balance.

Finally, the INVPOSTED field in the Transaction File must be changed to .T. (true) so that there is no chance of posting the same batch of transactions twice:

```
USE NWTXN
REPLACE ALL INVPOSTED WITH .T.
```

Again, if you can identify the new records, you can speed up this process:

```
USE NWTXN
GOTO RECORD 121
REPLACE REST INVPOSTED WITH .T.
```

Payments can be posted by using a similar sequence of commands. Note that payment entries, unlike the new invoice records, will be scattered throughout the Transaction File, not grouped together at the end. Testing the contents of the PMTPOSTED field is the only way to identify the payments to be posted:

```
SELECT 1
USE NWTXN
COPY TO NWTEMP FOR .NOT. PMTPOSTED
USE NWTEMP
SELECT 2
USE NWCUST INDEX NWCACCT
UPDATE ON ACCOUNT FROM NWTEMP RANDOM REPLACE YTDPMT WITH YTDPMT +
  NWTEMP->PMTAMOUNT, TOTPMT WITH TOTPMT + NWTEMP->PMTAMOUNT,
  BALANCE WITH BALANCE - NWTEMP->PMTAMOUNT
```

These file update operations correspond to Section B, Item 5 (Post invoice information to Customer File) and Section C, Item 1 (Update invoice and payment information) of the system outline.

Notice that UPDATE is useful in a different context from that of the REPLACE command described in the previous section. When each record in the file to be updated has one and only one match in another data base, the two files may be linked with SET RELATION and data transferred by means of the REPLACE command, since the RELATION ensures that the file providing the data is always positioned to the unique matching record.

UPDATE, on the other hand, is used when each record in the file to be updated may have any number of matching records in the file that will provide the data.

Accessing Three Files

By combining the techniques described in the preceding sections, you can work with more than two files at a time. However, a bit more strategic planning may be required to establish the relationships among the data bases. Because you may SET only one RELATION from a given work area, matching up the files may not be as automatic or straightforward as you might hope. Also, when there is more than one record in one file that corresponds to each record in another, your procedures should be designed to find these records in the most efficient way possible, as well as guaranteeing that you do not overlook any in the set of matching records.

These concepts are applied in printing customer invoices and statements in the National Widgets sample system. Printed formats are discussed in detail in Chapter 5, but it is clear at the outset that these two important documents require programming. The dBASE III PLUS report generator was designed to print columnar reports, not full-page formats. Although you can print data from two files together on a report, you cannot print formats like statements, which require laying out fields from one file (the Customer File) across the top half of the page, followed by a set of detail records from the other file (the individual invoices in the Transaction File). At command level you may have to settle for verifying that these files can be opened together and the required fields made available to the program you will eventually write.

For printing National Widgets' statements, the overall strategy will be to read through the Customer File and, for each customer, find the matching records in the Transaction File. (*Note:* The problem could also be approached from the opposite direction: read through the Transaction File and, for each customer's set of transactions, find the matching customer record.) SET RELATION may be used to link the Customer and Transaction files, but each customer record may have more than one matching entry in the Transaction File, and SET RELATION will automatically find only the first transaction record for each customer. We will then use LIST WHILE to display *all* of the customer's transactions. Figure 4-8 illustrates this dialog for one customer.

```
. SELECT 1
. USE NWCUST INDEX NWCACCT
. SELECT 2
. USE NWTXN INDEX NWTACCT
. SELECT NWCUST
. SET RELATION TO ACCOUNT INTO NWTXN
. FIND ABCPLUMB
. DISPLAY
      2  ABCPLUMB   ABC Plumbing                    1850 University Avenue
Berkeley             CA 94703 415 861-4543 Ed Williams             Kaypro 10,
Epson FX-100         12/02/85 12/11/86        0.00        0.00      796.41
796.41       0.00 Memo
. SELECT NWTXN
. LIST WHILE ACCOUNT = NWCUST->ACCOUNT
      1  ABCPLUMB   03/12/87 07302  138.15      0.00                      138.15
/ /                          .F. .F.
```

Figure 4-8. Displaying the Monthly Statement data

There is an important difference between specifying a condition with WHILE and using the same condition in a FOR clause. By itself, a FOR clause causes dBASE III PLUS to begin at the top of the file (or index) and read all the way through to the end, checking every record against the condition and processing only those passing the test. WHILE causes dBASE III PLUS to begin processing at the current position of the record pointer and to cease immediately when a record that does not satisfy the condition is found. If both a FOR and a WHILE clause are used in the same command, processing begins with the current record and stops when the condition in the WHILE clause is no longer true; within this group of records, only those satisfying the condition in the FOR clause are actually acted upon. In the example in Figure 4-8, the WHILE clause in the LIST command is the most efficient way to process only the desired transactions.

Printing invoices is a little more complicated. The most logical strategy would be to read through the Transaction File in sequence and, for each invoice transaction, find the one matching customer record and the set of matching order records. However, only one RELATION may be SET at once from the Transaction File work area. This command will be used in its area of greatest strength—to link the Transaction and Customer files—so that for each transaction the system automatically finds the single matching customer record. The Order File records that correspond to each Transaction File entry will be found with an explicit SEEK command. This strategy is illustrated for a single Transaction File record—that is, one invoice—in Figure 4-9.

Reorganizing Data Base Files

As demonstrated in the procedures in the preceding sections, two data base files may be combined by APPENDing records from one file into another. These examples illustrated one typical use of APPEND—to transfer records from a temporary file, which in the sample system was created by a TOTAL command—into the main working data base. APPEND is also commonly used to transfer records that are no longer accessed frequently from a current file into a historical or archive file; this speeds up processing in the current file while retaining the data for reporting purposes.

Frequently, when all or part of one file is APPENDed to another, the same set of records must then be deleted from the first file so that information is not duplicated in the two data bases. On other occasions an entire file must be emptied out and reinitialized—without first storing the records in another file—to prepare for a new set of entries. The DELETE command may be used to delete all or some of the records in a data base, and as we have seen, ZAP provides a very fast way to purge and reinitialize a file.

Both APPEND and DELETE permit the addition of a FOR clause that enables you to add or purge records selectively. In the DELETE command, which operates on only one data base, the condition in the FOR clause may be any legitimate logical expression, such as you might use in a LIST command. With APPEND, you may only use fields that are common to both files in the FOR clause. This is because dBASE III PLUS carries out the APPEND command by first adding each record to the new file; any fields not present in this file are lost in the process. The record is then tested to see if it satisfies the condition specified in the FOR clause; if not, it is overwritten by the next record APPENDed.

In the National Widgets sample system and in most accounting applications, these operations will form the heart of the end-of-period processing procedures. The sample application requires special processing at the end of each month and each year, as well as procedures that may be run on demand at any point during the year. In your own data bases, you may find similar operations that must be run weekly, quarterly, every fiscal period, every six months, or at intervals unique to your organization.

In the sample system the invoices that have been fully paid will be deleted from the Transaction File and transferred to the Transaction History File at the end of each month. Partial payments present a potential problem in this system: a payment can be posted only once, because the INVPOSTED field is set to .T. immediately after posting. If a second payment must be added into the amount already entered into a Transaction File record, the YTDPMT, TOTPMT, and BALANCE fields in the Customer File must be adjusted manually. Because the dollar amounts are low and National Widgets generally discourages partial payments, this is not a very serious problem. However, you must be careful that the end-of-month processing sequence removes a transaction from the current file only if it is completely paid *and* both the invoice and payment data have been posted. The paid and posted transactions will first be APPENDed to the Transaction History File and then DELETEd from the

```
. SELECT 1
. USE NWCUST INDEX NWCACCT
. SELECT 2
. USE NWTXN INDEX NWTINVC
. SET RELATION TO ACCOUNT INTO NWCUST
. SELECT 3
. USE NWORDER INDEX NWOINVC
. SELECT NWTXN
. DISPLAY
      1  ABCPLUMB    03/12/87 07302  138.15     0.00                         138.15
/ /                           .F.  .F.
. SELECT NWCUST
. DISPLAY
      2  ABCPLUMB    ABC Plumbing                      1850 University Avenue
Berkeley             CA 94703 415 861-4543 Ed Williams                  Kaypro 10,
Epson FX-100         12/02/85 12/11/86       0.00         0.00      796.41
796.41         0.00 Memo
. SELECT NWORDER
. SEEK NWTXN->INVOICE
. LIST WHILE INVOICE = NWTXN->INVOICE
      1  ABCPLUMB    07302 DISK    101-45            2     0.00      0.00  0.00
0.00     0.00
      2  ABCPLUMB    07302 FORMS   803-20            1     0.00      0.00  0.00
0.00     0.00
      3  ABCPLUMB    07302 RIBBON 240-51             2     0.00      0.00  0.00
0.00     0.00
```

Figure 4-9. Displaying the invoice data

current Transaction File:

```
USE NWTXNHST INDEX NWTHACCT, NWTHINVC
APPEND FROM NWTXN FOR INVAMOUNT = PMTAMOUNT .AND. INVPOSTED .AND. PMTPOSTED
USE NWTXN
DELETE FOR INVAMOUNT = PMTAMOUNT .AND. INVPOSTED .AND. PMTPOSTED
```

At the end of the year, the Transaction and Order History files must be emptied and the year-to-date fields in the Customer File reset to zero. As described previously, the fastest way to delete all of the records in a file is to use ZAP. Before you ZAP the history files, make an archival backup on floppy disks of the two DBF files. There is no need to preserve the indexes; they can always be recreated from the data base files if necessary. The following steps perform end-of-year processing for the National Widgets system:

```
USE NWTXNHST INDEX NWTHACCT, NWTHINVC
ZAP
USE NWORDHST INDEX NWOHACCT, NWOHINVC
ZAP
USE NWCUST
REPLACE ALL YTDINV WITH 0, YTDPMT WITH 0
```

The end-of-month and end-of-year processing sequences correspond to Section C, Item 9 (Update Transaction History File); Section B, Item 7 (Purge and reinitialize Order History File); Section C, Item 10 (Purge and reinitialize Transaction History File); and Section A, Item 3 (Zero customer year-to-date totals) in the system outline.

Deleting customers who have had no activity in the past year—Section B, Item 3 (Archive and delete inactive customers) in the system outline may also be included in the end-of-year processing sequence, although this step should be made flexible enough to run at any time, using any cutoff date. If you are familiar with the use of the dBASE III PLUS date functions and date comparisons, you might try setting up this procedure yourself; the final version will appear in Chapter 12.

This chapter modeled at command level all of the data entry, editing, and update procedures in the National Widgets sample system. In the most important part of this testing we established the relationships among the data bases and defined the ways in which these files are used together. Although most of the operations detailed in this chapter will undergo a substantial metamorphosis to reach their final form in the completed system, the work we have done here provides the foundation for all of the data input and processing functions in the system. Chapter 5 applies the same methodology to producing the system's printed output.

5

PRINTING LABELS AND REPORTS AT COMMAND LEVEL

You have probably used the dBASE III PLUS built-in report writer to print columnar reports with one line of data per record, perhaps with calculated columns and one or two levels of column subtotals as well as grand totals. A variety of mailing label formats can also be produced by dBASE III PLUS without special programming. In this chapter we will employ some of the less obvious capabilities of the report generator to produce attractively formatted reports and demonstrate the most efficient ways to control report selection criteria. Detailed discussions of several of the printed formats from the sample application will illustrate the general principles. These techniques adequately perform many of the mailing and reporting functions in the National Widgets sample system. If you are creating this system as a case study, you may want to test your understanding of the concepts presented in this chapter by setting up some of the remaining reports enumerated in the system outline in Figure 1-6.

USING THE LABEL GENERATOR

The hardest step in designing a label format is to measure the label stock carefully so that the fields are printed in the right places. Using the menu-driven CREATE LABEL command is a simple matter of filling out two screens of information accessed through pull-down menus: the "Options" screen, which describes the label dimensions and layout, and the "Contents" screen, which allows you to specify the data to be printed on each line of the label. You may choose one of five standard label layouts on the Options screen by pressing RETURN with the "Predefined size" option selected. If necessary, you can then change the width, height, left margin, lines between labels, number of labels across, and spaces between labels to match your own requirements.

For the National Widget one-up labels, the 3 1/2 × 15/16 × 1 predefined format will work with only one change—the left margin must be reset to five spaces to make it easier to line up the labels in the printer. These are the layout options:

Predefined size	3 1/2 × 15/16 × 1
Label width	35
Label height	5
Left margin	5
Lines between labels	1
Spaces between labels	0
Labels across page	1

The contents of the first three lines of the label are very straightforward—the CONTACT, COMPANY, and ADDRESS fields will be printed on these lines. On the fourth line, the CITY, STATE, and ZIP fields are combined by using the expression TRIM(CITY) + ", " + STATE + " " + ZIP so that they print in the standard format with no extra spaces between them. (See Chapter 9 and Appendix C for more details on TRIM and other dBASE III PLUS functions.) Figure 5-1 illustrates the one-up labels printed from the National Widgets Customer File.

There is no predefined format for printing four-up labels, but you can begin with any of the five standard layouts and modify the options to match the National Widgets label forms:

Label width	30
Label height	5
Left margin	5
Lines between labels	1
Spaces between labels	3
Labels across page	4

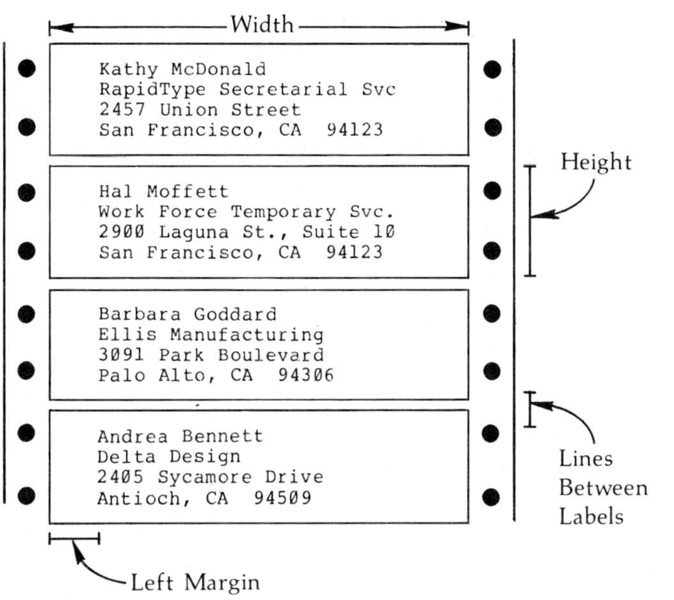

Figure 5-1. One-up mailing labels

The contents options are exactly the same as in the one-up label format. The dBASE III PLUS label printer is able to suppress empty lines if one of the fields is blank, even if you are printing labels four across, which offers a distinct advantage over the mail-merge modules of many word processors. Figure 5-2 illustrates the National Widgets four-up mailing labels.

When you print labels or reports, the order in which the records are printed may be controlled by sorting or, more commonly, by indexing the file. Selection criteria may be specified by including a scope, a FOR clause, a WHILE clause, or any reasonable combination of these three in your LABEL or REPORT command. In the National Widgets sample system, the Customer File is opened with the ZIP index in order to print labels in ZIP code order. To print one-up labels for all customers whose overall total orders exceed $500, you could use

```
USE NWCUST INDEX NWCZIP
LABEL FORM NWCUST1 TO PRINT FOR TOTINV > 500
```

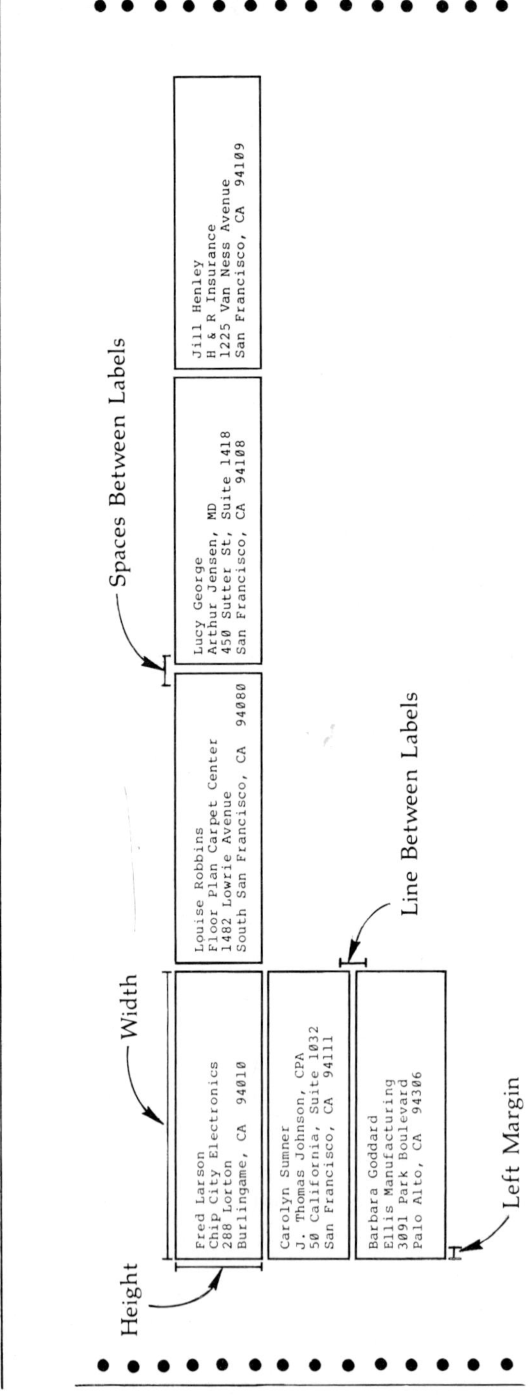

Figure 5-2. Four-up mailing labels

National Widgets routinely sends selective mailings to customers who own certain types of equipment. Since more than one item may have been entered into the EQUIPMENT field, you cannot use a condition like EQUIPMENT = "IBM" in the FOR clause. When dBASE III PLUS compares two character strings, it begins the comparison at the left and examines both strings up to the length of the shorter. Thus, if the EQUIPMENT field contains the text "Apple IIe, IBM PC", the condition EQUIPMENT = "Apple" will be true, but EQUIPMENT = "IBM" will not. You can, however, test for the occurrence of one character string anywhere within another by using the $ (*substring*) operator. The $ is often pronounced "is a substring of" or, more colloquially, "is contained in." Thus, you could print labels for all customers who own an IBM computer and have more than $500 in total orders with

```
USE NWCUST INDEX NWCZIP
LABEL FORM NWCUST1 TO PRINT FOR "IBM" $ EQUIPMENT .AND. TOTINV > 500
```

Using a FOR clause to specify selection criteria allows you the flexibility to write conditions that test any field or combination of fields in the record, but it does not always result in the fastest processing. This is because adding a condition to a command does not narrow the scope of the records processed by dBASE III PLUS. In the LABEL command just described, the test in the FOR clause is applied to each and every record in the data base, and only the ones that pass are printed. Even if no records satisfy the condition, "printing" the labels will occupy as much time as dBASE III PLUS requires to read through the entire file in indexed order.

If your selection criteria are based on the index key field, you can process the file much more quickly, which can be advantageous in many situations. For example, when you print mailing labels in ZIP code order, you will frequently find that you need to select by ZIP. You might want to target a particular geographical area by specifying a range of ZIP codes to be included in a mailing. In the event that the printer jams in the middle of a long label run, you would want to be able to restart the job where it was interrupted instead of having to reprint the whole set of labels.

In the first example from the sample system, mailing labels were printed for customers with more than $500 in total orders. In order to continue printing these labels after a printer jam, you can take advantage of the fact that the Customer File is indexed by ZIP and use FIND to position the record pointer at the first record you want to print (or at least close to this record if the ZIP codes are not unique):

```
USE NWCUST INDEX NWCZIP
FIND 94101
```

If you then included the condition FOR TOTINV > 500 in the LABEL command, the use of the FOR clause would cause dBASE III PLUS to begin processing at the top of the index, thus nullifying the effect of the FIND command. You can, however, use the REST scope (as we did in the file update procedures in Chapter 4) to process records selectively, beginning with the current position of the record pointer:

```
LABEL FORM NWCUST1 TO PRINT REST FOR TOTINV > 500
```

It may seem at first that the scope and FOR clauses are contradictory, but you can use them together. The scope, REST, takes precedence and determines the range of records that will be processed by dBASE III PLUS. Of those records, only the ones matching the condition in the FOR clause will actually be printed.

USING THE REPORT GENERATOR

Many of the reports in the National Widgets system may be printed without programming, by using the dBASE III PLUS report generator. The page formats for the Transaction Reference List, Invoice Register, Aging report, and Cash Receipts Listing are all very straightforward; they require just one printed line per record, with column totals for the numeric fields. If you are following this case study as a tutorial, you might try creating these report forms to review the use of the report generator. Assuming that the relevant FRM files exist, these reports may be used to illustrate a few more niceties regarding indexing, selection criteria, and performing calculations within a report.

Just as we began printing labels with a particular ZIP code, you might want to start the Invoice Register with a specific invoice number by opening the Transaction File (or Transaction History File) with the invoice number index, FINDing the beginning invoice number, and specifying the REST scope to encompass the rest of the file:

```
USE NWTXNHST INDEX NWTHINVC
FIND 07000
REPORT FORM NWINVREG TO PRINT REST
```

The addition of a simple FOR clause allows you to select only open invoices:

```
REPORT FORM NWINVREG TO PRINT REST FOR INVAMOUNT - PMTAMOUNT > 0
```

For the Aging report you can use the date arithmetic capabilities of dBASE III PLUS to calculate the age of an invoice in days by subtracting the invoice date from the current date. Recall that when you load dBASE III PLUS, the program obtains the current date—the date you entered when you booted the operating system—from DOS. This date is available to you in the form of the "current date" function, DATE( ). The contents of the age column in your report could therefore be specified as DATE( ) − INVDATE, which would yield the number of days that have elapsed since the invoice date.

You might want to use a date other than the current date as the basis for the aging if, for example, you printed the report on April 5 but wished to list the customers' status as of March 31. To do this, you could create a memory variable, which we'll call MAGEDATE, containing the aging date, and specify this variable instead of DATE( ) in the report column, which would be entered as MAGEDATE − INVDATE. To print the report, you would use

```
USE NWTXN INDEX NWTINVC
STORE CTOD("03/31/87") TO MAGEDATE
REPORT FORM NWAGING TO PRINT FOR INVAMOUNT - PMTAMOUNT > 0
```

You can also use date comparisons to print the Cash Receipts Listing for one day in order to replace or compare it to handwritten bank deposit slips:

```
USE NWTXN INDEX NWTINVC
REPORT FORM NWCASH TO PRINT FOR PMTDATE = CTOD("03/29/87")
```

For a range of dates you could use

```
REPORT FORM NWCASH TO PRINT FOR PMTDATE >= CTOD("03/01/87") .AND.
  PMTDATE <= CTOD("03/31/87")
```

For a report that is printed infrequently, you may choose *not* to maintain the index on a daily basis. Although dBASE III PLUS allows you to open as many as seven indexes with a data base, APPENDing and EDITing records will slow down somewhat in a large file with many indexes open. If a report is printed only two or three times a year, with an index that has no other use in the system, you can simply rebuild the index from scratch immediately before printing the report. For example, the National Widgets System Order Summary by inventory category and part number may be produced by a simple dBASE III PLUS report with two levels of subtotals. To print subtotals by CATEGORY and within CATEGORY, by

PARTNUMBER, the Order History File must be indexed by CATEGORY + PARTNUMBER, but this index is used solely for the purpose of printing this report. The Order Summary might also be a good candidate for the "summary only" option, which will not print every detail order record, but only the subtotals (by CATEGORY) and sub-subtotals (by PARTNUMBER).

The report generator was designed to produce this type of report, as the examples in the dBASE III PLUS manual illustrate, but you can also use the report generator to print more than one line of data per record or to print fields from two files at a time.

To print more than one line of data per record, specify a column width narrower than the contents of the column, and the data will wrap around onto a second line. Because dBASE III PLUS will not break a word in the middle, you can fit long character fields or memo fields into a report column of any width. You can also use this "word wrap" feature to print several separate fields in one column by combining them into a single expression. There are two methods of ensuring that the line breaks occur in the right places.

If the expressions to be printed on each line of a given column are fixed in length, you can simply concatenate them, with enough extra blank spaces added to each component to fill the report column completely. For example, to print the contact name, telephone number, and equipment fields in one column on the National Widgets Customer Reference List, you can specify the column width as 25 spaces (the width of the CONTACT and EQUIPMENT fields) and add enough blank spaces to the phone number to make it fill the column:

```
CONTACT + "(" + AREACODE + ") " + TELEPHONE + "           " + EQUIPMENT
```

If you revise your report and adjust the column width, you will have the minor inconvenience of adding or deleting spaces from these expressions. In other cases, you will be printing variable length text, such as TRIM(CITY) + "," + STATE + " " + ZIP in an address column. The most straightforward solution to both of these problems is to add semicolons (;) to the column contents expressions. When dBASE III PLUS encounters a semicolon, it breaks the line immediately. This technique was used in the Customer Reference List illustrated in Figure 5-3. The contents of the CONTACT, TELEPHONE, and EQUIPMENT column would be specified as

```
CONTACT + ";(" + AREACODE + ") " + TELEPHONE + ";" + EQUIPMENT
```

Note that the semicolon need not be a separate part of the expression—it may occur anywhere within a character string. The ADDRESS column is printed with

```
COMPANY + ";" + ADDRESS + ";" + TRIM(CITY) + ", " + STATE + "   " + ZIP
```

No matter which of these two methods you use, you can print additional fields on the same report lines without disrupting the alignment of the columns, and dBASE III PLUS will properly count the split lines so that your reports are paginated correctly. The only problem is that dBASE III PLUS will assign a default column width equal to the combined length of the fields, not only when you first CREATE the report, but also if you use MODIFY REPORT to alter the column contents. Each time you make a minor change, you will have to remember to reset the column width.

Remember that only character fields may be concatenated in this way. If your expressions contain date or numeric fields, they must be converted to characters by using the DTOC (date-to-character) or STR (numeric-to-string) conversion functions. The dates on the Customer Reference List were printed with the expression

```
"FIRST: " + DTOC(FIRSTORDER) + ";LAST:  " + DTOC(LASTORDER)
```

The year-to-date and total columns could be specified as

```
"INV: " + STR(YTDINV,10,2) + ";PMT: " + STR(YTDPMT,10,2)
```

and

```
"INV: " + STR(TOTINV,10,2) + ";PMT: " + STR(TOTPMT,10,2) +
  ";      ----------;BAL: " + STR(TOTINV - TOTPMT,10,2)
```

You could also print the numeric fields with the TRANSFORM function, which enables you to use any valid PICTURE to control the display format precisely. (PICTUREs, most commonly used in format files and programs to format and validate data, are discussed in more detail in Chapter 8.) The following expression prints the total column with commas inserted in the numbers, and with the balance enclosed in parentheses if it is negative:

```
"INV: " + TRANSFORM(TOTINV,"9,999,999.99") + ";PMT: " +
  TRANSFORM(TOTPMT,"9,999,999.99") + ";      ----------;BAL: " +
  TRANSFORM(TOTINV - TOTPMT,"@( 9,999,999.99")
```

```
Page No.      1
03/16/86
                                        NATIONAL WIDGETS, INC.
                                       CUSTOMER REFERENCE LIST

ACCOUNT ID  ADDRESS                         CONTACT / PHONE / EQUIP      ORDER DATES       YEAR-TO-DATE        TOTAL
----------  ----------------------------    -------------------------    ---------------   -----------------   -----------------

ABCPLUMB    ABC Plumbing                    Ed Williams                  FIRST: 12/02/85   INV:       151.33   INV:       947.74
            1850 University Avenue          (415) 861-4543               LAST:  03/12/87   PMT:         0.00   PMT:       796.41
            Berkeley, CA  94703             Kaypro 10, Epson FX-100                                                 ------------
                                                                                                               BAL:       151.33

ANDERSON                                    John Anderson                FIRST: 08/08/85   INV:         0.00   INV:       279.52
            3420 19th Street                (415) 563-8961               LAST:  12/01/86   PMT:         0.00   PMT:       279.52
            San Francisco, CA  94114        Apple IIe                                                               ------------
                                                                                                               BAL:         0.00

ARONOFF                                     Gina Aronoff                 FIRST: 10/09/86   INV:         0.00   INV:       232.50
            601 First Street                (707) 745-1813               LAST:  12/15/86   PMT:         0.00   PMT:       232.50
            Benicia, CA  94510              Apple IIc, Imagewriter                                                  ------------
                                                                                                               BAL:         0.00

CHIPCITY    Chip City Electronics           Fred Larson                  FIRST:   /  /     INV:         0.00   INV:         0.00
            288 Lorton                      (415) 348-6801               LAST:    /  /     PMT:         0.00   PMT:         0.00
            Burlingame, CA  94010           Osborne Exec, Epson MX-80                                               ------------
                                                                                                               BAL:         0.00

DELTADESGN  Delta Design                    Andrea Bennett               FIRST: 09/15/86   INV:         0.00   INV:       138.15
            2405 Sycamore Drive             (415) 754-7373               LAST:  09/15/86   PMT:         0.00   PMT:       138.15
            Antioch, CA  94509              Macintosh, Imagewriter                                                  ------------
                                                                                                               BAL:         0.00

ELLISMFG    Ellis Manufacturing             Barbara Goddard              FIRST: 10/18/85   INV:        98.29   INV:       767.29
            3091 Park Boulevard             (415) 494-1421               LAST:  02/18/87   PMT:        98.29   PMT:       767.29
            Palo Alto, CA  94306            IBM PC, Okidata 84                                                      ------------
                                                                                                               BAL:         0.00

FLOORPLAN   Floor Plan Carpet Center        Louise Robbins               FIRST: 11/20/86   INV:       205.08   INV:       389.26
            1482 Lowrie Avenue              (415) 871-3204               LAST:  02/05/87   PMT:       205.08   PMT:       389.26
            South San Francisco, CA  94080  NorthStar Advantage                                                     ------------
                                                                                                               BAL:         0.00

GREENTHUMB  Green Thumb Landscaping         Celia Lopez                  FIRST: 08/15/86   INV:       185.86   INV:       533.59
            1240 Hearst                     (415) 549-8901               LAST:  03/23/87   PMT:         0.00   PMT:       347.73
            Berkeley, CA  94702             Kaypro 4, Okidata 92                                                    ------------
                                                                                                               BAL:       185.86

HOMEMOVIES  Home Movies Video Rentals       Mark Vogel                   FIRST: 09/12/86   INV:         0.00   INV:       248.15
            2982 College Avenue             (415) 843-1148               LAST:  09/12/86   PMT:         0.00   PMT:       248.15
            Berkeley, CA  94705             Columbia, NEC 2010                                                      ------------
                                                                                                               BAL:         0.00

HRINSURANC  H & R Insurance                 Jill Henley                  FIRST: 07/12/85   INV:         0.00   INV:       538.43
            1225 Van Ness Avenue            (415) 398-1441               LAST:  10/27/86   PMT:         0.00   PMT:       538.43
            San Francisco, CA  94109        DEC Rainbow                                                             ------------
                                                                                                               BAL:         0.00
```

```
Page No.      2
03/16/86
                                        NATIONAL WIDGETS, INC.
                                        CUSTOMER REFERENCE LIST

ACCOUNT ID  ADDRESS                        CONTACT / PHONE / EQUIP    ORDER DATES      YEAR-TO-DATE       TOTAL
----------  -----------------------------  -------------------------  ---------------  -----------------  -----------------

IMAGEMAKER  The Image Makers               Lisa Burns                 FIRST: 11/12/86  INV:        0.00   INV:       389.50
            1900 Powell St, Suite 832      (415) 653-1250             LAST:  11/12/86  PMT:        0.00   PMT:       389.50
            Emeryville, CA  94608          IBM PC, NEC 7710                                                    ------------
                                                                                                          BAL:         0.00

JENSEN      Arthur Jensen, MD              Lucy George                FIRST: 03/26/85  INV:       69.52   INV:       677.94
            450 Sutter St, Suite 1418      (415) 397-8250             LAST:  03/20/87  PMT:        0.00   PMT:       608.42
            San Francisco, CA  94108       Compaq Deskpro, Brother                                             ------------
                                                                                                          BAL:        69.52

JOHNSON     J. Thomas Johnson, CPA         Carolyn Sumner             FIRST: 06/27/86  INV:      102.01   INV:       270.43
            50 California, Suite 1032      (415) 433-6488             LAST:  02/24/87  PMT:      102.01   PMT:       270.43
            San Francisco, CA  94111       IBM XT, Epson MX-100                                                ------------
                                                                                                          BAL:         0.00

KELLY       Kelly and Sons Furniture       Richard Kelly              FIRST:   /  /    INV:        0.00   INV:         0.00
            14800 Bancroft Avenue          (415) 357-7482             LAST:    /  /    PMT:        0.00   PMT:         0.00
            San Leandro, CA  94578         Eagle PC, TI 820                                                    ------------
                                                                                                          BAL:         0.00

KLEIN       Carol Klein, M.D.              Judy Barnes                FIRST: 10/14/85  INV:      106.70   INV:       800.43
            3204 Telegraph Avenue          (415) 891-2204             LAST:  04/02/87  PMT:        0.00   PMT:       693.73
            Oakland, CA  94609             IBM PC, Diablo 630                                                  ------------
                                                                                                          BAL:       106.70

LEWIS       Lewis and Associates           Joan Mills                 FIRST: 10/14/85  INV:        0.00   INV:       366.81
            408 Grand Avenue               (415) 839-5014             LAST:  09/19/86  PMT:        0.00   PMT:       366.81
            Oakland, CA  94610             Corona PC, NEC 3510                                                 ------------
                                                                                                          BAL:         0.00

MTK         M.T.K. Industries              Leslie Cohen               FIRST: 06/24/85  INV:        0.00   INV:     1,042.85
            1400  61st Street              (415) 655-7200             LAST:  12/11/86  PMT:        0.00   PMT:     1,042.85
            Emeryville, CA  94608          IBM XT, Epson FX-100                                                ------------
                                                                                                          BAL:         0.00

PHOENIX     Phoenix Construction                                      FIRST: 04/28/86  INV:        0.00   INV:       249.57
            3214 Pacheco Blvd.             (415) 939-8610             LAST:  07/07/86  PMT:        0.00   PMT:       249.57
            Martinez, CA  94553            Vector 3005, TI820                                                  ------------
                                                                                                          BAL:         0.00

QUICKPRINT  Quick Print, Inc.              Sarah Bernstein            FIRST: 05/17/85  INV:        0.00   INV:       358.73
            2532 Milvia                    (415) 865-3091             LAST:  09/23/85  PMT:        0.00   PMT:       358.73
            Berkeley, CA  94704            Corona PC, Okidata 92                                               ------------
                                                                                                          BAL:         0.00

RAPIDTYPE   RapidType Secretarial Svc      Kathy McDonald             FIRST:   /  /    INV:        0.00   INV:         0.00
            2457 Union Street              (415) 861-4048             LAST:    /  /    PMT:        0.00   PMT:         0.00
            San Francisco, CA  94123       Xerox 820, Diablo 620                                               ------------
                                                                                                          BAL:         0.00
```

Figure 5-3. The Customer Reference List

```
Page No.      3
03/16/86
                                    NATIONAL WIDGETS, INC.
                                   CUSTOMER REFERENCE LIST

ACCOUNT ID  ADDRESS                        CONTACT / PHONE / EQUIP    ORDER DATES        YEAR-TO-DATE         TOTAL
----------  -----------------------------  -------------------------  ---------------    -----------------    -----------------

SHAPEUP     Shape Up Fitness Center        Jeanne Lee                 FIRST: 02/14/86    INV:         0.00    INV:       435.42
            2832 MacDonald Avenue          (415) 236-7687             LAST:  11/12/86    PMT:         0.00    PMT:       435.42
            Richmond, CA  94804            Apple II, Okidata 83                                                    ------------
                                                                                                           BAL:         0.00

WESTJAN     Western Janitorial Svc.        Gail Armstrong             FIRST:   /  /      INV:         0.00    INV:         0.00
            3640 Mt. Diablo Blvd.          (415) 283-7150             LAST:    /  /      PMT:         0.00    PMT:         0.00
            Lafayette, CA  94549           Kaypro 10, Epson MX-100                                                 ------------
                                                                                                           BAL:         0.00

WHITNEY     Financial Planning Svcs.       James Whitney              FIRST:   /  /      INV:         0.00    INV:         0.00
            1800 Peralta, Suite 18         (415) 791-7474             LAST:    /  /      PMT:         0.00    PMT:         0.00
            Fremont, CA  94536             Eagle PC, Daisywriter                                                   ------------
                                                                                                           BAL:         0.00

WORKFORCE   Work Force Temporary Svc.      Hal Moffett                FIRST: 10/02/86    INV:         0.00    INV:       158.13
            2900 Laguna St., Suite 10      (415) 563-3492             LAST:  10/02/86    PMT:         0.00    PMT:       158.13
            San Francisco, CA  94123       Vector 5005                                                             ------------
                                                                                                           BAL:         0.00

YORKPUMP    York Pump, Inc.                Sharon Fern                FIRST:   /  /      INV:       136.14    INV:       136.14
            632 Charcot Avenue             (408) 946-9975             LAST:  02/03/87    PMT:         0.00    PMT:         0.00
            San Jose, CA  95131            Compupro                                                                ------------
                                                                                                           BAL:       136.14
```

Figure 5-3. The Customer Reference List (*continued*)

Although it is possible to carry out a numerical calculation within a column, you cannot request column subtotals or totals for any numeric field that is printed as part of a character string, because the expression constituting the contents of the column is not a number. This is also true of single numeric fields formatted with TRANSFORM, although strictly speaking, this function does not convert a number to character data.

Another set of dBASE III PLUS functions enable you to make simple decisions and print fields conditionally. The MAX and MIN functions allow you to print the greater or lesser, respectively, of two numeric expressions. The IIF function, which works much like the @IF function in Lotus 1-2-3 and other spreadsheet programs, allows you to evaluate any logical condition and display one value if the condition is true and another if it is false. For example, you could print two different descriptions in a report column, depending on a customer's year-to-date balance, with

```
IIF(BALANCE > 0, "Has ordered this year", "No orders this year")
```

Another way to enhance dBASE III PLUS reports is to print fields from two files at once. Some examples from the National Widgets system include printing a customer's full company name as well as the account number on the Invoice Register or Aging report, or adding the item description from the Inventory File to the Order Summary printed from the Order File. To do this, you simply open both of the files together and link them with SET RELATION before you CREATE or print the report. Just as in the file update procedures described in Chapter 4, fields in the unselected file are referenced by a combination of the file alias and field name. Thus, the company name column would be specified as NWCUST-> COMPANY. This is the sequence of commands that prints the Invoice Register:

```
SELECT 1
USE NWCUST INDEX NWCACCT
SELECT 2
USE NWTXN INDEX NWTINVC
SET RELATION TO ACCOUNT INTO NWCUST
REPORT FORM NWINVREG TO PRINT
```

Accessing Special Printer Features

If you own a printer that can switch type style, character pitch, line spacing, or other print attributes under software control, you can make use of many of these special features in dBASE III PLUS reports. Some common applications include fitting a wide report onto a narrow page by printing it in compressed print (16.5 characters per inch) on a dot matrix printer, switching between 10- and 12-pitch on a letter-quality printer, using a high-density dot-matrix correspondence quality mode for the final copy of a report, and printing portions of a mailing label or report in boldface or with underlining.

Printers, both dot matrix and letter quality, are generally controlled by two types of commands: single control characters and *escape sequences* (command sequences beginning with ESC, the character whose ASCII code is 27). For example, double-strike printing on the Epson FX series of printers is initiated with ESC-G and cancelled with ESC-H; and CTRL-O turns on compressed print. You will find a complete list of the commands used to access these special features in your printer manual.

To send a command sequence like ESC-G to the printer, you cannot simply turn on the printer with CTRL-P (or CTRL-PRTSC) and then press the ESC key followed by the G key. ESC has its own meaning within dBASE III PLUS, namely, to cancel the command or operation in progress. Instead, you must express the control characters in terms of their decimal ASCII codes, using the CHR function. CHR may be read as "the character whose ASCII code is...." (A good ASCII table can be helpful if your printer manual does not list the control sequences as decimal numbers.) To send the ESC-G sequence to the printer at command level (after turning on the printer with CTRL-P), you could use the following:

```
? CHR(27) + "G"
```

If you wished to print an entire report in a particular type style, character pitch, or other print attribute, you could simply toggle on the printer and send it the appropriate control code sequence before giving the REPORT or LABEL command. When the report is complete, you could return the printer to its default state either by turning it off or by using the CHR function to send it the commands that cancel the attributes you have set.

To a certain extent, these attributes may also be varied within a printed format. The contents of a report column or label line may consist of any dBASE III PLUS expression, including functions. For example, to print the company name field on a label in double-strike mode, you could specify this line in the label form as

```
CHR(27) + "G" + COMPANY + CHR(27) + "H"
```

On four-up labels, however, the printer control characters will disrupt the vertical alignment of the labels. This is because dBASE III PLUS counts the four characters (ESC, G, ESC, and H) among those sent to the printer to form the COMPANY line on the label, although they are not actually printed on the page. Similarly, with many printers, if you use this technique to highlight a report column, you may find that other fields on the same report line also share the specified print attribute or do not line up with the column headings.

If you try to use an expression where dBASE III PLUS expects a literal character string, the expression will be printed literally on the page instead of having the desired effect on the printer. This means that you cannot include printer control commands in report page titles or column headings. Nor do you have control over any text, such as subtotal headings and the subtotals themselves, printed automatically by dBASE III PLUS, which will always take on whatever print attributes that are in effect right before they are printed.

In order to print any of these headings in a different print mode, you must include the printer control command in the data printed immediately before the heading. To print the page title and column headings in double-strike mode, you must issue the command to initiate this print attribute before you begin printing the report. You could then include the command to return to normal print at the beginning of the first data column (the first item printed after the page heading) and the command to initiate double-strike at the end of the last data column (the last item printed before the page heading on all pages after page 1). Note that if the report contains subtotals, the subtotal headings and the subtotals themselves will also be printed in double-strike mode—and they will not align correctly with the columns of numbers they summarize.

INTERFACING WITH A WORD PROCESSOR

In Chapter 17 we will write a program to print personalized letters with dBASE III PLUS, but if you own a word processor with mail-merge capability, you may wish to use it instead. In dBASE III PLUS you can copy a data base file to two ASCII text file formats, *delimited* and *SDF* (System Data Format), as well as four other external formats, for exchanging information with word processors and other programs.

In a *delimited* file the fields are separated by commas, and character fields are surrounded (delimited) by some punctuation mark. The standard delimiter is the double quotation mark ("), but you can specify a different delimiter if you wish. Each record ends with a carriage return, so when you use the dBASE III PLUS or DOS TYPE command to display the contents of the file, each record will appear to begin on a new line on the screen. Programs that read and write delimited files identify the fields by counting commas from the beginning of the record: Field 1 incorporates all characters up to the first comma; field 2, all characters between the first and second; and so on. The quotes surrounding character fields are necessary to distinguish embedded commas (as in "John Smith, Jr.") from those used as field separators. Similarly, if a field is left blank, the comma that would normally follow this field remains as a place holder, so that the next field is not mistaken for the missing item. The delimited format can be read by WordStar/MailMerge, Microsoft Word, and Volkswriter Deluxe, among others.

SDF is a term used by dBASE III PLUS to describe what is more commonly called a "fixed-length record." In this format (as in the DBF file itself), there are no field separators. Each field occupies a fixed number of characters and is identified by its starting position in the record. If a particular item of data occupies less than the full field width, it is padded with blank spaces. (Character fields are usually left-justified in the field width, while numeric fields are right-justified.) As in the delimited format, each record is terminated by a carriage return. The PeachText 5000 word processor can read this format; fixed-length records are also used by many other data bases and accounting programs.

The SDF and delimited formats are most useful for interfacing with word processors, but dBASE III PLUS can also create *DIF* files (for VisiCalc), *SYLK* files (used by Multiplan and other Microsoft programs), Lotus 1-2-3 *WKS* (worksheet) files, and PFS:FILE format data files. In all of the spreadsheet formats, each record in the dBASE III PLUS data base becomes a row, with the fields lined up in columns. The EXPORT command is used to write PFS files, and the other five formats are produced by adding the TYPE clause to a COPY command (which would otherwise produce another DBF file). The syntax for this command is

COPY TO *file name* TYPE *file type*

The *file type* may be DELIMITED, SDF, DIF, SYLK, or WKS. For example, you could copy the National Widgets Customer File to an SDF file with

```
USE NWCUST
COPY TO NWLETTER TYPE SDF
```

You might assume that the resulting file would have the extension .SDF, but in fact both SDF and delimited files are given the extension .TXT (for "text").

When you create a delimited file, you may override the default delimiters by specifying your own. This command replaces the standard double quotation mark with slashes:

```
COPY TO NWLETTER TYPE DELIMITED WITH /
```

You can also choose to insert a single blank space between fields in place of the commas and delimiters with

```
COPY TO NWLETTER TYPE DELIMITED WITH BLANK
```

The order in which the data records are COPYed can be controlled either by sorting or, more commonly, indexing the data base you are going to COPY. You can also specify the fields to be included; they will be written to the external file in the order they are listed in the COPY command. You are restricted to COPYing whole fields, however—expressions like FIRSTNAME + LASTNAME or TRIM(CITY) are not permitted. Finally, you can include a scope, a FOR clause, and a WHILE clause to specify the range of records to be COPYed. In the National Widgets system, you could create a delimited file called NWIBM1.TXT, in ZIP code order, containing only the name and address fields, for customers who have IBM computers, with

```
USE NWCUST INDEX NWCZIP
COPY TO NWIBM1 TYPE DELIMITED FIELDS COMPANY, ADDRESS, CITY, STATE, ZIP,
  CONTACT FOR "IBM" $ EQUIPMENT
```

This file is illustrated in Figure 5-4, and an SDF file, NWIBM2.TXT, created by using the same index and selection criteria, is shown in Figure 5-5.

```
. USE NWCUST INDEX NWCZIP

. COPY TO NWIBM2 TYPE SDF FIELDS COMPANY, ADDRESS, CITY, STATE , ZIP, CONTACT FOR "IBM" $ EQUIPMENT
     5 records copied

. TYPE NWIBM2.TXT

J. Thomas Johnson, CPA   50 California, Suite 1032San Francisco      CA94111Carolyn Sumner
Ellis Manufacturing      3091 Park Boulevard     Palo Alto          CA94306Barbara Goddard
M.T.K. Industries        1400  61st Street       Emeryville         CA94608Leslie Cohen
The Image Makers         1900 Powell St, Suite 832Emeryville         CA94608Lisa Burns
Carol Klein, M.D.        3204 Telegraph Avenue   Oakland            CA94609Judy Barnes
```

Figure 5-4. A delimited file

```
. USE NWCUST INDEX NWCZIP

. COPY TO NWIBM1 TYPE DELIMITED FIELDS COMPANY, ADDRESS, CITY, STATE, ZIP, CONTACT FOR "IBM" $ EQUIPMENT

     5 records copied

. TYPE NWIBM1.TXT

"J. Thomas Johnson, CPA","50 California, Suite 1032","San Francisco","CA","94111","Carolyn Sumner"
"Ellis Manufacturing","3091 Park Boulevard","Palo Alto","CA","94306","Barbara Goddard"
"M.T.K. Industries","1400  61st Street","Emeryville","CA","94608","Leslie Cohen"
"The Image Makers","1900 Powell St, Suite 832","Emeryville","CA","94608","Lisa Burns"
"Carol Klein, M.D.","3204 Telegraph Avenue","Oakland","CA","94609","Judy Barnes"
```

Figure 5-5. An SDF file

6

EVALUATING THE NEW SYSTEM

The testing you have done at command level should clarify the flow of data through the system and the relationships among the data base files. You should have defined the sequence of events to be used to start up the system for the first time and identified many of the problems that will be encountered in making the transition from the manual system to the computer. You should also have gained an understanding of the advantages and limitations of working at the dot prompt and of some reasons for writing programs in the dBASE III PLUS language.

If you have carefully documented your command level testing, you will have a set of notes on paper or on disk that enable you to evaluate how closely your initial design meets the requirements of the final system. The system outline that served as a checklist during the command level testing phase can also guide your evaluation of your efforts. A review of your notes should enable you to answer these questions:

- Do the file structures accommodate the required data and support the relationships among the files?
- Can you can enter data into all the files and retrieve records for display, editing, or deletion?
- What characteristics of the behavior of dBASE III PLUS at command level would you want to change?
- Which procedures work well and benefit from the flexibility of working at command level?
- What command sequences are used repeatedly?

- Which command sequences take a long time to run or would do so with large files?
- What data validations are needed to preserve the integrity of the data bases?
- Are there calculations that are difficult or impossible to perform at command level?
- Are there reports or printed formats that are impossible to create with the built-in report and label generators?

This evaluation will guide you in making revisions to the file structures, personalizing the dBASE III PLUS environment to make your work at command level more comfortable and efficient, and determining how much programming is necessary or desirable to make the system faster, more powerful, easier to use, and less vulnerable to damage through operator errors.

REVISING FILE STRUCTURES

Entering a sampling of data from the real system into the data base files will help you identify the changes that must be made to your initial file structures. Most of these will be minor: changing field lengths, adding fields you have overlooked, deleting unnecessary fields, and changing field types to accommodate the data that must be entered. But in some cases you may find that your preliminary studies uncover some basic design flaws that require you to redesign the data base structures and complete another round of command level testing.

For example, in the National Widgets system, major problems may have surfaced in the Order and Transaction files and in the relationship between them. If you had created only one file intended to contain one record per invoice, with multiple sets of identical fields to record the items ordered, you would have discovered the awkwardness of dealing with an order that has too many line items to fit in one record and the inefficiency of this structure if most orders did not fill all of the fields. But if you had designed the file to accommodate one line item per record, with fields for the invoice number, date, and dollar totals, your testing would have revealed a different set of problems. This way of structuring the file makes it difficult to calculate and store the invoice subtotal, tax, and shipping charges and to enter one payment to cover all of the line item records that make up an invoice. The design chosen for the National Widgets files eliminates all of these problems; but if the accounting system had to accommodate a great many partial payments, credit memos, and refunds, the Transaction File setup would be deemed inadequate.

With dBASE III PLUS the structure of a file can easily be changed without losing any data you have already entered. To fully understand the implications of changing the structure of a file that contains data, you need to know a little about how the data is stored in a data base file. At the beginning of the file, a *header* contains the number of records in the file, the date of last update, the total record length, and the name, type, and length of each of the fields. Following the header, the data is stored as fixed-length records in which each field—and therefore, each record—occupies a fixed number of bytes (characters), with no extra spaces or special markers either between fields or between records. If the data you enter into a field is shorter than the full field length specified when the file was created, it is padded with blank spaces.

In order to add, delete, lengthen, or shorten fields safely, you would also need some way of making the corresponding changes in each of the data records so that they match the new structure. When you use MODIFY STRUCTURE, dBASE III PLUS makes a temporary copy of the file structure (with no data in it) for you to modify. When you have completed your changes, the data from the old file is appended into the new structure, which then assumes your original file name, while the old file is renamed with the extension .BAK (for backup). If the data base contains memo fields, a separate backup file is made for the DBT file that contains the memo text, with the extension .TBK (for text backup). In a large data base, the process of APPENDing the records into the new structure and copying the memo text file can take some time.

Whenever one file is APPENDed into another, the fields are matched up by name, so you can safely move a field to a new position in the structure without losing data. If you lengthen a field, the old data is padded with spaces. Shortening a character field results in truncating entries that will not fit in the new field length; for numeric fields, the field is filled with asterisks if the old value is too long. New fields added to the structure will be blank in all of the records, since dBASE III PLUS will find no matching field in the old structure to supply the data; and if you delete a field, the data from that field will of course be lost. MODIFY STRUCTURE also handles data type conversions intelligently: you can change a field type from numeric to character or vice versa, provided that the contents are compatible with the new data type; and you can change a character field that looks like a date to a true date or turn a date back into a character field. You can also change field names, but only if you observe certain rules: you may not add or delete fields, change field lengths or types, or move fields around in the structure at the same time.

If you are not sure which changes are permissible, take note of the message displayed at the bottom of the MODIFY STRUCTURE screen when you press CTRL-W or CTRL-END to save the new structure. If you have made any alterations that might cause data to be lost, dBASE III PLUS will warn you, "Database records will be APPENDED from backup fields of the same name only!!" "Database records will be COPIED from backup for all fields" tells you that you have made no potentially destructive changes. If you have changed field names, dBASE III PLUS will ask you to verify that data should in fact be transferred to the new file based on the field positions in the structure, rather than by name, with the query "Should data be COPIED from backup for all fields? (Y/N)".

In the sample system, because our advance planning was so thorough, only minor changes to the Customer File structure are required at this point. Some of the company names and addresses do not fit comfortably into the field lengths provided. Also, since the sales tax rate is determined by the customer's geographic location, this information should be stored in the Customer File so that it may be looked up and entered automatically into the Transaction File instead of being entered by the operator.

To accommodate these factors, the following changes must be made in the Customer File:

- Lengthen the COMPANY field to 30 characters
- Change the name of the ADDRESS field to ADDRESS1
- Add a second address line field called ADDRESS2
- Add a sales tax rate field called TAXRATE.

Since the changes to the Customer File include renaming a field as well as adding and lengthening fields, the structure must be modified in two steps. In the first step you can lengthen the COMPANY field and add the second address line (ADDRESS2) and tax rate (TAXRATE) fields, and in the second step you can rename the original ADDRESS field to ADDRESS1. The new structure for the Customer File is shown in Figure 6-1. After you have made these changes to the file structure, you will have to rebuild all of the indexes associated with the file—in this case, NWCACCT.NDX and NWCZIP.NDX. You must also revise any printed

```
. USE NWCUST INDEX NWCACCT, NWCZIP

. LIST STRUCTURE TO PRINT

Structure for database: C:NWCUST.dbf
Number of data records:       25
Date of last update   : 03/29/86
Field  Field Name  Type       Width    Dec
    1  ACCOUNT     Character     10
    2  COMPANY     Character     30
    3  ADDRESS1    Character     25
    4  ADDRESS2    Character     25
    5  CITY        Character     20
    6  STATE       Character      2
    7  ZIP         Character      5
    8  AREACODE    Character      3
    9  TELEPHONE   Character      8
   10  CONTACT     Character     25
   11  EQUIPMENT   Character     25
   12  TAXRATE     Numeric        5      2
   13  FIRSTORDER  Date           8
   14  LASTORDER   Date           8
   15  YTDINV      Numeric       10      2
   16  YTDPMT      Numeric       10      2
   17  TOTINV      Numeric       10      2
   18  TOTPMT      Numeric       10      2
   19  BALANCE     Numeric       10      2
   20  COMMENTS    Memo          10
** Total **                     260


. DISPLAY STATUS TO PRINT

Currently Selected Database:
Select area:  1, Database in Use: C:NWCUST.dbf   Alias: NWCUST
    Master index file:  C:NWCACCT.ndx  Key: account
           Index file:  C:NWCZIP.ndx  Key: ZIP
            Memo file:  C:NWCUST.dbt

File search path:
Default disk drive: C:
Print destination:  PRN:
Margin =      0
Current work area =    1

Press any key to continue...

*** INTERRUPTED ***
```

Figure 6-1. The Customer File

formats—in this case, the Customer Reference List and the two mailing label formats—that use the affected fields. You may also want to take the time to edit the data you have already entered into the file to conform to the new structure.

PERSONALIZING THE WORKING ENVIRONMENT

If your previous work with dBASE III PLUS has not already done so, these preliminary experiments will solidify your preferences regarding the default working environment. For example, data entry fields are displayed in inverse video, and when you fill up a field, the program beeps and automatically advances the cursor to the next item. These and many other characteristics of dBASE III PLUS, as well as the meanings of nine of the ten programmable function keys, can be altered with SET commands to suit your personal preferences. (See Appendix B for a list of all of the options you can SET.) A typical combination of SET commands might be

```
SET INTENSITY OFF
SET BELL OFF
SET CONFIRM ON
SET TYPEAHEAD TO 500
SET HISTORY TO 50
SET DEFAULT TO C
SET DELETED ON
SET DELIMITER ON
SET DELIMITER TO "[]"
SET FUNCTION 2 TO "USE NWCUST;"
```

The options you SET remain in effect only during the current work session. You can, however, save your own personalized default settings in a file called CONFIG.DB, which must be located in the directory from which you load the dBASE III PLUS program. These settings are automatically placed in effect whenever you start up dBASE III PLUS, although you can later override them with individual SET commands. The options listed in the previous example would appear as follows in CONFIG.DB:

```
INTENSITY = OFF
BELL = OFF
CONFIRM = ON
TYPEAHEAD = 500
HISTORY = 50
DEFAULT = C
DELETED = ON
DELIMITER = ON
DELIMITER = "[]"
F2 = USE NWCUST;
```

Note that the syntax used in CONFIG.DB differs in several respects from the equivalent SET commands. (See Appendix D for an explanation of the correct syntax for CONFIG.DB entries and a list of all of the options you can control through this file.)

You can further customize the working environment by assigning your own meanings to any of the programmable function keys except F1 (the HELP key), so you can issue frequently used commands with a single keystroke. You might, for example, redefine the F2 key to open a file:

```
SET FUNCTION 2 TO "USE NWINVENT INDEX NWICATPT;"
```

The semicolon in the command string symbolizes a carriage return, so this command includes the RETURN required to execute it. If you want one function key to contain a sequence of commands, you can use more than one semicolon within the command string:

```
SET FUNCTION 3 TO "USE NWCUST;LIST;"
```

A function key assignment need not be a complete command; it may represent any sequence of keystrokes. You might want to use the LIST command to look at the same set of fields from a data base with different selection criteria controlling which records are displayed. You could use SET FIELDS to suppress the display of the unwanted fields, but you would then have to SET FIELDS OFF to DISPLAY or EDIT the entire record. Instead, you could use a function key to store the constant portion of your command:

```
SET FUNCTION 4 TO "LIST ACCOUNT, BALANCE FOR "
```

When you press F4, dBASE III PLUS supplies the first part of the command (LIST ACCOUNT, BALANCE FOR) and you can complete it by typing your condition and pressing RETURN.

Another way to create a short abbreviation for a long command is to use the dBASE III PLUS macro capability. Simply store your command in a character variable with a short name:

```
STORE "USE NWCUST INDEX NWCACCT, NWCZIP" TO C
```

To use the macro, you would type

```
&C
```

Remember, the ampersand that identifies the expression &C as a macro tells dBASE III PLUS to substitute the value of the variable that follows for the variable itself. Thus, &C means "Use the value of the variable called C." Typing &C at the dot prompt is equivalent to typing the string of characters that make up the contents of the variable C. Since dBASE III PLUS permits up to 256 active memory variables totaling up to 31,000 bytes, you can use macros to create a customized command library far larger than the nine commands accessible through the special function keys. If you store many commands in memory variables to be used in this way, you will probably want to save them in a memory file on disk with

SAVE TO *memory file name*

The variables may be retrieved for use in subsequent work sessions with

RESTORE FROM *memory file name*

ADVANTAGES AND LIMITATIONS OF WORKING AT COMMAND LEVEL

One of the most important conclusions to be drawn from working at the dot prompt concerns both the power and the limitations of the dBASE III PLUS built-in commands. You will identify which operations can easily be accomplished at command level, which ones are clearly impossible without programming, and which can be made faster, more accurate, or easier to use by writing programs. The programs in a dBASE III PLUS system can be as informal as a simple menu that opens the necessary data bases and then calls built-in commands like APPEND, BROWSE, and REPORT, or they can be as complex as a complete *turnkey* system that uses custom programs for all of its functions.

The main advantage of the built-in commands is that any user willing to learn dBASE III PLUS may add to or modify the system without the aid of a programmer. The strongest reasons for writing programs fall into three groups:

- Automating frequently used or time-consuming command sequences
- Creating an easy-to-use system for operators who are unfamiliar with dBASE III PLUS
- Overcoming the limitations of the dBASE III PLUS built-in commands.

A basic familiarity with using dBASE III PLUS at command level, coupled with an understanding of the office environment and the people who will be using the application, should help you arrive at the right combination for your system.

Automation

Even for the most knowledgeable operators, running certain procedures at the dot prompt is inefficient because someone must be present at all times to issue commands. You will have to type the same commands over and over again in the course of a complete processing cycle, and no matter how well you understand the system, it is always possible to make a careless error that can seriously damage the data base. Because you must often check the results of one command before you can give the next, you will spend a frustrating amount of time just waiting and watching the screen. Writing programs to batch commands together will enable you to run time-consuming processes like PACKing and REINDEXing all of the files unattended, or perhaps overnight.

User-Friendly System

Even without knowing how to CREATE the file structures, build the indexes, and define the REPORT and LABEL forms, an operator working completely at command level must know a great deal about dBASE III PLUS and about the way an application is set up. In order to continue running the system the way we did as the file update procedures were explained in Chapter 4, the user must have a good understanding of dBASE III PLUS command syntax and know the names of all of the files, fields, and report and label forms. The operator must also remember which indexes go with each data base, the field(s) the indexes are based on, and when it is necessary to open each of the indexes.

If you used a CATALOG to document the development process, as suggested in Chapter 3, the resulting CATALOG data base can not only provide you with a list of the names of the files required by your application, but also help users choose the right file in a given context. Figure 6-2 illustrates the structure of a CATALOG data base, in this case one called NW.CAT; and Figure 6-3 lists the contents of this data base after

```
. USE NW.CAT

. LIST STRUCTURE TO PRINT

Structure for database: C:NW.cat
Number of data records:        24
Date of last update    : 03/29/86
Field  Field Name  Type        Width    Dec
    1  PATH        Character      70
    2  FILE_NAME   Character      12
    3  ALIAS       Character       8
    4  TYPE        Character       3
    5  TITLE       Character      80
    6  CODE        Numeric         3
    7  TAG         Character       4
** Total **                      181
```

Figure 6-2. The structure of a catalog file

carrying out the procedures described in Chapters 4 and 5. To use this CATALOG in a subsequent work session, you would open the file with

```
SET CATALOG TO NW
```

Whenever a CATALOG is open, only files contained in the CATALOG are displayed in the lists presented by the ASSIST menus. Working at the dot prompt, you can use a *CATALOG query clause* in many dBASE III PLUS commands that open files to request a list of available files of the specified type. For example, typing USE ? opens a window displaying a list of the data base files in the current CATALOG. You can scroll through the list of files to view the descriptions entered into the TITLE field in the CATALOG file. SET INDEX TO ? calls up a list of the index files *associated with the data base in the current work area;* as you move the cursor through the list of indexes, another window displays the key expressions.

When a file update procedure involves working with a set of two or more related data base files, you may use a VIEW to simplify the process of opening the files and establishing the relationships. The VIEW, which is saved in a file with a .VUE extension, includes information on which data bases and indexes should be opened and the work area selected. You may also optionally specify a single format file, a single FILTER condition, a list of the fields to be made available for display and updating. You can create or edit a VIEW in a prompted full-screen mode with CREATE

```
. USE NW.CAT

. LIST SUBSTR(PATH,1,2Ø), FILE_NAME, ALIAS, TYPE, SUBSTR(TITLE,1,6Ø), CODE, TAG

Record#  SUBSTR(PATH,1,2Ø)     FILE_NAME     ALIAS     TYPE SUBSTR(TITLE,1,6Ø)                                            CODE TAG
      1  C:NWINVENT.dbf        NWINVENT.dbf NWINVENT dbf  Inventory File                                                   1
      2  NWICATPT.ndx          NWICATPT.ndx NWICATPT ndx  CATEGORY+PARTNUMBER                                              1
      3  C:NWCUST.dbf          NWCUST.dbf   NWCUST   dbf  Customer File                                                    2
      4  NWCACCT.ndx           NWCACCT.ndx  NWCACCT  ndx  account                                                          2
      5  NWCZIP.ndx            NWCZIP.ndx   NWCZIP   ndx  ZIP                                                              2
      6  C:nworder.dbf         NWORDER.dbf  NWORDER  dbf  Order File                                                       3
      7  nwoinvc.ndx           NWOINVC.ndx  NWOINVC  ndx  INVOICE                                                          3
      8  C:nwordtmp.dbf        NWORDTMP.dbf NWORDTMP dbf  Temporary Transaction File (created by totalling orders)         4
      9  C:NWTXN.dbf           NWTXN.dbf    NWTXN    dbf  Transaction File                                                 5
     1Ø  NWOACCT.ndx           NWOACCT.ndx  NWOACCT  ndx  ACCOUNT + INVOICE                                                3
     11  C:NWORDHST.dbf        NWORDHST.dbf NWORDHST dbf  Order History File                                               6
     12  NWOHACCT.ndx          NWOHACCT.ndx NWOHACCT ndx  ACCOUNT+INVOICE                                                  6
     13  NWOHINVC.ndx          NWOHINVC.ndx NWOHINVC ndx  INVOICE                                                          6
     14  C:NWTEMP.dbf          NWTEMP.dbf   NWTEMP   dbf  Temporary File for Posting Invoices and Payments                 7
     15  C:NWTXNHST.dbf        NWTXNHST.dbf NWTXNHST dbf  Transaction History File                                         8
     16  NWTHACCT.ndx          NWTHACCT.ndx NWTHACCT ndx  ACCOUNT+INVOICE                                                  8
     17  NWTHINVC.ndx          NWTHINVC.ndx NWTHINVC ndx  INVOICE                                                          8
     18  C:NWCUST1.lbl         NWCUST1.lbl  NWCUST   lbl  One-up Mailing Labels for Customer File                          2
     19  C:TEST4.lbl           NWCUST4.lbl  NWCUST4  lbl  Four-up Mailing Labels for Customers                             2
     2Ø  C:NWINVREG.frm        NWINVREG.frm NWINVREG frm  Invoice Register                                                 8
     21  C:NWAGING.frm         NWAGING.frm  NWAGING  frm  Aging Report                                                     5
     22  C:NWCASH.frm          NWCASH.frm   NWCASH   frm  Cash Receipts Report                                             5
     23  C:NWCASH.frm          NWCASH.frm   NWCASH   frm  Cash Receipts Report                                             5
     24  C:NWCUSTRF.frm        NWCUSTRF.frm NWCUSTRF frm  Customer Reference List                                          2
```

Figure 6-3. The National Widgets System catalog file

VIEW or MODIFY VIEW, or you create the VIEW "on the fly" by opening all of the required files, issuing the appropriate SET commands, and then typing

CREATE VIEW *view file name* FROM ENVIRONMENT

You invoke a VIEW with

SET VIEW TO *view file name*

For example, in Chapter 4 we opened the Order and Inventory files together and linked them with SET RELATION in order to read the EQUIPMENT and PRICE fields into the Order File from the matching inventory records. You could create a VIEW called NWORDINV.VUE to open these files and establish the RELATION with the following commands:

```
SELECT 1
USE NWINVENT INDEX NWICATPT
SELECT 2
USE NWORDER
SET RELATION TO CATEGORY + PARTNUMBER INTO NWINVENT
CREATE VIEW NWORDINV FROM ENVIRONMENT
```

To use this VIEW, you would type

```
SET VIEW TO NWORDINV
```

Using this VIEW allows you to accomplish with a single command—the SET VIEW command—a task that would otherwise require five, and it enables a less knowledgeable user to easily open a set of files that you have created. However, it provides no help with the next step in this particular update process—the REPLACE command that fills in the EQUIPMENT and PRICE fields. VIEWs also impose further restrictions on several other dBASE III PLUS commands. With a VIEW in effect, you are limited to a single format file and a single FILTER condition, whereas dBASE III PLUS normally permits one of each per work area. Also, although you may SET only one RELATION *from* a given work area, you can SET RELATION *into* the same file from two different data bases. Through a VIEW, however, you can only create a "straight chain" of RELATIONs, so you could not open the Customer, Transaction, and Order files together, and SET RELATION into the Customer File from each of the other two data bases to provide access to the company name field.

As described in Chapter 4, you can use the SET FIELDS command to specify the set of fields accessible through DISPLAY, LIST, EDIT, and many other dBASE III PLUS commands. If more than one data base is open, you may include fields from all active files in the field list by specifying the file alias. Successive SET FIELDS commands add to the list of active fields, so you may select more fields than will fit within the 254-character command length limit. When you are working with a single data base, this command enables you to avoid retyping a lengthy list of field names many times. If more than one file is open, you cannot only display, but also modify, fields from any work area with the EDIT, CHANGE, BROWSE, and REPLACE commands. For example, with the Order and Inventory files opened together as described previously, you could use the following field list to display the Inventory File DESCRIP, COST, and PRICE fields for reference as you browse through the Order File and, if necessary, change a COST or PRICE to update the inventory data:

```
SET FIELDS TO ACCOUNT, INVOICE, CATEGORY, PARTNUMBER, EQUIPMENT, QUANTITY
SET FIELDS TO PRICE, SUBTOTAL, DISCRATE, DISCOUNT, INVAMOUNT
SET FIELDS TO NWINVENT->DESCRIP, NWINVENT->COST, NWINVENT->PRICE
```

This field list could be incorporated into the NWORDINV.VUE file described previously, so that invoking this VIEW creates a highly customized environment for editing the Order File.

Although these commands can be convenient for experienced users and helpful to novices, using them safely and without confusion still requires care, foresight, and understanding, both on the part of the expert setting up a VIEW, and also, unfortunately, by the users of the system. For example, if you set up the NWORDINV.VUE VIEW to edit the Order File, the users must understand that when the Inventory File is selected or if records are APPENDed to either data base, the field list is ignored, and all of the fields are displayed.

Working at the dot prompt, the user must also have a clear picture of the order in which procedures must be carried out. In the sample system, for example, the user must remember which calculations to perform before posting transactions and which reports must be printed before end-of-month or end-of-year processing clears the data from the current files.

Without programming, dBASE III PLUS provides only limited ways in which data may be validated or checked for accuracy and appropriateness. The program will allow you to enter only numbers into numeric fields; it permits only "true," "false," "yes," or "no" in logical fields; and it will reject as impossible dates like 13/42/87. However, the National Widgets model system provides numerous examples of the shortcomings of command level data entry. The dBASE III PLUS program cannot detect errors such as an invalid state abbreviation or an order date not in the current year, and it cannot force you to enter code fields or state abbreviations in uppercase only.

Although you can link two files on the basis of a common key field for lookups, you cannot use this relationship to prevent you from APPENDing a record to the Order File for an item that is missing from the Inventory File or for an order made by a customer who has not yet been entered into the Customer File. The NWORDINV.VUE VIEW described previously does not help with this problem, because of the way in which SET RELATION works. When a new record is APPENDed, the fields used to link the two files (CATEGORY and PARTNUMBER) are blank in the Order File, so the Inventory File is positioned at the end-of-file. Filling in these fields does not move the record pointer in the Order File, so the Inventory File pointer is not repositioned to the matching record.

If you delete a customer record, dBASE III PLUS can neither automatically delete all of the matching transaction records nor warn you that because active transactions exist, the customer should not be deleted. While you may have decided that the part numbers and customer account codes must be unique, dBASE III PLUS will not prevent you from APPENDing records with duplicate entries in these fields.

Although you cannot prevent these data entry problems, you can detect and even remedy some of them afterward. For example, you can convert all previously entered account codes to uppercase with

```
REPLACE ALL ACCOUNT WITH UPPER(ACCOUNT)
```

SET RELATION allows you to detect mismatches between two files. For example, to find records in the Order File for which there are no matching Customer File records, you can use the following:

```
SELECT 1
USE NWCUST INDEX NWCACCT
SELECT 2
USE NWORDER
SET RELATION TO ACCOUNT INTO NWCUST
LIST ACCOUNT, NWCUST->ACCOUNT, INVOICE, CATEGORY, PARTNUMBER
```

Whenever the Order File is positioned at a record for which there is no match in the Customer File, the record pointer in NWCUST will be positioned at the end-of-file, just as if you had used SEEK to attempt to find the matching record yourself. In the LIST command in the previous example, you can easily identify these invalid order records, because NWCUST—>ACCOUNT will be blank. You can take this technique one step further and list to the printer (for reference when you go back to correct your mistakes) *only* the problem records:

```
LIST ACCOUNT, INVOICE, CATEGORY, PARTNUMBER FOR NWCUST->ACCOUNT = " "
   TO PRINT
```

Because you can SET only one RELATION at a time, you cannot simultaneously open the Inventory File to check whether the part number is on file, so you must validate the part number in a separate step:

```
SELECT 1
USE NWINVENT INDEX NWICATPT
SELECT 2
USE NWORDER
SET RELATION TO CATEGORY + PARTNUMBER INTO NWINVENT
LIST ACCOUNT, INVOICE, CATEGORY, PARTNUMBER FOR NWINVENT->PARTNUMBER = " "
  TO PRINT
```

These extra steps are time-consuming, and they must be carried out by someone with a thorough understanding of dBASE III PLUS. This type of validation—and working at command level in general—is best suited for an organization that has at least one employee who is interested and able to invest the time to become conversant with dBASE III PLUS command level operation and who will run the system, supervise processing, or at least be readily available for advice and guidance. If your system must be used by a number of different people, many of whom have a low level of computer confidence or sophistication, it is to everyone's advantage to develop a set of easy-to-use, crash-proof custom programs.

Limitations

Most of the methods worked out in Chapter 4 for updating the data bases in the National Widgets system involved batch processing. Although records were added, edited, and deleted individually (in at least some of the data bases), all of the numerical calculations and transfers of information among the files were carried out by using procedures that were essentially separate from the data entry process. Using this kind of batch posting, you cannot, for example, enter a payment and see it immediately reflected in the customer's balance, and handling practical complexities like special sale prices and partial payments becomes cumbersome and time-consuming.

Using dBASE III PLUS built-in commands like REPLACE, UPDATE, and TOTAL does allow a nonprogrammer to perform relatively sophisticated manipulations of data contained in one or two files. But you can gain a great deal in speed and flexibility by substituting your own programs for these and the other dBASE III PLUS commands that process an entire data base at once. For example, if a file update procedure involved lookups in two other files based on SETting a RELATION into each, followed by a REPLACE step and an UPDATE, you would end up reading through the entire file four times. A program would allow you to open all three files together and accomplish all four steps with only one pass through the file being updated.

The report generator imposes limitations severe enough to present major problems even in a relatively simple application. While you can print multiple report lines per record, the method outlined in Chapter 5 for controlling field placement on the page is at best indirect. You can link two files with SET RELATION and thus draw data from two files for a report, but there is no way to print full-page formats like personalized letters or layouts like customer invoices and statements consisting of some fields from one file, followed by a set of matching records from another. By using a chain of RELATIONs, you can print data from three files on a report. For example, you could use the following to print an order listing that includes the invoice date (from the Transaction File) and the customer name (from the Customer File):

```
SELECT 1
USE NWCUST INDEX NWCACCT
SELECT 2
USE NWTXN INDEX NWTINVC
SET RELATION TO ACCOUNT INTO NWCUST
SELECT 3
USE NWORDER INDEX NWOINVC
SET RELATION TO INVOICE INTO NWTXN
REPORT FORM NWORDLST TO PRINT
```

However, because you can SET only one RELATION at a time from any given work area, you could not use two RELATIONS to print the item description (from the Inventory File) as well as the customer name (from the Customer File) on the order listing. To include both of these fields on the report, you would have to resort to adding a redundant field to the Order File. You might, for example, put in a DESCRIP field, which could be filled in at the same time the PRICE and EQUIPMENT fields are looked up in the Inventory File. The report could then be printed with one RELATION to access the Customer File fields.

The computations you can perform in a report are limited to accumulating two levels of subtotals—insufficient for many applications—and carrying out calculations within a record. Printing relatively simple statistics like counts or averages for the subtotal groups is beyond the capability of the report generator.

You also have little control over the format of the printed page. You cannot relocate the date or page number, move the titles, or print more than four lines of page or column titles. You cannot change the format of the subtotal group headings or even move the SUBTOTAL label down to the same line as the numbers themselves; and if you object to the term "SUB-SUBTOTAL" for the second level of subtotals, there is no way to change it. Although you have some access to your printer's special features, these cannot be utilized in all of the component parts of the report. You can add fields together and use a variety of functions to control the display format of character and numeric fields, but if you use the TRANSFORM function to insert commas or dollar signs or display negative numbers enclosed in parentheses (instead of using a trailing minus sign), you cannot accumulate column totals or subtotals for these fields. Of course, the dBASE III PLUS programming language provides for all these options and more.

II

AUTOMATING THE SYSTEM

Part II introduces the dBASE III PLUS programming language. The first examples will combine sequences of commands you have already used at the dot prompt into simple batch-type programs. These programs provide an easy transition to automating applications so that they can be run by operators who do not understand all of the component commands. Time-consuming procedures may be run unattended, and the system's more knowledgeable users will be freed from the tedium of typing the same command sequences over and over again. To make the system even easier to use and provide more extensive data formatting and validation capabilities, format files will be used to draw custom data entry screens for the full-screen APPEND and EDIT commands and later from within dBASE III PLUS programs.

Part II also introduces the basic programming structures that will form the building blocks for more complex programs. With these structures your programs can advance far beyond what is possible at command level. In these chapters you will learn to do the following:

- Collect input from the operator
- Display output on the screen or printer
- Read and process records from data bases one at a time
- Perform calculations and store the results
- Make decisions based on data base fields or user input
- Repeat a set of program steps
- Call one program from within another.

In Chapters 12 and 13, these components are combined into a menu-driven system for the National Widgets sample application. Along with the specific programming techniques, Part II will continue to emphasize planning and strategy. Also presented is a standard set of naming and notational conventions that will greatly increase the readability of your programs and make them easier for you and other programmers to maintain and modify. If you have never programmed before, you should study the chapters on programming structures and memory variables carefully. If you have experience with other higher-level languages, the basic programming structures will be familiar to you, and you may want to concentrate on the examples as prototypes for the kinds of operations typically performed on the data base files in any application.

7

WRITING SIMPLE PROGRAMS TO AUTOMATE PROCEDURES

Chapter 6 outlined the goals to be accomplished by writing dBASE III PLUS programs. This chapter will first tackle automation (setting up procedures that can be run unattended) because in this area you can realize the greatest gains without having to learn very much about programming. You will not even have to learn any new dBASE III PLUS commands to begin writing useful programs.

This chapter introduces the concept of dBASE III PLUS programming and shows how the dBASE III PLUS editor or an external word processor may be used to write programs. Using examples drawn from the National Widgets system procedures developed at command level in Chapters 4 and 5, you will write short programs to automate frequently used procedures, like printing reports, so that these procedures may be run by typing a single command. Time-consuming operations such as performing calculations, updating data bases, and building indexes will be combined into programs that carry out these tasks with minimal user involvement. Every dBASE III PLUS user can benefit substantially from learning to write programs like these, which make any dBASE III PLUS application more automatic, less dependent on the expertise of the users, and more efficient in its use of the operator's time and computer time.

INTRODUCING dBASE III PLUS PROGRAMMING

A *program* is a set of instructions that direct the computer to carry out a series of operations in a specified order. These instructions must be formulated according to strict rules of grammar and syntax so that the computer can "understand" them. In your command level work with dBASE III PLUS, you have already gained a basic familiarity with the syntax of many dBASE III PLUS commands, and you have "programmed" the computer by typing the set of instructions required to carry out a procedure one by one at the dot prompt. Combining commands into dBASE III PLUS programs that the computer can execute in sequence is only a small conceptual step from typing each command yourself.

In its simplest form, a *dBASE III PLUS program* is nothing more than an ordinary text file consisting of a series of dBASE III PLUS commands, each one typed just as you would enter it at the dot prompt and each ending with a RETURN. If you have ever worked with SUBMIT files under the CP/M operating system or BATCH files on an MS-DOS computer, this concept should already be familiar. A dBASE III PLUS program is normally given the extension .PRG, which identifies the text file to dBASE III PLUS as a program. If you adhere to this convention, you do not have to type the extension along with the file name in any dBASE III PLUS command that expects a program name. To run a program from the dot prompt, you type

DO *program name*

When dBASE III PLUS executes the program, it simply reads the lines in sequence from the text file and carries out the commands just as if you had typed each one yourself at the dot prompt.

Notational and Typographical Conventions

Before you begin writing programs, you should consider the benefits of establishing a set of notational and typographical conventions. The command lines in a dBASE III PLUS program, like those you issue from the dot prompt, may be typed in any combination of upper- and lowercase letters. In the dBASE III PLUS programs in this book, lowercase letters will be used for dBASE III PLUS command words and uppercase will be used for file, field, and memory variable names—although the dBASE III PLUS manual and many other books use the opposite convention—because this system makes the variable and file names stand out when you read a program.

Double quotation marks (") will be used to delimit character strings, but just as in your work at command level, you may also use single quotation marks (') or square brackets ([ ]) in dBASE III PLUS programs. The single quotation mark, since it is an unshifted character on the keyboard, is the easiest to type of the three allowable delimiters. If you use single quotation marks, remember that you must use the same symbol—the left-pointing apostrophe character found immediately to the right of the semicolon on most keyboards—at the beginning and the end of the character string, even if your keyboard also has a right-pointing apostrophe. When one of these characters is included *within* a string as punctuation, use a different delimiter pair around that particular string (as in the prompt message "Enter today's date: ").

A program will be more readable if you spell out all dBASE III PLUS command verbs in full, although at the dot prompt you can abbreviate commands to the first four characters. Extra spaces are permitted anywhere within a command line, and you may use blank lines to set off groups of commands as discrete functional units. In the programs in this book, extra spaces are used for clarity between the component parts of expressions, for example, (PRICE – COST) / PRICE. Extra spaces follow the commas in lists of file or field names, for example, ACCOUNT, COMPANY, CONTACT, TELEPHONE.

Comments form an important part of a program's internal documentation. An entire line may be identified as a comment by beginning the line with either an asterisk (*) or the word NOTE. You may also place a comment after any program statement on the same line by preceding it with two ampersands (&&). Comments are ignored by dBASE III PLUS when a program is executed, so they may be used to separate functional modules or to write notes for your own reference or for other programmers who may need to understand or modify your system. In a separate comment line, the * or NOTE need not be placed at the left margin; comment lines may be indented to match the sections of code they describe. Excessive use of comments will slow down program execution slightly, but unless your comments are verbose, the difference in speed is negligible compared to the benefits you will reap when you return to a program after several months, when the logic is no longer fresh in your mind, to add a module or make a change.

You should begin each program with a few comment lines that state the name of the program, a brief description of its purpose, the author, the date written, and the latest modification date. Including this information in the text of the program ensures that it is always visible when you edit the program or examine a printed copy of the code. In longer programs some programmers also include a more comprehensive description of the changes made in each revision, but this kind of documentation is usually more easily maintained on paper, by retaining and annotating your original printed listing whenever you make extensive changes.

Comparing a Command Level Procedure With a dBASE III PLUS Program

As a first example, we will compare the command level procedure devised in Chapter 5 to print the National Widgets Invoice Register with a program that does the same thing. Recall that in order to print fields from both the Customer File and the Transaction File, the two data bases must be opened in two dBASE III PLUS work areas and linked with SET RELATION. This is the command sequence used at the dot prompt:

```
SELECT 1
USE NWCUST INDEX NWCACCT
SELECT 2
USE NWTXN INDEX NWTINVC
SET RELATION TO ACCOUNT INTO NWCUST
REPORT FORM NWINVREG TO PRINT
```

These instructions could be combined into a program by creating a text file, NWINVREG.PRG, containing *exactly the same six commands.* This program is listed in Figure 7-1. Note that three comment lines were added to identify the program and that the commands were altered to conform to the guidelines suggested earlier for the use of upper- and lowercase letters. To run the program, you would type at the dot prompt

```
DO NWINVREG
```

Writing the program, like printing the report from the dot prompt, requires familiarity with dBASE III PLUS in general and with the National Widgets system files in particular, including

```
* NWINVREG.PRG
* PROGRAM TO PRINT THE NATIONAL WIDGETS INVOICE REGISTER
* WRITTEN BY:  M.LISKIN         5/10/85

select 1
use NWCUST index NWCACCT
select 2
use NWTXN index NWTINVC
set relation to ACCOUNT into NWCUST
report form NWINVREG to print
```

Figure 7-1. A program to print the National Widgets Invoice Register

- The names of the Customer and Transaction files.
- The name of the Transaction File index that enables you to print the report in numerical order by invoice number.
- The syntax of the USE command.
- How to open two files in two work areas.
- How to link two files with SET RELATION.
- The name of the Customer File index used to link the Customer and Transaction files with SET RELATION.
- The name of the common field used to link the Customer and Transaction files with SET RELATION.
- The name of the report form.
- The syntax of the REPORT command.

Once you have written the program, you only have to remember its name to run it.

Using the MODIFY COMMAND Editor To Write dBASE III PLUS Programs

You can write dBASE III PLUS programs with any word processor or text editor that can produce an ordinary ASCII text file, but for your convenience a rudimentary editor is provided with dBASE III PLUS. This editor is essentially the same dBASE III PLUS Word Processor used to enter and edit memo field text, with the addition of a few commands for reading and writing external files. You invoke the editor by typing

MODIFY COMMAND *program name*

As with other dBASE III PLUS commands that read or write disk files, if you do not include the file name in the command, dBASE III PLUS prompts you to enter it. You need not specify the extension if you use the standard .PRG. If you are actually writing a dBASE III PLUS program, there is no reason to deviate from the default .PRG extension, but as you will see in Chapter 8, the dBASE III PLUS editor may also be used to edit other types of files, such as format files.

The MODIFY COMMAND editor makes use of all the standard dBASE III PLUS full-screen edit mode commands. The command keys and their specific meanings in MODIFY COMMAND are listed in Table 7-1. As in other full-screen edit modes, you save your changes on disk and exit to the dot prompt with CTRL-W or the equivalent CTRL-END. Either ESC or CTRL-Q exits without saving the edited version of the file.

Although it is more than adequate for typing the short programs in this chapter, MODIFY COMMAND lacks the variety of cursor movement commands and advanced text editing facilities that are found in most program editors and word processors and that are especially useful for writing, editing, and debugging longer and more complex programs. In particular, there is no search and replace capability, although there is a search command; and you cannot designate a group of lines to be copied, moved, or deleted as a block.

The length of the files you can edit with MODIFY COMMAND is limited to 5000 characters. Since one dBASE III PLUS program may call another, splitting a program into smaller pieces to avoid the length limit does not present an insurmountable obstacle, but it can be inconvenient. In addition, even before you near the 5000-character limit, the editor's response time slows so much that a fast typist can easily outstrip the program and lose characters.

MODIFY COMMAND assumes a line length of 65 characters or columns and will word-wrap lines at column 66. In doing so, the editor, like many word processors, inserts a *soft* carriage return that dBASE III PLUS can differentiate from the *hard* carriage return generated when you press the RETURN key. A dBASE III PLUS command may be up to 254 characters in length and must end with a hard return. You can always tell

Table 7-1. Command Keys Used in the MODIFY COMMAND Editor

Command Key(s)	Function
CTRL-E or UP ARROW	Move the cursor one line up
CTRL-X or DOWN ARROW	Move the cursor one line down
CTRL-S or LEFT ARROW	Move the cursor one character to the left
CTRL-D or RIGHT ARROW	Move the cursor one character to the right
CTRL-A or HOME	Move the cursor one word to the left
CTRL-F or END	Move the cursor one word to the right
CTRL-Z or CTRL-LEFT ARROW	Move the cursor to the left edge of the line
CTRL-B or CTRL-RIGHT ARROW	Move the cursor to the right edge of the line
CTRL-C or PGDN	Move forward to display the next 18 lines
CTRL-R or PGUP	Move backward to display the previous 18 lines
CTRL-G or DEL	Delete the character at the cursor position without leaving a gap in the line
BACKSPACE	Delete the character to the left of the cursor without leaving a gap in the line
CTRL-T	Delete characters from the cursor position to the end of the word (including the following space)
CTRL-Y	Delete the entire line containing the cursor
CTRL-V or INS	Turn insert mode on (if it is off) or off (if it is on)
CTRL-N or RETURN (with insert mode on)	Insert a carriage return at the cursor position
CTRL-KB	Reformat from the cursor position to the next carriage return to conform to a right margin of 66 characters
CTRL-KF	Search for a character string
CTRL-KL	Repeat the previous search
CTRL-KW	Write the entire file being edited to another file
CTRL-KR	Read another entire file into the file being edited
CTRL-Q or ESC	Exit to the dot prompt without saving changes to disk
CTRL-W or CTRL-PGUP or CTRL-END	Save changes and exit to the dot prompt

the difference between the hard returns you have typed and the soft returns inserted by the editor: a hard return is displayed as a < in column 79 of the screen. Although it is convenient for entering free-form memo text, the word-wrap feature can be a nuisance when you are writing a program to draw a screen image wider than 66 characters. Also, automatic word-wrap makes it difficult to indent lines consistently, a drawback in longer and more complex programs where a consistent scheme for indenting certain lines can make the program much easier to read and understand.

Defeating the dBASE III PLUS editor's word-wrap requires some extra work, but it can be done. You can break a line at any point by typing a semicolon (;), pressing RETURN, and resuming the command on the next line. The semicolon prevents dBASE III PLUS from interpreting the hard return as a signal to end the command. (You cannot do this at the dot prompt, where dBASE III PLUS instead uses horizontal scrolling to allow you to type and view long commands.) You can use a semicolon to break any line before you reach column 66; or after dBASE III PLUS wraps the line, you can delete the soft carriage return (located immediately to the right of the last character on the line, not in column 79) with DEL or CTRL-G. This leaves a long line that extends beyond the right-hand edge of the screen. You can leave the line this way or, with INSERT turned ON, insert a semicolon and a RETURN anywhere you wish. As long as you do not reformat with CTRL-KB, the line will remain exactly as you have adjusted it.

When you use these techniques, remember that any characters appearing to the right of the semicolon on the same screen line will be ignored, so be sure to press RETURN before you continue typing your command. Also, since the command continues with the very first character on the following line, make sure that you do not inadvertently omit any required spaces between the words in a command. For example, the following line will generate an error message because there is no space between REST and FOR:

```
REPORT FORM NWINVREG TO PRINT REST;
FOR INVAMOUNT - PMTAMOUNT > 0
```

This command could be written correctly either as

```
REPORT FORM NWINVREG TO PRINT REST ;
FOR INVAMOUNT - PMTAMOUNT > 0
```

or

```
REPORT FORM NWINVREG TO PRINT REST;
 FOR INVAMOUNT - PMTAMOUNT > 0
```

The MODIFY COMMAND editor does not provide a way to print a program, but you can do this from within dBASE III PLUS in two ways. For a short program you can simply use SHIFT-PRTSC from within MODIFY COMMAND to dump the contents of the screen to the printer. You can also use the TYPE command at the dot prompt to print the contents of any ASCII text file. By default the dBASE III PLUS TYPE command (like its MS-DOS counterpart) displays the file on the screen; to route the output to the printer, you may either toggle the printer on with CTRL-P or add the phrase TO PRINT to the command. Because TYPE does not assume that you are listing a *program,* you must specify the full name, including extension, of the file you wish to print:

```
TYPE NWINVREG.PRG TO PRINT
```

Although TYPE is more than adequate for short programs, this command provides no way to paginate a long listing or print headings or page numbers. The only control you have over the format of the printed listing is to change the left margin with

SET MARGIN TO *left margin*

Using a Word Processor to Write dBASE III PLUS Programs

As mentioned previously, you can use any word processor or text editor that can create a pure ASCII text file to write dBASE III PLUS programs. These include editors specifically intended for programming, like EDLIN and the IBM Personal Editor, as well as a number of popular word processors, such as WordStar, WordPerfect, Microsoft Word, PeachText, and Volkswriter.

You may have to consult the user's manual for your word processor to find out how to create a file with no special headers or command codes. For example, if you use WordStar, you must open and edit a program in non-document mode. With Microsoft Word you must select the (F)ormatted (N)o option when you use the (T)ransfer (S)ave command to write the program to the disk. With PeachText, you must turn off the compression of multiple spaces into tab characters with (M)ode (B)lank packing (N)o when you write programs that draw formatted screens, because dBASE III PLUS cannot reconvert tabs to spaces, and they will be displayed on the screen as graphics characters. With WordPerfect, you must press CTRL-F5 and then select option 1—"Save current document as a DOS text file"—from the Document Conversion and Locking Screen.

In other cases, producing an ASCII text file is not so easy, and you may decide to work with MODIFY COMMAND instead. Many programs, especially those designed to emulate dedicated word processors (MultiMate and DisplayWrite, for example), require the use of a separate utility program to convert a word processing document to an ASCII text file. The conversion must, of course, be repeated every time you edit the file to change the program.

If you are in doubt as to whether your word processor can create ASCII files, you can use the DOS or dBASE III PLUS TYPE command to examine a file created with the software. An ASCII text file contains only the normal printable character set (letters, numbers, and punctuation marks), and you should see only the commands that you have actually typed into the file. Some word processors store a special header section at the beginning of each document, which is as indecipherable to dBASE III PLUS (and, probably, to you) as the dBASE III PLUS file structure information stored at the beginning of a data base file would be to the word processor.

If you have enough RAM in your computer, you can use the RUN command to access your word processor from within dBASE III PLUS. In addition to the 256K minimum required by dBASE III PLUS, you will need enough additional memory to load COMMAND.COM (about 18K under MS-DOS version 2) and also the word processor. If you are using a copy of WordStar called WS.COM, you could run this program with

```
RUN WS
```

If you cannot place both the word processor and the dBASE III PLUS overlay file (dBASE.OVL) on the same disk because of the limited disk capacity of floppy-based systems or the way your word processor is copy-protected, you will have to do some disk swapping. Make sure the disk containing COMMAND.COM and the word processor is in the drive when you give the RUN command; after you exit from the word processor, dBASE III PLUS will request the disk with the DBASE.OVL file when it is needed.

When you edit a dBASE III PLUS program with a word processor, be sure to specify the .PRG file extension. Many word processors have their own default extensions (often .DOC for document), which you must override to make your file recognizable to dBASE III PLUS as a program. If your word processor does not allow you to supply your own file extension, or if you forget occasionally, you can rename the program afterward:

```
RENAME NWCSTAT1.DOC TO NWCSTAT1.PRG
```

If you are sure that you will always want to use an external word processor to edit programs, you may add a line to your CONFIG.DB file to cause MODIFY COMMAND to invoke the word processor instead of the dBASE III PLUS editor:

TEDIT = *program name*

For example, to substitute WordStar for the MODIFY COMMAND editor, you would use

```
TEDIT = WS
```

The same memory requirements that govern the use of the RUN command apply here, and just as with RUN, the word processor disk must be present in the drive when you type MODIFY COMMAND. If you specify a file name in the MODIFY COMMAND command, it will be passed to the word processor. Of course, if the word processor permits you to save a file without exiting from the program, you can also edit additional files before returning to dBASE III PLUS. Also note that a program like WordStar must be reinstalled—to start up in non-document mode by default—to avoid automatically choosing the wrong editing mode and introducing non-ASCII characters into your programs.

You will probably prefer the flexibility of using the RUN command to the convenience of "permanently" substituting a word processor for the dBASE III PLUS editor: you can use the word processor to write a long new program or make large-scale changes in an existing file but still use the dBASE III PLUS MODIFY COMMAND editor, which loads faster, for writing short programs or fixing typos.

If you find it inconvenient to use your word processor as a program editor, consider purchasing a RAM-resident utility program (like Side-Kick) that has a Notepad editor. These programs can generally write straight ASCII files, and they are small enough not to require a great deal of RAM. Also, because they are always present in memory, accessing the editor and your program file is extremely fast.

AUTOMATING FREQUENTLY USED PROCEDURES: A SIMPLE CALCULATION PROGRAM

The NWINVREG.PRG program is useful because it reduces to a single command the five required to print a report from the dot prompt; so printing is easier for an operator who is unfamiliar with the intricacies of dBASE III PLUS command syntax. Procedures that perform calculations or update files are also well suited to this type of automation, since they often involve lengthy or complex command sequences. In the National Widgets sample system, the steps required to process a batch of newly entered Order File records can be combined into a program, NWO-CALC.PRG (National Widgets Order File Calculation Program), listed in Figure 7-2. This program opens the Order and Inventory files, links them with SET RELATION so that the PRICE and EQUIPMENT fields may be read from the Inventory File into the Order File records, and calculates the SUBTOTAL, DISCOUNT, and INVAMOUNT fields.

Note that the test for missing Inventory File records described in Chapter 6 was incorporated into this program:

```
LIST ACCOUNT, INVOICE, CATEGORY, PARTNUMBER TO PRINT
 FOR NWINVENT->PARTNUMBER = " "
```

This test depends on the fact that once you have linked the Order File to the Inventory File with SET RELATION through CATEGORY + PART-NUMBER (the common fields), the Inventory File is automatically positioned to the record containing the same combination of CATEGORY and PARTNUMBER as the record that dBASE III PLUS is pointing to in the Order File. If no matching record exists, the Inventory File is not positioned at any valid record, and the NWINVENT—>PARTNUMBER field (as well as any other field in the Inventory File) will be blank.

```
* NWOCALC.PRG
* PROGRAM TO FILL IN CALCULATED FIELDS IN NATIONAL WIDGETS ORDER FILE
* WRITTEN BY:    M.LISKIN        5/10/85

select 1
use NWINVENT index NWICATPT
select 2
use NWORDER
set relation to CATEGORY+PARTNUMBER into NWINVENT
replace all EQUIPMENT with NWINVENT->EQUIPMENT,;
  PRICE with NWINVENT->PRICE, SUBTOTAL with PRICE * QUANTITY,;
  DISCOUNT with DISCRATE * SUBTOTAL / 100,;
  INVAMOUNT with SUBTOTAL - DISCOUNT
list ACCOUNT, INVOICE, CATEGORY, PARTNUMBER to print;
  for NWINVENT->PARTNUMBER = " "
close databases
```

Figure 7-2. A program to perform Order File calculations

When you begin writing programs, you may assume that because the computer is doing all the work, nothing could possibly go wrong. Tests like the one just described reduce the likelihood that a serious problem will go unnoticed, but you cannot test for every possible contingency. For example, although missing Inventory records will be flagged, the NWO-CALC.PRG program cannot determine whether the price derived from the Inventory File is the correct one to use for a particular order. If certain order records must use a special sale price, you will have to change the PRICE field and recalculate the SUBTOTAL, DISCOUNT, and INVAMOUNT for these records.

The CLOSE DATABASES command at the end of the program closes all data base and index files open in any of the ten work areas. (Remember that the USE command closes only the file and indexes in the currently selected work area.) Closing the files protects against loss of data in case of a power failure or in the event that another user shuts down the computer after your program has finished without first closing the files or exiting from dBASE III PLUS with a QUIT command, which closes all open data bases. When a program opens more than one file, including a CLOSE DATABASES command is particularly important. In dBASE III PLUS a file cannot be open in more than one work area at a time, to prevent your making conflicting sets of changes in the two areas. If, after your program finished, another operator, working in area 1, tried to open the NWORDER file already open in area 2, dBASE III PLUS would issue the error message "File is already open." This could confuse someone who is unfamiliar with your program and does not thoroughly understand how to work with multiple files.

AUTOMATING LENGTHY PROCEDURES

Writing simple programs allows you to automate lengthy command sequences and time-consuming procedures so they may be run unattended, or perhaps overnight, thus reducing the amount of time you must spend waiting for a command to be executed so that you can type the next. Placing a complex sequence of commands into a program also lessens the chance that a careless error will corrupt the integrity of the data files.

Recall the command level procedure developed for the National Widgets system in Chapter 4 to generate Transaction File records from a batch of Order File entries:

```
USE NWORDER INDEX NWOINVC
TOTAL ON INVOICE TO NWORDTMP
USE NWTXN INDEX NWTACCT, NWTINVC
APPEND FROM NWORDTMP
DELETE FILE NWORDTMP.DBF
USE NWORDHST INDEX NWOHACCT, NWOHINVC
APPEND FROM NWORDER
USE NWORDER INDEX NWOACCT, NWOINVC
ZAP
```

This procedure first uses the TOTAL command to summarize all of the individual Order File records for each invoice into a single record in the temporary file NWORDTMP.DBF. The temporary file is APPENDed to the Transaction File, NWTXN.DBF, and then deleted. Since National Widgets wishes to maintain up to a full year's history of all items ordered, the records in the Order File are APPENDed to the Order History File, NWORDHST.DBF, before the ZAP command empties the Order File to prepare for a new batch of entries.

The larger the Order File, the longer the TOTAL command will take to execute. The same is true of the APPEND steps, especially since both NWTXN.DBF and NWORDHST.DBF are opened with more than one index and dBASE III PLUS must update each of the named indexes to reflect the newly APPENDed records. Automating this procedure by combining the steps into the NWOPOST1.PRG program listed in Figure 7-3 not only eliminates the tedium of typing the commands and waiting for each one to be executed, but it also helps to protect the accuracy of the crucial financial data contained in the data bases. Consider the implications of omitting either of the APPEND steps by mistake: an entire batch of orders would be lost from the Order History File, or worse, from the current Transaction File, which maintains National Widgets' accounts receivable records.

Monitoring a Program's Progress

When you type commands one by one at the dot prompt with TALK ON, dBASE III PLUS displays messages to inform you of the actions the program has taken in response to your commands. For potentially long-running commands like APPEND, COPY, or INDEX, these status messages provide a running display of the number of records or the percentage of the file processed so you can estimate how much more time will be required to complete the operation. When you automate lengthy procedures by combining the steps into dBASE III PLUS programs, you must not only provide a way to monitor the progress of the individual

```
* NWOPOST1.PRG
* PROGRAM TO CREATE INVOICE TRANSACTIONS FROM ORDERS,
*   AND ADD ORDERS TO ORDER HISTORY FILE
* WRITTEN BY:  M.LISKIN     5/10/85

use NWORDER index NWOINVC
total on INVOICE to NWORDTMP
use NWTXN index NWTACCT, NWTINVC
append from NWORDTMP
use NWORDHST index NWOHACCT, NWOHINVC
append from NWORDER
use NWORDER index NWOACCT, NWOINVC
zap
use
```

Figure 7-3. An order-posting program

commands, but also a way to keep track of how many program steps have already been executed.

When you run a program, dBASE III PLUS displays the same status messages on the screen that it would if you had typed the commands one at a time from the dot prompt. Figure 7-4 illustrates what the screen looks like as the order posting program, NWOPOST1.PRG, processes a small batch of Order File records. If you compare this display with the program listing in Figure 7-3, you can easily match each message to the command that generated it; but while the program is running, the screen may not seem very informative. You can suppress the display completely with SET TALK OFF, but if the program will be running for any length of time, this is inadvisable. The status display at least indicates that *something is happening*, making it less likely that an operator who is unacquainted with your program will reboot, thinking the system is hung up.

You can obtain an even more explicit record of the program's activity by using SET ECHO ON to echo each command line in the program to the screen as it is executed. You could type this command from the dot prompt before you run the program, but it is more expedient to enter it into the program. The SET ECHO OFF command at the end of the program ensures that in your subsequent work at command level, you won't see each command repeated after you type it. The new version of the program, NWOPOST2.PRG, is listed in Figure 7-5, and Figure 7-6 illustrates the appearance of the screen when you run the program.

```
. DO NWOPOST1

     38 Record(s) totalled
     11 Records generated
     11 records added
     38 records added
.
```

Figure 7-4. Running the order-posting program

```
* NWOPOST2.PRG
* PROGRAM TO CREATE INVOICE TRANSACTIONS FROM ORDERS,
*   AND ADD ORDERS TO ORDER HISTORY FILE
* WRITTEN BY:  M.LISKIN     5/10/85
* REVISED BY:  M.LISKIN     5/11/85


set echo on
use NWORDER index NWOINVC
total on INVOICE to NWORDTMP
use NWTXN index NWTACCT, NWTINVC
append from NWORDTMP
use NWORDHST index NWOHACCT, NWOHINVC
append from NWORDER
use NWORDER index NWOACCT, NWOINVC
zap
use
set echo off
```

Figure 7-5. The revised order-posting program

```
. DO NWOPOST2

set echo on
use NWORDER index NWOINVC
total on INVOICE to NWORDTMP
     38 Record(s) totalled
     11 Records generated
use NWTXN index NWTACCT, NWTINVC
append from NWORDTMP
     11 records added
delete file NWORDTMP.DBF
File has been deleted
use NWORDHST index NWOHACCT, NWOHINVC
append from NWORDER
     38 records added
use NWORDER index NWOACCT, NWOINVC
zap
use
set echo off
.
```

Figure 7-6. Running the revised order-posting program

A Program to Reindex The Data Bases

If you have ever worked with a data base file containing more than a few hundred records, you understand that constructing a new index for a large file can be slow, even on a hard disk. In any dBASE III PLUS application, at least two situations requiring indexing can be improved by combining the separate steps into programs. The first, an obvious candidate for this type of automation, is building an index that is used only for the purpose of printing a report, and then running the report. While indexing is generally safe to run unattended, it is more risky to print the report with no one physically present. If the paper or ribbon jams, you can lose more than your report—it is not uncommon to burn out the printhead on a dot-matrix printer this way. Writing a program to construct all of the indexes required for a number of reports is a safer approach. This program could be run overnight, and all of the reports printed the following day. (Of course, if you make further changes to a data base before printing one of the reports, you must be careful to include the required index among those named in your USE command, to avoid having to rebuild it.)

Second, every dBASE III PLUS system should have, as part of its disaster recovery procedures (which will be discussed in more detail later), a program to rebuild *all* of the indexes associated with *all* of the data bases. This program would allow you to return easily to normal operation after an operator either inadvertently or intentionally (to save time during high-volume data entry) opens a data base without one or more of its indexes. You may already have reindexed a data base at command level, using a sequence of steps like this:

```
USE NWCUST INDEX NWCACCT, NWCZIP
REINDEX
```

The REINDEX command is handy because it does not require that you remember the expressions that make up the index keys; you need only know the names of the indexes associated with the data base. This is possible because the key expression is stored at the beginning of the index file, where it can be read by dBASE III PLUS. However, REINDEX is not always the best way to regenerate the index. If an index is damaged by a hardware or disk failure, dBASE III PLUS may not be able to read the key expression from the damaged file, and you must instead use the same command that created the index in the first place:

INDEX ON *key expression* TO *index file name*

Using this construction in the reindexing program also allows it to be used as part of the recovery procedure if a more drastic hardware or software failure requires all of the data bases to be recopied from the backup disks. (Since the indexes may be recreated from scratch, you can save time in your daily routine by not backing up the index files.) The program in Figure 7-7, NWREIND1.PRG, rebuilds all of the indexes normally used with the National Widgets system data bases. As you write a similar program to reindex the files in your own applications, you can refer to the file structure and status listings printed earlier (like those in Chapter 2) to find any index keys you have forgotten.

```
* NWREIND1.PRG
* PROGRAM TO REINDEX ALL NATIONAL WIDGETS SYSTEM DATA BASES
* WRITTEN BY:   M.LISKIN          5/11/85

set echo on

use NWCUST
index on ACCOUNT to NWCACCT
index on ZIP to NWCZIP

use NWINVENT
index on CATEGORY + PARTNUMBER to NWICATPT

use NWTXN
index on ACCOUNT + INVOICE to NWTACCT
index on INVOICE to NWTINVC

use NWORDER
index on ACCOUNT + INVOICE to NWOACCT
index on INVOICE to NWOINVC

use NWTXNHST
index on ACCOUNT + INVOICE to NWTHACCT
index on INVOICE to NWTHINVC

use NWORDHST
index on ACCOUNT + INVOICE to NWOHACCT
index on INVOICE to NWOHINVC

use
set echo off
```

Figure 7-7. A program to reindex all of the National Widgets system data bases

A Program to Compile Statistics

The final program presented in this chapter extends beyond the standard procedures developed in Chapter 4 to perform file maintenance operations. This program, NWCSTAT1.PRG, will compile statistics on National Widgets' customers based on the type of computer equipment they own. It will count the number of customers in each category and accumulate year-to-date and total orders, as well as year-to-date and overall average dollars per customer, for all owners of IBM, Apple, Kaypro, and COMPAQ computers. At command level you could use the COUNT, SUM, and AVERAGE commands to compile the desired statistics. Figure 7-8 illustrates the dialog with dBASE III PLUS (your commands and the dBASE III PLUS responses) for just one of the categories.

These statistics represent the kind of management information that is very difficult to obtain by hand—exactly the type of ad hoc inquiry at which dBASE III PLUS excels. But in a large file, the immediacy of the query process is diminished by the fact that computing the totals can be time-consuming. Each COUNT, SUM, or AVERAGE command causes dBASE III PLUS to read through the entire data base, testing each record against the condition in the FOR clause to determine whether it should be included in the statistics. Using one SUM or AVERAGE command to process two fields (a maximum of 16 is permitted) maximizes the efficiency of these commands. Nevertheless, accumulating the desired statistics for four categories of customers requires 12 complete passes through the file. Placing the same commands into a dBASE III PLUS program enables you to calculate the totals without typing each command individually and waiting for the results.

When you use COUNT, SUM, or AVERAGE from within a program, you need a way to save the computed results; if the program has many steps, the output of the first few commands will scroll off the screen before the final numbers have been calculated. One way to do this is to record the output of the program on the printer with SET PRINT ON. To save the results in a text file on disk instead, you can use SET ALTERNATE TO NWCSTAT1, followed by SET ALTERNATE ON.

The statistics computed by the SUM, COUNT, and AVERAGE commands may also be preserved in memory variables, which you can examine at your convenience with DISPLAY MEMORY and use in subsequent calculations. This technique is illustrated in Figure 7-9. Storing the calculated results in memory variables also allows the program to be written much more efficiently. The example in Figure 7-8 was intended to illus-

```
. USE NWCUST
. COUNT FOR "IBM" $ EQUIPMENT
      5 records
. SUM YTDINV, TOTINV FOR "IBM" $ EQUIPMENT
      5 records summed
        417.21        3380.71
. AVERAGE YTDINV, TOTINV FOR "IBM" $ EQUIPMENT
      5 records averaged
     83.44      676.14
```

Figure 7-8. Using COUNT, SUM, and AVERAGE to compile statistics

trate all three of the dBASE III PLUS statistical commands, but using SUM, COUNT, and AVERAGE entails doing some extra work, because the AVERAGE is simply the sum divided by the count. However, if you have saved the counts and sums, the averages can be calculated and displayed with

```
? MYSUMIBM/MCOUNTIBM, MTSUMIBM/MCOUNTIBM
```

When a dBASE III PLUS program terminates, the names and values of all memory variables created within the program are RELEASEd (erased

```
. USE NWCUST
. COUNT TO MCOUNTIBM FOR "IBM" $ EQUIPMENT
      5 records
. SUM YTDINV, TOTINV TO MYSUMIBM, MTSUMIBM FOR "IBM" $ EQUIPMENT
      5 records summed
        417.21        3380.71
. DISPLAY MEMORY
MCOUNTIBM    pub    N           5  (         5.00000000)
MYSUMIBM     pub    N      417.21  (       417.21000000)
MTSUMIBM     pub    N     3380.71  (      3380.71000000)
    3 variables defined,       27 bytes used
  253 variables available,   5973 bytes available
```

Figure 7-9. Saving the counts and sums in memory variables

from working memory). One way to overcome this limitation is to save the variables on disk with

SAVE TO *memory variable file*

The memory variables may be retrieved later with

RESTORE FROM *memory variable file*

The accuracy of the COUNT command can be affected by errors made during data entry. Several people (or the same person at different times) may have entered data using various mixtures of upper- and lowercase letters (for example, in the EQUIPMENT field, "Kaypro", "KAYPRO", or "KayPro") into the file. You can circumvent this problem by using the UPPER function to convert the contents of the EQUIPMENT field to uppercase (or the LOWER function to convert to lowercase) for the purpose of the comparison. Doing this does not change the actual data stored in the Customer File; the uppercase version of the EQUIPMENT field is simply used in the comparison with the uppercase string specified in the FOR clause.

If you also doubt the consistency of the spelling, you can search for less than the full name. For example, if you suspect that you may have entered both "Osborne" and "Osborn" into the file, you could use

```
COUNT TO MCOUNTOSB FOR "OSBORN" $ UPPER(EQUIPMENT)
```

The equivalent, using the LOWER function, would be

```
COUNT TO MCOUNTOSB FOR "osborn" $ lower(EQUIPMENT)
```

Of course, more drastic misspellings like "Ozborn" would be harder to detect. The completed program, NWCSTAT1.PRG, which lists the memory variables to the printer and saves them in a memory file called NWCSTAT1.MEM, is shown in Figure 7-10.

Once you have decided not to allow the prospect of writing programs to intimidate you, you can look through your own applications for command sequences that lend themselves to this type of automation. If you used a paper log or an ALTERNATE file to record your work sessions at command level, these logs can supply the successful command sequences

```
* NWCSTAT1.PRG
* PROGRAM TO CALCULATE COUNTS AND YEAR-TO-DATE AND OVERALL TOTAL INVOICE
*   AMOUNTS AND AVERAGES FOR CUSTOMERS WHO OWN IBM EQUIPMENT
* WRITTEN BY:  M.LISKIN      5/11/85


set echo on
use NWCUST

count to MCOUNTIBM for "IBM" $ UPPER(EQUIPMENT)
sum YTDINV, TOTINV to MYSUMIBM, MTSUMIBM for "IBM" $ UPPER(EQUIPMENT)

count to MCOUNTAPP for "APPLE" $ UPPER(EQUIPMENT)
sum YTDINV, TOTINV to MYSUMAP, MTSUMAPP for "APPLE" $ UPPER(EQUIPMENT)

count to MCOUNTKAY for "KAYPRO" $ UPPER(EQUIPMENT)
sum YTDINV, TOTINV to MYSUMKAY, MTSUMKAY for "KAYPRO" $ UPPER(EQUIPMENT)

count to MCOUNTCOM for "COMPAQ" $ UPPER(EQUIPMENT)
sum YTDINV, TOTINV to MYSUMCOM, MTSUMCOM for "COMPAQ" $ UPPER(EQUIPMENT)

save to NWCSTATS
list memory to print
use
set echo off
```

Figure 7-10. A program to compile statistics for customers who own IBM equipment

that will make up the programs. You can even avoid having to retype the commands by editing a copy of the ALTERNATE file to remove the dBASE III PLUS dot prompts, the text displayed on the screen by dBASE III PLUS, and any extraneous commands.

If you are creating the National Widgets case study, you can examine the system outline in Figure 1-6 and review the procedures developed in Chapters 4 and 5 to find additional operations that may be automated with the kind of short programs illustrated in this chapter. As an exercise, you might try writing programs to post invoice and payment data from the Transaction File to the Customer File and to carry out the end-of-month and end-of-year procedures.

8

CREATING CUSTOM DATA ENTRY SCREENS

In Chapter 7 we took the first step toward automating a dBASE III PLUS data base system by combining sets of commands into simple programs. These programs are a convenience for any user and an absolute necessity in an environment in which not every operator is familiar with dBASE III PLUS command syntax. In this chapter we will begin to make the system even more accessible to novice users by creating customized data entry screens. These screens also help improve the accuracy of the information in the data base by applying validation tests to some of the fields and by automatically formatting others to ensure consistency.

As you know from your work at command level, in the standard data entry screen used by the dBASE III PLUS full-screen APPEND, EDIT, INSERT, and CHANGE commands, the field names in the data base are aligned on the left side of the screen as prompts. Normally, dBASE III PLUS displays the field names as light characters on a dark background, with the fields themselves in inverse video (dark characters on a bright background). This chapter will describe how to improve on the standard dBASE III PLUS data entry screen in the following ways:

- By customizing the screen colors or monochrome display attributes for both data and background text.
- By controlling the manner in which data is distinguished from background text.

- By designing more attractive screen layouts than the default data entry screen.
- By drawing lines and boxes with graphics characters.
- By using prompts that are longer and more descriptive than the field names.
- By presenting informative messages to guide the user in filling out the screen.
- By selecting which fields in a data base may be viewed and which may be altered by the operator.
- By displaying fields differently from the raw form in which they are stored in the data base.
- By guaranteeing that data entered into numeric and date fields falls within an allowable range.
- By controlling the type of data that may be entered into a field.
- By ensuring that character fields requiring embedded punctuation are entered consistently.
- By displaying and entering long character fields in a smaller screen window.

You can achieve these goals in dBASE III PLUS by using SET commands (to control the screen colors or monochrome display attributes) and format files. A *format file* is a special kind of dBASE III PLUS program, consisting solely of commands that display or collect data on the screen. With format files you can create custom screen layouts and introduce additional data formatting and validation capabilities. As will be shown in Chapter 12, a format file may be used not only at command level, but also from within a dBASE III PLUS program. If format files do not satisfy all of your data entry requirements, the same data display and collection commands that make up the format files in this chapter may also be used to construct more sophisticated custom data entry programs.

CONTROLLING SCREEN DISPLAY COLORS AND ATTRIBUTES

The use of inverse video in the default dBASE III PLUS data entry screen highlights the data so that it stands out from the background text and indicates the maximum field lengths, but it can be visually tiring during a long data entry session. You can alter the visual attributes of the screens used for full-screen editing with the SET INTENSITY, SET COLOR, and SET DELIMITERS commands.

The SET INTENSITY command determines whether background text is displayed differently from data entered by the operator. SET COLOR allows for separate control of the foreground and background colors used for both displayed and entered data. SET DELIMITERS enables you to define a set of punctuation marks to bracket the data fields on the screen, so that even with INTENSITY OFF and no special colors assigned, the field lengths are clearly delineated. The options that you SET with these commands govern the appearance of the screen when you work with the standard dBASE III PLUS full-screen commands and also apply to screens drawn by a format file or, as you will see in Part IV, a data entry program.

Controlling Color With SET COLOR

The SET COLOR command can change screen colors or, on a monochrome monitor, display attributes, to suit your personal preferences. SET COLOR gives you separate control over three distinct regions on the screen: the *standard display area,* the *enhanced display area,* and the *border.* These three areas are shown in Figure 8-1, which illustrates the appearance of the screen when a customer record in the National Widgets Customer File, NWCUST.DBF, is being edited.

With SET COLOR you can assign any single color to the border, the part of the screen that lies outside of the 25-line-by-80-character display area used by dBASE III PLUS. For the standard and enhanced areas, which are defined not by physical location on the screen *but by their usage,* you may control both the foreground and background colors. The colors assigned to the standard area are used for all text displayed by dBASE III PLUS, including the commands you type, dBASE III PLUS's responses and status messages, and field name prompts in the full-screen edit modes. The colors in the enhanced area are used for all data entered by the user. Despite the choice of terminology, the enhanced area need not be brighter than the standard area; you may assign to either area any pair of foreground and background colors.

The format for the SET COLOR command follows.

SET COLOR TO *standard foreground/standard background, enhanced foreground/standard background, border*

On a monochrome monitor the SET COLOR command allows you to select, instead of colors, the monochrome display attributes: normal video, underlining, or reverse video. The colors or monochrome attributes are expressed as letter codes. All of the codes and their meanings for the standard IBM monochrome and color monitors are summarized in Table 8-1. The addition of an asterisk (*) to a color abbreviation causes the display to flash, and a plus sign (+) produces high-intensity rather than low-intensity color.

If you leave out any of the five possible options in the SET COLOR command, the defaults—black for the border, white foreground on a black background for the standard area, and black foreground on a white background (inverse video) for the enhanced area—are used. These default values are the same for both color and monochrome display

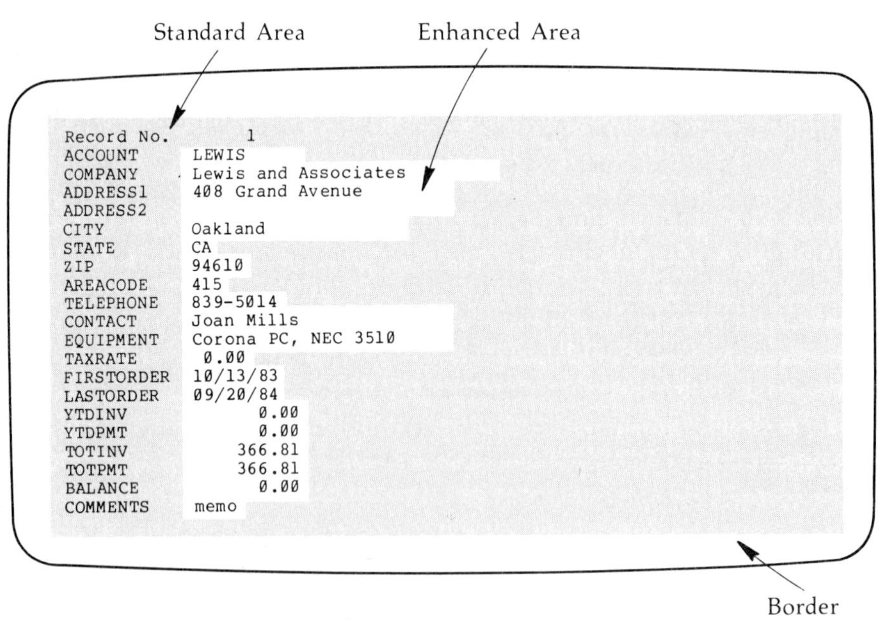

Figure 8-1. The dBASE III PLUS screen areas

Table 8-1. Color and Monochrome Attribute Codes

Color	Low Intensity	High Intensity
Black	N	
Blue	B	B+
Green	G	G+
Cyan	BG	BG+
Red	R	R+
Magenta	RB	RB+
Brown	GR	
Yellow		GR+
White	W	W+
Blank	X	
Monochrome Attribute	**Low Intensity**	**High Intensity**
Light	W	W+
Dark	N	
Inverse	I	I+
Underlined	U	U+

screens. A little experimentation at command level is the best way to determine the combination of colors or attributes that you find most comfortable and visually pleasing.

As an example (one that is not very attractive), the following command would set the standard colors used for text displayed by dBASE III PLUS to high-intensity white letters on a blue background, the enhanced colors used for entered data to red letters on a black background, and the border to green:

```
SET COLOR TO W+/B, R/N, G
```

In CONFIG.DB you would use

```
COLOR = W+/B, R/N, G
```

On a monochrome monitor, you could set the standard color to low-intensity reverse video and the enhanced color to high-intensity underlined letters with the command that follows.

```
SET COLOR TO I, U+
```

In these two examples, since the enhanced background and border colors were omitted, the default black will be used.

Surrounding Data Fields With Delimiters

Assigning different colors to the standard and enhanced areas with the SET COLOR option makes it easier to distinguish data to be entered by the operator from background text and data fields displayed by dBASE III PLUS. For the operator's convenience, the different colors also clearly emphasize the maximum field lengths. Instead of or in addition to color, you may wish to use one or two delimiters to set off data entry fields. The beginning and ending delimiter may be the same—for example, a colon (:) or vertical bar (|)—or they may be different. One common choice is a matching set of brackets ([and] or < and >). By default dBASE III PLUS does not use delimiters, so you must first activate this feature:

SET DELIMITERS ON

The actual delimiter character(s) are specified with

SET DELIMITERS TO *delimiter(s)*

If you feel that the delimiters are sufficient to differentiate between the standard and enhanced areas, you may use SET INTENSITY OFF to eliminate the difference in color between these areas. With INTENSITY OFF, the colors assigned to the standard display area—or the default colors, if you have not altered them with a SET COLOR command—are also used for the enhanced area. Thus, the sequence of commands you would use at the dot prompt to turn off the default inverse video and assign the square brackets as delimiters is

```
SET INTENSITY OFF
SET DELIMITERS ON
SET DELIMITERS TO "[]"
```

Or, in the CONFIG.DB file,

```
INTENSITY = OFF
DELIMITERS = ON
DELIMITERS = "[]"
```

DISPLAYING AND COLLECTING DATA ON THE SCREEN

The most powerful tool dBASE III PLUS provides for controlling the display and collection of data on the screen is the @...SAY...GET command. This command may be used in format files and in dBASE III PLUS programs to control precisely the placement and format of text and data displayed on the screen or printed on paper and to format and validate data entered by the operator. The complete syntax for this command is

@ *row, column* SAY *expression* GET *expression* PICTURE *picture* FUNCTION *function* RANGE *minimum value, maximum value*

This section describes the row and column coordinate system; it also explains the use of the SAY clause to display data and of the GET clause to enter data. The PICTURE, FUNCTION, and RANGE clauses used for formatting and validation will be discussed in the following section on combining @...SAY...GET commands into format files.

The dBASE III PLUS display screen has 25 rows (lines), numbered from 0 at the top to 24 at the bottom, and 80 columns, numbered from 0 to 79 from left to right. Lines 22 through 24 are normally reserved for the dBASE III PLUS status display. You can free these lines for your own use with SET STATUS OFF, which relocates some of the messages normally included in the status bar on line 22 to line 0. With STATUS OFF, line 0 is used for the INSERT and CAPS indicators, the *DEL* indicator that appears when a deleted record is edited, and certain other error messages, such as "Invalid date (press SPACE)," which appears if you enter an illegal value like 13/44/85 into a date field. If you absolutely must use line 0, you can also SET SCOREBOARD OFF to suppress all of these status messages; but it is preferable to leave the SCOREBOARD ON for the convenience of the user, and use this line sparingly, if at all, in your format files and programs.

Displaying Text and Data Fields

Using row and column coordinates, you can position text or enter data anywhere on the screen. All text placed on the screen with SAY, *including data fields,* is displayed using the standard (not enhanced) colors or monochrome attributes and without surrounding delimiters. Although the @...SAY command is intended for use within format files and dBASE III PLUS programs, you can also type this command at the dot prompt, so you can try the examples in this chapter and experiment with your own variations.

The following command displays the message "Welcome to the world of dBASE III PLUS" on line 10 (the eleventh line from the top of the screen), beginning at column 15:

```
@ 10,15 SAY "Welcome to the world of dBASE III PLUS"
```

To display the EQUIPMENT field from the Customer File at line 5, column 10, you would use

```
@ 5,10 SAY EQUIPMENT
```

With dBASE III PLUS you can SAY not just a single character string or data field, but *any syntactically correct expression.* You can also combine a character field, specified by name, with a prompt message, which is simply an arbitrary character string enclosed in quotes:

```
@ 5,10 SAY "Type of Computer Equipment: " + EQUIPMENT
```

Data types may not be mixed directly in an expression, so in order to display a numeric field or date this way, you must use the STR or DTOC (date-to-character) conversion function to convert the field to a character string so it may be concatenated with the prompt message:

```
@ 5,10 SAY "Customer Balance: " + STR(BALANCE,10,2)
```

or

```
@ 5,10 SAY "Most Recent Order Date: " + DTOC(LASTORDER)
```

You can avoid using the conversion functions and achieve the same results with two separate SAY commands:

```
@ 5,10 SAY "Most Recent Order Date: "
@ 5,34 SAY LASTORDER
```

Collecting Data Into Fields

The GET clause collects data into a field, with or without an accompanying message displayed by SAY. To present the words "Customer's Company Name" as a prompt at column 5 of line 10 on the screen and collect the operator's entry into the COMPANY field in the Customer File, you could use

```
@ 10,5 SAY "Customer's Company Name" GET COMPANY
```

If the field named in the GET clause is empty, the prompt specified in the SAY clause will be followed by a highlighted bar of the background color you have chosen for the enhanced area (with INTENSITY ON) or a set of delimiters (with DELIMITERS ON) indicating the position of the field. If the field already contains data, the current value is displayed within the delimiters for the operator to change:

```
Customer's Company Name [ABC Plumbing                    ]
```

Remember that the Customer File (or any other data base containing a field called COMPANY) must be open or a memory variable called COMPANY must exist in order for the command in this example to make sense. If no field or memory variable named COMPANY is available, the command will generate a "Variable not found" error message. When you are debugging your own programs or format files, look for misspelled field names or failure to open the right data base as the most likely cause for this error message.

dBASE III PLUS automatically supplies one space between the text displayed by SAY and the data field specified in the GET clause. If you want additional spaces, you may include them in the prompt:

```
@ 10,5 SAY "Customer's Company Name     " GET COMPANY
```

You may also GET a field without SAYing a message; for example:

```
@ 10,15 SAY "Telephone Number" GET AREACODE
@ 10,40 GET TELEPHONE
```

These two commands will result in this display:

```
Telephone Number  [415]   [861-4543]
```

CREATING CUSTOM SCREENS WITH FORMAT FILES

A *format file* is a text file consisting only of @...SAY...GET commands and, optionally, READ commands and comment lines. The file is identified to dBASE III PLUS as a format file by the extension .FMT. Format files may be used to enter and edit records with the dBASE III PLUS full-screen APPEND, EDIT, INSERT, and CHANGE commands, and they may also be invoked from within a dBASE III PLUS program. Through a format file you can design your own data entry forms, which can include multiple screen "pages," borders, headings, messages, and more descriptive prompts than the field names. You can use PICTUREs and FUNCTIONs to format data fields and validate numeric and date fields by restricting entries to a permissible RANGE of values. You can select the fields you wish to display, and you can control the ones that may be altered by the operator. It is possible to display and update information from two data bases by linking them with SET RELATION. Like dBASE III PLUS programs, format files may be created with MODIFY COMMAND or any other text editor that can produce a plain ASCII file. You open a format file with

SET FORMAT TO *format file name*

Once invoked, the format file replaces the default data entry screen used by the APPEND, EDIT, CHANGE and INSERT commands. All of the standard cursor movement and editing commands behave the same as in any of the other full-screen edit modes. The SET INTENSITY, SET COLOR, and SET DELIMITER commands have the same effects on the appearance of displayed text and entered data as they do when used with the standard dBASE III PLUS screens. Only one format file may be open in any work area, although, as noted previously, this format file may access fields from more than one data base. To cancel the format file in use in the current work area and return to the standard dBASE III PLUS screen, you can use either SET FORMAT TO or CLOSE FORMAT. The USE command, which closes the data base in the current work area, and the CLOSE ALL and CLOSE DATABASES commands, which close all open data bases, also close the corresponding format files.

A format file need not include all of the fields in a data base, and you do not have to allow entry in all of the ones that you do display. If new records are APPENDed with such a format file, any fields not collected with GET commands will simply remain blank. You can therefore use format files to control the fields that are accessible for a particular purpose or to a particular operator. Figure 8-2 illustrates a very simple format file, NWCUST1.FMT, which permits the user to enter and edit the name and address fields in the National Widgets Customer File and displays the BALANCE field without allowing it to be altered.

Note that extra spaces within the command lines have been inserted into the @...SAY...GET commands in NWCUST1.FMT to align the corresponding components of each command vertically, making the format file easy to read. The @...SAY...GET commands may be used to place data on the screen in any order. The format files in this chapter draw the screens from top to bottom and from left to right, combining the SAY commands that display the prompts with the GET commands

```
* NWCUST1.FMT
* FORMAT FILE FOR CUSTOMER FILE UPDATE AND INQUIRY
* WRITTEN BY:      M.LISKIN       05/23/85

@  5,10 say "National Widgets Customer File Update and Inquiry"
@  6,10 say "-------------------------------------------------"
@ 10,10 say "Account Code" get ACCOUNT
@ 12,10 say "Company Name" get COMPANY
@ 13,10 say "Address     " get ADDRESS1
@ 14,23                    get ADDRESS2
@ 15,10 say "City        " get CITY
@ 15,50 say "State"        get STATE
@ 15,63 say "Zip Code"     get ZIP
@ 18,10 say "Balance " + str(BALANCE,10,2)
```

Figure 8-2. A simple format file for the National Widgets Customer File

used to collect the fields. This approach requires less counting of spaces when you are designing the screen and results in a format file that is easy to understand and modify. However, you may prefer to draw the borders first, position the prompts with SAY commands, and use separate GET commands to read in the fields. We will see in Part IV that the latter strategy is more readily adapted for use in custom data entry *programs.*

Figure 8-3 illustrates the screen as it appears when you edit a typical customer record through the NWCUST1.FMT format file. To use this format file to edit customer records, you would type

```
USE NWCUST INDEX NWCACCT, NWCZIP
SET FORMAT TO NWCUST1
EDIT
```

VALIDATING AND FORMATTING DATA

Under the control of a format file containing the simple @...SAY...GET commands just described, dBASE III PLUS performs the same validation tests it does using the normal APPEND and EDIT screens: only numbers and a minus sign may be entered into numeric fields, only valid calendar dates are accepted in date fields, and the only permissible entries into logical fields are .T. (T, t, Y, or y) and .F. (F, f, N, or n). The addition of

```
National Widgets Customer File Update and Inquiry
-------------------------------------------------


Account Code [ABCPLUMB  ]

Company Name [ABC Plumbing                    ]
Address      [1850 University Avenue    ]
             [                          ]
City         [Berkeley            ]     State [CA]   Zip Code [94703]


Balance       0.00
```

Figure 8-3. Using NWCUST1.FMT to edit a customer record

RANGE and PICTURE clauses to the @...SAY...GET command allows for a much wider variety of validation tests and format transformations to be applied to data entered or displayed through format files.

The RANGE clause specifies a range of acceptable values for a date or numeric variable. To limit the sales tax rate entered into the TAXRATE field in the National Widgets Customer File to a number between 0 and 10, you could use

```
@ 10,10 SAY "Sales tax rate (percent)" GET TAXRATE RANGE 0, 10
```

If the operator types in a value outside of this range, dBASE III PLUS displays the message "Range is 0.00 to 10.00 (press SPACE)" on line 0 of the screen. Pressing the space bar clears the error message, but the cursor will not advance to the next field until a legitimate value has been entered. For dates, the minimum and maximum values must be expressed as character strings—to distinguish a date such as 12/31/85 from the numeric expression 12 divided by 31 divided by 85—converted to dates with the CTOD (character-to-date) function:

```
@ 10,10 SAY "Most recent order date" GET LASTORDER RANGE CTOD("01/01/87"),
CTOD("12/31/87")
```

The RANGE clause affects only newly entered or changed data. If the command in the previous example were part of a format file, an existing 1986 entry of 07/11/86 in the LASTORDER field would not generate an error message when you edited the record, but any attempt to type this date into the field would result in the error message "Range is 01/01/87 to 12/31/87."

PICTURE clauses allow you to exercise tight control over the appearance of displayed fields and the type and format of the data that may be entered into a field. The PICTURE is expressed as a character string (enclosed in any of the standard character delimiters), which may contain two types of formatting instructions, functions and/or a template.

A *function* consists of the symbol @ followed by one or more characters that identify the purpose of the function. Functions are used to control the overall display or entry format for a field. For example, the "@C" function causes CR (credit) to be displayed after a positive number, and "@X" displays DB (debit) after a negative number. All of the PICTURE functions are listed in Table 8-2. You may also combine the individual functions. For example, the following command causes dBASE III PLUS to display CR after the BALANCE field if it is greater than 0 and DB if it is less than 0:

```
@ 10,10 SAY BALANCE PICTURE "@CX"
```

Table 8-2. Function Symbols Used in the PICTURE Clause of the @...SAY...GET Command

Symbol	Data Types	Meaning in a SAY Clause	Meaning in a GET Clause
C	N	Display CR (credit) after positive numbers	None
D	N	Display DB (debit) after positive numbers	None
(	N	Display negative numbers in parentheses	None
B	N	Display numbers left-justified	Display numbers left-justified (data is stored right-justified)
Z	N	Display a zero value as blank spaces (but including any decimal point)	Display a zero value as blank spaces (data is stored as 0)
D	C,N,D	Display in American date format (MM/DD/YY)	Display in American date format (dates are stored in format determined by SET DATE option)
E	C,N,D	Display in European date format (DD/MM/YY)	Display in European date format (dates are stored in format determined by SET DATE option)
A	C	None	Permit only alphabetic characters
!	C	Display data in uppercase	Convert entered data to uppercase
R	C	None	Extra characters in template portion of the PICTURE are used for display only and do not become part of the data
S*n*	C	Display the first *n* characters of the data	Scroll the data through a space *n* characters wide

Functions may also be specified in a separate FUNCTION clause. Using this syntax, you would write the previous example as

```
@ 10,10 SAY BALANCE FUNCTION "@CX"
```

Functions like "@C" and "@X" may be used only with SAY to display data. Other functions may be used for input as well. The "@A" function allows only alphabetic characters—not numbers or punctuation marks—to be entered into a field. Any other keystrokes will be ignored, just as dBASE III PLUS disregards alphabetic characters typed into numeric fields. Used with SAY, the "@!" function displays a field in uppercase, regardless of how the data was actually entered; the same function in a GET clause converts lowercase characters to uppercase before storing the data in the field. The @S function allows you to scroll a long character field through a smaller input "window," using the standard full-screen edit keys to navigate through the field. For example, you could update a 200-character field called NOTES in a 50-character space with the following:

```
@ 10,10 SAY "Enter notes" GET NOTES FUNCTION "@S50"
```

While a function controls the display or entry of data field by field, a template is even more precise. A *template* is a set of symbols, one for each character position in the data field, which specify, character by character, the display format or the type of data to be entered into the field. For example, each ! in a template converts the character displayed or entered in the corresponding position to uppercase. An A allows only an alphabetic character to be entered, and a 9 permits only digits or a minus sign. Table 8-3 lists all of the dBASE III PLUS template symbols and their meanings.

Templates are commonly used to format numeric fields with commas for a more readable display. The commas specified in the template are inserted into the data field; any commas that do not have a digit on both sides are suppressed. Thus, to display the value 1200 as " 1,200.00", you could use the command

```
@ 10,10 SAY BALANCE PICTURE "9,999,999.99"
```

When a template is used in a GET clause, any symbols it contains,

Table 8-3. Template Symbols Used in the PICTURE Clause of the @...SAY...GET Command

Symbol	Data Types	Meaning in a SAY Clause	Meaning in a GET Clause
A	C	Display character unchanged	Permit only alphabetic character
X	C	Display character unchanged	Permit entry of any character
!	C	Display character in uppercase	Convert alphabetic character to uppercase
L	C	Display character unchanged	Permit only T,t,Y,y,F,f,N,n
	L	Display character unchanged	Permit only logical value
Y	L,C	Display character unchanged	Permit only T,t,Y,y,F,f,N,n
9	C	Display character unchanged	Permit only a numeric digit
	N	Display character unchanged	Permit numeric digit or minus sign
#	C	Display character unchanged	Permit numeric digit, space, minus sign, or decimal point
	N	Display character unchanged	Permit numeric digit, space, or minus sign
$	N	Display character if present, or "$" in place of a space	None
*	N	Display character if present, or "*" in place of a space	None
,	C	Display "," if digit present on both sides	Insert "," into data
	N	Display "," if digit present on both sides	None
OTHER	C	Display symbol in place of data character With "@R" function, symbol is inserted into data field	Insert symbol into data With "@R" function, symbol is displayed only
	N	Symbol is inserted into data field	None

other than the standard template characters listed in Table 8-3, are entered automatically into the field. During data entry the cursor will pass over these character positions. For example, the picture "999-9999" may be used to format the TELEPHONE field in the National Widgets

Customer File as three digits, a dash (supplied automatically by dBASE III PLUS), and four more digits.

A PICTURE may include both a function and a template. The function must come first and must be separated by a single space from the template symbols that follow. For example, you might use the PICTURE "@(9,999,999.99" to display the BALANCE field with inserted commas, surrounded by parentheses if it is negative. Extra characters used in templates with GET commands become part of the data stored in the field only for character fields. If you do not want the symbols stored in a character field, you can include the "@R" ("raw") function in the PICTURE.

As pointed out earlier, you may type @...SAY commands at the dot prompt. You can also experiment with GETs at command level. When you type an @...SAY...GET command at the dot prompt, the expression in the SAY clause and the data field named after the GET are simply displayed on the screen. To actually move the cursor into the field and enter data, you must type a READ command. Employing READ to activate one or more @...SAY...GET commands will be explained more fully in Chapter 12, but you may wish to use this technique now to explore the effects of the various functions and template symbols.

A Custom Screen for Entering Invoice Data

Chapter 4 illustrated the use of the CHANGE command to enter data into selected fields in the National Widgets Transaction File:

```
CHANGE FIELDS PMTDATE, PMTAMOUNT, REFERENCE, ACCOUNT, INVDATE, INVOICE
```

This command may be replaced by the format file, NWTXNPMT.FMT, illustrated in Figure 8-4, which allows data to be entered into the payment fields of the transaction records. Note that the format file allows you to *display* and *collect* fields from more than one data base, just as the SET FIELDS command gives you this capability at command level. The NWTXNPMT.FMT format file displays the customer's full company name, read from the Customer File, next to the ACCOUNT code. Since this field is displayed with SAY, it cannot be altered through this format file. However, the customer's address and the name of the contact person are presented with GETs below the payment fields, to provide the convenience of being able to note an address change at the same time a pay-

```
* NWTXNPMT.FMT
* FORMAT FILE FOR ENTERING PAYMENTS INTO TRANSACTION FILE
* WRITTEN BY:  M.LISKIN        03/28/86

@  1,10 say "NATIONAL WIDGETS, INC. -- PAYMENT ENTRY"
@  2,10 say "---------------------------------------"
@  5,10 say "Customer:            " + ACCOUNT
@  5,40 say NWCUST->COMPANY
@  7,10 say "Invoice Number:     " + INVOICE
@  7,40 say "Invoice Date:  " + dtoc(INVDATE)
@ 10,10 say "Payment Date       " get PMTDATE
@ 11,10 say "Payment Amount     " get PMTAMOUNT
@ 12,10 say "Payment Reference" get REFERENCE
@ 12,50 say "Use this field for a check"
@ 13,50 say "number or credit card number"
@ 15,10 say "Address            " get NWCUST->ADDRESS1
@ 16,28 get NWCUST->ADDRESS2
@ 17,28 get NWCUST->CITY
@ 17,56 get NWCUST->STATE
@ 17,65 get NWCUST->ZIP
@ 19,10 say "Contact            " get NWCUST->CONTACT
```

Figure 8-4. A format file for entering payment data into the National Widgets Transaction File

ment is entered.

In order to use this format file, the Transaction File and Customer File must be opened in two dBASE III PLUS work areas and linked through the ACCOUNT field with SET RELATION:

```
SELECT 1
USE NWCUST INDEX NWCACCT
SELECT 2
USE NWTXN INDEX NWTINVC
SET RELATION TO ACCOUNT INTO NWCUST
SET FORMAT TO NWTXNPMT
```

The Transaction File is opened with the invoice number index, which allows you to SEEK a particular record by invoice number. You then use EDIT to enter the payment information on the screen drawn by the format file. Since the format file does not permit you to alter the contents of the ACCOUNT or INVOICE field, there is no need to open the index (NWTACCT.NDX) based on the combination of these two fields. (Allowing these fields to be changed could seriously damage the integrity of the information in the data bases, since there are records in the Order File with the same invoice number as any given Transaction File record, and there may be many records throughout the system with the same account code.)

The SET RELATION command that links a record in the Transaction File to the matching Customer File record depends only on the index that accesses the Customer File by account number (NWCACCT.NDX) and therefore works regardless of the order in which the transactions are processed.

A Custom Screen for Updating The Customer File

When you create a format file as simple as NWTXNPMT.FMT, you can easily visualize the appearance of the screen as you type the @...SAY...GET commands. In designing a more complex screen, planning the screen on graph paper or CRT layout forms, or using your word processor to type an image of the screen layout, will minimize the time you spend later making trial-and-error adjustments to the placement of the fields. Even so, some experimentation will probably be required to perfect the screen. If you use CRT layout forms, you may find that the columns are numbered from 1 to 80 rather than from 0 to 79. If this is the case, you will either have to forego the use of column 0 or remember to make the appropriate adjustments in the coordinates when you create the format file.

Another way to create a format file is to use the dBASE III PLUS screen editor invoked by typing CREATE SCREEN or MODIFY SCREEN. This editor allows you to create borders, type your field prompts and other constant text directly on a screen "blackboard," and then fill in the SAY and GET commands that display and collect the data, including PICTURE, FUNCTION, and RANGE clauses. You may want to experiment with the screen editor to determine whether the ability to move fields around the screen makes up for the inconvenience of having to choose each option from a pull-down menu.

The preliminary sketch for a format file for the National Widgets Customer File, which includes the prompts, message text, field lengths, and PICTURES, is shown in Figure 8-5.

The format file itself, NWCUST2.FMT, is listed in Figure 8-6. This format file includes all of the fields in NWCUST.DBF and therefore accommodates all Customer File entry, editing, and inquiry functions.

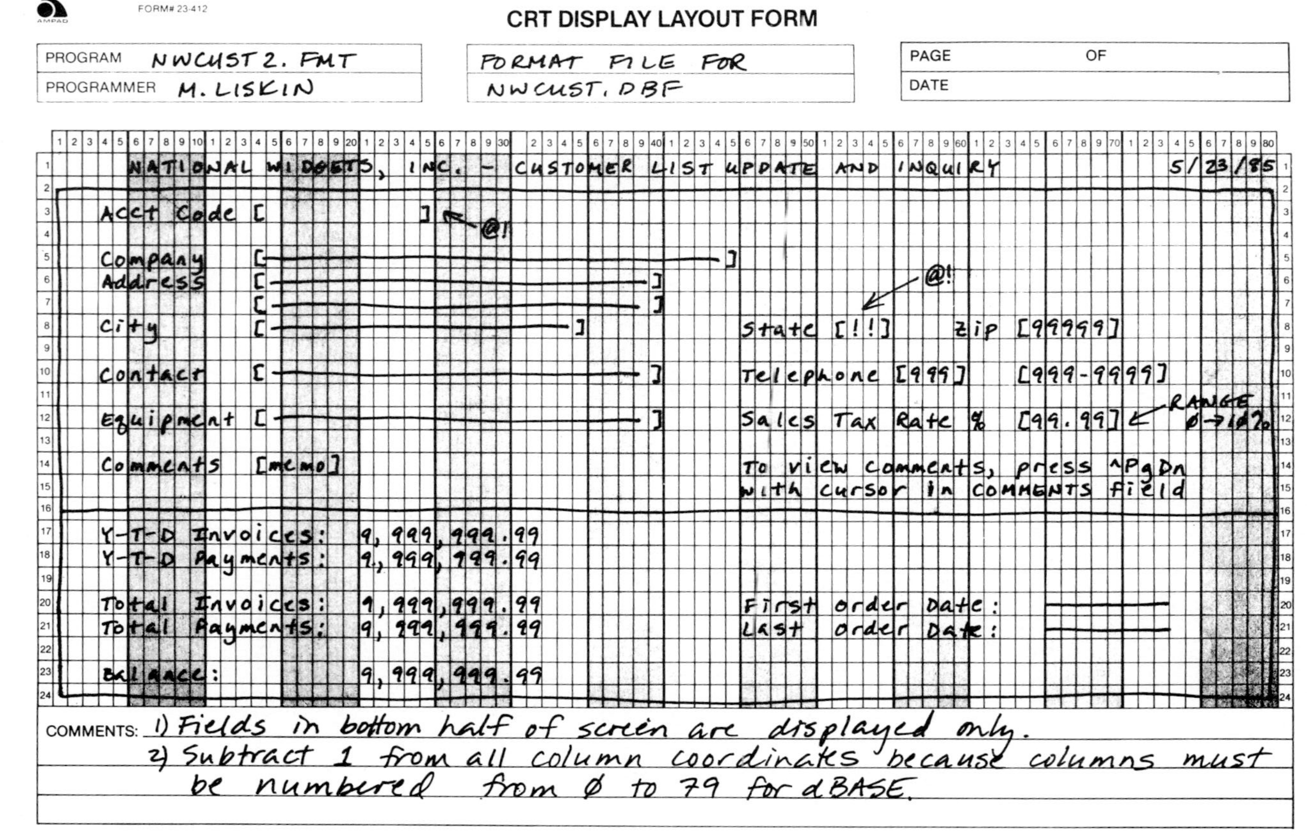

FORM# 23-412

CRT DISPLAY LAYOUT FORM

PROGRAM NWCUST2.FMT
PROGRAMMER M. LISKIN

FORMAT FILE FOR
NWCUST.DBF

PAGE OF
DATE

```
1  NATIONAL WIDGETS, INC. - CUSTOMER LIST UPDATE AND INQUIRY          5/23/85
3   Acct Code [          ] <- @!
5   Company   [-------------------------------]
6   Address   [---------------------------]
7             [---------------------------]              @!
8   City      [----------------------]        State [!!]   Zip [99999]
10  Contact   [---------------------------]   Telephone [999]   [999-9999]
12  Equipment [---------------------------]   Sales Tax Rate %  [99.99] <- RANGE 0->10%
14  Comments  [memo]                          To view comments, press ^PgDn
15                                            with cursor in COMMENTS field
17  Y-T-D Invoices:   9,999,999.99
18  Y-T-D Payments:   9,999,999.99
20  Total Invoices:   9,999,999.99            First order Date: ________
21  Total Payments:   9,999,999.99            Last order Date:  ________
23  Balance:          9,999,999.99
```

COMMENTS: 1) Fields in bottom half of screen are displayed only.
2) Subtract 1 from all column coordinates because columns must be numbered from 0 to 79 for dBASE.

Figure 8-5. The preliminary sketch for a format file, NWCUST2.FMT

```
* NWCUST2.FMT
* FORMAT FILE FOR CUSTOMER FILE INQUIRY AND UPDATE
* WRITTEN BY:     M.LISKIN      Ø5/23/85

@  1, 5 say "NATIONAL WIDGETS, INC. - CUSTOMER LIST UPDATE AND INQUIRY"
@  1,7Ø say date()
@  2, Ø say "+---------------------------------------"
@  2,4Ø say "---------------------------------------+"
@  3, Ø say "|  Acct Code" get ACCOUNT picture "@!"
@  3,79 say "|"
@  4, Ø say "|"
@  4,79 say "|"
@  5, Ø say "|  Company   " get COMPANY
@  5,79 say "|"
@  6, Ø say "|  Address   " get ADDRESS1
@  6,79 say "|"
@  7, Ø say "|            " get ADDRESS2
@  7,79 say "|"
@  8, Ø say "|  City      " get CITY
@  8,45 say "State" get STATE picture "@!"
@  8,59 say "Zip" get ZIP picture "99999"
@  8,79 say "|"
@  9, Ø say "|"
@  9,79 say "|"
@ 1Ø, Ø say "|  Contact   " get CONTACT
@ 1Ø,45 say "Telephone" get AREACODE picture "999"
@ 1Ø,63 get TELEPHONE picture "999-9999"
@ 1Ø,79 say "|"
@ 11, Ø say "|"
@ 11,79 say "|"
@ 12, Ø say "|  Equipment" get EQUIPMENT
@ 12,45 say "Sales Tax Rate % " get TAXRATE range Ø, 1Ø
@ 12,79 say "|"
@ 13, Ø say "|"
@ 13,79 say "|"
@ 14, Ø say "|  Comments " get COMMENTS
@ 14,45 say "To view comments, press ^PgDn"
@ 14,79 say "|"
@ 15, Ø say "|"
@ 15,45 say "with cursor in COMMENTS field"
@ 15,79 say "|"
@ 16, Ø say "+---------------------------------------"
@ 16,4Ø say "---------------------------------------+"
@ 17, Ø say "|  Y-T-D Invoices:" + transform(YTDINV, "9,999,999.99")
@ 17,79 say "|"
@ 18, Ø say "|  Y-T-D Payments:" + transform(YTDPMT, "9,999,999.99")
@ 18,79 say "|"
@ 19, Ø say "|"
@ 19,79 say "|"
@ 2Ø, Ø say "|  Total Invoices:" + transform(TOTINV, "9,999,999.99")
@ 2Ø,45 say "First Order Date:   "+dtoc(FIRSTORDER)
@ 2Ø,79 say "|"
@ 21, Ø say "|  Total Payments:" + transform(TOTPMT, "9,999,999.99")
@ 21,45 say "Last  Order Date:   "+dtoc(LASTORDER)
@ 21,79 say "|"
@ 22, Ø say "|"
@ 22,79 say "|"
@ 23, Ø say "|  Balance:       " + transform(BALANCE, "@( 9,999,999.99")
@ 23,79 say "|"
@ 24, Ø say "+---------------------------------------"
@ 24,4Ø say "---------------------------------------+"
```

Figure 8-6. A complete format file for the National Widgets Customer File

The appearance of the screen when this format file is used to edit a typical record is illustrated in Figure 8-7. To avoid the word-wrap problem while creating the format file with MODIFY COMMAND, the wide borders and heading were entered in two sections, keeping each line in the file shorter than 67 characters.

This file makes use of some of the more common functions and template characters. The "@!" function guarantees that the STATE and ACCOUNT fields contain only uppercase letters. While not an absolute necessity for the STATE field, consistent entry in uppercase in a code field like ACCOUNT, which uniquely identifies each record, is essential. The PICTUREs used with the AREACODE and TELEPHONE fields permit only digits to be entered and automatically supply the dash (-) in the phone number.

Displaying the fields in the bottom half of the screen with SAY commands rather than collecting them with GETs provides a small measure of security: these fields, which are updated by the process of entering and posting transactions, should not be changed by the operator. (Of course, a user who is familiar with dBASE III PLUS could close the format file and use EDIT, BROWSE, or REPLACE to alter any field in the data base.) The date fields were converted to character strings with the DTOC function in order to concatenate them with the prompt messages. Note that the TRANSFORM function was used to display the numeric fields with inserted commas and to surround the BALANCE field with parentheses if it is negative. You could have achieved the same effect by using two separate SAY commands for each numeric field—one for the prompt message and another, containing a PICTURE clause, for the field.

dBASE III PLUS supports the full IBM PC character set including graphics characters. In MODIFY COMMAND (and in many editors and word processors as well), you can enter graphics or foreign language characters directly into a format file by typing their decimal ASCII codes, using the ALT key with the numbers on the numeric keypad. (The numbers on the top row of keys in the main typewriter portion of the keyboard will *not* work.) For example, you could display a degree sign on the screen by entering it as ALT-248 (hold the ALT key down and press the 2, then the 4, and then the 8 on the numeric keypad).

You can also use graphics characters to create continuous horizontal and vertical lines on the screen. For example, you could draw a thick horizontal line by using the graphics character whose ASCII code is 220. For a horizontal line more than a few characters long, it is easier to use the REPLICATE function, which repeats any character string a specified

```
                                              INSERT
     NATIONAL WIDGETS, INC. - CUSTOMER LIST UPDATE AND INQUIRY         07/08/85
+---------------------------------------------------------------------------+
| Acct Code [ABCPLUMB  ]                                                    |
|                                                                           |
| Company   [ABC Plumbing                     ]                             |
| Address   [1850 University Avenue  ]                                      |
|           [                        ]                                      |
| City      [Berkeley           ]      State [CA]    Zip [94703]            |
|                                                                           |
| Contact   [Ed Williams              ]  Telephone [415]   [861-4543]       |
|                                                                           |
| Equipment [Kaypro 10, Epson FX-100  ]  Sales Tax Rate %   [  .  ]         |
|                                                                           |
| Comments  [memo]                       To view comments, press ^PgDn     |
|                                        with cursor in COMMENTS field     |
+---------------------------------------------------------------------------+
| Y-T-D Invoices:           0.00                                            |
| Y-T-D Payments:           0.00                                            |
|                                                                           |
| Total Invoices:         796.41         First Order Date:    12/01/83      |
| Total Payments:           0.00         Last  Order Date:    12/11/84      |
|                                                                           |
| Balance:                  0.00                                            |
+---------------------------------------------------------------------------+
```

Figure 8-7. Using NWCUST2.FMT to edit a customer record

number of times, than to type repeatedly the ASCII code 220 on the numeric keypad. The following command would draw a line 50 characters long starting at row 10, column 15:

```
@ 10,15 SAY REPLICATE(CHR(248),50)
```

A variation of the @...SAY command allows you to draw lines or boxes composed of the thin, continuous single- and double-line graphics characters. A box is defined by its upper left and lower right corners, and is composed of single-line graphics characters unless you include the DOUBLE keyword in the command. If the two row coordinates are the same, the "box" is reduced to a horizontal line. Vertical lines are created by using the same column coordinate. You could draw a double-lined box around the entire screen (leaving line 0 blank) with

```
@ 1,0 TO 24,79 DOUBLE
```

A format file for the Customer File, NWCUST3.FMT, that includes graphics characters is listed in Figure 8-8.

```
* NWCUST3.FMT
* FORMAT FILE FOR CUSTOMER FILE INQUIRY AND UPDATE
* WRITTEN BY:     M.LISKIN      03/28/86

@  2, 0 to 24,79 double
@  1, 5 say chr(17) +;
            " NATIONAL WIDGETS, INC. - CUSTOMER LIST UPDATE AND INQUIRY " +;
            chr(16)
@  1,70 say date()
@  3, 3 say "Acct Code" get ACCOUNT picture "@!"
@  5, 3 say "Company   " get COMPANY
@  6, 3 say "Address   " get ADDRESS1
@  7, 3 say "          " get ADDRESS2
@  8, 3 say "City      " get CITY
@  8,45 say "State" get STATE picture "@!"
@  8,59 say "Zip" get ZIP picture "99999"
@ 10, 3 say "Contact   " get CONTACT
@ 10,45 say "Telephone" get AREACODE picture "999"
@ 10,63 get TELEPHONE picture "999-9999"
@ 12, 3 say "Equipment" get EQUIPMENT
@ 12,45 say "Sales Tax Rate % " get TAXRATE range 0, 10
@ 14, 3 say "Comments " get COMMENTS
@ 14,45 say "To view comments, press ^PgDn"
@ 15,45 say "with cursor in COMMENTS field"
@ 16, 1 to 16,78
@ 17, 3 say "Y-T-D Invoices:" + transform(YTDINV, "9,999,999.99")
@ 18, 3 say "Y-T-D Payments:" + transform(YTDPMT, "9,999,999.99")
@ 20, 3 say "Total Invoices:" + transform(TOTINV, "9,999,999.99")
@ 20,45 say "First Order Date:    " + dtoc(FIRSTORDER)
@ 21, 3 say "Total Payments:" + transform(TOTPMT, "9,999,999.99")
@ 21,45 say "Last  Order Date:    " + dtoc(LASTORDER)
@ 23, 3 say "Balance:        " + transform(BALANCE, "@( 9,999,999.99")
```

Figure 8-8. A format file that uses graphics characters

Although using the graphics characters allows you to create more attractive screens, it may be preferable to rely on the standard characters (−, =, |, and +) for drawing borders and lines. Unless you have an IBM Graphics Printer (or a completely compatible model), your printer will not reproduce the graphics symbols as they appear on the screen. Since DOS is unable to translate the graphics characters into a symbol set universally available on all printers, using any characters with ASCII codes below 32 or above 127 in a screen prevents you from using SHIFT-PRTSC to dump an exact image of the screen to any printer, dot-matrix or letter-quality—a facility that is a very fast, convenient way to make a quick printout of one or two records from a data base in an attractive format.

If your data base has too many fields to fit on one screen, you can create a multiple-page format file by placing a READ command at each point where a new screen "page" begins. When you use the format file, the PGDN key clears the screen and then moves forward to display the next page, and PGUP moves back to the previous page.

Advantages and Disadvantages Of Format Files

Format files allow you to design custom data entry screens for use with the dBASE III PLUS full-screen APPEND, EDIT, INSERT, and CHANGE commands. You can draw attractively formatted screens with descriptive prompts and instructions for the user, and you can exert stringent control over the format, type, and, to some extent, contents of data entered by the operator. Although a format file like NWCUST2.FMT is considerably longer than any of the programs in Chapter 6, its structure is much simpler. The hardest task in creating a format file is designing a pleasing screen layout—perhaps by making a preliminary sketch on paper—before you begin.

A format file enables you to access memo fields with @...SAY...GET commands, just as you can using the standard APPEND and EDIT screens. When the cursor is in the memo field, pressing CTRL-PGDN invokes the built-in dBASE III PLUS "word processor" used for entering and editing memo text, and CTRL-PGUP returns you to the format file screen to fill in the rest of the fields. Although this may seem obvious and natural, it deserves emphasis because *only through a format file* does @...SAY...GET allow you to access memo fields. The same command, executed from within a dBASE III PLUS *program* that draws a formatted screen, may not be used to collect data into a memo field.

Format files represent a significant improvement over the standard dBASE III PLUS data entry screens, but they have serious limitations. Although you can create multiple page screens, each "page" must occupy the entire screen. If you want certain text or data to remain on the screen for the operator's reference—for example, the border around the screen or the customer account code and company name—you must repeat the commands that display these items after each READ command.

While they do provide more formatting and validation capabilities than the standard APPEND and EDIT input screens, format files do not permit all of the desirable types of data validation outlined in Chapter 6. Because you may only SET one RELATION at a time from a given work area, you are limited, as with reports, to displaying and updating information from two data base files at once. A format file cannot contain any dBASE III

PLUS commands other than @...SAY...GET and READ, so you cannot perform instant calculations or make decisions based on data entered into the fields. In the National Widgets sample system, if you were using a format file to edit records in the Order File, you could use SET RELATION to link this file to the Inventory File by the combination of CATEGORY + PARTNUMBER and display the full item description and price on the screen. You could not, however, simultaneously display the customer's company name stored in the Customer File, read the price automatically into the Order File record, or calculate the net order amount on the spot.

Format files will not help you overcome all of the limitations of the dBASE III PLUS APPEND command. They do not provide a means to test for the entry of duplicate records, and you cannot *selectively* carry over certain fields from one record to the next or establish default values for fields like AREACODE or STATE if these are largely constant throughout a data base. (SET CARRY ON carries over *all* of the fields from each new record to serve as the default values for the next). Although you can display or update inventory data while *editing* an order record, the same format file used to *append* new records to the Order File cannot prevent the operator from entering an order for an item that is missing from the Inventory File. This is largely due to the way that SET RELATION works: the record pointer in the file accessed through the RELATION is only repositioned when the record pointer moves in the selected work area. When a new record is APPENDed, the common fields, CATEGORY and PARTNUMBER, are blank, and the Inventory File is positioned to the end-of-file, where it remains even after you fill in these fields in the order record.

In Part IV, the @...SAY...GET command will be used to construct custom data entry programs in order to accomplish all of these objectives.

9

PROGRAMMING STRUCTURES

Chapter 7 described how to begin automating a dBASE III PLUS system by writing some simple programs consisting of command sequences to be executed one after the other, just as if they had been entered at the dot prompt. Since the programs employed only commands that you already knew from your work at command level, they represented an easy introduction to programming in the dBASE III PLUS language. But even experienced programmers will find that such short programs make useful additions to any data base system. Programs that open two data bases together and print a report or reindex all of the data base files will form essential components of the final version of the National Widgets sample system—and most of the dBASE III PLUS applications you design yourself. But although these simple programs have great practical utility, they barely tap the power of the dBASE III PLUS language, which offers many of the capabilities of other higher-level languages like BASIC or Pascal.

This chapter will begin with a brief review of how to use functions and how to build syntactically correct dBASE III PLUS expressions. We have already employed some complex expressions in the command level procedures, short programs, and format files developed thus far, and you may have used others in your own work at the dot prompt. Readers who have had little formal mathematical training should read this section closely.

The dBASE III PLUS programs in Chapter 7 operate only on information read from one or more data base files. Since you can write many useful programs without requesting any keyboard input, the subject of collecting and processing input from the user will be deferred to Chapter 11. But most programs must communicate some results to the operator, so this chapter presents several methods for displaying or printing the output of a dBASE III PLUS program.

Finally, this chapter will introduce the fundamental programming structures, often called *loops,* that are used in the dBASE III PLUS language to make decisions and repeat program steps. If you are new to the world of programming, you should read this material very carefully—the structures described here will form the core of all of your dBASE III PLUS programs. Most of the examples in this and the next few chapters are complete programs that you may type in and test with the data in the National Widgets sample files or modify to test with fields from your own data bases. If you already have experience with a higher-level language, you will probably want to skim through the chapter and focus on the exact syntax of the commands and the descriptions of typical uses for these structures in dBASE III PLUS programs.

EXPRESSIONS AND FUNCTIONS

In your work with dBASE III PLUS at command level, you have undoubtedly constructed expressions of moderate complexity and made use of at least a few functions. In the command level simulation of the National Widgets system, the TRIM function was used to remove trailing blank spaces from the CITY field before this field was printed on mailing labels, and in the NWCSTAT1.PRG program in Chapter 7, the UPPER function was used to convert a character field to all uppercase for comparison to an arbitrary character string. This section will summarize some of the formal rules for using functions and for constructing syntactically correct dBASE III PLUS expressions.

An *expression* may consist of data base fields, memory variables, constants, functions, and operators. An expression always evaluates to a single quantity of a specified data type (character, numeric, date, or logical). Although an expression may consist of more than one data type, data types must be combined according to certain rules; if you violate the rules, the error message "Data type mismatch" will result.

The mathematical operators + (addition), − (subtraction), * (multiplication), / (division), and ^ (exponentiation, also written as **) may be used with numeric data. Addition and subtraction also apply to dates: subtracting two dates yields the number of days between the two, and adding a number (assumed to be days) to a date or subtracting a number from a date yields another date the specified number of days in the future or past. However, you cannot add two dates together.

Character strings may also be added, or *concatenated*, with +, which combines the two strings directly. If you use − instead, dBASE III PLUS combines all of the trailing blanks from both strings and places them at the end of the resulting string, a process described in the original dBASE II manual as "string concatenation with blank squash." There is another specialized operator for character strings: $ (substring), which searches for one string within another and yields the logical value .T. (true) if the first string is found anywhere within the second.

The relational operators = (equal to), <> (not equal to), < (less than), > (greater than), <= (less than or equal to), and >= (greater than or equal to) are used to compare two expressions, resulting in the logical value .T. if the comparison is true or .F. if it is false. The three logical operators .AND., .OR., and .NOT. behave as they do in Boolean logic. When two expressions are combined with .AND., the result has the value .T. only if both expressions are true, while combining two expressions with .OR. yields a true result if either (or both) of the component expressions is true. .NOT. operates on a single logical expression and returns .T. if the original expression was false and .F. if it was true.

A *function* is a specialized operator provided in the dBASE III PLUS language in addition to those just enumerated. A function performs a specific transformation on a certain kind of input, yielding a specific type of output. You can think of a function as a kind of machine that, when given the right raw materials as input, performs a very specific operation and cranks out a predictable product as output. A dBASE III PLUS function is written as the name of the function followed by the input(s) enclosed in parentheses. For example, the SQRT function takes as its input a number and returns as output the "square root" of the number—a quantity that, when multiplied by itself, yields the original number. The TRIM function takes as input any character string—a character field, memory variable, or more complex character type expression—and returns the same character string, minus any trailing blank spaces. The expression TRIM(CITY) would thus yield "Berkeley" if the National Widgets Customer File were positioned at a record whose CITY field contained the character string "Berkeley   ".

If a function requires more than one input, the inputs must be listed (separated with commas, like any other dBASE III PLUS list) in the correct order within the parentheses. The SUBSTR function, which extracts a substring (a portion of a longer character string), has three inputs: the character string it operates on, a number representing the starting position of the substring, and the length of the substring. The expression SUBSTR(COMPANY,5,8), which you might read as "the substring of the COMPANY field that begins with the fifth character and is eight characters long," would have the value "Plumbing" if the National Widgets Customer File were positioned at a record with "ABC Plumbing" in the COMPANY field.

As you can see from the previous example, the data type of a function's output may differ from the data type of some or all of its inputs; two of the inputs to the SUBSTR function are numbers, while the output of the function is a character string. In fact, many of the dBASE III PLUS functions are provided solely to convert data of one type to another, when the context requires a particular data type. You have already seen how the DTOC (date-to-character) function converts a date to a character string so it may be concatenated with a prompt message in an expression like this:

```
"FIRST ORDER DATE: " + DTOC(FIRSTORDER)
```

Similarly, the STR (number-to-string) and TRANSFORM functions may be used to display a character string followed by a numeric field, as we did in the reports in Chapter 5. This function requires three inputs: the numeric expression to be converted, the total length of the character string to create (including the decimal point, if any), and the number of decimal places to include. These last two inputs usually match the specifications for the numeric expression on which the function operates, but this is not an absolute requirement. You could, for example, display the sales tax rate with four decimal places with this expression:

```
"SALES TAX RATE: " + STR(TAXRATE,7,4) + " PERCENT"
```

For more complex formatting, you can instead use the TRANSFORM function, which accepts as input a numeric expression and a PICTURE, and results in a display (or printout) equivalent to that produced by using an @...SAY command to display the same expression with the same PICTURE.

Not all functions require input specified by the user. For example, the DELETED( ) function is a logical function that has the value .T. when the data base in use is positioned at a record that has been marked for deletion. Nevertheless, the pair of parentheses that identify *all* dBASE III PLUS functions must be included to clearly identify this function as a function, not to be confused with a data base field or memory variable called DELETED. Although there is nothing within the parentheses, the DELETED function does have input, but the input is provided by the current record in the data base in use, not by the programmer. Similarly, the DATE( ) and TIME( ) functions read as inputs the DOS system date and time and return, respectively, a calendar date and a character string containing the current time.

The expression consisting of a function name with the function's inputs enclosed in parentheses is synonymous with the output of the function and may be used anywhere that an expression of that data type is permitted. Functions may be used with data base fields, memory variables, and constants to build more complex expressions. One function may also serve as the input to another function. For example, the CDOW (character day-of-week) function takes a date as input and returns as output a character string containing the name of the day of the week. Thus, on July 5, 1987, the expression CDOW(DATE( )) would yield the character string "Sunday".

The dBASE III PLUS language offers a wealth of functions for performing mathematical calculations, manipulating character strings and dates, transforming information of one data type to another, obtaining information about the data base in use in the selected work area, and determining what hardware and operating system software are present. We will make use of many of these functions in the remainder of the National Widgets system programs. A complete list of functions and examples of their usage may be found in Appendix C.

When you build complex expressions, you must be aware of the fact that dBASE III PLUS expressions are not simply evaluated from left to right. Within an expression, dBASE III PLUS performs the indicated operations in the following order:

- Evaluation of functions
- Exponentiation
- Multiplication and division, from left to right
- Numeric addition and subtraction, from left to right
- Character string concatenation
- Evaluation of relational operators, from left to right

- Evaluation of logical operators, in the following order: .NOT., .AND., .OR.

A complex expression may be scanned many times in order to adhere to this *precedence* of operations. In order to override the default order in which expressions are evaluated, you must use parentheses. Any expression containing parentheses is evaluated starting within the innermost set of parentheses and working outward. For example, consider a simple expression intended to calculate the profit margin, as a percent, on an inventory item:

```
PRICE - COST / PRICE * 100
```

Because all multiplication and division operations are carried out before any subtractions, this expression is evaluated by dividing COST by PRICE, multiplying this number by 100, and subtracting the result from PRICE. To force dBASE III PLUS to do the calculation correctly (subtract COST from PRICE, divide the difference by PRICE, and then multiply the result by 100), you must add parentheses, as follows:

```
(PRICE - COST) / PRICE * 100
```

As a final example, consider a condition you might use in a FOR clause to print labels for all customers who own either IBM *or* COMPAQ equipment *and* whose invoices total more than $500.

```
LABEL FORM NWCUST1 TO PRINT FOR TOTINV > 500 .AND.
  ("IBM" $ UPPER(EQUIPMENT) .OR. "COMPAQ" $ UPPER(EQUIPMENT))
```

If the parentheses were omitted from this expression, the precedence of .AND. over .OR. would result in selecting all customers whose total invoices exceed $500 and who own IBM equipment, as well as all COMPAQ owners.

DISPLAYING AND PRINTING INFORMATION

Most dBASE III PLUS programs convey some information to the operator by displaying it on the screen or printing it on paper. Even the simple program written in Chapter 7 to compute counts, sums, and averages displayed status messages while it ran and presented the calculated results on the screen. All of the dBASE III PLUS commands (including LIST, DISPLAY, REPORT, and LABEL) that you may use at the dot prompt to display data may also be used from within a program. In addition, the ? and @...SAY commands allow you to send as output any valid dBASE III PLUS expression, either to the screen or to the printer, and the TEXT ...ENDTEXT structure is used to output a block of text without interpretation by dBASE III PLUS. Before using any of these commands, you may wish to use CLEAR to clear the screen.

Using ? to Display Data

The ? command displays information on the next available line on the screen or printer. A ? command may include a list of expressions, separated by commas, which will be displayed or printed with a single space between each pair. You may have already used ? at command level, as we did in Chapter 7, to perform a calculation and display the result:

```
? MSUMIBM / MCOUNTIBM
```

This command is especially useful at the dot prompt, where you can use it to test a complex expression or function before incorporating it into a report or program. If you need several tries before you arrive at the correct formula, it is much easier to experiment at command level, using the HISTORY feature to avoid having to retype each attempt from scratch, than to edit your report form or program many times.

Used by itself (with no list of expressions), ? displays or prints a blank line. The ?? command is used to display more than one expression on the same line with no intervening spaces. Figure 9-1 lists a short program, DISP1.PRG, which illustrates some of these variations by displaying several fields from the first record of the National Widgets Customer File. Running this program results in the screen display shown in Figure 9-2. The DISP1.PRG program initially CLEARs the screen and opens the Customer File. The first ? command simply displays the message "This is the National Widgets Customer File." The next ? command, since it includes no expressions to display, produces a blank line on the screen. The program then uses two different methods to display the character string "Company Name:" and the field called COMPANY.

```
* DISP1.PRG
* PROGRAM TO ILLUSTRATE THE USE OF THE ? AND ?? COMMANDS
* WRITTEN BY:  M.LISKIN       6/10/85

clear
use NWCUST
? "This is the National Widgets Customer File"
?
?  "Company Name:", COMPANY
?
?  "Company Name:"
?? COMPANY
?
?  "Balance:"
?? BALANCE
```

Figure 9-1. A program to illustrate the use of the ? and ?? commands

The second variant, which uses ? to display the prompt, followed by ?? to display the COMPANY field, allows you to place other program steps between the two display commands. If you need spaces between the two expressions, however, you must remember to insert them yourself. The spacing problem is very easy to overlook when you display a numeric field next to a prompt, as we have done in DISP1.PRG with the BALANCE field, especially if the program is tested with a record in which the numeric value does not completely fill the field. In this example, the easi-

```
This is the National Widgets Customer File

Company Name: Lewis and Associates

Company Name:Lewis and Associates

Balance:       0.00
.
```

Figure 9-2. Running the DISP1.PRG program

est way to correct the spacing would be to include the extra space in the character string that forms the prompt, as in "Company Name: " or "Balance: ".

The output of ? commands is automatically sent to the terminal. From within a program, just as at command level, you may toggle the printer on with SET PRINT ON and turn it off with SET PRINT OFF. When SET PRINT ON/OFF was introduced in Chapter 3, it was used to *duplicate* the console display on paper as an aid to documenting your command level experiments. When you write a program to print information on paper, you often do *not* want the same data sent to the screen. The SET CONSOLE OFF command suppresses the screen display; you may turn it back on with SET CONSOLE ON. The program in Figure 9-3, DISP2.PRG, clears the screen, displays an opening message, prints the company name and balance from the first record in the Customer File, and then displays a closing message on the screen.

Using @...SAY in a Program

The ? command is best suited to displaying status messages or printing information one line after another with no special formatting. In Chapter

```
* DISP2.PRG
* PROGRAM TO ILLUSTRATE THE USE OF ? TO SEND OUTPUT TO THE PRINTER
* WRITTEN BY:  M.LISKIN       6/10/85


clear
use NWCUST
? "This is the National Widgets Customer File"
?
set console off
set print on

?  "Company Name:", COMPANY
?
?  "Balance:", BALANCE

set print off
set console on

? "This program printed a customer's company name and balance"
```

Figure 9-3. A program to illustrate the use of ? to send output to the printer

8 the @...SAY...GET command was used to create format files for use with APPEND, EDIT, or CHANGE. You may also use @...SAY...GET in dBASE III PLUS programs, with all of the same PICTURE, FUNCTION, and RANGE options to display data on a formatted screen, collect input from the operator, and control precisely the placement of data on the printed page.

Beyond the capabilities discussed in Chapter 8, several variants of the @...SAY command are more useful in dBASE III PLUS programs than in format files. You may clear all or part of a line on the screen with

@ *row, column*

This command erases the specified row, beginning with the specified column; using 0 for the column number clears the entire row. To clear a rectangular area of the screen that lies below and to the right of a particular point, you can use

@ *row, column* CLEAR

Chapter 8 described how to draw a double- or single-lined box on the screen with @ *row, column*. You can clear a rectangular area with

@ *row, column* CLEAR TO *row, column*

The format files in Chapter 8 used exact row and column numbers in all of the @...SAY...GET commands, but you may also use any valid numeric expressions to specify the coordinates. If the memory variable MR has the value 10 and the variable MC has the value 5, you could display a message beginning at column 5 of row 10 with

```
@ MR,MC SAY "This is a message"
```

For additional flexibility, you may also use the ROW( ) and COL( ) functions, which keep track of the current cursor position on the screen, and the corresponding PROW( ) and PCOL( ), which store the print head position. The values taken on by these functions are updated whenever the cursor or print head moves, so you can position a message five spaces to the right of the last item displayed with the following command:

```
@ ROW(), COL()+5 SAY "This is a message"
```

@...SAY normally displays data on the screen, but you can direct the output to the printer with SET DEVICE TO PRINT, which automatically turns off the screen display. To route the output of @...SAY commands back to the screen, you can use SET DEVICE TO SCREEN. The program in Figure 9-4, DISP3.PRG, uses @...SAY commands to produce output similar to that of DISP2.PRG.

Although a series of @...SAY commands may place text and data fields on the screen in any order, you must be careful when you print to proceed from top to bottom and, within each line, from left to right. If you use a row number lower than the row coordinate in a previous @...SAY command, dBASE III PLUS will eject the page and position the paper to the proper row number on the next sheet of paper before printing the data. This is frequently done inadvertently, especially when you are converting a program that draws a screen to one that prints the same format on paper, but you can also use this feature to your advantage to force a page eject at the end of one form before you begin printing the next.

Remember that the SET PRINT ON/OFF commands affect only sequential output, such as data displayed by the ? command (and other

```
* DISP3.PRG
* PROGRAM TO ILLUSTRATE THE USE OF @ .. SAY TO DISPLAY AND PRINT OUTPUT
* WRITTEN BY:  M.LISKIN        6/10/85


clear
use NWCUST
@ row(), 0 say "This is the National Widgets Customer File"

set device to print

@ prow(), 0          say "Company Name:"
@ prow(), pcol()+1 say COMPANY

@ prow()+2, 0          say "Balance:"
@ prow(),   pcol()+1 say BALANCE

set device to screen

@ row()+2, 0 say "This program printed a customer's company name and balance"
```

Figure 9-4. A program to illustrate the use of @...SAY to display and print output

dBASE III PLUS built-in commands like LIST or DISPLAY). These commands do not differentiate between the screen and the printer—each line of output is simply displayed or printed on the next available line—so the software permits either or both of these output devices to be in use at any given moment, and you must use independent SET commands to control the status of the printer and screen. For the formatted output produced by @...SAY, however, the printer and console are not assumed to be equivalent. As mentioned previously, data may be placed on a screen display, but not on the printed page, in any order. Since most paper is larger than the 25-line-by-80-column screen, many of the row and column coordinates in your printed formats will lie outside the boundaries of the screen. The SET DEVICE command therefore *selects* between these two output devices rather than allowing both to be active at once.

Displaying Blocks of Text With TEXT...ENDTEXT

The ? and @...SAY commands are useful for displaying individual lines of text, creating formatted screens, and filling out printed forms. If you want to display or print a large block of text, such as a sign-on message, a help screen, or the text of a personalized letter, you may also use TEXT ...ENDTEXT. This structure begins with a line containing only the word TEXT and ends with ENDTEXT. All of the lines between TEXT and ENDTEXT are output to the screen or printer without processing or interpretation, which results in a slightly faster "drawing" of the screen than the equivalent series of ? or @...SAY commands. The program in Figure 9-5, DISP4.PRG, illustrates the use of TEXT...ENDTEXT to display a screen that might be used as a sign-on message for the first program in the National Widgets system.

In DISP4.PRG, the CLEAR command erases the screen in order to display the block of text starting on line 1. Because of the three blank lines following the word TEXT, the top border of the box will appear on line 4 (the fifth line) of the screen. Text enclosed in a TEXT...ENDTEXT structure always begins on the next available screen (or printer) line, and the screen will scroll until the entire text passage has been displayed. You must make sure that your block of text will fit on the screen; if there are too many lines, the beginning of the text may scroll off the top of the screen before the operator can read it.

```
* DISP4.PRG
* PROGRAM TO ILLUSTRATE THE USE OF TEXT ... ENDTEXT TO DRAW A SCREEN
* WRITTEN BY:  M.LISKIN       6/10/85

clear
text

          +=======================================================+
          |                                                       |
          |                    *** Welcome ***                    |
          |                                                       |
          |                        to the                         |
          |                                                       |
          |       National Widgets Accounts Receivable System     |
          |                                                       |
          +=======================================================+


endtext
```

Figure 9-5. A program to illustrate the use of TEXT...ENDTEXT to draw a screen

MAKING DECISIONS WITH IF...ELSE...ENDIF

If a dBASE III PLUS system is to emulate your manual processing, it must be able to make decisions. The most basic decision-making process is testing to see whether a condition is true, and if it is, taking some action. In the National Widgets office, the owner might tell the bookkeeper, "If a customer owes us money, type a message on the monthly statement that says 'Please pay the outstanding balance promptly.'" When you write a statement-printing program, this program must make the same decision for each record in the Customer File.

Your work at command level has already provided a brief introduction to dBASE III PLUS's ability to make decisions by testing records against a condition specified in a FOR clause. By adding a FOR clause to a LIST, REPORT, COPY, or other dBASE command, you are saying, in effect: "Look at each record in the data base. If the condition following the word FOR is true, process the record. If the condition is not true, ignore the record." In Chapter 5, the IIF function was used to test a condition and, based on the outcome of the test, one of two different expressions was printed on a report.

As you can see from these examples, the need to make a choice is often signaled—in both the English language and many programming languages—by the use of the word "if." You can test a condition in a dBASE III PLUS program with the IF structure, which reads much like the English language equivalent. The simplest format for this structure is as follows:

if *condition*
  commands to execute if the condition is true
endif *comment*

The IF structure begins with the word IF, followed on the same line by the condition to be tested, and ends with the ENDIF line. As in a FOR clause, the *condition* may be any dBASE III PLUS expression that may take on the logical value .T. (true) or .F. (false). Between IF and ENDIF you may place one or more dBASE III PLUS commands, all of which will be executed if the condition is true. dBASE III PLUS ignores any text after the word ENDIF on the same line, so you may use this area to write a comment that will remind you (or other programmers reading your code) of what condition the IF loop is testing. In short programs such as the examples in this chapter, the comment may seem redundant, but when there are many statements between the IF and ENDIF, this practice makes it much easier to recognize the beginning and end of the IF structure when you are reading, modifying, or debugging a program.

In the National Widgets statement-printing program, you could test a customer's balance with the following IF structure:

```
if BALANCE > 0
   ? "Please pay the outstanding balance promptly"
endif                  [ BALANCE > 0 ]
```

Although an IF structure like this would normally form only a small part of a larger program, these three lines do constitute a complete dBASE III PLUS program. If you use MODIFY COMMAND or a word processor to type these three lines into a file called IFTEST1.PRG, you can run the program from the dot prompt, provided that a variable called BALANCE—either a data base field or memory variable—is available. The easiest way to test this is to open the NWCUST file, position the data base to any record you like, and type

```
DO IFTEST1
```

Figure 9-6 illustrates a typical dialog with dBASE III PLUS that tests the performance of this program with three selected customers. This figure illustrates a general strategy for supplying input to a program to make sure that it does what you intended. By looking at a printed Customer Reference List or using a LIST command (LIST ACCOUNT, COMPANY, BALANCE), we have found customers with balances greater than, equal to, and less than zero. (If your sample data does not provide you with all of the possibilities you wish to test, you can temporarily change the values of the relevant fields in a few records.) Before running IFTEST1.PRG for each of these customers, we have displayed the customer record to show the BALANCE, so it will be clear whether or not the program has performed as expected.

This type of IF. . .ENDIF structure tells dBASE III PLUS what to do if a certain condition is true. As you can see from Figure 9-6, if the condition is *not* true, *no* action will be taken. In certain situations, you may need to supply an alternate course of action. In our example, the owner might tell the bookkeeper, "If a customer owes us money, type a message on the statement that says 'Please pay the outstanding balance promptly,' or else

```
. USE NWCUST
. GOTO RECORD 3
. ? BALANCE
     85.74
. DO IFTEST1
Please pay the outstanding balance promptly
. GOTO RECORD 4
. ? BALANCE
      0.00
. DO IFTEST1
. GOTO RECORD 6
. ? BALANCE
    -10.00
. DO IFTEST1
.
```

Figure 9-6. Running the IFTEST1.PRG program

type the message, 'Thank you for your prompt payment.'" This two-way decision may be expressed in a dBASE III PLUS program like this:

if *condition*
  commands to execute if the condition is true
else
  commands to execute if the condition is false
endif

Like ENDIF, the word ELSE must appear on a line by itself. All of the commands between the IF and ELSE lines will be executed if the condition in the IF statement is true. Otherwise, the statements between ELSE and ENDIF will be executed. Translated into this format, in a program called IFTEST2.PRG, the amended statement-printing instructions would read

```
if BALANCE > 0
   ? "Please pay the outstanding balance promptly"
else
   ? "Thank you for your prompt payment"
endif                [ BALANCE > 0 ]
```

The same kind of dialog with dBASE III PLUS that was used to test the performance of IFTEST1.PRG is illustrated for this program in Figure 9-7.

You could carry out exactly the same test with the IIF function. This single command is equivalent to the IFTEST2.PRG program:

```
IIF(BALANCE > 0,"Please pay the outstanding balance promptly",
    "Thank you for your prompt payment")
```

The version that uses the IIF function will execute slightly faster. It is also more compact, which some programmers consider clearer and more efficient, while others find the denser expression harder to read and understand. Used at command level in a LIST or REPORT, IIF provides a decision-making capability that would otherwise be unavailable, but it is limited by the fact that a command may not exceed 254 characters in length. In a program, the IF structure, which can include any number of program statements, is far more powerful and flexible.

The statements within the IF...ELSE...ENDIF structure may be *any* dBASE III PLUS commands, including another IF loop. Placing one programming structure within another is called *nesting*. With nested IF loops,

```
. USE NWCUST
. GOTO RECORD 3
. ? BALANCE
     85.74
. DO IFTEST2
Please pay the outstanding balance promptly
. GOTO RECORD 4
. ? BALANCE
     0.00
. DO IFTEST2
Thank you for your prompt payment
. GOTO RECORD 6
. ? BALANCE
    -10.00
. DO IFTEST2
Thank you for your prompt payment
.
```

Figure 9-7. Running the IFTEST2.PRG program

you can test for more than two possible outcomes of a condition:

```
if condition 1
  commands to execute if condition 1 is true
else
  if condition 2
    commands to execute if condition 2 is true
  else
    commands to execute if condition 2 is false
  endif    (condition 2)
endif    (condition 1)
```

Although the third possibility is phrased "commands to execute if condition 2 is false," these steps, like *all* of the lines following the first ELSE, are executed *only* if condition 1 is also false. In the National Widgets example, the owner may have instructed the bookkeeper, "If a customer owes us money, type a message on the statement that says 'Please pay the outstanding balance promptly,' or else, if the balance is zero, type the message, 'Thank you for your prompt payment,' or else—that is, if the balance is less than zero—type the message, 'Your credit balance can be applied to future orders.'"

In a dBASE III PLUS program, IFTEST3.PRG, this test could be written

```
if BALANCE > 0
   ? "Please pay the outstanding balance promptly"
else
   if BALANCE = 0
      ? "Thank you for your prompt payment"
   else
      ? "Your credit balance can be applied to future orders"
   endif                [ BALANCE = 0 ]
endif                   [ BALANCE > 0 ]
```

The test dialog with dBASE III PLUS for this program is illustrated in Figure 9-8.

Another way to test for three possible outcomes of a condition is to use three separate IF loops, as follows:

```
if BALANCE > 0
   ? "Please pay the outstanding balance promptly"
endif                   [ BALANCE > 0 ]
if BALANCE = 0
   ? "Thank you for your prompt payment"
endif                   [ BALANCE = 0 ]
if BALANCE < 0
   ? "Your credit balance can be applied to future orders"
endif                   [ BALANCE < 0]
```

```
. USE NWCUST
. GOTO RECORD 3
. ? BALANCE
     85.74
. DO IFTEST3
Please pay the outstanding balance promptly
. GOTO RECORD 4
. ? BALANCE
      0.00
. DO IFTEST3
Thank you for your prompt payment
. GOTO RECORD 6
. ? BALANCE
    -10.00
. DO IFTEST3
Your credit balance can be applied to future orders
```

Figure 9-8. Running the IFTEST3.PRG program

In a program with more than three tests, this construction, illustrated in IFTEST4.PRG, may execute somewhat faster, but it can make the program harder to read and understand, since there is no indication that the three separate IF loops are related in any way. In the version with nested IF loops, it is clearer that the program is testing for several possible variations of the same data.

MAKING MULTIPLE-CHOICE DECISIONS WITH DO CASE

Either separate or nested IF structures may be used to choose among three or more alternatives. However, if you know that only one of a number of possibilities will be true, you can instead use the DO CASE structure, which is easier to read and will execute somewhat faster. This is the form of the DO CASE structure:

```
do case
      case condition 1
            commands to execute if condition 1 is true
      case condition 2
            commands to execute if condition 2 is true
      more cases
      otherwise
            commands to execute if none of the other conditions is true
endcase
```

This structure begins with the DO CASE line and ends with ENDCASE. These statements, and each individual CASE, must be placed on separate lines in the program. *dBASE III PLUS assumes that only one of the conditions in the CASE structure will be true.* When a DO CASE structure is processed, each of the conditions in the CASE statements is evaluated in turn. When a true condition is found, dBASE III PLUS executes the commands between this CASE and the next and then skips all of the remaining lines in the CASE structure, resuming execution with the command following the ENDCASE statement. The optional OTHERWISE clause, which must follow the last CASE, specifies the actions to take if none of the preceding conditions is true.

The following DO CASE structure could be used to replace the nested IFs in the statement-printing program:

```
do case
   case BALANCE > 0
      ? "Please pay the outstanding balance promptly"
   case BALANCE = 0
      ? "Thank you for your prompt payment"
   case BALANCE < 0
      ? "Your credit balance can be applied to future orders"
endcase
```

This example used three CASEs, rather than two CASEs and an OTHERWISE clause, to emphasize that there are exactly three possibilities for the BALANCE field. In this example and in many of the programs we will write, the conditions in the CASE statement test the same variable, but it is not required that the conditions be related to each other in any way.

Any program that uses a DO CASE structure can also be written with an equivalent series of nested IFs or separate IFs. When you are choosing one among three or more possibilities, the DO CASE structure is preferable, since it will run slightly faster and it will greatly improve the readability of the program. By definition, only one CASE may be true, so anyone reading the program will immediately understand that you are choosing one among a list of possibilities rather than conducting a series of independent tests. With deeply nested IF loops, it is more difficult to see at a glance which loops are completely enclosed within other structures and thus determine which alternatives the program is considering.

REPEATING PROGRAM STEPS WITH DO WHILE

The DO WHILE structure allows you to repeat a set of program steps as long as a specified condition is true. The general form for this structure is

do while *condition*
  commands to execute as long as the condition is true
enddo

If the condition in the DO WHILE statement is true when dBASE III PLUS begins processing the loop, the statements between DO WHILE

```
* COUNTER1.PRG
* PROGRAM TO ILLUSTRATE THE USE OF THE DO WHILE LOOP
* WRITTEN BY:  M.LISKIN       6/10/85

set talk off
store 1 to MCOUNT

do while MCOUNT <= 10

  ? "COUNT =", MCOUNT
  store MCOUNT + 1 to MCOUNT

enddo           [ MCOUNT <= 10 ]

? "This program counted from 1 to 10"
```

Figure 9-9. A program to illustrate the use of the DO WHILE loop

and ENDDO are executed, after which the condition is evaluated again. If it is still true, all of the statements within the loop are executed again. This process is repeated until the condition eventually becomes false, at which time execution resumes with the first program statement after ENDDO. As in the IF structure, dBASE III PLUS ignores any text on the same line as ENDDO, so you may use this area for a comment that restates the condition controlling the loop.

The program in Figure 9-9, COUNTER1.PRG, illustrates this structure. This program counts from 1 to 10, displaying the numbers on the screen as it proceeds. The SET TALK OFF command was included so that the STORE commands do not echo the new values for MCOUNT to the terminal; this variable is displayed with the ? command. The program first creates the memory variable MCOUNT and gives it a value of 1. Within the loop the value of MCOUNT is displayed and then incremented. When the value of MCOUNT reaches 11, the condition in the DO WHILE statement (MCOUNT <= 10) is no longer true, and dBASE III PLUS proceeds to the first statement following ENDDO and displays the final message on the screen.

If the condition in the DO WHILE statement is *not* true when dBASE III PLUS first reads this command, the steps within the loop will not be processed even once. You can illustrate this by changing the initialization of the memory variable MCOUNT in the COUNTER1.PRG program to

```
store 20 to MCOUNT
```

If you do not ensure that the condition in the DO WHILE statement eventually becomes false, the program will never stop processing the same set of steps. For example, removing the "store MCOUNT + 1 to MCOUNT" line from COUNTER1.PRG causes the program to display "COUNT = 1" over and over. The only way out of this "endless loop" is to press the ESC key to interrupt processing. (If you try this, remember to reset the initial STORE command so that MCOUNT is initialized with a value of 1, not 20.)

Remember also that dBASE III PLUS only evaluates the condition in the DO WHILE statement at the beginning of each pass through the loop. If the condition becomes false midway through, the rest of the commands will still be executed. *Only when dBASE III PLUS reaches the ENDDO line and returns to the DO WHILE statement to reevaluate the condition will the program exit the loop.* You can, however, use the EXIT command to get out of a DO WHILE loop at any point. If, for example, you wished the value of MCOUNT to be 10, not 11, when the counter program terminates, you could rewrite the program as illustrated by COUNTER2.PRG, which is listed in Figure 9-10.

The DO WHILE structure is commonly used in dBASE III PLUS to carry out the same set of steps for some or all of the records in a data base using DO WHILE .NOT. EOF( ). EOF( ) is the dBASE III PLUS end-

```
* COUNTER2.PRG
* PROGRAM TO ILLUSTRATE THE USE OF THE DO WHILE LOOP
* WRITTEN BY:   M.LISKIN        6/10/85


set talk off
store 1 to MCOUNT

do while MCOUNT <= 10

  ? "COUNT =", MCOUNT

  if MCOUNT = 10
     exit
  else
     store MCOUNT + 1 to MCOUNT
  endif

enddo          (MCOUNT <= 10)

? "This program counted from 1 to 10"
```

Figure 9-10. A program to illustrate the use of the EXIT command

```
* LISTER1.PRG
* PROGRAM TO ILLUSTRATE THE USE OF DO WHILE .NOT. EOF()
* WRITTEN BY:  M.LISKIN        6/10/85

set talk off
use NWCUST index NWCACCT

do while .not. eof()

   ? ACCOUNT, COMPANY, EQUIPMENT
   skip

enddo          [ not end-of-file ]

? "This program listed the Customer File"
```

Figure 9-11. A program to illustrate the use of DO WHILE .NOT. EOF( ) to process every record in a data base

of-file function, a logical function that has the value .F. if the record pointer is positioned at any record in a data base. When a sequential command like LIST or REPORT terminates, or when you attempt to SKIP past the last record (or last indexed record, if the file was opened with an index), the EOF( ) function assumes the value .T.

Figure 9-11 illustrates a simple program, LISTER1.PRG, which reads through the Customer File in account number order and displays the ACCOUNT, COMPANY, and EQUIPMENT fields from each record. Note that the DO WHILE loop in this program does exactly the same thing as the command:

```
LIST ACCOUNT, COMPANY, EQUIPMENT
```

If you forget the SKIP command—a very easy mistake to make—the condition in the DO WHILE statement never becomes false and the program will continue to display the first record in the file until you interrupt with the ESC key. You should also avoid the other common pitfall: placing a command (like LIST or INDEX) that processes an entire data base immediately prior to the loop. These commands leave the data base positioned at the end-of-file, in which case the condition in the DO WHILE statement is never true and the statements in the loop are not executed even once.

Within a DO WHILE structure, you may use the LOOP command to bypass the remaining steps in the loop and return immediately to the DO

```
* LISTER2.PRG
* PROGRAM TO PROCESS SELECTED RECORDS USING THE LOOP COM
* WRITTEN BY:  M.LISKIN       6/10/85

set talk off
use NWCUST index NWCACCT

do while .not. eof()

   if CITY <> "San Francisco"
      skip
      loop
   endif

   ? ACCOUNT, COMPANY, EQUIPMENT
   skip

enddo          [ not end-of-file ]

? "This program listed customers in San Francisco"
```

Figure 9-12. A program to illustrate the use of the LOOP command to process selected records

WHILE statement to reevaluate the condition. For example, if you wanted to display San Francisco customers only, you could rewrite LISTER1.PRG so that it first checks the contents of the CITY field, as shown in the LISTER2.PRG program in Figure 9-12. If the field does *not* contain the character string "San Francisco", the program will immediately SKIP to the next record and go back to the top of the loop. This program is equivalent to the LISTER3.PRG program in Figure 9-13, which tests to see whether the CITY field *does* contain the text "San Francisco". If so, the record is displayed; if not, the program proceeds to the next command after the IF loop, the SKIP command. Either of these versions of the program has the same effect as typing at the dot prompt:

```
LIST ACCOUNT, COMPANY, EQUIPMENT FOR CITY = "San Francisco"
```

A short program like this one does not highlight the usefulness of the LOOP command. However, if the DO WHILE loop contains many steps, structuring the program this way places the condition that determines whether or not a record is processed at the top of the loop, where it is obvious to any reader of the program. In a longer DO WHILE loop, the

```
* LISTER3.PRG
* PROGRAM TO PROCESS SELECTED RECORDS USING AN IF LOOP
* WRITTEN BY:   M.LISKIN        6/10/85

set talk off
use NWCUST index NWCACCT

do while .not. eof()

   if CITY = "San Francisco"
      ? ACCOUNT, COMPANY, EQUIPMENT
   endif

   skip

enddo            [ not end-of-file ]

? "This program listed customers in San Francisco"
```

Figure 9-13. A program to illustrate the use of an IF loop to process selected records

speed of execution may also significantly increase if you use LOOP to bypass interpretation of all of the remaining steps in the loop for records that should not be processed.

GENERAL PROGRAM STRUCTURE

A short program that illustrated the use of nested IF loops was presented earlier in this chapter. In general, any dBASE III PLUS programming structure may be used inside any other structure. There is no limit on how deeply you may nest loops, but too many loops within other loops can make your programs very hard to decipher. When you nest loops, you must be careful that each loop is completely enclosed within another. For example, the following loop is correct:

```
if condition 1
   do while condition 2
      program statements
   enddo
endif
```

```
* PROGRAM1.PRG

clear
? "This is Program 1"
?
do PROGRAM2

? "This is Program 1 again"

return


* PROGRAM2.PRG

? "This is Program 2"
?
do PROGRAM3

? "This is Program 2 again"

return


* PROGRAM3.PRG

? "This is Program 3"
?
return to master
```

Figure 9-14. Three programs to illustrate how one dBASE III program may call another

This version is wrong:

```
if condition 1
  do while condition 2
     program statements
endif
  enddo
```

One dBASE III PLUS program may call another with the same DO command you would use at the dot prompt. When the called program terminates, the calling program resumes execution with the line following the DO command. Note that a program ends when the last command in the program has been executed, but you can end the program at any point with a RETURN statement. Although it is not required, a RETURN should be placed at the end of every program. If PROGRAM1 calls PROGRAM2, which calls PROGRAM3, a RETURN statement in PROGRAM3 will transfer control back to PROGRAM2. When PROGRAM2 terminates, dBASE III PLUS will return to PROGRAM1; and PROGRAM1, which was called from the dot prompt, will return to the dot prompt when it ends. You can return directly from PROGRAM3 (or any other program in such a chain) to PROGRAM1 with RETURN TO MASTER.

Figure 9-14 lists three very simple programs that illustrate these concepts. When you run PROGRAM1, the following screen will appear:

```
This is Program 1

This is Program 2

This is Program 3

This is Program 1 again
.
```

Note that the message "This is Program 2 again" is never displayed, because PROGRAM3 uses RETURN TO MASTER to jump directly back to PROGRAM1 instead of returning to the program that called it.

10

PROGRAMMING STRATEGY

When you write short dBASE III PLUS programs that combine command sequences you have already tested at the dot prompt, you may well find that most of your programs work as intended on the first or second try; but as you begin to build longer and more complex programs, planning, strategy, and documentation become more important. Whether or not you have experience with other programming languages, try to resist the temptation to write an entire program at the computer the moment you first conceive it. Outlining a program on paper beforehand and developing long programs in stages will greatly reduce the amount of time you must spend debugging. If you are a beginner, the techniques for planning and documentation discussed in this chapter will ease your transition to writing longer and more sophisticated programs. This chapter also summarizes the standard nomenclature and notational conventions introduced in earlier chapters. Adhering to this or a similar set of guidelines will make your programs easier to read and understand, both for you and for other programmers who may eventually modify your system.

USING PSEUDOCODE TO PLAN A PROGRAM

In this and later chapters, we will make extensive use of *pseudocode* as a planning tool. As the name suggests, pseudocode is an informal outline of the tasks a program must accomplish. When you write pseudocode, your style can range from something very much like colloquial English to a format that more closely resembles dBASE III PLUS command syntax. The level of detail may range from a very brief outline of the broad functions a program will execute to almost as many lines as the final program.

As an example, consider LISTER2.PRG, the program written in Chapter 9 to list selected records from the Customer File. You might describe the purpose of this program as follows: "List, in alphabetical order by account number, the account number, company name, and type of equipment for all customers in San Francisco." An informal pseudocode listing for the program might look like this:

```
open the customer file with the account number index
for each record in the file:
   if the city is San Francisco,
      display the account number, company name, and equipment fields

after reading all the records,
display a closing message
```

This rough sketch may be all an experienced programmer needs to write the complete program. This style of pseudocode is also appropriate for beginners as a first description, in non-technical terms, of a new program. Using the pseudocode as an outline that clarifies the actions a program must take, you can determine how to translate these operations into dBASE III PLUS commands. A second, more formal, pseudocode listing that suggests the programming structures to be used can then serve as a guide when you actually sit down to write the program. Here is a more detailed pseudocode version of LISTER2.PRG:

```
turn off TALK to suppress dBASE III PLUS status messages
open the customer file with the account number index

for each record in the file:

   if the city is not San Francisco,
      skip the record
      go back to the top of the loop
   endif

   display the account number, company name, and equipment fields
   skip to the next record
end of steps to do for each record in the file

display a closing message
```

In a short program like this, the pseudocode version contains as much detail as the real program. In other cases, the pseudocode will be much more concise; a single phrase may serve as a functional description of a 20-line segment of the program. This brief version is a reassuring way to break down a large project into smaller, more manageable pieces, which you can tackle one at a time, writing out each segment in more detailed pseudocode before you translate it into dBASE III PLUS program statements. For a more experienced programmer, the second, more detailed version may not be necessary—each line may represent a block of statements you have used many times in the past and understand intimately.

Figure 10-1 is a pseudocode outline of the Main Menu program we will write in Chapter 12 for the National Widgets system. In this listing the single line "set up the working environment" might eventually translate to a lengthy series of SET commands; and "ask for the user's selection" might become a routine that presents a prompt message, stores the user's selection in a memory variable, checks it for validity, and if it is not an allowable choice, displays an error message and asks the question again. This informal style of pseudocode will be used throughout this book as a planning tool; a more detailed type of pseudocode that closely parallels the structure of the program itself will be used to provide a line-by-line explanation of how a program works.

BUILDING A PROGRAM IN STAGES

Writing a large dBASE III PLUS program entails the same steps outlined previously for writing increasingly detailed pseudocode versions: begin with the big picture and work your way down to the finer details. Just as the command level testing phase of system development is intended to ensure that all of the necessary data entry, processing, and output functions can be carried out by the system, the first version of a program should strive for the same goals. Once you have verified that your program manipulates the data files correctly, you can add the details that make it more versatile, easy to use, and reliable.

For example, when you write a Main Menu program for your own application, you might postpone deciding exactly which SET commands you will eventually use. Instead of a fancy opening sign-on screen, you could just display the message "This is the sign-on screen," and since you will be the only one using the program in its initial form, you could omit

```
set up the working environment
present a sign on screen

do the following until the user chooses to exit:

   draw the menu screen
   ask for the user's selection

   process the selection:

     if the selection is "1":
        run the customer information menu program

     if the selection is "2":
        run the order processing menu program

     if the selection is "3":
        run the financial transactions menu program

     if the selection is "4":
        reindex all the data base files

     if the selection is "88":
        exit to the dBASE III PLUS dot prompt

     if the selection is "99":
        exit to MS-DOS operating system

     if an invalid selection is chosen:
         display an error message
         allow the user to try again

   after processing the selection:

   close any open data bases
   go back and ask for another selection
```

Figure 10-1. The Main Menu program in pseudocode

the group of commands that display an error message if the operator fails to select a valid choice. The first version of the program might simply draw the menu screen, collect the user's choice, and set up a DO CASE structure to process the selection.

Notice also that the Main Menu program calls other programs, some of which may not be available yet. These programs may be created in a very rudimentary form, just to verify that they are called correctly and that they return properly to the Main Menu. For example, option 1 in the Main Menu program calls the Customer Information Menu with DO NWCMENU. To test the Main Menu program, it is sufficient to create a version of NWCMENU.PRG that clears the screen, identifies itself, waits for your acknowledgment, and then returns to the Main Menu:

```
* NWCMENU.PRG
* DUMMY VERSION OF CUSTOMER INFORMATION MENU
* WRITTEN BY:  M.LISKIN       06/20/85


clear
? "This is the Customer Menu"
?
wait
return
```

NAMING AND NOTATIONAL CONVENTIONS

Throughout the development of the National Widgets sample system, this book has stressed the importance of adhering to a consistent nomenclature for files and fields and a set of standard notational conventions. As an application grows in size and complexity, you will come to appreciate the value of these conventions. Figure 10-2 summarizes the rules used in the National Widgets sample system, which you may use as presented or adapt to match your personal preferences. As you develop conventions to use in your own work with dBASE III PLUS, remember that the primary aims should be consistency and readability. Write down the rules you establish as guidelines for your own use when you create new files, variables, and programs, and for the benefit of other programmers who may modify or add to your application later.

All of your file names should be as descriptive as possible within the DOS restriction of eight characters for the first part of the name. All of the disk files associated with a particular system should share a common two- or three-character prefix. Data base file names should clearly indicate the purpose of the file, and index names should provide some clue as to which data base the index file accesses and what field or fields make up the index key. Similarly, a format file name should contain a reference to the name of the data base it allows you to update. Report form names should either describe the report (for example, NWINVREG.FRM for the National Widgets Invoice Register) or, in the case of a comprehensive reference list for a data base, indicate the file that supplies the data (NWCUSTRF.FRM for the Customer File Reference List).

Program names should indicate the purpose of the program. In a large system with several menus, you may want to include in some program

Type of File	Extension	Suggested File Name	Example
Data bases	DBF	System prefix + description	NW + CUST+.DBF
Data base text	DBT	System prefix + data base name (file name is assigned by dBASE III PLUS)	NW + CUST+.DBT
Index	NDX	System prefix + data base + key field(s)	NW + I + CAT + PT + .NDX
Format file	FMT	System prefix + data base + optional description	NW + TXN + PMT + .FMT
Report form	FRM	System prefix + data base + description or system prefix + description	NW + CUST + RF + .FRM NW + INVREG + .FRM
Label form	LBL	System prefix + data base + description	NW + CUST + 1 + .FRM
Memory variable	MEM	System prefix + description	NW + CSTATS + .MEM
Program	PRG	System prefix + data base + description	NW + C + STATS + .PRG
Procedure	PRG	System prefix + description	NW + PROC

File Names:

- Avoid punctuation within file names.
- Limit file names to the eight characters permitted by the MS-DOS operating system.
- Use a common two- or three-character prefix for all of the files in a system.
- Use the standard dBASE III PLUS file extensions.
- Include a reference to the data base in all index and format file names.

- Include a functional description of the purpose of the format file in the names of any format files that do not simply access all of the data base fields.
- Include a reference to the data base or a functional description of the purpose of the report in all report and label form names.
- Name programs according to their purpose, not by menu option number.

Field Names:

- Do not use any dBASE III PLUS command or function name as a field name.
- Use common English words or abbreviations.
- Don't shorten field names for convenience in typing at the expense of clarity.
- Avoid the permitted underscore (_) punctuation.
- Use the same name for fields that contain the same type of information in different data bases.

Memory Variable Names:

- Do not use any dBASE III PLUS command or function name as a memory variable name.
- Use the prefix M for all memory variables.
- Use a common two- or three-character prefix for groups of memory variables that are used together or that have a common purpose in the system.
- Identify the public memory variables in the system with a common prefix.
- When a memory variable directly corresponds to a data base field, use a name consisting of the M (or other) prefix plus the name of the field.

Figure 10-2. File, field, and memory variable name conventions for dBASE III PLUS systems

names one character that symbolizes the menu calling it. However, the common practice of naming files with menu option numbers—for example, NWC13.PRG for the program called by option 13 on the Customer Information Menu—makes it unnecessarily difficult to identify the program that performs a particular function, unless you keep a printed copy of the menu handy at all times.

Choose field names that describe the contents of the fields. Using names that resemble ordinary English words will help you remember them and make your commands and programs easier to type, read, and understand. Although dBASE III PLUS permits you to use an underscore (_) as punctuation to improve the readability of your field names, fast typists may want to avoid the inconvenience of typing a shifted character located in a far corner of the keyboard. If you hunt and peck with two fingers, however, typing the underscore may not slow you down significantly. When a field occurs in more than one file, use the same name to emphasize the relationship among the files and to make it easier to recognize a field's purpose by its name.

If certain abbreviations allow you to shorten your field names without obscuring their meanings, use them. For example, ADD1 may be as clear to you as ADDRESS1 for "first address line," and the shorter name will be easier to type. On the other hand, the name FN might suggest "first name" to you, but another, more mathematically oriented, user or programmer might read this as "function."

Unlike many other programming languages, dBASE III PLUS does not prohibit you from using reserved words—the command and function names—for fields or memory variables, but you should avoid this practice. For example, you might choose the name STATUS for a field that describes the status of an order or inventory item. But this would prevent you from using a LIST command to display only the STATUS field from each record, since LIST STATUS is a dBASE III PLUS command itself. Similarly, if you named a program CASE.PRG or WHILE.PRG, you would run into trouble when you attempted to call the program with DO CASE or DO WHILE.

Beginning all memory variable names with M makes it easy to distinguish them from data base fields; PUBLIC variables used to store system-wide options should use a different prefix, such as MP. When you create a memory variable that directly corresponds to a data base field, the best choice for the memory variable name is the name of the data base field preceded by M or MP. You could thus use MACCOUNT for a variable used to collect a customer account number or MPSTATE for a PUBLIC variable that stores the default state for new entries.

Internal Program Documentation

As you develop a program, both the general strategy and the details will be fresh in your mind and you will be able to see at a glance what any part of the program is doing or remember why you used a certain technique to accomplish a particular goal. Three months later, however, when you return to the same program to make a minor change, you may hardly recognize your own code. Sooner or later your system will probably be read and modified by other programmers—if you quit your job, move to another department, or decide to turn the maintenance of the system over to a colleague so you can move on to other projects. At some point you might want to hire an outside expert to develop some components of the system that you find too difficult or time-consuming to write yourself. And if you yourself are acting as an outside consultant, you can be sure that your client's employees will eventually begin to modify or add to your programs. In all of these situations, the more clearly written and comprehensively documented your programs are, the easier your system will be to maintain and enhance.

As stated in Chapter 7, the programs in this book use lowercase for all dBASE III PLUS command words and function names and uppercase for all file, field, and memory variable names. All dBASE III PLUS commands should be spelled out in full. Extra spaces within command lines should be used to align corresponding portions of a set of similar commands, and blank lines should be used to set off groups of lines that form functional units in a program. As shown in the examples in Chapter 9, extra spaces are also commonly used to indent the program lines contained within an IF, DO WHILE, or DO CASE structure. In an IF structure, the IF, ELSE (if any), and ENDIF should all be at the same level, and the enclosed program statements should be indented:

```
if condition
   program statements
else
   other program statements
endif
```

The same convention applies to DO WHILE loops:

```
do while condition
   program statements
enddo
```

In a DO CASE structure, the individual CASE statements should be one level in from the DO CASE, and the statements within each CASE indented one level from the CASE statement:

```
do case
   case condition 1
      program statements
   case condition 2
      program statements
   otherwise
      program statements
endcase
```

When you write programs with deeply nested loop structures—for example, a DO WHILE loop that contains a DO CASE that contains an IF—you will appreciate the way indentation makes it easier to identify the statements within a loop and to pick out the beginning and end of each structure. In the programs in this book, we will indent three spaces for each level, so that the statements within an IF loop line up with the beginning of the condition in the IF statement, and the body of a DO WHILE loop or DO CASE structure is aligned with the words WHILE or CASE. Many programmers prefer to indent more spaces at each level; but remember that as you write more complex programs, you may find yourself beginning many lines uncomfortably close to the right margin. Also, the further the lines are indented, the more difficult it is to scan a printed listing and visually align the beginning and end of a loop containing many program statements. Except in extremely short loops, you should include the optional comment in all ENDIF and ENDDO statements that echoes the condition in the matching IF or DO WHILE statement. Comments should be placed before the section of the program they refer to, indented to the same level as the first statement following the comment, or on the first line of the program segment.

These notational conventions make even a short program much easier to read. Figure 10-3 reproduces the LISTER.PRG program written in Chapter 9 to display National Widgets' customers in San Francisco. Figure 10-4 is a much less readable version of the same program. The notational conventions used in the dBASE III PLUS programs in the National Widgets system are summarized in Figure 10-5.

```
* LISTER2.PRG
* PROGRAM TO PROCESS SELECTED RECORDS USING THE LOOP COMMAND
* WRITTEN BY:  M.LISKIN       6/10/85


set talk off
use NWCUST index NWCACCT

do while .not. eof()

   if CITY <> "San Francisco"
      skip
      loop
   endif

   ? ACCOUNT, COMPANY, EQUIPMENT
   skip

enddo          [ not end-of-file ]

? "This program listed customers in San Francisco"
```

Figure 10-3. LISTER2.PRG in its most readable form

```
SET TALK OFF
USE NWCUST INDE NWCACCT
DO WHIL .NOT. EOF()
IF CITY<>"San Francisco"
SKIP
LOOP
ENDI
? ACCOUNT,COMPANY,EQUIPMENT
SKIP
ENDD
? "This program listed customers in San Francisco"
```

Figure 10-4. LISTER2.PRG in its most compact form

Programming Conventions:

- Use lowercase for all dBASE III PLUS command and function names.
- Use uppercase for all file, memory variable, and field names.
- Spell out all dBASE III PLUS command words in full.
- Use extra spaces within expressions and lists to improve readability.
- Use extra spaces within command lines to align corresponding portions of a sequence of similar commands.
- Use blank lines between command lines to set off groups of commands that form functional units.
- Use preceding comments to identify the function of a group of program lines or to explain a complex procedure.
- Indent separate comment lines to the same level as the program lines they refer to, or place comments on the first line of the program section.
- Begin each program with comments that identify the name, purpose, author, date written, and last modification date.
- Indent the lines within IF, DO WHILE, and DO CASE structures.
- Use a fixed number of characters (for example, three) for each level of indentation.

Figure 10-5. Notational conventions for dBASE III PLUS programs

DOCUMENTING THE DEVELOPING SYSTEM

The techniques described in the previous section are part of the process of *internally* documenting a program, using notational and stylistic conventions that make the program easier to understand just by reading the code. As you build a dBASE III PLUS application, you should also maintain a system notebook that documents the development process on paper.

The notebook will serve as a reference guide for you and other programmers as you add to the growing system and as an aid to writing the end-user documentation when the project is complete. This notebook should eventually contain

- Listings of the file structures and index keys.
- Report and label samples.
- Listings of the memory variables used for systemwide options.
- Listings of CATALOG files used to record the names of the files that comprise the application and the relationships among them.
- Screen prints and printouts of ALTERNATE files used to document command level testing.
- Pseudocode listings.
- Complete program and format file listings.
- Screen prints showing all formatted data entry screens.
- System initialization procedures and the data entry startup sequence.
- Backup and recovery procedures.

You should keep copies, both on disk and on paper, of each major program revision. During the development process, both the programmers and the users may change their minds many times about the details or even the overall goals of a program. Keeping a record of the changes will make it easier to revise and help the people involved to understand the evolution of the system.

11

USING MEMORY VARIABLES

Chapter 7 introduced the use of memory variables in dBASE III PLUS programs to save the results of calculations so that they are available for further manipulation. When you begin writing more complex programs, memory variables will be used for these purposes and many others, including accepting input from the operator, controlling the repetition of steps with DO WHILE loops, and storing data that must be shared by many programs in the system.

As the name suggests, a memory variable is a temporary quantity that exists in RAM during a work session with dBASE III PLUS. Unless you save memory variables on disk, their values are lost when you turn off the computer or exit from dBASE III PLUS. If you are familiar with other programming languages, memory variables will not be new to you—a computer program in any language must be able to store values for use within the program and allow you to refer to them by name. In the dBASE III PLUS language, memory variables are used for this purpose, but since many dBASE III PLUS programs operate largely on input from data base files, and in many cases write their output to a data base as well, you do not need to define as many temporary variables as you would in other languages.

Memory variables also have another important function in dBASE III PLUS applications: they store separate, unrelated quantities that are used throughout the system and do not necessarily belong to any one data base file. Whether you are a newcomer or an experienced programmer, you should pay close attention as you read this chapter not only to the syntax of the commands used to create memory variables, but also to the programming strategies and typical uses for memory variables illustrated in the examples.

INITIALIZING MEMORY VARIABLES

In the NWCSTAT1.PRG program written in Chapter 7 to compile statistics from the Customer File, the memory variables used to store the calculated results were created by the COUNT, SUM, and AVERAGE commands—all the program had to do was assign the names. In most of the remaining programs in this book, memory variables must be *initialized*—created explicitly by the programmer—before they are used to store data. Memory variables may take on four of the five data types allowed for data base fields: character, numeric, logical, and date. (Memo memory variables are *not* permitted.) Like data base field names, memory variable names may be up to ten characters in length and may contain an embedded underscore (_). Beginning all memory variable names with M will clearly distinguish them from data base fields in your programs.

A memory variable is created by naming it and assigning it a value with the STORE command or the assignment (=) operator. dBASE III PLUS determines the data type of the variable by the data type of the initial value. To create a numeric memory variable, called MX in this case, and assign it an initial value of 1, you could use either

```
STORE 1 TO MX
```

or

```
MX = 1
```

If you have used other programming languages, the "=" syntax may seem more familiar and more concise than the STORE usage. Beginners should be careful not to confuse this meaning of the equal sign with its meaning in a condition that tests whether two expressions are equal to each other. The command line MX = 1 does *not* test whether MX currently equals 1; rather, it *creates* a memory variable called MX and *assigns* to it the value 1. If you have worked extensively with dBASE II or are converting programs written for dBASE II to run under dBASE III PLUS, you might choose to retain the STORE construction, which is the only way to initialize memory variables in dBASE II. Even in a new dBASE III PLUS system, there is another advantage to the STORE syntax — you may use it to assign the same value to several variables simultaneously:

```
STORE 0 TO MCOUNT, MSUM, MAVERAGE
```

Unlike other higher-level languages (some implementations of BASIC, for example), dBASE III PLUS does not permit you to use the equivalent MCOUNT = MSUM = MAVERAGE = 0. You may use both the STORE and "=" constructions in the same program, but for the sake of consistency, it is best to adopt one or the other usage or at least use STORE in certain clearly defined contexts and = in others. In the remaining examples in this chapter, and throughout this book, STORE will be used primarily.

You may also assign a new value to an existing memory variable. This effectively erases the old memory variable and recreates it from scratch — dBASE III PLUS retains no record of the original value. The value assigned to a memory variable need not be a constant — you may use any legitimate dBASE III PLUS expression made up of constants, data base fields, functions, and other memory variables. Numeric memory variables are assumed to be integers ten digits in length, and by default they have no decimal places. To create a variable with one or more decimal places, you must include them in the initial value:

```
STORE 1.00 TO MX
```

Character memory variables assume the same length as the value you assign (up to the maximum permissible length of 254 for dBASE III PLUS character strings). Thus, the following command creates a character variable called MLASTNAME seven characters long, with the initial value "Johnson":

```
STORE "Johnson" TO MLASTNAME
```

If it were necessary to make MLASTNAME longer while retaining the same initial value, you could add the appropriate number of trailing blank spaces:

```
STORE "Johnson          " TO MLASTNAME
```

Logical memory variables are initialized by assigning them the logical values .T. (true) or .F. (false).

```
STORE .T. TO MCONTINUE
```

As you can see from these examples, data consisting only of numeric digits is assumed to be a number, text enclosed in any of the standard character string delimiters is assumed to be character data, and logical values are set off by the period (.) delimiters. Initializing date memory variables is not quite so straightforward, because dBASE III PLUS does not have a standard delimiter that identifies a date as a date. Instead, you must create a character string that "looks like" a date and use the CTOD (character-to-date) function to convert it to a true date:

```
STORE CTOD("04/30/84") TO MDATEPAID
```

If you need to create a memory variable without giving it any particular value, you must specify a *blank* initial value. For numeric variables, you can use 0:

```
STORE 0 TO MX
```

For character strings you can assign a string of blank spaces of the desired length. The easiest way to define a short string is to type in the spaces:

```
STORE "      " TO MCATEGORY
```

For longer strings you can use the SPACE function to avoid counting spaces, either when you write the program the first time or later when you are rereading it to determine exactly how long the variable is. This command creates a memory variable called MCOMPANY, which is 30 characters long:

```
STORE SPACE(30) TO MCOMPANY
```

To initialize a blank date memory variable, you specify a blank character string as the input for the CTOD function:

```
STORE CTOD("  /  /  ") TO MDATE
```

or

```
STORE CTOD(" ") TO MDATE
```

The rules for initializing memory variables are summarized in Table 11-1.

USING MEMORY VARIABLES TO STORE OPERATOR INPUT

Memory variables are commonly used in dBASE III PLUS programs to accept input from the operator and store it for later processing. The sample programs written in Chapter 8 to illustrate the dBASE III PLUS programming structures drew their input almost entirely from the information in data base files. In a complete dBASE III PLUS application, your programs will have to present the users with choices and then act on their selections. For example, the Main Menu program we will write in Chapter 12 must present a list of options and, based on the operator's selection, which will be stored in a memory variable, carry out one of the system's functions. An inquiry program for the Customer File must ask the operator to identify the customer to be displayed by account number and store the response in a memory variable to be used as the object of a SEEK command. There are four commands and one function that you may use in dBASE III PLUS to solicit input from the operator and store the data in a memory variable: the ACCEPT, INPUT, WAIT TO, and @ ... SAY ... GET commands and the INKEY( ) function.

Table 11-1. Initializing Memory Variables

Type	Value	Examples
C	Character string of the desired length, enclosed in quotes	"Johnson ", " "
N	Numeric value with the desired number of decimal places	10.375, 0.00
L	Logical value surrounded by periods	.T., .n.
D	Character string, converted to a date with the character-to-date function	CTOD("04/30/84"), CTOD(" ")

Using the ACCEPT Command

The ACCEPT command allows you to display a prompt message for the user and save the data entered in a character memory variable. The general form of the command is

ACCEPT *prompt message* TO *memory variable name*

The prompt message is optional but is usually included. For example, the following command asks for a customer account number:

```
ACCEPT "Customer Account Number: " TO MACCOUNT
```

You need not explicitly initialize a memory variable with a STORE command before using it to ACCEPT input. If the memory variable named in the ACCEPT command does not already exist, it is created automatically; if it does exist, the old value is replaced by the new one typed in by the operator. Just as when you initialize a memory variable with a STORE command, the length of the variable created is equal to the length of the user's input. In contrast to @ ... SAY ... GET, the ACCEPT command makes no provision for formatting or validating the data entered.

Using the INPUT Command

The INPUT command allows for the entry of any type of data — not just a character string — into a memory variable. Its syntax is similar to that of the ACCEPT command:

INPUT *prompt message* TO *memory variable name*

As with ACCEPT, the memory variable named in the INPUT command need not be initialized in advance; it is created automatically by dBASE III PLUS. The data type of the variable is determined by the data type of the expression entered by the operator. If the user types a number, a numeric variable will be created, and if the entry is surrounded with one of the standard character string delimiter pairs, a character memory variable results. INPUT allows the operator to enter not only a constant value, but also the result of evaluating *any* dBASE III PLUS expression—for example, 3 + (BALANCE / 2) or CTOD("05/31/87") TXNDATE—in response to the prompt. The user must understand which of the dBASE III PLUS data types fits the context; and because many users may not possess that understanding, your program must be structured to cope with any possible type of data entered. As with ACCEPT, the INPUT command does not allow you to format or validate the data entered.

Using WAIT to Enter Data

The WAIT command, which pauses program execution until any key is pressed, also offers the option to save the operator's keystroke in a memory variable. WAIT, by itself, displays the message "Press any key to continue ..." at the beginning of the next available screen line and pauses indefinitely until the operator presses a key. WAIT is often used after displaying an error message, a help screen, or a description of what to do next, to make sure that the user has time to read the screen before the program resumes execution. If you like, you can substitute your own message by including a prompt string in the WAIT command:

```
WAIT "Press any key to return to the Main Menu"
```

If you would like dBASE III PLUS to pause without displaying a message—perhaps because your program has already placed the message elsewhere on a crowded screen—you can specify a *null* character string (a string of length 0), expressed as a pair of delimiters with no text in between, as the prompt:

```
WAIT ""
```

In these forms of the WAIT command, the actual key pressed by the user is immaterial. If you like, you can save the operator's keystroke in a character memory variable with

WAIT *prompt message* TO *memory variable name*

This command is commonly used to draw a menu or display a list of choices, in which each option is identified by a single letter or number, and save the user's selection for further processing. Here is an example:

```
clear
? "You may print labels in order by:"
?
? "    (A)ccount Number"
? "    (F)irst Order Date"
? "    (Z)ip Code"
?
wait "Please enter your choice " to MCHOICE
```

Since WAIT reads only one character from the keyboard, you cannot use this command if you wish to identify some of your options with two-digit numbers or longer character strings. Also, the user's keystroke is acted on immediately; once typed, it cannot be examined or corrected.

When you use ACCEPT, INPUT, and WAIT, you must include in the prompt message any spaces to be displayed between the end of the message text and the position of the data entry cursor where the operator will type the response. (Recall that @ ... SAY ... GET supplies one space automatically.) With all three of these commands, if the user presses RETURN instead of typing one or more characters, dBASE III PLUS creates a character memory variable of length 0. You can test for this possibility by measuring the length of the memory variable with the LEN function:

```
IF LEN(MCHOICE) = 0
```

Using the INKEY( ) Function

The INKEY( ) function may be used to detect a single keystroke. This function evaluates to a number—the ASCII code for the first character in the typeahead buffer. Unlike ACCEPT, INPUT, and WAIT, this function does not pause program execution indefinitely; if the typeahead buffer is empty and no key is pressed at the instant the function is evaluated, it returns a value of 0. INKEY( ) is therefore most often used within a loop that continues to test the value of the function until a key is pressed. This loop is equivalent to the single command WAIT " " TO MX:

```
store 0 to MX
do while MX = 0
   store inkey() to MX
enddo
```

In most situations, you will in fact want your program to pause indefinitely, to give the user as much time as he or she needs to read and respond to the information on the screen. If this is the case, WAIT is a simpler and more direct way to accomplish your objective. The advantage of using INKEY( ) is that it permits you to carry out other program steps while also waiting for input from the user. You could, for example, display records from a data base one at a time and prompt the user to interrupt at any point with the following loop:

```
use NWCUST

store 0 to MX

clear
? "Press any key to interrupt this listing"
?
do while MX = 0 .and. .not. eof()
   ? ACCOUNT, COMPANY, TELEPHONE
   store inkey() to MX
   skip
enddo
```

Using @ ... SAY ... GET To Enter Memory Variables

In Chapter 7 the @ ... SAY ... GET command was used to build format files for collecting data through APPEND and EDIT. With a few minor differences, it may also be used in dBASE III PLUS programs. When @ ... SAY ... GET commands are used within a program, they simply draw the screen and present the current contents of the specified data base fields and memory variables. To allow for operator entry, you must follow one or more @ ... SAY ... GET commands with a READ. The effect is exactly the same as that of the other full-screen edit modes: the operator may move freely among the fields and make changes, using any of the standard cursor movement and editing commands. Bypassing the last item on the screen or pressing CTRL-W or CTRL-END activates the READ statement and thus processes all of the preceding GETs.

Unlike ACCEPT, INPUT, and WAIT TO, the @ ... SAY ... GET command cannot create a memory variable—the named variable must be initialized beforehand. Often, you will simply initialize the memory variable to 0 or blank spaces, but you might also choose to present the user with a default value, which may be accepted automatically or altered by using any of the full-screen edit commands. Figure 11-1 shows a simple program, MEMTEST.PRG, which initializes several memory variables, allows the user to enter new values, and then displays the results.

```
* MEMTEST.PRG
* PROGRAM TO ILLUSTRATE THE USE OF @ ... SAY ... GET TO ENTER VALUES FOR
*   SEVERAL MEMORY VARIABLES
* WRITTEN BY:  M.LISKIN       6/20/85

set talk off
store "          "     to MACCOUNT
store "415"            to MAREACODE
store "        "       to MPHONE
store ctod("  /  /  ") to MTXNDATE
store 0.00             to MTXNAMOUNT

clear
@  5,10 say "Please enter the following information:"
@  6,10 say "---------------------------------------"
@ 10,10 say "Customer Account Number " get MACCOUNT   picture "@!"
@ 12,10 say "Telephone Number        " get MAREACODE  picture "999"
@ 12,45                              get MPHONE     picture "999-9999"
@ 14,10 say "Transaction Date        " get MTXNDATE
@ 16,10 say "Transaction Amount      " get MTXNAMOUNT
read

display memory
return
```

Figure 11-1. Using @ ... SAY ... GET to enter values for memory variables

Because the memory variables collected with @ ... SAY ... GET commands have already been initialized, pressing RETURN to leave a blank variable unchanged results in a 0, a blank date, or a string consisting of blank spaces. Note that a blank character string is not the same as the null string created by pressing RETURN in response to an ACCEPT or INPUT command. Thus, the MEMTEST.PRG program could detect a blank account number, telephone number, or order date by comparing the appropriate variable to a character string consisting of a single blank space:

```
IF MACCOUNT = " "
```

Remember that when dBASE III PLUS compares two strings of unequal length, the comparison extends only to the number of characters in the string on the right, so you need not compare MACCOUNT to a string of ten spaces to determine if it is blank.

@ ... SAY ... GET offers the programmer several important advantages over ACCEPT, INPUT, WAIT TO, and INKEY( ). You may position prompts or messages and collect data exactly where you want on the screen; use RANGEs, PICTUREs, or FUNCTIONs to format entries or test input for validity; and offer the operator the use of all the standard full-screen editing commands when several variables are collected on one screen. The ability to position a prompt precisely not only allows you to draw a formatted screen more easily, but also to test a single entry, and if it is not one of a finite number of permissible values, to display an error message and redraw the prompt *in exactly the same place on the screen.* The following offers the user the same choices as the example used to illustrate the use of WAIT TO:

```
clear
store " " to MSELECT

? "You may print labels in order by:"
?
? "      (A)ccount Number"
? "      (F)irst Order Date"
? "      (Z)ip Code"

do while MSELECT <> "A" .and. MSELECT <> "F" .and. MSELECT <> "Z"
   @ 10,5 say "Please enter your selection" get MSELECT picture "!"
   read
enddo
```

By contrast, if your program repeated an ACCEPT or INPUT command until a correct value was entered, each successive attempt would cause the prompt message to advance to the next line on the screen, possibly causing the menu text to scroll off the top of the screen. In the programs in this book, @ ... SAY ... GET will be used almost exclusively to enter input into memory variables, and WAIT will be used to pause a program indefinitely until the user presses a key.

USING LOCAL MEMORY VARIABLES WITHIN A PROGRAM

Memory variables are used within dBASE III PLUS programs much as you might use them at command level, as a scratch pad on which to note items of information that you will need later in the program. In many cases, you will have no use for these variables outside of the program that creates them.

Local memory variables are frequently used to control the repetition of a set of steps with a DO WHILE loop. For example, the program

COUNTER2.PRG written in Chapter 9 used the variable MCOUNT to count the number of passes through the loop. This program is reproduced in Figure 11-2. The program gives the variable MCOUNT an initial value of 1 and increments this value by 1 on each pass through the DO WHILE loop. When the value of MCOUNT reaches 10, the condition in the IF structure becomes true, and the EXIT command terminates the loop and transfers control to the first statement following the ENDDO statement.

If you have little experience with programming, the syntax STORE MCOUNT + 1 TO MCOUNT may seem strange. Remember that dBASE III PLUS processes a STORE command by first evaluating the expression following the word STORE (MCOUNT + 1). The result (1 more than the original value of MCOUNT) is then placed into the specified memory variable, which is essentially *recreated with a new value.* The alternate syntax MCOUNT = MCOUNT + 1 does exactly the same thing—this expression does *not* mean that MCOUNT already has a value equal to itself plus one. (Of course, no such value exists.)

Memory variables may be used in a similar way to accumulate counts and totals. The program in Figure 11-3, TOTAL.PRG, counts the number

```
* COUNTER2.PRG
* PROGRAM TO ILLUSTRATE THE USE OF THE DO WHILE LOOP
* WRITTEN BY:  M.LISKIN        6/10/85


set talk off
store 1 to MCOUNT

do while MCOUNT <= 10

   ? "COUNT =", MCOUNT

   if MCOUNT = 10
      exit
   else
      store MCOUNT + 1 to MCOUNT
   endif

enddo          [ MCOUNT <= 10 ]

? "This program counted from 1 to 10"
```

Figure 11-2. A program that uses memory variables to control a DO WHILE loop

```
* TOTAL.PRG
* PROGRAM TO ACCUMULATE COUNTS AND TOTALS FOR SELECTED RECORDS
* WRITTEN BY:  M.LISKIN        6/20/85
* REVISED BY:  M.LISKIN        6/20/85


set talk off
use NWCUST index NWCACCT

store 0    to MCOUNT
store 0.00 to MTOTAL

do while .not. eof()

   if CITY <> "San Francisco"
      skip
      loop
   endif

   store MCOUNT + 1      to MCOUNT
   store MTOTAL + TOTINV to MTOTAL

   skip

enddo          [ not end-of-file ]

? "Totals for Customers in San Francisco"
display memory

return
```

Figure 11-3. A program that uses memory variables to accumulate totals

of customers in San Francisco and accumulates the total dollar value of these customers' invoices. This program uses exactly the same DO WHILE .NOT. EOF( ) loop as the LISTER2.PRG program written in Chapter 9 to read through the Customer File, and like LISTER2.PRG, the program skips customers who do not live in San Francisco. But instead of simply displaying information on the screen for the selected customers, TOTAL.PRG adds 1 to MCOUNT, the memory variable used to store the count, and adds the customer's TOTINV field to MTOTAL, the variable that accumulates the dollar total. When the last record has been processed and the DO WHILE loop terminates, the memory variables are displayed with DISPLAY MEMORY. In Chapter 15 the same technique will be used to write a much more efficient version of the NWCSTAT1.PRG program that compiles statistics on National Widgets' customers based on the type of equipment they own.

Memory variables may also be used to preserve information from one record in a data base after the dBASE III PLUS record pointer has been repositioned elsewhere in the file. In a report-printing program, for example, in order to print subtotals when the value of a particular field changes, you must be able to compare the contents of the field in one record with the value of the field in the next; then, if the field has changed, you must print a set of subtotals before printing the data from the next record. You may store in a memory variable the contents of the field in each record on which the subtotals are based, so that when you SKIP to the next record, the previous field value is available for the comparison.

In a later example we will write a data entry program that simulates the SET CARRY ON option. Used at command level with APPEND, the CARRY option causes the data from each record to be used as the default field values for the next entry, but CARRY has no effect on records added to a file one at a time with APPEND BLANK. You might also want to *selectively* carry over data from only some of the fields, which is impossible when you are working at the dot prompt.

The general solution to both of these problems is to store in memory variables the field values from each new entry for use in the next. After the APPEND BLANK command positions the record pointer to the new (blank) record, all or selected fields may be REPLACEd with the memory variables before the new record is presented to the operator for editing. This strategy is illustrated in the partial program in Figure 11-4, which adds records to the Customer File. (*Note:* Unlike most of the examples in this book, this is *not* a complete dBASE III PLUS program.)

This program opens the Customer File and initiates a DO WHILE loop controlled by the memory variable MCONTINUE, a logical variable initialized with the value .T. (In a complete program, you would have to provide a way for the user to indicate a desire to stop adding new records, at which time the program would change the value of MCONTINUE to .F. to cause the program to exit from the DO WHILE loop.) Three character memory variables, MCITY, MSTATE, and MAREACODE, store the operator's last entries into the CITY, STATE, and AREACODE fields in the data base. On each pass through the loop, a new record is added to the Customer File with APPEND BLANK, and the three fields of interest are immediately REPLACEd with the values of the corresponding memory variables.

The first time through the loop, these fields will take on the blank initial values of the memory variables. The next step, in a complete pro-

```
use NWCUST index NWCACCT, NWCZIP

store .T. to MCONTINUE
store " " to MCITY, MSTATE, MAREACODE

do while MCONTINUE

   append blank

   replace CITY     with MCITY
   replace STATE    with MSTATE
   replace AREACODE with MAREACODE

   * in a complete program, commands to edit these
   * and the other fields in the record would go here

   store CITY     to MCITY
   store STATE    to MSTATE
   store AREACODE to MAREACODE

   * in a complete program, you would also need a way
   * to enable the operator to stop adding new records
   * and exit the program

enddo
```

Figure 11-4. A partial program that uses memory variables to preserve data from a previous record

gram, would be to use @ ... SAY ... GET commands, followed by a READ, to allow the operator to edit all of the fields in the new record. Finally, the program STOREs the values entered into the CITY, STATE, and AREACODE fields in MCITY, MSTATE, and MAREACODE. The next time through the loop, these values will replace the blank fields in the newly APPENDed record and will therefore appear on the screen as default values for the three fields.

All of the preceding examples illustrate uses of memory variables that are local to one dBASE III PLUS program. After you exit from the program that adds Customer File records, you have no use for the variables used to store the operator's last entries into the STATE, CITY, and AREA-CODE fields. Because this is usually the case, dBASE III PLUS considers all variables created within a program to be PRIVATE, or local, to that program unless you explicitly declare them PUBLIC. PRIVATE variables are automatically RELEASEd—their values are erased from memory—when the program that creates them terminates.

You may have at most 256 memory variables active at one time. By default you are also limited to a total of 6000 bytes in memory variables, but this limit may be increased to any value up to 31K with an entry in CONFIG.DB. Unlike many of the other CONFIG.DB settings, this is not an option you can also SET from the dot prompt; it must be known to dBASE III PLUS when the program first loads, so that the required amount of RAM can be set aside. For example, you could reserve 24K of memory for memory variables with this entry in CONFIG.DB:

```
MVARSIZ = 24
```

If you are running short of memory space, you can erase the values of one or more variables with the RELEASE command. Variables may be selectively RELEASEd by listing them individually:

```
RELEASE MACCOUNT, MCONTINUE, MCOUNT
```

If the names of the variables have something in common, they can also be released in groups, based on a match or failure to match a given pattern. The following command will RELEASE all variables whose names begin with the letters MX:

```
RELEASE ALL LIKE MX*
```

This command will RELEASE all variables *except* the ones that begin with MX:

```
RELEASE ALL EXCEPT MX*
```

In a large system that uses many memory variables, the automatic RELEASE of PRIVATE variables is usually desirable, as it obviates the need to RELEASE the variables explicitly at the end of each program. If you do need to preserve the values of some or all of the variables, you can either SAVE them in a memory file on disk, as in the NWCSTAT1.PRG program written in Chapter 7, or you can declare them PUBLIC.

USING PUBLIC MEMORY VARIABLES

Although memory variables are commonly used in dBASE III PLUS programs to provide temporary storage, certain variables, which we'll call "systemwide" options, should be available to any program in an application. Some typical examples from the National Widgets system might be the default state and area code for new entries in the Customer File, the next available invoice or check number, the disk drive to use for data files or indexes, the screen colors or monochrome attributes for the standard and enhanced display, and the company name to print on invoices, envelopes, or reports.

If you are a beginning programmer writing dBASE III PLUS programs for use by one company on one particular computer system, you might simply write many of these quantities into the programs as constants. Isolating them as memory variables, however, makes it easier to modify your programs for other hardware and other organizations and gives the users more control over these options without recourse to programming.

For example, assume that you have written a set of programs to run on a floppy disk system with two drives. The programs and report forms are stored, along with the dBASE III PLUS overlay file, on one disk in drive A:, and the data files and indexes are located on another disk in drive B:. Because of this separation of programs and data, you cannot simply SET DEFAULT TO B, so all of the programs must open files with statements like USE B:NWCUST INDEX B:NWCACCT, B:NWCZIP. If the application is later transferred to a hard disk system in which all of the files are located on drive C:, every one of the references to drive B: must be changed to C: or removed entirely since all files now reside on the default drive. If the disk drive designation had been stored in a memory variable, the value of the variable could simply have been changed—in one place—to effect the transition to the new hardware. Furthermore, you could provide a program that allows the user to alter the value of this variable without having to change the programs at all. These considerations are a convenience and a timesaver in your own applications and a necessity if you are writing systems that will be used in more than one installation.

In order to make a memory variable available to any program in the system, it must be declared PUBLIC. Memory variables must be declared PUBLIC *before* they are initialized. *This is the only instance in which the name of an uninitialized variable may be used in a command that does not itself create the variable*. Here is a small portion of a program that creates some PUBLIC variables and assigns them initial values:

```
public MPAREACODE, MPSTATE, MPDATA, MPINDEX, MPCOMPANY

store "415"                     to MPAREACODE
store "CA"                      to MPSTATE
store "C:"                      to MPDATA, MPINDEX
store "National Widgets, Inc." to MPCOMPANY
```

Since these variables must be saved from one work session to the next, they should be given a common prefix, so that as a group they may be saved to a memory file with one command. In this book the prefix MP will represent "memory variables, public." These variables may be saved in the file NWMEMORY.MEM with

```
SAVE ALL LIKE MP* TO NWMEMORY
```

USING PARAMETERS TO PASS DATA BETWEEN PROGRAMS

Chapter 9 illustrated how one dBASE III PLUS program may call another with a DO command. When one dBASE III PLUS program calls another, memory variables created within the calling program are available to the called program (and any programs it calls). If the called program changes the value of one of these variables, the change is passed back to the calling program, although any variables created *within* the called program are lost when the program terminates. Information may also be passed from one dBASE III PLUS program to another as *parameters*.

When one program calls another, you specify the parameters to be passed to the called program in the DO command:

DO *program name* WITH *parameter list*

The parameters may consist of any dBASE III PLUS expressions made up of constants, memory variables, data base fields, and functions. In the called program, the values of the parameters are stored in local memory variables, which are initialized by listing them in a PARAMETERS statement:

PARAMETERS *parameter list*

This statement must be the first *executable command* (the first non-comment line) in the program—in other words, the first thing you must do in the program is identify the input it will receive from the calling program. Note that this statement differs from the standard initialization of memory variables with STORE or =, in that it does not specify the data types of the variables or assign them initial values. When the program is called, the parameters assume the data type of the corresponding parameters passed by the calling program.

The parameters in the two programs need not have the same names. *The correspondence is established by the order in which the parameters appear in the DO command and the PARAMETERS statement.* Thus, parameters allow you to write standard routines with "generic" variable names. These programs may then be called with different sets of constants, fields, and memory variables appropriate to the context of the calling programs.

Figure 11-5 lists SUM.PRG, a simple program that calculates the sum of two numbers. The two numbers are passed as parameters to SUM.PRG, where they are stored in the memory variables MX and MY. The sum is computed as MX + MY and stored in the variable MSUM, which is passed back to the calling program. Figure 11-6 lists CALL-SUM.PRG, a program that calls the SUM program in two different ways. Figure 11-7 is a detailed pseudocode version of CALLSUM.PRG that explains, line by line, what the program does.

The first time SUM.PRG is called, the parameters passed by CALL-SUM. PRG consist of two constants (3 and 4) and a memory variable (MANSWER). The variable MANSWER must be initialized before listing it as a parameter in the DO command, but since it will acquire its value from the SUM program, it is given an initial value of 0. In SUM.PRG, the first parameter, MX, takes on the value 3—the first parameter named in the DO command. MY assumes the value of the second parameter, 4. The third parameter, MSUM, calculated as MX + MY, corresponds to the third parameter passed by CALLSUM.PRG. Thus, MANSWER takes on the value of MSUM when SUM.PRG terminates and control returns to CALLSUM.PRG.

The second time, SUM.PRG is called with three memory variables as

```
* SUM.PRG
* PROGRAM TO CALCULATE THE SUM OF TWO NUMBERS
* WRITTEN BY:  M.LISKIN        5/31/85

parameters MX, MY, MSUM

store MX + MY to MSUM

return
```

Figure 11-5. A program that calculates the sum of two numbers

parameters. MCREDIT corresponds to MX, the first parameter in SUM.PRG, MDEBIT to MY, and MBALANCE to MSUM. *It is up to you to keep track of which variables provide input to the called program and which will return values to the calling routine.* The first time SUM.PRG is called, only the third parameter, MANSWER, is a memory variable—the values of the two constants 3 and 4 may not be changed by any dBASE III PLUS program. The second time, however, all three parameters are memory variables, whose values may be changed in the called program. If, for example,

```
* CALLSUM.PRG
* PROGRAM TO ILLUSTRATE WAYS OF CALLING ONE DBASE III PROGRAM FROM ANOTHER
*   AND PASSING PARAMETERS BETWEEN THE TWO
* WRITTEN BY:  M.LISKIN        5/31/85

clear
store 0 to MANSWER
do SUM with 3, 4, MANSWER
? "The sum of 3 and 4 is:", MANSWER
?

store 100.00 to MCREDIT
store -75.25 to MDEBIT
store 0.00   to MBALANCE
do SUM with MCREDIT, MDEBIT, MBALANCE
? "Total credits: ", MCREDIT
? "Total debits:  ", MDEBIT
? "The balance is:", MBALANCE

return
```

Figure 11-6. A program that calls SUM.PRG in two different ways

```
clear the screen
initialize the variable MANSWER, which will contain the sum of the two numbers,
  with a value of 0
call the SUM program with the parameters 3, 4, and MANSWER
display the value of MANSWER
display a blank line

initialize the variable MCREDIT with a value of 100.00
initialize the variable MDEBIT with a value of -75.25
initialize the variable MBALANCE, which will contain the sum of MCREDIT
  and MDEBIT, with a value of 0.00
call the SUM program with the parameters MCREDIT, MDEBIT, and MBALANCE
display the value of MCREDIT
display the value of MDEBIT
display the value of MBALANCE
```

Figure 11-7. The CALLSUM.PRG program in pseudocode

SUM.PRG altered the value of MX, the change would be passed back to MCREDIT, a highly undesirable occurrence.

Since the memory variables created in a program are always available to those programs it calls, parameters are never *required.* But using parameters gives you the advantage of being able to build up a library of useful routines that may be called by a variety of programs in different contexts, with differently named variables as parameters. This technique may be confusing to a beginning dBASE III PLUS programmer, and you may choose to avoid the use of parameters in the first few systems you write. When you are ready to begin using parameters, you can extract procedures from the programs you have already written and modify them to accept input via parameters. These routines may then form the building blocks for any new data base systems you design.

12

A MENU PROGRAM FOR THE SYSTEM

The short programs written in Chapter 7 represented the first step toward automating a dBASE III PLUS application. Because they group commands together to be executed in sequence without operator intervention, programs like these can free a knowledgeable dBASE III PLUS user from the tedium of retyping the same commands over and over and waiting for long-running commands to be executed. Because they can be run by an operator who does not understand the syntax of the commands they contain, these programs also allow dBASE III PLUS to be used more effectively in the average office setting, in which not every staff member is familiar with dBASE III PLUS.

In this chapter we will coordinate the components of the dBASE III PLUS system developed in Chapters 4 through 11 by writing a set of menu programs. As you may know from working with accounting or other applications software, a *menu* is a list of options presented on the screen, with each option identified by a short code followed by a longer description of its purpose. To carry out any of the operations listed on the menu, the operator simply types the short code. The addition of a menu program makes a data base application significantly easier to use. It insulates the user from the open-ended and intimidating dot prompt, offering instead a screen that presents a discrete set of possible choices. With the option descriptions couched in the terminology of the user's business or profession, it is easier not only to use each menu selection, but also to remember the sequence in which the operations should be carried out.

The menu programs in this chapter make use of all of the dBASE III PLUS programming structures introduced in Chapter 9 to display text on the screen, accept input from the operator, and make decisions based on this input. Although the menus will be quite a bit longer than any of the programs written thus far, they should be easy to construct, since they draw extensively on the command level procedures and short programs that we have already developed. Many of these procedures will be incorporated unchanged into the menu programs, while others will be enhanced by the addition of more informative prompts and status messages. To lend additional flexibility, user-specified selection criteria will be incorporated into procedures that produce printed output.

ORGANIZING THE MENU PROGRAMS

In very informal pseudocode, this is what a menu program must do:

do the following until the user chooses to exit:

draw the screen image for the menu

let the user choose one of the options

depending on the user's choice, take the appropriate action

A system outline like the one developed in Chapter 1 for the National Widgets system (see Figure 1-6) is an excellent guide to creating menus. You can see from the outline that the National Widgets system has too many options to be presented on one screen. We will therefore create a main menu that calls three submenus. Since the outline breaks down the components of the system into broad functional areas, it also suggests the most logical organization for the menus.

How the procedures in a system are divided among the menus depends on the nature of the information processed by the system, the work flow in the office, and the people who will use the computer. In a smaller application that manipulates only one fundamental type of data, like a mailing list system, all of the data base entry and update procedures might be placed on one menu screen, and all of the options that produce printed output on another. In a system composed of several distinct functional areas—for example, in the National Widgets system, customer information, order processing, and financial transactions—the menus should be divided along the same lines. Often, different staff members must work with different parts of the system, and the programs will seem less confusing if each user can move quickly to a particular menu and see only the options relevant to his or her job responsibilities. This approach also lends itself well to the creation of a security system in which access to each of the submenus is controlled by a different password. Finally, structuring the menus according to functional areas allows you to easily expand the system to include another major division by adding one more option to the Main Menu that calls a new submenu. In the sample system, inventory management might be implemented in this way. If one of the individual menus eventually grows too large and unwieldy, it may then be divided into separate file management and report menus.

A MAIN MENU PROGRAM

The Main Menu program for the National Widgets sample system will call three submenus, which handle customer information, order processing, and financial transactions. The Main Menu also includes operations that cross these functional boundaries and might thus be labeled *system utilities*. An example is the program written in Chapter 7 to reindex all of the data bases. (If there were more of these procedures, they might merit a separate Utility Menu.) The relationship among the menus is illustrated schematically in Figure 12-1.

Since it is the first entry point into the system, the Main Menu customizes the working environment with SET commands and then displays a sign-on screen before presenting the list of choices to the user. The sign-on screen displays the current date so that the operator may verify that the date was set when the operating system was first booted; it might also include the name of the organization for which the system was written, the programmer's name or company name, and a copyright notice. Figure 12-2 describes in pseudocode what the Main Menu program for the National Widgets system must do.

The program, NWMENU1.PRG, is listed in Figure 12-3. (The name of this program and the name of the Customer Information Menu program include the "1" because new versions will be presented in later chapters.) The first command, CLEAR ALL, closes all CATALOGs, data bases, indexes, and format files; releases all memory variables; and selects work

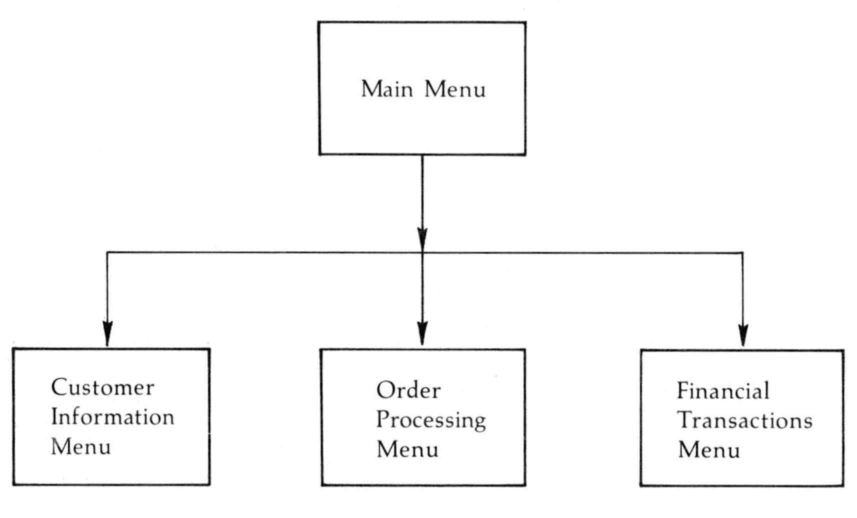

Figure 12-1. The relationships among the menus

area 1. You should begin any Main Menu program with this command, which restores dBASE III PLUS to the default startup condition, since you have no way of knowing what files the user may have opened prior to running the menu. The user may also have issued SET commands from the dot prompt or created a CONFIG.DB file containing settings that are inappropriate for your application. All of the options of interest should therefore be SET explicitly in the Main Menu, even if the values chosen correspond to the dBASE III PLUS defaults.

The SET options in NWMENU1.PRG fall into two groups: those that are almost always used in any menu-driven system (SET TALK OFF, SET STATUS OFF, SET SAFETY OFF, and SET DELETED ON), and those that may vary with the personal preferences of the programmer and users.

SET TALK OFF suppresses the messages dBASE III PLUS normally displays in response to your commands. When status messages are *required*, your own programs can provide them or you can temporarily turn TALK back ON. For the most part, however, you will not want your for-

```
customize the working environment with SET commands
present a sign-on screen with TEXT ... ENDTEXT
display the current date

do the following until the user chooses to exit:
   draw the screen image for the menu with TEXT ... ENDTEXT
   choices are:
        1 - Customer Information
        2 - Order Processing
        3 - Financial Transactions
        4 - Reindex All Data Bases
       88 - Exit to dBASE III PLUS
       99 - Exit to Operating System

   ask for the user's selection

   if the selection is "1":
      run the customer information menu program

   if the selection is "2":
      run the order processing menu program

   if the selection is "3":
      run the financial transactions menu program


   if the selection is "4":
      run the NWREIND1 program

   if the selection is "88":
      restore SET options to their defaults
      exit to dBASE III PLUS dot prompt

   if the selection is "99":
      exit to MS-DOS operating system

   otherwise
      display an error message

end of steps to do until the user chooses to exit
```

Figure 12-2. The Main Menu program in pseudocode

matted screens or printouts disrupted by the display of the record pointer's new position after a SKIP command or the echo of the values STOREd to memory variables.

SET STATUS OFF turns off the status bar and message area that normally occupy the last three lines of the screen, freeing these lines for use in your menus and data base update screens.

SET SAFETY OFF allows a program to overwrite disk files without asking for confirmation from the operator. At command level the SAFETY feature protects against the inadvertent destruction of an exist-

```
* NWMENU1.PRG
* FIRST VERSION OF MAIN MENU PROGRAM FOR ACCOUNTS RECEIVABLE SYSTEM
* WRITTEN BY:  M.LISKIN       04/11/86

clear all
set talk off
set status off
set safety off
set deleted on

set default to c
set bell off
set confirm off
set delimiters on
set delimiters to "[]"
set intensity on
set color to W, W+

clear
@  6,10 to 12,70 double
@  8,27 say "  National Widgets, Inc."
@ 10,27 say "Accounts Receivable System"

@ 15,24 say "Today is " + cdow(date()) + ", " + cmonth(date()) + " " + ;
            str(day(date()),2) + ", " + str(year(date()),4)
@ 16,0
wait "                          Press any key to display the Main Menu"


do while .T.

   clear
   text

             National Widgets, Inc.  -  Accounts Receivable System

                                 Main Menu


                      ( 1) - Customer Information Menu

                      ( 2) - Order Processing Menu

                      ( 3) - Financial Transaction Menu

                      ( 4) - Reindex All Data Bases



                      (88) - Exit to dBASE III PLUS Command Level

                      (99) - Exit to MS-DOS Operating System
   endtext

   @  1, 0 to 24,79 double
   @  3, 1 to  3,78
   @  5, 1 to  5,78
   @ 22, 1 to 22,78
```

Figure 12-3. The Main Menu program

```
   store Ø to MSELECT
   @ 23,27 say "Please enter your selection    " get MSELECT picture "99"
   read

   do case

      case MSELECT = 1
         do NWCMENU1

      case MSELECT = 2
         do NWOMENU

      case MSELECT = 3
         do NWTMENU

      case MSELECT = 4
         do NWREIND1

      case MSELECT = 88
         clear
         set talk on
         set status on
         set safety on
         set deleted off
         cancel

      case MSELECT = 99
         clear
         quit

      otherwise
         @ 23,1Ø say "Not a valid selection -- Press any key to try again"
         wait ""

   endcase

enddo          [ .T. ]

return
```

Figure 12-3. The Main Menu program (*continued*)

ing disk file caused by using the same name in a command that creates a new file. In a menu-driven system, however, the programmer should assume the responsibility for ensuring that files are overwritten only when intended, so that the users do not encounter bewildering choices.

For example, a program might build an index called NWCDATE.NDX especially for the purpose of printing a customer listing by last order date. If a copy of the index remains on the disk from the last run and SAFETY is ON, dBASE III PLUS will display the message "NWCDATE.NDX already exists, overwrite it? (Y/N)." When confronted with a dire warning like this, a naive operator will usually make the safest response and answer no, which results in the even more confusing query, "Cancel, Ignore, or Suspend? (C, I, or S)." Answering "C" or "S" exits from the program and returns the user to the dot prompt. Answering "I" causes dBASE III PLUS to ignore the error condition and continue, which prevents the new index from being constructed; printing the report with the old index may result in the omission of some of the records in the file, or worse, a "Record is out of range" or "End of file encountered" error message.

SET DELETED ON causes dBASE III PLUS to ignore records that have been marked for deletion, so that they do not appear in reports or label runs, are not displayed in LIST commands, and are not included in the statistics calculated by commands like COUNT or SUM. With DELETED ON the system behaves in every respect as if the deleted records are not present at all, except that you may still access a deleted record with a direct GOTO by record number.

The remaining SET options control the behavior of dBASE III PLUS in the full-screen edit modes, the default disk drive, the use of delimiters, and the screen colors or monochrome display attributes. These options may be adjusted to reflect the personal preferences of the programmer and, more important, the users of the system. In the National Widgets sample system, the following SET commands were chosen:

SET DEFAULT TO C establishes drive C: as the default disk drive.

SET BELL OFF and SET CONFIRM OFF control the actions taken by dBASE III PLUS when a user's entry fills a field completely in one of the full-screen edit modes. SET BELL OFF turns off the bell or beep normally emitted under these conditions, and SET CONFIRM OFF causes the cursor to advance automatically to the next field, so that the operator does not have to press RETURN.

SET DELIMITERS ON and SET DELIMITERS TO "[]" assign the square brackets as delimiters for the full-screen edit modes.

SET INTENSITY ON and SET COLOR TO W, W+ set the display attributes on a color or monochrome monitor to low-intensity white for the background area used for displayed data and high-intensity white for the enhanced area used for data entered by the operator.

The sign-on screen in the sample application consists only of the National Widgets company name and a title for the system, which are displayed and surrounded by a double-line border with @ ... SAY commands. Next, the dBASE III PLUS date functions are used to present the current date in the more readable form "Today is Friday, June 19, 1987" rather than the usual "Today is 06/19/87". This long expression illustrates how functions may be combined to produce a single character string for display purposes. These are the component parts of the expression:

"Today is" is simply a character string constant.

CDOW(DATE()) applies the CDOW (character day of the week) function to the DATE() (current date) function, to yield the name of the day of the week—in this example, "Friday".

", " is another character string constant, which adds a comma and a space between the day of the week and the month.

CMONTH(DATE()) applies the CMONTH (character month) function to the DATE() (current date) function, to give the name of the month—"June".

STR(DAY(DATE()),2) uses the DAY function to extract the day—19—from the current date in the form of a number. This numeric result is then converted to a character string of length 2 with the STR function.

", " is another character string constant.

STR(YEAR(DATE()),4) uses the YEAR function to extract the year—1987—from the current date; the year is converted to a character string of length 4 with the STR function.

Following the date display the WAIT command presents a message for the operator and causes dBASE III PLUS to pause until a key is pressed. Once these preliminaries have been completed, the program establishes a loop to draw the menu screen, ask the user for a selection, and carry out the appropriate program steps. It is clear that the repetition of steps can be carried out with a DO WHILE loop, but the condition to use in the DO WHILE statement may not be intuitively obvious. The way the condition is stated in the pseudocode suggests one way to set up this loop: you could create a logical variable, perhaps called MCONTINUE, initialized with a value of .T., and use DO WHILE MCONTINUE to begin the loop. When the user chooses one of the exit options, the program could STORE

.F. TO MCONTINUE to prevent another pass through the loop. This method was illustrated in the partial program in Figure 11-4. However, there is a more elegant technique that does not involve creating an extra memory variable. Writing the loop statement as DO WHILE .T. says, in effect, "Do the following steps while .T. is true." Of course, the logical value .T. is *always* true, so this construction sets up an endless loop that will execute forever unless you provide another way to exit. You can exit a DO WHILE loop in any of the following ways:

EXIT causes dBASE III PLUS to exit immediately from the DO WHILE loop and proceed to the first program statement after the ENDDO.

RETURN causes dBASE III PLUS to exit immediately from the current program and return control to the calling program (or it returns control to the dot prompt if the program was invoked from the dot prompt).

CANCEL causes dBASE III PLUS to exit immediately from the current program and return to the dot prompt.

```
* NWCMENU1.PRG
* FIRST VERSION OF CUSTOMER INFORMATION MENU FOR ACCOUNTS RECEIVABLE SYSTEM
* WRITTEN BY:  M.LISKIN       04/11/86

do while .T.

   clear
   text

             National Widgets, Inc.  -  Accounts Receivable System

                          Customer Information Menu

                    ( 1) - Add New Customers
                    ( 2) - Inquire, Edit, Delete, Recall Customers

                    (10) - Print Customer Reference List
                    (11) - Print Rolodex Cards
                    (12) - Customer Equipment Profile

                    (20) - Print Mailing Labels 1-Up
                    (21) - Print Mailing Labels 4-Up
                    (22) - Copy to Word Processor Format
```

Figure 12-4. The Customer Information Menu program

```
                    (30) - Zero Year-to-Date Totals
                    (31) - Archive and Delete Inactive Customers

                    (99) - Return to Main Menu
   endtext

   @  1, 0 to 24,79 double
   @  3, 1 to  3,78
   @  5, 1 to  5,78
   @ 22, 1 to 22,78

   store 0 to MSELECT
   @ 23,27 say "Please enter your selection   " get MSELECT picture "99"
   read

   do case

      case MSELECT = 1
         use NWCUST index NWCACCT, NWCZIP
         set format to NWCUST2
         append

      case MSELECT = 2
         do NWCEDIT

      case MSELECT = 10
         use NWCUST index NWCACCT
         report form NWCUSTRF to print

      case MSELECT = 11
         do NWCCARD1

      case MSELECT = 12
         do NWCSTAT1

      case MSELECT = 20
         do NWCLABL1

      case MSELECT = 21
         do NWCLABL4

      case MSELECT = 22
         do NWCCOPY

      case MSELECT = 30
         do NWCZERO

      case MSELECT = 31
         do NWCDELET

      case MSELECT = 99
         return

      otherwise
         @ 23,10 say "Not a valid selection -- Press any key to try again"
         wait ""

   endcase

   close databases

enddo          [ .T. ]

return
```

Figure 12-4. The Customer Information Menu program *(continued)*

QUIT exits from the current program and from dBASE III PLUS to the operating system.

The Main Menu program for the National Widgets system provides two exits: to dBASE III PLUS and to the operating system.

Within the DO WHILE loop, the program CLEARs the screen and draws the menu with a combination of a TEXT ... ENDTEXT structure to display the options and @ ... SAY commands to draw the borders. In the National Widgets system, the use of graphics characters will be avoided in any screens that the user is likely to want to print using SHIFT-PRTSC, such as data base update screens. Continuous line borders will, however, be used to dress up screens that would rarely be printed, such as menus and sign-on screens.

The screen could have been created entirely with a series of ? @ ... SAY commands. TEXT ... ENDTEXT was chosen primarily because it facilitates the process of modifying the menu program to accommodate future changes without having to count lines, measure column positions, or make sure that no quotation marks are inadvertently left out of the character strings that form the menu image. If you do combine TEXT ... ENDTEXT with @ ... SAY commands, make sure to place the TEXT ... ENDTEXT structure first, so that the text displayed this way does not overwrite the characters placed on the screen with @ ... SAY.

The prompt inviting the operator to choose an option is dropped into the menu screen at the proper location with an @ ... SAY ... GET command, and the user's selection is saved in a memory variable called MSELECT. Since numeric memory variables are created with a default length of ten digits, but the highest option number on the screen is a two-digit number, the "99" PICTURE limits the length of the user's entry. In this program the choices are all numbers, but MSELECT could have been made a character variable to accommodate letters or combinations of letters and numbers. The two exit options were given the numbers 88 and 99 to emphasize the distinction between these and the other choices and make it less likely that the operator would select one by mistake and exit from the system prematurely.

Processing the user's choice is an obvious candidate for a DO CASE structure, since the selection will always be one of a finite number of possibilities. Any entry other than the six legitimate selections is handled by an OTHERWISE clause, which displays an error message and pauses the program until the user acknowledges the message by pressing a key;

it then returns to the top of the loop to redraw the menu. The first three CASEs invoke other programs—the three submenus—and the fourth calls the NWREIND1.PRG program. If the user chooses to exit to dBASE III PLUS command level, the program resets TALK, STATUS, SAFETY, and DELETED to the default states and exits to the dot prompt with CANCEL. The option that exits to the operating system simply clears the screen and then QUITs to MS-DOS. When the user returns to the Main Menu from one of the submenus or from the reindexing program, execution resumes with the first statement after the ENDCASE. Since this is ENDDO, the program returns immediately to the top of the loop and reevaluates the condition in the DO WHILE statement. Of course, .T. is still true, so the statements in the loop are executed again to redraw the menu and ask for another selection.

The menu, like any other dBASE III PLUS program, may be invoked from the dot prompt with a DO command:

```
DO NWMENU1
```

However, if the command used to load dBASE III PLUS includes the name of a dBASE III PLUS program, the program will be run immediately, bypassing the dot prompt. From MS-DOS you can go directly to the National Widgets Main Menu program with

```
DBASE NWMENU1
```

The system's three submenus all share the same basic structure (except, of course, that the SET options and the date display are not necessary). As much as possible you should strive for consistent format in your menus. Using the same region of the screen for the same type of information helps the operators become accustomed to looking for status messages, error messages, and command prompts in familiar locations. Similar options should also have similar numbers. For example, the path from a file update menu to a report menu might be given the same number as the return path. You can also use blocks of numbers to group related functions and make it easier for the users to learn the arbitrary option numbers. For example, if the basic file update operations are numbered from 1 to 6, you might jump directly to the numbers 10 through 19 for printing reports, 20 to 29 for mailing functions, and 30 to 39 for file deletion and purge procedures.

THE CUSTOMER INFORMATION MENU

We will use the customer information module of the National Widgets system to illustrate a variety of ways in which simple procedures and short programs may be integrated into a menu system. The menu program, NWCMENU1.PRG, is listed in Figure 12-4. Like the Main Menu, this program sets up an endless loop with DO WHILE .T. Inside this loop the menu screen is displayed, the user's choice is collected into a memory variable, and the selection is processed with a DO CASE structure. The only exit from the loop is provided by option 99, which returns control to the Main Menu with a RETURN command. After the ENDCASE statement, the CLOSE DATABASES command ensures that after each procedure terminates, all the data base files, indexes, and format files it may have opened are closed, and all changes to the files are written to the disk, so the next option selected begins with a clean

Any number of program statements may be included in a CASE, and in a small system like this one, all of the required procedures may easily be incorporated whole into the menu. On the other hand, many programmers prefer *always* to have each CASE call a separate program or procedure (procedure files will be introduced in Chapter 22), leaving the menu shorter, cleaner, and easier to understand. This rationale assumes that when you read the menu program, your attention is focused on the big picture; the details of *how* the options work are available, if and when you need this information, in the separate programs or procedures called by the menu. Exactly where to draw the line is a matter of discretion. In NWCMENU1.PRG the decisions are based on two factors. In most instances, if only a few steps are required they are included in the menu, while lengthy command sequences are written as separate programs. If, however, this first version of the system uses only a few commands that will later become a more complex procedure, using a separate program right from the start makes it easier to elaborate on the individual options later without changing the menu program.

The Customer Information Menu Options

We will examine the individual CASEs in the National Widgets Customer Information Menu one by one, beginning with those that can be accomplished with the fewest commands and the least new programming.

Option 1, "Add New Customers," uses APPEND, together with the format file, NWCUST2.FMT, written in Chapter 8. The three steps—opening the data base with the required indexes, naming the format file, and invoking the APPEND command—do not require a separate program; they are included in the menu itself.

Option 10, "Print Customer Reference List," is equally straightforward. The menu program must simply open the Customer File with the account number index and print the report using the report form NWCUSTRF.FRM designed in Chapter 5.

Option 12, "Customer Equipment Profile," calls the NWCSTAT1 program written in Chapter 7 to compile statistics on National Widgets' customers based on the type of computer equipment they own.

At first glance it would seem that option 30, "Zero Year-to-Date Totals," could be accomplished with two command lines:

```
use NWCUST
replace all YTDINV with 0, YTDPMT with 0
```

If the Customer File is large, however, the REPLACE step may take some time to run, and unless an indication of the computer's progress is displayed on the screen, it may appear to the user that nothing is happening. The program in Figure 12-5, NWCZERO.PRG, solves this problem by first displaying a reminder of which option is running and then using SET TALK ON to temporarily restore the standard dBASE III PLUS status message that continuously monitors the number of records REPLACEd. NWCZERO.PRG also attempts to preserve the integrity of the data base by disabling the ESC key with SET ESCAPE OFF, so that the user cannot easily interrupt the process, leaving some of the records with nonzero values in the year-to-date fields. (This precaution makes it less likely that an operator will casually or accidentally interrupt the program, but it is inadvisable if you suspect that the people using the system will resort to turning off the computer if they are unable to stop a program in any other way.) Before returning to the menu, the program must SET TALK OFF and SET ESCAPE ON to restore the working environment to its original state.

Option 31 of the Customer Information Menu, "Archive and Delete Inactive Customers," uses a similar strategy to keep the user informed of the progress of some potentially long-running commands. The program in Figure 12-6, NWCDELET.PRG, copies to a backup file, NWOLDCST, those customers who have not placed an order in over a year and then

```
* NWCZERO.PRG
* PROGRAM TO ZERO CUSTOMER YEAR-TO-DATE TOTALS
* WRITTEN BY:  M.LISKIN        6/18/85

use NWCUST

set talk on
set escape off

clear
@ 10,10 say "Zeroing year-to-date totals -- Please do not interrupt"
replace all YTDINV with 0, YTDPMT with 0

set talk off
set escape on

return
```

Figure 12-5. A program to zero customer year-to-date totals

deletes them from the Customer File. The criteria in the COPY and DELETE commands make use of dBASE III PLUS's ability to calculate elapsed time (in days) between two dates: if LASTORDER DATE() is greater than 365 days (one year), the customer will be purged from the file. For faster processing these two steps are carried out with no indexes open.

If you try this program, you will see that records with a blank LASTORDER date are *not* deleted. Instead of considering an empty field equivalent to a very early date, dBASE III PLUS treats the field as if the data is not available and therefore should not be tested at all. If this interpretation does not suit your purposes, you could state the condition as

```
for date() - LASTORDER > 365 .or. dtoc(LASTORDER) = "  "
```

This illustrates an important lesson. During the testing stages of a data base application, it is essential to examine the relevant data bases carefully before and after running a new program, so that you know exactly how every possible type of missing or erroneous data will affect the results.

After the DELETE step the program opens the two Customer File indexes with SET INDEX TO NWCACCT, NWCZIP before the PACK command permanently removes the deleted records (and automatically rebuilds all open indexes). PACK also deletes any records previously marked individually for deletion by the users; if this is *not* what you want, the PACK step should be made a separate program. Before you PACK the file, you might choose to print the deleted records for a final proofreading. To do this, you can use the DELETED( ) function. Recall that this logical function has the value .T. whenever the dBASE III PLUS record pointer is positioned at a deleted record. You could therefore create a menu option that prints only the deleted customers in the standard Customer Reference List format by using this command sequence:

```
set deleted off
report form NWCUSTRF to print for deleted()
set deleted on
```

```
* NWCDELET.PRG
* PROGRAM TO ARCHIVE AND DELETE CUSTOMERS WITH NO ORDERS FOR ONE YEAR
* WRITTEN BY:  M.LISKIN       6/18/85

use NWCUST

set talk on
set escape off

clear
@ 10,10 say "Copying inactive customers to archive file NWOLDCST.DBF"
@ 12,10 say "                  Please do not interrupt"
copy to NWOLDCST for date() - LASTORDER > 365

clear
@ 10,10 say "Deleting inactive customers from Customer File"
@ 12,10 say "               Please do not interrupt"
delete for date() - LASTORDER > 365

set index to NWCACCT, NWCZIP
pack

set talk off
set escape on

return
```

Figure 12-6. A program to archive and delete inactive customers

User-Specified Selection Criteria

On the Customer Information Menu, options 20 and 21 print, respectively, one-up and four-up mailing labels, in the NWCUST1.FMT and NWCUST4.FMT label formats described in Chapter 5. At command level you could print one-up labels in ZIP code order for all customers with

```
USE NWCUST INDEX NWCZIP
LABEL FORM NWCUST1 TO PRINT
```

A quick look at the system outline in Figure 1-6 will remind you that mailing labels and personalized letters must be printed for selected groups of customers as well as for the entire file. The two mailing label programs, NWCLABL1.PRG (listed in Figure 12-7) and NWCLABL4.PRG (listed in Figure 12-8), introduce a general method for allowing the user to specify report selection criteria. In this case, these programs select customers by type of computer equipment. Figure 12-9 explains in pseudo-

```
* NWCLABL1.PRG
* PROGRAM TO PRINT 1-UP MAILING LABELS FOR ALL CUSTOMERS
*   OR SELECTED CUSTOMERS (BY TYPE OF EQUIPMENT)
* WRITTEN BY:  M.LISKIN        6/18/85

use NWCUST index NWCZIP

clear
store space(25) to MEQUIPMENT
@ 10,10 say "Enter type of equipment for customers in this mailing: "
@ 14,10 say "(or press <RETURN> to include ALL customers)"
@ 12,20 get MEQUIPMENT picture "@!"
read

if MEQUIPMENT <> " "
   set filter to trim(MEQUIPMENT) $ upper(EQUIPMENT)
   goto top
endif

label form NWCUST1 to print

set filter to

return
```

Figure 12-7. A program to print one-up labels for selected customers

```
* NWCLABL4.PRG
* PROGRAM TO PRINT 4-UP MAILING LABELS FOR ALL CUSTOMERS
*   OR SELECTED CUSTOMERS (BY TYPE OF EQUIPMENT)
* WRITTEN BY:  M.LISKIN       6/18/85

use NWCUST index NWCZIP

clear
store space(25) to MEQUIPMENT
@ 10,10 say "Enter type of equipment for customers in this mailing: "
@ 14,10 say "(or press <RETURN> to include ALL customers)"
@ 12,20 get MEQUIPMENT picture "@!"
read

if MEQUIPMENT <> " "
   set filter to trim(MEQUIPMENT) $ upper(EQUIPMENT)
   goto top
endif

label form NWCUST4 to print

set filter to

return
```

Figure 12-8. A program to print four-up labels for selected customers

```
open the customer file with the zip code index

clear the screen
initialize the memory variable MEQUIPMENT with 25 blank spaces
display a message: which type of equipment must a customer have
   to be included in this mailing?
display a message: press <RETURN> to leave MEQUIPMENT blank if
   you want to include all customers
collect the user's answer into the memory variable MEQUIPMENT


if MEQUIPMENT was not left blank
   establish a filter to include only those records where
      MEQUIPMENT (trimmed to remove trailing blank spaces)
      is contained in the EQUIPMENT field (converted to upper case)
   position the record pointer to the first record which satisfies
      the condition in the filter

print labels using a label form (NWCUST1.LBL or NWCUST4.LBL)

cancel the filter

return to the menu
```

Figure 12-9. The label-printing program in pseudocode

code the way these programs work.

In each program the Customer File is opened with the ZIP code index. The operator is asked to specify the type of equipment used by customers to be included in the mailing. The memory variable MEQUIPMENT, initialized with 25 blank spaces to match the length of the EQUIPMENT field, stores the entry, which is converted to uppercase with "@!" PICTURE. A message on the screen instructs the operator to press RETURN to leave MEQUIPMENT blank if no selection is desired. After the READ command, MEQUIPMENT is tested to determine whether it is still blank. If not, the selection criteria are established with the command SET FILTER TO TRIM(MEQUIPMENT) $ UPPER(EQUIPMENT).

With a FILTER in effect, the system behaves as if the data base contains only those records that satisfy the condition in the SET FILTER command, much as SET DELETED ON causes dBASE III PLUS to process only non-deleted records. At command level SET FILTER allows you to avoid typing the same FOR clause many times. In a program SET FILTER provides the means to establish selection criteria *conditionally*—the rest of the program steps will execute exactly the same whether or not you have actually SET a FILTER. In this example the FILTER restricts the records processed to those in which the user's entry into the variable MEQUIPMENT is contained in the EQUIPMENT field (converted to uppercase for purposes of comparison to match the memory variable). The FILTER remains in effect until canceled at the end of the program with SET FILTER TO.

The GOTO TOP command that follows the SET FILTER command is necessary because although the FILTER instructs dBASE III PLUS to exclude all records that do not satisfy the specified condition, the SET FILTER command does not automatically reposition the data base to the first such record. In NWCLABL1.PRG, opening the Customer File with the ZIP code index leaves the file positioned at the first record in ZIP code order. Without the GOTO TOP, this first record would be printed regardless of whether it met the conditions specified in the SET FILTER command. When you explicitly reposition the record pointer with GOTO TOP, dBASE III PLUS moves not to the first indexed record, but to *the first indexed record that matches the FILTER condition,* thus ensuring that only the desired records are selected.

In this version of the system, personalized letters and envelopes are printed by a word processing program that reads the delimited file format described in Chapter 5. Figure 12-10 lists a program, NWCCOPY.PRG, that copies some of the fields from all or selected customer records to a

```
* NWCCOPY.PRG
* PROGRAM TO COPY ALL OR SELECTED CUSTOMERS (BY TYPE OF EQUIPMENT)
*   TO DELIMITED FILE TO PRINT LETTERS OR ENVELOPES USING WORD PROCESSOR
* WRITTEN BY:  M.LISKIN       6/18/85

use NWCUST index NWCZIP

clear
store Ø to MTOTINV
@ 1Ø, 5 say "Enter minimum total invoices for customers in this mailing: ";
        get MTOTINV
@ 12,1Ø say "(or press <RETURN> to include ALL customers)"
read

@ 15, 5 say;
  "Copying customers to word processing format -- Please do not interrupt"

if MTOTINV > Ø
   set filter to TOTINV >= MTOTINV
   goto top
endif

set talk on
copy to NWCUST type delimited fields COMPANY, ADDRESS1, ADDRESS2, CITY,;
   STATE, ZIP, CONTACT, AREACODE, TELEPHONE, TOTINV

set talk off
set filter to

return
```

Figure 12-10. A program to copy selected customers to a delimited file

delimited file called NWCUST.TXT. Like the mailing label programs, NWCCOPY.PRG opens the Customer File with the ZIP code index so that records are copied to the delimited file in ZIP code order. This time the selection is based on the total dollar value of the customers' invoices, so the user is asked to enter the minimum value for this field for records to be included in the mailing. The amount is stored in the numeric memory variable MTOTINV. Just as in the mailing label program, a FILTER establishes the selection criteria if the user has specified a non-zero value for MTOTINV. To produce a status message that allows the operator to monitor the progress of the COPY command, the program displays the message "Copying customers ... " and uses SET TALK ON to provide a running count of how many records have been copied. Not all of the fields in the Customer File will be printed in the personalized letters, so the COPY command lists only the required fields. Finally, the program cancels the FILTER with SET FILTER TO and turns off the display of dBASE III PLUS status messages with SET TALK OFF before returning to the menu.

Using Format Files For Printed Output

One of the limitations of working with dBASE III PLUS at command level is its inability to print full-page formats easily. Producing invoices or statements that combine data from two or more files will require more complex programs, but for printouts like Rolodex or index cards, you may use a format file to lay out the fields from a single record on one page. The problem is that format files process one record at a time. With APPEND and EDIT, this is exactly what you want, but there is no built-in command that enables you to use a format file to print all of the records in a data base automatically. Instead, you must write a program that uses a DO WHILE loop to read through the data base and print each record individually. Like the series of @...SAY...GET commands to which it is equivalent, a format file may be activated from within a program by a READ command.

A format file, NWCCARDS.FMT, for printing the National Widgets Customer File on 3 × 5 cards is listed in Figure 12-11. This format is designed for printing at 10 characters per inch horizontally (for a total width of 50 characters) and 6 lines per inch vertically (18 lines per card). Although this format file does not include any PICTURE clauses, you may use the same functions and templates to format printed output as were used in Chapter 7 for displaying data on the screen.

The program, NWCCARD1.PRG, that uses the format file is listed in Figure 12-12. This program opens the Customer File with the account number index to print the cards in alphabetical order. The selection criteria are established by using the same method as in the label-printing and word processor interface programs. In this case, records are selected by first order date, making use of the ability of dBASE III PLUS to compare two dates and determine which is greater (that is, later). As always the date variable must be initialized and tested to see if it is blank via the character string equivalent. With this program a complete set of cards could be printed once, and then a new set that included only new customers added since the last printing could be produced periodically.

```
* NWCCARDS.FMT
* FORMAT FILE TO PRINT CUSTOMER ROLODEX OR INDEX CARDS
* WRITTEN BY:  M.LISKIN       6/18/85

@  2, 5 say ACCOUNT
@  2,30 say "(" + AREACODE + ") " + TELEPHONE
@  4,10 say COMPANY
@  5,10 say ADDRESS1
@  6,10 say ADDRESS2
@  7,10 say trim(CITY) + ", " + STATE + "  " + ZIP
@  9,10 say "CONTACT:      "  + CONTACT
@ 11,10 say "EQUIPMENT:    "  + EQUIPMENT
@ 13,10 say "FIRST ORDER: " + dtoc(FIRSTORDER)
```

Figure 12-11. A format file for printing Rolodex or index cards

```
* NWCCARD1.PRG
* PROGRAM TO PRINT ROLODEX OR INDEX CARDS
*   USING FORMAT FILE NWCCARDS.FMT
* WRITTEN BY:  M.LISKIN       6/18/85

use NWCUST index NWCACCT

clear
store ctod("  /  /  ") to MFIRSTORD
@ 10,10 say "Print only customers whose first order date is AFTER ";
        get MFIRSTORD
@ 12,10 say "(or press <RETURN> to include ALL customers)"
read

if dtoc(MFIRSTORD) <> "  /  /  "
   set filter to FIRSTORDER > MFIRSTORD
   goto top
endif

set format to NWCCARDS
set device to print
@  0, 0 say chr(27) + "C" + chr(18)

do while .not. eof()
   read
   skip
enddo

set filter to
@  0, 0 say chr(27) + "C" + chr(66)
set device to screen

return
```

Figure 12-12. A program to print Rolodex or index cards

The format file is opened with SET FORMAT TO NWCCARDS, and the output is directed to the printer with SET DEVICE TO PRINT. The DO WHILE loop processes all of the records in the file. Inside the loop the READ command activates the format file to print the data from the current record, after which SKIP repositions the record pointer to the next record. After all of the records have been processed, the output of @... SAY...GET commands is redirected to the screen with SET DEVICE TO SCREEN so that the menu program may ask the user for another selection.

This program presents an additional complication. Recall that when dBASE III PLUS sends data to the printer by means of a series of @... SAY commands, a row coordinate lower than the one in the previous @... SAY causes the printer to eject the paper to the top of the next page. If your printer is set up for a 66-line page (6 lines per inch on paper 11 inches long), the form length must be reset to 18 lines to print 3 × 5 cards. Although some printers allow you to set the form length with a dial on the front panel, it is best to control the printer through software, so that the operator does not have to remember to reset the form length before and after printing cards. The printer control string immediately following the SET DEVICE TO PRINT command in NWCCARDS.PRG sets the form length to 18 lines on Epson dot-matrix printers. (If you own another printer, you can look up the correct codes to use in the printer manual.) After all the records have been processed, the printer is reset to the standard 66-line form length.

A Program to Find and Edit A Customer Record

The most complex program in this chapter, NWCEDIT.PRG, finds a particular customer record and edits it. Although it is easy to draw the edit screen with the same format file (NWCUST2.FMT) used in the APPEND option, editing records in a data base is more complicated than APPENDing new entries, because you must first find the record you wish to edit. At command level you could do this with GOTO if you knew the record number or, more likely, use SEEK to search the index for the desired record. The edit program must parallel this process, and it must properly handle the situation in which SEEK fails to find the requested record. Figure 12-13 outlines the general strategy in pseudocode.

The complete program, NWCEDIT.PRG, is listed in Figure 12-14. The

```
open the customer file with the account number and zip indexes

do the following until the user chooses to exit:

   ask for a customer account number

   if the account number is left blank:
      exit the program and return to the menu

   otherwise:
      search account number index for the customer

      if the customer is found:

         open the format file
         edit the customer record
         close the format file

      otherwise:

         display an error message

      endif          [ customer found ]

   endif        [ account number left blank ]

end of steps to do until the user chooses to exit
```

Figure 12-13. Pseudocode version of a program to find and edit a customer record

Customer File is opened with both the account number and ZIP code indexes, since either of these key fields may be changed by the user. The account number index is named first so that it may be used as the basis of the SEEK command. Next, the program uses SET DELETED OFF to allow deleted records to be viewed, edited, or recalled. As in the Main Menu program, DO WHILE .T. is used to set up an "endless" loop to ask the user for an account number, look for the customer, and edit the record.

Within the loop a message is displayed requesting a customer account number, and the user's input is stored in the memory variable MACCOUNT. The PICTURE ensures that the entry is automatically converted to uppercase. If the account number is left blank, a RETURN command exits to the Main Menu. Otherwise SEEK is used to search the index for a match on MACCOUNT. This variable must be TRIMmed so that the program can search for a partial account number. Recall that when dBASE III PLUS compares two character strings, the comparison

```
* NWCEDIT.PRG
* PROGRAM TO FIND AND EDIT RECORDS IN NWCUST.DBF,
*   USING NWCUST2.FMT TO DRAW THE INPUT SCREEN
* WRITTEN BY:  M.LISKIN        4/11/86

use NWCUST index NWCACCT, NWCZIP
set deleted off

do while .T.

   clear
   store "          " to MACCOUNT
   @ 10,10 say "Enter customer account number " get MACCOUNT picture "@!"
   @ 12,10 say "(Or press <RETURN> to quit)"
   read

   if MACCOUNT = " "

      set deleted on
      return

   else

      seek trim(MACCOUNT)
      if found()
         set format to NWCUST2
         edit
         set format to
      else
         @ 15,10 say trim(MACCOUNT) + " is not in the Customer File"
         wait "               Press any key to try again"
      endif                [ customer found ]

   endif             [ MACCOUNT = " " ]

enddo          [ .T. ]

return
```

Figure 12-14. A program to find and edit a customer record

extends for a number of characters equal to the length of the string on the right. At command level, if you SEEK "JOHN", you will find JOHNSON (that is, if there is no record with the account number JOHN). However, if JOHN is entered into a memory variable initialized with ten blank spaces, you are actually SEEKing "JOHN   ", which does *not* match JOHNSON.

If the desired record exists in the file, the FOUND( ) function will have the value .T. If SEEK fails to find a matching record, FOUND( ) will be .F., and the program must test for this possibility and display an error message rather than attempt to EDIT the nonexistent record. If the SEEK succeeds, the format file is opened with SET FORMAT TO NWCUST2 before invoking EDIT. As always, the operator can use PGUP and PGDN to browse through the records in the file and CTRL-U to delete or recall records. Exiting from EDIT by pressing CTRL-END, CTRL-W, or ESC returns control to the NWCEDIT.PRG program, where the format file is closed with SET FORMAT TO. This is the end of the steps enclosed by the DO WHILE loop; so whether or not a record was found, the program goes back to the top of the loop to clear the screen and ask the operator for another account number. The format file must be opened before each EDIT command and closed afterward, so that on the next pass through the loop, the READ command collects the user's entry into MACCOUNT instead of activating the format file.

This completes the first version of the customer information module of the National Widgets sample system. If you are following along with this case study as a tutorial, you might want to apply the same strategy to the creation of the Order Processing and Financial Transactions menus. Although some of these operations, such as printing invoices and statements, clearly cannot be accomplished without more sophisticated programs, most of the data entry, editing, and file update procedures can be created much as we have illustrated in this chapter for the Customer File. Since most of the printed reports are within the capabilities of the dBASE III PLUS report generator, you should be able to produce much of the printed output as well. If you are building your own application, you might instead choose to apply the same principles to creating a simple menu-driven system of your own.

13

EVALUATING THE SYSTEM

Chapter 12 described how a set of menu programs may be used to integrate the procedures developed during the command level testing phase with some simple programs. To illustrate these concepts, two of the four menus that will eventually make up the National Widgets system were created—the Main Menu, which is the user's entry point into the application, and the Customer Information Menu. The two remaining menus—the Order Processing Menu and the Financial Transactions Menu—may be constructed in much the same way. These programs, NWOMENU.PRG and NWTMENU.PRG, are presented in Figures 13-1 and 13-2 as they might look in this first version of the system. Most of the components of these menus consist of command sequences that have already been developed and new format files and short programs similar to the ones called by the Customer Information Menu. A few of the options, however, will require more sophisticated programming techniques.

This chapter will evaluate the work done in Chapters 1 through 12. We will measure the gains made over working with dBASE III PLUS at command level, define the remaining limitations of the relatively simple programs written in these chapters, and compare the current version of the National Widgets system to the original design specifications to see how closely the users' requirements have been met. Using the original system outline in Figure 1-6 as a framework, Figure 13-3 relates the functions of the system to the menus and procedures that carry out the corresponding operations in the dBASE III PLUS application.

```
* NWOMENU.PRG
* ORDER PROCESSING MENU PROGRAM FOR ACCOUNTS RECEIVABLE SYSTEM
* WRITTEN BY:  M.LISKIN        04/11/86


do while .T.

   clear
   text
             National Widgets, Inc.  -  Accounts Receivable System

                              Order Processing Menu

               ( 1) - Add New Orders
               ( 2) - Inquire, Edit, Delete, Recall Orders
               ( 3) - Calculate Discount and Extended Price

               (10) - Print Current Order List by Invoice Number
               (11) - Print Order Reference List by Invoice Number
               (12) - Print Order Reference List by Customer

               (20) - Print Orders for Warehouse
               (21) - Print Invoices

               (30) - Create Invoice Transactions and Update Order History
               (31) - Post Invoice Data to Customer File
               (32) - Purge and Reinitialize Order History File

               (99) - Return to Main Menu
   endtext

   @  1, 0 to 24,79 double
   @  3, 1 to  3,78
   @  5, 1 to  5,78
   @ 22, 1 to 22,78

   store 0 to MSELECT
   @ 23,22 say "Please enter your selection   " get MSELECT picture "99"
   read

   do case

      case MSELECT = 1
         use NWORDER index NWOACCT, NWOINVC
         set format to NWORDER
         append

      case MSELECT = 2
         do NWOEDIT

      case MSELECT = 3
         do NWOCALC

      case MSELECT = 10
         use NWORDER index NWOINVC
         report form NWORDRFI to print

      case MSELECT = 11
         do NWORDRFI
```

Figure 13-1. The Order Processing Menu program

```
      case MSELECT = 12
         do NWORDRFA

      case MSELECT = 20
         do NWORDWH

      case MSELECT = 21
         do NWINVPRT

      case MSELECT = 30
         do NWOPOST

      case MSELECT = 31
         do NWIPOST

      case MSELECT = 32
         use NWORDHST index NWOHACCT, NWOHINVC
         zap

      case MSELECT = 99
         return

      otherwise
         @ 23,10 say "Not a valid selection -- Press any key to try again"
         wait ""

   endcase

   close databases

enddo          [ .T. ]

return
```

Figure 13-1. The Order Processing Menu program (*continued*)

```
* NWTMENU.PRG
* FINANCIAL TRANSACTION MENU PROGRAM FOR ACCOUNTS RECEIVABLE SYSTEM
* WRITTEN BY:  M.LISKIN       04/11/86


do while .T.

   clear
   text

             National Widgets, Inc.  -  Accounts Receivable System

                         Financial Transaction Menu

               ( 1) - Inquire, Edit, Delete, Recall Invoices
               ( 2) - Inquire, Edit, Delete, Recall Payments
```

Figure 13-2. The Financial Transactions Menu program

```
            (10) - Print Current Transaction List
            (11) - Print Transaction History List
            (12) - Print Invoice Register
            (13) - Print Cash Receipts Listing
            (14) - Print Aging Report
            (15) - Print Order Summary by Category
            (16) - Print Order Summary by Type of Equipment
            (17) - Print Accounting Summary
            (20) - Print Statements
            (30) - Update Transaction History File
            (31) - Purge and Reinitialize Transaction History File

            (99) - Return to Main Menu
endtext

@  1, 0 to 24,79 double
@  3, 1 to  3,78
@  5, 1 to  5,78
@ 22, 1 to 22,78

store 0 to MSELECT
@ 23,22 say "Please enter your selection   " get MSELECT picture "99"
read

do case

   case MSELECT = 1
      do NWTEDITI

   case MSELECT = 2
      do NWTEDITP

   case MSELECT = 10
      use NWTXN index NWTACCT
      report form NWTXNREF to print

   case MSELECT = 11
      do NWTXNREF

   case MSELECT = 12
      do NWINVREG

   case MSELECT = 13
      do NWCASHRC

   case MSELECT = 14
      do NWAGING

   case MSELECT = 15
      do NWORDSMC

   case MSELECT = 16
      do NWORDSME

   case MSELECT = 17
      do NWACTSUM

   case MSELECT = 20
      do NWSTPRT
```

Figure 13-2. The Financial Transactions Menu program (*continued*)

```
        case MSELECT = 30
           do NWTHUPD

        case MSELECT = 31
           use NWTXNHST index NWTHACCT, NWTHINVC
           zap

        case MSELECT = 99
           return

        otherwise
           @ 23,10 say "Not a valid selection -- Press any key to try again"
           wait ""

     endcase

     close databases

  enddo          [ .T. ]

  return
```

Figure 13-2. The Financial Transactions Menu program (*continued*)

Outline of National Widgets Accounts Receivable System

I. Customer Information—all functions carried out through the Customer Information Menu

1. Update Individual Customer Information
   (add, inquire, change, delete)
   Menu Option: 1 and 2
   Procedure: APPEND, using NWCUST2.FMT, to add customers
   NWCEDIT.PRG, using NWCUST2.FMT, to inquire, change, or delete
2. Archive and Delete Inactive Customers
   Menu Option: 31
   Procedure: NWCDELET.PRG
3. Zero Customer Year-to-Date Totals
   Menu Option: 30
   Procedure: NWCZERO.PRG

Figure 13-3. Evaluating the first version of the National Widgets Accounts Receivable System by comparison with the original outline

4. Customer Lists
   Menu Option: Customer ledger cards
   a. Customer Reference List
      Menu Option: 10
      Procedure: NWCUSTRF.FRM
      Comments: Option prints all customers. We could print new customers since a specified date or customers with no activity since a specified date with a program (similar to NWCLABL1.PRG) that asks for the cutoff date, establishes the selection criteria with SET FILTER, and prints the report using NWCUSTRF.FRM.
      We still cannot print financial transactions from NWTXN.DBF on the same report.
   b. Rolodex or Index Cards
      Menu Option: 11
      Procedure: NWCCARD1.PRG, which uses NWCCARDS.FMT
      Comments: Program prints all customers or new customers since a specified date. We could print one customer at a time with a program (similar to NWCEDIT.PRG) that asks for a customer account number, finds the customer, and prints a card using NWCCARDS.FMT.
5. Customer Profiles
   Menu Option: 12
   Procedure: NWCSTAT1.PRG
   Comments: Program profiles customers by type of equipment. We still cannot profile customers by product category, which is not stored in NWCUST.DBF.
6. Mailings to Customers
   a. Print Mailing Labels for All Customers
      Menu Option: 20 and 21
      Procedure: NWCLABL1.PRG or NWCLABL4.PRG

Figure 13-3. Evaluating the first version of the National Widgets Accounts Receivable System by comparison with the original outline (*continued*)

b. Print Mailing Labels for Selected Customers
Menu Option: 20 and 21
Procedure: NWCLABL1.PRG or NWCLABL4.PRG
Comments: Program prints customers selected by type of equipment. We could write similar programs to select by last order date or total orders. We still cannot select by product category, which is not stored in NWCUST.DBF.

c. Print Personalized Letters for Selected Customers
Menu Option: 22
Procedure: NWCCOPY.PRG and word processing program
Comments: Program prints customers selected by total orders. We could write similar programs to select by type of equipment or last order date. We still cannot select by product category, which is not stored in NWCUST.DBF.

d. Print Envelopes for Christmas Cards
Menu Option: 22
Procedure: NWCCOPY.PRG and word processing program

II. Order Processing—all functions carried out through the Order Processing Menu

1. Update Individual Customer Information (add, inquire, change, delete)
Menu Option: 1 and 2
Procedure: APPEND, using NWORDER.FMT* to add orders
NWOEDIT.PRG* to inquire, change, or delete
NWOCALC.PRG to calculate line item totals
Comments: NWOEDIT.PRG* (similar to NWCEDIT.PRG) would ask for an order by invoice number. The program might LIST all matching order records, then allow the user to access one by record number for editing with NWORDER.FMT.

2. Print Order Reference List
Menu Option: 10, 11, and 12

Figure 13-3. Evaluating the first version of the National Widgets Accounts Receivable System by comparison with the original outline (*continued*)

Procedure: NWOREFI.FRM* to print all current orders from NWORDER.DBF using NWOINVC.NDX
NWORDRFI.PRG* to print orders using NWOREFI.FRM*, from NWORDHST.DBF using NWOHINVC.NDX
NWORDRFA.PRG* to print orders using NWOREFA.FRM*, from NWORDHST.DBF using NWOHACCT.NDX
Comments: Two different report forms allow for subtotalling by customer and invoice or by invoice alone. Programs that print from NWORDHST.DBF would ask for one customer to print, or a starting invoice number.

3. Print Orders for Warehouse
Menu Option: 20
Procedure: NWORDWH.PRG*
Comments: This is a full-page format (similar to an invoice), including data from NWORDER.DBF and NWTXN.DBF.
We still cannot print this format.

4. Print Invoices
Menu Option: 21
Procedure: NWINVPRT.PRG*
Comments: This is a full-page format including data from NWCUST.DBF, NWORDER.DBF, and NWTXN.DBF.
We still cannot print this format.

5. Post Invoice Information to Customer File
Menu Option: 31
Procedure: NWIPOST.PRG*
Comments: This program would use the UPDATE command as described in Chapter 4 to post invoice and payment data from NWTXN.DBF to NWCUST.DBF.

6. Update Order History File
Menu Option: 30
Procedure: NWOPOST.PRG

7. Purge and Reinitialize Order History File
Menu Option: 32
Procedure: ZAP command

Figure 13-3. Evaluating the first version of the National Widgets Accounts Receivable System by comparison with the original outline *(continued)*

III. Financial Transactions—all functions carried out through the Financial Transaction Menu

1. Update Transaction (Invoice and Payment) Information (add, inquire, change, delete)
   Menu Option: 1 and 2
   Procedure: NWTEDITI.PRG* to edit invoice data
   NWTEDITP.PRG* to edit payment data (invoice records are created by NWOPOST.PRG)
   Comments: NWTEDITI.PRG* (similar to NWCEDIT.PRG) would ask for an invoice by number, to be edited with a format file, NWTXNINV.FMT*, which would allow access only to invoice fields.
   NWTEDITP.PRG* (similar to NWCEDIT.PRG) would ask for an invoice by number, to be edited with a format file, NWTXNPMT.FMT, which allows access only to payment fields.
2. Print Transaction Reference List
   Menu Option: 10 and 11
   Procedure: NWTXNREF.FRM* to print all current transactions from NWTXN.DBF using NWTACCT.NDX
   NWTXNREF.PRG* to print transactions using NWTXNREF.FRM*, from NWTXNHST.DBF using NWTHACCT.NDX
   Comments: Program would ask for one customer to print, or print all transactions, subtotalled by customer.
3. Print Invoice Register
   Menu Option: 12
   Procedure: NWINVREG.PRG*
   Comments: Program would ask for a starting invoice number, then use NWINVREG.FRM* to print the report.
4. Print Cash Receipts Listing
   Menu Option: 13
   Procedure: NWCASHRC.PRG*
   Comments: Program would ask for starting and ending payment dates, then use NWCASHRC.FRM* to print the report.

Figure 13-3. Evaluating the first version of the National Widgets Accounts Receivable System by comparison with the original outline (*continued*)

5. Print Aging Report
   Menu Option: 14
   Procedure: NWAGING.PRG*
   Comments: Program would open NWCUST.DBF and NWTXN.DBF, link the files with SET RELATION, and then use NWAGING.FRM to print the report for all invoice transactions that have not been paid in full.
6. Print Customer Statements
   Menu Option: 20
   Procedure: NWSTPRT.PRG*
   Comments: This is a full-page format including data from NWCUST.DBF and NWTXN.DBF.
   We still cannot print this format.
7. Order Summary
   Menu Option: 15 and 16
   Procedure: NWORDSMC.PRG* to print summary by category. NWORDSME.PRG* to print summary by type of equipment.
   Comments: NWORDSMC.PRG* would index NWORDHST.DBF by CATEGORY, ask for a category, and then print the report using NWORDSMC.FRM*, which would subtotal by category. NWORDSME.PRG* would index NWORDHST.DBF by EQUIPMENT, ask for the type of equipment, and then print the report using NWORDSME.FRM*, which would subtotal by type of equipment.
   Either program would allow the user to print all of the records in NWORDHST.DBF.
8. Accounting Summaries
   Menu Option: 17
   Procedure: NWACTSUM.PRG*
   Comments: This program must summarize data from NWORDHST.DBF, NWINVENT.DBF, NWTXN.DBF, and NWTXNHST.DBF. We still cannot write this program.

Figure 13-3. Evaluating the first version of the National Widgets Accounts Receivable System by comparison with the original outline (*continued*)

9. Update Transaction History File
   Menu Option: 30
   Procedure: NWTHUPD.PRG*
   Comments: This program performs the steps described in Chapter 4 for end-of-month processing.
10. Purge and Reinitialize Transaction History File
   Menu Option: 31
   Procedure: ZAP command

*Note: These programs, format files, and report forms have *not* yet been created, but could be using the techniques described in Chapters 1 through 12.

Figure 13-3. Evaluating the first version of the National Widgets Accounts Receivable System by comparison with the original outline (*continued*)

GAINS OVER COMMAND LEVEL OPERATION

With the addition of the menus, the system has made significant gains with respect to two of the three major reasons enumerated in Chapter 7 for writing dBASE III PLUS programs automation and user-friendliness. By automating frequently used or long-running commands, even simple batch-type programs enhance any data base system. These programs free the users from repeatedly typing the same lengthy command sequences, a tedious process that also has the potential to corrupt the data base through careless errors. And because they may be run unattended, these programs allow both human and computer resources to be used more effectively within an organization.

Writing programs allows many of the component procedures in a system to be carried out by operators who know little about dBASE III PLUS or the details of the specific application. The names of all the data bases, indexes, format files, report and label forms, and memory variable files are written into the programs, so the operator need not remember them. In a menu-driven system, the operators do not even need to know the function of each type of file, and they need absolutely no knowledge of dBASE III PLUS command syntax to use the application.

Instead, the menu prompts may describe in English the tasks the options perform. If a system is written specifically for one organization, the descriptions can be completely customized to conform closely to the terminology used in the office, no matter how idiosyncratic it is. The layout of the menus and the presentation of the options can suggest the order in which the operations must be performed, in order to emulate the manual processing system and to preserve the integrity of the data bases.

REMAINING LIMITATIONS

The system created in the first twelve chapters is still less than ideal in several important ways. We have done little to overcome many of the limitations of working at the dot prompt and using the standard report and label generators to produce the system's printed output. The simple programs written thus far perform no data validation beyond the capabilities of dBASE III PLUS at command level. Most of the file update procedures, while they may run without operator intervention, use the same REPLACE, COUNT, SUM, TOTAL and UPDATE commands that can be typed at the dot prompt, and they are equally inefficient in the way they process the files. In many cases — the program that calculates customer statistics is a good example — these commands must make many passes through a data base to perform the desired calculations or file updates.

We have yet to print full-page formats like order forms, invoices, and statements; reports that include data from more than two files; reports requiring more than two levels of subtotals; or reports that accumulate statistics other than column totals, such as counts and averages. Report forms like NWCUSTRF.FRM have pushed the report generator to its limits, but the appearance of the system's printed output could be further improved by providing more flexible access to the printer's special features and by controlling the page layout more precisely. In addition to performing complex calculations, it would be desirable to introduce into columnar reports the variety of data display formats available through PICTUREs, such as inserting commas in numeric fields, while still being able to perform calculations on the data thus displayed. (Recall that the dBASE III PLUS report generator cannot compute subtotals on numeric fields formatted with the TRANSFORM function.)

In Chapter 12 a format file, accessed from a very simple program, was used to print Rolodex cards from the Customer File. Because a format file may include only @ ... SAY ... GET commands and comment lines, it is impossible to print certain fields conditionally. Using the IIF function, you could suppress the display of the headings "CONTACT:", "EQUIPMENT", and "FIRST ORDER:" if the corresponding fields were blank, but it is impossible to eliminate the blank lines that result from a missing COMPANY or ADDRESS2 field. Another alternative is to print the cards by using a label form, but using this method *all* blank lines would be eliminated, including the ones we have deliberately included above and below the address block and between the CONTACT, EQUIPMENT, and FIRST ORDER lines.

The label printing and word processor interface programs in Chapter 12 illustrate a generally applicable technique for soliciting input from the operator and acting on that input. However, the specific method used, while easy to program, rapidly becomes cumbersome if too many different selection criteria are necessary. For example, the label-printing programs process selected customers according to the type of computer equipment they own. But National Widgets also wants to select for label runs by last invoice date or total invoices. Another variation of the program could be written for each of these selections, but since we already have two programs (one for one-across labels and one for four-across labels), this would result in a total of *six* label-printing programs. With many possible selection criteria, the number of separate programs in the system and the number of menu options would increase dramatically.

In a small system with clearly defined requirements this is a viable alternative, especially because it requires very little programming expertise. You can see from Figure 13-3, however, that in a typical data base application, printing the same basic report format with different selection criteria is the rule rather than the exception. With a half dozen variations of the same basic program, modifying any of the programs would necessitate making the same change in all of them. Furthermore, the users may want to *combine* different selection criteria—for example, in the National Widgets system, to produce mailing labels for all owners of IBM equipment who have more than $500 in total invoices and whose last order was more than six months ago. Chapter 16 will demonstrate how to write a single program that allows the user to specify multiple selection criteria for a report.

The remaining, and most serious, fundamental problem with this first version of the system is that many of the procedures in the sample application do not closely parallel the normal work flow in the manual system they are intended to replace. Consider as a detailed example the way in which orders are processed in the National Widgets system. When you use option 1 from the Order Processing Menu, the individual line items on each customer order form must be entered into the Order File, with the invoice number assigned by the operator. The invoice number and customer account number must be entered into each of the Order File records that will eventually make up one invoice, although you can SET CARRY ON to make this process easier. In a separate step, option 3 is used to fill in prices from the Inventory File and calculate discounts and extended prices; if a nonstandard price is charged, the operator must remember to retrieve the appropriate order record (using option 2) and make the change. Transaction File entries are created by option 30, which uses the TOTAL command to summarize the order records as we did at the dot prompt in Chapter 4. (Since this version of the system cannot print invoices, the Order File records are no longer needed, so they are appended to the Order History File and deleted to prepare for the next batch of entries.) The user must then remember to switch to another menu—the Financial Transactions Menu—and use option 1 to fill in the invoice date, tax rate, and shipping charges and to calculate the final net invoice amount.

Chapter 16 will present an order entry program that emulates the manual processing of National Widgets' orders. For each order the customer account number will be entered only once and checked against the Customer File to make sure the customer has already been entered into the system. The program will then create an invoice record in the Transaction File, supplying the next sequential invoice number automatically. The operator will then enter the individual line items on the order into the Order File. The category and part number will be validated and the prices obtained from the Inventory File as the items are entered; the operator will have the option to override the standard prices with manual entries. The discount and extended price fields will be calculated instantly and added into the invoice subtotals. The operator must fill in the shipping charges and a prepayment, if any; the tax rate will be obtained from the Customer File. Finally, the system will total the invoice. Although the invoice will not actually be printed until later, this program reduces to a single operation a procedure that at command level requires a carefully prescribed sequence of many steps. The user will find it very similar to typing the invoices manually.

Although the system as it stands could be improved considerably, it would be a mistake to underestimate the significance of what has already been accomplished. For many applications a system like this is complete and fully usable in its present form. For example, the Customer Information Menu, used in conjunction with a word processing program with mail-merge capability, is an excellent model for a simple mailing list system. Attaining this goal required some knowledge of programming, but at a level that is not much more demanding than working with dBASE III PLUS at the dot prompt. Almost any user who has some familiarity with dBASE III PLUS, regardless of prior programming experience, can create systems like this one, and any dBASE III PLUS application that you have been using at command level could be substantially improved by this type of implementation. Parts III and IV of this book will expand on the programming concepts introduced thus far to give you the tools to meet the requirements of almost any dBASE III PLUS application you may encounter.

REFINING THE SYSTEM

In Part III the fundamental dBASE III PLUS programming structures are combined into longer and more sophisticated programs that perform many operations more efficiently than the built-in commands used in the simple batch-type programs in Part II. These programs will overcome many of the limitations of working at the dot prompt uncovered during the command level testing phase of system development, and they more closely emulate the manual procedures they are intended to replace. A variety of techniques will be presented for working with multiple files, validating data entered by the user, and producing printed formats like letters, invoices, statements, and reports with subtotals and statistics. As the programs become more complicated, testing and debugging methods are introduced that enable you to make sure that your programs manipulate the data correctly and to find the causes of the errors you will inevitably make.

14

TESTING AND DEBUGGING

The programs presented in Parts I and II of this book illustrate dBASE III PLUS programming structures and demonstrate some straightforward ways to carry out the file update, inquiry, and reporting operations essential to any data base application. These programs may be less complex, flexible, and easy to use than the ones that will ultimately form the National Widgets system, but all of them are basically correct: they run without errors and work as intended. If you have been following the development of this case study as a tutorial or writing similar programs for your own data base application, you have probably discovered that most programs do not work perfectly on the first try. Even if you are an accurate typist, you may occasionally have entered a command line incorrectly and encountered a "Syntax error" message when you tried to run the program. In other cases, a program may have run to completion without generating an error message but still produced incorrect results.

In a ten-line program, a careful rereading of the listing will usually enable you to locate the problem. As you write longer and more complicated programs, you increase the potential for making not only careless typing mistakes, but also fundamental errors in the logic or structure of a program. Subsequent chapters will introduce more sophisticated programming techniques, but first this chapter will discuss two separate but related concepts: testing and debugging. *Testing* consists of providing a program with a wide range of input to make sure that it runs without generating syntax errors and that it manipulates the data correctly under a variety of conditions. When a problem does occur, *debugging* is the process of identifying and correcting it.

SYNTAX ERRORS

The most common errors you will make—and the easiest to find and correct—are *syntax errors.* When you first learn the dBASE III PLUS language, you may make many genuine mistakes, such as using the wrong command verb or forgetting an essential phrase or punctuation mark. An advanced user's syntax errors are usually caused by misspelling a dBASE III PLUS command word, function name, data base field name, or memory variable name, or by combining variables and functions illegally in a complex algebraic expression. Very often, these are simply typographical errors, but it is also easy to forget the field names in a data base you do not regularly work with if you do not have a printed copy of the structure.

At the dot prompt, dBASE III PLUS responds to syntax errors by displaying a message identifying the type and location of the problem. If the first word of your command line is not one of the command verbs recognized by dBASE III PLUS, you will be told just that:

```
. LSIT ACCOUNT, COMPANY, TELEPHONE
*** Unrecognized command verb.
         ?
LSIT ACCOUNT, COMPANY, TELEPHONE
```

If one of the other words in the command is unrecognizable, dBASE III PLUS responds with as specific an error message as possible. To help you pinpoint the exact source of the problem, dBASE III PLUS repeats the command line on the screen and positions a question mark where the line ceased making sense. For example, if you misspell a field or memory variable name in a list of expressions, the error message is usually "Variable not found," and the question mark is positioned above or just to the right of the erroneous variable name.

In the following example, the name of the AREACODE field was mistyped:

```
. LIST ACCOUNT, COMPANY, AREACDE, TELEPHONE
Variable not found.
                                    ?
LIST ACCOUNT, COMPANY, AREACDE, TELEPHONE
Do you want some help? (Y/N)
```

Answering Y invokes a one-screen summary of the syntax and usage of the command verb. Figure 14-1 shows the help screen for the LIST command that would be displayed if you accepted the offer of help after

```
                          LIST
                          ====

Syntax      :  LIST [<scope>] [<expression list>] [FOR <condition>]
                    [WHILE <condition>] [OFF] [TO PRINT]

Description :  Displays the contents of a database file.
               Used alone, it displays all records.  Use the scope and
               FOR/WHILE clauses to list selectively.  The expression
               list can be included to select fields or a combination
               of fields, such as Cost * Rate.  OFF suppresses the record
               numbers.



HELP        |<C:>|NWCUST     |              |Rec: 1/25        |Ins    |   Caps
 Previous screen - PgUp. Previous menu - F10. Exit with Esc or enter a command.
                  ENTER > [                    ]
```

Figure 14-1. The help screen for the LIST command

typing the above command. If you recognize immediately that you have simply misspelled a field name, you can refuse the help screen, use UP ARROW to retrieve the command line from HISTORY, edit the command, and resubmit it. The SET HELP option, which is ON by default, governs whether or not dBASE III PLUS includes the query "Do you want some help? (Y/N)" in its response to syntax errors. If you are an expert dBASE III PLUS user and a poor typist, you can use SET HELP OFF to avoid having to answer N to this question every time you incorrectly type a command. If you ever do need a reminder of the syntax of a particular command, you can still request the help screen from the dot prompt with

HELP *command verb*

You might also want to SET HELP OFF if you run dBASE III PLUS on floppy disks and have removed from your work disk the HELP.DBS file that contains the text of the help screens in order to gain additional disk space. When working on 360K floppies, even a novice dBASE III PLUS user might decide to refer to the printed command reference card for help rather than sacrificing the 70K of disk space occupied by the help file.

Deciphering some of the syntax error messages is easier if you understand a little about how dBASE III PLUS *parses,* or interprets, commands. Each command line is scanned from left to right, and interpretation stops immediately when an error is encountered. The first word in every command must be one of the verbs recognized by dBASE III PLUS, so if you misspell the verb, dBASE III PLUS knows exactly what is wrong with your command. All constants—character strings enclosed in quotes, numbers, and logical fields surrounded by periods—are processed literally, and every other word is tested to see if it is a recognizable dBASE III PLUS *keyword* (a function name or command component, such as FOR, WHILE, or DELIMITED). All words not recognized as keywords are tested to see if they are field names in the data base file in use in the selected work area or active memory variables. Thus, forgetting to use quotation marks to delimit a character string results in a "Variable not found" message:

```
. LIST FOR CITY = Berkeley
Variable not found.
                          ?
LIST FOR CITY = Berkeley
Do you want some help? (Y/N)
```

In this command, LIST is a known command verb and FOR is a recognized keyword. Neither "CITY" nor "Berkeley" is found in the dBASE III PLUS vocabulary, but "CITY" is a field name in the data base in use—the National Widgets Customer File. dBASE III PLUS assumes that "Berkeley" is also a data base field or memory variable against which your condition is being tested to determine if its contents are the same as the contents of the CITY field. If a field or variable called "Berkeley" existed, this would be a perfectly reasonable condition to use in a FOR clause, so dBASE III PLUS cannot determine that you actually meant to type a character string constant. Since no field or memory variable called "Berkeley" exists, it makes sense to display the "Variable not found" error message. On the other hand, if you forget the second of the pair of delimiters surrounding a character string, dBASE III PLUS assumes that you intended to type a character string and gives you a more specific description of the error:

```
. LIST FOR CITY = "Berkeley
Unterminated string.
                           ?
LIST FOR CITY = "Berkeley
Do you want some help? (Y/N)
```

You will find that many of the other common error messages are also self-explanatory, if a bit terse. For example, "Unbalanced parenthesis" identifies an unequal number of left and right parentheses in an expression. Even when it is impossible to describe precisely the nature of the error, dBASE III PLUS still attempts to identify the problem word in the command:

```
. LIST ACCOUNT, COMPANY, TELEPHONE FR AREACODE = "415"

Syntax error.
                                      ?
LIST ACCOUNT, COMPANY, TELEPHONE FR AREACODE = "415"
Do you want some help? (Y/N)
```

or

```
. USE NWCUST IND NWCACCT
Unrecognized phrase/keyword in command.
            ?
USE NWCUST IND NWCACCT
Do you want some help? (Y/N)
```

Another very common error message, "Data type mismatch," results from constructing an expression that mixes data types incorrectly, attempting to REPLACE a field with an expression of the wrong data type, or comparing two expressions of different types. Incorrect expressions involving a variable and a constant (rather than two fields or memory variables) may instead yield the "Invalid operator" error message.

In the following example, the expression in the FOR clause compares AREACODE, a character field, to 415, which is a number:

```
. LIST ACCOUNT, COMPANY, TELEPHONE FOR AREACODE = 415
Data type mismatch.
                                                    ?
LIST ACCOUNT, COMPANY, TELEPHONE FOR AREACODE = 415
Do you want some help? (Y/N)
```

Thus, the entire FOR clause is incomprehensible, but dBASE III PLUS cannot determine whether the fault lies in the field or the constant. The position of the question mark, to the right of the condition in the FOR clause, reflects this fact. Since dBASE III PLUS cannot always determine *exactly* which word in a command is incorrect, the position of the question mark may not lead you directly to the problem. However, interpretation of a command stops as soon as an error is found, so you need never look to the right of the question mark in the error message. Consider a more complex condition involving the AREACODE field:

```
. LIST ACCOUNT, COMPANY, TELEPHONE FOR YTDINV > 0 .AND. AREACODE = 415
Data type mismatch
                                                                ?
LIST ACCOUNT, COMPANY, TELEPHONE FOR YTDINV > 0 .AND. AREACODE = 415
Do you want some help? (Y/N)
```

The question mark in this example is located very close to the exact source of the problem, in a much more helpful spot than it would be if you had reversed the two halves of the condition:

```
. LIST ACCOUNT, COMPANY, TELEPHONE FOR AREACODE = 415 .AND. YTDINV > 0
Data type mismatch
                                                       ?
LIST ACCOUNT, COMPANY, TELEPHONE FOR AREACODE = 415 .AND. YTDINV > 0
Do you want some help? (Y/N)
```

Your first reaction to this error message might be to suspect YTDINV. But the position of the question mark means only that dBASE III PLUS was not able to determine that something was wrong until it passed the logical operator .AND. in the command. If you are not sure what is wrong in an expression like this, you can test each part of the condition independently at the dot prompt. You need not retype the full LIST command in order to find the error. If you position the data base to any valid record, you can display the entire condition or either of its component parts:

```
. ? YTDINV > 0
.F.
. ? AREACODE = 415
Data type mismatch.
                  ?
? AREACODE = 415
```

In this dialog dBASE III PLUS was able to show you the value of the expression YTDINV > 0, which, like any condition, is a logical expression with a value of .T. or .F. (.F. for the particular record in this example). The expression AREACODE = 415, on the other hand, produced the same error message generated by the original command. A similar approach can help find an error in a complex expression made up of constants, data base fields, and memory variables. Breaking down the expression into its component parts and displaying each part separately, or building up an expression in stages, is often the best way to find a problem when the dBASE III PLUS error message is not particularly helpful. All of the dBASE III PLUS error messages and their most likely causes are listed in Appendix F.

When an error occurs within a dBASE III PLUS program, execution pauses, and dBASE III PLUS displays the incorrect line along with the same error message that the erroneous command would generate if you had typed it at the dot prompt. Because one program may call another, the error listing also traces the chain of programs leading to the one that contains the faulty command. Just as at command level, an examination of the error display will usually lead you to the source of the problem. *Whenever you test or debug a program, you should have a complete set of program listings available for reference, as well as printouts of the structure and contents of any data bases processed by the program, in the appropriate indexed or sequential order.* For all but the most obvious errors, you must be able to see the bad command line in context and know what data the program was attempting to process when it crashed in order to find and correct the bug.

Consider the NWCZERO.PRG program written in Chapter 12, which used the following command to reset the National Widgets Customer File year-to-date invoice and payment fields to zero at the end of the year:

```
replace all YTDINV with 0, YTDPMT with 0
```

If you misspelled the YTDINV field name as YTINV, running the program would result in the following display:

```
          Zeroing year-to-date totals -- Please do not interrupt
Variable not found.
                       ?
replace all YTINV with 0, YTDPMT with 0
Called from - C:NWCZERO.PRG
Called from - C:NWCMENU1.PRG
Called from - C:NWMENU1.PRG
Cancel, Ignore, or Suspend? (C, I, or S)
```

Recall that the "Zeroing year-to-date totals..." message is displayed by the NWCZERO.PRG program before it executes the REPLACE command that caused the error. The bad command is displayed on the screen, with the question mark indicating the location of the problem. The tracing of program flow begins with the program that contains the error, NWCZERO.PRG, and informs you that this program was called from NWCMENU1.PRG (the Customer Information Menu program), which was in turn called from NWMENU1.PRG (the Main Menu program).

Whether or not you have SET HELP OFF, errors in a dBASE III PLUS program do not result in an offer of help. Instead, you are given the choice of three courses of action: Cancel, Ignore, or Suspend. Typing the letter C to choose Cancel terminates the program, releases all PRIVATE memory variables, and returns you to the dot prompt. Selecting Ignore causes dBASE III PLUS to bypass the line with the error and continue with the next command in the program. Choosing Suspend pauses execution and returns you to the dot prompt without releasing any memory variables; you can type any commands you wish and then pick up where you left off with the RESUME command, or you can terminate the program by typing CANCEL.

If you realize you have made a serious error, you will probably want to cancel the program, correct the error, and try running it again. If you have made a trivial mistake like omitting the closing quote in the "Zeroing year-to-date totals..." message, you might choose to ignore the "Unterminated string" error message and continue. Since this error affects only the screen display, not the way in which the program manipulates the data, you can correct it later rather than interrupting the current test run.

If you are not sure what has caused the error, the best strategy is to suspend execution and track down the source of the problem by using the techniques outlined earlier in this chapter. Just as in your work at the dot prompt, errors caused by misspelling a command word or field name, or by omitting a quotation mark or parenthesis, are usually easy to identify and fix. When you suspend a program, any data bases opened by your program remain positioned exactly where they were when the program crashed, so you may dissect a faulty expression and test its component parts with ? commands. For example, in debugging the NWCZERO.PRG program, the following dialog would pinpoint the cause of the problem:

```
          Zeroing year-to-date totals -- Please do not interrupt
Variable not found.
                    ?
replace all YTINV with 0, YTDPMT with 0
Called from - C:NWCZERO.PRG
Called from - C:NWCMENU1.PRG
Called from - C:NWMENU1.PRG
Cancel, Ignore, or Suspend? (C, I, or S) Suspend
Do suspended



. ? YTINV
Variable not found.
        ?
? YTINV
```

Since you intended YTINV to be a field in the current data base, your next step might be to use LIST STRUCTURE to remind yourself of which data base is open and how the field names are spelled. Once you realize that the field name should have been spelled YTDINV, you can type the command correctly at the dot prompt:

```
replace all YTDINV with 0, YTDPMT with 0
```

When the command is complete, you can use RESUME to continue execution with the next command line.

In a more complex program, particularly one that opens more than one data base, you might also want to DISPLAY the current record, or DISPLAY STATUS to make sure that the right indexes are open and that the correct work area is selected. Another very common oversight, especially when you modify or add to an existing program, is to use a memory variable in a calculation without prior initialization, which also results in the "Variable not found" error message. As mentioned in Chapter 11, all memory variables created within a program are RELEASEd when a program terminates, so it is generally better to suspend rather than cancel a program when you are not sure what has caused an error. This allows you to examine the values of all of the memory variables with DISPLAY MEMORY or the values of selected variables with ? commands. If you do decide to terminate the program to correct the error, you can type CANCEL at the dot prompt.

dBASE III PLUS DEBUGGING TOOLS

Sometimes when a program crashes because of a fundamental error in logic rather than a simple syntax error, you may reread the listing over and over without discovering the cause of the problem. To help you track down the more elusive bugs in your programs, dBASE III PLUS provides five SET options—SET TALK, SET ECHO, SET DEBUG, SET STEP, and SET DOHISTORY—that enable you to trace the execution of a program as it runs.

SET TALK ON turns on the dBASE III PLUS status messages that inform you of the actions taken in response to your commands. As pointed out in Chapter 12, the TALK display is useful at command level but is generally undesirable in a program; the messages will disrupt your formatted screens and might not be comprehensible to users who are unfamiliar with dBASE III PLUS command syntax. Most menu-driven systems therefore SET TALK OFF in the first menu. When you debug a program, however, the TALK messages—especially the echo of the values you STORE to memory variables or REPLACE into data base fields, and the display of the new current record number after a SKIP command—can be invaluable aids in uncovering the source of an error in logic.

SET ECHO ON echoes each command line to the display screen as the program runs, so you can trace the execution of a program line by line. The program lines scroll by as fast as they are carried out, but you can pause the program at any point with CTRL-NUMLOCK or CTRL-S (as you can whenever you run a dBASE III PLUS program) and then resume with RETURN or CTRL-Q. Commands that are not actually processed are not echoed. For example, the statements in an IF structure are not echoed if the condition in the IF statement evaluates to .F. Combined with SET TALK ON, the ECHO option is particularly useful for finding errors in the structure or logic of a program that contains nested DO WHILE or IF loops. As mentioned earlier, a printed copy of the program and the relevant data bases is essential to understanding the display produced by SET ECHO ON.

SET DEBUG ON routes the output produced by the ECHO option to the printer instead of to the screen. This is especially handy when you test a program that draws a formatted screen, since the echoed command lines can be hard to see and can obscure other information your program displays on the screen. For programs that do not produce much screen output, it is usually unnecessary.

SET STEP ON causes a program to operate in single-step mode. Command lines are executed one at a time, and after each line, dBASE III PLUS pauses and displays the message "Press SPACE to step, S to suspend, or Esc to cancel..." Pressing the space bar causes dBASE III PLUS to proceed to the next command, the ESC key terminates the program and returns you to the dot prompt, and S suspends execution temporarily and returns you to the dot prompt. Just as when you suspend execution after a syntax error message, you can type any commands you like and then use RESUME to continue running the program. With ECHO and TALK also ON, the SET STEP ON option provides an alternative to stopping and starting the program manually with CTRL-S and CTRL-Q. Running a program in single-step mode gives you precise control—you can pause or stop the program at any line, not just when a faulty command line generates a syntax error.

SET DOHISTORY ON causes program lines, as well as commands executed from the dot prompt, to be recorded in HISTORY. When a program crashes due to a syntax error, you can LIST HISTORY to identify the line that caused the error; this will be the second-to-last command in the list (just before the LIST HISTORY command). If you wish, you can also edit the command, resubmit it, and then RESUME the program. This correction does not actually change the program; it simply allows you to substitute the correct command for the erroneous line in the program. To permanently fix the problem, you must edit the program file. When you are debugging a sizeable program, SET DOHISTORY ON can be a more straightforward and less confusing way to find the problem than running the program with ECHO ON. If you use this feature, you will almost always want to SET ECHO OFF and increase the number of commands saved in HISTORY beyond the default of 20.

All of these SET commands may be typed at the dot prompt before a program is run, or they can be temporarily placed in the program itself. If the program you are testing is called from a menu, make sure that the SET commands in the menu program, especially SET TALK OFF, do not override the options you SET at command level. You may also run into the same problem if you are testing a program that already contains a SET TALK ON and a subsequent SET TALK OFF command, such as the NWCZERO.PRG program used as an example in the previous section. In this case, you can remove the SET TALK OFF line or disable it by inserting an asterisk (*) at the beginning of the line you wish to disable. Since the asterisk is used in the dBASE III PLUS language to identify comment lines, any statement beginning with this comment marker will not be executed. Later, the program may be restored to its original form by removing the asterisks. You might want to distinguish these temporary comment markers from ordinary comment lines that must remain in the program by using more than one asterisk or by placing the asterisk(s) at the left margin rather than indenting them. Note that any of the five debugging options may be SET ON or OFF anywhere in a program, so if you have narrowed down the source of a problem to a particular section of code, you may SET TALK ON, SET ECHO ON, SET DEBUG ON, SET STEP ON, and/or SET DOHISTORY ON just before the problem area, and then SET the same options off immediately afterward.

Some of these debugging techniques will be demonstrated by using the TOTAL.PRG program, written in Chapter 11, that illustrated the use of memory variables to accumulate totals. This program is reproduced in its correct form in Figure 14-2. Suppose that you had forgotten the SKIP command right before the ENDDO. If you run the program this way (you might want to try this yourself), the computer will appear to hang up.

```
* TOTAL.PRG
* PROGRAM TO ACCUMULATE COUNTS AND TOTALS FOR SELECTED RECORDS
* WRITTEN BY:  M.LISKIN        6/20/85
* REVISED BY:  M.LISKIN        6/20/85


set talk off
use NWCUST

store 0    to MCOUNT
store 0.00 to MTOTAL

do while .not. eof()

   if CITY <> "San Francisco"
      skip
      loop
   endif

   store MCOUNT + 1      to MCOUNT
   store MTOTAL + TOTINV to MTOTAL

   skip

enddo          [ not end-of-file ]

? "Totals for Customers in San Francisco"
display memory

return
```

Figure 14-2. A program that uses memory variables to accumulate totals

There will be no evidence of disk activity, but because you can interrupt the program by pressing the ESC key, you can rule out a hardware failure or a bug in dBASE III PLUS as a likely cause of the problem. Running the program with TALK and ECHO ON (with a comment marker temporarily disabling the SET TALK OFF command) results in the display in Figure 14-3. (To save space in the listing, the program was interrupted with ESC much earlier than it would be in a typical trial run.)

Notice that an IF or DO WHILE command is always executed—the condition must always be evaluated—and therefore echoed to the terminal. If the condition is true, the following statements are also executed, so they appear on the monitor as well. If the condition is false, the commands that are passed over are not displayed. Under these conditions an ENDIF statement is also suppressed, which can be a bit confusing, but ENDDO is always echoed to the terminal. In a program with many nested DO WHILE loops, you can follow the ECHO display more easily if you have included in each ENDDO statement a comment that reiterates the condition in the matching DO WHILE command.

The listing of the test run in Figure 14-3 shows that the first two records were skipped, leaving the data base positioned at record 3, which you can confirm as the first record with "San Francisco" in the CITY field with a LIST command, or by referring to a printout of the Customer File. The next time through the loop, *and every subsequent time,* the condition in the IF statement tested false, so the SKIP and LOOP commands were not executed. However, record 4 has "Oakland," not "San Francisco," in the CITY field, which alone should suggest that the program never reached the fourth record in the file. You could confirm this by using a DISPLAY command to show you the current position of the record pointer after pressing ESC to interrupt the program.

You might also have observed from the TALK display that no more record numbers were displayed after record 3, or you might have noticed that the value of MTOTAL echoed after each STORE command was an exact multiple of the TOTINV amount in record 3. If you let the program run long enough, you will see MCOUNT increase beyond 25, the number of records in the sample data base.

As you may already have gathered from this discussion, debugging is far from an exact science. Although a systematic approach and the habit of logical thinking are definite assets, instinct and intuition also come into play. The TALK and ECHO options are especially helpful because they allow you to display as much information as possible while a program runs, thus increasing the chances that you will discover a clue to the source of the problem.

When you are completely at sea, using SET STEP ON allows you to trace a program step by step and suspend operation at any time to examine the contents of the data bases or the values of key memory variables. You can also compare the data manipulated by a program to the printed listings, which provide the ultimate reference to the contents of a data base. To do this, temporarily insert strategically placed DISPLAY commands to display the entire record being processed or ? commands to show you the values of selected fields. Unless you have also SET STEP ON, you may want to use a WAIT command after each DISPLAY so that you have time to study or print the screen before allowing the program to continue. Placing these temporary commands at the left margin, rather than indenting them, will make them easier to find and remove later.

Assume that running the TOTAL.PRG program as illustrated in Figure 14-3 did not give you enough information to determine the source of the

```
use NWCUST

store Ø to    MCOUNT
Ø
store Ø.ØØ to MTOTAL
Ø.ØØ

do while .not. eof()

   if CITY <> "San Francisco"
      skip
Record No.       2
      loop

   if CITY <> "San Francisco"
      skip
Record No.       3
      loop

   if CITY <> "San Francisco"

   store MCOUNT + 1       to MCOUNT
          1
   store MTOTAL + TOTINV to MTOTAL
        279.52

enddo            [ not end-of-file ]

   if CITY <> "San Francisco"

   store MCOUNT + 1       to MCOUNT
          2
   store MTOTAL + TOTINV to MTOTAL
        559.Ø4

enddo            [ not end-of-file ]

   if CITY <> "San Francisco"

   store MCOUNT + 1       to MCOUNT
          3
   store MTOTAL + TOTINV to MTOTAL
        838.56

enddo            [ not end-of-file ]

   if CITY <> "San Francisco"

   store MCOUNT + 1       to MCOUNT
          4
   store MTOTAL + TOTINV to MTOTAL
       1118.Ø8

enddo            [ not end-of-file ]

   if CITY <> "San Francisco"
```

Figure 14-3. Running TOTAL.PRG with TALK and ECHO ON

```
    store MCOUNT + 1       to MCOUNT
          5
    store MTOTAL + TOTINV to MTOTAL
        1397.60

enddo           [ not end-of-file ]
*** INTERRUPTED ***
Called from - C:total.prg
Cancel, Ignore, or Suspend? (C, I, or S) Suspend
Do suspended
```

Figure 14-3. Running TOTAL.PRG with TALK and ECHO ON *(continued)*

problem. Placing a temporary DISPLAY command just before the IF statement would allow you to check every time the condition is evaluated to see whether the program's decision is correct. A similar command immediately preceding a STORE command enables you to verify the calculation. In a data base with many fields, it is usually less confusing to use a ? command to display only the fields you really need to see, rather than DISPLAYing the whole record. Be sure to include enough information to identify uniquely the record being processed and to evaluate the program's performance. The record number itself may be displayed using the RECNO() function. Figure 14-4 lists a version of the TOTAL.PRG program with two temporary ? commands, one before the IF loop and one before the STORE command. Figure 14-5 shows the display obtained by running the program with TALK and ECHO ON. The ? commands leave no doubt that the same record is being processed over and over again.

You can include memory variables in the temporary DISPLAY or ? commands inserted for debugging purposes; or to see all of the active memory variables, you can use DISPLAY MEMORY (perhaps followed by WAIT) or LIST MEMORY TO PRINT. You can also type these commands at the dot prompt when a program crashes, or at the point of interruption when you press ESC (for example, to get out of an endless loop), as long as you remember to suspend rather than cancel execution. If you need to see the values of your memory variables after a program terminates normally, you can place a temporary DISPLAY MEMORY command immediately before the RETURN, or you can make all or some of the variables PUBLIC. You can do this either by temporarily placing a PUBLIC declaration at the beginning of the program before any of the variables are initialized or by typing the PUBLIC command at the dot prompt before running the program. For example, to make the memory variables created in the TOTAL.PRG program available after the program runs to completion, you could use

```
PUBLIC MCOUNT, MTOTAL
```

Sometimes, in spite of your best efforts, a program fails for a reason you cannot fathom, or it performs erratically, depending on the contents of the data base. When this happens, reread the listing carefully and look for fundamental errors in program structure:

- Does each IF, DO WHILE, DO CASE, TEXT, ELSE, CASE, OTHERWISE, ENDIF, ENDDO, ENDCASE, and ENDTEXT statement occur on a separate line ending with a carriage return?

```
* TOTAL.PRG
* PROGRAM TO ACCUMULATE COUNTS AND TOTALS FOR SELECTED RECORDS
* WRITTEN BY:  M.LISKIN       6/20/85
* REVISED BY:  M.LISKIN       6/20/85


set talk off
use NWCUST

store 0    to MCOUNT
store 0.00 to MTOTAL

do while .not. eof

? ACCOUNT, CITY, TOTINV

   if CITY <> "San Francisco"
      skip
      loop
   endif

? ACCOUNT, CITY, TOTINV
   store MCOUNT + 1      to MCOUNT
   store MTOTAL + TOTINV to MTOTAL

enddo          [ not end-of-file ]

? "Totals for Customers in San Francisco"
display memory

return
```

Figure 14-4. The TOTAL.PRG program with two temporary ? commands

```
use NWCUST

store 0 to    MCOUNT
0
store 0.00 to MTOTAL
0.00

do while .not. eof()

? ACCOUNT, CITY, TOTINV
LEWIS      Oakland                    366.81

   if CITY <> "San Francisco"
      skip
Record No.      2
      loop

? ACCOUNT, CITY, TOTINV
ABCPLUMB   Berkeley                   934.56

   if CITY <> "San Francisco"
      skip
Record No.      3
      loop

? ACCOUNT, CITY, TOTINV
ANDERSON   San Francisco              279.52

   if CITY <> "San Francisco"

? ACCOUNT, CITY, TOTINV
ANDERSON   San Francisco              279.52
   store MCOUNT + 1      to MCOUNT
          1
   store MTOTAL + TOTINV to MTOTAL
        279.52

enddo            [ not end-of-file ]

? ACCOUNT, CITY, TOTINV
ANDERSON   San Francisco              279.52

   if CITY <> "San Francisco"

? ACCOUNT, CITY, TOTINV
ANDERSON   San Francisco              279.52
   store MCOUNT + 1      to MCOUNT
          2
   store MTOTAL + TOTINV to MTOTAL
        559.04

enddo            [ not end-of-file ]

? ACCOUNT, CITY, TOTINV
ANDERSON   San Francisco              279.52

   if CITY <> "San Francisco"
```

Figure 14-5. Using temporary ? commands to test TOTAL.PRG (with TALK and ECHO ON)

```
? ACCOUNT, CITY, TOTINV
ANDERSON   San Francisco            279.52
*** INTERRUPTED ***
Called from - C:TOTAL.prg
Cancel, Ignore, or Suspend? (C, I, or S) Suspend
Do suspended
```

Figure 14-5. Using temporary ? commands to test TOTAL.PRG (with TALK and ECHO ON) *(continued)*

- Are all IF, DO WHILE, and DO CASE structures nested properly? (Does each loop fall entirely within another loop?)
- Are ENDIF, ENDDO, ENDTEXT, or ENDCASE statements omitted or misspelled?
- Are any loop terminators paired with the wrong loop-beginning statements? (For example, does a DO WHILE loop end with ENDIF?)

These errors are usually easiest to spot on a printed program listing. In a long or complex program, drawing lines to connect the beginning and ending statements of each loop, working outward from the innermost in a series of nested loops, can help clarify the way the loops are nested and uncover structural errors. In a large program you can use your word processor's search feature to detect mismatched or missing loop terminators. For example, you could search repeatedly for "DO WHILE," counting as you go, and repeat the process with "ENDDO" to make sure there is an ENDDO for each DO WHILE statement. If your word processor counts the number of successful replacements in a global search and replace command, you can take advantage of this feature by searching for "DO WHILE," replacing every occurrence with "DO WHILE" just to obtain the count, and then doing the same thing with "ENDDO."

As a last resort in difficult cases, you might also try simulating the execution of the program by tracing the code, line by line, working from printed program listings and data base reference lists. Carrying out all of the calculations yourself as if you were the computer can be a tedious but revealing exercise when a program contains an obscure error in logic.

SETTING UP TESTING CONDITIONS

The debugging techniques discussed so far will help you discover the cause when a program halts with a syntax error, stops prematurely before all of the records in a file have been processed, or runs forever. But just because a program generates no syntax errors and appears to complete normally does *not* mean that it has produced the right results. Again using TOTAL.PRG as an example, suppose you had omitted the LOOP command within the IF statement that tests to see if a customer is located in San Francisco. This version of the program appears to run normally and displays a total and a count when it finishes:

```
Totals for Customers in San Francisco
MCOUNT       priv  N          14  (         14.00000000)          C:TOTAL.prg
MTOTAL       priv  N        5125.01  (       5125.01000000)       C:TOTAL.prg
    2 variables defined,        18 bytes used
  254 variables available,    5982 bytes available
```

Do not be too quick to accept these numbers as correct! One of the reasons for testing an application with a small amount of sample data is that you can identify unreasonable output when you are familiar with the data. You might, for example, know the 25 sample customers in the National Widgets system well enough to suspect the output of the TOTAL command when it states that 14 customers (more than half) are in San Francisco. In a small sample file, you can check a program's output by hand or even more easily by typing commands at the dot prompt. In this case, you can SET TALK ON and use the built-in COUNT and SUM commands at the dot prompt to verify the statistics computed by TOTAL.PRG:

```
. USE NWCUST
. SUM TOTINV FOR CITY = "San Francisco"
      6 records summed
      1907.82
```

The result of running this version of the TOTAL.PRG program with TALK and DEBUG ON and with the same temporary ? commands used earlier is illustrated in Figure 14-6. In this listing the first record, in which the CITY field contains "Oakland", is SKIPped, leaving the data base positioned at record 2. The CITY field in record 2, displayed right before the STORE, contains "Berkeley", but MCOUNT is incremented and the

```
use NWCUST

store 0 to    MCOUNT
0
store 0.00 to MTOTAL
0.00

do while .not. eof()

? ACCOUNT, CITY, TOTINV
LEWIS      Oakland                        366.81

   if CITY <> "San Francisco"
      skip
Record No.       2
   endif

? ACCOUNT, CITY, TOTINV
ABCPLUMB   Berkeley                       934.56
   store MCOUNT + 1       to MCOUNT
          1
   store MTOTAL + TOTINV to MTOTAL
        934.56

   skip
Record No.       3

enddo             [ not end-of-file ]

? ACCOUNT, CITY, TOTINV
ANDERSON   San Francisco                  279.52

   if CITY <> "San Francisco"

? ACCOUNT, CITY, TOTINV
ANDERSON   San Francisco                  279.52
   store MCOUNT + 1       to MCOUNT
          2
   store MTOTAL + TOTINV to MTOTAL
       1214.08

   skip
Record No.       4

enddo             [ not end-of-file ]

? ACCOUNT, CITY, TOTINV
KLEIN      Oakland                        790.70

   if CITY <> "San Francisco"
      skip
Record No.       5
   endif

? ACCOUNT, CITY, TOTINV
MTK        Emeryville                    1042.85
   store MCOUNT + 1       to MCOUNT
          3
```

Figure 14-6. Using temporary ? commands to test TOTAL.PRG (with TALK and DEBUG ON)

```
   store MTOTAL + TOTINV to MTOTAL
       2256.93

   skip
Record No.      6

enddo              [ not end-of-file ]
*** INTERRUPTED ***
Called from - C:total.prg
Cancel, Ignore, or Suspend? (C, I, or S) Suspend
Do suspended
```

Figure 14-6. Using temporary ? commands to test TOTAL.PRG (with TALK and DEBUG ON) (*continued*)

TOTINV field is added into MTOTAL. This pinpoints the source of the problem: the CITY field in this record was never tested to see if it contained "San Francisco".

The output of the TOTAL.PRG program was easy to duplicate using COUNT and SUM commands at the dot prompt. In other cases, you may have to use a combination of built-in commands and manual calculations to check the results of a program, but you should never neglect this crucial step. It is especially important to prove the correct performance of programs that produce no visible output to signal potential problems—for example, a program that posts transaction data to the Customer File.

Whenever a more complex expression than CITY = "San Francisco" is used in a condition, you should examine the results to make sure that the right records are selected. This test must be carried out in a way that does not depend on the way the expression is constructed, since the point is to determine whether the expression is correct. Instead, you might LIST the relevant fields from the data base and manually perform the required calculations for the appropriate records to see if the program's output is correct.

When you test a program, make sure that your sample data provides a wide range of input encompassing all of the possibilities that will exist in the final data base. If a program tests the contents of a particular field, make sure that each file includes some records in which the field is blank, some that satisfy the condition, and some that do not, even if the users of the application are convinced some of these values can't occur in the real system. Recall the NWCDELET.PRG program written in Chapter 12 to delete inactive customers from the National Widgets Customer File. This program deletes records in which the LASTORDER date is more than one year earlier than the current date:

```
DELETE FOR DATE() - LASTORDER > 365
```

When you test this program, the data in the sample file should include some records in which DATE() − LASTORDER is less than 365 days, some in which this expression is exactly equal to 365, some in which it is greater, and at least one in which LASTORDER is blank. As mentioned in Chapter 12, records with a blank LASTORDER field are *not* deleted by NWCDELET.PRG. You might not have noticed this if you didn't include a blank LASTORDER date in the test data. Devising strategic test conditions is especially important in assessing whether a program is able to cope with "impossible" values such as negative numbers, or in finding instances where you have used the wrong comparison operator in a condition (for example, "less than" when you really needed "less than or equal to").

Any program that accepts input from the operator should be tested by entering every conceivable type of wrong or implausible data to verify that the program does not crash and that you have provided adequate validation tests. Whenever a SEEK or FIND command is used, you must make sure the program properly handles the situation in which a matching record is not found. For example, the NWCEDIT.PRG program written in Chapter 12 to find and edit a customer record must be tested to ensure that it can handle an attempt to search for a customer who is not present in the Customer File.

No matter how conscientiously you approach the testing process, it can be difficult for any programmer to thoroughly test his or her own work. You should use real test data from the existing manual system, because your own familiarity with the purpose of a program can lead you to supply only input that works with the program structure. A sampling of real data from the manual system will better duplicate all of the challenges your programs must meet. One of the goals of the testing phase is to deliver fully debugged programs to the system's users so that they need never see a "Syntax error" message or a report with incorrect totals. However, it is often true that only the ultimate users of the system will enter a wide enough range of data and make all of the data entry mistakes necessary to uncover every bug. For this reason, one of the users of the application should try out your programs in the experimental stages. And a cooperative person who is unacquainted with both the manual system and your program is often best suited to find out how user-friendly and crash-proof a program is, because he or she will enter the widest range of erroneous input.

15

MAKING THE SYSTEM MORE EFFICIENT AND FLEXIBLE

This chapter will use the programming structures described in Chapter 9 to show you how to write dBASE III PLUS programs that process a data base far more efficiently and that offer more flexibility to the system's users than the batch-type programs that made up most of the examples in Part I. Additional error checking and validation capabilities will also be introduced to make the programs easier to use and harder to crash. In the process of accomplishing these goals, the chapter will develop a set of standard techniques that will be used throughout the remaining programs in this book and that may also form the components of your own dBASE III PLUS applications. Beginning programmers should pay special attention to the way the dBASE III PLUS programming structures are combined to build longer programs. Whether or not you have programmed in other languages, you should study the programs in this chapter carefully: they attain a level of sophistication comparable to any real-world data base system, and they perform functions required in almost any dBASE III PLUS application.

From now on it is assumed that any programs you write will eventually be called from one of the menus that guide the user through an application. Certain commands that might be included in a program intended to be run from the dot prompt—for example, SET TALK OFF at the beginning and SET TALK ON or CLOSE DATABASES at the end—will therefore be omitted. In the National Widgets system these commands are already present in the menu programs. If you are designing your own application, your menus should contain these commands as well. For testing purposes, however, you may want to run a program directly from the dot prompt. If you do this, you must remember to SET TALK OFF before running your program, if necessary, and CLOSE DATABASES afterward. You can reduce the tedium of typing these commands frequently by assigning them to function keys or storing them in character string variables to be invoked as macros, as described in Chapter 6.

PROCESSING A DATA BASE FILE MORE EFFICIENTLY

The NWCSTAT1.PRG program written in Chapter 7 compiled statistics on National Widgets' customers according to the type of equipment they own. This program used exactly the same built-in COUNT and SUM commands you could type at command level to read through the Customer File and save the statistics in memory variables. Although placing the commands in a program makes better use of the operator's time by allowing the procedure to be run without supervision, it is relatively inefficient in the way it processes the Customer File. Just as at command level, each COUNT or SUM command causes dBASE III PLUS to read through the entire data base, with the FOR clause determining which records are included in the totals. Compiling the statistics for four categories of customers thus requires eight complete passes through the file. In a sample data base with 25 records this is not a serious problem, but if you had 2000 customers, you might grow impatient.

Using the programming structures described in Chapter 9, you can rewrite NWCSTAT1.PRG so that it accumulates all of the desired statistics on a single pass through the Customer File. Like the original, the new version of the program will use memory variables to store the counts and sums, but this time the program will control the values of these variables explicitly. For each record in the file the program must check the EQUIPMENT field and, based on the contents of this field, increment the appropriate count variable and add the customer's invoice totals into the appropriate sum variables. Here is a pseudocode outline of a program that uses this strategy to process just one category of equipment, IBM:

```
open the Customer File (no index necessary)
initialize a memory variable for the count with a value of 0
initialize memory variables for the year-to-date total and overall total
   with a value of 0.00
```

```
for each record in the file:

  if the customer has "IBM" in the EQUIPMENT field:
    increment the count variable
    add the year-to-date invoices into the year-to-date total variable
    add the total invoices into the overall total variable

  skip to the next record

after all records have been processed,
clear the screen

display the count and sums
calculate and display the averages
```

Of course, the complete program must accumulate statistics for owners of Apple, COMPAQ, and Kaypro computers as well. Although the pseudocode outline uses the word "if" in the test for the customer's type of equipment, the fact that the program must contend with four mutually exclusive possibilities suggests that a DO CASE structure is more appropriate than four IF loops. Using this basic structure as a point of departure, several other improvements can be added to make the program more user-friendly and to improve the quality and utility of the output.

Since we have dispensed with the COUNT and SUM commands that, with TALK ON, give the user a running status display of how many records have been processed, it is important to provide some other way to monitor the program's progress. Exactly what type of status message to display, in this or any other potentially long-running program, deserves serious consideration. When a program processes a file in indexed order—for example, if the Customer File were opened with the ACCOUNT index—the best kind of status message is usually something like "Working on:", followed by the index key field(s) and several other fields from the current record. An operator who is reasonably familiar with the data base should be able to see at a glance from this display how far the program has progressed. In the National Widgets Customer File, or any other name and address list processed in alphabetical order, this would be especially easy.

You have already seen, however, that if the order in which the records are processed is immaterial, opening a file with no indexes allows the program to run faster. When a file is read in sequential order, the status message should report the total number of records in the file and identify by number the record currently being processed, so the user sees something like this: "Working on Customer Record 102 of 2500." Both of these numbers are readily available for use in your programs through dBASE III PLUS functions—RECCOUNT() evaluates to the total number of records in the file, and RECNO() yields the record number of the record currently being processed.

Sometimes a program must access a data base in indexed order, but the index key fields do not provide an obvious clue as to how many records have been processed. In a case like this, the "Working on Record 102 of 2500" format for the status message would be much more informative; but since the records are not processed in sequential order, you cannot simply display the record numbers. Instead, you could use a memory variable as a counter and display the value of this variable in the status message along with the total number of records in the file. The counter variable, which you might call MCOUNT, should be initialized with a value of 1 at the beginning of the program and incremented with STORE MCOUNT + 1 to MCOUNT on each pass through the DO WHILE loop that processes all of the records in the file.

The new version of the customer statistics program will also improve the quality of the information it provides by counting not only the four categories National Widgets is specifically interested in, but also all of the customers who do not fall into any of these categories. Since only one pass through the file is required no matter how many separate totals are accumulated, the addition of this miscellaneous category will not slow down the program appreciably, and it can provide valuable management information. If too many records fall into this category, the users might want to investigate whether one or more of the machines represented deserve a separate count. The final version of the program, NWCSTAT2.PRG, is listed in Figure 15-1, with a detailed pseudocode explanation in Figure 15-2.

The program opens the Customer File with no indexes and positions the fixed portion of the status message text on the screen. Because this display does not change except for the current record number, it is placed on the screen only once, before the beginning of the DO WHILE loop that processes the entire file. Note that the RECCOUNT() function is numeric, so it must be converted to a character string with the STR function in order to concatenate it with the constant text in the status message. The empty space in the text of the message will have the current record number filled in on each pass through the loop. The two STORE commands initialize memory variables to contain the counts for the five categories of customers and the year-to-date and overall totals. The latter

```
* NWCSTAT2.PRG
* PROGRAM TO COMPILE CUSTOMER STATISTICS BASED ON TYPE OF EQUIPMENT OWNED
* WRITTEN BY:  M.LISKIN       4/20/86

use NWCUST

store 0    to MCOUNTIBM, MCOUNTAPP, MCOUNTKAY, MCOUNTCOM, MCOUNTMSC
store 0.00 to MYSUMIBM, MYSUMAPP, MYSUMKAY, MYSUMCOM, MYSUMMSC,;
              MTSUMIBM, MTSUMAPP, MTSUMKAY, MTSUMCOM, MTSUMMSC

clear
@ 10,10 say "Compiling Customer Statistics -- Please Do Not Interrupt"
@ 12,10 say "Working on Record            of " + str(reccount(),5)

do while .not. eof()

   @ 12,27 say recno()

   do case

      case "IBM" $ UPPER(EQUIPMENT)
         store MCOUNTIBM + 1      to MCOUNTIBM
         store MYSUMIBM + TOTINV to MYSUMIBM
         store MTSUMIBM + TOTINV to MTSUMIBM

      case "APPLE" $ UPPER(EQUIPMENT)
         store MCOUNTAPP + 1      to MCOUNTAPP
         store MYSUMAPP + TOTINV to MYSUMAPP
         store MTSUMAPP + TOTINV to MTSUMAPP

      case "KAYPRO" $ UPPER(EQUIPMENT)
         store MCOUNTKAY + 1      to MCOUNTKAY
         store MYSUMKAY + TOTINV to MYSUMKAY
         store MTSUMKAY + TOTINV to MTSUMKAY

      case "COMPAQ" $ UPPER(EQUIPMENT)
         store MCOUNTCOM + 1      to MCOUNTCOM
         store MYSUMCOM + TOTINV to MYSUMCOM
         store MTSUMCOM + TOTINV to MTSUMCOM

      otherwise
         store MCOUNTMSC + 1      to MCOUNTMSC
         store MYSUMMSC + TOTINV to MYSUMMSC
         store MTSUMMSC + TOTINV to MTSUMMSC

   endcase

   skip

enddo

save to NWCSTAT2

clear
@  1,20 say "Customer Statistics by Type of Equipment Owned"
@  2,20 say "----------------------------------------------"
@  5, 0 say "Equipment    Customers"
@  5,25 say "YTD Total    YTD Average         Overall    Overall Avg"
@  8, 0 say "  IBM"
```

Figure 15-1. The new customer statistics program

```
@  8,10 say MCOUNTIBM
@  8,25 say MYSUMIBM               picture "99,999.99"
@  8,40 say MYSUMIBM / MCOUNTIBM picture "99,999.99"
@  8,55 say MTSUMIBM               picture "99,999.99"
@  8,70 say MTSUMIBM / MCOUNTIBM picture "99,999.99"
@ 10, 0 say "  Apple"
@ 10,10 say MCOUNTAPP
@ 10,25 say MYSUMAPP               picture "99,999.99"
@ 10,40 say MYSUMAPP / MCOUNTAPP picture "99,999.99"
@ 10,55 say MTSUMAPP               picture "99,999.99"
@ 10,70 say MTSUMAPP / MCOUNTAPP picture "99,999.99"
@ 12, 0 say "  Kaypro"
@ 12,10 say MCOUNTKAY
@ 12,25 say MYSUMKAY               picture "99,999.99"
@ 12,40 say MYSUMKAY / MCOUNTKAY picture "99,999.99"
@ 12,55 say MTSUMKAY               picture "99,999.99"
@ 12,70 say MTSUMKAY / MCOUNTKAY picture "99,999.99"
@ 14, 0 say "  Compaq"
@ 14,10 say MCOUNTCOM
@ 14,25 say MYSUMCOM               picture "99,999.99"
@ 14,40 say MYSUMCOM / MCOUNTCOM picture "99,999.99"
@ 14,55 say MTSUMCOM               picture "99,999.99"
@ 14,70 say MTSUMCOM / MCOUNTCOM picture "99,999.99"
@ 16, 0 say "  Other"
@ 16,10 say MCOUNTMSC
@ 16,25 say MYSUMMSC               picture "99,999.99"
@ 16,40 say MYSUMMSC / MCOUNTMSC picture "99,999.99"
@ 16,55 say MTSUMMSC               picture "99,999.99"
@ 16,70 say MTSUMMSC / MCOUNTMSC picture "99,999.99"

@ 20,20 say "Press <SHIFT-PRTSC> to print this screen"
@ 22,20 say "Press any key to return to the Main Menu"

wait ""

return
```

Figure 15-1. The new customer statistics program (*continued*)

variables are initialized as 0.00 so that they may contain dollar amounts, including pennies.

Within the DO WHILE loop the four discrete possibilities in the EQUIPMENT field are tested with a DO CASE structure. As in the original version of the program, the EQUIPMENT field is converted to uppercase for the comparison. If a customer does not fall into one of the four standard categories, the OTHERWISE clause adds the customer's data into the miscellaneous category statistics. After all of the records in the file have been processed, the memory variables are saved on disk and the statistics are displayed with @ ... SAY commands. Creating a set of memory variables for the averages is not necessary, since @ ... SAY may be used to display the result of evaluating an expression like MTSUMIBM

```
open the customer file (no index necessary)

initialize  memory variables for the counts to 0
initialize memory variables for the year-to-date totals
   and overall totals to 0.00

clear the screen
display a status message, including the total number of records in the file

for each record in the file:

   display the current record number as part of the status message

   if the customer has "IBM" in the EQUIPMENT field:
      increment the IBM count variable
      add the year-to-date invoices into the IBM year-to-date total variable
      add the total invoices into the IBM overall total variable

   if the customer has "APPLE" in the EQUIPMENT field:
      increment the Apple count variable
      add the year-to-date invoices into the Apple year-to-date total variable
      add the total invoices into the Apple overall total variable

   if the customer has "KAYPRO" in the EQUIPMENT field:
      increment the Kaypro count variable
      add the year-to-date invoices into the Kaypro year-to-date total variable
      add the total invoices into the Kaypro overall total variable

   if the customer has "COMPAQ" in the EQUIPMENT field:
      increment the Compaq count variable
      add the year-to-date invoices into the Compaq year-to-date total variable
      add the total invoices into the Compaq overall total variable

   if the customer has none of the above in the EQUIPMENT field:
      increment the Miscellaneous count variable
      add the year-to-date invoices into the Misc. year-to-date total variable
      add the total invoices into the Misc. overall total variable

   skip to the next record

end of steps to do for each record in the file

save the statistics in a memory variable file on disk

clear the screen
display the counts and totals
calculate and display the averages

display a message explaining how to print the screen
display a message explaining how to exit the program
wait until a key is pressed
exit the program
```

Figure 15-2. The new customer statistics program in pseudocode

/MCOUNTIBM. All of the information fits easily on one screen, so the program need not make any special provision for printing the statistics. Instead, it displays a message reminding the operator that SHIFT-PRTSC may be used to obtain a hard copy. When you design programs like this for your own applications, you will find that the summary screens are complex enough to merit a sketch on paper before you begin writing the program.

ADDING FLEXIBILITY AND INPUT VALIDATION

The programs in Chapter 12 introduced the concept of asking the operator a question and storing the response in a memory variable for use later in the program. This technique was used in the label-printing and word processor interface programs in the National Widgets system for selective mailings to customers based on the type of computer equipment they own or the total dollar amount of their previous purchases. Each of these programs asks an essentially open-ended question and makes no attempt to validate the user's entry. If the selection criteria are not satisfied by any of the records in the file, the programs will run normally but produce no printed output.

This is often the only reasonable way to proceed. For example, the NWCLABL1.PRG program allows the user the flexibility of entering *any* type of equipment. Because the Customer File is processed in random order with respect to the EQUIPMENT field, the program must use a FOR clause or FILTER to test each record against the specified condition and exclude those that do not satisfy the condition. The program cannot identify whether any matching customers exist until every record in the file has been read.

In other cases, it *is* possible to validate the user's entry and refuse to go on until a correct response has been entered. When a condition depends on the index key field(s), you have much more control, for two reasons: you know in advance the order in which the records will be processed, and you can access any record by key in a matter of seconds. If, for example, you allowed the user to specify a single ZIP code for which to print labels, you could use a SEEK command to determine very quickly whether any customers with the specified ZIP code exist. However, indexing does not provide a workable solution to the problem of selecting by type of equipment. Building the index, which is not needed for any other purpose in the system, may take a long time in a large file. Also, the user must be permitted to enter a character string that may appear *anywhere* within the EQUIPMENT field, whereas FIND and SEEK both require that you specify the beginning of the field.

While you would rarely want to print mailing labels for a single ZIP code, consider the more realistic problem of allowing the user to start the NWCLABL1.PRG program, or any other dBASE III PLUS program that produces a lengthy report, at some point other than the beginning of the file. This might be necessary because of a paper jam or because the operator decided to interrupt a long-running print job in order to use the computer for some more urgent task. Under these circumstances it would be highly desirable to restart the report from the point of interruption rather than reprint the entire set of labels. Chapter 5 demonstrated a general method for accomplishing this at command level. Since the labels are printed in ZIP code order, you can use a FIND or SEEK command to quickly position the data base to the first record with any specified ZIP code. For example, to begin with ZIP code 94101, you could use

```
SEEK "94101"
LABEL FORM NWCUST1 TO PRINT REST
```

To incorporate this technique into a program, you must ask the operator for the starting ZIP code and store the answer in a memory variable to use as the object of the SEEK:

```
store "     " to MZIP
clear
@ 10,10 say "Enter starting zip code:" get MZIP picture "99999"
read
seek MZIP
label form NWCUST1 to print rest
```

If the operator enters a value for MZIP that does not exist in the index, the SEEK command leaves the data base positioned at the end-of-file and the program returns immediately to the menu without printing any labels. The reason for this may not be obvious to an inexperienced user, but unlike the selection by type of equipment, this problem can easily be remedied. Since the program may test the value of the EOF() function or the FOUND() function to determine the outcome of the SEEK, you can apply the same technique introduced in the NWC-EDIT.PRG program in Chapter 12 for asking a question, testing the answer, and, if it is wrong, asking the question again. In pseudocode, here is what the program must do:

```
do the following until a correct ZIP code is found:
  ask for the beginning ZIP code
  search the index for the ZIP code
  if the ZIP code is found,
    exit this loop and begin printing labels
  otherwise,
    display an error message
    go back and ask the question again
  end of steps to do until a correct ZIP code is found
  begin printing labels
```

The easiest way to structure this validation procedure is to set up an "endless" loop with DO WHILE .T. and use an EXIT command to get out of the loop when a correct ZIP code is entered. Within the loop the user's choice for the starting ZIP code is stored in a memory variable, which is used as the object of a SEEK command. If the SEEK succeeds, the program EXITs from the loop and begins printing labels. If the SEEK fails, the value of the FOUND() function will be .F. Just as in NWCEDIT.PRG, this program must display an error message and use a WAIT command to pause execution until the user presses a key, after which the error message is erased and the loop statements are executed again.

The decision to permit the user to enter the starting ZIP code suggests another element that may easily be added to the program: the option to specify the ending ZIP code as well. This would allow for selective mailings to customers in a particular geographical area defined by a range of ZIP codes. The revised version of the label-printing program, NWCLABL2.PRG, is listed in Figure 15-3. This program illustrates the method for soliciting the beginning and ending ZIP codes. These two entries are stored in the memory variables MZIPBEGIN and MZIPEND. Notice that neither of these variables is initialized with a blank value. Instead, MZIPBEGIN acquires the value of the ZIP field in the first record in the Customer File in ZIP code order, since that is where the data base is positioned when the USE command opens the file with the ZIP code index. With MZIPBEGIN initialized in this way, the lowest ZIP code in the file will appear as the default value presented by the @ ... SAY ... GET command.

Thus the operator does not need to know the first ZIP code to begin printing from the very beginning of the file. If the value of MZIPBEGIN is not changed by the operator, the first record in ZIP code order is used as the object of the SEEK. If the user is resuming where a previous print run left off, the new starting ZIP code can be found on the set of labels

```
* NWCLABL2.PRG
* PROGRAM TO PRINT 1-UP MAILING LABELS FOR ALL CUSTOMERS
*   OR SELECTED CUSTOMERS (BY TYPE OF EQUIPMENT)
*   FOR A RANGE OF ZIP CODES
* WRITTEN BY:  M.LISKIN        4/25/86

use NWCUST index NWCZIP

store ZIP         to MZIPBEGIN
store "99999"     to MZIPEND
store space(25)   to MEQUIPMENT

clear
@ 10,10 say "Enter type of equipment for customers in this mailing"
@ 14,10 say "(or press <RETURN> to include ALL customers)"
@ 12,20 get MEQUIPMENT picture "@!"
read

do while .T.

   @ 16,10 say "Enter starting zip code:" get MZIPBEGIN picture "99999"
   @ 17,10 say "Enter ending   zip code:" get MZIPEND   picture "99999"
   read

   seek trim(MZIPBEGIN)

   if found()
      exit
   else
      @ 19,10 say "There is no customer with that zip code"
      @ 20,10 say "Press any key to reenter the zip code"
      wait ""
      @ 19,10
      @ 20,10
   endif

enddo

if MEQUIPMENT <> " "
   set filter to trim(MEQUIPMENT) $ upper(EQUIPMENT)
   goto top
endif

label form NWCUST1 to print while ZIP <= MZIPEND

set filter to

return
```

Figure 15-3. A program to print labels for a range of ZIP codes

already printed. The ending ZIP code need not be specified exactly. Since the labels are printed in ZIP code order, a WHILE clause in the LABEL command ensures that printing will cease as soon as a record is reached in which the ZIP code is higher than MZIPEND. To make it easy for the user to print the entire file, MZIPEND is therefore initialized with the highest possible value, "99999."

This version of the label-printing program illustrates a method of validation that looks up the user's entry in a data base file. *Any* value may be entered, as long as a matching record is found in the data base. In other cases a program must ask a question and permit only a few possible answers, all of which are known in advance to the programmer. The simplest case, and one of the most common, requires asking a yes or no question. For example, assume that in the National Widgets system, mailings are infrequent enough that the decision has been made *not* to maintain the ZIP code index automatically. Instead, the index will be rebuilt immediately prior to printing the labels. The necessary commands can be included in the label-printing program:

```
use NWCUST
index on ZIP to NWCZIP
```

If the program must be run several times consecutively—perhaps for different groups of customers selected by type of equipment—rebuilding the index unconditionally wastes time, since no new records will be added or ZIP codes changed between label runs. Ideally, the program should ask the user whether it is necessary to rebuild the index, after displaying an appropriate explanation of how to come to the right decision. Here is the easiest way to ask the question:

```
use NWCUST
store .T. to MREINDEX
clear
@ 10,10 say "Do you need to reindex the Customer File by ZIP code?";
        get MREINDEX picture "Y"
read

if MREINDEX
   index on ZIP to NWCZIP
else
   set index to NWCZIP
endif
```

In this partial program the Customer File is opened with no index. A logical memory variable, MREINDEX, is created to store the user's response to the question "Do you need to reindex...." If the user answers Y, the index is rebuilt. Otherwise the program opens the existing ZIP code index. The "Y" PICTURE, which may also be used with character variables, automatically converts the user's entry to uppercase and permits only two possible entries: Y and N.

To illustrate the importance of restricting the range of permissible responses to a question, suppose that you had written the program like this:

```
use NWCUST
store " " to MREINDEX
clear
@ 10,10 say "Do you need to reindex the Customer File by ZIP code?";
        get MREINDEX picture "!"
read

if MREINDEX = "Y"
   index on ZIP to NWCZIP
else
   set index to NWCZIP
endif
```

While this program segment asks for a yes or no answer, it does nothing to prevent the operator from entering a character other than Y or N. Obviously, it would have been better to include a reminder of the two possible choices in the prompt, but there are two more serious problems. First, although the "!" PICTURE converts the entry to uppercase so the program does not have to test for both Y and y, *any* other character will be interpreted as "no." If the user means to type Y but presses U by mistake, the file will not be reindexed. The program must therefore keep asking the question until either a Y or N is entered.

The "Y" PICTURE provides an easy way to accomplish this objective, and it will be used in this book whenever a program must ask a yes or no question. However, there is another more general solution to the problem. The method, which was introduced in Chapter 11, uses a DO WHILE loop:

```
use NWCUST
store " " to MREINDEX
clear
do while MREINDEX <> "Y" .and. MREINDEX <> "N"
   @ 10,10 say "Do you need to reindex the Customer File by ZIP code? (Y/N)";
           get MREINDEX picture "!"
   read
enddo
```

The condition in the DO WHILE statement ensures that the steps within the loop—the process of asking the question and collecting the answer into the memory variable MREINDEX—are repeated as long as

MREINDEX is not equal to "Y" and not equal to "N." To the operator it will seem that the cursor refuses to leave the field until a correct answer is entered (just as when you use the "Y" PICTURE). In most cases, the reason for this behavior is self-evident, so if the program clearly indicates the possible choices (note the addition of the options (Y/N) to the prompt), an error message need not be displayed for every wrong entry.

This statement of the loop condition guarantees that when the program exits the DO WHILE loop, MREINDEX has one of the two permissible values. But there is a more elegant way of stating the condition that can be generalized for alternatives other than "yes" and "no" and for cases in which a program must choose one of four or five options:

```
do while .not. MREINDEX $ "YN"
```

This statement means "do the following while it is not true that MREINDEX is a substring of (is contained in) the character string 'YN'." Since the condition MREINDEX $ "YN" is true if MREINDEX is either "Y" or "N," the condition .NOT. MREINDEX $ "YN" will have the opposite value. Thus, the loop is executed as long as MREINDEX is neither "Y" nor "N". When you have many possibilities, this construction is a very concise and readable way to specify the condition:

```
do while .not. MOPTION $ "ABCDE"
```

This is exactly equivalent to

```
do while MOPTION <> "A" .and. MOPTION <> "B" .and. MOPTION <> "C" .and.
   MOPTION <> "D" .and. MOPTION <> "E"
```

Using the "$" construction rather than the equivalent set of "<>" comparisons makes it much more obvious that the condition refers to five possible values of the same variable rather than five separate, unrelated conditions linked with .AND.

Although it is ultimately impossible to ensure that the user will always make the correct decision about reindexing the file, there is one additional technique you can use to help determine whether reindexing is necessary: you can check whether the ZIP code index is present on the disk already. If not, the program should not ask the user's permission; it should rebuild the index automatically. The FILE function is used to test for the existence of the index file. The expression FILE("NWCZIP.NDX") has the value .T. if the file is present and .F. if it is not.

Figure 15-4 lists NWCLABL3.PRG, a new version of the label-printing program that incorporates all of these enhancements. First, a message is displayed describing the circumstances under which the index file should be rebuilt. If the ZIP code index is present on the disk, MREINDEX is initialized with the value .T., and the program asks the operator whether or not to reindex the Customer File by ZIP. If the index is not found, the question is never asked, so MREINDEX retains its initial value .T. If either the program or the user chooses to reindex the data base, a message informs the user of this decision and temporarily turns TALK ON to monitor the process. The order in which the program asks the questions is important: the file must be reindexed before the program tries to SEEK the starting ZIP code.

```
* NWCLABL3.PRG
* PROGRAM TO PRINT 1-UP MAILING LABELS FOR ALL OR SELECTED CUSTOMERS
*   ACCORDING TO USER-SPECIFIED SELECTION CRITERIA
*   THE CUSTOMER FILE IS REINDEXED BY ZIP IF NECESSARY
* WRITTEN BY:  M.LISKIN       4/25/86

use NWCUST

clear
text

                              *** CAUTION ***

          The Customer File must be reindexed by ZIP CODE if you have
          added new customers or changed any zip codes in the file
          since the last time the file was reindexed.
endtext

store .T. to MREINDEX

if file("NWCZIP.NDX")
   @  8,10 say "Do you need to reindex the Customer File by ZIP code?";
           get MREINDEX picture "Y"
   read
endif

if MREINDEX
   @ 10,10 say "Reindexing Customer File by ZIP -- Please do not interrupt"
   set talk on
   index on ZIP to NWCZIP
   goto top
   set talk off
```

Figure 15-4. A label-printing program that reindexes the file if necessary

```
else
   set index to NWCZIP
endif

store ZIP     to MZIPBEGIN
store "99999" to MZIPEND

do while .T.

   @ 15,10 say "Enter starting zip code:" get MZIPBEGIN picture "99999"
   @ 16,10 say "Enter ending   zip code:" get MZIPEND   picture "99999"
   read

   seek trim(MZIPBEGIN)

   if found()
      exit
   else
      @ 18,10 say "There is no customer with that zip code"
      @ 19,10 say "Press any key to reenter the zip code"
      wait ""
      @ 18,10
      @ 19,10
   endif

enddo

store space(25) to MEQUIPMENT
@ 18,10 say "Enter type of equipment for customers in this mailing"
@ 19,10 say "(or press <RETURN> to include ALL customers)"
@ 20,20 get MEQUIPMENT picture "@!"
read

if MEQUIPMENT <> " "
   set filter to trim(MEQUIPMENT) $ upper(EQUIPMENT)
   goto top
endif

label form NWCUST1 to print while ZIP <= MZIPEND

set filter to

return
```

Figure 15-4. A label-printing program that reindexes the file if necessary (*continued*)

USING COMPLEX SELECTION CRITERIA

The label-printing programs in these examples select customers by type of computer equipment. But the system outline presented in Chapter 1 also notes that customers must be selected for mailings by product category, last order date, and total order amount. The programs in Chapter 12 used examples of criteria like these to illustrate selections based on character, numeric, and date fields. However, the National Widgets system requires a way to combine these criteria for a single mailing. To make matters more complicated, you might want to select not only people whose total orders have exceeded a certain dollar amount, but also people whose total orders are less than a specified amount, to solicit their business move actively. And although you would probably mail more often to people who have placed recent orders, you might target an occasional mailing to customers who have *not* ordered in a long time, perhaps in a last attempt to reinstate them before dropping inactive accounts at the end of the year. These criteria are similar to the selection by type of equipment—and distinctly different from specifying the range of ZIP codes to be included—in that they are not based on an index key and therefore require a sequential search of the file by using a FOR clause or FILTER.

The selection by product category requires reading two data base files together—the Customer File and the Order History File—since no category information is maintained in the Customer File. The subject of accessing multiple files will be discussed in detail in Chapter 16. In this chapter, the equipment, last order date, and last order amount criteria will be combined into a program that selects customers by any combination of the following factors:

- A certain type of equipment
- Total invoices between a specified maximum and minimum value
- Last order date between two specified dates.

To implement this flexible set of selection criteria, the program will use a macro to specify the FILTER condition. This version of the label-printing program will store the user's selection criteria in a character string variable that is built up in stages, based on the answers to questions asked by the program. This variable, expanded as a macro, will provide the condition to be used with SET FILTER. Figure 15-5 lists the portion of the program that asks the user to specify the criteria and establishes the filter.

Like the starting and ending ZIP codes described earlier, the variables that contain the minimum and maximum overall invoice totals and the earliest and latest dates to be included are initialized with values chosen to make it easy for the user to include the entire file by leaving the initial

```
store space(25)        to MEQUIPMENT
store 0.00             to MINVMIN
store 9999999.99       to MINVMAX
store ctod("01/01/01") to MDATEMIN
store ctod("12/31/99") to MDATEMAX

clear
@  4,10 say "Enter type of equipment for customers in this mailing: "
@  6,10 say "(or press <RETURN> to include ALL types of equipment)"
@  5,20 get MEQUIPMENT picture "@!"

@  9,10 say "Enter range of overall total invoices to include:"
@ 10,10 say "Minimum" get MINVMIN picture "9999999.99"
@ 10,40 say "Maximum" get MINVMAX picture "9999999.99"

@ 13,10 say "Enter range of last invoice dates to include:"
@ 14,10 say "Earliest" get MDATEMIN
@ 14,40 say "Latest"   get MDATEMAX
read

store "TOTINV >= MINVMIN .and. TOTINV <= MINVMAX .and. " +;
      "LASTORDER >= MDATEMIN .and. LASTORDER <= MDATEMAX" to MCONDITION

if MEQUIPMENT <> " "
   store MCONDITION + " .and. trim(MEQUIPMENT) $ upper(EQUIPMENT)";
         to MCONDITION
endif

set filter to &MCONDITION
goto top
```

Figure 15-5. Using a macro to establish variable selection criteria

values unchanged. Combining these criteria with the equipment selection is a little more complicated. As in the earlier version of the program, the operator is instructed to leave MEQUIPMENT blank if no selection by equipment is desired. After the selection screen is filled in, the expression that forms the fixed portion of the selection criteria is stored in the variable MCONDITION. If the MEQUIPMENT variable was not left blank, the selection by equipment is *added* onto the existing value of the variable MCONDITION. Finally, the filter is established by using a macro to expand the value of MCONDITION. Thus,

```
set filter to &MCONDITION
```

is exactly the same as

```
set filter to TOTINV >= MINVMIN .and. TOTINV <= MINVMAX .and.;
              LASTORDER >= MDATEMIN .and. LASTORDER <= MDATEMAX .and.;
              trim(MEQUIPMENT) $ upper(EQUIPMENT)
```

In this example, most of the elements in the filter were constant. You might wonder why the program did not use a more straightforward IF test:

```
if MEQUIPMENT = " "
   set filter to TOTINV >= MINVMIN .and. TOTINV <= MINVMAX .and.;
                 LASTORDER >= MDATEMIN .and. LASTORDER <= MDATEMAX
else
   set filter to TOTINV >= MINVMIN .and. TOTINV <= MINVMAX .and.;
                 LASTORDER >= MDATEMIN .and. LASTORDER <= MDATEMAX .and.;
                 trim(MEQUIPMENT) $ upper(EQUIPMENT)
endif
```

The use of the variable MCONDITION to contain the expression that specifies the selection criteria affords much more flexibility than the IF test. This technique can easily be expanded to include more possibilities, many of which may be conditional, like the test for type of equipment. This technique will be used in all of the programs in this book that must select according to more than one non-index key field.

16

ACCESSING MULTIPLE FILES

This chapter introduces dBASE III PLUS programs that access information from more than one data base file. Like the programs in Chapter 15, these programs provide options that make the application more flexible for the users, as well as additional error checking and validation capabilities to help preserve the integrity of the data bases. These programs are a great improvement over the batch-type programs written in Part II because they more closely simulate the paper forms and, more important, the work flow of the manual system that the application replaces. These programs will be easier to use because they may be called from a menu and ask questions that require no knowledge of dBASE III PLUS command syntax. Furthermore, the underlying file structures and indexes are more deeply buried, so that understanding the cycle of processing will no longer require a detailed knowledge of how the files are designed.

ESTABLISHING THE RELATIONSHIPS BETWEEN THE FILES

In working at command level and in the simple programs written in Part II SET RELATION was used extensively to link two data bases through a common key field. SET RELATION will still be used in more complex programs. This command offers the advantage of clearly stating the relationship between two data bases early in the program, when the files are first opened. There are two serious limitations, however. First, you may SET only one RELATION from any given work area. Second, if there is more than one record in the second file (the one accessed through the RELATION) with an index key that matches the current record in the first file, SET RELATION positions the second data base to the first matching record, with no indication that there is more than one. This does not prohibit you from using SET RELATION to link the two files, as long as you understand that you cannot *automatically* access all of the matching records as a set.

The beauty of using SET RELATION at command level is that it allows you to link two files *with one command* so that subsequent commands like LIST or REPORT, which process many records sequentially from one data base, automatically position the second file to the matching records without any further instructions from the operator. Chapter 4 illustrated for a single record the equivalence of SET RELATION to using a SEEK command to find the matching record in the second file yourself. At command level the SEEK command sequence is not very useful. Because you must type a separate SEEK command to find the match for each record in a file, you cannot use this method with commands like LIST, LABEL, or REPORT, which operate on entire data bases. However, in dBASE III PLUS programs you would use global commands like LIST much less frequently than using DO WHILE loops to process records one at a time.

One-to-One Relationships

Either at command level or in a dBASE III PLUS program, SET RELATION is the most convenient way to establish a one-to-one relationship between two files. Figure 16-1 shows LISTORD1.PRG, a modified version of the LISTER1.PRG program written in Chapter 9 to illustrate the use of a DO WHILE loop that simulates the dBASE III PLUS LIST command. This program displays three fields from each of the records in the National Widgets Order File.

If you wanted to display the customer's full company name instead of the account number, you could use SET RELATION to link the Order File to the Customer File via the common ACCOUNT field. This is illustrated in the second version of the order listing program, LISTORD2.PRG, in Figure 16-2. Since you can SET only one RELATION at a time from any

```
* LISTORD1.PRG
* PROGRAM TO LIST SELECTED FIELDS FROM THE ORDER FILE
* WRITTEN BY:  M.LISKIN       7/18/85

set talk off
use NWORDER index NWOACCT

do while .not. eof()

   ? ACCOUNT, CATEGORY, PARTNUMBER
   skip

enddo          [ not end-of-file ]

return
```

Figure 16-1. A program to list selected fields from the Order File

```
* LISTORD2.PRG
* PROGRAM TO LIST SELECTED FIELDS FROM THE ORDER FILE
*   USING SET RELATION TO FIND THE MATCHING CUSTOMER INFORMATION
* WRITTEN BY:  M.LISKIN       7/18/85

select 1
use NWCUST  index NWCACCT

select 2
use NWORDER index NWOACCT
set relation to ACCOUNT into NWCUST

do while .not. eof()

   ? NWCUST->COMPANY, CATEGORY, PARTNUMBER
   skip

enddo          [ not end-of-file ]

return
```

Figure 16-2. A program to list selected fields from the Order and Customer files

given work area, you cannot use this method to also display the item description from the Inventory File. For each record in the Order File you must select the Inventory File and use SEEK to search the index for a match on the combination of the CATEGORY and PARTNUMBER fields in the Order File record. The program can then select the Order File again and display the required fields from all three files. This strategy is illustrated in the LISTORD3.PRG program in Figure 16-3. The decision to use SET RELATION for the link to the Customer File and SEEK to find the match in the Inventory File was arbitrary. You could do it the other way around, as in the LISTORD4.PRG program in Figure 16-4. Or you could use SEEK for both the customer and inventory information, as

```
* LISTORD3.PRG
* PROGRAM TO LIST SELECTED FIELDS FROM THE ORDER FILE
*   USING SET RELATION TO FIND THE MATCHING CUSTOMER INFORMATION
*   AND SEEK TO FIND THE MATCHING INVENTORY INFORMATION
* WRITTEN BY:  M.LISKIN        7/18/85

set talk off

select 1
use NWINVENT index NWICATPT

select 2
use NWCUST   index NWCACCT

select 3
use NWORDER  index NWOACCT
set relation to ACCOUNT into NWCUST

select NWORDER

do while .not. eof()

   select NWINVENT
   seek NWORDER->CATEGORY + NWORDER->PARTNUMBER

   select NWORDER
   ? NWCUST->COMPANY, CATEGORY, PARTNUMBER, NWINVENT->DESCRIP

   skip

enddo          [ not end-of-file ]

return
```

Figure 16-3. A program to list selected fields from the Order, Customer, and Inventory files

```
* LISTORD4.PRG
* PROGRAM TO LIST SELECTED FIELDS FROM THE ORDER FILE
*   USING SET RELATION TO FIND THE MATCHING INVENTORY INFORMATION
*   AND SEEK TO FIND THE MATCHING CUSTOMER INFORMATION
* WRITTEN BY:  M.LISKIN       7/18/85

set talk off

select 1
use NWINVENT index NWICATPT

select 2
use NWCUST   index NWCACCT

select 3
use NWORDER  index NWOACCT
set relation to CATEGORY + PARTNUMBER into NWINVENT

select NWORDER

do while .not. eof()

   select NWCUST
   seek NWORDER->ACCOUNT

   select NWORDER
   ? NWCUST->COMPANY, CATEGORY, PARTNUMBER, NWINVENT->DESCRIP

   skip

enddo          [ not end-of-file ]

return
```

Figure 16-4. A program to list selected fields from the Order, Customer, and Inventory files

shown in the final version of the order listing program, LISTORD5.PRG, in Figure 16-5.

These variations were presented to stress the complete equivalence between using SET RELATION to find a matching record and finding the same record with a SEEK command. In both methods the two files to be linked contain a common field, and the file in which you are searching for the match is indexed on this field. The programs in this book will use SET RELATION whenever a file must be linked to only one other data base. When two or more links must be established from a single work area, SEEK will usually be used instead, to emphasize the fact that the files are being treated consistently, so that you will not later wonder why SET

```
* LISTORD5.PRG
* PROGRAM TO LIST SELECTED FIELDS FROM THE ORDER FILE
*   USING SEEK TO FIND THE MATCHING CUSTOMER AND INVENTORY
INFORMATION
* WRITTEN BY:  M.LISKIN       7/18/85

set talk off

select 1
use NWINVENT index NWICATPT

select 2
use NWCUST   index NWCACCT

select 3
use NWORDER  index NWOACCT

select NWORDER

do while .not. eof()

   select NWCUST
   seek NWORDER->ACCOUNT

   select NWINVENT
   seek NWORDER->CATEGORY + NWORDER->PARTNUMBER

   select NWORDER
   ? NWCUST->COMPANY, CATEGORY, PARTNUMBER, NWINVENT->DESCRIP

   skip

enddo         [ not end-of-file ]

return
```

Figure 16-5. A program to list selected fields from the Order, Customer, and Inventory files

RELATION was chosen in one case rather than the other. In your own programs you may use any combination of the two methods that seems reasonable. The conventions you adopt should be included in the written notation and usage guidelines described in Chapter 10.

One-to-Many Relationships

Linking two files that have a one-to-many relationship is a little more complicated. As illustrated in the series of programs just presented, you may use either SET RELATION or SEEK to find one record in a file that matches the current record in another, but neither command will help you identify an entire group of matching records. Once you have found the first match, however, you can access the set with a condition in a WHILE clause. Recall that unlike a FOR clause, WHILE causes any sequential commands, like LIST or REPORT, to begin processing a data base with the current record and to continue only as long as the condition remains true. If you use a DO WHILE loop instead of a built-in command like LIST, the effect is the same.

Figure 16-6 illustrates a sequence of commands you can use at the dot prompt to demonstrate this technique. In this example, the National Widgets Customer and Order files are opened together and linked by the common ACCOUNT field with SET RELATION. A SEEK command is used to find a particular customer, ELLISMFG. (You might have used GOTO instead if you knew the record number.) With the Customer File positioned to the record for ELLISMFG, SET RELATION automatically positions the Order File to the first record for this customer. The condition in the LIST command means "while the ACCOUNT field in the current work area (the Order File) is the same as the ACCOUNT field in the record at which the Customer File is positioned." Since the Order File is indexed by ACCOUNT (as it must be for SET RELATION to work), all of a customer's order records are grouped together in indexed order, so when the first order for another customer is encountered and the condition in the WHILE clause is no longer true, you can be sure that all of

```
. SELECT 1
. USE NWORDER INDEX NWOACCT
. SELECT 2
. USE NWCUST INDEX NWCACCT
. SET RELATION TO ACCOUNT INTO NWORDER
. SEEK "ELLISMFG"
. DISPLAY
     14  ELLISMFG    Ellis Manufacturing              3091 Park Boulevard
                        Palo Alto             CA 94306 415 494-1421 Barbara
Goddard              IBM PC, Okidata 84                10/18/83    / /          89.90
     0.00      758.90       669.00          0.00 Memo
. SELECT NWORDER
. LIST CATEGORY, PARTNUMBER, QUANTITY, PRICE WHILE ACCOUNT = NWCUST->ACCOUNT
      4  FORMS  820-20      1    21.95     21.95
      5  DISK   101-65      1    48.00     48.00
      6  STOR   481-20      1    19.95     19.95
```

Figure 16-6. A one-to-many relationship between two files

ELLISMFG's orders have been displayed.

You might wonder why the condition in the LIST command was not stated more directly:

```
LIST CATEGORY, PARTNUMBER, QUANTITY, PRICE WHILE ACCOUNT = "ELLISMFG"
```

At the dot prompt you probably *would* use this command when you work with a specific customer. But within a dBASE III PLUS program in which the condition is used to control a DO WHILE loop, stating the condition more generally allows the same program statements to work for *any* customer record.

DISPLAYING INFORMATION FROM THREE FILES

The techniques discussed in the previous section may be combined to write a customer and order inquiry program that displays some information from the Customer File — the company name and address — with all of the customer's orders. For each order record, the program will display the full item description from the Inventory File, in addition to the category and part number. Here is a brief pseudocode outline of what the program must do:

```
open the Customer, Order, and Inventory files
do the following until the user chooses to exit:
    ask for a customer account number
    find the customer
    display the name and address fields
    find the matching order records
    for each order record find the matching inventory record
    display the selected fields from the Order and Inventory files
end of steps to do until the user chooses to exit
close the data bases
```

The first version of the program, NWCORD1.PRG, is listed in Figure 16-7, with a detailed pseudocode explanation in Figure 16-8. In this program SET RELATION is used for both links between data bases: the Customer File is linked to the Order History File through the ACCOUNT

```
* NWCORD1.PRG
* PROGRAM TO FIND A CUSTOMER AND ALL ORDERS
* WRITTEN BY:  M.LISKIN       04/25/86


select 1
use NWINVENT index NWICATPT

select 2
use NWORDHST index NWOHACCT
set relation to CATEGORY + PARTNUMBER into NWINVENT

select 3
use NWCUST   index NWCACCT
set relation to ACCOUNT into NWORDHST

do while .T.

   clear
   select NWCUST
   store "          " to MACCOUNT

   * FIND THE CUSTOMER
   do while .T.

      @  1, 0 say "Customer account number" get MACCOUNT picture "@!"
      @  1,40 say "(or press <RETURN> to exit)"
      read
      if MACCOUNT = " "
         return
      endif

      seek trim(MACCOUNT)

      if found()
         exit
      else
         @ 15,10 say "There is no customer with account number " + MACCOUNT
         @ 16,10 say "Press any key to reenter the account number"
         wait ""
         @ 15,10
         @ 16,10
      endif

   enddo                  [ customer not found yet ]

   * DISPLAY CUSTOMER INFORMATION
   @  3, 0 say COMPANY
   @  4, 0 say ADDRESS1
   @  5, 0 say ADDRESS2
   @  6, 0 say trim(CITY) + ", " + STATE + "  " + ZIP
   @  7, 0 say "(" + AREACODE + ") " + TELEPHONE
   @  3,56 say "Y-T-D INV: " + transform(YTDINV,"9,999,999.99")
   @  4,56 say "TOTAL INV: " + transform(TOTINV,"9,999,999.99")
   @  6,56 say "BALANCE:   " + transform(BALANCE,"9,999,999.99")

   * FIND AND DISPLAY MATCHING ORDER HISTORY RECORDS
   select NWORDHST
   if .not. found()
      @ 10,10 say "There are no orders for this customer"
   else
```

Figure 16-7. A customer and order inquiry program

```
      @  9, 0 say "CATEGORY   ITEM"
      @  9,48 say "QUANT     PRICE      DISC       TOTAL"
      @ 10, 0 say replicate("-",79)
      list off CATEGORY, " ", PARTNUMBER, "  ", NWINVENT->DESCRIP, "  ",;
               QUANTITY, PRICE, DISCOUNT, " ", INVAMOUNT;
               while ACCOUNT = NWCUST->ACCOUNT
   endif

   @ 22,10 say "You may press <SHIFT> <PRTSC> to print this screen"
   @ 23,10 say "Press any other key to search for another customer"
   wait ""

enddo                  [ main loop ]

close databases

return
```

Figure 16-7. A customer and order inquiry program (*continued*)

field so that the Order History File is always positioned automatically to the first of a customer's group of order records; and the Order History File is linked to the Inventory File through the combination of CATEGORY + PARTNUMBER to make the full item description (the DESCRIP field) available when an order record is displayed.

After opening the three data bases and establishing the relationships among them, the program sets up an "endless" loop with DO WHILE .T. to ask the operator for a customer account number and to display the customer's name, address, and order information. Within this loop another DO WHILE loop performs the steps described in the pseudocode outline as "ask for a customer account number" and "find the customer." This section of the program uses a method almost identical to that used in the label-printing programs in Chapter 15 to ask for and validate the starting ZIP code. The user is asked for a customer account number, and the entry is collected into a memory variable, MACCOUNT, initialized with ten blank spaces. A message on the screen reminds the operator how to exit the program by pressing RETURN to leave the account number blank. After the @ ... SAY ... GET command, the program checks to see if this variable is still blank; if so, a RETURN command exits the program.

If the user has typed in an account number, a SEEK command searches the index for the customer. MACCOUNT is TRIMmed so that the operator may type in part of the account number if all ten characters are not required to identify the customer uniquely or if the user has

```
open the inventory file with the category/partnumber index

open the order history file with the account number index
link this file to the inventory file by category + partnumber

open the customer file with the account number index
link this file to the order history file by account number

do the following until the user chooses to exit:

   clear the screen
   select the customer file
   initialize a memory variable, MACCOUNT, for the customer account number

   do the following until a valid customer account number is entered:

      ask for a customer account number

      if the account number is left blank
         exit the program
      endif

      search the index for the account number
      if the account number is found:
         exit from this loop
      otherwise
         display an error message
         wait until a key is pressed
         erase the error message
      endif

   end of steps to do until a valid customer account number is entered

   display the company name, address, and telephone number
   display the year-to-date invoices, total invoices, and balance

   select the order history file
   if there are no order records for the customer:
      display a message: "There are no orders for this customer"
   otherwise
      display column headings for the order listing
      list the order fields and inventory file description field
               while the account field matches the customer file account field
   endif

   display a message explaining how to print the screen
   wait until a key is pressed

end of steps to do until the user chooses to exit

close all open data bases

exit from the program
```

Figure 16-8. The customer and order inquiry program in pseudocode

forgotten the full account number. If the SEEK command finds the customer, the program EXITs the DO WHILE loop. If the SEEK fails to find a customer, an error message is displayed, and a WAIT command pauses the program. When the user acknowledges the message by pressing a key, the program erases the error message and returns to the top of the loop to ask for an account number again.

Once a customer record has been found, the company name and address fields and some of the dollar totals are displayed with @ ... SAY commands. Next the Order History File is selected. If there are no order records for the customer, SET RELATION positions the record pointer at the end-of-file. Just as if you had used SEEK and failed to find an order record, EOF( ) is .T. and FOUND( ) is .F. The program tests the value of the FOUND( ) function (you could also have used IF EOF( ) instead of IF .NOT. FOUND( )) and informs the operator if there are no orders. Otherwise, a set of column headings is displayed, and the same LIST command used at command level displays the desired fields from the Order History File and the DESCRIP field from the matching Inventory File record.

Extra spaces were included between some of the fields displayed by LIST (which normally places only one space between the items) to improve the appearance of the screen. (When you write your own programs of this type, you will find that achieving a pleasing screen layout and matching the column headings to the data generally require either a sketch on graph paper or varying amounts of trial and error.) After the orders have been displayed, a WAIT command pauses the program, and a message tells the operator how to search for another customer and how to use SHIFT-PRTSC to obtain a hard copy of the data on the screen. Figure 16-9 illustrates the display for ELLISMFG.

This version of the program works fine with small sample data files. But one remaining problem will surface when you run it with a full set of data. If there are too many order records to fit on one screen, the display will scroll without pause, pushing the customer name and address fields and possibly some of the order records off the top of the screen. In order to solve this problem, the convenient LIST command must be abandoned in favor of a DO WHILE loop that displays the order records one by one, counting lines as it goes. When the screen is full, the program must pause to allow the operator to read or print the screen and then display the next set of records. The completed program, NWCORD2.PRG, is shown in Figure 16-10; the pseudocode outline for the new section is shown in Figure 16-11. The DO WHILE loop is controlled by the same condition used in the LIST command to process only the records in which the

```
Customer account number [ELLISMFG  ]    (or press <RETURN> to exit)

Ellis Manufacturing                                     Y-T-D INV:       89.90
3091 Park Boulevard                                     TOTAL INV:      758.90

Palo Alto, CA  94306                                    BALANCE:          0.00
(415) 494-1421

CATEGORY  ITEM                                    QUANT  PRICE    DISC    TOTAL
-------------------------------------------------------------------------------
 FORMS    820-20   3-1/2 x 1" Labels, 1-up            1  21.95    0.00    21.95
 DISK     101-65   5-1/4" DSDD Soft Sector            1  48.00    0.00    48.00
 STOR     481-20   Locking Disk Storage Tray          1  19.95    0.00    19.95




          You may press <SHIFT> <PRTSC> to print this screen
          Press any other key to search for another customer
```

Figure 16-9. Using the customer and order inquiry program

account number matches the Customer File record:

```
do while ACCOUNT = NWCUST->ACCOUNT
```

The program displays orders in groups of ten, using a line counter variable called MLINE that is initialized with a value of 1 before the beginning of the loop and incremented each time an order record is displayed. The value of MLINE is tested at the top of the DO WHILE loop. If MLINE is greater than 10, a message is displayed for the operator and a WAIT command pauses the display. When a key is pressed, the program clears the bottom half of the screen and resets the value of MLINE to 1 before displaying the next order.

A few of the details should be noted. The @ 11,0 CLEAR command, which erases the bottom half of the screen before the eleventh order is displayed, leaves the cursor positioned at line 11, column 0. Since the ? command displays data on the *next* available line, the data from the

```
* NWCORD2.PRG
* PROGRAM TO FIND A CUSTOMER AND ALL ORDERS
* WRITTEN BY:  M.LISKIN       04/25/86


select 1
use NWINVENT index NWICATPT

select 2
use NWORDHST index NWOHACCT
set relation to CATEGORY + PARTNUMBER into NWINVENT

select 3
use NWCUST   index NWCACCT
set relation to ACCOUNT into NWORDHST

do while .T.

   clear
   select NWCUST
   store "          " to MACCOUNT

   * FIND THE CUSTOMER
   do while .T.

      @  1, 0 say "Customer account number" get MACCOUNT picture "@!"
      @  1,40 say "(or press <RETURN> to exit)"
      read
      if MACCOUNT = " "
         return
      endif

      seek trim(MACCOUNT)

      if found()
         exit
      else
         @ 15,10 say "There is no customer with account number " + MACCOUNT
         @ 16,10 say "Press any key to reenter the account number"
         wait ""
         @ 15,10
         @ 16,10
      endif

   enddo                   [ customer not found yet ]

   * DISPLAY CUSTOMER INFORMATION
   @  3, 0 say COMPANY
   @  4, 0 say ADDRESS1
   @  5, 0 say ADDRESS2
   @  6, 0 say trim(CITY) + ", " + STATE + "  " + ZIP
   @  7, 0 say "(" + AREACODE + ") " + TELEPHONE
   @  3,56 say "Y-T-D INV: " + transform(YTDINV,"9,999,999.99")
   @  4,56 say "TOTAL INV: " + transform(TOTINV,"9,999,999.99")
   @  6,56 say "BALANCE:   " + transform(BALANCE,"9,999,999.99")


   * FIND AND DISPLAY MATCHING ORDER RECORDS
   select NWORDHST
   if .not. found()
      @ 10,10 say "There are no orders for this customer"
```

Figure 16-10. The revised customer and order inquiry program

```
else
   @  9, 0 say "CATEGORY  ITEM"
   @  9,48 say "QUANT    PRICE     DISC      TOTAL"
   @ 10, 0 say replicate("-",79)

   store 1 to MLINE
   do while ACCOUNT = NWCUST->ACCOUNT

      * PAUSE AND CLEAR SCREEN AFTER EACH 10 ORDERS
      if MLINE > 10
         @ 22,10 say "You may press <SHIFT> <PRTSC> to print this screen"
         @ 23,10 say "Press any other key to continue displaying orders"
         wait ""
         @ 11, 0 clear
         @ 10,79
         store 1 to MLINE
      endif

      ? CATEGORY, "  ", PARTNUMBER, "  ", NWINVENT->DESCRIP, "  ",;
        QUANTITY, PRICE, DISCOUNT, " ", INVAMOUNT
      skip
      store MLINE + 1 to MLINE

   enddo                    [ account matches customer account ]

endif                   [ customer found ]

@ 22,10 say "You may press <SHIFT> <PRTSC> to print this screen"
@ 23,10 say "Press any other key to search for another customer"
wait ""

enddo                [ main loop ]

close databases

return
```

Figure 16-10. The revised customer and order inquiry program (*continued*)

eleventh order record would be placed on line 12, not line 11, as in the first screen of orders. To resolve this inconsistency, the cursor is positioned on line 10 (to the right of any displayed text so as not to disrupt the screen display) with @ 10,79, before the next ? command presents the data from the next order record.

Notice also that in this program, the line of dashes displayed with @ 10,0 SAY REPLICATE("-",79) is only 79 characters long. If you had used 80 dashes, the cursor would have been positioned in the first column of line 11 (column 0) after this @ ... SAY command rather than in the last column (column 79) of line 10. The ? command that displays the first order record would therefore have placed this record on line 12. As with the second screenful of orders, you could correct this with an @ 10,79

```
initialize the line counter variable, MLINE, with a value of 1

do the following while the account field matches the customer file account:

   if ten orders have been displayed
      display a message for the operator
      wait until a key is pressed
      clear the bottom half of the screen
      position the cursor on line 10
      reset the line counter to 1
   endif

   display the order fields and description from the inventory file record

   skip to the next record in the file
   increment the line counter

end of steps to do while the account field matches the customer file account
```

Figure 16-11. The line-counting routine in pseudocode

command immediately following the command that draws the dashed line. Or, in both cases, you could have allowed the display to begin on line 12. The purpose of this discussion is simply to point out a few of the myriad small details that you should be aware of in order to ensure that your programs present a consistent and pleasing display for the users.

It might also seem strange to check the value of MLINE *before* displaying each line of data. The first time through the DO WHILE loop, MLINE is not greater than 10, so this variable need not be checked before processing the first record. Applying some of the testing principles described in Chapter 14 reveals the reason for this decision. In order to determine whether the NWCORD2.PRG program functions correctly, these possibilities must be tested:

- A nonexistent customer
- A customer who has no orders
- A customer who has fewer than ten orders
- A customer who has more than ten orders
- A customer who has exactly ten orders
- The last customer in the Order File.

The last two cases are the easiest to overlook and the ones most likely to cause problems. Consider how the program would perform for a customer with exactly ten orders if the test for MLINE were placed *after* the display of each order record. After the tenth order MLINE would be incremented, and the SKIP command would reposition the data base to the next record—a record for another customer. Because the value of MLINE would be 11 at this point, the message "Press any other key to continue displaying orders" would be displayed. Yet when the user pressed a key and the program returned to the top of the DO WHILE loop, the condition in the DO WHILE statement would no longer be true. The program would therefore exit the loop and display the final message "Press any other key to search for another customer," leaving the operator wondering why more order records were promised and not delivered. Moving the test to the top of the loop ensures that the program tests to see if the pause is necessary only after it has SKIPped to the next record and determined that there is another order to display.

You should also test the behavior of a program at the end-of-file, although in this case, you will find no problems. When the SKIP command positions the data base to the "blank" record beyond the end-of-file, ACCOUNT is no longer equal to NWCUST—>ACCOUNT, so the program properly exits from the DO WHILE loop.

SELECTIONS BASED ON DATA IN TWO FILES

As pointed out earlier in this chapter, linking two files with SET RELATION enables you to draw upon fields from both files in commands that act on an entire data base, such as LIST, LABEL, or REPORT. What may not be obvious is that the RELATION need not be based only on fields present in both files—you may in fact use any legitimate dBASE III PLUS expression. This flexibility can be used to good advantage to add the selection by product category to the National Widgets label-printing program.

A typical product category selection might be expressed in English this way: "Print labels for all customers who have ordered products in the DISK category." To find these customers, the program must read through the Customer File, and for each record, search the Order History File for records with the matching customer account number and the specified category (in this case, DISK). Linking the files by account number would be simple—this field is common to both files, and there is already an account number index for each—but you cannot SET RELATION based on ACCOUNT + CATEGORY, because there is no CATEGORY field in the Customer File. However, the program must ask the user which category to include in the mailing, and store this entry in a memory variable; the SET RELATION command can thus link the two files based on the combination of this memory variable and the customer account number.

To support this relationship, the Order History File will be indexed on the combination of CATEGORY + ACCOUNT. With the category stored in a memory variable called MCATEGORY, you could establish the linkage as follows:

```
use NWCUST
set relation to MCATEGORY + ACCOUNT into NWORDHST
```

With this RELATION in effect, dBASE III PLUS automatically positions the Order History File to the first record in which the contents of the CATEGORY field matches MCATEGORY and in which the ACCOUNT field matches the ACCOUNT field in the current Customer File record. Note that SET RELATION does not give you any clues as to *how many* matching order records there may be. In some contexts, this restriction limits the usefulness of SET RELATION in dBASE III PLUS programs, but in this case, it is irrelevant how many times a customer has ordered DISK products: a label should be printed as long as there is at least one order. If there is no matching order record, the Order History File will be positioned at the "blank" record past the end-of-file, and NWORDHST—>ACCOUNT will be blank. You could thus print labels for all customers who have ordered products in the "DISK" category with

```
label form NWCUST1 to print for NWORDHST->ACCOUNT <> " "
```

This technique is incorporated into the label-printing program, NWCLABL5.PRG, listed in Figure 16-12. The program begins by opening both data bases and displaying a message that informs the user under what circumstances it is necessary to rebuild each of the indexes. As in NWCLABL3.PRG, the program checks to see whether each of the index files exists; if so, the user is asked whether or not to reindex, and the answers are stored in two logical memory variables, MREINDEXC and MREINDXO. If either index is missing, it is automatically rebuilt without asking the user's permission.

```
* NWCLABL5.PRG
* PROGRAM TO PRINT 1-UP MAILING LABELS FOR ALL OR SELECTED CUSTOMERS
*   ACCORDING TO USER-SPECIFIED SELECTION CRITERIA
*   INCLUDING PRODUCT CATEGORY READ FROM ORDER HISTORY FILE
*   THE CUSTOMER FILE IS REINDEXED BY ZIP IF NECESSARY
* WRITTEN BY:  M.LISKIN       4/25/86

select 1
use NWCUST

select 2
use NWORDHST

clear
text
                              *** CAUTION ***

          The Customer File must be reindexed by ZIP CODE if you have
          added new customers or changed any zip codes in the file
          since the last time the file was reindexed.

          The Order History File must be reindexed by CATEGORY if you
          have added new records or changed any category codes in the
          file since the last time the file was reindexed.
endtext

* ASK WHETHER TO REBUILD REQUIRED INDEXES IF THEY ARE ALREADY PRESENT
* IF NOT PRESENT, REBUILD THEM WITHOUT ASKING

store .T. to MREINDEXC, MREINDEXO

if file("NWCZIP.NDX")
   @ 13,10 say "Do you need to reindex the Customer File by ZIP code?";
           get MREINDEXC picture "Y"
   read
endif

if file("NWOHCAT.NDX")
   @ 15,10 say "Do you need to reindex the Order History File by CATEGORY?";
           get MREINDEXO picture "Y"
   read
endif

* REINDEX CUSTOMER FILE IF NECESSARY OR OPEN EXISTING INDEX IF NOT
select NWCUST
if MREINDEXC
   @ 18,10 say "Reindexing Customer File by ZIP -- Please do not interrupt"
   set talk on
   index on ZIP to NWCZIP
   goto top
   set talk off
else
   set index to NWCZIP
endif

select NWORDHST
if MREINDEXO
   @ 21, 5 say;
     "Reindexing Order History File by CATEGORY -- Please do not interrupt"
```

Figure 16-12. A label-printing program that selects by product category

```
      set talk on
      index on CATEGORY + ACCOUNT to NWOHCAT
      goto top
      set talk off
   else
      set index to NWOHCAT
   endif

   * ENTER RANGE OF ZIP CODES, VALIDATE STARTING ZIP

   select NWCUST
   store ZIP       to MZIPBEGIN
   store "99999"   to MZIPEND
   clear

   do while .T.

      @  1,10 say "Enter starting zip code:" get MZIPBEGIN picture "99999"
      @  2,10 say "Enter ending   zip code:" get MZIPEND   picture "99999"
      read

      seek trim(MZIPBEGIN)

      if found()
         exit
      else
         @ 22,10 say "There is no customer with that zip code"
         @ 23,10 say "Press any key to reenter the zip code"
         wait ""
         @ 22,10
         @ 23,10
      endif

   enddo

   * ENTER CUSTOMER SELECTION CRITERIA
   store space(25)         to MEQUIPMENT
   store "      "          to MCATEGORY
   store 0.00              to MINVMIN
   store 9999999.99        to MINVMAX
   store ctod("01/01/01")  to MDATEMIN
   store ctod("12/31/99")  to MDATEMAX

   clear
   @  4,10 say "Enter type of equipment for customers in this mailing:"
   @  5,20 get MEQUIPMENT picture "@!"
   @  6,10 say "(or press <RETURN> to include ALL equipment types)"
   @  9,10 say "Enter range of overall total invoices to include:"
   @ 10,10 say "Minimum" get MINVMIN picture "9999999.99"
   @ 10,40 say "Maximum" get MINVMAX picture "9999999.99"

   @ 13,10 say "Enter range of last invoice dates to include:"
   @ 14,10 say "Earliest" get MDATEMIN
   @ 14,40 say "Latest"   get MDATEMAX
   read

   * ENTER PRODUCT CATEGORY, VALIDATE IN ORDER HISTORY FILE
   select NWORDHST
```

Figure 16-12. A label-printing program that selects by product category *(continued)*

```
   do while .T.
   @ 16,10 say "Enter product CATEGORY:" get MCATEGORY picture "@!"
   @ 17,10 say "(or press <RETURN> to include ALL categories)"
   read
   if MCATEGORY = " "
      exit
   endif

   seek MCATEGORY

   if found()
      exit
   else
      @ 22,10 say "There are no orders with that category"
      @ 23,10 say "Press any key to reenter the zip code"
      wait ""
      @ 22,10
      @ 23,10
   endif
enddo

* CONSTRUCT FILTER CONDITION AND PRINT LABELS
select NWCUST

store "TOTINV >= MINVMIN .and. TOTINV <=MINVMAX .and. " +;
      "LASTORDER >= MDATEMIN .and. LASTORDER <=MDATEMAX" to MCONDITION

if MEQUIPMENT <> " "
   store MCONDITION + " .and. trim(MEQUIPMENT) $ upper(EQUIPMENT)";
         to MCONDITION
endif

if MCATEGORY <> " "
   set relation to MCATEGORY + ACCOUNT into NWORDHST
   store MCONDITION + " .and. NWORDHST->ACCOUNT <> ' '" to MCONDITION
endif

set filter to &MCONDITION
goto top

label form NWCUST1 to print while ZIP <= MZIPEND

set filter to

return
```

Figure 16-12. A label-printing program that selects by product category (*continued*)

Next, the beginning and ending ZIP codes are collected, with the beginning ZIP code validated just as in NWCLABL3.PRG. The user's selections for the type of equipment, the minimum and maximum total invoice amount, and the earliest and latest value for the most recent order date are collected as illustrated in Figure 15-5. Next, the Order History File is SELECTed and the user's choice of product category entered and validated using the same program structure introduced for the starting

ZIP code. This validation, which ensures that the user does not enter a nonexistent product category (or one that is present in the Inventory File but has never been ordered), is the reason that the Order History File was indexed by CATEGORY + ACCOUNT rather than ACCOUNT + CATEGORY, which would also have served to link the two data bases in the desired manner. If a category is filled in, the phrase " .and. NWORDHST—> ACCOUNT <>' ' " is added to the prior value of the variable, MCONDITION, that stores the selection criteria.

TRANSFERRING DATA BETWEEN FILES

Using the same types of linkages illustrated in the NWCORD2.PRG and NWCLABL5.PRG programs, you can not only read and display but also transfer data between files. Recall the sequence of commands used at the dot prompt or in simple batch-type programs to post invoice data to the Customer File:

```
SELECT 1
USE NWTXN
COPY TO NWTEMP FOR .NOT. INVPOSTED
USE NWTEMP
SELECT 2
USE NWCUST INDEX NWCACCT
UPDATE ON ACCOUNT FROM NWTEMP RANDOM REPLACE LASTORDER WITH NWTEMP->INVDATE,
  YTDINV WITH YTDINV + NWTEMP->INVAMOUNT, TOTINV WITH TOTINV +
  NWTEMP->INVAMOUNT, BALANCE WITH BALANCE + NWTEMP->INVAMOUNT
USE NWTXN
REPLACE ALL INVPOSTED WITH .T.
```

Payments were posted by using a similar set of commands:

```
USE NWTXN
COPY TO NWTEMP FOR .NOT. PMTPOSTED
SELECT 2
USE NWTEMP
SELECT 1
USE NWCUST INDEX NWCACCT
UPDATE ON ACCOUNT FROM NWTEMP RANDOM REPLACE YTDPMT WITH YTDPMT +
  NWTEMP->PMTAMOUNT, TOTPMT WITH TOTPMT + NWTEMP->PMTAMOUNT,
  BALANCE WITH BALANCE + NWTEMP->PMTAMOUNT
USE NWTXN
REPLACE ALL PMTPOSTED WITH .T.
```

In order to post both invoices and payments, six complete passes through the Transaction File are required: one to copy the unposted invoice records to a temporary file, one to perform the UPDATE operation, one to reset the INVPOSTED field to .T., and the analogous three steps for the payment data. This procedure can be replaced by a program that reads through the Transaction File once and updates the appropriate fields in the matching customer record. Once the data has been posted, the Transaction File INVPOSTED and PMTPOSTED fields can be reset to T. so that the record is not posted again the next time the program is run. Here is a brief pseudocode outline of what the program must do:

```
open the customer and transaction files
for each record in the transaction file:
    if the invoice data has not been posted,
        update the Customer File invoice fields
        reset the invoice "posted" status field to .T.
    if the payment data is present and has not been posted,
        update the Customer File payment fields
        reset the payment "posted" status field to .T.
end of steps to do for each record in the transaction file
```

The transaction posting program, NWTPOST.PRG, is listed in Figure 16-13, and the detailed pseudocode outline is shown in Figure 16-14. The program opens the Customer File with the account number index so that this file may be linked to the Transaction File with SET RELATION. The Transaction File is opened without an index, to speed up processing. This program uses the standard method introduced in the NWCSTAT2.PRG program to display a status message that monitors the number of Transaction File records processed.

After the program opens the files, a DO WHILE loop processes the Transaction File records in sequence. The program must skip over any transaction records in which both the invoice and payment data have already been posted. The pseudocode outline shows that the program must test each record individually to determine whether the invoice data or the payment data should be posted, so no special provisions are required to skip over completely posted transactions. However, this is a relatively inefficient way to skip these transactions, since dBASE III PLUS must process both of the IF tests and the unnecessary REPLACE command for these records.

One way to solve this problem is to use a SET FILTER command

```
* NWTPOST.PRG
* PROGRAM TO POST TRANSACTION DATA (INVOICES AND PAYMENTS) TO CUSTOMER FILE
* WRITTEN BY:  M.LISKIN       4/25/86


select 1
use NWCUST index NWCACCT

select 2
use NWTXN
set relation to ACCOUNT into NWCUST

clear
@ 10,10 say "Posting Invoices and Payments -- Please Do Not Interrupt"
@ 12,10 say "Working on Record            of " + str(reccount(),5)

do while .not. eof()

   @ 12,27 say recno()

   * SKIP TRANSACTION IF BOTH INVOICE AND PAYMENT DATA HAVE BEEN POSTED
   if INVPOSTED .and. PMTPOSTED
      skip
      loop
   endif

   * IF THERE IS NO MATCHING CUSTOMER RECORD, PRINT THE TRANSACTION
   select NWCUST

   if .not. found()
      set print on
      set console off
      select NWTXN
      display
      set print off
      set console on
      skip
      loop
   endif

   select NWTXN

   * IF INVOICE DATA HAS NOT BEEB POSTED
   * POST INVOICE DATA, MARK INVOICE AS POSTED
   if .not. INVPOSTED
      replace NWCUST->YTDINV with NWCUST->YTDINV + NWTXN->INVAMOUNT,;
              NWCUST->TOTINV with NWCUST->TOTINV + NWTXN->INVAMOUNT,;
              NWCUST->BALANCE with NWCUST->BALANCE + NWTXN->INVAMOUNT
      replace NWCUST->LASTORDER with INVDATE,INVPOSTED with .T.
   endif

   * IF PAYMENT DATA IS PRESENT AND NOT POSTED,
   * POST PAYMENT DATA, MARK PAYMENT AS POSTED
   if PMTAMOUNT > 0 .and. .not. PMTPOSTED
      replace NWCUST->YTDPMT with NWCUST->YTDPMT + NWTXN->PMTAMOUNT,;
              NWCUST->TOTPMT with NWCUST->TOTPMT + NWTXN->PMTAMOUNT,;
              NWCUST->BALANCE with NWCUST->BALANCE - NWTXN->INVAMOUNT
      replace PMTPOSTED with .T.
   endif
```

Figure 16-13. The transaction posting program

```
   skip
enddo
return
```

Figure 16-13. The transaction posting program (*continued*)

(placed before the beginning of the DO WHILE loop) to exclude the completely posted transactions:

```
set filter to .not. INVPOSTED .or. .not. PMTPOSTED
```

This FILTER causes dBASE III PLUS to process only records in which either .NOT. INVPOSTED or .NOT. PMTPOSTED is .T.; that is, at least one of these fields has the value .F. With a FILTER in effect, dBASE III PLUS behaves as if the excluded records do not exist, so the record numbers for these entries will not appear in the status display. Nevertheless, each record must be tested against the condition in the SET FILTER command, so if the Transaction File contains many completely posted records, there will be long pauses between record numbers, partially defeating the purpose of the status display. Since the early records are most likely to have been posted already, it may take quite a while for the very first record number to appear on the screen, which can be quite disconcerting.

There is a method for displaying a continuous status message while still processing the Transaction File efficiently. The program can display the record number and then, if the transaction has been completely posted, immediately skip to the next record and bypass the remaining steps within the DO WHILE loop:

```
if INVPOSTED .and. PMTPOSTED
   skip
   loop
endif
```

For each record that *is* processed, the program selects the Customer File, which is automatically positioned to the matching customer record by the SET RELATION command. Although the Transaction File should

```
open the customer file with the account number index

open the transaction file
link this file to the customer file by account number

clear the screen
display a status message

for each record in the transaction file

   display the record number

   if the invoice has been posted and the payment has been posted
      skip the record
      go back to the top of the loop
   endif

   select the customer file

   if there is no customer that matches the transaction record
      turn on the printer
      turn off the console
      select the transaction file
      print the current record
      turn off the printer
      turn on the console
      skip to the next record
      go back to the top of the loop
   endif

   select the transaction file

   if the invoice data has not been posted
      replace the customer last order date with the invoice date,
      add the invoice amount into the year-to-date invoice total,
          overall invoice total, and balance fields
      reset the invoice "posted" status field to "true"
   endif

   if payment data exists and has not been posted
      add the payment amount into the year-to-date payment total,
          and overall payment total
      subtract the payment amount from the balance fields
      reset the payment "posted" status field to "true"
   endif

   skip to the next record

end of steps to do for each record in the transaction file

exit from the program
```

Figure 16-14. The transaction posting program in pseudocode

never contain an entry with no matching customer record, allowing such a contingency to go undetected is such a serious problem that the posting program and any other program like it must contend with this possibility. NWTPOST.PRG therefore tests to see if a customer record was found. If not, the printer is turned on, the console turned off, the Transaction File SELECTed, and the offending record printed in its entirety with a DISPLAY command. The printer is then turned off and the console turned back on, and the program SKIPs to the next record and returns to the top of the loop. This technique results in a relatively crude listing, but it does identify the problem records; if necessary, this routine could later be replaced by the commands to produce a more aesthetically pleasing report.

If the INVPOSTED field in the Transaction File is *not* .T., the invoice fields are posted to the customer record exactly as was done with the UPDATE command, and the INVPOSTED field is reset to .T. If payment data is actually present (the PMTAMOUNT field is greater than 0) and has not been posted, the payment fields in the Customer File are updated and the PMTPOSTED field is reset to .T. Notice that you may not only display but also REPLACE fields from any open file, as long as the file alias is included in all references to fields not in the currently selected work area. If you prefer, you could SELECT each file in turn before performing the REPLACE commands. Using this technique, the payment posting sequence would look like this:

```
if PMTAMOUNT > Ø .and. .not. PMTPOSTED
   select NWCUST
   replace YTDPMT with YTDPMT + NWTXN->PMTAMOUNT,;
           TOTPMT with TOTPMT + NWTXN->PMTAMOUNT,;
           BALANCE with BALANCE - NWTXN->INVAMOUNT
   select NWTXN
   replace PMTPOSTED with .T.
endif
```

This method has the advantage of keeping the REPLACE commands shorter and more concise, so you can fit more REPLACEments into a single command, but it has the potential to enter incorrect data into your files if you forget a SELECT command. This oversight simply generates a syntax error—the cause of which should be easy to find and fix—if the named field is not present in the currently selected file. If, however, the field name duplicates one in the selected work area, the REPLACE command will be performed and the program will appear to complete normally—making this type of error very difficult to notice and track down.

A PROGRAM TO ENTER ORDERS AND CREATE INVOICE TRANSACTIONS

As indicated in Chapter 13, the way that order records were entered and invoice transactions generated in the command level simulation of the National Widgets system left much to be desired, although the procedures developed did make it possible to verify that the file structures would adequately accommodate the required data. The last and longest program in this chapter is an order entry program designed to improve the way the Order and Transaction files are updated. This program will perform extensive data validation, which is impossible at command level, and it requires very little knowledge of dBASE III PLUS on the part of the operator. Unlike the command level procedures, it will also closely simulate the way in which orders are processed manually in the National Widgets office. Chapter 18 will present the companion program that prints the invoices. Here is an informal pseudocode outline of what the order entry program must do:

```
open the Inventory, Order, Transaction, and Customer files
do the following until the user chooses to exit:
    enter the customer account number
    look up the customer in the Customer File
    display the address, balance, and equipment fields
    ask the operator to confirm that this is the right customer
    create an invoice transaction record with the next available invoice
        number
    do the following until the user chooses to stop:
        create an order record
        enter the item category and part number
        look up the item in the Inventory File
        display the description and price
        enter the discount rate
        calculate the subtotal, discount, and net invoice amount
        add the totals into the corresponding fields in the transaction
            record
    end of order line-item entry steps
```

enter the shipping charge, tax rate, and prepayment data (if any)
calculate the tax and net invoice amount
increment the next available invoice number

end of steps to do until user chooses to exit

save the memory variable containing the next available invoice number

Filling in the details of this outline will draw on many of the components developed earlier in this chapter and in Chapter 15. For example, the first three lines of pseudocode within the main loop—"enter the customer account number," "look up the customer in the customer file," and "display the address, balance, and equipment fields"—can be accomplished with the same section of code used in the NWCORD2.PRG program to display the Customer File data. The complete program, NWORDENT.PRG, is listed in Figure 16-15; the detailed pseudocode outline is shown in Figure 16-16.

The order entry program opens all four of the main data base files in the National Widgets system. Although it would appear that the program could use SET RELATION to link the Transaction File to the Customer File by the common ACCOUNT field and to link the Order File to the Inventory File by the combination of CATEGORY + PARTNUMBER, this would necessitate adding records to the files in a way that reduces both the flexibility and security of the system. Instead, SEEK commands are used to find the matching records in the related data bases.

After the files are opened, the program sets up an "endless" loop with DO WHILE .T. to enter invoices until the user chooses to exit. To prohibit entering an order for a customer who is not already in the Customer File, the program begins by asking the operator to enter a customer account number and by validating the entry with a SEEK command, exactly as in the NWCORD2.PRG program. As before, the operator may exit from the program by leaving the account number blank.

Once the operator enters a valid customer account number, the program displays the company name, address, and telephone number with the customer's year-to-date and total invoices, type of equipment, and balance. This is the first of several points in the program when the operator must be given a way to exit without entering a record into one of the data bases. In this case, the program asks for confirmation before adding an invoice record to the Transaction File.

The operator might want to cancel the entry at this point because the name and address displayed indicated that the wrong customer account

```
* NWORDENT.PRG
* ORDER ENTRY PROGRAM
* WRITTEN BY:  M.LISKIN        04/25/86

select 1
use NWINVENT index NWICATPT

select 2
use NWORDER  index NWOACCT, NWOINVC

select 3
use NWTXN    index NWTACCT, NWTINVC

select 4
use NWCUST   index NWCACCT

do while .T.

   clear
   select NWCUST
   store "           " to MACCOUNT

   * FIND THE CUSTOMER AND ENTER A TRANSACTION RECORD
   do while .T.

      @  1, 0 say "Customer account number" get MACCOUNT picture "@!"
      @  1,40 say "(or press <RETURN> to exit)"
      read
      if MACCOUNT = " "
         save all like MP* to NWMEMORY
         return
      endif

      seek trim(MACCOUNT)

      if found()
         exit
      else
         @ 15,10 say "There is no customer with account number " + MACCOUNT
         @ 16,10 say "Press any key to reenter the account number"
         wait ""
         @ 15,10
         @ 16,10
      endif

   enddo             [ enter customer ]

   * DISPLAY CUSTOMER INFORMATION
   @  3, 0 say COMPANY + "      (" + AREACODE + ") " + TELEPHONE
   @  4, 0 say ADDRESS1
   @  5, 0 say ADDRESS2
   @  6, 0 say trim(CITY) + ", " + STATE + "  " + ZIP
   @  7, 0 say "EQUIPMENT: " + EQUIPMENT
   @  3,56 say "Y-T-D INV: " + transform(YTDINV,"9,999,999.99")
   @  4,56 say "TOTAL INV: " + transform(TOTINV,"9,999,999.99")
   @  6,56 say "BALANCE:   " + transform(BALANCE,"9,999,999.99")
   @  8, 0 say replicate("-",79)
```

Figure 16-15. The order entry program

```
* CONFIRM THE CUSTOMER
store .T. to MCONTINUE
@ 15,10 say "Enter an invoice for this customer? (Y/N)" get MCONTINUE;
            picture "Y"
read
@ 15, 0
if .not. MCONTINUE
   loop
endif

* ADD A TRANSACTION RECORD
select NWTXN
append blank
replace ACCOUNT with NWCUST->ACCOUNT, INVDATE with date(),;
        INVOICE with str(MPINVOICE,5), TAXRATE with NWCUST->TAXRATE
@  9, 0 say "INVOICE DATE   " get INVDATE
@  9,45 say "INVOICE NUMBER"  get INVOICE picture "99999"
read

* ENTER ORDER LINE ITEMS
do while .T.

   select NWORDER
   @ 10, 0 clear
   store "          " to MCATEGORY, MPARTNUM
   store 0          to MQUANTITY
   @ 11, 0 say "CATEGORY"    get MCATEGORY picture "@!"
   @ 11,20 say "PART NUMBER" get MPARTNUM  picture "999-99"
   read
   if MCATEGORY = " "
      exit
   endif

   * VALIDATE THE ITEM IN INVENTORY
   select NWINVENT
   seek MCATEGORY + MPARTNUM
   if found()
      @ 11,45 say DESCRIP
      store PRICE to MPRICE
   else
      @ 15,10 say "There is no such inventory item"
      @ 16,10 say "Press any key to reenter the CATEGORY and PART NUMBER"
      wait ""
      @ 15,10
      @ 16,10
      loop
   endif

   * CANCEL THE LINE ITEM IF QUANTITY IS 0
   select NWORDER
   @ 13, 0 say "QUANTITY ORDERED   " get MQUANTITY picture "9999"
   @ 14, 0 say "UNIT PRICE         " get MPRICE picture "9999.99"
   read
   if MQUANTITY = 0
      @ 17,10 say "This item has been cancelled"
      @ 18,10 say "Press any key to enter another item"
      wait ""
      @ 17,10
```

Figure 16-15. The order entry program (*continued*)

```
         @ 18,10
         loop
      endif

      * ADD AN ORDER LINE ITEM RECORD
      append blank
      replace ACCOUNT with NWCUST->ACCOUNT, INVOICE with NWTXN->INVOICE,;
              CATEGORY with NWINVENT->CATEGORY, PARTNUMBER with;
              NWINVENT->PARTNUMBER, EQUIPMENT with NWINVENT->EQUIPMENT
      replace QUANTITY with MQUANTITY, PRICE with MPRICE, SUBTOTAL with;
              QUANTITY * PRICE

      @ 15, 0 say "SUBTOTAL          $" + transform(SUBTOTAL,"9,999.99")
      @ 17, 0 say "DISCOUNT RATE      " get DISCRATE
      read
      replace DISCOUNT with SUBTOTAL * DISCRATE / 100, INVAMOUNT with;
              SUBTOTAL - DISCOUNT
      @ 18, 0 say "DISCOUNT          " + transform(DISCOUNT,"9,999.99")
      @ 20, 0 say "NET INVOICE AMT $" + transform(INVAMOUNT,"9,999.99")

      * UPDATE TRANSACTION FIELDS TO REFLECT ORDER LINE ITEM
      replace NWTXN->SUBTOTAL with NWTXN->SUBTOTAL + NWORDER->SUBTOTAL,;
              NWTXN->DISCOUNT with NWTXN->DISCOUNT + NWORDER->DISCOUNT

      @ 22,20 say "Press any key to enter another item"
      wait ""

   enddo                  [ Enter order line items ]

   * COMPLETE TRANSACTION ENTRY
   select NWTXN
   @ 10, 0 clear
   @ 11, 0 say "SUBTOTAL          $" + transform(SUBTOTAL,"9,999.99")
   @ 12, 0 say "DISCOUNT           " + transform(DISCOUNT,"9,999.99")
   @ 14, 0 say "SHIPPING CHARGE   " get SHIPPING
   @ 15, 0 say "SALES TAX RATE     " get TAXRATE
   read
   replace TAX with (SUBTOTAL - DISCOUNT) * TAXRATE / 100, INVAMOUNT with;
           SUBTOTAL - DISCOUNT + TAX + SHIPPING
   @ 16, 0 say "SALES TAX          " + transform(TAX,"9,999.99")
   @ 18, 0 say "NET INVOICE AMT $" + transform(INVAMOUNT,"9,999.99")
   * ENTER PRE-PAYMENT DATA
   @ 20, 0 say "PRE-PAYMENT AMT " get PMTAMOUNT
   read
   if PMTAMOUNT > 0
      replace PMTDATE with date()
      @ 20,45 say "PAYMENT DATE" get PMTDATE
      @ 21,45 say "REFERENCE   " get REFERENCE
      read
   endif

   @ 22,20 say "Press any key to enter another invoice"
   wait ""

   * INCREMENT NEXT AVAILABLE INVOICE NUMBER
   store MPINVOICE + 1 to MPINVOICE

enddo                 [ main loop ]

return
```

Figure 16-15. The order entry program (*continued*)

```
open the inventory file with the category/part number index

open the order file with the account number and invoice number indexes

open the transaction file with the account number and invoice number indexes

open the customer file with the account number index

do the following until the user chooses to exit:

   clear the screen
   select the customer file
   initialize a memory variable, MACCOUNT, for the customer account number


   do the following until a valid customer account number is entered:

      ask for a customer account number

      if the account number is left blank,
         save the public memory variables on disk
         exit the program
      endif

      search the index for the account number
      if the account number is found,
         exit from this loop
      otherwise
         display an error message
         wait until a key is pressed
         erase the error message
      endif

   end of steps to do until a valid customer account number is entered

   display the company name, address, telephone number, and type of equipment
   display the year-to-date invoices, total invoices, and balance

   initialize a memory variable, MCONTINUE, with the value .T.
   display a message: "Enter an invoice for this customer? (Y/N)"
   collect the user's entry into the variable MCONTINUE
   if the user answered "No",
      go back to the top of the loop to re-enter the customer
   endif

   select the transaction file
   append a blank record
   replace the account number with the customer's account number, the date
      with today's date, the invoice number with the next available invoice
      number, and the tax rate with the customer's tax rate
   collect the invoice date from the user
   collect the invoice number from the user


   do the following until the user chooses to exit:

      select the order file
      clear the screen from line 10 down
      initialize memory variables for the category, part number, and quantity
      collect the category from the user
      collect the part number from the user
      if the category is left blank,
         exit from the order entry loop
      endif
```

Figure 16-16. The order entry program in pseudocode

```
    select the inventory file
    search the index for the item by category and partnumber
    if the item is found,
       display the item description
       store the standard price to a memory variable, MPRICE
    otherwise,
       display an error message
       wait until a key is pressed
       clear the error message
       go back to the top of the order entry loop
    endif

    select the order file
    collect the quantity ordered from the user
    collect the price from the user
    if the quantity entered is 0,
       display a message: "This item has been cancelled"
       wait until a key is pressed
       clear the error message
       go back to the top of the order entry loop
    endif

    append a blank record
    replace the account number with the customer's account number,
       the invoice number with the invoice number from the transaction
       record, the category, part number, and equipment with the inventory
       record category, part number, and equipment, the quantity with the
       quantity entered by the user, the price with the price entered by the
       user, and the subtotal with the quantity multiplied by the price

    display the subtotal
    collect the discount rate from the user
    replace the discount with the subtotal multiplied by the discount rate,
       (converted to a percent by dividing by 100), and replace the net
       invoice amount with the subtotal minus the discount
    display the discount
    display the net invoice amount
    select the transaction file
    replace the subtotal with the current subtotal plus the subtotal from the
       order record (the subtotal for the current line item), and replace the
       discount with the current discount plus the discount from the
       order record (the discount for the current line item)

    display a message: "Press any key to enter another item"
    wait until a key is pressed

end of order entry loop

select the transaction file
clear the screen from line 10 down
display the subtotal
display the discount
collect the shipping charge from the user
collect the tax rate from the user
replace the tax with the result of subtracting the discount from the
   subtotal, and multiplying the result by the tax rate (converted to a
   percent by dividing by 100, and replace the net invoice amount with the
   subtotal minus the discount plus the tax plus the shipping charge
display the tax
display the net invoice amount

collect the pre-payment amount from the user
```

Figure 16-16. The order entry program in pseudocode *(continued)*

```
   if the pre-payment amount is not 0,
      replace the payment date with today's date
      collect the payment date from the user
      collect the payment reference from the user
   endif

   display a message: "Press any key to enter another invoice"
   wait until a key is pressed

   increment the next available invoice number

end of steps to do until the user chooses to exit
```

Figure 16-16. The order entry program in pseudocode (*continued*)

number had been entered. Including the dollar totals provides some insight into the customer's order history and credit status; if a large balance is outstanding, the operator may decide not to allow the customer to place another order without prepayment. Displaying the EQUIPMENT field makes it more likely that the operator will notice the discrepancies between the item ordered and the equipment with which it will be used. Including this field on the screen can thus help to flag part numbers that were incorrectly transcribed on the manual order forms and also reduce the chance that the operator will enter the wrong part number into the computer and fail to notice the error. The choice of which fields to display in this type of program should be made carefully; the fields will make a big difference in how helpful the system is perceived to be. If the operator chooses not to continue with the entry, a LOOP command causes the program to return to the top of the main DO WHILE loop and ask for another customer account number.

If the operator confirms the invoice entry, the program SELECTs the Transaction File and appends a blank record. This sequence of events prohibits the use of SET RELATION to link the Transaction and Customer files, because the customer must be found and displayed before a transaction record even exists. A REPLACE command fills in the fields that are already known. The ACCOUNT and TAXRATE fields are taken from the Customer File, and the current date, expressed using the DATE() function, is entered in the INVDATE field. In this case (unlike the NWTPOST.PRG example) it really is necessary to SELECT the file to be updated. Although you may REPLACE fields in any open data base, you may only APPEND records to the data base in the currently selected work area.

The memory variable MPINVOICE, which stores the next available invoice number, is the first of the systemwide public memory variables that will be used in the National Widgets system. The program increments the value of MPINVOICE after each new invoice is entered, so it is best to make this variable numeric and use the STR function to convert it to a character string in the REPLACE command. You must create MPINVOICE with a STORE command before you can test the order entry program for the first time by running it from the dot prompt. At the end of every order entry session, the program saves the new value on disk. If you run the program from the dot prompt rather than from a menu program, you must first RESTORE the systemwide memory variables:

```
RESTORE FROM NWMEMORY
```

The next step is to enter the individual items the customer has ordered into the Order File. Since a given invoice may contain one or many items, another DO WHILE loop allows the user to continue entering order records until he or she chooses to exit. Once again, the operator's entry must be validated—in this case, by looking up the item in the Inventory File—and the program must also provide a way out in case the wrong item is entered by mistake. Two memory variables, MCATEGORY and MPARTNUM, collect the category and part number that identify the item ordered. Leaving the MCATEGORY field blank signals that the last item has been entered and the order is complete; an EXIT command provides a way out of the DO WHILE loop that adds records to the Order File. This data entry sequence ensures that a blank record cannot be APPENDed to this file until we are sure a line item with a valid CATEGORY and PARTNUMBER actually exists. For the same reason, SET RELATION cannot be used to link the Order File to the Inventory File to validate the Order File entries; each item must be looked up in the Inventory File *before* APPENDing a record to the Order File. Instead, the program selects the Inventory File and uses SEEK to search the index for the combination of MCATEGORY + MPARTNUM. If the item does not exist in the Inventory File, an error message is displayed and the LOOP command returns control to the top of the order entry loop to allow the operator to reenter MCATEGORY and MPARTNUM. When a valid inventory item has been entered, the description is displayed for the benefit of the operator and the PRICE stored in a memory variable,

MPRICE, to serve as the item's default price.

The program still has not added a record to the Order File, so as to provide one last chance to abort the entry. The order quantity is collected into the memory variable MQUANTITY, and the variable (MPRICE) that contains the price read from the Inventory File is presented for the operator to accept or change. After these two entries the program tests to see if MQUANTITY has been left blank (0). If so, the entry is cancelled, a message is displayed informing the operator of this fact, and a LOOP command returns control to the top of the order record entry loop to reenter MCATEGORY and MPARTNUM. This second chance to exit provides an extra measure of safety, in case the user enters a valid—but wrong—part number and notices the error when the item description is displayed. If a non-zero order quantity is entered, the program APPENDs a blank record to the Order File and fills in the available fields. The ACCOUNT field comes from the Customer File; the INVOICE number from the Transaction File; the CATEGORY, PARTNUMBER, and EQUIPMENT fields from the Inventory File; and the QUANTITY, PRICE, and SUBTOTAL fields from the memory variables MQUANTITY and MPRICE.

No hard and fast rules can be defined to govern how far to allow the operator to proceed and still escape without entering an order record. This judgment must be made on the basis of previous programming experience, combined with an understanding of the organization and operators using the application. In another setting, we might have decided to collect *all* of the order fields into memory variables and ask the operator to confirm the entire line item (with a question like "Are you sure this item is OK?") before APPENDing the record.

The program displays the SUBTOTAL without allowing it to be changed and then asks for the discount rate. The DISCOUNT is calculated, displayed, and subtracted from the SUBTOTAL to yield the value for the INVAMOUNT field, the net order amount to be printed on the invoice. This completes the Order File record, and the dollar totals from the latest order line item are added into the corresponding Transaction File invoice fields. Finally, the program displays a message and pauses before returning to the top of the loop for another order entry.

When the operator exits from the order line-item entry loop (by leaving MCATEGORY and MPARTNUMBER blank), the Transaction File invoice record must be completed. The bottom half of the screen is cleared to make room for the transaction data, and the SUBTOTAL and DISCOUNT fields are displayed. The operator enters the SHIPPING charge and may change the sales tax rate read in from the Customer File if necessary. The TAX and INVAMOUNT (net invoice amount) fields are calculated and displayed, and the operator is given the opportunity to enter a prepayment. Only if a non-zero amount is filled in does the program REPLACE the payment date (PMTDATE) with the current date and allow the operator to alter this date and enter a payment reference (like a check or credit card number). Again, note that it is not *necessary* to SELECT the Transaction File in order to REPLACE these fields. This time the decision was based on the fact that the SELECT commands reflect the logical stages of the program: first, the Customer File is selected to validate the account number, then a transaction record is added, then a series of Order File records are entered, and finally, the Transaction File record is completed.

After completing the invoice, the program displays a message and pauses until the operator presses a key. Since an invoice was added to the file, the memory variable, MPINVOICE, which contains the next available invoice number, is incremented before the program returns to the top of the main loop to ask for another customer account number for the next invoice. After the user exits from the main loop by leaving the customer account number blank, all of the system's public memory variables (only MPINVOICE, so far) are saved to the memory file NWMEMORY.MEM, so that the next time the program is used, the correct beginning invoice number is available.

The programs in this chapter have made major refinements in the development of the National Widgets system. The error-checking techniques introduced here help preserve the integrity of the files by preventing erroneous data from being entered, and the programs come very close to simulating the work flow and paper forms in the manual system. An operator using the NWCORD2.PRG to inquire into a customer's order history will appreciate the resemblance of the screen to the familiar customer ledger cards.

Using the same kinds of programming structures, you should be able to write a similar program that displays on the screen exactly the same information contained on the ledger cards. If anything, this program would be simpler than NWCORD2.PRG, since it must access only two files, the Customer File and the Transaction History File, rather than three. The order entry program, the longest and most complex we have written so far, turns the order entry procedure, which at command level requires a thorough understanding of dBASE III PLUS as well as the particular files that make up the system, into a process that could easily be carried out by anyone in the office.

17

PROGRAMS TO PRINT REPORTS

The programs in this chapter and Chapter 18 overcome some of the shortcomings and limitations of the dBASE III PLUS report generator enumerated in Chapter 6. These programs will improve the appearance of your reports by allowing you to add print enhancements throughout the report, control the page layout more precisely, and format data with PICTURE clauses as well as the TRANSFORM function. You will also be able to print reports that draw data from more than two files and to produce full-page formats like letters, invoices, and statements, all of which are impossible with the standard dBASE III PLUS report generator. Using the techniques described in these chapters, you will be able to do the following:

- Print columnar reports that include fields from more than two data bases.
- Print full-page formats that include fields from two or more data base files.
- Print fields conditionally based on their contents.
- Print on single sheets of paper or envelopes as well as continuous forms.
- Print statistics other than column totals.

- Control the display format of numeric fields and still print totals, subtotals, and other statistics for these fields.
- Control the placement and format of the date, page number, page title, and column headings.
- Print page footers as well as headers.
- Use special print enhancements anywhere in a report, including in the page title and column headings.

The programs in this chapter produce reports based primarily on information contained in a single data base, although they will continue to apply the techniques introduced in Chapter 16 for looking up data in other files. This chapter describes two basic types of reports: full-page formats like index cards, letters, and envelopes, which lay out the fields from one record on one printed page, and columnar reports like those produced by the report generator, which require numerical calculations to print subtotals, totals, and other statistics.

As the sample programs in this book become longer and more complex, the discussion will focus more closely on the details of the National Widgets application. It is natural for beginning programmers who are following the development of this system as a case study to concentrate at first on the intricacies of the program structures and the specific methods used to achieve the desired results. Although the program descriptions may seem to be too concerned with the detailed requirements of a single organization, you will find that the relationships among the data bases and the types of reports produced are typical of many business data bases. When you design your own systems, you can consider the programs presented in this and the following chapter to be prototypes for the kinds of reports found in almost any data base application. The programs in these two chapters introduce standard techniques for carrying out operations such as asking the operator which record(s) to print, controlling the page layout and field placement, and accumulating totals and other statistics. These procedures may be viewed as building blocks that you can assemble in many different ways, depending on the requirements of your own data base applications.

A PROGRAM TO PRINT ROLODEX OR INDEX CARDS

Chapter 12 presented a program to print Rolodex or index cards for National Widgets' customers. This program controlled the layout of the fields on the cards through a format file. Incorporating the very same @ ... SAY commands that comprise the format file into the program that prints the cards affords two important advantages over calling the format file from the program: you can perform calculations more complicated than these expressed by the type of explicit algebraic formula permitted in an @ ... SAY command, and you can print fields conditionally with more flexibility than is possible when using only the IIF function.

For example, in the National Widgets Customer File, if the COMPANY or ADDRESS2 field is not filled in, a blank line is printed by the format file. The extra line produced by a blank COMPANY line would probably not be noticed because of its position between the ACCOUNT field and the first address line, but an empty ADDRESS2 field leaves an unsightly gap in the address. Also, if the CONTACT, EQUIPMENT, or FIRSTORDER field is left blank, the format file still prints the heading ("CONTACT:", "EQUIPMENT:", or "FIRST ORDER:"), and if the AREACODE or TELEPHONE field is missing, the parentheses intended to surround the area code are printed nonetheless. These might not be perceived as serious problems in the National Widgets system, partly because the field headings serve as reminders that some of this data should be obtained from the customer and entered into the data base. But in other contexts conditional printing is very important.

One way to avoid printing the heading if a field is blank is to use the IIF function. For example, you could substitute the following three commands for the @ ... SAY commands in the NWCCARDS.FMT format file that print the CONTACT, EQUIPMENT, and FIRSTORDER fields:

```
@  9,10 say IIF(CONTACT = " ", "", "CONTACT:      " + CONTACT)
@ 11,10 say IIF(EQUIPMENT = " ", "", "EQUIPMENT:    " + EQUIPMENT)
@ 13,10 say IIF(dtoc(FIRSTORDER) = " ", "", "FIRST ORDER: " + dtoc(FIRSTORDER))
```

In these @ ... SAY commands, the conditions in the IIF functions test each field to see if it is blank by comparing the field contents to a single blank space. (Recall that FIRSTORDER, which is a date field, must be converted to a character string with the DTOC function before the comparison can be made.) If the field is blank, a null string is printed; otherwise, the heading and the field are printed together.

The IIF function provides an elegant solution to this simple problem; however, you may not always be able to use it. A complex condition coupled with a lengthy expression to be printed may result in an @ ... SAY command longer than the maximum length of 254 characters permitted for any dBASE III PLUS command. If you need to choose among more than two alternatives, using a series of nested IF loops or a DO CASE structure provides more flexibility and is more readable than the equivalent set of nested IIF functions. The IIF function also cannot help with the problem of suppressing a blank line in the middle of the customer name and address block, since the format file always prints ADDRESS1 and city/state/ZIP on lines 5 and 7, respectively.

You might also have considered printing the cards with a label format, since the dBASE III PLUS label generator automatically suppresses blank lines if any fields on the label are empty. dBASE III PLUS can print "mailing labels" up to 16 lines deep, with up to 16 lines between labels, so with the right combination of label height and number of lines between labels, you can accommodate cards or other continuous forms up to 32 lines long. However, the label printer will eliminate *all* blank lines within a label, including the ones deliberately placed between some of the fields to achieve a more attractive and readable printed format.

Modifying the original NWCCARDS.PRG program to eliminate the format file is easy: just delete all references to the format file and substitute the same @ ... SAY commands used in NWCCARDS.FMT for the READ command that activated the format file. Figure 17-1 lists a program, NWCCARD2.PRG, that is exactly equivalent to the original combination of NWCCARD1.PRG and NWCCARDS.FMT presented in Chapter 12. If you compare this program to the listing in Figure 12-12, you will see that the SET FORMAT TO NWCCARDS line has been removed, and in place of the READ command are the @ ... SAY commands from the format file, unchanged except for the extra spaces inserted to match the indentation within the DO WHILE loop.

If you are developing the sample system or paralleling the process with your own application, the easiest way to make the required changes is to edit a copy of the NWCCARD1.PRG program with a word processor or

```
* NWCCARD2.PRG
* PROGRAM TO PRINT ROLODEX OR INDEX CARDS
*   USING FORMAT FILE NWCCARDS.FMT
* WRITTEN BY:  M.LISKIN        7/28/85

use NWCUST index NWCACCT

clear
store ctod("  /  /  ") to MFIRSTORD
@ 10,10 say "Print only customers whose first order date is AFTER ";
        get MFIRSTORD
@ 12,10 say "(or press <RETURN> to include ALL customers)"
read

if dtoc(MFIRSTORD) <> "  /  /  "
   set filter to FIRSTORDER > MFIRSTORD
   goto top
endif

set device to print
@  0, 0 say chr(27) + "C" + chr(18)

do while .not. eof()

   @  2, 5 say ACCOUNT
   @  2,30 say "(" + AREACODE + ") " + TELEPHONE
   @  4,10 say COMPANY
   @  5,10 say ADDRESS1
   @  6,10 say ADDRESS2
   @  7,10 say trim(CITY) + ", " + STATE + "  " + ZIP
   @  9,10 say "CONTACT:      "   + CONTACT
   @ 11,10 say "EQUIPMENT:    "   + EQUIPMENT
   @ 13,10 say "FIRST ORDER: "    + dtoc(FIRSTORDER)

   skip

enddo

set filter to
@  0, 0 say chr(27) + "C" + chr(66)
set device to screen

return
```

Figure 17-1. A program to print Rolodex or index cards

MODIFY COMMAND and incorporate the entire format file into the program. You can then delete the comment lines and use a global search and replace command to add the leading spaces to the @ ... SAY commands. (With the MODIFY COMMAND editor, you can use CTRL-KR to read in the format file, but you must adjust each line manually, since there is no search and replace capability.)

To suppress a heading when the corresponding field is blank, you can use an IF loop that checks whether the field is *not* blank by comparing it to a character string consisting of a single blank space. For example, for the

CONTACT field, the test would look like this:

```
if CONTACT <> " "
   @  9,10 say "CONTACT:      " + CONTACT
endif
```

If CONTACT is not blank, both the heading and the field are printed. If CONTACT is blank, no action is taken. The EQUIPMENT and FIRSTORDER fields could be handled similarly:

```
if EQUIPMENT <> " "
   @ 11,10 say "EQUIPMENT:    " + EQUIPMENT
endif

if dtoc(FIRSTORDER) <> " "
   @ 13,10 say "FIRST ORDER: " + dtoc(FIRSTORDER)
endif
```

In all three cases, if the field is printed, it is always printed in the same position on the card; and if it is blank, nothing else is printed in its place. Thus, skipping blank CONTACT and EQUIPMENT fields results only in a larger gap between the address and the first order date, which is not a very serious problem. Within the address block, however, omitting the ADDRESS2 field must *not* result in a blank line between ADDRESS1 and the city/state/ZIP line. If ADDRESS2 is blank, the program should not only skip printing this field, but also print the next field in a different place. Here is the simplest way to accomplish this:

```
@  2, 5 say ACCOUNT
@  2,30 say "(" + AREACODE + ") " + TELEPHONE
@  4,10 say COMPANY
@  5,10 say ADDRESS1
if ADDRESS2 = " "
   @  6,10 say trim(CITY) + ", " + STATE + "  " + ZIP
else
   @  6,10 say ADDRESS2
   @  7,10 say trim(CITY) + ", " + STATE + "  " + ZIP
endif
```

This method works well for the National Widgets index cards because the program need not test for a blank COMPANY field, so only two variations are possible within the address block. However, if you were printing four or five address fields, any one of which might be blank, keeping track of all of the possible combinations would result in a very confusing and convoluted set of nested IF loops. A more general solution uses the PROW( ) and PCOL( ) functions, which monitor the current print head row and column position. Using these functions, you can print each item

```
* NWCCARD3.PRG
* PROGRAM TO PRINT ROLODEX OR INDEX CARDS
* WRITTEN BY:  M.LISKIN        6/18/85

use NWCUST index NWCACCT

clear
store ctod("  /  /  ") to MFIRSTORD
@ 10,10 say "Print only customers whose first order date is AFTER ";
        get MFIRSTORD
@ 12,10 say "(or press <RETURN> to include ALL customers)"
read

if dtoc(MFIRSTORD) <> "  /  /  "
   set filter to FIRSTORDER > MFIRSTORD
   goto top
endif

set device to print

@  0, 0 say chr(27) + "C" + chr(18)

do while .not. eof()

   @  2, 5 say ACCOUNT

   @  2,30 say ""
   if TELEPHONE <> " "
      if AREACODE <> " "
         @  2,pcol() say "(" + AREACODE + ") "
      endif
      @  2,pcol() say TELEPHONE
   endif

   @  3, 0 say " "
   if COMPANY <> " "
      @  prow() + 1,10 say COMPANY
   endif
   @  prow() + 1,10 say ADDRESS1
   if ADDRESS2 <> " "
      @  prow() + 1,10 say ADDRESS2
   endif
   @  prow() + 1,10 say trim(CITY) + ", " + STATE + "  " + ZIP

   if CONTACT <> " "
      @  9,10 say "CONTACT:      " + CONTACT
   endif

   if EQUIPMENT <> " "
      @ 11,10 say "EQUIPMENT:    " + EQUIPMENT
   endif

   if dtoc(FIRSTORDER) <> " "
      @ 13,10 say "FIRST ORDER: " + dtoc(FIRSTORDER)
   endif

   @ 15,10 say "YTD INVOICES:   " + transform(YTDINV, "9,999,999.99")
   @ 16,10 say "TOTAL INVOICES: " + transform(TOTINV, "9,999,999.99")

   skip
```

Figure 17-2. An improved program to print Rolodex or index cards

```
enddo                    [ not end-of-file ]

set filter to
@  0, 0 say chr(27) + "C" + chr(66)
set device to screen

return
```

Figure 17-2. An improved program to print Rolodex or index cards (*continued*)

of data on the next available line or at the next available column on the current line without having to know the exact line or column number. A new version of the index card-printing program, NWCCARD3.PRG, listed in Figure 17-2, illustrates this technique.

This program, like NWCCARD2.PRG, prints the ACCOUNT field at row 2, column 5. The telephone number, if present, will be printed on the same line. If the area code is missing, the telephone number should be printed anyway; but if the telephone number is blank, the area code, even if it has been filled in, should be omitted. The NWCCARD3.PRG program uses the PCOL( ) function to print either or both of the two components of the phone number. Whether or not the area code is included, the telephone number must begin at a fixed position on the card (column 30), so the program positions the print head to the correct column with

```
@  2,30 say ""
```

Two nested IF loops are then used to print the combination of AREACODE and TELEPHONE. If TELEPHONE is not blank, the AREACODE is tested; and if it is filled in, it is printed beginning at the current print head position, at column 30 of row 2. Next, TELEPHONE is printed at the current print position; this will be column 30 if the AREACODE field was blank or column 36 if printing the AREACODE, with parentheses and one trailing space, moved the print head over six spaces. If this seems confusing, you might try tracing through the loop yourself and counting spaces for the various combinations of blank AREACODE and TELEPHONE fields.

The same basic strategy is used to print the address block. A blank space is printed on row 3 to force at least one empty line between the ACCOUNT field and the beginning of the address. If the COMPANY field is not blank, it is printed on row 4. *Once any field has been printed conditionally, you can no longer use absolute row numbers to print the remaining address lines, since the program cannot determine whether any of the optional lines were actually printed.* ADDRESS1 (which the program assumes is never blank) is therefore printed at the coordinates PROW( )+1,10, which means one line past the current printer row; that is, on the next line on the card. The second address line, which may be blank, and the city/state/ZIP line, which is always present, are also printed by using relative row coordinates.

In this program the decision was made always to print the CONTACT, EQUIPMENT, and FIRSTORDER fields in the same places on the card no matter how many lines the address occupies, so the program returns to using absolute row coordinates for these fields. Notice also that two more fields, YTDINV and TOTINV, were added to the cards and formatted with the TRANSFORM function to insert commas every three digits for improved readability. Figure 17-3 illustrates the first few cards printed by this program.

A PROGRAM TO PRINT ENVELOPES

Using @ ... SAY commands allows you to position fields anywhere on the page and to format data fields with PICTUREs. Alternative, if you only need to print several lines of data one after the other, you can use the ? command, which, like an @ ... SAY command with a relative row coordinate expressed as PROW( ) + 1, places the data on the next available printer line. This method will be demonstrated in a program that prints addresses on envelopes, replacing the word processor used in the first version of the National Widgets system for customer mailings. Using dBASE III PLUS to print the envelopes eliminates the need to copy a large portion of the file to the text file format required by the word processor, thus saving both time and disk space.

```
ABCPLUMB                    (415)  861-4543

     ABC Plumbing
     1850 University Avenue
     Berkeley, CA  94703

     CONTACT:      Ed Williams

     EQUIPMENT:    Kaypro 10, Epson FX-100

     FIRST ORDER: 12/01/83

     YTD INVOICES:           385.56
     TOTAL INVOICES:       1,181.97
- - - - - - - - - - - - - - - - - - - - - - -

ANDERSON                    (415)  563-8961

     3420 19th Street
     San Francisco, CA  94114


     CONTACT:      John Anderson

     EQUIPMENT:    Apple IIe

     FIRST ORDER: 08/08/83

     YTD INVOICES:             0.00
     TOTAL INVOICES:         279.52
- - - - - - - - - - - - - - - - - - - - - - -

ARONOFF                     (707)  745-1813

     601 First Street
     Benicia, CA  94510


     CONTACT:      Gina Aronoff

     EQUIPMENT:    Apple IIc, Imagewriter

     FIRST ORDER: 10/09/84

     YTD INVOICES:             0.00
     TOTAL INVOICES:         232.50
- - - - - - - - - - - - - - - - - - - - - - -

CHIPCITY                    (415)  348-6801

     Chip City Electronics
     288 Lorton
     Burlingame, CA  94010

     CONTACT:      Fred Larson
```

Figure 17-3. Customer index cards

So far all of the reports in this book have required continuous-form paper. The standard report and label generators do not provide an option to instruct dBASE III PLUS to pause at the end of each page so that the operator can insert another sheet of paper into the printer. This is reasonable for lengthy data base reports; the cost of a tractor feed for most printers is well worth the time and frustration it will save you in hand-feeding hundreds of single sheets. However, for small mailings consisting of personalized letters and envelopes, it would not be unusual for a small business or nonprofit organization to print on single sheets of letterhead or ordinary envelopes. The envelope-printing program will therefore ask the operator whether single envelopes are being hand-fed into the printer. If so, the program must pause before printing each address and display a message prompting the operator to insert the next envelope.

A general-purpose envelope-printing program also should not assume that the return address is preprinted on the envelopes. As with the MPINVOICE variable introduced in Chapter 16, the user's company name and address may be stored in a set of public memory variables so they are available to be printed on envelopes, letters, or reports. You can use the following command sequence at the dot prompt to add these new variables to the memory file, NWMEMORY.MEM, created in Chapter 16:

```
RESTORE FROM NWMEMORY
STORE "National Widgets, Inc." TO MPCOMPANY
STORE "843 Parker Street" TO MPADDRESS1
STORE "Berkeley, CA  94710" TO MPADDRESS2
STORE "" TO MPADDRESS3
SAVE TO NWMEMORY
```

Although the third address line is not needed for National Widgets, it is provided to accommodate companies with a two-line street address. When you test the envelope-printing program by running it from the dot prompt, you must first use RESTORE to make these variables available to your program:

```
RESTORE FROM NWMEMORY
```

In pseudocode, here is what the envelope-printing program must do:

open the Customer File with the ZIP code index

ask whether to print on single envelopes
ask whether to print the return address

for each record in the Customer File:

if printing on single envelopes,
    ask the operator to insert an envelope
    wait until a key is pressed

if necessary, print the return address

print the customer address
eject the envelope from the printer

end of steps to do for each record in the file

The complete program, NWCENV.PRG, is listed in Figure 17-4; a detailed pseudocode outline is shown in Figure 17-5.

```
* NWCENV.PRG
* PROGRAM TO PRINT ENVELOPES FOR CUSTOMERS
* WRITTEN BY:  M.LISKIN        05/07/86

clear
use NWCUST index NWCZIP

store .T. to MSINGLE, MRETURNADD
@ 10,10 say "Are you printing on single envelopes? (Y/N)";
        get MSINGLE picture "Y"
@ 12,10 say "Do you want to print a return address? (Y/N)";
        get MRETURNADD picture "Y"
read

set margin to 45
set console off
set print on

do while .not. eof()

   if MSINGLE
      set print off
      set console on
      @ 15,10 say "Insert an envelope, then press any key to begin printing"
      wait ""
      @ 15, 0
      set console off
      set print on
   endif                  [ print on single envelopes ]

   if MRETURNADD
      set margin to 5
      ? MPCOMPANY
      ? MPADDRESS1
      ? MPADDRESS2
      ? MPADDRESS3
```

Figure 17-4. A program to print envelopes

```
      ?
      ?
      ?
      ?
      ?
      ?
      ?
      set margin to 45
   endif                    [ print return address ]

   ? CONTACT
   if COMPANY <> " "
      ? COMPANY
   endif
   ? ADDRESS1
   if ADDRESS2 <> " "
      ? ADDRESS2
   endif
   ? trim(CITY) + ", " + STATE + "  " + ZIP

   eject

   skip

enddo                       [ not end-of-file ]

set margin to 0
set print off
set console on

return
```

Figure 17-4. A program to print envelopes (*continued*)

The program opens the Customer File with the ZIP code index and initializes two logical memory variables in which to store the answers to two yes-or-no questions: whether to print on single envelopes and whether to print the return address. Next, three SET commands are used to prepare for printing the envelope. SET MARGIN TO 45 establishes the left margin for printing the customer name and address. If your application requires more than one size envelope, it would be better to store this value in a public memory variable than to write it explicitly into the program. (This strategy will be used in the letter-printing program in the next section.) SET CONSOLE OFF turns off the console so that the information printed on the envelope is not also displayed on the screen, and SET PRINT ON routes to the printer the output of the ? commands that follow.

```
clear the screen
open the customer file with the zip code index

initialize two memory variables, MSINGLE and MRETURNADD,
   with the value .T.

display a message: "Are you printing on single envelopes? (Y/N)"
collect the user's entry into MSINGLE
display a message: "Do you want to print a return address? (Y/N)"
collect the user's entry into MRETURNADD

set the left margin to 45
turn the console off
turn the printer on

for each record in the customer file:

   if printing on single envelopes,
      turn the printer off
      turn the console on
      display a message: "Insert an envelope, then press any key to begin
                         printing"
      wait until a key is pressed
      erease the message
      turn the console off
      turn the printer on
   endif                 [ printing on single envelopes ]

   if printing the return addresses
      set the left margin to 5
      print the company name
      print the return address
      print 7 blank lines
      set the left margin to 45
   endif                 [ print return address ]

   print the contact name
   if the company name is not blank
      print the company name
   endif
   print the first address line
   if the second address line is not blank
      print the second address line
   endif
   print the city, state, and zip code
   eject the envelope from the printer

   skip to the next record

enddo                    [ not end-of-file ]

set the left margin to 0
turn the print off
turn the console on

exit from the program
```

Figure 17-5. The envelope-printing program in pseudocode

Within the DO WHILE loop that processes all of the records in the Customer File, the program first tests whether the user has chosen to print on single envelopes. If so, a prompt message is displayed and a WAIT command pauses the program until the operator presses a key to indicate that the envelope is in place. The two SET commands, SET PRINT OFF and SET CONSOLE ON, are necessary to reverse the status of these options set outside the DO WHILE loop, so that the "Insert an envelope . . ." message appears on the screen and *not* on the printer. Following the WAIT command, the console is turned off again and the printer turned on again to print the customer name and address on the envelope. The program erases the prompt line while the envelope is being printed, which makes it obvious to the operator that the message is not a static part of the screen; it appears only when dBASE III PLUS is ready for the next envelope.

If the operator has requested that the program print the return address, the left margin is reset to 5 spaces with SET MARGIN TO 5 and the company name and address memory variables are printed, followed by seven blank lines to advance the envelope a little more than an inch (if you are printing at 6 lines per inch) to the correct position for the customer name and address. The left margin is then reset to 45 characters and the name and address block printed with IF loops to suppress a blank COMPANY or ADDRESS2 field. Finally, an EJECT command ejects the envelope from the printer. Since the program does not reset the page length, the printer will assume a 66-line page, although the typical business envelope is no more than 25 lines deep. If you find the long form feed annoying, you can add a printer control command to the program to reset the form length as in the index card-printing program.

The NWCENV.PRG program lacks the flexibility of the programs in Chapter 15. You might want this program to solicit selection criteria from the user, ask whether or not to rebuild the ZIP code index, or allow the operator to specify a range of ZIP codes to be included in the mailing. These amenities were omitted from NWCENV.PRG for two reasons. First, the program was kept as short as possible so as not to obscure its fundamental structure or new features. Second, many of these options would be useful additions to quite a few of the programs in the system. In Part IV these frequently used routines will be extracted and placed in separate programs or in a procedure file, so that they may be called by any other programs in the application.

A PROGRAM TO PRINT PERSONALIZED LETTERS

It is only a short step from printing envelopes to printing an entire letter. Except for the placement on the page, the return address and inside address can be printed in the same way they were printed on an envelope. There are two easy ways to print the body of the letter: you can use a TEXT ... ENDTEXT structure, or you can create a data base with a memo field to store the text of the letter.

The first version of the letter-printing program, NWCLTR1.PRG, uses the TEXT ... ENDTEXT method. Since the size and page layout are likely to vary more than the dimensions of an envelope, the default left margin for letters is stored in a public memory variable, MPLMARGIN, rather than written into the program. This variable can be created and added to the set of public variables stored in NWMEMORY.MEM from the dot prompt before you run the program for the first time:

```
RESTORE FROM NWMEMORY
STORE 10 TO MPLMARGIN
SAVE TO NWMEMORY
```

Chapter 21 will present a program that enables the users to enter or change all of the system's public memory variables; but for convenience, the letter-printing program allows the operator to confirm the default value or change the left margin each time the program is run. The program also asks the user to enter a few other variables: the date to print on the letter; the closing signature; and an optional second closing line, such as "Enclosures."

Using a dBASE III PLUS program rather than a word processor is best suited to situations in which the text of the letter changes infrequently and no print enhancements are required. Although you can use print control commands in dBASE III PLUS (as we did in the index card-printing program to change the form length) to set the character pitch, vertical spacing, or type font for an entire section of a letter, you cannot underline or boldface individual words. Using ? or @ ... SAY commands, you can print fields from a data base in a letter, but you cannot insert a field into the middle of a sentence and reformat the surrounding text, as you can with most mail-merge programs.

The TEXT ... ENDTEXT structure containing the body of the letter should be placed in a separate file rather than in the letter-printing program itself, so that people who are unfamiliar with dBASE III PLUS can edit the text more easily. If you must load the entire program into your editor or word processor every time a minor change in the text is required, the chances increase that accidentally altering a command or deleting a line will render the program useless. NWCLTEXT.PRG, the program that prints the body of National Widgets' year-end sale announcement letter, is listed in Figure 17-6. The text of the letter may be created with MODIFY COMMAND or with a word processor. If you use a word processor, be careful not to insert any of the word processor's

```
* NWCLTEXT.PRG
* PROGRAM TO PRINT THE TEXT OF LETTERS TO CUSTOMERS
* WRITTEN BY:  M.LISKIN           05/07/86

text
Dear Friends:


    We are writing to let you know about our special year-end
sale on all computer supplies and accessory products.  National
Widgets had a really good year in 1987, thanks to YOU, our valued
customers, and we want to celebrate the holiday season by passing
along some terrific values to you.

    Floppy disks from all manufacturers are on sale at 15% off
our normally low prices, and all TrueData products, including
disks and magnetic tape cartridges, are 20% off.  Be sure to
check out the enclosed list of special items which make
ideal gifts for the computer owners among your friends and
business associates, including:

                        * Dust Covers
                        * Glare Screens
                        * Cleaning Kits
                        * Terminal stands

    We're also enclosing a description of our new line of
ergonomically designed computer furniture and workstations.
These attractive units can make the long hours you spend at
your terminal speed by in comfort.

      Here's hoping that 1987 has been as good a year for you as
it has been for us, and that 1988 will bring even greater business
success and personal happiness!



Sincerely,
endtext

return
```

Figure 17-6. A program to print the text of a letter

embedded print commands, which will be incomprehensible to dBASE III PLUS. The program that prints the letter, NWCLTR1.PRG, is listed in Figure 17-7, and Figure 17-8 illustrates a typical letter produced by this program.

```
* NWCLTR1.PRG
* PROGRAM TO PRINT LETTERS FOR CUSTOMERS
*   USING TEXT ... ENDTEXT FOR THE BODY OF THE LETTER
* WRITTEN BY:  M.LISKIN        07/28/85

clear
use NWCUST index NWCZIP

store date()     to MDATE
store space(25)  to MCLOSE1, MCLOSE2
store .T.        to MSINGLE, MRETURNADD

@  3,10 say "Enter date to print       " get MDATE
@  5,10 say "Enter left margin         " get MPLMARGIN picture "99"
@  6,10 say "Enter closing signature   " get MCLOSE1
@  7,10 say "Enter second closing line " get MCLOSE2

@ 10,10 say "Are you printing on single sheets of paper? (Y/N)";
        get MSINGLE picture "Y"
@ 12,10 say "Do you want to print a return address? (Y/N)";
        get MRETURNADD picture "Y"
read

set margin to MPLMARGIN
set console off
set print on

do while .not. eof()

   if MSINGLE
      set print off
      set console on
      @ 18,10 say;
        "Insert a sheet of paper, then press any key to begin printing"
      wait ""
      @ 18,0
      set console off
      set print on
   endif                  [ print on single sheets ]

   if MRETURNADD
      ? MPCOMPANY
      ? MPADDRESS1
      ? MPADDRESS2
      ? MPADDRESS3
   endif                  [ print return address ]
```

Figure 17-7. A program to print personalized letters using TEXT ... ENDTEXT for the body of the letter

```
    ? cmonth(MDATE) + str(day(MDATE),3) + ", " + str(year(MDATE),4)
    ?
    ?
    ?
    ?
    ?
    ?

    ? CONTACT
    if COMPANY <> " "
       ? COMPANY
    endif
    ? ADDRESS1
    if ADDRESS2 <> " "
       ? ADDRESS2
    endif
    ? trim(CITY) + ", " + STATE + "  " + ZIP
    ?

    do NWCLTEXT

    ?
    ?
    ?
    ?
    ? MCLOSE1
    ? MCLOSE2

    eject

    skip

enddo                      [ not end-of-file ]

set margin to 0
set print off
set console on

return
```

Figure 17-7. A program to print personalized letters using TEXT ... ENDTEXT for the body of the letter *(continued)*

Using a data base to store the text of a letter is more appropriate if you have many different letters that are printed frequently, and the users of the system are already familiar with how to enter and edit memo field text. Since each letter may require different margins and a different closing signature, it makes sense also to include fields for these items in the data base. In addition, the file should contain a character field for a brief description of each letter. The structure for this data base, NWLETTER.DBF, is listed in Figure 17-9.

The program, NWCLTR2.PRG, that prints letters with this data base,

```
National Widgets, Inc.
943 Parker Street
Berkeley, CA  94710

December 1, 1987



Louise Robbins
Floor Plan Carpet Center
1482 Lowrie Avenue
South San Francisco, CA  94080

Dear Friends:

    We are writing to let you know about our special year-end
sale on all computer supplies and accessory products.  National
Widgets had a really good year in 1987, thanks to YOU, our valued
customers, and we want to celebrate the holiday season by passing
along some terrific values to you.

    Floppy disks from all manufacturers are on sale at 15% off
our normally low prices, and all TrueData products, including
disks and magnetic tape cartridges, are 20% off.  Be sure to
check out the enclosed list of special items which make
ideal gifts for the computer owners among your friends and
business associates, including:

                        * Dust Covers
                        * Glare Screens
                        * Cleaning Kits
                        * Terminal stands

    We're also enclosing a description of our new line of
ergonomically designed computer furniture and workstations.
These attractive units can make the long hours you spend at
your terminal speed by in comfort.

      Here's hoping that 1987 has been as good a year for you as
it has been for us, and that 1988 will bring even greater business
success and personal happiness!



Sincerely,



All of the Folks at
National Widgets, Inc.
```

Figure 17-8. A personalized letter printed by NWCLTR1.PRG

is listed in Figure 17-10. The program begins by opening the NWLETTER.DBF file and displaying the record numbers and descriptions with a DISPLAY ALL command. DISPLAY ALL was chosen instead of LIST so that the display will pause if there are more records than will fit on one screen. The user is allowed to choose a letter by number, and the selection is stored in the memory variable MLETTERREC. The RANGE clause in the @ ... SAY ... GET command limits the user's entry to a number between 0 and the total number of records in the NWLETTER.DBF file. If the user enters 0, the program returns to the menu, while any other choice positions the NWLETTER.DBF file to the selected record. As in NWCLTR1.PRG, the operator may set the date to be printed on the letters and specify whether to print on single sheets of paper and whether a return address is required.

The left margin is set to the value of the LMARGIN field in NWLETTER.DBF with a SET MARGIN command, and the display width for memo fields is set to the value of the RMARGIN field by using SET MEMOWIDTH. (This way of defining the "right margin" as the line width rather than the absolute right margin column number is also used by many word processors and text editors.) If the text of the letter is entered by means of the dBASE III PLUS memo field editor, with the lines formed into paragraphs by the editor's word-wrap feature, dBASE III PLUS can always reformat the memo text to the specified width. If

```
. USE NWLETTER

. LIST STRUCTURE TO PRINT

Structure for database: C:NWLETTER.dbf
Number of data records:       0
Date of last update   : 05/06/86
Field  Field Name  Type       Width    Dec
    1  DESCRIP     Character     50
    2  LMARGIN     Numeric        2
    3  RMARGIN     Numeric        2
    4  CLOSE1      Character     25
    5  CLOSE2      Character     25
    6  LETTERTEXT  Memo          10
** Total **                     115
```

Figure 17-9. The structure of the letter file

```
* NWCLTR2.PRG
* PROGRAM TO PRINT LETTERS FOR CUSTOMERS
*   USING A MEMO FIELD FOR THE BODY OF THE LETTER
* WRITTEN BY:  M.LISKIN       05/07/86

select 1
use NWLETTER

clear
@  1, 0 say "Available letters are:"
@  2, 0
display all DESCRIP

store 0 to MLETTERREC
@ 24, 0 say "Please enter your choice, or 0 to quit";
        get MLETTERREC range 0, RECCOUNT()
read
if MLETTERREC = 0
   return
else
   goto MLETTERREC
endif

clear
store date() to MDATE
store .T.    to MSINGLE, MRETURNADD

@  3,10 say "Enter date to print       " get MDATE

@ 10,10 say "Are you printing on single sheets of paper? (Y/N)";
        get MSINGLE picture "Y"
@ 12,10 say "Do you want to print a return address? (Y/N)     ";
        get MRETURNADD picture "Y"
read

set margin to LMARGIN
set memowidth to RMARGIN

select 2
use NWCUST index NWCZIP

set console off
set print on

do while .not. eof()

   if MSINGLE
      set print off
      set console on
      @ 18,10 say;
        "Insert a sheet of paper, then press any key to begin printing"
      wait ""
      @ 18,0
      set console off
      set print on
   endif                 [ print on single sheets ]

   if MRETURNADD
      ? MPCOMPANY
```

Figure 17-10. A program to print personalized letters using a memo field for the body of the letter

```
      ? MPADDRESS1
      ? MPADDRESS2
      ? MPADDRESS3
   endif                 [ print return address ]

   ? cmonth(MDATE) + str(day(MDATE),3) + ", " + str(year(MDATE),4)
   ?
   ?
   ?
   ?
   ?
   ?

   ? CONTACT
   if COMPANY <> " "
      ? COMPANY
   endif
   ? ADDRESS1
   if ADDRESS2 <> " "
      ? ADDRESS2
   endif
   ? trim(CITY) + ", " + STATE + "  " + ZIP
   ?

   select NWLETTER
   ? LETTERTEXT

   ?
   ?
   ?
   ?
   ? CLOSE1
   ? CLOSE2
   eject

   select NWCUST
   skip
enddo                      [ not end-of-file ]

set margin to 0
set print off
set console on

return
```

Figure 17-10. A program to print personalized letters using a memo field for the body of the letter (*continued*)

each line ends with a hard carriage return, as it might if text typed with another editor or word processor were read into the memo field with CTRL-KR, the lines will be printed correctly only if the right margin is wider than the text.

Next, the Customer File is opened with the ZIP code index and the program begins printing letters. The NWLETTER.DBF file is SELECTed to print the contents of the LETTERTEXT field, because a memo field may not be specified by alias; after finishing each letter, the program SELECTs the Customer File again to prepare to print the next.

Both of these letter-printing programs assume that the entire letter will fit on a single sheet of paper. In order to print multiple pages with the TEXT ... ENDTEXT method, you must either create two separate programs, one for the text to be printed on the first page of the letter, and another for the second page, or use two TEXT ... ENDTEXT structures in the NWCLTEXT.PRG program. Using a data base for the text of the letters, you can include two (or more) memo fields in the data base for the text of the letters. The first field will then become page 1 of the letter, the second page 2, and so on. In either case, the letter-printing program must use an EJECT command (and, if you are printing on single sheets, a WAIT) between the pages.

A PROGRAM TO PRINT A MULTILINE REPORT

In Chapter 5 a Customer Reference List was designed with the dBASE III PLUS report generator. This report exemplified a format requiring more than the one line of data per record easily handled by the report generator. In this section, a program will be presented to print this and other similar reports. The program offers two immediate advantages: it allows for more precise control over the page layout and the display format of the data. Also, as in the other programs in this chapter, the Customer Reference List program can suppress the empty lines printed by the report generator if some of the fields in the data base are left blank, and it can make even more sophisticated conditional print decisions. In addition, this program represents the first step toward an entirely different type of report that will be introduced in Chapter 18—one that lists all of the customer information *and* all of the customer's invoice and payment transactions (in other words, all of the information on the manual ledger cards).

You already know how to use @ ... SAY commands to print the fields from the Customer File in the same layout produced by the NWCUSTRF.FRM report form. This program must address two new problems: printing page headers and footers and keeping track of how far down the page the printer has advanced, in order to eject the paper to the top of the next sheet at the proper time rather than printing over the perforations between pages. For some reports, including the National Widgets Customer Reference List, you could easily calculate when to begin a new page. If the top margin, including page heading, used nine lines, and the bottom margin, which contains the footing, were six lines deep, this would leave 51 lines (66 − (9 + 6) = 51) for data. Since each customer record occupies four lines and one blank line should be printed between records, ten customer records will fit on each page. You might therefore structure the program with two nested DO WHILE loops:

```
open the Customer File
do the following until you reach the end of the file:
    print the page heading
    initialize a counter with a value of 1
    do the following while the counter is less than or equal to 10:
        print a customer record
        increment the counter
        skip to the next customer record
    end of steps to do while the counter is less than or equal to 10
    print the page footing
    eject the paper
end of steps to do until you reach the end of the file
```

Since all of the row coordinates in the @ ... SAY commands can be specified with the relative PROW( ) function, there is no need to count lines explicitly. However, this approach breaks down when transaction detail must be added to the report, because different customers will have varying numbers of transactions, making it impossible to predict the exact number of how many lines to allocate for each record. A more general strategy involves using as a line counter a memory variable that always contains the number of the next available line on which data may be printed. Before printing each line, the program could check the counter and, if it has reached a specified value, print the page footer, eject the paper, increment the page number, and print the heading for the new page.

However, it is not necessary or even desirable to check the counter every time a line is printed. In this type of report, you would not want to split across a page boundary the group of lines that make up a customer record; so it is only necessary to test the line counter once per record. To leave a one-inch margin at the bottom of a 66-line page, the program should begin a new page if the line counter is higher than 56; this way, no customer record would extend past line 60.

In general, the program works like this:

```
open the Customer File with the account number index
for each record in the Customer File:
    if we are past line 56,
        print a page footer
        eject the paper
        increment the page number
        print a page heading
    print the data from the customer record
end of steps to do for each record in the file
```

The complete program, NWCREF1.PRG, is listed in Figure 17-11; the detailed pseudocode outline is shown in Figure 17-12. Note how the program ensures that the page header, but not the page footer, is printed before the first data record is processed. Since the header is printed whenever the line counter reaches 56, the counter variable, MLINE, is initialized with a value higher than 56, which forces dBASE III PLUS to print the heading before the first data record. However, the footer—which in this case consists of a short notation on line 64 identifying the designer of the report—is only printed if the line counter does not still have its initial value, 65. Since the test for when to print the page header ensures that no customer data will ever be printed this low on the page, MLINE will never have the value 65 after any customer data has been printed. Thus, the footer is printed at the bottom of page 1, but *not* before the first page of the report is printed.

No EJECT command is needed to advance the paper to the top of the next page when the line counter reaches 56. Whenever a program attempts to print on a line with a number lower than the row coordinate in the previous @ ... SAY command, dBASE III PLUS first sends a form-feed command to the printer, so that the data is printed on the specified line on the new page. Printing the first line of the page heading on line 1

```
* NWCREF1.PRG
* PROGRAM TO PRINT CUSTOMER REFERENCE LIST
* WRITTEN BY:  M.LISKIN        7/28/85

use NWCUST index NWCACCT

store 65 to MLINE
store 1  to MPAGE

set device to print

do while .not. eof()

   * PRINT PAGE HEADER
   if MLINE > 56
      * IF A PAGE OF DATA HAS BEEN PRINTED, PRINT PAGE FOOTER
      if MLINE <> 65
         @ 64, 0 say "Prepared by Miriam Liskin"
      endif
      @  1,   0 say cmonth(date()) + str(day(date()),3) + ", " +;
                    str(year(date()),4)
      @  1,123 say "PAGE " + str(MPAGE,3)
      @  3, 55 say "NATIONAL WIDGETS, INC."
      @  4, 54 say chr(27) + "E" + "CUSTOMER REFERENCE LIST" + chr(27) + "F"
      @  7,   0 say "ACCOUNT ID   ADDRESS                              " +;
                    "CONTACT / PHONE / EQUIP      ORDER DATES           " +;
                    "YEAR-TO-DATE            TOTAL"
      @  8,   0 say "----------   ------------------------------- " +;
                    "------------------------   ---------------       " +;
                    "----------------    -----------------"
      store MPAGE + 1 to MPAGE
      store 10        to MLINE
   endif                               [ past line 56 ]

   * CONSTRUCT NAME AND ADDRESS VARIABLE
   store "" to MADDRESS
   if COMPANY <> " "
      store COMPANY to MADDRESS
   endif
   store MADDRESS + ADDRESS1 + "      " to MADDRESS
   if ADDRESS2 <> " "
      store MADDRESS + ADDRESS2 + "      " to MADDRESS
   endif
   store MADDRESS + trim(CITY) + ", " + STATE + "   " + ZIP to MADDRESS
   store left(MADDRESS + space(120), 120) to MADDRESS

   * PRINT CUSTOMER DATA
   @ MLINE,       0 say chr(27) + "E" + ACCOUNT + chr(27) + "F"
   @ MLINE,      13 say substr(MADDRESS,1,30)
   @ MLINE,      45 say CONTACT
   @ MLINE,      73 say "FIRST: " + dtoc(FIRSTORDER)
   @ MLINE,      92 say "INV: " + transform(YTDINV, "9,999,999.99")
   @ MLINE,     113 say "INV: " + transform(TOTINV, "9,999,999.99")
   @ MLINE + 1, 13 say substr(MADDRESS,31,30)
   @ MLINE + 1, 45 say "(" + AREACODE + ") " + TELEPHONE
   @ MLINE + 1, 73 say "LAST:  " + dtoc(LASTORDER)
   @ MLINE + 1, 92 say "PMT: " + transform(YTDPMT, "9,999,999.99")
```

Figure 17-11. A program to print a Customer Reference List

```
      @ MLINE + 1,113 say "PMT: " + transform(TOTPMT, "9,999,999.99")
      @ MLINE + 2, 13 say substr(MADDRESS,61,30)
      @ MLINE + 2, 45 say EQUIPMENT
      @ MLINE + 2,118 say "------------"
      @ MLINE + 3, 13 say substr(MADDRESS,91,30)
      @ MLINE + 3,118 say TOTINV - TOTPMT picture "9,999,999.99"

      store MLINE + 5 to MLINE

      skip

   enddo                    [ not end-of-file ]

   @ 64, 0 say "Prepared by Miriam Liskin"
   eject
   set device to screen

   return
```

Figure 17-11. A program to print a Customer Reference List (*continued*)

triggers this automatic page eject for all except the first page, when despite the value of the line counter (65), there has been no "previous" @ ... SAY command. Remember that the dBASE III PLUS report generator performs a page eject before beginning a report (unless you include the NOEJECT keyword in your REPORT command), in case a previous output command—LIST TO PRINT, for example—has left the printer positioned in the middle of a page. If you wish to simulate this behavior, you can include an EJECT in your report-printing programs before the DO WHILE loop that processes all of the records in the file.

The page header is similar to the one produced by the NWCUSTRF.FRM report form, except that the NWCREF1.PRG program prints the page number at the right-hand edge of line 1 and the date at the left. A combination of dBASE III PLUS date functions transforms a date in the form 07/31/87 to July 31,1987. The page number variable, MPAGE, is converted to a character string so it may be concatenated easily with the prompt "PAGE ". The report title consists of the same two lines as the original report form, although in a program you are not limited to the four lines of page titles allowed by the dBASE III PLUS report generator, and the lines need not be centered. Similarly, the column titles could occupy more than four lines, and you could, if you wished, draw a continuous line of dashes across the page below the column titles. (This is impossible with the report generator, which automatically places one space between

```
open the customer file with the account number index

initialize a variable, MLINE, for the line counter, with a value of 65
initialize a variable, MPAGE, for the page number, with a value of 1

route output to the printer

for each record in the customer file:

   if we are past line 56,
      if the line counter is not 65 (i.e., we have printed a page of data)
         print the page footer
      endif
      print the page header
      increment the page number
      reset the line counter to 10
   endif                            [ we are past line 56 ]

   initialize a memory variable, MADDRESS, for the customer address
   if the company field is not blank,
      store the company name in MADDRESS
   endif
   add the first address line plus 5 spaces to the value of MADDRESS
   if the second address line is not blank,
      add the second address line plus 5 blank spaces to the value of MADDRESS
   endif
   add the city, state, and zip fields to the value of MADDRESS
   add 120 blank spaces to the value of MADDRESS, and then store the first
       120 characters of MADDRESS to MADDRESS

   print the fields from the customer file on lines MLINE, MLINE + 1,
       MLINE + 2, and MLINE + 3

   add 5 to the line counter, MLINE

   skip to the next record

enddo                         [ not end-of-file ]

print the page footer
eject the paper
route output to the screen

exit from the program
```

Figure 17-12. The Customer Reference List program in pseudocode

columns and does not allow any portion of a column heading to span two columns.) The last line of the page heading is printed on line 8, and line 9 will be left blank; so after printing the heading, MLINE is reset to 10, the line on which the next customer record should begin. At the same time the value of MPAGE is incremented in preparation for printing the heading on the next page.

In this example, the report title is printed in boldface. This is accomplished by adding the required printer control commands (expressed as

ASCII characters by using the CHR function) to the beginning and end of the character string that makes up the title:

```
@  4,54 say CHR(27) + "E" + "CUSTOMER REFERENCE LIST" + CHR(27) + "F"
```

The particular codes used in NWCREF1.PRG activate and terminate "emphasized" print on Epson dot-matrix printers. If you have a different printer, you can look up the appropriate control codes in your printer manual. Note that the E in the command (ESCAPE-E) that initiates the special print mode is an ordinary uppercase E that could also have been included in the character string that forms the title:

```
@  4,54 say CHR(27) + "ECUSTOMER REFERENCE LIST" + CHR(27) + "F"
```

The E was instead placed in a separate character string to make it clearer to anyone reading the program that this character is part of a special print command, not a typographical error in the page title.

If the program were to emulate the report form exactly, the next step would be a series of @ ... SAY commands to print the customer fields on the next four lines on the page. However, like the other programs in this chapter, the Customer Reference List program should suppress blank lines in the customer company name and address section. This is more difficult than the same operation in the programs that printed index cards, envelopes, and letters, because other fields are printed on each of the four address lines. Because @ ... SAY commands must print fields from left to right on each line, and from the top of the page to the bottom, the program must know in advance exactly which fields will be printed on each line.

To resolve this problem, the NWCREF1.PRG program constructs a single memory variable, MADDRESS, that contains all four address lines, each beginning at a fixed position, with the nonblank fields first. Four substrings of this variable yield the four separate address lines that must be printed on the report. MADDRESS is initialized as a null string and built up in stages. If the COMPANY field is not blank, it becomes the new value of MADDRESS; if it is blank, MADDRESS is still 0 characters in length after this first IF loop. Since there is always a first address line, the ADDRESS1 field is appended unconditionally to the current value of MADDRESS. If it is not blank, ADDRESS2 is then added onto the current value of MADDRESS, and the CITY, STATE, and ZIP fields follow. If you use this technique to combine fields of unequal lengths (as in this example), make sure that each component of the combined memory variable is the same length — that of the longest field it might contain. In NWCREF1.PRG, all of the address lines added to MADDRESS are filled out to the length of the COMPANY field (30 characters) with blank spaces.

In order to extract the four 30-character substrings to be printed on the report, MADDRESS must be at least 120 characters long; but at this point it might be almost any length, because it may or may not contain the COMPANY and ADDRESS2 fields, and also because the CITY field is TRIMmed. To resolve this problem, 120 blank spaces are added to the current value of MADDRESS and then the LEFT function is used to extract the first (left-most) 120 characters. This way, the steps that actually print the data do not have to include a check to see how long MADDRESS is. The variable is constructed so that all of the nonblank fields are at the beginning. Thus, the program can simply print the four 30-character substrings of MADDRESS beginning at positions 1, 31, 61, and 91. Since no other fields will be printed *below* the address, it makes no difference if the last one or two substrings consist only of blank spaces.

Note that the four address lines are all printed by using the SUBSTR function, to emphasize that they are completely equivalent, rather than by using the LEFT function for the first 30 characters and RIGHT for the last. In contrast, the LEFT function used in constructing MADDRESS simply shortens and clarifies the last STORE command in the sequence. Also, the last two steps in this procedure — adding the CITY, STATE, and ZIP fields to the address, adding 120 blank spaces, and extracting the first 120 characters of the resulting string — could have been combined into one, unless you feel the denser expression makes the program harder to understand:

```
store left(MADDRESS + trim(CITY) + ", " + STATE + "  " + ZIP +;
      space(120), 120) to MADDRESS
```

The series of @ ... SAY commands that print the rest of the fields is long but straightforward. This program uses the relative coordinates MLINE + 1, MLINE + 2, and MLINE + 3 for the line numbers within each customer record. After printing each group of four lines, MLINE is updated in a single step by adding 5 to its current value — 4 for the lines already printed, plus 1 for the blank line between the records. You could instead increment the counter after printing each line:

```
store MLINE + 1 to MLINE
```

This method allows you to always specify the line number in exactly the same way, as MLINE, whereas the relative coordinates make it easier to see at a glance how many lines of data are printed per record.

The NWCREF1.PRG program prints the account number in the same emphasized print used for the page title by adding the same print commands to the @ ... SAY command used to print the ACCOUNT field. After printing the data for each customer, the program SKIPs to the next record in the file. After all of the records have been printed, the page footer is printed on the last page of the report, an EJECT command forces the sheet of paper out of the printer, and the output of @ ... SAY commands is returned to the console with SET DEVICE TO SCREEN.

The hardest task in writing this type of program is designing an attractive and easy-to-read page layout. If you are working from an existing report form, you can use it as a point of departure for the report. However, certain changes in the format of the data—for example, using PICTUREs or the TRANSFORM function to insert commas in numeric fields—will necessitate reformatting the report to accommodate the wider columns required by these fields. The dBASE III PLUS report generator can help you with the task of determining the column coordinates to use in the @ ... SAY commands in your programs. You can route the output of any dBASE III PLUS report to a disk file with the TO FILE option. For example, this command sequence "prints" the Customer Reference List designed in Chapter 5 to a disk file called NWCUSTRF.TXT:

```
USE NWCUST INDEX NWCACCT
REPORT FORM NWCUSTRF TO FILE NWCUSTRF
```

You can then edit the resulting text file, NWCUSTRF.TXT, with a word processor or the MODIFY COMMAND editor to see how changes affect the appearance of the report. You can even read the column heading lines into the program directly: simply add quotation marks and break the long lines into shorter strings so they do not extend beyond the screen's right margin or wrap around, obscuring the program's indentation and loop structure. If you need to move or widen a column, you can make these changes in one line of the text file; and if your word processor displays the cursor column and row position, you can read off the row coordinates of the fields by moving the cursor across a line.

Remember that most word processors call the first column on the screen column 1, whereas dBASE III PLUS begins numbering the columns with 0; so you must either forego the use of column 0 in your programs or remember to subtract 1 from each column position. A RAM-resident notepad utility like SideKick is particularly useful for this task, since you can load the text file into the notepad and load the dBASE III PLUS program that must print the same format into your editor and flip quickly between the two. This trick can be a valuable timesaver even for reports that cannot be printed by the report generator because they require complex calculations or more than two levels of subtotals. You can create a simplified version of the report with the desired column widths and headings, print it to disk, and then use the resulting text file as a guide to the layout of the fields in the program with which you will print the report.

PRINTING REPORTS WITH SUBTOTALS AND STATISTICS

While the dBASE III PLUS report generator can easily produce reports with one line of data per record and one or two levels of subtotals, the dBASE III PLUS programs presented in this section offer significant advantages. Through examples of the National Widgets Order Reference Lists, the section will demonstrate methods for printing fields from more than two files and calculating statistics other than column totals. The first program will print the National Widgets Order Reference List in numerical sequence by invoice number. This report lists all the records in the Order File and subtotals for each invoice. In addition to the subtotals and grand totals, the program calculates and prints the total number of invoices and the average invoice amount. You can use the techniques introduced in this program to produce reports that require more complex calculations and to print components of other types of reports, such as the detail sections of invoices, statements, and the complete Customer List with transactions.

Here is one overall strategy for printing a report with one level of subtotals:

```
open the Order History, Inventory, and Customer files
initialize memory variables to accumulate the subtotals, grand totals,
    and number of invoices
initialize memory variables for the current invoice number and
    customer account number

for each record in the Order History File:
```

if we are past line 56,

print a page footer
eject the paper
increment the page number
print a page header

print the data from the order record and matching inventory record
add the order data into the subtotals

skip to the next record in the file

if the invoice number has changed,
print the subtotals
add the subtotals into the grand totals
increment the invoice counter
zero the subtotals to prepare for the next invoice
reset the current invoice number and customer account number

end of steps to do for each record in the file

print the grand totals and statistics

A program that illustrates this method, NWOREFI1.PRG, is listed in Figure 17-13; the detailed pseudocode outline is shown in Figure 17-14. Figure 17-15 illustrates the appearance of the final report.

```
* NWOREFI1.PRG
* PROGRAM TO PRINT ORDER SUMMARY WITH SUBTOTALS BY INVOICE NUMBER
* WRITTEN BY:  M.LISKIN       7/28/85

select 1
use NWCUST   index NWCACCT

select 2
use NWINVENT index NWICATPT

select 3
use NWORDER  index NWOINVC
set relation to CATEGORY + PARTNUMBER into NWINVENT

store 0.00    to MINVSUB, MINVDISC, MINVAMT, MSUB, MDISC, MAMT
store INVOICE to MINVOICE
store ACCOUNT to MACCOUNT
```

Figure 17-13. A program to print the Order Reference List with subtotals by invoice number

```
store 0        to MCOUNT
store 1        to MPAGE
store 65       to MLINE

set device to print

do while .not. eof()

   * PRINT PAGE HEADER
   if MLINE > 56
      * IF A PAGE OF DATA HAS BEEN PRINTED, PRINT PAGE FOOTER
      if MLINE <> 65
         @ 64, 0 say "Prepared by Miriam Liskin"
      endif
      @  1,  0 say cmonth(date()) + str(day(date()),3) + ", " +;
                   str(year(date()),4)
      @  1,123 say "PAGE " + str(MPAGE,3)
      @  3, 55 say "NATIONAL WIDGETS, INC."
      @  4, 47 say "ORDER REFERENCE LIST BY INVOICE NUMBER"
      @  7,  0 say "CATEGORY   PART NUMBER   ITEM DESCRIPTION              " +;
                   "EQUIPMENT   QUANTITY      PRICE   SUBTOTAL    " +;
                   "DISC RATE   DISCOUNT   INV AMOUNT"
      @  8,  0 say "--------   -----------   -------------------------     " +;
                   "---------   --------   ---------   --------    " +;
                   "---------   ---------   ----------"
      store MPAGE + 1 to MPAGE
      store 10        to MLINE
   endif                [ we are past line 56 ]


   * PRINT ORDER FIELDS
   @ MLINE,  0 say CATEGORY
   @ MLINE, 11 say PARTNUMBER
   @ MLINE, 25 say NWINVENT->DESCRIP
   @ MLINE, 53 say EQUIPMENT
   @ MLINE, 67 say QUANTITY
   @ MLINE, 76 say PRICE     picture "9,999.99"
   @ MLINE, 87 say SUBTOTAL  picture "9,999.99"
   @ MLINE,100 say DISCRATE
   @ MLINE,110 say DISCOUNT  picture "9,999.99"
   @ MLINE,123 say INVAMOUNT picture "9,999.99"
   store MLINE + 1 to MLINE

   * ADD ORDER AMOUNTS INTO INVOICE SUBTOTALS
   store MINVSUB  + SUBTOTAL  to MINVSUB
   store MINVDISC + DISCOUNT  to MINVDISC
   store MINVAMT  + INVAMOUNT to MINVAMT

   skip

   * IF INVOICE NUMBER HAS CHANGED, PRINT SUBTOTALS
   if INVOICE <> MINVOICE

      * FIND MATCHING CUSTOMER RECORD
      select NWCUST
      seek MACCOUNT
      if COMPANY <> " "
         store trim(COMPANY) to MCOMPANY
      else
         store trim(CONTACT) to MCOMPANY
      endif
      select NWORDER
```

Figure 17-13. A program to print the Order Reference List with subtotals by invoice number (*continued*)

```
        * PRINT INVOICE SUBTOTALS
        @ MLINE,     87 say "--------              --------      --------"
        @ MLINE + 1, 2 say "TOTALS FOR INVOICE " + MINVOICE +;
          "  (" + trim(MACCOUNT) + " - " + MCOMPANY + ")"
        @ MLINE + 1, 86 say MINVSUB  picture "99,999.99"
        @ MLINE + 1,109 say MINVDISC picture "99,999.99"
        @ MLINE + 1,122 say MINVAMT  picture "99,999.99"
        store MLINE + 3 to MLINE

        * ADD SUBTOTALS INTO GRAND TOTALS
        store MCOUNT + 1        to MCOUNT
        store MSUB    + MINVSUB  to MSUB
        store MDISC   + MINVDISC to MDISC
        store MAMT    + MINVAMT  to MAMT

        * ZERO SUBTOTAL FIELDS
        store 0.00              to MINVSUB, MINVDISC, MINVAMT
        * RESET CURRENT INVOICE NUMBER AND CUSTOMER ACCOUNT NUMBER
        store INVOICE           to MINVOICE
        store ACCOUNT           to MACCOUNT

     endif                  [ the invoice number has changed ]

  enddo                     [ not end-of-file ]

  * PRINT GRAND TOTALS
  @ MLINE,     87 say "========              ========      ========"
  @ MLINE + 1,  0 say "GRAND TOTALS:"
  @ MLINE + 1, 86 say MSUB  picture "99,999.99"
  @ MLINE + 1,109 say MDISC picture "99,999.99"
  @ MLINE + 1,122 say MAMT  picture "99,999.99"
  @ MLINE + 3,  0 say "AVERAGE FOR " + str(MCOUNT,4) + " INVOICES:"
  @ MLINE + 3,122 say MAMT/MCOUNT picture "99,999.99"

  @ 64, 0 say "Prepared by Miriam Liskin"
  eject
  set device to screen

  return
```

Figure 17-13. A program to print the Order Reference List with subtotals by invoice number *(continued)*

```
open the customer file with the account number index

open the inventory file with the category/part number index

open the order file with the invoice number index
link this file to the inventory file by category + partnumber
```

Figure 17-14. The Order Reference List program in pseudocode

```
initialize memory variables for the invoice subtotals and grand totals
initialize a memory variable, MINVOICE, for the current invoice number
   with the invoice number from the first order record
initialize a memory variable, MACCOUNT, for the current customer account number
   with the account number from the first order record
initialize a memory variable, MCOUNT, for the invoice count with a value of Ø
initialize a memory variable, MPAGE, for the page number with a value of 1
initialize a memory variable, MLINE, for the line counter with a value of 65

route the output to the printer

for each record in the order file:

   if we are past line 56
      if the line counter is not 65 (i.e., we have printed a page of data
         print the page foooter
      endif
      print the page header
      increment the page counter
      reset the line counter to 1Ø
   endif                 [ we are past line 56 ]

   print the order fields and the description from the inventory record

   increment the line counter
   add the invoice subtotal, discount, and invoice amount into the
      invoice subtotals

   skip to the next record

   if the invoice number has changed,

      select the customer file
      find the customer for this order
      if the company name is not blank,
         store the company name to the variable MCOMPANY
      otherwise
         store the contact name to the variable MCOMPANY
      endif
      select the order file
      print a row of dashes under each column to be subtotalled
      print the text "TOTALS FOR INVOICE " plus the current invoice number
         plus the customer account number and the variable MCOMPANY
      print the subtotal, discount, and invoice amount subtotals
      add 3 to the line counter

      increment the invoice counter
      add the invoice subtotals into the grand totals
      zero the invoice subtotals
      reset the current invoice number
      reset the current customer account number

   endif                 [ the invoice number has changed ]

enddo                    [ not end-of-file ]

print a row of dashes under each column to be totalled
print the text "GRAND TOTALS:"
print the grand totals
print the text "AVERAGE FOR " plus the invoice count plus the text " INVOICES:"
calculate the average by dividing the total invoice amount by the invoice
   count, and print the average
```

Figure 17-14. The Order Reference List program in pseudocode *(continued)*

```
print the page footer
eject the page
route the output to the screen

exit from the program
```

Figure 17-14. The Order Reference List program in pseudocode (*continued*)

This program begins by opening the three required files and linking the Order File to the Inventory File with SET RELATION. As discussed in Chapter 16, you could instead have used SET RELATION to find the matching customer record for each order and SEEK to retrieve the inventory record. In this case, SET RELATION was chosen for the Inventory File because this lookup must be done once for each order record, whereas access to the customer record is needed less frequently—only once for the group of orders that make up an invoice. The program therefore lets dBASE III PLUS work "behind the scenes" to obtain the inventory information and uses SEEK to find the matching customer record.

The program must keep track of several additional details. It must determine when the invoice number has changed in order to stop and print subtotals before continuing to print order detail lines. To accomplish this, a memory variable called MINVOICE is used to keep track of the data from the previous record in the file. This variable is initialized at the beginning of the program with the invoice number from the first (indexed) record in the Order File. You could update the value of MINVOICE for each record processed, but since the invoice number remains the same within each group of orders, it only needs to be updated when the invoice number has changed. Therefore, the logical place to update the value of MINVOICE is just after printing a set of subtotals. The variable MACCOUNT keeps track of the customer account number for the group of orders that make up an invoice so the program can SEEK the appropriate customer record and print the company name on the report. The ACCOUNT field changes when (and only when) the invoice number changes, so this variable is updated at the same time as MINVOICE.

```
May 11, 1987                                                                                          PAGE  1

                                              NATIONAL WIDGETS, INC.
                                       ORDER REFERENCE LIST BY INVOICE NUMBER

CATEGORY   PART NUMBER   ITEM DESCRIPTION            EQUIPMENT  QUANTITY      PRICE   SUBTOTAL  DISC RATE   DISCOUNT  INV AMOUNT
--------   -----------   -------------------------   ---------  --------  ---------   --------  ---------  ---------  ----------

FORMS      820-20        3-1/2 x 1" Labels, 1-up                       1      21.95      21.95       0.00       0.00       21.95
DISK       101-65        5-1/4" DSDD Soft Sector                       1      48.00      48.00       0.00       0.00       48.00
STOR       481-20        Locking Disk Storage Tray                     1      19.95      19.95       0.00       0.00       19.95
                                                                                      --------             ---------   ---------
  TOTALS FOR INVOICE 06981   (ELLISMFG - Ellis Manufacturing)                            89.90                  0.00       89.90

DISK       102-10                                                      2      52.00     104.00       0.00       0.00      104.00
                                                                                      --------             ---------   ---------
  TOTALS FOR INVOICE 07039   (YORKPUMP - York Pump, Inc.)                               104.00                  0.00      104.00

ACCESS     541-22        Non-magnetic Copy Stand                       1      32.50      32.50       0.00       0.00       32.50
FORMS      803-32        9-1/2 x 11" White                             2      37.50      75.00       0.00       0.00       75.00
DISK       101-63        5-1/4" DSDD 10 Sector                         1      48.00      48.00       0.00       0.00       48.00
COVER      540-13                                                      1      29.97      29.97       0.00       0.00       29.97
                                                                                      --------             ---------   ---------
  TOTALS FOR INVOICE 07055   (FLOORPLAN - Floor Plan Carpet Center)                     185.47                  0.00      185.47

ACCESS     541-15        Terminal Swivel Mount                         1      92.50      92.50       0.00       0.00       92.50
                                                                                      --------             ---------   ---------
  TOTALS FOR INVOICE 07223   (JOHNSON - J. Thomas Johnson, CPA)                          92.50                  0.00       92.50

DISK       101-45        5-1/4" DSDD Soft Sector                       2      31.50      63.00       0.00       0.00       63.00
FORMS      803-20        14-1/2 x 11" Green Bar                        1      45.25      45.25       0.00       0.00       45.25
RIBBON     240-51        Epson MX/FX100              EPSON             2      14.95      29.90       0.00       0.00       29.90
                                                                                      --------             ---------   ---------
  TOTALS FOR INVOICE 07302   (ABCPLUMB - ABC Plumbing)                                  138.15                  0.00      138.15

DISK       101-45        5-1/4" DSDD Soft Sector                       2      31.50      63.00      10.00       6.30       56.70
STOR       481-10        5-1/4" Disk Case, Blue                        2       2.85       5.70       0.00       0.00        5.70
                                                                                      --------             ---------   ---------
  TOTALS FOR INVOICE 07401   (JENSEN - Arthur Jensen, MD)                                68.70                  6.30       62.40

ACCESS     533-12        Plexiglas Printer Stand                       1      39.95      39.95       0.00       0.00       39.95
FORMS      803-32        9-1/2 x 11" White                             2      37.50      75.00       0.00       0.00       75.00
STOR       481-30        Oak Disk Storage Case                         1      44.95      44.95      10.00       4.50       40.45
RIBBON     240-30        Okidata 80, 81, 82, 83      OKI               3       4.25      12.75       0.00       0.00       12.75
                                                                                      --------             ---------   ---------
  TOTALS FOR INVOICE 07418   (GREENTHUMB - Green Thumb Landscaping)                     172.65                  4.50      168.15

FORMS      803-21        14-1/2 x 11" White                            1      42.50      42.50       0.00       0.00       42.50
PRTWHL     360-10        Diablo Courier 10           DIABLO            1       8.75       8.75       0.00       0.00        8.75
PRTWHL     360-12                                                      1       8.75       8.75       0.00       0.00        8.75
RIBBON     270-51        Diablo Hytype II Multi      DIABLO            6       7.25      43.50      15.00       6.53       36.97
                                                                                      --------             ---------   ---------
  TOTALS FOR INVOICE 07538   (KLEIN - Carol Klein, M.D.)                                103.50                  6.53       96.97


Prepared by Miriam Liskin
```

Figure 17-15. The Order Reference List with subtotals by invoice number

A set of numeric memory variables accumulates the subtotals, grand totals, and counts. The report must add up the SUBTOTAL, DISCOUNT, and INVAMOUNT fields for each invoice; the corresponding memory variables are named MINVSUB, MINVDISC, and MINVAMT. Three more variables, MSUB, MDISC, and MAMT, are used for the grand totals, and MCOUNT contains the total number of invoices. The overall average dollar amount per invoice can be printed at the bottom of the report by dividing MAMT by MCOUNT.

The initialization of the line and page counters and the section of the report that prints the page header and footer should seem familiar: these routines are virtually identical to those used in the program that prints the Customer Reference List. Even though each record occupies only one line in the report, the program stops printing order records at line 56 to allow room for a subtotal. For each order record the required fields from the Order File and matching Inventory File record are printed with @ ... SAY commands, and MLINE is incremented. The three fields to be subtotaled are added into the memory variables that hold the invoice totals, and the program SKIPs to the next record in the file.

At this point, the program must check to see if the invoice number has changed by comparing the INVOICE field from the new record to MINVOICE (the invoice number from the previous group of order records). If the field has changed, the steps in the IF loop are executed and the text "TOTALS FOR INVOICE " is printed, followed by the invoice number, which is stored in the variable MINVOICE. Be careful to print the *memory variable* MINVOICE, not the INVOICE *field;* the SKIP command has already repositioned the data base to a new record with a different invoice number.

The program prints the customer's account number and company name in parentheses next to the subtotal text. A SEEK command can be used to retrieve the matching Customer File record, but there is one complication: National Widgets has quite a few customers who, as individuals or professionals, do not use a company name, and in these cases, the CONTACT field should be printed rather than leaving the space blank. The program therefore creates a memory variable called MCOMPANY to be printed in the subtotal line, and gives it the value of either the COMPANY field or the CONTACT field, depending on whether COMPANY is empty. The text identifying the subtotal line is printed at column 2 rather than directly under the CATEGORY field at column 0, to set it off slightly from the preceding lines of data. The legend is placed on the same line, MLINE + 1, as the subtotals, rather than directly below the data, where it is placed in standard dBASE III PLUS reports. The program also adds dashed lines below the columns of numbers that precede the subtotals. These few examples are illustrative of the ways in which a program can easily format a report more attractively than the dBASE III PLUS report generator.

After the subtotals are printed, the line counter is increased by 3 (to account for the two lines occupied by the dashes and subtotals and to skip one line before beginning the next group of orders), the subtotals are added into the grand totals, and the invoice count is incremented. Although this is the only point at which the invoice count could be updated, there is another way to accumulate the grand totals: you could add the data from each order record into the grand totals at the same time the subtotals are updated. The approach illustrated in NWOREFI1.PRG was chosen partly because it runs a little faster; only one STORE command is required per subtotal field per invoice, instead of one for every order record. Also, when you read the program, it is easier to identify the calculations performed as part of the subtotal processing.

Once the subtotals have been added into the grand totals, NWINVSUB, NWINVDISC, and NWINVAMT are zeroed to begin accumulating the subtotals for the next invoice. After the ENDDO statement, the program prints the grand totals and calculates and prints the average dollar value of the invoices included in the report. You should check the program's printed reports carefully to identify programming mistakes such as forgetting to zero NWINVSUB, NWINVDISC and NWINVAMT or zeroing the subtotals before you update the grand totals. Unless you look closely at the printed reports, you may not spot these bugs, since the program will appear to work. But an examination of the report will reveal the error: if you fail to zero the subtotals, the numbers in each set of subtotals will be higher than in the previous group, and if you zero the subtotals before adding them into the grand totals, the grand totals will be 0. As suggested earlier, NWOREFI1.PRG illustrates only one of the correct ways to write the Order Reference List program. This program reads through the file using one DO WHILE .NOT. EOF( ) loop, as if all records are equal. After reading each record, it pauses to determine whether the invoice number has changed, and if so, it prints a set of subtotals. An alternate approach might treat the file as if the records were grouped by invoice (as they are, if the file is accessed through the invoice number index) and use two nested DO WHILE loops, one to read through the file from beginning to end, and an inner loop to process each group of orders.

This method works as follows:

```
open the Order History, Inventory, and Customer files
initialize memory variables to accumulate the subtotals, grand totals,
   and number of invoices
initialize memory variables for the current invoice number and
   customer account number
for each record in the Order History File:
   for each record in the current invoice group:
      if we are past line 56,
         print a page footer
         eject the paper
         increment the page number
         print a page heading
      print the data from the order record and matching inventory
         record
      add the order data into the subtotals
      skip to the next record in the file
   end of steps to do for the current invoice group
   print the subtotals
   add the subtotals into the grand totals
   increment the invoice counter
   zero the subtotals to prepare for the next invoice
   reset the current invoice number and customer account number
end of steps to do for each record in the file
print the grand totals and statistics
```

A version of the order-printing program, NWOREFI2.PRG, that uses this method is listed in Figure 17-16. For this report neither program structure has a very strong advantage over the other; both are presented so you may choose the one that seems most logical and sensible to use in your own report-printing programs.

Printing Two Levels of Subtotals

Either of the two methods just described can be used to print two or more levels of subtotals. This will be illustrated with a program to print the National Widgets Order Reference List in alphabetical order by cus-

```
* NWOREFI2.PRG
* PROGRAM TO PRINT ORDER SUMMARY WITH SUBTOTALS BY INVOICE NUMBER
* WRITTEN BY:  M.LISKIN        7/28/85

select 1
use NWCUST   index NWCACCT

select 2
use NWINVENT index NWICATPT

select 3
use NWORDER  index NWOINVC
set relation to CATEGORY + PARTNUMBER into NWINVENT

store 0.00    to MINVSUB, MINVDISC, MINVAMT, MSUB, MDISC, MAMT
store INVOICE to MINVOICE
store ACCOUNT to MACCOUNT
store 1       to MPAGE
store 65      to MLINE

set device to print

do while .not. eof()

   * PROCESS ORDERS ON ONE INVOICE
   do while INVOICE = MINVOICE

      * PRINT PAGE HEADER
      if MLINE > 56
         * IF A PAGE OF DATA HAS BEEN PRINTED, PRINT PAGE FOOTER
         if MLINE <> 65
            @ 64, 0 say "Prepared by Miriam Liskin"
         endif
         @ 1,  0 say cmonth(MDATE) + str(day(MDATE),3) + ", " +;
                     str(year(MDATE),4)
         @ 1,123 say "PAGE " + str(MPAGE,3)
         @ 3, 55 say "NATIONAL WIDGETS, INC."
         @ 4, 47 say "ORDER REFERENCE LIST BY INVOICE NUMBER"
         @ 7,  0 say "CATEGORY   PART NUMBER   ITEM DESCRIPTION              " +;
                     "EQUIPMENT   QUANTITY      PRICE   SUBTOTAL    " +;
                     "DISC RATE   DISCOUNT   INV AMOUNT"
         @ 8,  0 say "--------   -----------   -------------------------     " +;
                     "---------   --------   ---------   --------   " +;
                     "---------   ---------   ----------"
         store MPAGE + 1 to MPAGE
         store 10        to MLINE
      endif              [ we are past line 56 ]

      * PRINT ORDER FIELDS
      @ MLINE,  0 say CATEGORY
      @ MLINE, 11 say PARTNUMBER
      @ MLINE, 25 say NWINVENT->DESCRIP
      @ MLINE, 53 say EQUIPMENT
      @ MLINE, 67 say QUANTITY
      @ MLINE, 76 say PRICE     picture "9,999.99"
      @ MLINE, 87 say SUBTOTAL  picture "9,999.99"
      @ MLINE,100 say DISCRATE
      @ MLINE,110 say DISCOUNT  picture "9,999.99"
      @ MLINE,123 say INVAMOUNT picture "9,999.99"
      store MLINE    + 1        to MLINE
```

Figure 17-16. An alternate program to print the Order Reference List with subtotals by invoice number

```
      * ADD ORDER AMOUNTS INTO INVOICE SUBTOTALS
      store MINVSUB  + SUBTOTAL  to MINVSUB
      store MINVDISC + DISCOUNT  to MINVDISC
      store MINVAMT  + INVAMOUNT to MINVAMT

      skip

   enddo                  [ invoice number has not changed ]

   * FIND MATCHING CUSTOMER RECORD
   select NWCUST
   seek MACCOUNT
   if COMPANY <> " "
      store trim(COMPANY) to MCOMPANY
   else
      store trim(CONTACT) to MCOMPANY
   endif
   select NWORDER

   * PRINT INVOICE SUBTOTALS
   @ MLINE,    87 say "--------                --------       --------"
   @ MLINE + 1, 2 say "TOTALS FOR INVOICE " + MINVOICE +;
     "  (" + trim(MACCOUNT) + " - " + MCOMPANY + ")"
   @ MLINE + 1, 86 say MINVSUB  picture "99,999.99"
   @ MLINE + 1,109 say MINVDISC picture "99,999.99"
   @ MLINE + 1,123 say MINVAMT  picture "99,999.99"
   store MLINE + 3 to MLINE

   * ADD INVOICE SUBTOTALS INTO GRAND TOTALS
   store MSUB  + MINVSUB  to MSUB
   store MDISC + MINVDISC to MDISC
   store MAMT  + MINVAMT  to MAMT

   * ZERO INVOICE SUBTOTALS
   store 0.00             to MINVSUB, MINVDISC, MINVAMT
   * RESET CURRENT INVOICE NUMBER AND CUSTOMER ACCOUNT NUMBER
   store INVOICE          to MINVOICE
   store ACCOUNT          to MACCOUNT

enddo                     [ not end-of-file ]

* PRINT GRAND TOTALS
@ MLINE,     87 say "========                ========       ========"
@ MLINE + 1,  0 say "GRAND TOTALS:"
@ MLINE + 1, 86 say MSUB  picture "99,999.99"
@ MLINE + 1,109 say MDISC picture "99,999.99"
@ MLINE + 1,123 say MAMT  picture "99,999.99"

@ 64, 0 say "Prepared by Miriam Liskin"
eject
set device to screen

return
```

Figure 17-16. An alternate program to print the Order Reference List with subtotals by invoice number (*continued*)

tomer, with subtotals by customer and, within each customer's group of orders, by invoice number. A program that prints this report, NWOREFA1.PRG, is listed in Figure 17-17, and the report produced by this program for a small Order History File is listed in Figure 17-18.

```
* NWOREFA1.PRG
* PROGRAM TO PRINT ORDER SUMMARY WITH SUBTOTALS BY CUSTOMER AND INVOICE NUMBER
* WRITTEN BY:  M.LISKIN        7/28/85

select 1
use NWCUST   index NWCACCT

select 2
use NWINVENT index NWICATPT

select 3
use NWORDHST index NWOHACCT
set relation to CATEGORY + PARTNUMBER into NWINVENT

store 0.00     to MINVSUB, MINVDISC, MINVAMT, MCUSTSUB, MCUSTDISC, MCUSTAMT,;
                  MSUB, MDISC, MAMT
store INVOICE to MINVOICE
store ACCOUNT to MACCOUNT
store 0       to MCUSTCOUNT, MCOUNT
store 1       to MPAGE
store 65      to MLINE

set device to print

do while .not. eof()

   * PRINT PAGE HEADER
   if MLINE > 54
      * IF A PAGE OF DATA HAS BEEN PRINTED, PRINT PAGE FOOTER
      if MLINE <> 65
         @ 64, 0 say "Prepared by Miriam Liskin"
      endif
      @  1,   0 say cmonth(date()) + str(day(date()),3) + ", " +;
                    str(year(date()),4)
      @  1,123 say "PAGE " + str(MPAGE,3)
      @  3, 55 say "NATIONAL WIDGETS, INC."
      @  4, 40 say "ORDER REFERENCE LIST BY CUSTOMER AND INVOICE NUMBER"
      @  7,  0 say "CATEGORY   PART NUMBER   ITEM DESCRIPTION            " +;
                    "EQUIPMENT   QUANTITY      PRICE   SUBTOTAL    " +;
                    "DISC RATE   DISCOUNT   INV AMOUNT"
```

Figure 17-17. A program to print the Order Reference List with subtotals by customer and invoice number

```
      @  8,  0 say "--------   -----------   -------------------------   " +;
                   "---------   --------  ---------   --------   " +;
                   "---------   ---------   ----------"
      store MPAGE + 1 to MPAGE
      store 10        to MLINE
   endif               [ we are past line 54 ]

   * PRINT ORDER FIELDS
   @ MLINE,  0 say CATEGORY
   @ MLINE, 11 say PARTNUMBER
   @ MLINE, 25 say NWINVENT->DESCRIP
   @ MLINE, 53 say EQUIPMENT
   @ MLINE, 67 say QUANTITY
   @ MLINE, 76 say PRICE      picture "9,999.99"
   @ MLINE, 87 say SUBTOTAL   picture "9,999.99"
   @ MLINE,100 say DISCRATE
   @ MLINE,110 say DISCOUNT   picture "9,999.99"
   @ MLINE,123 say INVAMOUNT picture "9,999.99"
   store MLINE + 1 to MLINE

   * ADD ORDER AMOUNTS INTO SUBTOTALS
   store MINVSUB  + SUBTOTAL  to MINVSUB
   store MINVDISC + DISCOUNT  to MINVDISC
   store MINVAMT  + INVAMOUNT to MINVAMT

   skip

   * IF INVOICE NUMBER HAS CHANGED, PRINT SUBTOTALS
   if INVOICE <> MINVOICE

      * PRINT INVOICE SUBTOTALS
      @ MLINE,     87 say "--------               --------      --------"
      @ MLINE + 1,  2 say "TOTALS FOR INVOICE " + MINVOICE
      @ MLINE + 1, 86 say MINVSUB  picture "99,999.99"
      @ MLINE + 1,109 say MINVDISC picture "99,999.99"
      @ MLINE + 1,122 say MINVAMT  picture "99,999.99"
      store MLINE + 3 to MLINE

      * ADD INVOICE SUBTOTALS INTO CUSTOMER SUBTOTALS
      store MCUSTCOUNT + 1        to MCUSTCOUNT
      store MCUSTSUB   + MINVSUB  to MCUSTSUB
      store MCUSTDISC  + MINVDISC to MCUSTDISC
      store MCUSTAMT   + MINVAMT  to MCUSTAMT

      * ZERO INVOICE SUBTOTALS
      store 0.00                  to MINVSUB, MINVDISC, MINVAMT
      * RESET CURRENT INVOICE NUMBER
      store INVOICE               to MINVOICE

   endif               [ invoice number has changed ]

   * IF CUSTOMER HAS CHANGED, PRINT SUBTOTALS
   if ACCOUNT <> MACCOUNT

      * FIND MATCHING CUSTOMER RECORD
      select NWCUST
      seek MACCOUNT
      if COMPANY <> " "
         store trim(COMPANY) to MCOMPANY
      else
         store trim(CONTACT) to MCOMPANY
      endif
      select NWORDHST
```

Figure 17-17. A program to print the Order Reference List with subtotals by customer and invoice number (*continued*)

```
    * PRINT CUSTOMER SUBTOTALS
    @ MLINE,     87 say "--------               --------     --------"
    @ MLINE + 1,  2 say "TOTALS FOR CUSTOMER " + trim(MACCOUNT) + " - " +;
                        MCOMPANY
    @ MLINE + 1, 86 say MCUSTSUB  picture "99,999.99"
    @ MLINE + 1,109 say MCUSTDISC picture "99,999.99"
    @ MLINE + 1,122 say MCUSTAMT  picture "99,999.99"
    @ MLINE + 3,  2 say "AVERAGE FOR " + str(MCUSTCOUNT,4) + " INVOICES:"
    @ MLINE + 3,122 say MCUSTAMT / MCUSTCOUNT picture "99,999.99"
    store MLINE + 6 to MLINE

    * ADD CUSTOMER SUBTOTALS INTO GRAND TOTALS
    store MCOUNT + MCUSTCOUNT to MCOUNT
    store MSUB   + MCUSTSUB   to MSUB
    store MDISC  + MCUSTDISC  to MDISC
    store MAMT   + MCUSTAMT   to MAMT
    * ZERO CUSTOMER SUBTOTALS
    store 0.00                to MCUSTSUB, MCUSTDISC, MCUSTAMT
    store 0                   to MCUSTCOUNT
    * RESET CURRENT CUSTOMER ACCOUNT NUMBER
    store ACCOUNT             to MACCOUNT

  endif                 [ customer has changed ]

enddo                   [ not end-of-file ]

* PRINT GRAND TOTALS
@ MLINE,     87 say "========               ========     ========"
@ MLINE + 1,  0 say "GRAND TOTALS:"
@ MLINE + 1, 86 say MSUB  picture "99,999.99"
@ MLINE + 1,109 say MDISC picture "99,999.99"
@ MLINE + 1,122 say MAMT  picture "99,999.99"
@ MLINE + 3,  0 say "AVERAGE FOR " + str(MCOUNT,4) + " INVOICES:"
@ MLINE + 3,122 say MAMT / MCOUNT picture "99,999.99"
@ 64, 0 say "Prepared by Miriam Liskin"
eject
set device to screen

return
```

Figure 17-17. A program to print the Order Reference List with subtotals by customer and invoice number (*continued*)

The files are opened as in NWOREFI1.PRG, except that this program prints from the Order History File and uses the account number index instead of the invoice number index. The program requires an additional set of memory variables to accumulate the customer subtotals; these are identified by the prefix MCUST. The sections of the program that print the page heading and the order fields and add these fields into the invoice level subtotals are taken directly from NWOREFI1.PRG.

The routines that print the subtotals are a bit different. The customer name need not be printed with the invoice subtotals; logically, it should be included in the customer level subtotal text. Notice also that the invoice level subtotals are added not into the grand totals, but into the customer level subtotals, which are later added into the grand totals. After printing the invoice level subtotals, the program checks to determine if the customer account number has also changed. If so, the customer level subtotals and average are printed, and the customer subtotals are added into the grand totals and zeroed out. Finally, the variable MACCOUNT is reset so it contains the account number for the current order record.

A few pitfalls may not be apparent from this sample program. First, *the order in which the program checks to determine if the two subtotal fields have changed is very important.* Since the program prints subtotals for each invoice within each customer's set of order records, it must *first* check to see if the invoice number has changed. If you tested the ACCOUNT field first, found that the customer had changed, and performed the customer level subtotal processing, the invoice subtotals for the last group orders for each customer would not be printed or zeroed out. These numbers would therefore be included in the subtotals for the next customer's first invoice.

Second, in most cases, the test to determine if the field controlling the inner level of subtotals has changed must also check the field controlling the outer level of subtotals. In this example, the invoice numbers are unique, so the invoice number could never be the same for two different customers. Consider, however, a program to print orders with subtotals by CATEGORY within ACCOUNT, using an index based on the combination ACCOUNT + CATEGORY. Obviously the program must check to see if the CATEGORY has changed *before* testing the ACCOUNT field, just as NWOREFA1.PRG tests to determine if the invoice number has changed before checking the customer ACCOUNT.

However, two consecutive order records—for two different customers—might have the same value in the CATEGORY field. In this case, the first test, which checks whether the category has changed, would fail, so the category subtotals would not be printed, added into the customer subtotals, or zeroed out. The change in the customer ACCOUNT field would be detected, so the program would print the customer subtotals in the right place, but these subtotals would not include the customer's last category of orders. Instead, the subtotals for this group of orders would appear as part of the next customer's first set of subtotals. You can avoid this potential problem by printing the inner level of subtotals (in

```
May 11, 1987                                                                                        PAGE  1

                                               NATIONAL WIDGETS, INC.
                                     ORDER REFERENCE LIST BY CUSTOMER AND INVOICE NUMBER

CATEGORY  PART NUMBER  ITEM DESCRIPTION           EQUIPMENT  QUANTITY     PRICE  SUBTOTAL  DISC RATE  DISCOUNT  INV AMOUNT
--------  -----------  -------------------------  ---------  --------  --------  --------  ---------  --------  ----------

DISK      1Ø1-45       5-1/4" DSDD Soft Sector                      2     31.5Ø     63.ØØ       Ø.ØØ      Ø.ØØ       63.ØØ
FORMS     8Ø3-2Ø       14-1/2 x 11" Green Bar                       1     45.25     45.25       Ø.ØØ      Ø.ØØ       45.25
RIBBON    24Ø-51       Epson MX/FX1ØØ             EPSON             2     14.95     29.9Ø       Ø.ØØ      Ø.ØØ       29.9Ø
                                                                                   --------             --------    --------
  TOTALS FOR INVOICE Ø73Ø2                                                           138.15                 Ø.ØØ      138.15

FORMS     8Ø3-2Ø       14-1/2 x 11" Green Bar                       1     45.25     45.25       Ø.ØØ      Ø.ØØ       45.25
                                                                                   --------             --------    --------
  TOTALS FOR INVOICE Ø83Ø2                                                            45.25                 Ø.ØØ       45.25

                                                                                   --------             --------    --------
  TOTALS FOR CUSTOMER ABCPLUMB - ABC Plumbing                                        183.4Ø                 Ø.ØØ      183.4Ø

  AVERAGE FOR    2 INVOICES:                                                                                           91.7Ø

FORMS     82Ø-2Ø       3-1/2 x 1" Labels, 1-up                      1     21.95     21.95       Ø.ØØ      Ø.ØØ       21.95
DISK      1Ø1-65       5-1/4" DSDD Soft Sector                      1     48.ØØ     48.ØØ       Ø.ØØ      Ø.ØØ       48.ØØ
STOR      481-2Ø       Locking Disk Storage Tray                    1     19.95     19.95       Ø.ØØ      Ø.ØØ       19.95
                                                                                   --------             --------    --------
  TOTALS FOR INVOICE Ø6981                                                            89.9Ø                 Ø.ØØ       89.9Ø

FORMS     82Ø-2Ø       3-1/2 x 1" Labels, 1-up                      1     21.95     21.95       Ø.ØØ      Ø.ØØ       21.95
STOR      481-2Ø       Locking Disk Storage Tray                    1     19.95     19.95       Ø.ØØ      Ø.ØØ       19.95
                                                                                   --------             --------    --------
  TOTALS FOR INVOICE Ø8981                                                            41.9Ø                 Ø.ØØ       41.9Ø

                                                                                   --------             --------    --------
  TOTALS FOR CUSTOMER ELLISMFG - Ellis Manufacturing                                 131.8Ø                 Ø.ØØ      131.8Ø

  AVERAGE FOR    2 INVOICES:                                                                                           65.9Ø

ACCESS    541-22       Non-magnetic Copy Stand                      1     32.5Ø     32.5Ø       Ø.ØØ      Ø.ØØ       32.5Ø
FORMS     8Ø3-32       9-1/2 x 11" White                            2     37.5Ø     75.ØØ       Ø.ØØ      Ø.ØØ       75.ØØ
DISK      1Ø1-63       5-1/4" DSDD 1Ø Sector                        1     48.ØØ     48.ØØ       Ø.ØØ      Ø.ØØ       48.ØØ
COVER     54Ø-13                                                    1     29.97     29.97       Ø.ØØ      Ø.ØØ       29.97
                                                                                   --------             --------    --------
  TOTALS FOR INVOICE Ø7Ø55                                                           185.47                 Ø.ØØ      185.47

FORMS     8Ø3-32       9-1/2 x 11" White                            2     37.5Ø     75.ØØ       Ø.ØØ      Ø.ØØ       75.ØØ
COVER     54Ø-13                                                    1     29.97     29.97       Ø.ØØ      Ø.ØØ       29.97
                                                                                   --------             --------    --------
  TOTALS FOR INVOICE Ø8Ø55                                                           1Ø7.5Ø                 Ø.ØØ      1Ø7.5Ø

                                                                                   --------             --------    --------
  TOTALS FOR CUSTOMER FLOORPLAN - Floor Plan Carpet Center                           292.97                 Ø.ØØ      292.97

  AVERAGE FOR    2 INVOICES:                                                                                          146.49

Prepared by Miriam Liskin
```

Figure 17-18. The Order Reference List with subtotals by customer and invoice number

this example, the CATEGORY subtotals) whenever either subtotal field changes, using a test like this:

```
if CATEGORY <> MCATEGORY .or. ACCOUNT <> MACCOUNT
```

Note also that no special actions are required to force the last group of subtotals to print. This is because when the program SKIPs past the last record in the file, dBASE III PLUS considers that the record pointer is positioned at a new blank record, so the tests to determine if either of the subtotal fields has changed will evaluate to .T. rather than generate an error message.

When you run this program, you may notice a few other glitches. With the right combination of records in the Order File, a customer subtotal may be printed uncomfortably close to the bottom of a page. If the last of one customer's orders falls on line 56, seven more lines must be printed (the invoice level subtotals, the customer level totals and average, and two blank lines). This results in only three blank lines for the bottom margin, and leaves no space between the last summary line printed and the page footer (which is always printed on line 64). The easiest way to avoid this awkward spacing is to begin a new page at line 52 or 54 rather than 56. These examples demonstrate the importance of running a program with a realistic sampling of data in order to discover all of the potential problems.

In a large data base, you might also need a substitute for the dBASE III PLUS report generator's subtotal headings that precede each subtotal group. When an invoice contains only a few line items, printing the invoice number *after* the group of order records is acceptable; but if a customer had four pages of orders, you would want to identify the customer first. How to do this may not be obvious. You might consider testing to determine if the account number has changed *before* printing each order line item rather than after. However, MACCOUNT cannot be reset at this time, because it is needed later in the program to determine when to print the subtotals. But unless you change the value of MACCOUNT, the heading will print again on the next—and every other—pass through the loop. Another possibility is to unconditionally print the customer subtotal heading on the first page of the report, right after the page heading. Then, after printing each customer's subtotals, the program could skip a few lines and print the heading for the next customer. As long as you place this step in an IF loop that ensures that the heading is not printed at the end-of-file, this method works, but it repeats the same section of code twice and makes the logical structure of the program less clear.

Structuring the program with nested DO WHILE loops, as demonstrated in NWOREFI2.PRG, provides a neater solution to this problem. Three nested loops are required to print two levels of subtotals: one to process all of the records in the file, one to process each customer's group of order records, and the innermost loop to process the orders that make up each invoice.

This is the general strategy:

```
open the Order History, Inventory, and Customer files
initialize memory variables to accumulate the subtotals, grand totals,
  and number of invoices
initialize memory variables for the current invoice number and
  customer account number

for each record in the Order History File:

  print the customer subtotal heading

  for each record in the current customer group:

    for each record in the current invoice group:

      if we are past line 56,
        print a page footer
        eject the paper
        increment the page number
        print a page heading

      print the data from the order record and matching inventory
        record

      add the order data into the subtotals
      skip to the next record in the file

    end of steps to do for the current invoice group

    print the invoice subtotals
    add the invoice subtotals into the customer totals
    increment the invoice counter
    zero the invoice subtotals to prepare for the next invoice
    reset the current invoice number

  end of steps to do for the current customer group

  print the customer subtotals
  add the customer subtotals and invoice counter into the grand totals
  zero the customer subtotals to prepare for the next customer
  reset the current customer account number
```

end of steps to do for each record in the file

print the grand totals and statistics

This strategy also leaves a few loose ends to be cleaned up. Because the commands that print the customer subtotal heading occur earlier in the program than the steps that test the line counter to see if it is time to begin a new page, the first customer's subtotal heading will be printed above the page heading on page 1. To solve this problem, the page heading routine must be duplicated before the DO WHILE .NOT. EOF( ) loop. Also, with the right combination of data, one of the customer headings may be printed by itself as the last line on a page. The program should therefore check the line counter just before printing this heading and begin a new page if necessary. Once again, it is necessary to repeat the lines that print the page heading, so the loop structure of the program must be altered to overcome this difficulty.

Whenever the same group of program statements is used more than once within the same program or by many programs in a system (as suggested in the discussion of soliciting report selection criteria from the user), these steps should be contained in a separate program or procedure. Figure 17-19 lists a program, NWOREFA2.PRG, that uses the nested DO WHILE loop structure previously described to print the same report as NWOREFA1.PRG. This program assumes the presence of a separate program, NWHEAD.PRG, that prints the page heading, and another short program, NWFOOT.PRG, that prints the footer. In each of the Order Reference List programs, the commands to print the page footer were also duplicated (the footer must also be printed before the final EJECT command, after the DO WHILE .NOT. EOF( ) loop terminates). This may not have stood out as a major problem because in these examples, the footer consists of only one line. You might try writing the NWHEAD.PRG and NWFOOT.PRG programs by extracting the header and footer lines from NWOREFA1.PRG. In Chapter 18 a program similar to NWHEAD.PRG will be developed to print the page heading on a new version of the Customer Reference List, and in Part IV general-purpose procedures will be designed for printing all of the report headers and footers in a dBASE III PLUS system.

```
* NWOREFA2.PRG
* PROGRAM TO PRINT ORDER SUMMARY WITH SUBTOTALS BY CUSTOMER AND INVOICE NUMBER
* WRITTEN BY:  M.LISKIN       7/28/85

select 1
use NWCUST   index NWCACCT

select 2
use NWINVENT index NWICATPT

select 3
use NWORDHST index NWOACCT
set relation to CATEGORY + PARTNUMBER into NWINVENT

store 0.00     to MINVSUB, MINVDISC, MINVAMT, MCUSTSUB, MCUSTDISC, MCUSTAMT,;
                  MSUB, MDISC, MAMT
store INVOICE to MINVOICE
store ACCOUNT to MACCOUNT
store 0        to MCUSTCOUNT, MCOUNT
store 1        to MPAGE
store 65       to MLINE

set device to print

* PRINT PAGE HEADER
do NWHEAD

do while .not. eof()

   * FIND MATCHING CUSTOMER RECORD
   select NWCUST
   seek MACCOUNT
   if COMPANY <> " "
      store trim(COMPANY) to MCOMPANY
   else
      store trim(CONTACT) to MCOMPANY
   endif
   if MLINE > 54
      do NWHEAD
   endif
   @ MLINE + 2, 0 say "INVOICES FOR " + trim(MACCOUNT) + " - " + MCOMPANY + ":"
   store MLINE + 4 to MLINE

   select NWORDHST

   * PROCESS ONE CUSTOMER'S INVOICES
   do while ACCOUNT = MACCOUNT

      * PROCESS GROUP OF ORDERS ON ONE INVOICE
      do while INVOICE = MINVOICE
```

Figure 17-19. A program to print the Order Reference List with subtotals by customer and invoice number with nested DO WHILE loops

```
         * PRINT PAGE FOOTER, HEADER
         if MLINE > 54
            do NWFOOT
            do NWHEAD
         endif

         * PRINT ORDER RECORDS
         @ MLINE,  0 say CATEGORY
         @ MLINE, 11 say PARTNUMBER
         @ MLINE, 25 say NWINVENT->DESCRIP
         @ MLINE, 53 say EQUIPMENT
         @ MLINE, 67 say QUANTITY
         @ MLINE, 76 say PRICE      picture "9,999.99"
         @ MLINE, 87 say SUBTOTAL   picture "9,999.99"
         @ MLINE,100 say DISCRATE
         @ MLINE,110 say DISCOUNT   picture "9,999.99"
         @ MLINE,123 say INVAMOUNT picture "9,999.99"
         store MLINE + 1 to MLINE

         * ADD ORDER AMOUNTS INTO INVOICE SUBTOTALS
         store MINVSUB  + SUBTOTAL  to MINVSUB
         store MINVDISC + DISCOUNT  to MINVDISC
         store MINVAMT  + INVAMOUNT to MINVAMT

         skip

      enddo                   [ invoice number has not changed ]

      * PRINT INVOICE SUBTOTALS
      @ MLINE,      87 say "--------               --------       --------"
      @ MLINE + 1,  2 say "TOTALS FOR INVOICE " + MINVOICE
      @ MLINE + 1, 86 say MINVSUB  picture "99,999.99"
      @ MLINE + 1,109 say MINVDISC picture "99,999.99"
      @ MLINE + 1,122 say MINVAMT  picture "99,999.99"
      store MLINE + 3 to MLINE

      * ADD INVOICE SUBTOTALS INTO CUSTOMER SUBTOTALS
      store MCUSTCOUNT + 1          to MCUSTCOUNT
      store MCUSTSUB   + MINVSUB    to MCUSTSUB
      store MCUSTDISC  + MINVDISC   to MCUSTDISC
      store MCUSTAMT   + MINVAMT    to MCUSTAMT

      * ZERO INVOICE SUBTOTALS
      store 0.00                    to MINVSUB, MINVDISC, MINVAMT
      * RESET CURRENT INVOICE NUMBER
      store INVOICE                 to MINVOICE
   enddo                      [ customer account number has not changed ]

   * PRINT CUSTOMER SUBTOTALS
   @ MLINE,      87 say "--------               --------       --------"
   @ MLINE + 1,  2 say "TOTALS FOR " + trim(MACCOUNT) + " - " + MCOMPANY
   @ MLINE + 1, 86 say MCUSTSUB  picture "99,999.99"
   @ MLINE + 1,109 say MCUSTDISC picture "99,999.99"
   @ MLINE + 1,122 say MCUSTAMT  picture "99,999.99"
   @ MLINE + 3,  2 say "AVERAGE FOR " + str(MCUSTCOUNT,4) + " INVOICES:"
   @ MLINE + 3,122 say MCUSTAMT / MCUSTCOUNT picture "99,999.99"
   store MLINE + 6 to MLINE
```

Figure 17-19. A program to print the Order Reference List with subtotals by customer and invoice number with nested DO WHILE loops (*continued*)

```
    * ADD CUSTOMER SUBTOTALS INTO GRAND TOTALS
    store MCOUNT + MCUSTCOUNT to MCOUNT
    store MSUB   + MCUSTSUB   to MSUB
    store MDISC  + MCUSTDISC  to MDISC
    store MAMT   + MCUSTAMT   to MAMT

    * ZERO CUSTOMER SUBTOTALS
    store 0.00               to MCUSTSUB, MCUSTDISC, MCUSTAMT
    * RESET CURRENT CUSTOMER ACCOUNT NUMBER
    store ACCOUNT            to MACCOUNT

enddo                       [ not end-of-file ]

* PRINT GRAND TOTALS
@ MLINE,     87 say "========             ========      ========"
@ MLINE + 1,  0 say "GRAND TOTALS:"
@ MLINE + 1, 86 say MSUB  picture "99,999.99"
@ MLINE + 1,109 say MDISC picture "99,999.99"
@ MLINE + 1,122 say MAMT  picture "99,999.99"
@ MLINE + 3,  0 say "AVERAGE FOR " + str(MCOUNT,4) + " INVOICES:"
@ MLINE + 3,122 say MAMT / MCOUNT picture "99,999.99"

* PRINT PAGE FOOTER
do NWFOOT

eject
set device to screen

return
```

Figure 17-19. A program to print the Order Reference List with subtotals by customer and invoice number with nested DO WHILE loops (*continued*)

As you can see, except for the simplest tasks, there are often several ways to write a procedure or to structure an entire program. Although there are many wrong ways to write a particular program, it is not true that only one correct—or even best—way exists. The discussions of the programs in this chapter outlined some alternatives and their respective advantages and described test conditions that may reveal the superiority of some structures over others in certain settings. Although some programmers feel that the only true test of a program is that it works, writing code that is easy to understand and modify is also important. This is often hard to judge until the entire system nears completion, and sometimes the best way to structure a program depends on personal preference and style. In your own work, if you arrive at a method that differs from the examples presented here and that holds up under rigorous testing, trust your own skills and instincts. Your way may be as good as or better than the technique presented here.

18

PRINTING REPORTS FROM MULTIPLE FILES

The programs in this chapter print reports based on two or more data bases and emulate many of the paper forms in the National Widgets manual system. These programs combine the methods used in Chapter 16 to establish the relationships between the files with the overall program structures introduced in the last chapter to produce full-page formats like invoices and statements. As in Chapter 17, the discussion focuses on detailed examples from the National Widgets system. As you read the program descriptions, consider how the report layouts and programming structures presented here might be applied to other data base systems. In your own applications, you are likely to face many of these same problems as well as others that are comparable in complexity, although different in kind.

PRINTING A CUSTOMER LIST WITH TRANSACTIONS

One advantage of computerizing an application is that once the information is entered, it may be used in various calculations and viewed in multiple formats without expending further human energy. The programs presented so far have addressed many of the requirements for entering data and updating totals based on the new entries. However, the system now suffers from one of the inconveniences of the manual system that National Widgets hoped to eliminate by converting to dBASE III PLUS: having to read two or more reports to find information that logically belongs in a single printed format. For each National Widgets customer, you have to look at one report for the customer information, another for the financial transactions, and a third for the customer's order history. Faced with this situation, the user is likely to complain that although the computer generates statistics that would be too difficult to compile by hand, it is easier to obtain basic information from the manual ledger cards. This essential information includes customer contact names, telephone numbers, past-due balances, and payment records, all of which are referred to in the day-to-day operation of the business.

Creating reports that print data from more than one file can help to solve this problem. For example, the National Widgets Customer Reference List program written in Chapter 17 can be expanded to include financial transactions. For each customer the new Customer Reference List program will first print all of the information from the Customer File in the same format as NWCREF1.PRG, and then print all of the customer's invoice data from the Transaction History File with invoice and payment subtotals. The appearance of the report is illustrated in Figure 18-1. This report effectively replaces the manual ledger cards: although it does not physically resemble the cards, the report contains all of the personal and financial information on file for each customer. You will find an analog for this report in any data base system with a file—here, the Customer File—in which each record has multiple matching entries in another—in this case, the Transaction File.

Unlike the manual ledger cards, however, an existing copy of a dBASE III PLUS report cannot be updated easily. To maintain up-to-date printouts, you must reprint each report and replace the old copy with the new. In some ways this is less efficient than the manual system, in which the same set of ledger cards may last for years. But while it requires more computer time and wastes more paper, printing the report requires less time and attention from the users than updating ledger cards; a person must simply be present in case the paper jams. If printing the report were to become too time-consuming, you could write the program so that it asks the user for a cutoff date and prints only those customers with transaction activity after the specified date. Thus, the entire report could be printed twice a year and update reports printed monthly. Each month the new set of report pages could be added to the front of the binder or folder containing all of the reports. To look up a customer, you would start with

```
July 31, 1987                                                                                PAGE  1

                                              NATIONAL WIDGETS, INC.
                                              CUSTOMER REFERENCE LIST

ACCOUNT ID  ADDRESS                         CONTACT / PHONE / EQUIP   ORDER DATES        YEAR-TO-DATE       TOTAL
----------  ------------------------------  ------------------------  ---------------    ----------------   ----------------

ABCPLUMB    ABC Plumbing                    Ed Williams               FIRST: 12/02/85    INV:     385.56   INV:     1,181.97
            1850 University Avenue          (415) 861-4543            LAST:  03/12/87    PMT:     104.24   PMT:     1,038.80
            Berkeley, CA  94703             Kaypro 10, Epson FX-100                                                 ------------
                                                                                                                          143.17

           INVOICE  DATE        SUBTOTAL  DISCOUNT        TAX   SHIPPING  INV AMOUNT  PMT DATE  PMT AMOUNT  REFERENCE
           -------- --------  ---------- --------   --------  ---------- ----------  --------  ----------  ---------------
           07302      /  /        138.15     0.00       0.00       0.00      138.15    /  /          0.00
           10403    04/30/87       96.00     0.00       6.24       2.00      104.24  06/12/87      104.24  Check #1406
           12112    05/20/87      117.25     7.47       7.14       3.50      120.42    /  /          0.00
           14318    06/12/87       19.95     0.00       1.30       1.50       22.75    /  /          0.00
                              ---------- --------   --------  ---------- ----------            ----------
                                  371.35     7.47      14.68       7.00      385.56                104.24

==========================================================================================================================

ANDERSON    3420 19th Street                John Anderson             FIRST: 08/08/85    INV:       0.00   INV:       279.52
            San Francisco, CA  94114        (415) 563-8961            LAST:  12/01/86    PMT:       0.00   PMT:       279.52
                                            Apple IIe                                                               ------------
                                                                                                                            0.00

==========================================================================================================================

ARONOFF     601 First Street                Gina Aronoff              FIRST: 10/09/86    INV:       0.00   INV:       232.50
            Benicia, CA  94510              (707) 745-1813            LAST:  12/15/86    PMT:       0.00   PMT:       232.50
                                            Apple IIc, Imagewriter                                                  ------------
                                                                                                                            0.00

==========================================================================================================================

CHIPCITY    Chip City Electronics           Fred Larson               FIRST:   /  /      INV:       0.00   INV:         0.00
            288 Lorton                      (415) 348-6801            LAST:    /  /      PMT:       0.00   PMT:         0.00
            Burlingame, CA  94010           Osborne Exec, Epson MX-80                                               ------------
                                                                                                                            0.00

==========================================================================================================================

DELTADESGN  Delta Design                    Andrea Bennett            FIRST: 09/15/86    INV:       0.00   INV:       138.15
            2405 Sycamore Drive             (415) 754-7373            LAST:  09/15/86    PMT:       0.00   PMT:       138.15
            Antioch, CA  94509              Macintosh, Imagewriter                                                  ------------
                                                                                                                            0.00

==========================================================================================================================

ELLISMFG    Ellis Manufacturing             Barbara Goddard           FIRST: 10/18/85    INV:      89.90   INV:       767.29
            3091 Park Boulevard             (415) 494-1421            LAST:  02/18/87    PMT:       0.00   PMT:       669.00
            Palo Alto, CA  94306            IBM PC, Okidata 84                                                      ------------
                                                                                                                           89.90

Prepared by Miriam Liskin
```

Figure 18-1. The Customer Reference List with transactions

the latest set of update pages and work your way back toward the older reports.

The decision to print the report this way should not be made lightly, since it affects the way the program must be structured. If you wanted to print all customers, regardless of transaction activity, the program would have to read through the Customer File, print the customer information, and then look for the matching records (if any) in the Transaction History File. If you wanted to print only customers with activity after a certain date, the program would check the Transaction History File before printing the customer data and, if there were no transactions, skip to the next customer. A much more efficient way to process the files would be to read through the Transaction History File in order of customer account number and, if a transaction is found within the specified time frame, find the matching customer record and then print the data from both files. This method of reading two files will be demonstrated later in this chapter in the statement-printing program, so the first strategy, printing every customer record, will be used for the Customer Reference List.

In any program of this type, even if you routinely printed all of the records in the main file—in this case, the Customer File—you would frequently want to print just one record (with the matching transactions) or a few selected records. You might do this to update the printed listing for a particularly active account or to provide a hard copy of the data on a few crucial customers to someone else in the organization. Since this type of report can be very long, the program should also provide the option to restart the report from any specified point in case a print session is interrupted. This may be done using the same general technique illustrated in the label-printing programs in Chapter 12, with one additional provision: to produce a report with consecutively numbered pages, you must also allow the operator to enter the starting page number.

Here is the basic strategy:

```
open the Customer and Transaction History files

ask whether to print customers one at a time
if not,
    ask for the starting account number and page number

for each record in the Customer File:

    if we are printing customers one at a time,
        ask for a customer account number
```

```
        print the data from the customer record
        initialize memory variables for the transaction totals
        select the Transaction History File
        if there are transaction records,
           print a heading for the transaction data
        for each record in the Transaction History File:
           print the data from the transaction history record
           add the data into the transaction totals
        end of steps to do for each record in the Transaction History File
        draw a line across the page
        if the transaction totals are not zero,
           print the transaction totals
        if we are printing customers one at a time,
           eject the paper
        otherwise
           skip to the next record in the file
     end of steps to do for each record in the Customer File
```

The program, NWCREF2.PRG, is listed in Figure 18-2. The only new concept in this program is the method for printing all or selected customers within the same loop structure that prints the entire file. The routine that asks the operator which single customer to print is inside the DO WHILE loop so that these steps may be repeated until the operator chooses to exit by leaving the account number blank. However, this portion of the program is executed only if the user has chosen to print customers one at a time. If you are printing customers one by one, dBASE III PLUS does not process the file in sequence from beginning to end. In fact, it is important *not* to SKIP to the next record after printing each customer: if the operator chose to print the last customer in the file, the SKIP would make the EOF( ) function true, and the program would return to the menu instead of making another pass through the loop and asking for another customer.

The program begins by opening the Customer and Transaction History files and linking them through the ACCOUNT field with SET RELATION. Next, the user is asked whether customers should be printed one at a time, and the selection is stored in the memory variable MONE (pro-

```
* NWCREF2.PRG
* PROGRAM TO PRINT CUSTOMER REFERENCE LIST
* WRITTEN BY:  M.LISKIN       7/28/85

select 1
use NWTXNHST index NWTHACCT

select 2
use NWCUST   index NWCACCT
set relation to ACCOUNT into NWTXNHST

clear
store .F. to MONE
@ 10,10 say "Do you want to print customers one at a time? (Y/N)";
        get MONE picture "Y"
read

store 1  to MPAGE
store 65 to MLINE

* IF NOT PRINTING CUSTOMERS ONE AT A TIME,
* ASK FOR STARTING CUSTOMER AND PAGE NUMBER
if .not. MONE

   * BY DEFAULT, START WITH FIRST CUSTOMER
   store ACCOUNT to MACCOUNT

   do while .T.
      @ 12,10 say "Enter first customer to print" get MACCOUNT picture "@!"
      read
      if MACCOUNT = " "
         return
      endif
      seek trim(MACCOUNT)
      if found()
         @ 14,10 say "Enter starting page number" get MPAGE picture "999"
         read
         exit
      else
         @ 20,10 say trim(MACCOUNT) + "is not in the Customer File"
         @ 21,10 say "Press any key to reenter the customer"
         wait ""
         @ 20,10
         @ 21,10
      endif
   enddo

endif                        [ not printing one customer at a time ]

set device to print

do while .not. eof()

   * IF PRINTING CUSTOMERS ONE AT A TIME, ASK WHICH CUSTOMER TO PRINT
   if MONE
      store "          " to MACCOUNT
      set device to screen
      do while .T.
         @ 12,10 say "Enter customer to print" get MACCOUNT picture "@!"
         read
         if MACCOUNT = " "
            return
         endif
```

Figure 18-2. A program to print the Customer Reference List with transactions

```
         seek trim(MACCOUNT)
         if found()
            set device to print
            exit
         else
            @ 20,10 say trim(MACCOUNT) + "is not in the Customer File"
            @ 21,10 say "Press any key to reenter the customer"
            wait ""
            @ 20,10
            @ 21,10
         endif
      enddo
   endif                    [ printing one customer at a time ]

   if MLINE > 56
      * IF A PAGE OF DATA HAS BEEN PRINTED, PRINT PAGE FOOTER,
      * GO TO NEXT PAGE, PRINT PAGE HEADER
      if MLINE <> 65
         * PRINT PAGE FOOTER
         do NWCFOOT
      endif
      * PRINT PAGE HEADER
      do NWCHEAD
   endif

   * CONSTRUCT NAME AND ADDRESS VARIABLE
   store "" to MADDRESS
   if COMPANY <> " "
      store COMPANY to MADDRESS
   endif
   store MADDRESS + ADDRESS1 + "      " to MADDRESS
   if ADDRESS2 <> " "
      store MADDRESS + ADDRESS2 + "      " to MADDRESS
   endif
   store MADDRESS + trim(CITY) + ", " + STATE + "  " + ZIP to MADDRESS
   store left(MADDRESS + space(120), 120)                 to MADDRESS

   * PRINT CUSTOMER DATA
   @ MLINE,      0 say ACCOUNT
   @ MLINE,     13 say substr(MADDRESS,1,30)
   @ MLINE,     45 say CONTACT
   @ MLINE,     73 say "FIRST: " + dtoc(FIRSTORDER)
   @ MLINE,     92 say "INV: " + transform(YTDINV, "9,999,999.99")
   @ MLINE,    113 say "INV: " + transform(TOTINV, "9,999,999.99")
   @ MLINE + 1, 13 say substr(MADDRESS,31,30)
   @ MLINE + 1, 45 say "(" + AREACODE + ") " + TELEPHONE
   @ MLINE + 1, 73 say "LAST:  " + dtoc(LASTORDER)
   @ MLINE + 1, 92 say "PMT: " + transform(YTDPMT, "9,999,999.99")
   @ MLINE + 1,113 say "PMT: " + transform(TOTPMT, "9,999,999.99")
   @ MLINE + 2, 13 say substr(MADDRESS,61,30)
   @ MLINE + 2, 45 say EQUIPMENT
   @ MLINE + 2,118 say "------------"
   @ MLINE + 3, 13 say substr(MADDRESS,91,30)
   @ MLINE + 3,118 say TOTINV - TOTPMT picture "9,999,999.99"
   store MLINE + 5 to MLINE

   * INITIALIZE VARIABLES FOR TRANSACTION SUBTOTALS
   store 0.00       to MSUB, MDISC, MTAX, MSHIP, MINV, MPMT

   * PRINT TRANSACTIONS
   select NWTXNHST
   * IF THERE ARE TRANSACTIONS...
   if found()
```

Figure 18-2. A program to print the Customer Reference List with transactions (*continued*)

```
      * IF APPROACHING BOTTOM OF THE PAGE
      if MLINE > 56
         * PRINT PAGE FOOTER
         do NWCFOOT
         * PRINT PAGE HEADER
         do NWCHEAD
      endif
      * PRINT TRANSACTION DETAIL COLUMN HEADINGS
      do NWTHEAD
   endif

   * PROCESS GROUP OF TRANSACTIONS FOR ONE CUSTOMER
   do while ACCOUNT = NWCUST->ACCOUNT

      * IF APPROACHING BOTTOM OF THE PAGE...
      if MLINE > 56
         * PRINT PAGE FOOTER
         do NWCFOOT
         * PRINT PAGE HEADER
         do NWCHEAD
         * PRINT TRANSACTION DETAIL COLUMN HEADINGS
         do NWTHEAD
      endif

      * PRINT TRANSACTION FIELDS
      @ MLINE, 10 say INVOICE
      @ MLINE, 20 say INVDATE
      @ MLINE, 31 say SUBTOTAL  picture "99,999.99"
      @ MLINE, 43 say DISCOUNT  picture "99,999.99"
      @ MLINE, 57 say TAX
      @ MLINE, 69 say SHIPPING
      @ MLINE, 79 say INVAMOUNT picture "99,999.99"
      @ MLINE, 91 say PMTDATE
      @ MLINE,103 say PMTAMOUNT picture "99,999.99"
      @ MLINE,115 say REFERENCE
      store MLINE + 1 to MLINE

      * ADD TRANSACTION AMOUNTS INTO SUBTOTALS
      store MSUB  + SUBTOTAL  to MSUB
      store MDISC + DISCOUNT  to MDISC
      store MTAX  + TAX       to MTAX
      store MSHIP + SHIPPING  to MSHIP
      store MINV  + INVAMOUNT to MINV
      store MPMT  + PMTAMOUNT to MPMT

      skip

   enddo                     [ ACCOUNT = customer account ]

   * IF SUBTOTALS ARE PRESENT (I.E., THERE ARE TRANSACTIONS), PRINT THEM
   if MINV > Ø
      @ MLINE,     31 say "---------   ---------   --------   ---------   " +;
                          "----------               -----------"
      @ MLINE + 1, 31 say MSUB  picture "99,999.99"
      @ MLINE + 1, 43 say MDISC picture "99,999.99"
      @ MLINE + 1, 55 say MTAX  picture "9,999.99"
      @ MLINE + 1, 67 say MSHIP picture "9,999.99"
      @ MLINE + 1, 79 say MINV  picture "99,999.99"
      @ MLINE + 1,103 say MPMT  picture "99,999.99"
      store MLINE + 3 to MLINE
   endif
```

Figure 18-2. A program to print the Customer Reference List with transactions (*continued*)

```
    @ MLINE, 0 say replicate("=", 132)
    store MLINE + 2 to MLINE
    select NWCUST

    * IF PRINTING CUSTOMERS ONE AT A TIME, EJECT PAGE
    * OTHERWISE, SKIP TO NEXT CUSTOMER RECORD
    if MONE
       do NWCFOOT
       eject
    else
       skip
    endif

enddo                        [ .not. eof() ]

do NWCFOOT
eject
set device to screen

return
```

Figure 18-2. A program to print the Customer Reference List with transactions (*continued*)

nounced as "M-one," not "moan"). The line and page counters are initialized, and if customers will *not* be printed one at a time, the program asks the operator for the starting customer account number. The variable MACCOUNT, which stores the answer to this question, is initialized with the contents of the ACCOUNT field from the first record in the Customer File, so that by default, the program begins printing with the first customer. If the operator types in a different account number, it is validated with a SEEK command to make sure that the customer exists. Once a valid account number has been entered, the operator is asked for the starting page number, which defaults to 1. Although the program does not allow the operator to request a nonexistent customer, it is the operator's responsibility to enter an appropriate combination of page number and customer account number.

Within the main DO WHILE loop, if customers are being printed one at a time, the operator selects which customer to print. You might consider allowing the operator to enter the page number here as well, so that the printout could be inserted in proper sequence into a previously printed report as a replacement page. In the NWCREF2.PRG program, the decision was made not to print page numbers at all when customers are printed one at a time. After this IF loop, the Customer File is always positioned at the next record to be printed, because the operator has selected the customer individually, because it is the first pass through the loop and the data base is positioned at the first record to be printed, or because one or more customer records have already been printed and the program has returned to the top of the loop. This is also the first of three instances in which the program checks to determine if it must begin a new page and print a page header. The three instances are

- Before printing each customer record.
- Before printing the transaction column headings, so that they do not appear alone at the bottom of a page.
- Before printing each transaction record.

To make matters more complicated, the second and third cases *also* require the transaction column headings to be printed. Also, in the first instance, the program must check the value of MLINE to determine whether to print the page footer, but this test is not necessary in the second and third cases. Once any customer or transaction record has been printed, MLINE cannot still have its initial value of 65—if the value of this variable is greater than 56, at least one full page of data must have been printed. To provide the flexibility to handle all of these situations, the commands that print the page header, page footer, and column headings will be placed in three separate programs that are called by the main program. (Later these separate programs will become procedures.) These three programs are listed in Figures 18-3, 18-4, and 18-5.

The Customer File fields are printed exactly as in the original

```
* NWCFOOT.PRG
* PROGRAM TO PRINT PAGE FOOTER ON CUSTOMER REFERENCE LIST
* WRITTEN BY:  M.LISKIN       5/07/86

@ 64, 0 say "Prepared by Miriam Liskin"

return
```

Figure 18-3. A program to print the Customer Reference List page footer

```
* NWCHEAD.PRG
* PROGRAM TO PRINT PAGE HEADER ON CUSTOMER REFERENCE LIST
* WRITTEN BY:  M.LISKIN       7/28/85

@  1,  0 say cmonth(date()) + str(day(date()),3) + ", " +;
              str(year(date()),4)
if .not. MONE
   @  1,123 say "PAGE " + str(MPAGE,3)
endif
@  3, 55 say "NATIONAL WIDGETS, INC."
@  4, 54 say "CUSTOMER REFERENCE LIST"
@  7,  0 say "ACCOUNT ID   ADDRESS                               " +;
              "CONTACT / PHONE / EQUIP     ORDER DATES          " +;
              "YEAR-TO-DATE          TOTAL"
@  8,  0 say "----------   -------------------------------  " +;
              "-------------------------   ---------------     " +;
              "-----------------    ------------------"
store MPAGE + 1 to MPAGE
store 10        to MLINE

return
```

Figure 18-4. A program to print the Customer Reference List page header

NWCUSTRF.PRG program, after which the program must print the customer's transactions. The memory variables that accumulate the transaction totals are reset to zero, and the Transaction History File is selected. Because the two files are linked with SET RELATION, the Transaction

```
* NWTHEAD.PRG
* PROGRAM TO PRINT TRANSACTION COLUMN HEADINGS ON CUSTOMER REFERENCE LIST
* WRITTEN BY:  M.LISKIN       7/28/85

@ MLINE + 1, 10 say "INVOICE   DATE         SUBTOTAL    DISCOUNT          " +;
                    "TAX     SHIPPING    INV AMOUNT   PMT DATE    " +;
                    "PMT AMOUNT   REFERENCE"
@ MLINE + 2, 10 say "--------  --------    ---------   ---------    " +;
                    "--------   ---------    ----------    --------   " +;
                    "-----------   ---------------"
store MLINE + 4 to MLINE

return
```

Figure 18-5. A program to print the transaction detail column headings

History File will be positioned at a valid record and the FOUND( ) function will have the value .T. if the customer has one or more transactions. It is important to carry out the test for existing transactions *before* calling NWTHEAD.PRG to print the transaction column headings. If there are no transactions, no column titles should be printed, but the program cannot just select the Customer File and loop back to the top of the main DO WHILE loop to print the next customer. It must first draw a line across the page to separate the two adjacent customer records and either print the page footer and EJECT the paper to the top of the next page (if the program is printing customers one at a time) or SKIP to the next record (if the entire file is being printed). Before printing the column headings, the program also checks the value of MLINE to determine if it must begin a new page so that the transaction column titles are never printed alone on the last few lines of a page.

The DO WHILE loop that prints the transaction data need not be placed within the same IF loop that tests for the presence of transactions, because the condition in the DO WHILE statement (ACCOUNT = NWCUST—>ACCOUNT) ensures that the steps within this loop are not executed even once unless a transaction that matches the customer record exists. The program prints the transaction records and updates the subtotals in a manner similar to the Order Reference List programs presented in Chapter 17. If there are no transactions, these memory variables still have their initial zero values after the inner DO WHILE loop terminates; the program tests for this possibility and prints the subtotals only if transactions exist. Whether or not transactions have been printed, the program draws a double line across the page and selects the NWCUST file to prepare to print the next customer. When printing single customers, the program ejects the page from the printer; otherwise, the program SKIPs to the next record in the file.

A PROGRAM TO PRINT STATEMENTS

Printing statements is very similar to printing the Customer Reference List with transactions although their page layouts are different. In both cases, fields from one record in the Customer File are printed with a set of matching transactions. If anything, setting up the page format for statements is easier. In the National Widgets system, each statement requires only one page, since no customer would ever have more than a few outstanding transactions. In a larger business, or a different type of application that used a page format similar to that of a statement, you could test the value of the line counter variable before printing each transaction, just as in the Customer Reference List program. When necessary, the program could advance to a new page and print the transaction detail column headings on the new page. Depending on the context, you might or might not also want to reprint all of the customer data on the second page of the statement (which would work much like printing a page header).

In the National Widgets system, statements will be printed on plain 8 1/2- × 11-inch paper; by changing the @ ... SAY commands that print the fields and resetting the page length with printer control commands, you could easily adapt the program to a form of any size or shape. Since only current transactions are of interest, the report is printed from the Transaction File rather than the Transaction History File. In any given month, statements probably will *not* be required for most customers, so instead of reading through the Customer File in sequence (which was necessary to print the Customer Reference List), the statement-printing program will work from the Transaction File and find the matching customer for each group of transactions.

The statement includes subtotals for only two Transaction File fields, INVAMOUNT and PMTAMOUNT, but some additional calculations are required to perform the desired aging of unpaid invoices. Separate subtotals must be accumulated for invoices that fall into four standard aging categories: current, 0-30 days past due, 31-60 days past due, and over 60 days past due. The operator must supply the date from which to age each invoice. This will not necessarily be either the current date or the last day of the month, since one month's statements might not be printed until the following month. Any invoices that are dated within 30 days of the cutoff date entered by the operator are considered current, consistent with National Widgets' net 30-day payment terms. Invoices within 30 to 60 days of the cutoff date are in the 0-30 days past-due category, and so on.

This is the general approach:

open the Customer and Transaction files

ask whether to print customers one at a time
if not,

```
        ask for the starting account number
    for each group of records in the Transaction file:
        if we are printing customers one at a time,
            ask for a customer account number
        print the data from the matching customer record
        initialize memory variables for the transaction and aging totals
        print a heading for the transaction data
        for each record in the Transaction File for the current customer:
            print the data from the transaction record
            add the data into the transaction totals
            add the data into the correct aging total
        end of steps to do for each record in the Transaction File
        print the transaction invoice and payment totals and balance
        print the aging totals
        print a message depending on the balance and aging totals
        eject the paper
    end of steps to do for each group of records in the Transaction File
```

The statement-printing program, NWSTPRT.PRG, is listed in Figure 18-6; the detailed pseudocode outline is shown in Figure 18-7. Figure 18-8 illustrates a statement produced by NWSTPRT.PRG. The program begins by opening the Customer and Transaction files. The files cannot be linked with SET RELATION because of the condition that controls the DO WHILE loop used to process each group of Transaction File records that matches the current record in the Customer File. If the Customer File were also positioned as dBASE III PLUS advanced the record pointer through the Transaction File, the condition ACCOUNT = NWCUST—> ACCOUNT would always be true, and the program would print all of the transactions in the file on one statement. If you prefer to use SET RELATION, you could store the customer account number in a memory variable, perhaps called MACCOUNT, right before the DO WHILE loop, and use the condition ACCOUNT = MACCOUNT in the DO WHILE statement. In NWSTPRT.PRG, however, an explicit SEEK is used to find the customers' transactions.

```
* NWSTPRT.PRG
* PROGRAM TO PRINT CUSTOMER STATEMENTS
* WRITTEN BY:  M.LISKIN       7/28/85

select 1
use NWCUST index NWCACCT

select 2
use NWTXN  index NWTACCT

clear
store date() to MAGEDATE
@  6,10 say "Enter the date to use as the basis for the aging" get MAGEDATE
read

store .F. to MONE
@ 10,10 say "Do you want to print customers one at a time? (Y/N)";
        get MONE picture "Y"
read

* IF NOT PRINTING CUSTOMERS ONE AT A TIME,
* ASK FOR STARTING CUSTOMER AND PAGE NUMBER
if .not. MONE

   * BY DEFAULT, START WITH FIRST CUSTOMER
   store ACCOUNT to MACCOUNT

   do while .T.
      @ 12,10 say "Enter first customer to print" get MACCOUNT picture "@!"
      read
      if MACCOUNT = " "
         return
      endif
      seek trim(MACCOUNT)
      if found()
         exit
      else
         @ 20,10 say trim(MACCOUNT) + "has no current transactions"
         @ 21,10 say "Press any key to reenter the customer"
         wait ""
         @ 20,10
         @ 21,10
      endif
   enddo

endif                           [ not printing one customer at a time ]

set device to print

do while .not. eof()

   * IF PRINTING CUSTOMERS ONE AT A TIME, ASK WHICH CUSTOMER TO PRINT
   if MONE
```

Figure 18-6. A program to print customer statements

```
      store "          " to MACCOUNT
      set device to screen
      do while .T.
         @ 12,10 say "Enter customer to print" get MACCOUNT picture "@!"
         read
         if MACCOUNT = " "
            eject
            return
         endif
         seek trim(MACCOUNT)
         if found()
            set device to print
            exit
         else
            @ 20,10 say trim(MACCOUNT) + "has no current transactions"
            @ 21,10 say "Press any key to reenter the customer"
            wait ""
            @ 20,10
            @ 21,10
         endif
      enddo
   endif                  [ printing one customer at a time ]

   * PRINT RETURN ADDRESS
   @  5,(85 - len(trim(MPCOMPANY)))  / 2 say MPCOMPANY
   @  6,(85 - len(trim(MPADDRESS1))) / 2 say MPADDRESS1
   @  7,(85 - len(trim(MPADDRESS2))) / 2 say MPADDRESS2
   @  8,(85 - len(trim(MPADDRESS3))) / 2 say MPADDRESS3
   @ 11,34                               say "S T A T E M E N T"
   @ 12,34                               say "-----------------"

   * FIND MATCHING CUSTOMER RECORD,
   * CONSTRUCT NAME AND ADDRESS VARIABLE
   select NWCUST
   seek NWTXN->ACCOUNT
   store "" to MADDRESS
   if COMPANY <> " "
      store COMPANY to MADDRESS
   endif
   store MADDRESS + ADDRESS1 + "     " to MADDRESS
   if ADDRESS2 <> " "
      store MADDRESS + ADDRESS2 + "     " to MADDRESS
   endif
   store MADDRESS + trim(CITY) + ", " + STATE + "  " + ZIP to MADDRESS
   store left(MADDRESS + space(120), 120)                  to MADDRESS

   * PRINT CUSTOMER DATA
   @ 25, 8 say substr(MADDRESS,1,30)
   @ 25,52 say cmonth(MAGEDATE) + str(day(MAGEDATE),3) + ", " +;
               str(year(MAGEDATE),4)
   @ 26, 8 say substr(MADDRESS,31,30)
   @ 27, 8 say substr(MADDRESS,61,30)
   @ 28, 8 say substr(MADDRESS,91,30)

   * PRINT TRANSACTION DETAIL COLUMN HEADERS
   @ 32, 8 say;
     "INVOICE      INV DATE       AMOUNT       PMT DATE        AMOUNT"
   @ 33, 8 say;
     "---------------------------------------------------------------"
   store 35   to MLINE
```

Figure 18-6. A program to print customer statements (*continued*)

```
* INITIALIZE VARIABLES FOR TRANSACTION SUBTOTALS
store 0.00 to MINV, MPMT, MCURR, MPAST0, MPAST30, MPAST60

select NWTXN

* PROCESS GROUP OF TRANSACTIONS FOR ONE CUSTOMER
do while ACCOUNT = NWCUST->ACCOUNT

   * PRINT TRANSACTION FIELDS
   @ MLINE, 8 say INVOICE
   @ MLINE,21 say INVDATE
   @ MLINE,33 say INVAMOUNT picture "99,999.99"
   if PMTAMOUNT > 0
      @ MLINE,49 say PMTDATE
      @ MLINE,61 say PMTAMOUNT picture "99,999.99"
   endif
   store MLINE + 1 to MLINE

   * ADD TRANSACTION AMOUNTS INTO SUBTOTALS
   store MINV  + INVAMOUNT     to MINV
   store MPMT  + PMTAMOUNT     to MPMT
   store INVAMOUNT - PMTAMOUNT to MBAL

   * ADD TRANSACTION BALANCE INTO CORRECT AGING CATEGORY SUBTOTAL
   if MBAL > 0
      do case
         case MAGEDATE - INVDATE <= 30
            store MCURR + MBAL   to MCURR
         case MAGEDATE - INVDATE <= 60
            store MPAST0 + MBAL  to MPAST0
         case MAGEDATE - INVDATE <= 90
            store MPAST30 + MBAL to MPAST30
         otherwise
            store MPAST60 + MBAL to MPAST60
      endcase
   endif

   skip

enddo                    [ ACCOUNT = customer account ]


* PRINT TRANSACTION SUBTOTALS
@ MLINE,     33 say "---------                         ---------"
@ MLINE +  1,33 say MINV picture "99,999.99"
@ MLINE +  1,61 say MPMT picture "99,999.99"

* PRINT AGING SUBTOTALS
@ 53, 8 say "CURRENT CHARGES:"
@ 53,33 say MCURR   picture "99,999.99"
@ 54, 8 say "0  - 30 DAYS PAST DUE:"
@ 54,33 say MPAST0  picture "99,999.99"
@ 55, 8 say "30 - 60 DAYS PAST DUE:"
@ 55,33 say MPAST30 picture "99,999.99"
@ 56, 8 say "OVER 60 DAYS PAST DUE:"
@ 56,33 say MPAST60 picture "99,999.99"

* CALCULATE AND PRINT BALANCE
store MINV - MPMT to MBALANCE
@ 57,33 say "========="
```

Figure 18-6. A program to print customer statements (*continued*)

```
   @ 58, 8 say "BALANCE DUE:"
   @ 58,33 say MBALANCE picture "99,999.99"

   do case
      case MBALANCE < 0
         @ 61,15 say "YOUR CREDIT BALANCE CAN BE APPIED TO FUTURE ORDERS
      case MBALANCE = 0
         @ 61,15 say "THANK YOU FOR YOUR PROMPT PAYMENT"
      case MPAST60 > 0
         @ 61,15 say "YOUR ACCOUNT IS SERIOUSLY DELINQUENT"
         @ 62,15 say "PLEASE PAY THE PAST DUE BALANCE PROMPTLY"
      otherwise
         @ 61,15 say "PLEASE PAY THE OUTSTANDING BALANCE PROMPTLY"
   endcase

   * IF PAST END-OF-FILE AND PRINTING CUSTOMERS ONE AT A TIME,
   * REPOSITION RECORD POINTER TO TOP OF FILE SO PROGRAM DOESN'T TERMINATE
   if eof() .and. MONE
      goto top
   endif

enddo                     [ not end-of-file ]

eject
set device to screen

return
```

Figure 18-6. A program to print customer statements (*continued*)

```
open the customer file with the account number index

open the transaction file with the account number index

clear the screen
initialize a memory variable, MAGEDATE, for the aging date, with today's date
   display a message: "Enter the date to use as the basis for the aging"
   collect the user's entry into MAGEDATE

initialize a memory variable, MONE, with the value .F.
display a message: "Do you want to print customers one at a time? (Y/N)"
collect the user's entry into MONE

if we are not printing customers one at a time

   initialize a memory variable, MACCOUNT, for the customer account number
   do the following until a valid customer account number is entered:
      ask for a customer account number
      if the account number is left blank
         exit from the program
      endif
```

Figure 18-7. The statement-printing program in pseudocode

```
      search the index for the account number
      if the account number is found,
         exit from this loop
      otherwise,
         display an error message
         wait until a key is pressed
         erase the error message
      endif
   end of steps to do until a valid customer account number is entered

endif                      [ not printing one customer at a time ]

route the output to the printer

for each record in the transaction file

   if we are printing customers one at a time,
      initialize a memory variable, MACCOUNT, for the customer account number
      route the output to the screen
      do the following until a valid customer account number is entered:
         ask for the customer account number
         if the account number is left blank
            eject the paper
            exit from the program
         endif
         search the index for the account number
         if the account number is found,
            route the output to the printer
            exit from this loop
         otherwise,
            display an error message
            wait until a key is pressed
            erase the error message
         endif
      end of steps to do until a valid customer account number is entered
   endif                  [ printing one customer at a time ]

   print the company name centered on the page
   print the return address centered on the page
   print "S T A T E M E N T" centered on the page
   print "-----------------" centered on the page

   select the customer file
   search the index for the account number to be printed
   construct the customer name and address block
   print the customer name and address block

   print the transaction column titles

   initialize a memory variable, MLINE, for a line counter with the value 35
   initialize memory variables for the invoice, payment, and aging totals

   select the transaction file

   do the following while the account number matches the customer account

      print the invoice number, date, and amount
      if the payment amount is filled in,
         print the payment date and amount

      increment the line counter
      add the invoice and payment amounts into the totals
      store the balance due in a memory variable, MBAL
```

Figure 18-7. The statement-printing program in pseudocode (*continued*)

```
      if there is a balance due,
         if the invoice was printed less than 30 days ago
            add the balance due into the current total
         if the invoice was printed 30 - 60 days ago
            add the balance due into the  urrent total
         if the invoice was printed 60 - 90 days ago
            add the balance due into the current total
         if the invoice was printed more than 90 days ago
            add the balance due into the over 60 day total
      endif

      skip to the next record

   enddo                  [ ACCOUNT = customer account ]

   print the transaction totals

   print the aging totals

   store the overall balance due to a memory variable, MBALANCE
   print the balance due

   if the customer has a credit balance
      print "YOUR CREDIT BALANCE CAN BE APPIED TO FUTURE ORDERS
   if the customer has a zero balance
      print "THANK YOU FOR YOUR PROMPT PAYMENT"
   if the customer has a past 60 days due balance
      print "YOUR ACCOUNT IS SERIOUSLY DELINQUENT"
            "PLEASE PAY THE PAST DUE BALANCE PROMPTLY"
   otherwise
      print "PLEASE PAY THE OUTSTANDING BALANCE PROMPTLY"

   if we are past the end-of-file and we are printing customers one at a time,
      position the data base to the first indexed record
   endif

end of steps to do for each record in the file

eject the page
route the output to the screen

exit from the program
```

Figure 18-7. The statement-printing program in pseudocode (*continued*)

After opening the data bases, the program asks for the date to be used as the basis for the aging calculations, and the user's entry is collected into the memory variable MAGEDATE. This variable is initialized with the current date, which the operator can override. The routines that ask the user whether to print statements one at a time, collect the starting customer account number, and ask which customer to print are identical to those used in the Customer Reference List program, with one exception: the SEEK command looks up the customer account number in the

```
                    National Widgets, Inc.
                      943 Parker Street
                     Berkeley, CA  94710


                      S T A T E M E N T
                      -----------------






ABC Plumbing                                       July 31, 1987
1850 University Avenue
Berkeley, CA  94703


INVOICE       INV DATE       AMOUNT       PMT DATE       AMOUNT
---------------------------------------------------------------
10403         04/30/87       104.24       06/12/87       104.24
12112         05/20/87       120.42
14318         06/12/87        22.75
                          ---------                   ---------
                             247.41                      104.24






CURRENT CHARGES:                 0.00
0  - 30 DAYS PAST DUE:          22.75
30 - 60 DAYS PAST DUE:         120.42
OVER 60 DAYS PAST DUE:           0.00
                            =========
BALANCE DUE:                   143.17

       PLEASE PAY THE OUTSTANDING BALANCE PROMPTLY
```

Figure 18-8. A customer statement

Transaction File instead of the Customer File. The fact that there may be more than one matching Transaction File record is immaterial at this point; as long as there is *at least one* record, it is acceptable to request a statement for the customer. To suit the context, the wording of the message displayed if the SEEK fails has been changed slightly, to "This customer has no current transactions."

When a valid customer is found or, if all customers are to be printed, when the data base is positioned at the first of the next customer's group of transactions, the program prints the memory variables containing the user's company name and address, together with the word STATEMENT as a page header. For added flexibility, you might decide to ask the user whether or not to print the company name and address, just as printing the return address was optional in the letter-printing program in Chapter 17. If you occasionally print on letterhead, you could also add to this program the option to print on single sheets of paper.

For National Widgets' statements, the return address will be centered on the page. To make the program as general as possible, this is done by measuring the length of each address line and calculating its starting position on the page rather than writing the column coordinates for National Widgets into the program. The following expression calculates the column coordinate used in the @ ... SAY command that prints the company name:

```
(85 - len(trim(MPCOMPANY))) / 2
```

This expression is easiest to understand if you work outward from the innermost set of parentheses. First, the MPCOMPANY variable is TRIMmed to remove trailing blanks. The LEN function evaluates to the length of the resulting character string, 22 for "National Widgets, Inc." This number is subtracted from 85 (the page width at 10 characters per inch) to yield the number of blank spaces, 63, that remain on the line after MPCOMPANY is printed. To center the heading, these 63 spaces must be divided evenly to the left and right of the company name, so 63 is divided by 2 to calculate the correct starting position for the variable. The word STATEMENT and the underlining are printed by using absolute coordinates, since this text will change very rarely.

The customer name and address fields are formed into an address block just as was done in the Customer Reference List program, and the statement date (the aging date rather than the current date, so that the customers will understand how the aging totals are calculated) is printed on the page by using the standard date conversion functions. Next, a heading is printed for the invoice data. So far, all of the fields have been printed in fixed positions on the page, using absolute row coordinates in the @ ... SAY commands. The first invoice transaction is always printed on line 35, but there is no way to know how many invoices there will be for a given customer; so a line counter is created to keep track of the next available line on the page. At the same time, memory variables are initialized to contain the invoice, payment, and aging totals.

To print the transaction detail, the program selects the Transaction File and sets up a loop that reads through the group of transaction records that match the current customer record. This may seem circular: a record from the Transaction File is used as the basis for the SEEK command that retrieves the customer record, which is then used to control the DO WHILE loop that reads through the Transaction File. As suggested earlier, you could instead use a memory variable to keep track of the account number for the customer being processed, but since the Customer File fields are required in any event, there is no need to create an extra memory variable. For each transaction the invoice number, date, and amount fields, which are always present, are printed unconditionally, but the payment fields are printed only if they are actually filled in, to avoid printing the confusing " / / " in the date column and 0.00 in the payment amount column. After printing each transaction, the program increments the line counter and adds the invoice and payment amounts into the memory variables MINV and MPMT, respectively.

Next, a DO CASE structure is used to add the net amount due on the invoice (the result of subtracting the payment amount from the invoice amount) into the proper aging category. For convenience, this amount is stored in the memory variable MBAL, although you could instead use the expression MINV − MPMT throughout. Since the DO CASE structure allows only one of the CASEs to be processed, writing the CASEs in the right order can simplify considerably the conditions that must be used. The first CASE tests whether the time elapsed since the invoice date is 30 days or less. If it is, all of the succeeding cases are skipped. If the second case, which selects invoices printed between 30 and 60 days ago, is processed at all, the invoice must be more than 30 days old, so there is no need to state the condition fully as

```
case MAGEDATE - MINVDATE <= 60 .and. MAGEDATE - MINVDATE > 30
```

When the SKIP command positions the Transaction File to the first record for a new customer, the inner DO WHILE loop terminates, and the program prints the invoice and payment totals and the aging information. Finally, the overall balance is calculated, stored in the variable MBALANCE, and printed. As before, MINV — MPMT is stored in a memory variable to avoid the awkwardness of using the longer expression, not only here, but also in the DO CASE structure that prints the closing messages on the statements. Again, be careful of the order in which the CASEs are listed. If the customer has a credit balance or a zero balance, these possibilities are detected first. Next, the program checks whether the customer has a balance over 60 days old. If so, a more strongly worded message is printed than that for customers processed by the OTHERWISE clause, which includes everyone who has an outstanding balance but no invoices more than 60 days old. This is a good example of a DO CASE structure in which the conditions in the individual CASEs do not all pertain to exactly the same variable or set of variables.

Notice that the balance is calculated by adding up the invoice and payment amounts from the individual transactions and subtracting the payments from the invoices. The balance is also available from the BALANCE field in the Customer File, but since the program does not rely on this number, correct statements could still be printed even if the user had neglected to post transactions.

As in the Customer Reference List program, dBASE III PLUS must be prevented from exiting the program after printing the last customer represented in the Transaction File when statements are printed one at a time. Recall that after printing the last customer, the SKIP command in the inner DO WHILE loop has positioned the Transaction File past the end-of-file. Although the outer loop is controlled by the condition .NOT. EOF( ), dBASE III PLUS has not yet reevaluated this condition, because it has not reached the ENDDO and returned to the top of the loop. If the record pointer is positioned at the end-of-file *and* the program is printing statements one at a time, the Transaction File is positioned at the arbitrarily chosen first indexed record, so that when the program returns to the top of the outer DO WHILE loop, .NOT. EOF( ) is still true.

When you write a program as complicated as this one, you are likely to make at least a few mistakes in logic and many careless syntax errors. The best way to debug a program like this, with many nested IF and DO WHILE loops, is to SET ECHO ON, SET TALK ON, and trace the execution of the program by following along with a printout of the program and a list of the current contents of each of the data bases. Even when the program appears to work, however, make sure that you set up testing conditions that verify its correct performance. Working from a listing of the contents of the Transaction File, you should use either a calculator or a series of SUM commands at the dot prompt to prove that the right totals and all of the appropriate transactions are printed on the statements and that the aging totals are calculated correctly. The easiest way to provide a range of dates to test the aging calculation thoroughly is to print the same customer statement but vary the aging date entered into the variable MAGEDATE.

A PROGRAM TO PRINT INVOICES

The National Widgets invoice-printing program must produce a page layout very similar to the statement format. Like the order entry program that supplies the data to be printed on the invoices, this program opens all four of the National Widgets system current files. The most difficult task is making sure that the program selects the right file at the right time. In the statement-printing program, the main loop was set up to read through the Transaction File so as not to waste time reading and skipping over customer records with no matching current transactions, although it is more natural to view each statement as representing one customer record. For printing invoices, however, the Transaction File record *is* the fundamental unit of information: the program prints one invoice per transaction record. It makes sense intuitively to structure the program to read through the Transaction File one record at a time and, for each record, find the matching Customer File record to print the name and address and the matching group of Order File records that make up the individual invoice line items. For each order record the item description can be looked up in the Inventory File. In this program both one-to-one relationships — matching up each transaction record with the right customer and each order record with the right inventory item — can be handled well by SET RELATION. Once these two relationships are established, the program must explicitly control the relationship only between each transaction record and the matching group of order records. The program, NWINVPRT.PRG, is listed in Figure 18-9, and a typical invoice is shown in Figure 18-10.

Just as in the statement-printing program, the user is asked for the date to be printed on the invoices and given the option to print invoices one at a time, for the entire Transaction File or beginning with a particular invoice number. The invoice header is very similar to the statement

```
* NWINVPRT.PRG
* PROGRAM TO PRINT CUSTOMER INVOICES
* WRITTEN BY:  M.LISKIN       7/28/85


select 1
use NWINVENT index NWICATPT

select 2
use NWCUST   index NWCACCT

select 3
use NWORDER  index NWOINVC
set relation to CATEGORY + PARTNUMBER into NWINVENT

select 4
use NWTXN  index NWTINVC
set relation to ACCOUNT into NWCUST

clear
store date() to MINVDATE
@  6,10 say "Enter the date to print on the invoices" get MINVDATE
read

store .F. to MONE
@ 10,10 say "Do you want to print invoices one at a time? (Y/N)";
        get MONE picture "Y"
read

* IF PRINTING INVOICES ONE AT A TIME,
* ASK FOR STARTING INVOICE NUMBER
if MONE

   * BY DEFAULT, START WITH FIRST INVOICE
   store INVOICE to MINVOICE

   do while .T.
      @ 12,10 say "Enter first invoice to print" get MINVOICE picture "99999"
      read
      if MINVOICE = " "
         save all like MP* to NWMEMORY
         return
      endif
      seek MINVOICE
      if found()
         exit
      else
         @ 20,10 say MINVOICE + "is not in the Transaction File"
         @ 21,10 say "Press any key to reenter the invoice number"
         wait ""
         @ 20,10
         @ 21,10
      endif
   enddo

endif                      [ not printing invoices one at a time ]

set device to print

do while .not. eof()
```

Figure 18-9. A program to print invoices

```
* IF PRINTING INVOICES ONE AT A TIME, ASK WHICH INVOICE TO PRINT
if MONE
   store "     " to MINVOICE
   set device to screen
   do while .T.
      @ 12,10 say "Enter invoice to print" get MINVOICE picture "99999"
      read
      if MINVOICE = " "
         eject
         return
      endif
      seek MINVOICE
      if found()
         set device to print
         exit
      else
         @ 20,10 say MINVOICE + "is not in the Transaction File"
         @ 21,10 say "Press any key to reenter the invoice number"
         wait ""
         @ 20,10
         @ 21,10
      endif
   enddo
endif                   [ printing invoices one at a time ]

* PRINT RETURN ADDRESS
@  5,(85 - len(trim(MPCOMPANY)))  / 2 say MPCOMPANY
@  6,(85 - len(trim(MPADDRESS1))) / 2 say MPADDRESS1
@  7,(85 - len(trim(MPADDRESS2))) / 2 say MPADDRESS2
@  8,(85 - len(trim(MPADDRESS3))) / 2 say MPADDRESS3
@ 11,36                               say "I N V O I C E"
@ 12,36                               say "-------------"
@ 13,36                               say "  NO.  " + INVOICE

* FIND MATCHING CUSTOMER,
* CONSTRUCT NAME AND ADDRESS VARIABLE
select NWCUST
store "" to MADDRESS
if COMPANY <> " "
   store COMPANY to MADDRESS
endif
store MADDRESS + ADDRESS1 + "     " to MADDRESS
if ADDRESS2 <> " "
   store MADDRESS + ADDRESS2 + "     " to MADDRESS
endif
store MADDRESS + trim(CITY) + ", " + STATE + "  " + ZIP to MADDRESS
store left(MADDRESS + space(120), 120)                  to MADDRESS

* PRINT CUSTOMER DATA
@ 20, 5 say substr(MADDRESS,1,30)
@ 20,60 say cmonth(MINVDATE) + str(day(MINVDATE),3) + ", " +;
            str(year(MINVDATE),4)
@ 21, 5 say substr(MADDRESS,31,30)
@ 22, 5 say substr(MADDRESS,61,30)
@ 23, 5 say substr(MADDRESS,91,30)

* PRINT ORDER DETAIL COLUMN HEADERS
@ 27, 5 say "CATEGORY  PART #   QUANT      PRICE    SUBTOTAL     " +;
             "DISC %  DISCOUNT    AMOUNT"
```

Figure 18-9. A program to print invoices (*continued*)

```
   @ 28, 5 say "-------------------------------------------------" +;
               "--------------------------"
   store 30 to MLINE

   * FIND FIRST MATCHING ORDER RECORD
   select NWORDER
   seek NWTXN->INVOICE

   * PROCESS GROUP OF ORDER RECORDS FOR ONE INVOICE
   do while INVOICE = NWTXN->INVOICE

      * PRINT ORDER FIELDS
      @ MLINE,     5 say CATEGORY
      @ MLINE,    15 say PARTNUMBER
      @ MLINE,    25 say QUANTITY
      @ MLINE,    31 say PRICE     picture "99,999.99"
      @ MLINE,    42 say SUBTOTAL  picture "99,999.99"
      @ MLINE,    55 say DISCRATE
      @ MLINE,    61 say DISCOUNT  picture "99,999.99"
      @ MLINE,    71 say INVAMOUNT picture "99,999.99"
      @ MLINE + 1, 7 say NWINVENT->DESCRIP

      store MLINE + 2 to MLINE

      skip

   enddo                  [ INVOICE = transaction file INVOICE ]

   * PRINT TRANSACTION FIELDS
   select NWTXN

   @ 53,50 say "SUBTOTAL:"
   @ 53,71 say SUBTOTAL  picture "99,999.99"
   @ 54,50 say "SALES TAX:"
   @ 54,71 say TAX       picture "99,999.99"
   @ 55,50 say "SHIPPING:"
   @ 55,71 say SHIPPING  picture "99,999.99"
   if PMTAMOUNT > 0
      @ 56,50 say "PREPAYMENT:"
      @ 56,71 say PMTAMOUNT picture "99,999.99"
   endif
   @ 57,71 say "========="
   @ 58,50 say "BALANCE DUE:"
   @ 58,71 say INVAMOUNT - PMTAMOUNT picture "99,999.99"
   if INVAMOUNT - PMTAMOUNT > 0
      @ 61,15 say "TERMS:  NET 30 DAYS.  YOUR PROMPT PAYMENT IS APPRECIATED."
   endif

   * IF NOT PRINTING INVOICES ONE AT A TIME,
   * SKIP TO NEXT TRANSACTION RECORD
   if .not. MONE
      skip
   endif

enddo                     [ not end-of-file ]

eject
set device to screen

return
```

Figure 18-9. A program to print invoices (*continued*)

```
                              National Widgets, Inc.
                                943 Parker Street
                               Berkeley, CA  94710


                                  I N V O I C E
                                  -------------
                                    NO. 14325



Home Movies Video Rentals                                   July 31, 1987
2982 College Avenue
Berkeley, CA  94705


CATEGORY  PART #   QUANT      PRICE   SUBTOTAL    DISC %  DISCOUNT     AMOUNT
---------------------------------------------------------------------------
DISK      101-45       2      31.50      63.00      0.00      0.00      63.00
  5-1/4" DSDD Soft Sector
PRTWHL    321-11       1      12.50      12.50      0.00      0.00      12.50
  NEC Courier 10
PRTWHL    321-18       1      15.00      15.00      0.00      0.00      15.00
  NEC Emperor P.S.
STOR      481-10       5       2.85      14.50      0.00      0.00      14.25
  5-1/4" Disk Case, Blue




                                            SUBTOTAL:                  104.75
                                            SALES TAX:                   6.81
                                            SHIPPING:                    2.50
                                                                    =========
                                            BALANCE DUE:               114.06

       TERMS:  NET 30 DAYS.  YOUR PROMPT PAYMENT IS APPRECIATED.
```

Figure 18-10. A customer invoice

header, except that the program begins printing detail line items higher on the page; this is because each item occupies two lines and there may be more line items than there are transactions on a typical statement. To print the line items, the Order File is selected and a SEEK command finds the first record that matches the invoice number from the Transaction File record, after which a DO WHILE loop prints all of the line items on the invoice. The order fields are printed across the page in columns, with the description from the Inventory File on a second line in order to fit all of the data on an 8 1/2- by 11-inch sheet of paper.

Unlike the statement-printing program, NWINVPRT.PRG uses the totals in the Transaction File rather than adding up the line items as it prints, since some of the required data—the sales tax and shipping charges—is available only from the Transaction File. After the last item has been printed, the program selects the Transaction File and prints the invoice subtotal, sales tax, shipping charges, and prepayment, if any. The balance due on the invoice is calculated and printed; and unless the order is prepaid, a message reminding the customer of National Widgets' payment terms is printed. Finally, if invoices are not being printed one at a time, the program SKIPs to the next record in the Transaction File. Like the Customer Reference List program (NWCREF2.PRG), the invoice-printing program must not execute this SKIP if the operator has elected to print single invoices, so that printing the last invoice in the file does not set EOF( ) to .T. and thus cause the program to terminate.

A PROGRAM TO PRINT ORDER STATISTICS

Chapter 16 presented a customer statistics program that made one pass through the Customer File and accumulated counts and totals in memory variables. This approach is well suited to handling a few discrete possibilities—in this instance, four possible entries in the EQUIPMENT field, plus a miscellaneous category. With more than a few categories, the increased number of CASEs and memory variables makes this type of program larger, slower, less efficient, and more difficult to understand and modify. Eventually you might even exceed the limit of 256 memory variables, but the structure of the program presents a more serious problem: with some data bases you may not even know in advance how many possibilities the program must take into account.

To solve this problem, you can create another data base, indexed on the field of interest, to contain the totals. For each record in the main file, the program can search for a match in the summary file. If a record is found, the program can add the data from the main file into the totals in the existing summary record; if not, a new record should be appended to the summary file. Finally, the totals can be printed from the summary file by using either a report form or a custom program.

This technique will be used to write a program that summarizes the National Widgets Order File data by inventory category. For each category the report prints the total number of orders, the total dollar value of the orders, and the number of times a customer ordered more than five of an item at one time. These statistics can give an overview of sales trends, keep management informed of the best- and worst-selling product lines, provide guidelines for inventory stocking quantities, and help the company evaluate its quantity discount policy.

This is the general strategy for structuring the program:

```
open the Order History and Order Summary files
for each record in the Order History File:
    look for a match on the category in the Order Summary File
    if there is no match in the Order Summary File,
        append a record to the Order Summary File
    add the order history fields into the order summary fields
end of steps to do for each record in the Order History File
print a report from the Order Summary File
```

This program structure enables you to open the Order History File with no indexes and read it in sequential order for the fastest processing. There is another, less obvious advantage to this program: it allows you to reprint the Order Summary Report without accumulating the totals again or to accumulate the totals without printing the report immediately (if, for example, your files are large and you do not trust your printer to run overnight).

Before writing the program, you must create the Order Summary File. In this example, there are three statistics of interest. Two of these—the total dollar value of the orders for each category and the total number of times an item from the category was ordered—are very straightforward. The third is a simple example of a conditional test: in order to help

National Widgets assess its quantity discount schedule, the program must count the number of orders in which the order quantity is five or more. To compile these statistics, the Order Summary File needs four fields—CATEGORY, ORDERS, QUANTORDER, and INVAMOUNT—and it must be indexed by CATEGORY.

The structure and index keys are listed in Figure 18-11. In this case, a simple report form is adequate for producing the printed output. The data base file, index, report form, and program have all been given the same name, NWOSTATS, so that whenever you look at the disk directory, you will recall that these files perform one function and that the data base and index exist solely for the purpose of printing the report.

```
. USE NWOSTATS

. LIST STRUCTURE TO PRINT

Structure for database : C:NWOSTATS.dbf
Number of data records :       7
Date of last update    : 08/06/85
Field  Field name  Type       Width    Dec
    1  CATEGORY    Character      6
    2  ORDERS      Numeric        6
    3  QUANTORDER  Numeric        6
    4  INVAMOUNT   Numeric       10      2
** Total **                      29



. DISPLAY STATUS TO PRINT

Currently Selected Database:
Select area:  1, Database in Use: C:NWOSTATS.dbf   Alias: NWOSTATS
    Master index file:  C:NWOSTATS.ndx  Key: CATEGORY
          Lock:

File search path:
Default disk drive: C:
Print destination:  LPT1:
Margin =      0
Current work area =    1

Press any key to continue...

*** INTERRUPTED ***
```

Figure 18-11. The Order Statistics File

The order statistics program is listed in Figure 18-12. The program begins by opening the Order Statistics File and asking the operator whether it is necessary to accumulate a new set of totals and whether or not to print the report. If the operator chooses to accumulate new statistics, the Order Summary File is quickly emptied with ZAP and the Order History File is opened and linked to the Order Statistics File through the CATEGORY field with SET RELATION. Using the standard method described in Chapter 15, the program displays a running status message that allows the operator to monitor the program's progress.

After these preliminaries, a DO WHILE loop is set up to process all of the records in the Order History File. The Order Statistics File is selected

```
* NWOSTATS.PRG
* PROGRAM TO COMPILE ORDER STATISTICS BASED ON INVENTORY CATEGORY
* WRITTEN BY:  M.LISKIN        7/28/85

select 1
use NWOSTATS index NWOSTATS

store .T. to MACCUM, MPRINT

clear
@  3,10 say "Do you want to accumulate new statistics? (Y/N)";
        get MACCUM picture "Y"
@  5,10 say "Do you want to print the report now? (Y/N)       ";
        get MPRINT picture "Y"
read

* IF ACCUMULATING NEW TOTALS...
if MACCUM

   zap

   select 2
   use NWORDHST
   set relation to CATEGORY into NWOSTATS

   @ 10,10 say "Compiling Order Statistics -- Please Do Not Interrupt"
   @ 12,10 say "Working on Record              of " + str(reccount(),5)

   do while .not. eof()

      @ 12,27 say recno()

      select NWOSTATS
```

Figure 18-12. A program to compile and print order statistics

```
        * IF NO RECORD EXISTS THAT MATCHES ORDER CATEGORY,
        * ADD ONE TO SUMMARY FILE
        if .not. found()
           append blank
           replace CATEGORY with NWORDHST->CATEGORY
        endif

        * ADD ORDER AMOUNTS INTO SUMMARY FILE FIELDS
        replace INVAMOUNT with INVAMOUNT + NWORDHST->INVAMOUNT,;
                ORDERS with ORDERS + 1
        if NWORDHST->QUANTITY >= 5
           replace QUANTORDER with QUANTORDER + 1
        endif

        select NWORDHST
        skip

     enddo             [ not eof() ]

  endif                [ accumulate new statistics ]

  * IF PRINTING REPORT...
  if MPRINT
     select NWOSTATS
     report form NWOSTATS to print
  endif

  return
```

Figure 18-12. A program to compile and print order statistics (*continued*)

for each order record. If no matching record is found, FOUND( ) is .F., and the program appends a new record to the Order Summary File and REPLACEs the CATEGORY field with the CATEGORY field from the Order History File. This happens once for each CATEGORY represented in the Order History File, for the first order record in which the category appears. For every subsequent record with the same contents in the CATEGORY field, SET RELATION will find an existing record in the Order Summary File. In either case, the order amount added into the INVAMOUNT field in the Order Summary File and the ORDERS field is incremented. If the order quantity is five or higher, the QUANTORDER field is also incremented. Having updated the summary statistics, the program selects the Order History File again and SKIPs to the next record.

After all the records in the file have been processed, the program checks to see whether the user has chosen to print the results immediately. If so, it prints the report illustrated in Figure 18-13. Notice that if

```
Page No.      1
05/12/87
                   NATIONAL WIDGETS, INC.
              ORDER HISTORY STATISTICS BY CATEGORY

                     NUMBER        QUANTITY          TOTAL
CATEGORY          OF ORDERS          ORDERS    ORDER VALUE
--------       ------------    ------------   ------------


ACCESS                    3               0         164.95
COVER                     2               0          62.47
DISK                      6               0         423.70
FORMS                    10               0         519.40
PRTWHL                    3               0          27.45
RIBBON                    4               1          92.37
STOR                      5               0          91.75
*** Total ***
                         33               1        1382.09
```

Figure 18-13. The Order Statistics report

the operator answers N to both of the initial questions, the program will do absolutely nothing. All of the processing steps are enclosed in an IF structure that depends on the value of MACCUM, and all of the output steps are within another IF structure that tests the value of MPRINT.

This program was deliberately kept simple to emphasize its structure, but the same general strategy may be applied to much more complicated calculations or more sophisticated conditional processing than the simple test for the order quantity in NWOSTATS.PRG. In many cases, since the file update portion of the program can perform very complex computations, the final report can be produced easily by the standard report generator. If necessary, however, the second section of the program, which produces the printed output (or displays the results on the screen, like the NWCSTAT2.PRG program from Chapter 15), can include the equivalent of one of the report-printing programs described in Chapter 17. The biggest advantage of this program, even when you are accumulating only simple totals and counts, is that its structure is independent of the number of categories and the specific values of the CATEGORY field for which you are accumulating statistics.

In this example, for the six possible values of the CATEGORY field currently represented in the National Widgets Order History File, the method used in NWCSTAT2.PRG would have worked just as well, until the company expanded its product line to include more categories. The strategy presented in NWOSTATS.PRG would work equally well for 6, 60, or 600 categories, provided that enough disk space was available for the Order Summary File. The limitation of this technique is that it matches up the two files based on the exact contents of the field or fields on which the subtotals are based. Therefore, you cannot rewrite a program like NWCSTAT2.PRG this way, because it does not total on the exact value of the EQUIPMENT field, but rather looks for an arbitrary sequence of characters contained anywhere within the field.

The programs in this and the previous chapter produced a variety of reports of several types found in almost any dBASE III PLUS application:

- Formats with one record per printed page (index cards or letters).
- Full-page formats with data from more than one file (invoices or statements).
- Columnar reports with subtotals, totals, and other statistics.
- Combination reports with multiple records in one fie for each record in another (like the Customer Reference List).
- Summary reports with the statistics compiled in an auxiliary data base.

These programs should be viewed as a set of prototypes for constructing your own report-printing programs. While many of the details will have to be changed to suit the particular requirements of any individual system, the overall program structures can be adapted readily to most of the printed formats you will need to produce.

Remember also that the programs in Part III have introduced many standard procedures used in various combinations for purposes of illustration. Some of these routines include

- Asking questions with a finite number of possible answers
- Allowing the user to enter selection criteria
- Allowing the user to restart a report beginning with a particular record
- Allowing the user to print or display a single record
- Printing on single sheets of paper

- Printing page headers and footers
- Centering text.

As you write your own dBASE III PLUS programs, you might begin to compile a list of these and other generally useful procedures that can be combined in different ways to lend flexibility to a system. In Part IV many of these routines will be rewritten in more general terms so that they may be called in many different contexts and placed in a procedure file so that they may be called by any of the programs that comprise a data base application.

IV

OPTIMIZING THE SYSTEM

Part IV describes ways to optimize and customize a dBASE III PLUS application to better serve the needs of both the users and the programmer. Additional data validation methods will be incorporated into the data base update and inquiry programs to help ensure that the information in the data bases is as complete and accurate as possible. Techniques are introduced for giving the users access to a wider range of report selection criteria without the need for programming. In addition, the users will gain more flexibility to customize the system to their hardware and operating system configuration and personal preferences. Decreasing the extent to which an application depends on a specific hardware and operating system environmment makes it easier and less costly for users to upgrade their system, because the programs will not have to be extensively rewritten. It also enables the programmer to use the same or similar routines in applications destined for different users.

The discussions in these chapters also emphasize ways to optimize the application development process and improve your productivity as a programmer and system designer. Many of the standard routines developed for the National Widgets sample system will be generalized and extracted into a procedure file so they may be called from any program in the application. Using procedure files streamlines an application by reducing redundancy and facilitates revising and maintaining the system. With the common routines isolated in procedures, many alterations can be effected by making the change in only one place — the procedure file — rather than editing all of the programs that use a routine. Once you have developed a library of general-purpose procedures, you will be able to construct new dBASE III PLUS systems more efficiently, since many procedures may be used with very few changes in all of the systems you design.

The additional complications introduced when several users must share hardware and software will be addressed in a chapter on networking and security. Methods will be described for implementing a password-protected security system to control access to dBASE III PLUS itself, and to the programs, program options, data bases, and data base fields in an application. Techniques will be presented for constructing applications to be used in a local area network (LAN) environment so that users may safely share hardware and software, and when necessary, update the same data base files simultaneously.

When you write an application comparable in size and complexity to an off-the-shelf software package, it is crucial to provide adequate printed documentation both for the users and for the programmers (including yourself) who may later have to modify or enhance the system. Guidelines will be presented for producing good documentation that will make your dBASE III PLUS systems easier to learn, use, and maintain.

19

DATA BASE UPDATE AND INQUIRY PROGRAMS

The programs written thus far have taken two fundamentally different approaches to entering new data into a dBASE III PLUS data base file and editing existing records. The first, presented in Chapter 12 with the first version of the National Widgets system, updated the Customer File by combining the native dBASE III PLUS APPEND and EDIT commands with a format file that drew a customized input screen. The second approach, exemplified by the order entry program described in Chapter 16, added records to two data bases and verified each of the entries with a series of validation and calculation steps.

Using a format file with APPEND or EDIT is best suited to updating a single data base that does not depend on information in any other files and does not require extensive validation. In the National Widgets system, the Customer File and the Inventory File are good examples of this type of data base. Entering orders, on the other hand, requires adding new records to both the Order and Transaction files and, in the process, looking up data in the Customer and Inventory data bases. The programs written in Chapter 12, which update the Customer File by using NWCUST2.FMT to draw the screen, perform only the relatively limited data validations possible through the @ ... SAY ... GET commands that make up the format file. In contrast, the order entry program validates many fields individually as they are entered and, for the most part, forbids the entry of erroneous data.

The disadvantages of designing a system using format files for data entry were summarized in Chapter 13. The main problems cited were the inability to perform calculations or conditional processing and the limited range of validation tests you can perform. Chapter 20 will describe a program that checks the data in all of the records in a file in a batch process, partially solving the validation problem. However, the options thus far provided for entering and editing customer records in the National Widgets system also make it difficult for users to switch easily and quickly between the APPEND and EDIT functions. In the current system the only way to verify the existence of a customer record while entering new customers into the file is to exit from the APPEND option, return to the Customer Information Menu, select the edit/inquiry program to search for the customer in question, and then go back to appending records. This is inconvenient enough that when in doubt, the users are likely to add the customer without first searching for a duplicate. The program cannot prevent this, since APPEND affords no way to test for or reject duplicate account numbers.

Ideally, a general-purpose update and inquiry program should allow the operator to add new records, search for a particular record, page forward or backward through the file, delete records, and recover previously deleted records. The NWCEDIT.PRG program written in Chapter 12 already provides most of these functions: the operator can search for a customer by account number, move to the next record with PGDN, go backward through the file with PGUP, and delete or recall records with CTRL-U. The only remaining requirement is the ability to add new customer records through the same program. This chapter will present two versions of an update and inquiry program for the Customer File, both of which use a format file to draw the input screen. Finally, to overcome the limitations of dBASE III PLUS format files, a third version of the customer update and inquiry program will substitute the equivalent series of @ ... SAY ... GET commands for the format file. In Chapter 20 this program will be further expanded to include more extensive data validation tests and to encompass data from a second file—the Transaction File.

A GENERAL-PURPOSE UPDATE AND INQUIRY PROGRAM

To add records to a data base through the same program that allows you to edit existing entries, we must abandon the APPEND command entirely. Instead, the program must add records to the file one at a time with APPEND BLANK and allow the user to fill in the fields with EDIT. Adding this capability to the NWCEDIT.PRG program written in Chapter 12 requires very little modification of the basic structure of the program. Currently, if the operator enters a customer account number that is not found in the NWCACCT.NDX index, the program displays an error message and asks the operator to reenter the account number. To add an APPEND option, you could change the program so it interprets the entry of a nonexistent account number as a request to add a new customer with the specified account number to the file. This new version of the edit program, NWCEDIT2.PRG, is listed in Figure 19-1; a pseudocode explanation is shown in Figure 19-2.

Like the original program, NWCEDIT2.PRG asks for a customer account number and uses SEEK to search the account number index for a match. If the record is not found, there are two possible explanations: the operator either made a mistake when entering the account number or wishes to add a new customer to the file. The program therefore asks whether or not to add the new customer record. If the answer is N, the program displays a message; and when the operator acknowledges the message by pressing a key, the LOOP command returns control to the top of the DO WHILE loop to clear the screen and ask for another account number. If the user answers Y to the offer to enter a new customer, a record is added to the file with APPEND BLANK. The program can already determine the account number for this customer—the value entered into MACCOUNT—so this field is filled in with a REPLACE command. At this point, the data base is positioned at a valid record (the newly appended record), just as it would be if a SEEK command had retrieved an existing customer. The only difference is that for a newly appended record, all of the fields except the account number are blank. In either case, the program opens the NWCUST2.FMT format file, uses EDIT to allow the operator to view or change the data, and then closes the format file.

IMPROVING THE UPDATE AND INQUIRY PROGRAM

From the user's point of view, the ability to enter and edit records through the same program is a definite improvement, but NWCEDIT2 .PRG affords the programmer no more control over the data entry

```
* NWCEDIT2.PRG
* PROGRAM TO FIND AND EDIT RECORDS IN NWCUST.DBF,
*   USING NWCUST2.FMT TO DRAW THE INPUT SCREEN
* WRITTEN BY:  M.LISKIN        5/09/86

use NWCUST index NWCACCT, NWCZIP
set deleted off

do while .T.

   clear
   store "          " to MACCOUNT
   @ 10,10 say "Enter customer account number " get MACCOUNT picture "@!"
   @ 12,10 say "(Or press <RETURN> to quit)"
   read

   if MACCOUNT = " "

      set deleted on
      return

   else

      seek trim(MACCOUNT)
      if .not. found()
         @ 15,10 say trim(MACCOUNT) + " is not in the Customer File"
         store .F. to MADD
         @ 17,10 say "Do you want to add this customer? (Y/N)";
                 get MADD picture "Y"
         read
         if MADD
            append blank
            replace ACCOUNT with MACCOUNT
         else
            wait "            Press any key to try again"
            loop
         endif
      endif              [ customer not found ]

      set format to NWCUST2
      edit
      set format to

   endif              [ MACCOUNT = " " ]

enddo           [ .T. ]

return
```

Figure 19-1. A program for adding and editing customer records

environment than the original NWCEDIT.PRG from which it is derived. The ultimate goal, which will be achieved in the next chapter, is to validate certain fields as the data is entered or changed. In order to do this, the program must prohibit the operator from freely paging forward or

```
open the customer file with the account number and zip indexes
allow deleted records to be viewed and edited

do the following until the user chooses to exit:

   clear the screen
   initialize a memory variable, MACCOUNT, for the customer account number
   ask for the customer account number

   if the account number is left blank,

      return to ignoring deleted records
      exit from the program

   otherwise,

      search the account number index for the customer

      if the customer is not found,
         display a message that the customer is not in the Customer File
         ask whether to add the customer to the file

         if the user says "no",
            display a message
            wait until a key is pressed
            return to the top of the program
         otherwise,
            append a blank record
            replace the ACCOUNT field with the new account number

      open the NWCUST2 format file
      edit the record
      close the format file

end of steps to do until the user chooses to exit
```

Figure 19-2. The program for adding and editing customer records in pseudocode

backward through the file, as he or she can by using EDIT. Instead, the program must process each record individually and force the user to enter correct (or at least plausible) data before moving on to another record. In many data bases you will also want to control more closely the circumstances under which records may be deleted. For example, in the National Widgets system, a customer record should not be deleted unless the balance is 0 and there have been no financial transactions in the current month.

The first version of the integrated data entry and update program uses a format file to draw the input screen, just as in NWCEDIT2.PRG. The design of the program reflects the two essentially separate steps it carries out: first, the program positions the dBASE III PLUS record pointer to the correct record in the data base and, second, it takes the appropriate action *on that record only.* Like NWCEDIT2.PRG, the new update program must allow the operator to enter a specific customer account number to be searched for and then use SEEK to position the data base to the desired record. In order to confine the subsequent editing process to the single record retrieved by the SEEK command, the program must use a READ command to activate the format file that draws the input screen instead of invoking the dBASE III PLUS EDIT command. Each READ command triggers the execution of the @ ... SAY ... GET commands in the format file *once,* thus allowing the operator to edit only the current record.

Abandoning the EDIT command also means losing the ability to edit memo fields and to delete or recover records with CTRL-U. The only real reason to retain the format file is for convenience, since it has already been created and some of the system's users may want to use it in their work with dBASE III PLUS at command level. If you are building a new system of your own, you could bypass this transitional step and go directly to the program structure outlined in the next section, which uses @ ... SAY ... GET commands placed directly in the program to collect the data.

Since the operator can no longer use the standard dBASE III PLUS full-screen edit commands to page forward or backward or to delete or recall records, the update program must provide substitutes for these functions. You can include all of these capabilities in the basic program by expanding the first portion of the program—the routine that positions the record pointer. The format file could then be opened and the READ command issued to collect the data. Table 19-1 lists the operations the update program must perform, together with the dBASE III PLUS commands the program will use to carry out these functions.

One way to structure the program would be to present a menu of choices similar to the list in Table 19-1 and allow the user to select commands by number or letter from the menu. As outlined in Chapters 12 and 13, menus can make a system easier for a dBASE III PLUS novice to use, but filling the screen with a menu is not always the best way to design a program. In a data entry program, displaying the menu and selecting an option should be as fast and unobtrusive as possible. For the National Widgets customer update and inquiry program, all of the options will be placed, in abbreviated form, on one line at the bottom of the data entry screen. The program assumes that the operator will want to use the SEARCH command more frequently than any of the others, and the

Table 19-1. The Update Program Functions

Function	dBASE III PLUS Command
ADD a new record	APPEND BLANK
SEARCH for a record by account number	SEEK
Page forward to the NEXT record	SKIP
Page backward to the PREVIOUS record	SKIP−1
DELETE the record on the screen	DELETE
RECOVER the (deleted) record on the screen	RECALL

option prompt is phrased accordingly:

```
Customer to edit / (N)ext / (P)rev / (D)el / (R)ecover / (A)dd
```

This prompt line invites the user to enter an account number to search for or to type a single letter representing one of the other command choices.

The complete program, NWCUPD1.PRG, is listed in Figure 19-3; the pseudocode explanation is shown in Figure 19-4, and a slightly modified version of the original format file, NWCUST4.FMT, in Figure 19-5. The format file was altered to make room for the two extra lines needed for the option line at the bottom of the screen. NWCUST2.FMT included a number of blank lines that made the screen more readable, many of which could have been removed, but since this program can no longer access the memo field, lines 14 and 15 (which displayed the memo field and the instructions for editing it) were deleted and all of the succeeding lines moved up.

The program begins by opening the Customer File with both indexes. The SET DELETED OFF command enables the user to view and recall deleted records. Within the DO WHILE .T. loop, the program clears line 23 on the screen and displays the option prompt. Line 23 is cleared because the screen is fairly crowded, and the program will also use this line for error messages. Rather than explicitly clearing every error message, the program assumes on each pass through the loop that there may already be text on this line, and erases it. The operator's entry is collected into the memory variable MACCOUNT, and a DO CASE structure processes the selection. As in NWCEDIT2.PRG, the operator can exit by leav-

```
* NWCUPD1.PRG
* PROGRAM TO INQUIRE, EDIT, ADD, AND DELETE CUSTOMERS
*   USING NWCUST4.FMT TO DRAW THE SCREEN
* WRITTEN BY:  M.LISKIN        05/09/86

use NWCUST index NWCACCT, NWCZIP

set deleted off

clear

do while .T.

   @ 23, 0
   store "          " to MACCOUNT
   @ 23,2 say;
    "Customer to edit / (N)ext / (P)rev / (D)el / (R)ecover / (A)dd" ;
    get MACCOUNT picture "@!"
   read
   if MACCOUNT = " "
      set deleted on
      return
   endif

   do case

      case MACCOUNT = "N "
         skip
         if eof()
            @ 23, 0
            @ 23,15 say "This is the last name -- Press any key to contin
            wait ""
            loop
         endif

      case MACCOUNT = "P "
         skip -1
         if bof()
            @ 23, 0
            @ 23,15 say "This is the first name -- Press any key to conti
            wait ""
            loop
         endif

      case MACCOUNT = "D "
         store .F. to MCONFIRM
         @ 23, 0
         @ 23,10 say "Are you sure you want to delete this customer? (Y/N
                 get MCONFIRM picture "Y"
         read
         if MCONFIRM
            delete
            @  3,65 say "* DELETED *"
            @ 23, 0
            @ 23,15 say trim(ACCOUNT) +;
                        " has been deleted -- Press any key to continue"
            wait ""
         endif
         loop
```

Figure 19-3. A customer update and inquiry program

```
      case MACCOUNT = "R "
         recall
         @ 23, 0
         @ 23,15 say trim(ACCOUNT) +;
                     " has been recovered -- Press any key to continue"
         wait ""
         loop

      case MACCOUNT = "A "
         store "          " to MACCOUNT
         @ 23, 0
         @ 23,10 say "Enter the account number for the new entry ";
                 get MACCOUNT picture "@!"
         read
         if MACCOUNT = " "
            loop
         endif
         seek MACCOUNT
         if found()
            @ 23, 0
            @ 23,10 say trim(MACCOUNT) +;
                        " is already on file -- Press any key to continue"
            wait ""
            loop
         else
            append blank
            replace ACCOUNT with MACCOUNT, STATE with MPSTATE,;
                    AREACODE with MPAREACODE, TAXRATE with MPTAXRATE
         endif

      otherwise
         seek trim(MACCOUNT)
         if .not. found()
            @ 23,0
            @ 23,15 say trim(MACCOUNT) +;
                        " not found -- Press any key to continue"
            wait ""
            loop
         endif

   endcase


   set format to NWCUST4
   read
   set format to

   if deleted()
      @  3,65 say "* DELETED *"
   endif

   if dtoc(LASTORDER) <> "  /  /  "
      store date() - LASTORDER to MDAYS
      @ 21,45 say "LAST ORDER WAS " + str(MDAYS,4) + " DAYS AGO"
   endif

enddo

return
```

Figure 19-3. A customer update and inquiry program (*continued*)

```
open the customer file with the account number and zip code indexes

allow deleted records to be viewed and edited

clear the screen

do the following until the user chooses to exit:

   clear line 23 on the screen
   initialize a memory variable, MACCOUNT, for the customer account number
   display the option prompt line
   collect the account number from the user
   if the account number is left blank,
      return to ignoring deleted records
      exit from the program
   endif

   do case

      if the user entered "N " (NEXT):
         skip to the next record in the file
         if you are past the end-of-file,
            clear line 23
            display a message: "This is the last name"
            wait until a key is pressed
            go back to the top of the loop
         endif

      if the user entered "P " (PREVIOUS):
         skip to the previous record in the file
         if you are past the beginning-of-file,
            clear line 23
            display a message: "This is the first name"
            wait until a key is pressed
            go back to the top of the loop
         endif

      if the user entered "D " (DELETE):
         initialize a memory variable, MCONFIRM, with the value .F.
         clear line 23
         ask whether the customer should be deleted
         collect the user's entry into MCONFIRM
         if the user answered "Y"
            delete the record
            display a message: "* DELETED *"
            clear line 23
            display a message identifying the deleted customer
            wait until a key is pressed
         endif
         go back to the top of the loop

      if the user entered "R " (RECALL):
         recall the (deleted) record
         clear line 23
         display a message identifying the recovered customer
         wait until a key is pressed
         go back to the top of the loop
```

Figure 19-4. The customer update and inquiry program in pseudocode

```
      if the user entered "A " (ADD):
         initialize a memory variable, MACCOUNT, for the account number
         clear line 23
         ask for the customer account number
         if the account number is left blank,
            go back to the top of the loop
         endif
         search the index for the account number
         if a record is found,
            clear line 23
            display a message:  "the customer is already on file"
            wait until a key is pressed
            go back to the top of the loop
         otherwise,
            append a blank record
            replace the account number with the variable MACCOUNT,
                    and the state, area code, and sales tax rate
                    with the default values
         endif

      otherwise,
         search the index for the account number
         if the account number is not found,
            clear line 23
            display an error message
            wait until a key is pressed
            go back to the top of the loop
         endif

   endcase

   open the format file
   edit the customer record
   close the format file

   if the current record is deleted,
      display a message: "* DELETED *"
   endif

   if the last order date is filled in,
      calculate the number of days elapsed since the last order
      display the number of days elapsed since the last order
   endif

end of steps to do until the user chooses to exit
```

Figure 19-4. The customer update and inquiry program in pseudocode (*continued*)

ing MACCOUNT blank, in which case the program SETs DELETED ON and RETURNs to the menu.

The program must be able to determine from the value of MACCOUNT whether the user has entered an account number to search for or one of the single-letter command options. For example, if N is entered,

```
* NWCUST4.FMT
* FORMAT FILE FOR CUSTOMER FILE INQUIRY AND UPDATE
* WRITTEN BY:     M.LISKIN      Ø5/23/85

@  1, 5 say "NATIONAL WIDGETS, INC. - CUSTOMER LIST UPDATE AND INQUIRY"
@  1,7Ø say date()
@  2, Ø say "+---------------------------------------"
@  2,4Ø say "---------------------------------------+"
@  3, Ø say "|  Acct Code" get ACCOUNT picture "@!"
@  3,79 say "|"
@  4, Ø say "|"
@  4,79 say "|"
@  5, Ø say "|  Company   " get COMPANY
@  5,79 say "|"
@  6, Ø say "|  Address   " get ADDRESS1
@  6,79 say "|"
@  7, Ø say "|            " get ADDRESS2
@  7,79 say "|"
@  8, Ø say "|  City      " get CITY
@  8,45 say "State" get STATE picture "@!"
@  8,59 say "Zip" get ZIP picture "99999"
@  8,79 say "|"
@  9, Ø say "|"
@  9,79 say "|"
@ 1Ø, Ø say "|  Contact   " get CONTACT
@ 1Ø,45 say "Telephone" get AREACODE picture "999"
@ 1Ø,63 get TELEPHONE picture "999-9999"
@ 1Ø,79 say "|"
@ 11, Ø say "|"
@ 11,79 say "|"
@ 12, Ø say "|  Equipment" get EQUIPMENT
@ 12,45 say "Sales Tax Rate % " get TAXRATE range Ø, 1Ø
@ 12,79 say "|"
@ 13, Ø say "|"
@ 13,79 say "|"
@ 14, Ø say "+---------------------------------------"
@ 14,4Ø say "---------------------------------------+"
@ 15, Ø say "|  Y-T-D Invoices:" + transform(YTDINV, "9,999,999.99")
@ 15,79 say "|"
@ 16, Ø say "|  Y-T-D Payments:" + transform(YTDPMT, "9,999,999.99")
@ 16,79 say "|"
@ 17, Ø say "|"
@ 17,79 say "|"
@ 18, Ø say "|  Total Invoices:" + transform(TOTINV, "9,999,999.99")
@ 18,45 say "First Order Date:    " + dtoc(FIRSTORDER)
@ 18,79 say "|"
@ 19, Ø say "|  Total Payments:" + transform(TOTPMT, "9,999,999.99")
@ 19,45 say "Last  Order Date:    " + dtoc(LASTORDER)
@ 19,79 say "|"
@ 2Ø, Ø say "|"
@ 2Ø,79 say "|"
@ 21, Ø say "|  Balance:       " + transform(BALANCE, "@( 9,999,999.99")
@ 21,79 say "|"
@ 22, Ø say "+---------------------------------------"
@ 22,4Ø say "---------------------------------------+"
```

Figure 19-5. The format file used by the customer update and inquiry program

the program should position the record pointer to the next record in the file rather than search for a customer whose account number is N. To make this distinction, you must test for the entry of *a single letter,* N. If the ACCOUNT field can never contain spaces, you can accomplish this by looking at the first two characters of MACCOUNT:

```
case MACCOUNT = "N "
```

You might wonder why the condition could not be stated as

```
case MACCOUNT = "N"
```

or

```
case trim(MACCOUNT) = "N"
```

When dBASE III PLUS compares two character strings, if the string to the right of the equal sign is shorter, the comparison extends only as far as the length of the shorter string. Either of the above conditions will therefore be true whenever an account number beginning with N (for example, NORTH or NATIONAL) is entered. If you ever needed to search for an account number consisting of the single letter N (a rather unlikely occurrence), you would have to test the full value of the variable MACCOUNT:

```
case MACCOUNT = "N         "
```

The other CASEs use comparable conditions to test for the other single command letters, P, D, R, and A. Because MACCOUNT is TRIMmed before it is used as the object of a SEEK, entering any *other* single letter causes the program to search for the first customer whose account number begins with the specified letter.

The NWCUPD1.PRG program is easiest to understand if you read it from the bottom up. If the operator has chosen any option except DELETE or RECOVER, the program must do exactly the same thing after the DO CASE structure that processes the operator's selection and, if necessary, repositions the data base to the correct record—namely, invoke the NWCUST4.FMT format file to edit the record. The format file is opened, used, and closed with these three lines:

```
set format to NWCUST4
read
set format to
```

As in NWCEDIT2.PRG, the format file is closed before returning to the top of the DO WHILE loop so that the READ command that follows the display of the option prompt collects the variable MACCOUNT rather than reactivating NWCUST4.FMT.

Next we will examine the operation of each of the command options. If the operator has entered N, the program SKIPs to reposition the data base to the "next" record in the file (that is, the next record in alphabetical order by account number). If the file was already positioned at the last record in the index, the SKIP command moves the record pointer past the end-of-file. The program tests for this contingency by looking at the value of the EOF( ) function and displaying an error message if EOF( ) is .T. After the operator acknowledges the message by pressing a key, the program returns to the top of the DO WHILE loop to ask for another option. The LOOP command is very important: if you did not use this command to bypass the steps after the ENDCASE, the program would attempt to edit the nonexistent blank record past the end-of-file.

The P CASE that moves backward to the previous record works much the same way. If the SKIP −1 command positions the data base before the beginning-of-file, the BOF( ) function is .T., and the program again displays an error message and LOOPs back to ask for another account number.

If the DELETE option is chosen, the program asks for confirmation before proceeding to DELETE the displayed record. If the operator answers Y to the request for confirmation, the program DELETEs the record, displays a message to that effect, and asks the operator to acknowledge the message by pressing a key. Abandoning the EDIT command also results in losing the standard dBASE III PLUS "Del" indicator that appears in the status bar on line 22 (or, with STATUS OFF, as in any program called from the National Widgets Main Menu, on line 0) when you EDIT a record that has been marked for deletion. The NWCUPD1.PRG program replaces this deletion flag with the message "* DELETED *." Rather than attempting to imitate the dBASE III PLUS "Del" flag exactly, the program positions the "* DELETED *" message on line 3, leaving line 0 free for the standard dBASE III PLUS "Ins" indicator and the error messages displayed if an invalid date or sales tax rate is entered.

Whether or not the user has allowed the deletion to take place, there is no need to edit the current record with the format file. The program assumes that the DELETE option would only be selected with a record already displayed on the screen (perhaps a dangerous assumption, as will be shown later). The program therefore LOOPs back to the top of the DO WHILE loop at the end of the D CASE.

The RECOVER option invokes the RECALL command to cancel the deletion of a record previously marked for deletion. Rather than echoing the dBASE III PLUS command verb RECALL, the option prompt uses the term RECOVER, because it is closer to the way this operation would normally be described in English. (RECALL might easily be misconstrued to mean "call up a customer from the file for display.") Recalling a record that should have remained deleted is safer than deleting a record by mistake, so the RECOVER option RECALLS the displayed record without first asking the operator's permission. In your own programs you might decide to require the same confirmation to recall a record that NWCUPD1.PRG requires before a deletion. You do not need to test whether the record to be RECOVERed is actually deleted; the RECALL command has no effect on a record that is not marked for deletion.

Just as in NWCEDIT2.PRG, a new customer is added into the file by appending a blank record and then filling in the fields with the format file. Again, the option prompt describes this function with a more familiar word (ADD) than the dBASE III PLUS command itself. The NWCUPD1.PRG program incorporates a test for duplicate account numbers, so that the same customer cannot be added into the file twice by mistake or the same account code assigned to two customers with similar company names. Before appending a blank record, the program asks the operator to enter the account number for the new customer. You can cancel the entry at this point by leaving the account number blank, which causes the program to LOOP back to the DO WHILE statement and present the option line again. If an account number is entered, the program uses SEEK to search the index for a matching ACCOUNT field.

Note that this time the variable MACCOUNT is *not* TRIMmed before the SEEK. Normally the TRIM function is used to remove the trailing blanks from a memory variable before the variable is used as the object of a SEEK or FIND command to allow you to find a match on the first part of the field. In this context, however, the user is *not* searching for an existing record and would never want to enter less than the full account number to be assigned to the new customer. If you did TRIM MAC-

COUNT, the user could not give a new customer an account number (WILLIAMS, for example) that matched the first few characters of any existing customer's account code (such as WILLIAMSON).

If the SEEK succeeds in finding a customer record with the same account number, the program displays an error message; if the new account number is unique, a blank record is added to the file and the ACCOUNT field REPLACEd with the memory variable MACCOUNT. The program uses three public memory variables to supply default values for the STATE, AREACODE, and TAXRATE fields. If you are experimenting with the National Widgets system, these variables should be added to the memory file NWMEMORY.MEM by typing the following sequence of commands at the dot prompt:

```
RESTORE FROM NWMEMORY
STORE "CA" TO MPSTATE
STORE "415" TO MPAREACODE
STORE 6.50 TO MPTAXRATE
SAVE ALL LIKE MP* TO NWMEMORY
```

If you test the update program by running it outside of the menu system, remember to use RESTORE FROM NWMEMORY to make these variables available.

Finally, if MACCOUNT does not contain the single letters N, P, D, R, or A, the operator must have intended to enter a customer account number (or partial account number) to be searched for. Just as in NWCEDIT2.PRG, the program TRIMs the account number, performs the SEEK, and displays an error message if the requested customer is not found. Although an OTHERWISE section is often used in a DO CASE structure to take care of all of the miscellaneous possibilities not handled by the other CASEs, in the NWCUPD1.PRG program the OTHERWISE section is the CASE that is likely to be used most frequently.

After the program processes the ENDCASE statement, the dBASE III PLUS record pointer should be positioned at a valid record in the Customer File. Whether the record was found by a SEEK command, newly added to the file with APPEND BLANK, or reached by a SKIP or SKIP −1, the program must do exactly the same thing in each case—edit the record. The options that should not result in displaying or editing a record (DELETE and RECOVER) both use a LOOP command to bypass this portion of the program. Similarly, the error conditions (moving past the end or beginning of the file, failing to find a record, or entering a duplicate account number) all LOOP back to the DO WHILE statement. The program therefore opens the format file, uses READ to activate the GETs and allow the operator to edit the record, and closes the format file again.

Before returning to the top of the DO WHILE loop to allow the operator to choose another option, the program must determine if the record on the screen is marked for deletion and, if so, display the "* DELETED *" indicator on line 3. (Although the program displays this message at the moment a record is deleted, a replacement for the usual dBASE III PLUS "Del" message must appear *whenever* a deleted record is displayed on the screen.) The NWCUPD1.PRG program also calculates the number of days since the customer's last order and displays this information next to the balance.

Evaluating the Update And Inquiry Program

The NWCUPD1.PRG program, in contrast to the separate APPEND and EDIT options used in the system presented in Chapter 12, allows the operator to use the system more easily and intuitively. Before entering a new record, the operator can easily verify that the customer is not already on file; and even if the user does not exercise this option, the program forbids the entry of duplicate account numbers. This program also introduces an example of how to perform a calculation and display data conditionally. Although the computation of the elapsed time since the last order could have been accomplished with an IIF function, more complicated calculations involving several steps cannot be handled within a format file.

The program still has a few problems. Although the NWCUPD1.PRG program incorporates some error checking, it does not test for every possible kind of erroneous input. Some problems will surface only when certain errors are made in a particular order. For example, if the user asks for the NEXT record when the data base is positioned at the last record in the index, the program correctly responds with a message that the record displayed is the last one in the file. However, the record pointer is no longer positioned at the last record, but past the end-of-file. If the user selects N again, the SKIP command generates the dBASE III PLUS error message "End of file encountered" before the program even reaches the error trap that displays the more helpful "This is the last name . . ." message and loops back to allow another try. The program exhibits similar behavior at the beginning of the file if the user tries to move backward to the PREVIOUS record with the BOF( ) function already set to .T. This problem also crops up if the operator first searches for a nonexistent customer account number and then asks for the NEXT record, because the failure of the SEEK leaves the data base positioned past the end-of-file. You can easily correct these anomalies by making sure that the SKIP commands in the NEXT and PREVIOUS option CASEs are only executed if the data base is positioned at a valid record with these tests:

```
if .not. eof()
   skip
endif
```

and

```
if .not. bof()
   skip N-1
endif
```

The program should also refuse to carry out a DELETE or RECALL command unless the data base is positioned at a valid record. In these CASEs, it would be easy to test the values of the EOF( ) and BOF( ) functions; if either were true, the program could display a message instructing the operator to search for a valid record first. This test is a step in the right direction, but it will not improve the behavior of the system if the operator chooses DELETE or RECOVER as the very first option upon entering the program. The data base is positioned by the initial USE command to the first indexed record; so if the operator chooses DELETE and answers Y to the request for confirmation, the first record in the file will be deleted. Since the record is not actually displayed on the screen, this may not be noticed immediately, and when someone eventually realizes that a customer has disappeared, the reason may not be readily apparent.

Similarly, RECOVER will RECALL the first record if it was previously deleted. Fortunately, there is a relatively simple solution to this problem: place a SKIP −1 command immediately after the USE command that opens the file. Although the attempt to move backward past the beginning-of-file sets the BOF( ) indicator to true, it leaves the file positioned at the first record (unlike SKIPping beyond the last record, which leaves you positioned at a blank record past the end-of-file). Thus, you can still choose NEXT as the first option to page through the records in indexed order. The discussion of all of these small problems may seem too detailed, but they illustrate the range of error checking that a program can and should perform so that operators unfamiliar with dBASE III

PLUS can use the system with ease.

This program, like all of the work done with the Customer File so far, fails to take into account the relationship between this file and the other data bases in the system. Consider the implications of deleting a customer record and leaving open transactions. It certainly makes sense to be able to delete a record from the Customer File while leaving intact the matching records in the Order History File and Transaction History File. Some of the historical reports compile statistics that do not depend on the customer—for example, totals based on the types of products ordered or the profitability of certain inventory categories. However, the update program should not allow a customer with a non-zero balance or current transactions to be deleted. Also, the program should not permit a customer account number to be changed, because this would make it impossible to match up the customer with Order History File and Transaction History File records entered under the old account number.

Another set of potential problems and design issues is difficult or impossible to resolve except by eliminating the format file and placing the GET commands that collect the data directly in the program. A relatively simple example is the way in which the program displays the "* DELETED *" indicator. Displaying this message *after* the operator has filled in the fields on the screen is less than ideal: it should really appear together with the data when the record is first displayed. You cannot place an IF loop in a format file, where only @ ... SAY ... GET commands are permitted, although you could substitute an IIF function. If the message were displayed between the SET FORMAT TO NWCUST4 and the READ command, it would be eradicated because the screen is always cleared when a format file is invoked.

The fundamental design philosophy of this program may or may not also present problems, depending on the way the update program is typically used. In some settings the operators rarely call up a record on the screen except to make a change, so the fact that the NWCUPD1.PRG program always places the cursor in the first field of any record displayed, enabling the user to edit the data, is just what you would want. In other cases, if the program were used primarily for on-screen inquiry, the users might find it inconvenient to have to press ESC or CTRL-END to terminate the editing process for each record displayed on the screen before being able to choose the next option. To solve this problem, the display and editing functions must be separated, so that the SEARCH, NEXT, and PREVIOUS options cause a record to be displayed *only*, and so that a new CHANGE option allows the displayed record to be edited.

Activating a format file with a READ command has removed one of the format file's major advantages—the ability to enter and edit memo fields—while retaining many of the disadvantages. When using a format file, it is impossible to ask for some of the fields, make a decision based on the data entered, and then collect the remaining fields. For example, you might want to check the STATE field and, if the STATE is "CA", use the sales tax rate stored in the memory variable MPTAXRATE as the default value for the TAXRATE field. Otherwise (for out-of-state customers), the default should be 0. You might even want to display certain fields conditionally, based on the contents of other fields. When using a format file, you must collect all of the data and allow dBASE III PLUS to save all of the fields at once. You cannot solve this problem by splitting the fields into two groups, to be edited either with two format files or a single multiple-page format file, because dBASE III PLUS always clears the screen before drawing the image defined by a format file or each page in a multi-page format file.

A NEW STRUCTURE FOR THE CUSTOMER UPDATE AND INQUIRY PROGRAM

Although many of the problems described in the previous section can be solved without eliminating the format file, they will all be tackled at once with a program that replaces NWCUST3.FMT with a TEXT ... ENDTEXT structure that draws the input screen mask and a series of @ ... SAY ... GET commands to collect the data. The program, NWCUPD2.PRG, is listed in Figure 19-6. This program opens both the Customer File and the Transaction File and links them with SET RELATION in order to check for any current transactions before allowing a customer record to be deleted. Again, the program uses SKIP −1 to skip backward in the Customer File and thus set the BOF( ) function to .T. This way, the error traps in the program will prevent the user from choosing as a first command option any operation that requires a record to be displayed on the screen. As in NWCUPD1.PRG, a SET DELETED OFF command allows deleted records to be viewed, edited, printed, or recalled.

This program separates the display of the screen image from the GET commands that actually collect the data. TEXT ... ENDTEXT is used to draw the screen, and then the program superimposes on this constant mask the data from the records to be displayed or edited. This approach speeds up the program by eliminating the time required in NWCUPD1.PRG

```
* NWCUPD2.PRG
* PROGRAM TO INQUIRE, EDIT, ADD, AND DELETE CUSTOMERS
* WRITTEN BY:  M.LISKIN       08/01/85

select 1
use NWTXN  index NWTACCT

select 2
use NWCUST index NWCACCT, NWCZIP
set relation to ACCOUNT into NWTXN
skip -1

set deleted off

do NWCSCRN

do while .T.

   @ 23, 0
   store " " to MOPTION
   @ 23, 0 say "(S)earch  (C)hange  (N)ext  (P)rev  (D)el  " +;
               "(R)ecover  (A)dd  (M)emo  e(X)it" get MOPTION picture "!"
   read

   do case

      case MOPTION = "X"
         set deleted on
         return

      case MOPTION = "S"
         store "          " to MACCOUNT
         @ 23, 0
         @ 23,10 say "Enter the account number to search for";
                 get MACCOUNT picture "@!"
         read
         if MACCOUNT = " "
            loop
         endif
         seek trim(MACCOUNT)
         if .not. found()
            @ 23, 0
            @ 23,15 say trim(MACCOUNT) +;
                        " not found -- Press any key to continue"
            wait ""
            loop
         endif

      case MOPTION = "C"
         if eof() .or. bof()
            @ 23, 0
            @ 23,15 say "You must SEARCH first -- Press any key to continue"
            wait ""
            loop
         endif

      case MOPTION = "N"
         if .not. eof()
            skip
         endif
```

Figure 19-6. The revised customer update and inquiry program

```
   if eof()
      @ 23, 0
      @ 23,15 say "This is the last name -- Press any key to continue"
      wait ""
      loop
   endif

case MOPTION = "P"
   if .not. bof()
      skip -1
   endif
   if bof()
      @ 23, 0
      @ 23,15 say "This is the first name -- Press any key to continue"
      wait ""
      loop
   endif

case MOPTION = "D"
   if eof() .or. bof()
      @ 23, 0
      @ 23,15 say "You must SEARCH first -- Press any key to continue"
      wait ""
      loop
   endif

   if BALANCE <> 0.00
      @ 23, 0
      @ 23,15 say "Balance is not 0.00 -- Press any key to continue"
      wait ""
      loop
   endif

   select NWTXN
   if found()
      @ 23, 0
      @ 23,10 say;
        "There are current transactions -- Press any key to continue"
      wait ""
      select NWCUST
      loop
   else
      select NWCUST
   endif

   store .F. to MCONFIRM
   @ 23, 0
   @ 23,10 say "Are you sure you want to delete this customer? (Y/N)";
         get MCONFIRM picture "Y"
   read

   if MCONFIRM
      delete
      @ 3,65 say "* DELETED *"
      @ 23, 0
      @ 23,15 say trim(ACCOUNT) +;
                   " has been deleted -- Press any key to continue"
      wait ""
   endif
   loop
```

Figure 19-6. The revised customer update and inquiry program (*continued*)

```
   case MOPTION = "R"
      if eof() .or. bof()
         @ 23, 0
         @ 23,15 say "You must SEARCH first -- Press any key to continue"
         wait ""
         loop
      endif

      recall
      @  3,65 say "           "
      @ 23, 0
      @ 23,15 say trim(ACCOUNT) +;
                  " has been recovered -- Press any key to continue"
      wait ""
      loop

   case MOPTION = "A"
      store "          " to MACCOUNT
      @ 23, 0
      @ 23,10 say "Enter the account number for the new entry";
              get MACCOUNT picture "@!"
      read

      if MACCOUNT = " "
         loop
      endif
      seek MACCOUNT
      if found()
         @ 23, 0
         @ 23,10 say trim(MACCOUNT) +;
                     " is already on file -- Press any key to continue"
         wait ""
         loop
      else
         append blank
         replace ACCOUNT with MACCOUNT, STATE with MPSTATE,;
                 AREACODE with MPAREACODE, TAXRATE with MPTAXRATE
      endif

   case MOPTION = "M"
      if eof() .or. bof()
         @ 23, 0
         @ 23,15 say "You must SEARCH first -- Press any key to continue"
         wait ""
         loop
      endif

      set format to NWCUST5.FMT
      edit
      set format to
      do NWCSCRN

   otherwise
      loop
endcase

if deleted()
   @ 3,65 say "* DELETED *"
else
```

Figure 19-6. The revised customer update and inquiry program (*continued*)

```
      @ 3,65 say "            "
   endif

   @  3,13 get ACCOUNT picture "@!"
   @ 14,18 get YTDINV picture "9,999,999.99"
   @ 15,18 get YTDPMT picture "9,999,999.99"
   @ 17,18 get TOTINV picture "9,999,999.99"
   @ 17,62 get FIRSTORDER
   @ 18,18 get YTDPMT picture "9,999,999.99"
   @ 18,62 get LASTORDER
   @ 20,18 get BALANCE picture "@( 9,999,999.99"
   clear gets

   if dtoc(LASTORDER) <> "  "
      store date() - LASTORDER to MDAYS
      @ 20,45 say "LAST ORDER WAS " + str(MDAYS,4) + " DAYS AGO"
   else
      @ 20,45 say space(30)
   endif

   @  5,13 get COMPANY
   @  6,13 get ADDRESS1
   @  7,13 get ADDRESS2
   @  8,13 get CITY
   @  8,51 get STATE picture "@!"
   @  8,63 get ZIP picture "99999"
   @ 10,13 get CONTACT
   @ 10,55 get AREACODE picture "999"
   @ 10,63 get TELEPHONE picture "999-9999"
   @ 12,13 get EQUIPMENT
   @ 12,63 get TAXRATE range 0, 10

   if MOPTION $ "CA"
      read
   else
      clear gets
   endif

enddo

return
```

Figure 19-6. The revised customer update and inquiry program (*continued*)

to redraw the screen for each record. The TEXT ... ENDTEXT structure that draws the screen image is placed in a separate file, NWCSCRN.PRG, listed in Figure 19-7, because this will keep the main program uncluttered and because this routine must be called from more than one place in NWCUPD2.PRG.

Even with the GETs moved to a separate part of the program, @ ... SAY commands could still be used to draw the screen. TEXT ... ENDTEXT was chosen primarily because this structure makes it much easier to design and modify a screen layout with a word processor or the MOD-

```
* NWCSCRN.PRG
* PROGRAM TO DRAW CUSTOMER FILE UPDATE AND INQUIRY SCREEN
* WRITTEN BY:  M.LISKIN       08/05/85

clear
text
     NATIONAL WIDGETS, INC. - CUSTOMER LIST UPDATE AND INQUIRY
+------------------------------------------------------------------------------+
|  Acct Code [          ]                                                      |
|                                                                              |
|  Company    [                              ]                                 |
|  Address    [                         ]                                      |
|             [                         ]                                      |
|  City       [                    ]        State [  ]    Zip [     ]          |
|                                                                              |
|  Contact    [                         ]   Telephone [   ]  [   -    ]       |
|                                                                              |
|  Equipment [                          ]   Sales Tax Rate %  [  .  ]          |
+------------------------------------------------------------------------------+
|  Y-T-D Invoices [            ]                                               |
|  Y-T-D Payments [            ]                                               |
|                                                                              |
|  Total Invoices [            ]            First Order Date [        ]        |
|  Total Payments [            ]            Last  Order Date [        ]        |
|                                                                              |
|  Balance        [            ]                                               |
+------------------------------------------------------------------------------+
endtext

@  1,70 say date()

return
```

Figure 19-7. The customer update and inquiry screen

IFY COMMAND editor than it is with @ ... SAY ... GET commands. Note that the brackets that delimit the data fields were included in the screen image. Since the Main Menu program uses SET DELIMITERS ON and specifies the delimiter characters with SET DELIMITERS TO "[ ]", a set of brackets is always supplied by dBASE III PLUS for each field collected with a GET. The brackets are duplicated in the TEXT ... ENDTEXT structure so that the screen remains constant in appearance from the moment it is drawn—even before the user has retrieved and displayed the first record. When you are designing a new screen, you may have to count spaces to determine where the delimiters go, but they also serve as a guide to exactly how much space each field occupies. This is especially helpful when you are trying to squeeze many fields into a crowded screen.

With the brackets included in the screen image, you could SET DELIMITERS OFF, at least within the update program, but the dBASE III PLUS delimiters were retained so that brackets are always displayed when the program solicits input from the user—for example, when the program asks a question such as "Are you sure you want to delete this customer?" If you do SET DELIMITERS OFF in your own programs, remember that the coordinates in the GET commands must be one column to the right of your screen's opening brackets. With DELIMITERS ON, the position of the GET must coincide with the position of the bracket so that the dBASE III PLUS delimiter overwrites yours.

The first portion of the program asks the user to make a choice and then processes it, much like NWCUPD1.PRG. The new program incorporates most of the desired improvements listed in the previous section. The option line now presents only completely equivalent choices: SEARCH, CHANGE, NEXT, PREVIOUS, DELETE, RECOVER, ADD, MEMO, and EXIT. (Some abbreviation was required to squeeze all of these choices into one line.) This program uses separate options for the SEARCH and CHANGE functions; a new choice, MEMO, was added to allow the operator to edit the memo field with a new format file. Since the program no longer asks for a customer account number by default, an explicit EXIT option is required to return to the menu. As in NWCUPD1.PRG, line 23 is cleared to make sure that no error message remains on this line whenever the option prompt is redisplayed. We will examine the options one by one.

The EXIT option requires only that the program SET DELETED ON before the RETURN command transfers control back to the Customer Information Menu, so that deleted records are ignored throughout the rest of the programs in the system. The NEXT and PREVIOUS options now test the status of the EOF( ) or BOF( ) functions before executing the SKIP commands. Similarly, the CHANGE, DELETE, RECOVER, and MEMO options verify whether or not the data base is positioned at a valid record, and if it is not, display an error message reminding the operator to search for a record first. In addition to asking for confirmation, the DELETE option performs two tests—to make sure that the BALANCE field is 0 and that no current transactions exist—before deleting a customer record. The test for transaction activity works because the Customer and Transaction Files are linked with SET RELATION. The FOUND( ) function will be true for the Transaction File if it contains any records that match the current customer record.

The SEARCH option does what the NWCUPD1.PRG did by default: it asks for a customer account number, uses SEEK to search the index for the matching account number, and displays an error message if no matching customer record is found. The new CHANGE option requires no special action in this part of the program, except to check that the data base is actually positioned at a valid record. The ADD option is identical to its counterpart in NWCUPD1.PRG.

In order to enter or edit text in the COMMENTS field, the MEMO option opens a new format file, NWCUST5.FMT, listed in Figure 19-8. The format file must be used with the EDIT command to make the memo field accessible. But once in EDIT there is no way to confine the operator to viewing or changing only one record. To prevent any of the fields *except* COMMENTS from being edited outside of the main program, the screen drawn by the format file contains only three fields—ACCOUNT, COMPANY, and COMMENTS—two of which (ACCOUNT and COMPANY) are displayed with @ ... SAY commands and may not be changed by the operator. When the operator returns to the main program by pressing ESC or CTRL-END, the format file is closed and the NWCSCRN.PRG program is called to redisplay the Customer File data entry screen. After the ENDCASE statement, the data from the current customer record is filled in on this screen.

This record may or may not be the one that was on the screen when the MEMO option was chosen, depending on whether or not the operator paged forward or backward while the format file was in effect. If this presents a problem, it is easy to modify the program to keep track of the record displayed at the time the MEMO option was selected. You can do this by storing the current value of the ACCOUNT field in a memory variable before the SET FORMAT TO NWCUST5 command and then using SEEK to reposition the data base to the same record when the for-

```
* NWCUST5.FMT
* FORMAT FILE FOR EDITING CUSTOMER FILE MEMO FIELD
* WRITTEN BY:     M.LISKIN      08/05/85

@  5,10 say trim(ACCOUNT) + " - " + COMPANY
@  8,10 say "Comments " get COMMENTS
@ 15,10 say "To view comments, press ^PgDn"
@ 17,10 say "To save changes and return to main screen, press ^End"
```

Figure 19-8. A format file to enter and edit memo fields

mat file is closed:

```
store ACCOUNT to MACCOUNT
set format to NWCUST5
edit
set format to
seek MACCOUNT
do NWCSCRN
```

You can also store the record number in a memory variable and use GOTO to reposition the record pointer:

```
store recno() to MRECORD
set format to NWCUST5
edit
set format to
goto MRECORD
do NWCSCRN
```

Just as in the earlier version of the update program, in this program the data base is always positioned after the ENDCASE statement at the record to be displayed or edited. A series of GET commands replaces the format file used in NWCUPD1.PRG for this purpose. If the record is deleted, the program displays the "* DELETED *" indicator. If not, since the program no longer clears the entire screen before each new record is displayed (the format file does this automatically), enough blank spaces are placed in the same position on the screen to erase a deletion indicator that may have been left from the last record. Notice that the RECOVER option must also eradicate the deletion indicator in the same way.

The NWCUST2.FMT, NWCUST3.FMT, and NWCUST4.FMT format files used @ ... SAY commands to display the fields that should not be changed through the customer update and inquiry program (the dollar totals and order dates, which must be updated only by posting transactions). Because the fields were displayed with SAY commands, they appeared in the background color (or monochrome attribute). In the sample system, this means low- rather than high-intensity characters. The NWCUPD2.PRG program displays all of the fields in the brighter intensity, to distinguish the data in the Customer File from the background text. There are two ways to accomplish this. One method uses a SET COLOR command to change the background color used for data displayed with SAY, and the other uses GET commands rather than SAYs to display the fields. The latter technique works because although the GET commands *display* the named fields, dBASE III PLUS does not actually allow the cursor to move into the fields to edit the data until a READ command is encountered. Instead of a READ, the NWCUPD2.PRG program uses CLEAR GETS, which causes dBASE III PLUS to "cancel" all pending GETS (those not yet processed by a READ). As a result, the fields are displayed in the foreground intensity used for entered data, but the operator is not allowed to edit them.

The items to be displayed in this manner must be placed on the screen first, followed by a CLEAR GETS. A second series of GETs and a READ command then allow the remaining fields to be viewed and edited. The fields must be presented in this reverse order because dBASE III PLUS processes only one group of GETs, together with a single READ, at a time. If the program first displayed the fields to be edited, issued the READ command, and then listed the rest of the GETs, the second group of fields would not even appear on the screen until after the operator moved the cursor past the last field (TAXRATE) to trigger the READ command. The order chosen displays all the fields at once, with the CLEAR GETS preventing the operator from editing the group of fields on the bottom half of the screen. Notice that the account number was included among the fields that may not be changed through this program, so that no mismatches between the Customer File and the Transaction and Order files can be made inadvertently.

Finally, the READ command itself is executed only if the operator has chosen the CHANGE or ADD option. If the program is displaying a record after a SEARCH, NEXT, or PREVIOUS command, or if it has just returned from the memo text screen, a CLEAR GETS command is used instead, so that *all* of the fields on the screen are displayed, and the cursor returns to the option line rather than moving into the screen to allow the operator to edit the data.

This version of the program lays the groundwork for other, more sophisticated data entry and inquiry programs. Using this basic structure, you can easily add multiple READs to collect the fields into groups and perform conditional tests, based on the values entered into each group of fields, to determine the way the remaining items are processed. The next chapter will discuss ways to add extensive validation tests to this program to make sure that the data entered into a file conforms to a fixed set of rules established by the users and the programmers.

20

DATA VALIDATION

The programs in this book have introduced progressively more exacting standards for validating data entered by the users. At the simplest level, dBASE III PLUS validates all numeric and date fields to guarantee that the values entered are at least reasonable, if not correct. Using @ ... SAY ... GET commands to collect data, either in a format file or in a dBASE III PLUS program, allows for a broader range of input formatting and validity checking through the use of PICTURE, FUNCTION, and RANGE clauses. In addition, the programs have demonstrated techniques for asking a question and making sure that the response is one of a finite number of possibilities, and for validating fields by using SEEK to look up the matching records in other files. This chapter will illustrate two general methods for incorporating these and other types of validation tests into your dBASE III PLUS programs to ensure that all of the data entered into a file conforms to a clearly defined set of criteria.

The tests you will want to perform on a given data base are often highly customized to the idiosyncratic requirements of your particular organization. In the National Widgets system, for example, the following rules might be defined for data entered into the Customer File:

- The ACCOUNT field must not be blank.
- Both COMPANY and CONTACT fields must not be left blank; that is, either a company name or the name of an individual must be entered to identify the customer.
- The first address line (ADDRESS1) must not be blank.

- The CITY field must not be blank.
- The STATE field must contain one of the 50 valid state postal abbreviations.
- The ZIP field must be filled completely with a five-digit number.
- If the customer's address is outside of California, the sales tax rate (TAXRATE) should be 0.
- If the customer's address is within California, the sales tax rate must be either 6.00 or 6.50.

These rules are typical of the validation tests commonly applied to name and address data bases. When designing a system, you may find that clearly defining the validation rules can be more difficult than implementing the tests. The users may have trouble articulating in precise terms the kind of human judgments they make without thinking. If you are an outside consultant or programmer, you may also find that understanding the rules or helping users define them requires you to learn a lot about the organization for which you are writing the programs. Determining *when* to perform the validation tests depends in part on the consequences of entering erroneous data into a file and also on your understanding of the setting in which the program will be used. There are three stages at which you might choose to validate the information entered into a data base file:

- As each field is entered or changed.
- After all of the fields in one record have been entered or changed.
- In a batch procedure periodically applied to an entire data base.

When data is displayed and collected by using a series of @ ... SAY ... GET commands followed by a READ, the field values are known to dBASE III PLUS (that is, available to your program for testing) only after the READ command is executed. This means that in order to test each field as it is entered, you must follow each GET command (that collects data into a field that must be validated) with a READ. Since you have no way of knowing how many tries it will take to enter the field correctly, the GET and READ commands must be placed in a DO WHILE loop that does not allow the user to advance to the next field until a correct value has been entered. This recalls the method used to keep repeating a question until one of a finite number of permissible responses has been entered. In a program for entering new records into a data base, the DO

WHILE loop would be very straightforward. For example, to make sure that the CITY field was not left blank, you could use

```
do while CITY = " "
   @  8,13 get CITY
   read
enddo
```

Since all of the fields in a newly appended record are blank, the program will always go through the loop at least once.

If the same DO WHILE loop were used for editing existing records, however, it would be impossible to change the CITY field, because if the field were not blank, the condition in the DO WHILE statement would never be true. Instead, you could substitute the following:

```
do while .T.
   @  8,13 get CITY
   read
   if CITY <> " "
      exit
   endif
enddo
```

Since .T. is always true, the loop is always executed at least once. If, after the READ command, the CITY field is not blank, the EXIT command transfers control to the first statement following ENDDO. Otherwise, the program returns to the top of the DO WHILE loop, retests the condition, and, since .T. is still true, makes another pass through the loop.

This approach is appropriate when the data entered into certain fields is required for decisions or calculations that must be made before other fields are collected or before records are added to or deleted from a data base. In these situations the user must not be allowed to continue until the relevant fields are correct. However, adding this type of validation to a program like the National Widgets Customer File update and inquiry program written in Chapter 19 would very likely meet with great resistance from the users. In the name and address block alone, nearly every field must be validated in some way. Since all of the fields should be displayed together when a record is first retrieved, the program would first have to GET all of the fields and then CLEAR GETS, as was done in the NWCUPD2.PRG program for the fields that must not ever be changed by the operator. A series of DO WHILE loops containing a second set of GETs and READs could then be used to collect and validate the individual fields.

The READ command, in addition to collecting data typed by the user into the fields named in the preceding GETs, also has the same effect as CLEAR GETS: it wipes out all knowledge of the GETs from dBASE III PLUS's memory and thereby prohibits the user from moving the cursor back into those fields on the screen. Performing the validations this way would not only slow down the data entry process; it also would effectively disable one of dBASE III PLUS's best features, the ability to use the full-screen edit commands to move freely among the fields on a screen while entering or editing a record.

The READ command has a SAVE option that appears to provide a partial solution to this problem: READ SAVE does not CLEAR the pending GETs. However, the *next* READ command encountered reactivates all of these previously executed GETs. This results in repositioning the cursor in the first of the fields thus displayed and forcing the user to step through all of the fields again, for a reason that is not readily apparent. In addition to this annoyance, there are two real dangers in using READ SAVE. First, if it takes the user many tries to enter correct data into the fields that are validated, it is possible to exceed the maximum number of GETs permitted between READ or CLEAR GETS commands, and the program will "crash." Since you can increase the number of GETS (128 by default) to 1023 with an entry in CONFIG.DB, this is an unlikely occurrence, even in a data base with many fields. The second and more serious problem is that while READ SAVE causes dBASE III PLUS to "remember" the screen positions of the GETs and the data to be displayed, moving the cursor back into a field collected with an @ ... SAY ... GET command within a DO WHILE loop does not repeat the execution of the DO WHILE loop. The data is therefore collected without validation.

In most settings the kind of instantaneous validation accomplished by collecting each field within its own DO WHILE loop is really not necessary. In the National Widgets system, for example, leaving an address field blank or entering an incorrect state abbreviation does not have nearly as serious a consequence as entering an order for a nonexistent customer or an order containing an invalid inventory part number. At the opposite end of the spectrum, you could allow records to be entered into the Customer File without any validation at all, as in the update and inquiry programs in Chapter 19, and then use a separate program to check every record in the file to make sure that it conforms to all of the rules defined earlier for acceptable entries.

This batch validation strategy is appropriate for organizations in which the operators are generally fast and accurate and there is little to be gained by slowing down the data entry process with on-the-spot validation tests. You might also use this approach in high-volume, high-speed input situations, such as the initial entry of hundreds or thousands of records into a new data base system. Batch validation is also appropriate when you have downloaded data from a mainframe or converted a file created by another program to a dBASE III PLUS data base. While such a file generally requires careful proofreading to catch more subtle errors, a batch validation program can be a very efficient first screening to ensure the reasonableness of the converted data.

The final alternative, allowing the operator to enter an entire record, and then checking all of the appropriate fields, is a good compromise between the two extremes. It is best suited for performing routine maintenance on existing data base files, when speed is less important because fewer entries are being made and the accuracy of the operators is less assured. In this chapter the two recommended validation strategies will be demonstrated by writing a batch validation program for the National Widgets Customer File and then adding the same validation tests to the update and inquiry program written in Chapter 19.

A BATCH VALIDATION PROGRAM

The basic strategy for any batch validation program is to read through the data base, apply the necessary tests to each record, and mark or print the ones that fail any of the tests. Since this can take a considerable amount of time if the file is large, it is generally best to print a listing of the records that do not pass every test rather than pausing when a problem is found and asking the operator to correct it. Printing the error listing allows the program to be run unattended (overnight, if you can trust your printer not to jam), and gives the users time to find the information that is missing or incorrect before returning to the update program to fix the problems.

The validation program must keep track of the results of all of the validation tests applied to each record. If a record passes all of the tests, it should not be printed at all; if it fails to conform to one or more of the criteria, only the invalid fields should appear on the listing. In order to make the report as informative as possible, the program should print at least the contents of the incorrect fields and perhaps a brief description of what is wrong with the data. If the STATE field was left blank, for example, the program might simply print "Blank" or "Missing." For an invalid state abbreviation, the program might print the erroneous STATE field and the explanation "INVALID."

To accommodate the variable error message text, the program creates a set of character memory variables to contain the error messages, reinitialized as null strings for each record processed. If a record fails one of the tests, an error message is stored in the appropriate variable. If all the variables are still blank after each test has been performed, this means that the record has passed the full complement of validation tests and should not be printed. For each record with at least one error, the program can simply print all of the memory variables, and only the nonblank ones will be visible.

A batch validation program for the National Widgets Customer File, NWCVALID.PRG, is listed in Figure 20-1; a typical error listing is shown in Figure 20-2. The program opens the Customer File with the account number index. Although reading the file in sequential rather than indexed order would result in somewhat faster processing, the index was used in this case so that the error listing is printed in the order most convenient for the users—alphabetical order by account number. Since the file is processing in alphabetical order, the best status message to allow the user to monitor the program's progress consists of the account number and company name rather than the record number. After opening the Customer File, the program reminds the operator to turn on the printer, since unlike the other menu options in the National Widgets system that print reports, it may not be clear to the uninitiated that the validation program will produce any printed output. Also in preparation for printing the report, the program initializes two memory variables, MLINE and MPAGE, to store the printed line and page numbers, respectively.

The first test the program performs determines whether the ACCOUNT field was left blank. If so, the record number—expressed as the RECNO( ) function converted to a character string ten characters long with the STR function—is stored in the variable MACCOUNT. When this variable is printed on the error listing, it will give the user some way to identify the problem record so it may be corrected or deleted. If either the ADDRESS1 or CITY fields is blank, the message "MISSING" is stored in the corresponding variable; and if neither the COMPANY nor the CONTACT field has been filled in, "BOTH MISSING" is stored in the variable MCOMPANY.

Checking the STATE field is a little more complicated. If the field is blank, the standard "MISSING" error message should be printed. If the STATE field was filled in, the program must test whether the two characters entered into the field form one of the 50 legitimate postal abbrevia-

```
* NWCVALID.PRG
* PROGRAM TO VALIDATE CUSTOMER FILE RECORDS
* WRITTEN BY:  M.LISKIN        Ø8/Ø5/85

use NWCUST index NWCACCT

clear
@ 1Ø,1Ø say "Make sure the printer is on, then press any key to continue"
wait ""

store 1  to MPAGE
store 65 to MLINE

clear
@ 1Ø,1Ø say "Validating Customer File -- Please do not interrupt"
@ 12,1Ø say "Working on:"

do while .not. eof()

   @ 12,25 say ACCOUNT + " - " + COMPANY

   store "" to MACCOUNT, MCOMPANY, MADDRESS, MCITY, MSTATE, MZIP, MTAXRATE

   if ACCOUNT = " "
      store str(recno(),1Ø) to MACCOUNT
   endif

   if COMPANY = " " .and. CONTACT = " "
      store "BOTH MISSING" to MCOMPANY
   endif

   if ADDRESS1 = " "
      store "MISSING" to MADDRESS
   endif

   if CITY = " "
      store "MISSING" to MCITY
   endif

   if STATE = " "
      store "MISSING" to MSTATE
   else
      if .not. STATE $ MPSTATES
         store STATE + " (INVALID)" to MSTATE
      endif
   endif

   if ZIP = " "
      store "MISSING" to MZIP
   else
      if len(trim(ZIP)) < 5
         store ZIP + " (INVALID)" to MZIP
      endif
   endif

   do case
      case STATE = "  " .or. MSTATE <> " "
         store "CHECK AFTER ENTERING STATE" to MTAXRATE
      case STATE = "CA"
         if TAXRATE <> 6.ØØ .and. TAXRATE <> 6.5Ø
            store str(TAXRATE,5,2) + " (SHOULD BE 6.ØØ OR 6.5Ø)" to MTAXRATE
         endif
      otherwise
         if TAXRATE > Ø
```

Figure 20-1. A batch validation program for the National Widgets Customer File

```
          store str(TAXRATE,5,2) + " (SHOULD BE 0.00)" to MTAXRATE
       endif
 endcase

 if len(MACCOUNT + MCOMPANY + MADDRESS + MCITY + MSTATE + MZIP + MTAXRATE);
       = 0
    skip
    loop
 endif

 if ACCOUNT <> " "
    store ACCOUNT to MACCOUNT
 endif

 set device to print

 if MLINE > 60
    @  1,  0 say cmonth(date()) + str(day(date()),3) + ", " +;
                 str(year(date()),4)
    @  1,123 say "PAGE " + str(MPAGE,3)
    @  3, 55 say "NATIONAL WIDGETS, INC."
    @  4, 50 say "CUSTOMER FILE RECORDS WITH ERRORS"
    @  7,  0 say "ACCOUNT        COMPANY OR CONTACT     ADDRESS LINE 1     " +;
                 "CITY        STATE              ZIP              " +;
                 "SALES TAX RATE"
    @  8,  0 say "----------     ------------------     --------------     " +;
                 "---------    --------------    --------------    " +;
                 "------------------------------"
    store MPAGE + 1 to MPAGE
    store 10        to MLINE
 endif                  [ we are past line 60 ]

 @ MLINE,  0 say MACCOUNT
 @ MLINE, 15 say MCOMPANY
 @ MLINE, 37 say MADDRESS
 @ MLINE, 55 say MCITY
 @ MLINE, 67 say MSTATE
 @ MLINE, 83 say MZIP
 @ MLINE,100 say MTAXRATE

 store MLINE + 1 to MLINE
 skip

 set device to screen

enddo

eject

return
```

Figure 20-1. A batch validation program for the National Widgets Customer File (*continued*)

tions. This may be done by creating a character string composed of all of the valid state abbreviations and using a substring comparison to test whether the STATE field is contained in this string. These abbreviations change rarely, so you might consider writing the complete character

```
August 18, 1985                                                                                    PAGE   1

                                            NATIONAL WIDGETS, INC.
                                       CUSTOMER FILE RECORDS WITH ERRORS

ACCOUNT       COMPANY OR CONTACT    ADDRESS LINE 1   CITY       STATE         ZIP             SALES TAX RATE
----------    ------------------    --------------   ---------  ------------- --------------  ------------------------------

        18                                                      MISSING                       CHECK AFTER ENTERING STATE
ANDERSON      BOTH MISSING                                      CS (INVALID)                  CHECK AFTER ENTERING STATE
CHIPCITY                            MISSING                                                    6.40 (SHOULD BE 6.00 OR 6.50)
FLOORPLAN                                                                     9408  (INVALID)
HOMEMOVIES                                           MISSING
```

Figure 20-2. The listing produced by the batch validation program

string into the program as a constant or initializing a memory variable with this character string at the beginning of the program. In other applications, if you used this basic method to test the entries in a special code field against a list of permissible values, it would be better to store the choices in a public memory variable, so the users could view, add, change, or delete codes as needed. To illustrate this technique, the state abbreviations will be stored in a public memory variable called MPSTATEABB.

There is one more complication to consider before creating this variable. Suppose that the first part of the variable MPSTATEABB looked like this:

```
"ALAKAZARCA"
```

These are the abbreviations for Alabama (AL), Alaska (AK), Arizona (AZ), Arkansas (AR), and California (CA). If the STATE field contains any one of these five abbreviations, it will pass this test:

```
if STATE $ MPSTATEABB
```

The problem is that many other combinations of two letters, none of which are valid state abbreviations—for example, KA, ZA, and RC—are also contained in MPSTATEABB. In order to ensure that only the 50 valid possibilities pass the test, the separate abbreviations that make up the variable MPSTATEABB must be separated by some character that would never be found in the field. MPSTATEABB could be constructed as

```
"AL-AK-AZ-AR-CA"
```

or

```
"AL/AK/AZ/AR/CA"
```

If you are following along with the development of the National Widgets system, you can add this variable to the PUBLIC variables stored in NWMEMORY.MEM with these commands at the dot prompt:

```
RESTORE FROM NWMEMORY
STORE "AL/AK/AZ/AR/CA/CZ/CO/CT/DE/DC/FL/GA/GU/HI/ID/IL/IN/IA/KS/KY/"+;
      "LA/ME/MD/MA/MI/MN/MS/MO/MT/NE/NV/NH/NJ/NM/NY/NC/ND/OH/OK/OR/"+;
      "PA/PR/+RI/SC/SD/TN/TX/UT/VT/VA/VI/WA/VW/WI/WY/" TO MPSTATEABB
SAVE ALL LIKE MP* TO NWMEMORY
```

The validation sequence for the STATE field begins by testing whether the field is blank. If it is, the message "MISSING" is stored in the variable MSTATE. If it is not, the program tests to see if the abbreviation is *not* one of the 50 legitimate possibilities with

```
if .not. STATE $ MPSTATEABB
```

If the STATE field is not one of the allowable abbreviations, the contents of the field plus the message "(INVALID)" are stored to MSTATE, so that when the user reads the report, it will be evident what data was entered into the field and what was wrong with the entry. The ZIP code is also tested in two steps. If it is blank, the error message variable MZIP assumes the value "MISSING". Otherwise, the ZIP field is TRIMmed. If the length of the TRIMmed field is less than five characters, an incomplete ZIP code was entered, and the program stores the partial ZIP code, along with the "(INVALID)" explanation, in MZIP. This program does *not* check the ZIP code to make sure that it contains only numbers, a test that would require examining the field one character at a time. Note also that you would not want to perform such a test if your file might contain any foreign addresses, which could legitimately have letters in the ZIP codes.

Next, the sales tax rate field, TAXRATE, is tested. For this field there are three possible error conditions. If the state is not California, the sales tax rate should be 0. For California customers the rate is either 6.00 or 6.50 percent, depending on the county, but the county is not currently stored in the Customer File, and adding it to the data base would serve no useful purpose outside of validating the sales tax rate. The best we can do, therefore, is to flag those records that contain an impossible tax rate. The third possibility to test for is less obvious. If the STATE field was left blank, there is no way to judge whether or not the sales tax rate is correct, so the program stores a reminder, "CHECK AFTER ENTERING STATE," to the error message variable MTAXRATE.

After you perform these tests, all of the error message variables will retain their original null values if no errors were found, and the program should SKIP to the next record in the file and then LOOP back to the top of the DO WHILE loop to validate the next record. To check the values of the variables, you could use an expression like this:

```
if MACCOUNT = "" .and. MCOMPANY = "" .and. MADDRESS = ""  .and.;
   MCITY = "" .and. MSTATE = "" .and. MTAXRATE = ""
```

With only six variables, this is perfectly acceptable, but this method quickly becomes unwieldy with a larger number of validation tests. Instead, the NWCVALID.PRG program concatenates all of the memory variables into one character string, and tests to see if the length of the string is 0:

```
if len(MACCOUNT + MCOMPANY + MADDRESS + MCITY + MSTATE + MZIP + MTAXRATE) = 0
```

If at least one of the error message variables is not blank, the account number from the problem record is stored in the variable MACCOUNT. At this point MACCOUNT always contains some means of identifying the record printed on the error listing—either the account number or, if the ACCOUNT field was blank, the record number—so that it may be found and corrected. Note that the contents of the account field could not have been stored in the variable MACCOUNT any earlier in the program without disrupting the test that determines whether or not the record should be printed by checking to determine if all of the memory variables, including MACCOUNT, are blank.

If the record must be printed, the program routes the output of @ ... SAY ... GET commands to the printer with SET DEVICE TO PRINT. The section of the program that prints the report resembles the programs already described in Chapters 16 and 17 for printing columnar reports. After printing the error messages, the program SKIPs to the next record in the file and returns the output of @ ... SAY ... GET commands to the console with SET DEVICE TO SCREEN so that the next customer's account number and company name may be displayed on the screen as part of the status message that allows the user to monitor the program's progress.

ADDING VALIDATION TO AN UPDATE AND INQUIRY PROGRAM

The alternative to the after-the-fact batch validation performed by the NWCVALID.PRG program is to check each record as it is entered or edited, so that erroneous data may not be entered into the file in the first place. The method for doing this nicely fits into the structure of the general-purpose update and inquiry program presented in Chapter 19. To implement this validation scheme, you can place the entire group of @ ... SAY ... GET commands that collect the fields, together with the necessary tests, into a DO WHILE loop that forces the operator to keep editing the record until it satisfies all of the validation criteria. On each pass through this loop, the program should display an error message next to each field in which the contents are unacceptable and then go through the data entry steps again. This method allows the operator to move freely among the fields using the standard dBASE III PLUS full-screen editing commands, while still forcing each record entered into the file to adhere to a specified set of rules. The only minor inconvenience is having to move the cursor through all of the preceding fields on the screen each time through the loop in order to change one incorrect item. We will have to accept this limitation, however, since dBASE III PLUS provides no easy way around it.

Figure 20-3 lists a new update and inquiry program, NWCUPD3.PRG, that applies this technique to the National Widgets Customer File, using many of the same validation tests as NWCVALID.PRG. The pseudocode explanation is listed in Figure 20-4. The first part of the program opens the Customer and Transaction files, draws the input screen, and positions the record pointer to the record to be displayed or edited in a manner very similar to the NWCUPD2.PRG program written in Chapter 19. In addition to the Customer and Transaction files, the program opens a new file, NWCODES.DBF, which is used to look up and validate the STATE and AREACODE fields.

```
* NWCUPD3.PRG
* PROGRAM TO INQUIRE, EDIT, ADD, AND DELETE CUSTOMERS
* WRITTEN BY:  M.LISKIN      08/01/85

select 1
use NWTXN   index NWTACCT

select 2
use NWCODES index NWCODES

select 3
use NWCUST  index NWCACCT, NWCZIP
set relation to ACCOUNT into NWTXN
skip -1

set deleted off
```

Figure 20-3. An update and inquiry program with validation tests

```
store " " to MCITY

do NWCSCRN

do while .T.

   @ 23, 0
   store " " to MOPTION
   @ 23, 0 say "(S)earch  (C)hange  (N)ext  (P)rev  (D)el  " +;
               "(R)ecover  (A)dd  (M)emo  e(X)it" get MOPTION picture "!"
   read

   do case

      case MOPTION = "X"
         set deleted on
         return

      case MOPTION = "S"
         store "          " to MACCOUNT
         @ 23, 0
         @ 23,10 say "Enter the account number to search for";
                 get MACCOUNT picture "@!"
         read
         it MACCOUNT = " "
            loop
         endif
         seek trim(MACCOUNT)
         if .not. found()
            @ 23, 0
            @ 23,15 say trim(MACCOUNT) +;
                        " not found -- Press any key to continue"
            wait ""
            loop
         endif

      case MOPTION = "C"
         if eof() .or. bof()
            @ 23, 0
            @ 23,15 say "You must SEARCH first -- Press any key to continue"
            wait ""
            loop
         endif

      case MOPTION = "N"
         if .not. eof()
            skip
         endif
         if eof()
            @ 23, 0
            @ 23,15 say "This is the last name -- Press any key to continue"
            wait ""
            loop
         endif

      case MOPTION = "P"
         if .not. bof()
            skip -1
         endif
```

Figure 20-3. An update and inquiry program with validation tests *(continued)*

```
      if bof()
         @ 23, 0
         @ 23,15 say "This is the first name -- Press any key to continue"
         wait ""
         loop
      endif

   case MOPTION = "D"
      if eof() .or. bof()
         @ 23, 0
         @ 23,15 say "You must SEARCH first -- Press any key to continue"
         wait ""
         loop
      endif

      if BALANCE <> 0.00
         @ 23, 0
         @ 23,15 say "Balance is not 0.00 -- Press any key to continue"
         wait ""
         loop
      endif

      select NWTXN
      if found()
         @ 23, 0
         @ 23, 5 say;
           "There are current transactions -- Press any key to continue"
         wait ""
         select NWCUST
         loop
      else
         select NWCUST
      endif

      store .F. to MCONFIRM
      @ 23, 0
      @ 23,10 say "Are you sure you want to delete this customer? (Y/N)";
              get MCONFIRM picture "Y"
      read

      if MCONFIRM
         delete
         set color to W+, W+
         @  3,65 say "* DELETED *"
         set color to W, W+
         @ 23, 0
         @ 23,15 say trim(ACCOUNT) +;
                     " has been deleted -- Press any key to continue"
         wait ""
      endif
      loop

   case MOPTION = "R"
      if eof() .or. bof()
         @ 23, 0
         @ 23,15 say "You must SEARCH first -- Press any key to continue"
         wait ""
         loop
      endif
```

Figure 20-3. An update and inquiry program with validation tests (*continued*)

```
         recall
         @  3,65 say "          "
         @ 23, 0
         @ 23,15 say trim(ACCOUNT) +;
                    " has been recovered -- Press any key to continue"
         wait ""
         loop

      case MOPTION = "A"
         store "          " to MACCOUNT
         @ 23, 0
         @ 23,10 say "Enter the account number for the new entry";
                 get MACCOUNT picture "@!"
         read

         if MACCOUNT = " "
            loop
         endif
         seek MACCOUNT
         if found()
            @ 23, 0
            @ 23,10 say trim(MACCOUNT) +;
                       " is already on file -- Press any key to continue"
            wait ""
            loop
         else
            append blank
            replace ACCOUNT with MACCOUNT, STATE with MPSTATE,;
                    CITY with MCITY, AREACODE with MPAREACODE,;
                    TAXRATE with MPTAXRATE
         endif

      case MOPTION = "M"
         if eof() .or. bof()
            @ 23, 0
            @ 23,15 say "You must SEARCH first -- Press any key to continue"
            wait ""
            loop
         endif

         set format to NWCUST5
         edit
         set format to
         do NWCSCRN

      otherwise
         loop

   endcase

   if deleted()
      set color to W+, W+
      @ 3,65 say "* DELETED *"
      set color to W, W+
   else
      @ 3,65 say "           "
   endif

   @  3,13 get ACCOUNT
   @ 14,18 get YTDINV picture "9,999,999.99"
```

Figure 20-3. An update and inquiry program with validation tests (*continued*)

```
@ 15,18 get YTDPMT picture "9,999,999.99"
@ 17,18 get TOTINV picture "9,999,999.99"
@ 17,62 get FIRSTORDER
@ 18,18 get YTDPMT picture "9,999,999.99"
@ 18,62 get LASTORDER
@ 20,18 get BALANCE picture "@( 9,999,999.99"
clear gets

if dtoc(LASTORDER) <> "  "
   store date() - LASTORDER to MDAYS
   @ 20,45 say "LAST ORDER WAS " + str(MDAYS,4) + " DAYS AGO"
else
   @ 20,45 say space(28)
endif

do while .T.

   store .T. to MVALID
   set color to W, W+

   @  5,13 get COMPANY
   @  6,13 get ADDRESS1
   @  7,13 get ADDRESS2
   @  8,13 get CITY
   @  8,51 get STATE picture "@!"
   @  8,63 get ZIP picture "99999"
   @ 10,13 get CONTACT
   @ 10,55 get AREACODE picture "999"
   @ 10,63 get TELEPHONE picture "999-9999"
   @ 12,13 get EQUIPMENT
   @ 12,63 get TAXRATE range 0, 10

   if MOPTION $ "CA"
      read
   else
      clear gets
   endif

   set color to W+, W+

   if ACCOUNT = " "
      delete
      @ 3,65 say "* DELETED *"
      exit
   endif

   if COMPANY = " " .and. CONTACT = " "
      store .F. to MVALID
      @  5, 1 say "*"
      @ 10, 1 say "*"
   else
      @  5, 1 say " "
      @ 10, 1 say " "
   endif

   if ADDRESS1 = " "
      store .F. to MVALID
      @  6, 1 say "*"
   else
      @  6, 1 say " "
   endif
```

Figure 20-3. An update and inquiry program with validation tests (*continued*)

```
if CITY = " "
   store .F. to MVALID
   @  8, 1 say "*"
else
   @  8, 1 say " "
endif

if STATE = " "
   store .F. to MVALID
   @  8,43 say "*"
   @  9,51 say space(20)
else
   select NWCODES
   seek "S" + NWCUST->STATE
   if found()
      @  8,43 say " "
      @  9,51 say DESCRIP
   else
      @  8,43 say "*"
      @  9,51 say space(20)
   endif
   select NWCUST
endif

if len(trim(ZIP)) < 5
   store .F. to MVALID
   @  8,57 say "*"
else
   @  8,57 say " "
endif

if AREACODE = " "
   @ 10,43 say " "
   @ 11,55 say space(20)
else
   select NWCODES
   seek "A" + NWCUST->AREACODE
   if found()
      @ 10,43 say " "
      @ 11,55 say DESCRIP
   else
      store .F. to MVALID
      @ 10,43 say "*"
      @ 11,55 say space(20)
   endif
   select NWCUST
endif

if STATE = "  " .or. (STATE <> "CA" .and. TAXRATE > 0) .or.;
   (STATE = "CA" .and. TAXRATE <> 6.00 .and. TAXRATE <> 6.50)
   store .F. to MVALID
   @ 12,43 say "*"
else
   @ 12,43 say " "
endif
```

Figure 20-3. An update and inquiry program with validation tests (*continued*)

```
      if MVALID
         exit
      else
         @ 23, 0
         @ 23,15 say 'Please correct the fields marked with a "*" '
         if .not. MOPTION $ "CA"
            store "C" to MOPTION
         endif
      endif

   enddo                          [ not validated ]

   set color to W, W+

   if MOPTION = "A"
      store CITY to MCITY
   endif

enddo

return
```

Figure 20-3. An update and inquiry program with validation tests (*continued*)

```
open the transaction file with the account number index

open the code file with the code type/code index

open the customer file with the account number and zip code indexes
link this file to the transacton file by account number
skip backward to set the BOF() function to .T.

allow deleted records to be viewed and edited

initialize a memory variable, MCITY, for the most recently entered CITY field

draw the input screen

do the following until the user chooses to exit:

   clear line 23 on the screen
   initialize a memory variable, MOPTION, for the user's command option
   display the option prompt line
   collect the command option from the user

   do case

      if the user entered "X " (EXIT):
         return to ignoring deleted records
         exit from the program
```

Figure 20-4. The update and inquiry program in pseudocode

```
if the user entered "S" (SEARCH):
   initialize a memory variable, MOPTION, for the customer account number
   clear line 23
   collect the account number from the user
   if the account number is left blank,
      go back to the top of the loop
   endif
   search the index for the account number
   if the account number is not found,
      clear line 23
      display an error message
      wait until a key is pressed
      go back to the top of the loop
   endif

if the user entered "C" (CHANGE):
   if you are past the end-of-file or beginning-of-file,
      clear line 23
      display an error message:  "You must search first"
      wait until a key is pressed
      go back to the top of the loop
   endif

if the user entered "N " (NEXT):
   if you are not already past the end-of-file,
      skip to the next record in the file
   endif
   if you are past the end-of-file,
      clear line 23
      display a message: "This is the last name"
      wait until a key is pressed
      go back to the top of the loop
   endif

if the user entered "P " (PREVIOUS):
   if you are not already past the beginning-of-file,
      skip to the previous record in the file
   endif
   if you are past the beginning-of-file,
      clear line 23
      display a message: "This is the first name"
      wait until a key is pressed
      go back to the top of the loop
   endif

if the user entered "D " (DELETE):
   if you are past the end-of-file or beginning-of-file,
      clear line 23
      display an error message:  "You must search first"
      wait until a key is pressed
      go back to the top of the loop
   endif

   if the balance is not zero,
      clear line 20
      display an error message: "Balance is not 0"
      wait until a key is pressed
      go back to the top of the loop
   endif
```

Figure 20-4. The update and inquiry program in pseudocode (*continued*)

```
      select the transaction file
      if there is a matching record for the customer,
         clear line 23
         display an error message: "There are current transactions"
         wait until a key is pressed
         select the customer file
         go back to the top of the loop
      otherwise,
         select the customer file
      endif

      initialize a memory variable, MCONFIRM with a valueof .F.
      clear line 23
      ask whether the customer should be deleted
      collect the user's entry into MCONFIRM
      if the user answered "Y",
         delete the record
         set the background color to high intensity
         display a message: "* DELETED *"
         set the background color to normal intensity
         clear line 23
         display a message identifying the deleted customer
         wait until a key is pressed
      endif
      go back to the top of the loop

   if the user entered "R " (RECALL):
      if you are past the end-of-file or beginning-of-file,
         erase the deletion indicator
         clear line 23
         display an error message:  "You must search first"
         wait until a key is pressed
         go back to the top of the loop
      endif

      recall the (deleted) record
      clear line 23
      display a message identifying the recovered customer
      wait until a key is pressed
      go back to the top of the loop

   if the user entered "A " (ADD):
      initialize a memory variable, MACCOUNT, for the account number
      clear line 23
      ask for the customer account number
      if the account number is left blank,
         go back to the top of the loop
      endif
      search the index for the account number
      if a record is found,
         clear line 23
         display a message:  "The customer is already on file"
         wait until a key is pressed
         go back to the top of the loop
      otherwise
         append a blank record
         replace the account number with the variable MACCOUNT,
                 the city with MCITY (the city from the previous entry),
                 and the state, area code, and sales tax rate
                 with the default values
      endif
```

Figure 20-4. The update and inquiry program in pseudocode (*continued*)

```
   if the user entered "M" (MEMO):
      if you are past the end-of-file or beginning-of-file,
         clear line 23
         display an error message:  "You must search first"
         wait until a key is pressed
         go back to the top of the loop
      endif

      open the format file
      edit the memo field
      close the format file
      redraw the input screen

   otherwise:
      go back to the top of the loop

endcase

if the current record is deleted,
   set the background color to high intensity
   display a message: "* DELETED *"
   set the background color to normal intensity
otherwise,
   erase any previously displayed "* DELETED *" message
endif

display the fields which must not be changed by the user
clear all pending GETs

if the last order date is filled in,
   calculate the number of days elapsed since the last order
   display the number of days elapsed since the last order
otherwise,
   erase any previously displayed calculation
endif

do the following until the record is validated

   initialize a memory variable, MVALID, to store the validation status
      of the record, with a value of .T.
   set the background color to normal intensity

   display the fields which may be changed by the user

   if the user selected the CHANGE or ADD options,
      collect the data
   otherwise,
      clear all pending GETs
   endif

   set the background color to high intensity

   if the account number is blank,
      delete the record
      display a message: "* DELETED *"
      exit from the validation loop
   endif

   if the company name and contact name are both blank,
      set the validation status of the record to false
      display a marker next to the company name
      display a marker next to the contact name
   otherwise,
      erase any previously displayed marker next to the company name
      erase any previously displayed marker next to the contact name
  endif
```

Figure 20-4. The update and inquiry program in pseudocode (*continued*)

```
if the first address line is blank,
   set the validation status of the record to false
   display a marker next to the first address line
otherwise,
   erase any previously displayed marker next to the first address line
endif

if the city is blank,
   set the validation status of the record to false
   display a marker next to the city
otherwise,
   erase any previously displayed marker next to the city
endif

if the state is blank,
   set the validation status of the record to false
   display a marker next to the state
   erase any previously displayed state name
otherwise,
   select the code file
   search the index for a state code matching the state entered into
      the customer file
   if a match is not found,
      display a marker next to the state
      erase any previously displayed state name
   otherwise,
      erase any previously displayed marker next to the state
      display the state name
   endif
   select the customer file
endif

if fewer than 5 digits were entered into the zip code field,
   set the validation status of the record to false
   display a marker next to the zip code
otherwise,
   erase any previously displayed marker next to the zip code
endif

if the area code is blank,
   erase any previously displayed marker next to the area code
   erase any previously displayed area code description
otherwise,
   select the code file
   search the index for an area code code matching the area code
      entered into the customer file
   if a match in not found,
      display a marker next to the area code
      erase any previously displayed area code description
   otherwise,
      erase any previously displayed marker next to the area code
      display the area code description
   endif
   select the customer file
endif

if the state is blank,
   or the state is not California and the tax rate is not zero,
   or the state is California and the tax rate is not 6.00 or 6.50
   set the validation status of the record to false
   display a marker next to the tax rate
otherwise,
   erase any previously displayed marker next to the tax rate
endif
```

Figure 20-4. The update and inquiry program in pseudocode (*continued*)

```
      if the record passed all the validation tests,
         exit the validation loop
      otherwise,
         clear line 23
         display a message: 'Please correct the fields marked with a "*" '
         if the user did not select the CHANGE or ADD option,
            set the option to CHANGE
         endif
      endif

   end of validation loop

   set the background color to normal intensity

   if the user selected the ADD option,
      store the city entered into the record in MCITY to use as the default
         for the next new record
   endif

enddo
```

Figure 20-4. The update and inquiry program in pseudocode (*continued*)

Apart from the data validation, this program incorporates several enhancements not included in the original. SET COLOR commands are used to highlight some of the messages displayed on the screen. Recall that the NWCUPD2.PRG program employed GET rather than SAY commands to display fields in the higher intensity selected for the foreground color used for entered data (followed by a CLEAR GETS command to prevent the user from being able to edit the fields). The NWCUPD3.PRG program also displays the "* DELETED *" indicator and the error markers in the higher intensity characters used for the foreground color, but it is less convenient to use GETs for this purpose than to use them for the data fields. One reason is that you can only GET data base fields and memory variables, not character string constants (by definition, the value of a constant cannot be changed, so it does not make sense to present it for editing with a GET command). The program would have to store the text to be displayed in a memory variable and then GET the variable. Also, with DELIMITERS ON, any variables displayed with GET commands are surrounded by a pair of delimiters (in the sample system, square brackets), so the program would have to SET DELIMITERS OFF before displaying highlighted messages and then SET DELIMITERS ON again.

In this program it is easier to use a SET COLOR command to assign the same video attribute to the foreground and background colors:

```
set color to W+, W+
```

The display colors are returned to normal with

```
set color to W, W+
```

The placement of these commands is a bit tricky. If you were to place the SET COLOR TO W, W+ command after the ENDCASE and before the display of the "* DELETED *" indicator, you could use SAY commands throughout the validation loop. However, it is preferable to retain the existing GETs that display the fields from NWCUST.DBF; in this way you can avoid having to adjust all of the column coordinates in the SAY commands so that the data does not overwrite the brackets drawn on the screen by NWCSCRN.PRG. Also, because the background color is used to display the delimiters, the brackets surrounding the fields that the user is allowed to edit would be highlighted, which users may consider an annoying inconsistency. In NWCUPD3.PRG, the display colors are set to normal at the top of the validation loop, reset to use bright for the background colors that display the error indicators, and then reset to normal after the validation loop.

Deciding which display method to use and which text to highlight in your own programs is up to you. The National Widgets examples were designed to produce the same display on any monochrome or color screen. If you have a color monitor, remember that you have more than two colors at your disposal. The color you choose for error messages and status indicators might be entirely different from those selected for the screen mask and data fields. It is best, however, to use a single color with the standard black background, so the spaces that will be used to eradicate previously displayed error indicators do not appear as blocks of color.

One of the advantages of the dBASE III PLUS APPEND command that was lost in the transition to more sophisticated data entry programs is the ability to use SET CARRY ON to assign the data entered into the fields in one record as the default values for the next. This is because records added to a file with APPEND BLANK are unaffected by the status of the CARRY option. The NWCUPD3.PRG program illustrates a technique for emulating CARRY, with one additional enhancement: the ability to selectively carry over certain fields. For example, if you were entering names into a mailing list from a set of labels sorted by ZIP code, the city might be the same for a large group of consecutive records, and you could avoid having to type the same city over and over. On the other hand, fields that would never be the same from one record to the next, like the name or street address, should remain blank in each newly appended record.

In this example, only the CITY field will be carried over. In order to do this, a memory variable, MCITY, is used to store the value of the CITY field from each new entry. Whenever a new record is added to the file, the CITY field is replaced with MCITY, and at the same time the systemwide defaults stored in public memory variables are plugged into the STATE, AREACODE, and TAXRATE fields. The value of MCITY is updated for each new entry into the data base; that is, if MOPTION = "A" after the validation loop terminates and the data in the new record has been accepted. Notice that MCITY must also be initialized at the start of the program—in this case, with a single blank space—so that the first time the operator chooses ADD, MCITY has a value, albeit a blank value, and the REPLACE command does not generate a "Variable not found" error message.

The easiest and most versatile way to set up the validation loop is to collect the fields and perform the tests in a second DO WHILE .T. loop. A memory variable called MVALID stores the overall status of the record. At the top of the DO WHILE loop this variable is given the value .T., and then, if the record fails any one of the validation tests, it is reset to .F. Thus, the program assumes at the beginning of each pass through the loop that the record was correctly entered; failure to satisfy even one of the validation conditions means that the record is not correct after all.

If a record does not pass all of the tests, the way it should be treated depends on how crowded the screen is, and on whether the cause of an error message will be obvious to the users. For example, in the Customer File, if the STATE field is flagged as incorrect, it should be obvious that the problem is an illegitimate state abbreviation, and it is generally easy to remember that some fields must not be left blank. In other cases, as with the sales tax rate, the operators may not readily grasp what is wrong if the field is marked as incorrect with no explanation. There may not be enough empty space on the input screen to display a detailed message like "Should be 6.00 or 6.50," which is used on the listing produced by NWCVALID.PRG if the sales tax rate was incompatible with the state. On the customer update screen there is room for an explicit error message next to some of the fields—the address fields, for example—but not others. On a very crowded screen you might only have room to place a marker, perhaps an arrow (—>) or an asterisk (*), next to each invalid field, and to display a message at the bottom of the screen informing the operator that the marked fields must be corrected.

The NWCUPD3.PRG program displays a highlighted asterisk next to each field that fails one of the validation tests. The program must also anticipate that the operator might make several passes through the loop before entering correct information in all of the fields; it must erase any previously displayed error indicators when a field is finally entered correctly. Each time one of the tests is performed, therefore, the program should display either the error message or enough blank spaces to erase a previously displayed message from the screen. After carrying out all of the tests, the program can check the overall status of the record by examining the value of MVALID. If this variable is still .T., it is safe to EXIT from the validation loop; if not, the program displays a message informing the operator that the indicated fields must be corrected.

When adding a new customer to the file or using the CHANGE option to edit an existing record, the operator is not permitted to exit the validation loop until all of the fields have been entered correctly. However, it would be a mistake to assume that previously entered records need not be validated. Consider what would happen if erroneous data had been entered into the file by using APPEND at command level, and a record displayed by the SEARCH, NEXT, or PREVIOUS option failed some of the tests. With MVALID set to false, the program would go through the validation loop again, but since it only processes the READ command (that is, allows the operator to change the data) if the ADD or CHANGE option was selected, there is no way to correct the invalid fields—or to exit from the loop. The program would therefore display the fields, perform the validation tests, and then loop back and display the fields again and again. If MVALID is false and MOPTION is neither C nor A, the NWCUPD3.PRG program therefore displays the standard reminder to correct the marked fields and then changes MOPTION to C, so that the next time through the validation loop, the READ command *is* executed. Although the user may have retrieved the record with no intention of making any changes, the program behaves in a consistent manner whenever incorrect data is displayed on the screen: it always forces the user to fix the errors.

Within the inner DO WHILE loop, the program displays the fields with GET commands. As in NWCUPD2.PRG, it executes either a READ command to allow the operator to edit the record (for a CHANGE or ADD) or CLEAR GETS (if the SEARCH, NEXT, or PREVIOUS option was selected). This program uses many of the same validation tests as the batch validation program, NWCVALID.PRG. One important difference is the way that a blank ACCOUNT field is handled. Of course, if all of the records in the Customer File had been added through the update and inquiry program, the ACCOUNT field could never be blank, because leaving this field empty would abort a new entry. The reason for validating this field at all is that during the early stages of initializing a data base system—perhaps while the programs were under development—customer records may have been added by using APPEND at command level. Although the batch validation program was intended to "clean up" the file after this kind of data entry, there is no guarantee that the users have actually run this program or made the suggested corrections to the data. Since the update program does not allow the operator to change the ACCOUNT field, it simply DELETEs any record in which this field is blank and immediately EXITs the validation loop.

The second difference from NWCVALID.PRG is the way the NWCUPD3.PRG program validates the STATE and AREACODE fields. Earlier chapters described methods for validating a field by searching for a matching record in another file. For example, in the order entry program, the customer account number was validated with a lookup in the Customer File, and the inventory item was validated by searching for a record with the same category and part number in the Inventory File. In both cases, the file used for the lookup already existed as an integral part of the application. In other situations you may need to set up a file like the NWCODES.DBF data base used in the NWCUPD3.PRG program just for the purpose of validating certain fields, most commonly fields in which codes are entered.

When the codes are very short and there are relatively few of them, you can simply store the permissible values in a memory variable, as was done with the state abbreviations in the first version of the customer update program, but this method becomes less convenient when the combined length of the codes exceeds the maximum length of 254 characters for a dBASE III PLUS character string variable. Other benefits accrue from placing the codes in a file: it is easier for the users to update the list of acceptable codes, and you have room to store a longer description of each code, which can then be displayed on the screen or printed on reports in addition to or instead of the abbreviation.

With only two types of codes to validate, you might consider setting up a separate file for each. In a larger system, however, you might have to validate a dozen different types of codes, and it is more efficient to combine them into a single file. In the National Widgets sample system, the code file will include three types of codes—state abbreviations, area codes, and inventory categories—although only the first two are used in the customer update program. At the very least this file requires three fields: one to distinguish among the different types of codes, one for the code itself, and one for the longer description. The structure for the code file, NWCODES.DBF, is listed in Figure 20-5, together with some of the data required to perform the Customer File validations.

One character is usually sufficient for the CODETYPE field. In the NWCODES.DBF file, S is entered into this field for state records, A for area code records, and C for inventory categories. Since several types of codes are stored together in one file, the CODE field must be as long as the longest of the codes, and the DESCRIP field must be able to accommodate the longest description. The CODE field in NWCODES.DBF is therefore six characters long (the length of the inventory category). The file is indexed on the combination of CODETYPE and CODE to enable you to search for any particular value of any of the types of codes. To validate a STATE field, for example, you would search the index for the combination S (the value entered into the CODETYPE field) plus the value of the STATE field:

```
seek "S" + NWCUST->STATE
```

For the area code you would use

```
seek "A" + NWCUST->AREACODE
```

In the National Widgets system, the CODETYPE field may seem unnecessary, since you would never find in the AREACODE field two characters that match one of the possible state abbreviations or part of an area code in the state field. In your own systems the code field entries in different data bases might overlap more. For example, you might use a single letter code to represent a customer's status—A for active, I for inactive, R for credit risk, and so on. In the Inventory File you might have another set of single-letter codes representing the status of an item, perhaps S for stocked, O for ordered as needed, and so on. If the code file were indexed only on CODE, an S entered into the Customer File status field would not generate an error message because S is a valid entry in the code file, yet S is not a valid customer status code. Using the CODETYPE field to distinguish between customer codes and inventory item codes resolves this problem.

Notice that in the NWCUPD3.PRG program, the STATE field must be

```
. USE NWCODES INDEX NWCODES

. LIST STRUCTURE TO PRINT

Structure for database : C:NWCODES.dbf
Number of data records :       15
Date of last update    : 08/18/85
Field  Field name  Type       Width    Dec
    1  CODETYPE    Character      1
    2  CODE        Character      6
    3  DESCRIP     Character     20
** Total **                      28



. DISPLAY STATUS TO PRINT


Currently Selected Database:
Select area:  1, Database in Use: C:NWCODES.dbf   Alias: NWCODES
    Master index file: C:NWCODES.ndx  Key: CODETYPE + CODE
          Lock:

File search path:
Default disk drive: C:
Print destination:  LPT1:
Margin =     0
Current work area =    1

Press any key to continue...

*** INTERRUPTED ***



. LIST

Record#  CODETYPE CODE   DESCRIP
      8  A        213    Los Angeles Area
      7  A        408    San Jose Area
      6  A        415    San Francisco Area
     10  C        ACCESS Accessories
     12  C        COVER  Dust covers
      9  C        DISK   Disks
     11  C        FORMS  Paper forms
     13  C        PRTWHL Print wheels
     14  C        RIBBON Printer ribbons
     15  C        STOR   Disk storage boxes
      1  S        AK     Alaska
      2  S        AL     Alabama
      4  S        AR     Arkansas
      3  S        AZ     Arizona
      5  S        CA     California
```

Figure 20-5. The code file

filled in, while the area code, and in fact the entire phone number, need not be entered, so the AREACODE field is validated only if it is not blank. For both fields validated with a lookup in the code file, when no matching record is found in NWCODES.DBF, the standard error indicator is displayed on the screen; when a match is found, the DESCRIP field is displayed for the operator's information. Displaying the description is valuable because it makes the screen more informative to a user who is unfamiliar with the codes, and because it increases the likelihood that the entry of a possible — but wrong — value for the code field will be noticed and corrected. For example, if 408 had been entered as the area code for a San Francisco customer, the message "San Jose Area" might remind another operator that the area code, although a valid possibility in the code file, should in fact be 415.

Although the discussion of the validation tests in the NWCVALID.PRG and NWCUPD3.PRG programs focused on the particular data entry rules defined for the National Widgets Customer File, these tests are typical, both in kind and in complexity, of the types of validations you might apply in other data base systems. When you are trying to decide how to validate a particular field, consider the strengths of each method we have described. When a field must take on one of a small number of permissible values that rarely change, these possibilities may be stored in a character string constant or a local memory variable. The data entered into the field can then be tested with the "$" operator to see if it is contained in this longer string. If the list of allowable entries changes more often, it is better to place these entries in a public memory variable, so they may more easily be updated by the users. With longer entries or more possibilities, placing the codes in a separate data base gives the users even more flexibility to edit or extend the list without having to alter the program.

21

GIVING THE USER MORE CONTROL

The last six chapters have gradually introduced more options for the users of the dBASE III PLUS programs in the National Widgets sample system. In the process, the programs have also grown in length and complexity, since they must ask more questions, offer more choices, and then validate the operator's responses. When you build your own dBASE III PLUS systems, you will find that even when your programs incorporate all of the requirements laid out in the initial system design, your job is far from finished. Without fully understanding the capabilities of dBASE III PLUS, the users cannot predict the demands they will eventually place on the system, and even if you are an experienced programmer, you cannot predict all of the users' needs unless you are intimately familiar with the workings of the organization. But once the staff begins to use the programs, new possibilities will suggest themselves.

This chapter addresses the important goal of giving users more power and flexibility to customize and adapt the system to their varying needs without programming. The users will gain more control over the system's printed output through the addition of a wider range of selection criteria to the programs that produce reports and labels. To complement the ability to begin printing at any point in the file, the chapter demonstrates a method for safely interrupting a print run and later resuming from the point of interruption. This chapter also presents the first of two setup programs that will allow users to customize the systemwide options stored in PUBLIC memory variables. These programs also introduce some new tricks for manipulating character string variables that may be applied in many other contexts as well. When you design your own dBASE III PLUS systems, you can adapt the techniques applied in these examples to the individual requirements of your applications.

PROVIDING FLEXIBLE SELECTION CRITERIA FOR REPORTS

The basic mailing label-printing program written in Chapter 12 was expanded in Chapter 15 to allow the user to specify selection criteria based on the EQUIPMENT, TOTINV, and LASTORDER fields in the Customer File. This new program collected the operator's selections for type of computer equipment, maximum and minimum total invoices, and earliest and latest values for the customer's last order date into a set of memory variables. These variables were then combined into a single character string memory variable, MCONDITION, that contained the selection criteria. Depending on whether or not the equipment type was filled in, MCONDITION might contain either of these two expressions:

```
TOTINV >= MINVMIN .and. TOTINV <= MINVMAX .and. LASTORDER >= MDATEMIN .and.
  LASTORDER <= MDATEMAX .and. trim(MEQUIPMENT) $ upper(EQUIPMENT)
```

or

```
TOTINV >= MINVMIN .and. TOTINV <= MINVMAX .and. LASTORDER >= MDATEMIN .and.
  LASTORDER <= MDATEMAX
```

The program used a SET FILTER command to limit processing to the records that passed all of the specified tests, as follows:

```
set filter to &MCONDITION
```

The initial values for the variables used to store the operator's entries for the maximum and minimum values of TOTINV (0.00 and 9999999.99) and the earliest and latest permissible values for LASTORDER (01/01/01 and 12/31/99) were defined so as to encompass any data that might possibly be entered into the file. Thus, accepting any of the defaults guaranteed that all of the records in the file would pass the corresponding portion of the test. Defining the default values this way made it easy to establish the selection criteria while allowing the user to ignore any of the five possible choices.

You can see how this general method might be extended to include more criteria by adding more tests to the expression stored in MCONDITION. This section will demonstrate a method for constructing this memory variable more efficiently, to maximize the number of tests that fit within the 254-character limit for a dBASE III PLUS command line. For those cases in which more criteria are required than can be accommodated by a single variable, a technique will be introduced for using two or more memory variables to store the selection criteria.

Creating a Single Selection Criteria Variable

Ideally, the program should offer the user the opportunity to select some or all of a number of different criteria for any particular mailing. However, it is not always possible, as demonstrated with the selection by type of equipment, to select initial values for the memory variables that allow them to be used safely in the SET FILTER command. As you increase the number of selection criteria, you may also run into another serious problem: the maximum permissible length for both character string variables and command lines is only 254 characters. The length of MCONDITION is therefore limited to 254 minus the length of the fixed portion of the command "SET FILTER TO ", or 254 − 14 = 240 characters. You might want your program to allow for selections based on, say, ten fields, but even if the user chose only three or four of these conditions, accounting for all ten possible selections in MCONDITION could easily result in an expression longer than 240 characters. The program must therefore examine the user's choices and include in MCONDITION only those variables that have actually been filled in. By comparing each memory variable to its initial value, the program can determine which criteria were entered by the user. The variable MCONDITION can then be built up in stages, incorporating tests for only those variables whose initial values were altered by the operator.

Figure 21-1 lists a partial program that illustrates this technique. MEQUIPMENT is initialized with 25 blank spaces, to match the length of the EQUIPMENT field. The two numeric variables are initialized with the smallest possible number, 0.00 (for MINVMIN), and the largest possible number, 9999999.99 (for MINVMAX), that might be found in the data base. After collecting these three variables with @ ... SAY ... GET commands, the program checks to see which ones have changed. Since

```
store ""           to MCONDITION
store space(25)    to MEQUIPMENT
store 0.00         to MINVMIN
store 9999999.99 to MINVMAX

clear

@  1,10 say "Enter type of equipment for customers in this mailing:"
@  2,10 say "(or press <RETURN> to include ALL equipment types)"
@  4,20 get MEQUIPMENT picture "@!"

@  7,10 say "Enter range of overall total invoices to include:"
@  9,10 say "Minimum" get MINVMIN picture "9999999.99"
@  9,40 say "Maximum" get MINVMAX picture "9999999.99"

read

if MEQUIPMENT <> " "
   store "trim(MEQUIPMENT) $ upper(EQUIPMENT) .and. " to MCONDITION
endif

if MINVMIN > 0
   store MCONDITION + "TOTINV >= MINVMIN .and. " to MCONDITION
endif

if MINVMAX < 9999999.99
   store MCONDITION + "TOTINV <= MINVMAX .and. " to MCONDITION
endif
```

Figure 21-1. Constructing variable selection conditions

accepting the initial value for any variable is tantamount to saying, "I don't want to select according to this criterion," the program adds the appropriate test to the value of MCONDITION only if a variable no longer contains its default value. Note that each phrase added to MCONDITION is followed by " .and. " to prepare for the addition of another test. If the user filled in all three variables, MCONDITION would look like this:

```
trim(MEQUIPMENT) $ upper(EQUIPMENT) .and. TOTINV >= MINVMIN .and.
  TOTINV <= MINVMAX .and.
```

If only the minimum total invoices had been entered, MCONDITION would have the following value:

```
TOTINV >= MINVMIN .and.
```

All that is required to turn the value of MCONDITION into a syntactically correct expression is to remove the last seven characters — the trailing " .and. ". Note that the necessity to be consistent and *always* provide seven extra characters at the end of MCONDITION is the reason that even the last possible phrase that could be added to MCONDITION is followed by " .and. ".

Before adjusting the value of MCONDITION, consider what would happen if the user failed to specify *any* selection criteria. If this were the case, MCONDITION would still have its initial value — a null string of length 0. The STORE command that truncates MCONDITION should therefore be performed only if the length of the variable is no longer 0:

```
if len(MCONDITION) > 0
   store left(MCONDITION, len(MCONDITION) - 7) to MCONDITION
endif
```

In this STORE command the length of the new value of MCONDITION is expressed as len(MCONDITION) − 7, or seven characters less than the full length of the variable.

It might seem more logical and straightforward simply to test the variable MCONDITION by comparing it to a null string. If you do this, be careful to state the test this way:

```
if "" <> MCONDITION
```

This will *not* work:

```
if MCONDITION <> ""
```

The reason is that when dBASE III PLUS compares two character strings, if the string on the right side of the comparison operator (in this case, <>) is shorter than the string on the left, the comparison extends only to the number of characters contained in the smaller string. If a null string appears to the right of the <>, no characters are compared, and the expression MCONDITION <> " " always has the value .T.

This method of building up the condition for the SET FILTER command allows only those criteria that are actually specified by the user to occupy space in MCONDITION. You can fit even more selection criteria into one variable by removing the unnecessary blank spaces that are normally inserted to improve the legibility of complex expressions. Since the value of MCONDITION is never seen by anyone — not even the programmer — the aesthetic factor is less important than the flexibility to construct a more complex condition. Remember that spaces are optional around arithmetic and logical operators (like +, −, $, and .AND.) and comparison operators (like =, < >, and <=). For even more efficiency you can also shorten the memory variable names, although this *will* make your program harder to understand. Figure 21-2 lists a new version of the partial program in Figure 21-1, rewritten to compress the expression contained in MCONDITION as much as possible. Note that without the spaces that formerly surrounded the .AND., the final STORE command must be adjusted to remove the last *five* characters of MCONDITION.

```
store ""            to MCONDITION
store space(25)     to ME
store 0.00          to MI1
store 9999999.99 to MI2

clear

@  1,10 say "Enter type of equipment for customers in this mailing:"
@  2,10 say "(or press <RETURN> to include ALL equipment types)"
@  4,20 get ME picture "@!"

@  7,10 say "Enter range of overall total invoices to include:"
@  9,10 say "Minimum" get MI1 picture "9999999.99"
@  9,40 say "Maximum" get MI2 picture "9999999.99"

read

if ME <> " "
   store "trim(ME)$upper(EQUIPMENT).and." to MCONDITION
endif

if MI1 > 0
   store MCONDITION + "TOTINV>=MI1.and." to MCONDITION
endif

if MI2 < 9999999.99
   store MCONDITION + "TOTINV<=MI2.and." to MCONDITION
endif

if len(MCONDITION) > 0
   store left(MCONDITION, len(MCONDITION) - 5) to MCONDITION
endif
```

Figure 21-2. The variable selection routine rewritten for maximum compression

Creating Two Selection Criteria Variables

Despite these precautions, the users may still fill in more conditions than will fit into 240 characters. To increase the space available to you for expressing selection criteria, you can use a FILTER for one condition and a FOR clause to specify another. For example, with a FILTER in effect, if you included a FOR clause in a LABEL FORM or REPORT FORM command, the FOR clause is superimposed on the FILTER and only those records that satisfy both conditions are printed. You can take advantage of this in your selection programs by creating two memory variables called MCOND1 and MCOND2, which can be used like this:

```
set filter to &MCOND1
label form NWCUST1 rest to print &MCOND2
```

The scope clause, REST, is included in the command so that printing may begin with a specified ZIP code and continue until the end of the file. You may instead prefer to specify the ending ZIP code, as in the label-printing program written in Chapter 15. With the ending ZIP code stored in the memory variable MZIPEND and a FOR clause stored in MCOND2, the command sequence would look like this:

```
set filter to &MCOND1
label form NWCUST1 to print while ZIP<=MZIPEND &MCOND2
```

The general strategy for constructing the variables MCOND1 and MCOND2 is an extension of the method used to build up MCONDITION in the previous example. For each test to be added to the growing set of conditions, the program must first check whether MCOND1 can accommodate the new phrase. If not, the program checks to see if there is room in MCOND2.

For example, the equipment type variable, ME, could be handled like this:

```
if ME <> " "
   if len(MCOND1 + "trim(ME)$upper(EQUIPMENT).and.") <= 240
      store MCOND1 + "trim(ME)$upper(EQUIPMENT).and." to MCOND1
   else
```

```
      if len(MCOND2 + "trim(ME)$upper(EQUIPMENT).and.") <= 203
         store MCOND2 + "trim(ME)$upper(EQUIPMENT).and." to MCOND2
      endif
   endif
endif
```

Some important details in this example should be noted. First, in the (unlikely) event that the user specifies no selection criteria, MCOND1 will still have its initial null value, and expanding the macro in SET FILTER TO &MCOND1 yields the command SET FILTER TO. This simply cancels any FILTER that might be in effect—exactly what you would want under the circumstances.

If all of the user's selection criteria fit in MCOND1, MCOND2 will retain its initial value. To ensure that the program also behaves correctly under these circumstances, the keyword FOR must *not* be written explicitly into the LABEL FORM command, because if MCOND2 were blank, the command "label form NWCUST1 to print while ZIP<=MZIPEND for" would generate a "Syntax error" message. One solution to this problem is to initialize MCOND2 with the value "FOR " and, after all of the selection criteria are entered, see if its length is still only four characters. If so, the program can STORE a null value to MCOND2 so that the LABEL FORM command reduces to "label form NWCUST1 to print while ZIP<=MZIPEND".

The maximum allowable length for the expression that forms the selection criteria stored in MCOND2 is therefore 203 characters: 254 minus the length of the fixed portion of the LABEL FORM command (47 characters for the first portion of the command, "label form NWCUST1 to print while ZIP<=MZIPEND ", and 4 characters for "for ", which is included in MCOND2 but which cannot be altered by the user).

The partial programs presented thus far have also failed to account for the possibility that the user may have specified more conditions than will fit in both MCOND1 and MCOND2. If all of the tests are written like these examples, the program will ignore the extra conditions without warning the user. To solve this problem, you can collect the user's selection criteria and construct the memory variables MCOND1 and MCOND2 in a DO WHILE loop just like the validation loop used in the NWCUPD3. PRG program written in Chapter 20. If too many selection criteria are specified, the program can display an error message such as "Too many selection criteria were entered" and return to the top of the loop to allow the user to reenter the criteria. With this program structure you may also perform any of the types of validation tests used in the NWCUPD3.PRG program on the memory variables that comprise the selection criteria. For example, if you allow the user to select by state, you could make sure that a valid state abbreviation is entered by comparing it with the public variable MPSTATES.

Establishing Ad Hoc Selection Criteria

There is another enhancement that is easy to add to the program and that tremendously increases the range of selection criteria available to a user who understands little about dBASE III PLUS command syntax—providing for ad hoc selection criteria. One major limitation of the program structure outlined in the previous section is that all of the selections are essentially separate, equal conditions linked with .AND. For other combinations of criteria, the dBASE III PLUS program may be easier to use, but it is considerably less flexible than working at command level. For example, to print labels for all customers who own IBM equipment *or* whose total invoices exceed $500, you could type the following at the dot prompt:

```
LABEL FORM NWCUST1 TO PRINT FOR "IBM" $ UPPER(EQUIPMENT) .OR. TOTINV > 500
```

Using the selection program, the only way to produce the same set of labels would be to run the program twice, once for each of the two conditions. If it is important to produce one continuous ZIP code sequence for bulk mailings, this can be more than a minor annoyance. In other cases, in which conditions must be combined with .AND., .OR., and .NOT., you may not be able to use the program at all. For example, the program could not print labels for all customers who own either IBM *or* COMPAQ equipment *and* whose invoices total more than $500. But you could do this at command level with the following:

```
LABEL FORM NWCUST1 TO PRINT FOR TOTINV > 500 .AND.
  ("IBM" $ UPPER(EQUIPMENT) .OR. "COMPAQ" $ UPPER(EQUIPMENT))
```

Adding to the selection program the capability to choose among a full range of conditions, linked in any order with .AND., .OR., or .NOT., is no mean feat. You could allow the user to choose the order in which the conditions are stated from a menu of numbered criteria, and to choose which logical operator (.AND. or .OR.) should be placed between any two conditions. You could even allow a condition to be negated by preceding it with .NOT. However, your program would also have to provide for grouping the components of the condition with parentheses to make sure that the tests are carried out in the right order, and this can be a tall order.

This process of analyzing the component parts of a command is, after all, what dBASE III PLUS does when it parses the expressions you type at the dot prompt. It also comes close to describing the operation of the full-screen CREATE QUERY command, which allows you to build up a FILTER condition and save it for future use in a .QRY file. Even if you could write the program, using it would require the same understanding of dBASE III PLUS syntax as using CREATE QUERY—only slightly less than the knowledge required for working at command level. You might instead consider simply calling CREATE QUERY from within the selection program, but there are two limitations to this approach. First, a .QRY file can be used only in a SET FILTER command, so it cannot be used to construct MCOND2. Second, for relatively straightforward selection criteria, a well-designed program is considerably easier to use than CREATE QUERY.

A reasonable compromise is to retain the program structure outlined earlier to handle the most common requirement—several separate conditions linked with .AND.—and also allow the operator to type in any arbitrary expression as an ad hoc selection that may be used in addition to or instead of the conditions stored in MCOND1 and MCOND2. Users who do not understand the rudiments of dBASE III PLUS syntax can ignore this feature.

As when working at the dot prompt, the user must be responsible for ensuring that the expression entered will select the desired records. However, you can use the TYPE function to examine an expression and determine if it is syntactically correct, so your program can at least prevent an erroneous entry from generating a "Syntax error" message when the condition is used. The TYPE function returns the data type (character, numeric, logical, memo, or date) of an expression as the single character C, N, L, M, or D. If the expression is invalid, because it is constructed incorrectly or because a variable name is misspelled or unavailable, dBASE III PLUS cannot determine the type, and the function evaluates to U (for undefined).

A label-printing program that incorporates all of these features is listed in Figure 21-3. This program, NWCLABL6.PRG, begins by opening the Customer File, asking whether it is necessary to reindex by ZIP, and requesting the beginning and ending ZIP codes, exactly like the label-printing program in Chapter 15. Next, the variables are initialized for the

```
* NWCLABL6.PRG
* PROGRAM TO PRINT 1-UP MAILING LABELS FOR ALL OR SELECTED CUSTOMERS
*   ACCORDING TO USER-SPECIFIED SELECTION CRITERIA
*   INCLUDING PRODUCT CATEGORY AND AD HOC SELECTIONS
*   THE CUSTOMER FILE IS REINDEXED BY ZIP IF NECESSARY
* WRITTEN BY:  M.LISKIN       4/25/86


select 1
use NWCUST

select 2
use NWORDHST

clear
text
                              *** CAUTION ***

          The Customer File must be reindexed by ZIP CODE if you have
          added new customers or changed any zip codes in the file
          since the last time the file was reindexed.

          The Order History File must be reindexed by CATEGORY if you
          have added new records or changed any category codes in the
          file since the last time the file was reindexed.
endtext

* ASK WHETHER TO REBUILD REQUIRED INDEXES IF THEY ARE ALREADY PRESENT
* IF NOT PRESENT, REBUILD THEM WITHOUT ASKING

store .T. to MREINDEXC, MREINDEXO

if file("NWCZIP.NDX")
   @ 13,10 say "Do you need to reindex the Customer File by ZIP code?";
           get MREINDEXC picture "Y"
   read
endif

if file("NWOHCAT.NDX")
   @ 15,10 say "Do you need to reindex the Order History File by CATEGORY?";
           get MREINDEXO picture "Y"
   read
endif

* REINDEX CUSTOMER FILE IF NECESSARY OR OPEN EXISTING INDEX IF NOT
select NWCUST
if MREINDEXC
   @ 18,10 say "Reindexing Customer File by ZIP -- Please do not interrupt"
   set talk on
   index on ZIP to NWCZIP
   goto top
   set talk off
else
   set index to NWCZIP
endif

* REINDEX ORDER HISTORY FILE IF NECESSARY OR OPEN EXISTING INDEX IF NOT
select NWORDHST
if MREINDEXO
   @ 21, 5 say;
     "Reindexing Order History File by CATEGORY -- Please do not interrupt"
```

Figure 21-3. The new label-printing program

```
   set talk on
   index on CATEGORY + ACCOUNT to NWOHCAT
   goto top
   set talk off
else
   set index to NWOHCAT
endif

* ENTER RANGE OF ZIP CODES, VALIDATE STARTING ZIP

select NWCUST
store ZIP        to MZIPBEGIN
store "99999"    to MZIPEND
clear

do while .T.

   @  1,10 say "Enter starting zip code:" get MZIPBEGIN picture "99999"
   @  2,10 say "Enter ending   zip code:" get MZIPEND   picture "99999"
   read

   seek trim(MZIPBEGIN)

   if found()
      exit
   else
      @ 22,10 say "There is no customer with that zip code"
      @ 23,10 say "Press any key to reenter the zip code"
      wait ""
      @ 22,10
      @ 23,10
   endif

enddo

* ENTER CUSTOMER SELECTION CRITERIA
store space(25)        to ME
store "      "         to MC
store 0.00             to MI1
store 9999999.99       to MI2
store ctod("01/01/01") to MD1
store ctod("12/31/99") to MD2
do while .T.

   store ""     to MCOND1
   store "for " to MCOND2
   clear

   @  1,10 say "Enter type of equipment for customers in this mailing:"
   @  2,10 say "(or press <RETURN> to include ALL equipment types)"
   @  4,20 get ME picture "@!"

   @  6,10 say "Enter range of overall total invoices to include:"
   @  7,10 say "Minimum" get MI1 picture "9999999.99"
   @  7,40 say "Maximum" get MI2 picture "9999999.99"

   @ 10,10 say "Enter range of last invoice dates to include:"
   @ 11,10 say "Earliest" get MD1
   @ 11,40 say "Latest"   get MD2

   read
```

Figure 21-3. The new label-printing program *(continued)*

```
* ENTER PRODUCT CATEGORY, VALIDATE IN ORDER HISTORY FILE
select NWORDHST

do while .T.

   @ 14,10 say "Enter product CATEGORY:" get MC picture "@!"
   @ 15,10 say "(or press <RETURN> to include ALL categories)"
   read
   if MC = " "
      exit
   endif

   seek MC

   if found()
      exit
   else
      @ 22,10 say "There are no orders with that category"
      @ 23,10 say "Press any key to reenter the zip code"
      wait ""
      @ 22,10
      @ 23,10
   endif

enddo

* CONSTRUCT FILTER CONDITION AND PRINT LABELS
select NWCUST

if ME <> " "
   if len(MCOND1 + "trim(ME)$upper(EQUIPMENT).and.") <= 240
      store MCOND1 + "trim(ME)$upper(EQUIPMENT).and." to MCOND1
   else
      if len(MCOND2 + "trim(ME)$upper(EQUIPMENT).and.") <= 203
         store MCOND2 + "trim(ME)$upper(EQUIPMENT).and." to MCOND2
      else
         @ 22,20 say "Too many selection criteria were entered"
         @ 23,20 say "Press any key to reenter the condition"
         wait ""
         loop
      endif
   endif
endif

if MI1 > 0
   if len(MCOND1 + "TOTINV>=MI1.and.") <= 240
      store MCOND1 + "TOTINV>=MI1.and." to MCOND1
   else
      if len(MCOND2 + "TOTINV>=MI1.and.") <= 203
         store MCOND2 + "TOTINV>=MI1.and." to MCOND2
      else
         @ 22,20 say "Too many selection criteria were entered"
         @ 23,20 say "Press any key to reenter the condition"
         wait ""
         loop
      endif
   endif
endif

if MI2 < 9999999.99
   if len(MCOND1 + "TOTINV<=MI2.and.") <= 240
```

Figure 21-3. The new label-printing program *(continued)*

```
         store MCOND1 + "TOTINV<=MI2.and." to MCOND1
      else
         if len(MCOND2 + "TOTINV<=MI2.and.") <= 203
            store MCOND2 + "TOTINV<=MI2.and." to MCOND2
         else
            @ 22,20 say "Too many selection criteria were entered"
            @ 23,20 say "Press any key to reenter the condition"
            wait ""
            loop
         endif
      endif
   endif

   if dtoc(MD1) <> "01/01/01"
      if len(MCOND1 + "LASTORDER>=MD1.and.") <= 240
         store MCOND1 + "LASTORDER>=MD1.and." to MCOND1
      else
         if len(MCOND2 + "LASTORDER>=MD1.and.") <= 203
            store MCOND2 + "LASTORDER>=MD1.and." to MCOND2
         else
            @ 22,20 say "Too many selection criteria were entered"
            @ 23,20 say "Press any key to reenter the condition"
            wait ""
            loop
         endif
      endif
   endif

   if dtoc(MD2) <> "12/31/99"
      if len(MCOND1 + "LASTORDER<=MD2.and.") <= 240
         store MCOND1 + "LASTORDER<=MD2.and." to MCOND1
      else
         if len(MCOND2 + "LASTORDER<=MD2.and.") <= 203
            store MCOND2 + "LASTORDER<=MD2.and." to MCOND2
         else
            @ 22,20 say "Too many selection criteria were entered"
            @ 23,20 say "Press any key to reenter the condition"
            wait ""
            loop
         endif
      endif
   endif

   if MC <> " "
      set relation to MC + ACCOUNT into NWORDHST
      if len(MCOND1 + "NWORDHST->ACCOUNT<>' '.and.") <= 240
         store MCOND1 + "NWORDHST->ACCOUNT<>' '.and." to MCOND1
      else
         if len(MCOND2 + "NWORDHST->ACCOUNT<>' '.and.") <= 203
            store MCOND2 + "NWORDHST->ACCOUNT<>' '.and." to MCOND2
         else
            @ 22,20 say "Too many selection criteria were entered"
            @ 23,20 say "Press any key to reenter the condition"
            wait ""
            loop
         endif
      endif
   endif

   if len(MCOND2) < 201
      store space(201 - len(MCOND2)) to MEXTRACOND
      @ 18, 5 say;
        "Enter extra selection conditions, or press <RETURN> to leave blank:"
```

Figure 21-3. The new label-printing program (*continued*)

```
      @ 19, 5 get MEXTRACOND picture "@S70"
      read
   endif

   if MEXTRACOND <> " "
      if type(MEXTRACOND) <> "L"
         @ 22, 5 say "Your extra selection conditions "+;
                     "are not a valid dBASE III PLUS expression"
         @ 23,20 say "Press any key to reenter the conditions"
         wait ""
         loop
      else
         store MCOND2 + "(" + trim(MEXTRACOND) + ")" to MCOND2
      endif
   endif

   store .F. to MOK
   @ 24,20 say "Are these selections OK? (Y/N)" get MOK picture "Y"
   read
   if MOK
      exit
   endif

enddo

if len(MCOND1) > 0
   store left(MCOND1, len(MCOND1) - 5) to MCOND1
endif

if len(MCOND2) = 4
   store "" to MCOND2
else
   if MEXTRACOND = " "
      store left(MCOND2, len(MCOND2) - 5) to MCOND2
   endif
endif

set filter to &MCOND1
goto top
label form NWCUST1 to print while ZIP<=MZIPEND &MCOND2

set filter to

return
```

Figure 21-3. The new label-printing program (*continued*)

"extra" ad hoc condition (MEXTRACOND) and the user's answers to all of the questions. Collecting and validating the entries is done within a DO WHILE loop that is repeated until the user confirms the selections and the TYPE function determines that the "extra" selection condition is in fact a syntactically correct dBASE III PLUS expression. Note that MCOND1 and MCOND2 are initialized within this loop, so that on each pass the program erases the conditions constructed on the previous try rather than adding onto them.

To keep this example short, no new selection criteria were added, and no validation tests are applied to any of the entries except MEXTRACOND. For each variable that has changed from its initial value, the appropriate phrase is added into either MCOND1 or MCOND2. If the new condition does not fit in either variable, an error message is displayed, and the user is given another chance to enter all of the selection criteria.

Next, the user is allowed to enter an "extra" condition into the memory variable MEXTRACOND. It is safe to assume that there will be more room left in MCOND2 than in MCOND1, but the exact length of MCOND2 depends on how many selection criteria have already been specified. As stated earlier, the fixed portion of the LABEL FORM command is 51 characters long, and the expression entered into MEXTRACOND will be surrounded by a pair of parentheses, so the space available for MEXTRACOND is 254 – 51 – 2 – the current length of MCOND2, or 201 – LEN(MCONDITION). The variable is collected by using the @S70 PICTURE so that, regardless of its length, it fits neatly on one line on the screen. If MCONDITION is shorter than 70 characters, the actual length determines the width of the input window.

Thus, MEXTRACOND is initialized and collected from the user only if MCOND2 is shorter than 201 characters. If the program determines that MEXTRACOND was not left blank, the expression is validated with the TYPE function. Since any valid dBASE III PLUS condition is a logical expression, the program tests to see if the TYPE function returns L. If it does not, an error message is displayed and the program returns to the top of the data entry loop to allow the operator to try again. The program requires that not just the extra condition, but *all* of the selection criteria be reentered to allow the user to rethink the selection strategy. Since the variables that hold the user's individual choices are initialized outside the DO WHILE loop, the operator's most recent selections will appear as defaults on each pass through the loop.

When the extra condition has been entered correctly, it is concatenated with MCOND2 to form the complete condition used in the LABEL FORM command. If you have so few selection possibilities that you are using only one variable (MCOND1) in your programs, you can perform the equivalent steps to add the "extra" condition onto the existing value of MCOND1 instead of MCOND2.

The user is given one last chance to confirm that the selections are not only syntactically correct, but also what he or she intended. If the answer to the "Are these selections OK?" query is Y, an EXIT command is used to escape from the data entry loop. Finally, the program tests to see if the variable MCOND1 has changed from its initial length of 0 characters; if so, the last five characters (the terminal .AND.) are removed. If not enough selection criteria were specified to require the use of MCOND2, this variable still has its initial value, "for ", and the program STOREs a null value in MCOND2 so that this variable has no effect on the LABEL FORM command. If an ad hoc condition was entered into MCONDITION, this condition forms the last part of MCOND2, and no adjustment to the length of this variable is required. If, however, MEXTRACOND is blank, and MCOND2 no longer has its initial length of four characters, the trailing .AND. is removed.

You may also wish to apply the same kinds of selection criteria to printed output produced by dBASE III PLUS programs—for example, the NWCREF2.PRG program that prints the Customer Reference List or the NWCLETTR.PRG program that prints personalized letters. A report-printing program could collect the user's selection criteria and store them in the variables MCOND1 and MCOND2 just as in the NWCLABL6.PRG program, and MCOND1 could be used in exactly the same way, by placing the same SET FILTER TO &MCOND1 command before the DO WHILE .NOT. EOF( ) loop that processes the data base record by record to print the report.

The second condition stored in MCOND2 must be handled slightly differently, since a FOR clause may only be used with the dBASE III PLUS commands that process an entire data base (such as LABEL, REPORT, and LIST). To control which records are printed by a dBASE III PLUS program, you must test each record individually at the top of the DO WHILE .NOT. EOF( ) loop, and for each one that does not match the specified condition, SKIP to the next record and bypass the remaining steps in the DO WHILE loop with a LOOP command.

This partial program illustrates the general strategy:

```
do while .not. eof()

   if .not. (&MCOND2)
      skip
      loop
   endif

   * steps to print records that satisfy the condition in MCOND2

   skip

enddo
```

In order for this structure to work, MCOND2 must be initialized as a null string. Note also that the condition expressed by MCOND2 describes the records that *should* be printed, but the condition is used to determine which records should be *skipped*. The condition is therefore negated with .NOT. in the IF statement. Because .NOT. takes precedence over .AND. and .OR., the parentheses around &MCOND2 are necessary to ensure that the .NOT. negates the entire condition expressed by MCOND2, not just the first phrase.

This method can readily be generalized to accommodate more selection criteria than can be stored in two variables. With a third set of criteria stored in a variable called MCOND3, the program would be structured like this:

```
do while .not. eof()

   if .not. (&MCOND2)
      skip
      loop
   endif

   if .not. (&MCOND3)
      skip
      loop
   endif

   * steps to print records that satisfy the conditions in MCOND2 and MCOND3

   skip

enddo
```

There is one remaining problem with this strategy. Depending on the number of selection criteria entered by the user, MCOND2 or MCOND3—or both—may still have their initial null values, and after the macro expression is expanded, the IF statement will read IF .NOT. ( ), which generates a "Syntax error" message.

You can solve this problem by testing the values of each of the variables used for the selection criteria before the beginning of the DO WHILE loop. Each variable that retains its original null value must be assigned instead an expression that is always true. When a true condition is negated with .NOT., it is always false; therefore this condition will never cause the program to skip a record. The most obvious expression that is always true is the logical value .T. itself. The test may be carried out as follows:

```
if len(MCOND2) = 0
   store ".T." to MCOND2
endif
```

When the value of MCOND2 is substituted for the macro &MCOND2, the IF statement reads IF .NOT. (.T.)—in other words, "if .T. is not true." Of course, the logical value .T. is always true, so the condition in the IF command is always false, and the SKIP and LOOP commands are never executed. This way, the program effectively ignores MCOND2 or MCOND3 if either is blank.

CUSTOMIZING THE SYSTEMWIDE OPTIONS

The last few chapters have introduced a set of PUBLIC memory variables used to store quantities that should be available to any program in the system. Some of these items, like MPINVOICE (the next available invoice number), are updated automatically by programs in the system—in this case, by the invoice-printing program—and the new values saved on disk for future use. Others, like MPSTATEABB, which contains the list of state postal abbreviations, rarely change; and many, like the company name and address, are generally entered only once, when the system is first installed.

This section will present the first of two "setup" programs that allow the users to enter and edit this set of variables and thus customize the systemwide options for their own needs and preferences without having to understand the dBASE III PLUS commands involved. This program will handle the group of PUBLIC memory variables that is unique to a particular application (although some of these, like the state abbreviations or company name and address, may be found in many dBASE III PLUS systems). The setup program does not add any new functions to the sample application; rather, it makes the users more independent of the programmers, and it allows you to design systems that are easier to adapt to the needs of more than one organization.

Chapter 24 will describe a similar program for updating a set of PUBLIC memory variables that store certain information about the user's hardware and operating system. These variables, which should be used in any dBASE III PLUS application that must run on more than one computer, will enable you to write programs that are relatively hardware-independent, since they may be customized by the user, without programming, for any system configuration supported by dBASE III PLUS.

This chapter also adds one new PUBLIC variable to the National

Widgets system, to store the inventory category codes and descriptions. The way the setup program updates the codes and descriptions stored in this variable demonstrates some versatile techniques for manipulating character strings that may be applied in other situations as well.

To change the values of any of the PUBLIC memory variables from the dot prompt, you would RESTORE the variables from the memory file, recreate the ones you wished to change with STORE commands, and SAVE the new values. For example, to assign a new default area code, you could use this sequence of commands:

```
RESTORE FROM NWMEMORY
STORE "408" TO MPAREACODE
SAVE ALL LIKE MP* TO NWMEMORY
```

This is easy enough for the area code, which is only three characters long, but it would be very tedious to retype the entire MPSTATE-ABB variable if you discovered that you had omitted one of the state abbreviations. A trick you can use to update this variable efficiently was suggested in Chapter 8, which pointed out that you can experiment with @ ... SAY at command level to determine the effects of the various PICTURE function and template symbols. What may not be so obvious is that you can also issue a GET command from the dot prompt. Just as when the command is used from within a program, one or more @ ... SAY ... GET commands must be activated by a READ before you can edit the data. If you need to lengthen the value of a character variable—for example, to add a new state abbreviation—you can do this by first appending a string of blank spaces and later TRIMming the variable, if necessary. The following sequence of commands lengthens MPSTATEABB, allows this variable and the default state and area code to be edited, and then TRIMs MPSTATEABB so that it does not contain any blank spaces and thus does not permit a blank state abbreviation to be entered into the Customer File:

```
RESTORE FROM NWMEMORY
STORE MPSTATEABB + SPACE(20) TO MPSTATEABB
CLEAR
@  1,0 SAY "STATE ABBREVIATIONS" GET MPSTATEABB PICTURE "@!"
@ 10,0 SAY "DEFAULT STATE" GET MPSTATE PICTURE "@!"
@ 12,0 SAY "DEFAULT AREA CODE" GET MPAREACODE PICTURE "999"
READ
STORE TRIM(MPSTATEABB) TO MPSTATEABB
SAVE ALL LIKE MP* TO NWMEMORY
```

If you wished to allow the state field to be left blank (to accommodate foreign addresses), MPSTATEABB would have to contain two blank spaces. These should be followed by a slash or placed somewhere other than at the end of the variable, so that they are not removed by the TRIM command. Note that the prompt messages displayed by SAY are unnecessary if you are sure you will remember which variable is which, and the PICTURE clauses may be omitted if you are careful to adhere to your guidelines for legitimate entries into these variables. Although this procedure is easy enough for someone familiar with dBASE III PLUS, every complete application that uses systemwide options stored in memory variables should include a program that allows the users to view and change the values of the variables without having to understand anything about dBASE III PLUS command syntax.

In many dBASE III PLUS applications, including the National Widgets sample system, the systemwide option variables are few and small enough that all of them may remain in memory at all times and still leave plenty of room for the local variables required by the programs in the system. When this is the case, you can save all of the variables on disk in one memory file—in this case, NWMEMORY.MEM—and issue a single RESTORE command from the Main Menu to load them into memory. Any variables created (or RESTOREd) in a dBASE III PLUS program are available to all other programs called by that program, so with this structure it is not strictly necessary that they be declared PUBLIC. In a system that requires more or larger variables to accommodate the required systemwide options, you may have to divide the variables into several sets, SAVEd in different memory files (with more descriptive names than NWMEMORY). In addition, it is usually more expedient to RESTORE the variables from the setup program rather than from the Main Menu, to make it easier to change or add variables, so it is better to declare them PUBLIC.

Whether or not you make the variables PUBLIC, you should assign them common prefixes so that it is easy to SAVE and, if necessary, RELEASE them in groups. The prefixes also readily identify the variables as systemwide options rather than local variables. (Unless they are declared PUBLIC, this is a distinction that has meaning only to the programmer, not to dBASE III PLUS.) If you have more than one set of variables, you might give them all a common two-letter prefix (like the MP in our sample application), followed by a third letter that identifies the group to which a variable belongs (for example, MPV for variables used to *validate* new records, or MPP for variables used to control *printing* functions).

The program that allows the users to alter the values of the systemwide options should also be able to create the variables if they do not already exist, so that a user who is not familiar with dBASE III PLUS can start up the application from scratch or recover from a disk crash that destroys the original memory variable file. Whichever program loads the variables into memory with a RESTORE command—preferably the setup program called from the Main Menu program—should first test for the existence of the memory file, so that the initial RESTORE command can never generate a "File does not exist" error message. If the memory variable file is missing, the program must create the variables with blank or default initial values.

Recall that a variable must be declared PUBLIC *before* it is initialized. If you do decide to declare the systemwide option variables PUBLIC, it is therefore important to do so before the RESTORE command. Be sure also to include the ADDITIVE keyword in the RESTORE command; otherwise, dBASE III PLUS will eradicate all knowledge of existing memory variable names (including those that are PUBLIC) before loading the new variables into memory from the named file. Although you can SAVE or RELEASE variables or declare them PRIVATE in groups based on their names, you must list each variable name explicitly in a PUBLIC declaration. (A command like PUBLIC ALL LIKE MP*, which would be very convenient, is *not* permitted.)

A Program to Customize The Systemwide Options

Figure 21-4 lists NWSETUP1.PRG, a program that allows the user to customize the application-specific systemwide options in the National Widgets sample system. This program may be invoked in two different ways: it is called automatically by the Main Menu program, and it may also be chosen by the user. If the NWMEMORY.MEM file is missing from the disk, the memory variables are initialized with a series of STORE commands. All of the numeric variables are initialized as 0, and most of the character variables are initialized with blank spaces, using either a literal character string or the SPACE function. If NWSETUP1.PRG was called automatically by the Main Menu and NWMEMORY.MEM already exists, the program RETURNs to the menu immediately after the RESTORE command. Thus, the user is only shown the variables for editing if he or she has explicitly chosen to run the setup program. The program tests this condition by examining the value of MSELECT, the memory variable created in NWMENU1.PRG to store the user's menu choice. This variable

```
* NWSETUP1.PRG
* PROGRAM TO UPDATE APPLICATION-SPECIFIC SYSTEMWIDE OPTIONS
* WRITTEN BY:  M.LISKIN       6/20/85

public MPCOMPANY, MPADDRESS1, MPADDRESS2, MPADDRESS3, MPSTATEABB, MCATEGORY,;
       MPSTATE, MPAREACODE, MPINVOICE, MPLMARGIN, MPTAXRATE, MPBACKUP

if file("NWMEMORY.MEM")
   restore from NWMEMORY additive
   if MSELECT = 0
      return
   endif
else
   store space(35)  to MPCOMPANY, MPADDRESS1, MPADDRESS2, MPADDRESS3
   store space(254) to MPSTATEABB, MPCATEGORY
   store "  "       to MPSTATE
   store "   "      to MPAREACODE
   store 0          to MPINVOICE, MPLMARGIN
   store 0.00       to MPTAXRATE
   store ctod(" ")  to MPBACKUP
endif

do NWSETUP2

clear

do while .T.

   store .T. to MVALID

   @  3, 5 say "Enter your company name and address:"
   @  4,10 say "Company" get MPCOMPANY
   @  5,10 say "Address" get MPADDRESS1
   @  6,18               get MPADDRESS2
   @  7,18               get MPADDRESS3

   set console off
   store MPSTATEABB + space(254) to MPSTATEABB
   set console on

   @  9, 5 say "Valid state abbreviations"  get MPSTATEABB picture "@!"
   @ 10, 5 say "(use slashes or dashes"
   @ 11, 5 say "to separate, and after"
   @ 12, 5 say "last abbreviation)"
   @ 15, 5 say "Default state abbreviation" get MPSTATE    picture "!!"
   @ 16, 5 say "Default area code         " get MPAREACODE picture "999"
   @ 17, 5 say "Default sales tax rate    " get MPTAXRATE  picture "99.99";
                                                           range 0, 10
   @ 18, 5 say "Default letter left margin" get MPLMARGIN  picture "99"
   @ 19, 5 say "Next invoice number       " get MPINVOICE  picture "99999"

   read

   set color to W+, W+

   if MPSTATE $ MPSTATEABB
      @ 15, 3 say " "
   else
      @ 15, 3 say "*"
      store .F. to MVALID
   endif

   set color to W, W+
```

Figure 21-4. A program to customize the application-specific systemwide options

```
   if .not. MVALID
      @ 24,15 say 'Please correct the items marked with a "*"'
   else
      store .F. to MOPTOK
      @ 24, 0
      @ 24,20 say "Are these options OK? (Y/N)" get MOPTOK picture "Y"
      read
      if MOPTOK
         exit
      endif
   endif

enddo

clear
@  2,10 say 'Enter up to 11 inventory category codes and descriptions:'
@  5,20 say '  Code                     Description'
@  6,20 say '--------             ----------------'

do while .T.

   set console off
   store MPCATEGORY + space(254) to MPCATEGORY
   set console on

   store 1 to MCOUNT
   do while MCOUNT <= 11
      store ltrim(str(MCOUNT,2)) to MCOUNTC
      store substr(MPCATEGORY, (MCOUNT - 1) * 23 + 2,  6)  to MCODE&MCOUNTC
      store substr(MPCATEGORY, (MCOUNT - 1) * 23 + 9, 15)  to MDESCRIP&MCOUNTC
      @ MCOUNT + 7, 5 say MCOUNT
      @ MCOUNT + 7,20 get MCODE&MCOUNTC picture "@!"
      @ MCOUNT + 7,40 get MDESCRIP&MCOUNTC
      store MCOUNT + 1 to MCOUNT
   enddo

   read

   store 1 to MCOUNT
   store "" to MPCATEGORY
   do while MCOUNT <= 11
      store ltrim(str(MCOUNT,2)) to MCOUNTC
      if MCODE&MCOUNTC <> " "
         store MPCATEGORY + "/"+MCODE&MCOUNTC + "/" + MDESCRIP&MCOUNTC;
               to MPCATEGORY
      endif
      store MCOUNT + 1 to MCOUNT
   enddo

   store .F. to MOPTOK
   @ 24, 0
   @ 24,20 say "Are these options OK? (Y/N)" get MOPTOK picture "Y"
   read
   if MOPTOK
      exit
   endif

enddo

store trim(MPSTATEABB) to MPSTATEABB
save all like MP* to NWMEMORY

return
```

Figure 21-4. A program to customize the application-specific systemwide options (*continued*)

will have the value 0 if the NWSETUP1.PRG was called automatically, before the user has chosen an option, or 11 if the user has selected the setup option. Note that to make this technique work, NWMENU1. PRG must be modified to initialize MSELECT prior to the call to NWSETUP1.PRG.

The basic strategy for the NWOPT1.PRG program is to present the variables to the user with @ ... SAY ... GET commands for editing and then SAVE the updated variables on disk. The variables are collected within a DO WHILE loop much like the validation loop used in the NWCUPD3.PRG program to enter and edit Customer File records. Just as in the Customer File update program, the memory variable MVALID, which is initialized with a value of .T. at the start of each pass through the loop, stores the overall status (valid or invalid) of the entire set of systemwide option variables. In this example, only one variable, the default state, is validated.

Entering the company name and return address is very straightforward. Before the user is allowed to edit the list of state abbreviations, the length of the variable MPSTATEABB is increased to 254 characters, so that new abbreviations may be added. This is necessary because the program will TRIM MPSTATEABB to conserve memory and prohibit the entry of a blank state field into the Customer File. In order to expand the variable to its maximum permissible length, a string of 254 blank spaces is added to the present value of MPSTATEABB. Adding the maximum number of blank spaces to *any* character string (other than a null string) results in the error message "***Execution error on + : concatenated string too large," which you may have encountered at command level if you tried to add together two character strings whose combined length exceeded 254 characters. Before reporting the error, however, dBASE III PLUS does add as many spaces as possible to the current value of MSTATEABB, thus increasing its length to 254 characters. The NWSETUP1.PRG program turns off the screen display with SET CONSOLE OFF prior to the STORE command, so that the error message does not appear on the screen, and returns the display to normal with SET CONSOLE ON immediately afterward. If this "invisible" error bothers you, you could calculate exactly how many spaces to add to MSTATEABB by subtracting the current length of the variable from 254:

```
store MPSTATEABB + space(254 - len(MPSTATEABB)) to MPSTATEABB
```

The default state (MPSTATE), area code (MPAREACODE), sales tax rate (MPTAXRATE), left margin for letters (MPLMARGIN), and next invoice number (MPINVOICE) present no special problems. A RANGE clause is used to limit the sales tax rate to a value between 0.00 and 10.00. After all the variables are collected, MPSTATE is validated by testing to see if it is contained in MPSTATEABB. If this entry (or in other applications, any of a number of variables that are validated) does not validate properly, a message instructing the user to correct the indicated item or items is displayed. Even if all of the fields pass, the program asks the user to confirm that they have in fact been entered correctly. Answering Y to the question "Are these options OK?" causes the program to EXIT the DO WHILE loop; otherwise, the program returns to the top of the loop to allow the user to reenter all of the variables.

A second DO WHILE loop is used to update the new variable, MPCATEGORY, which stores the inventory category codes and descriptions used in the National Widgets system. In Chapter 20 a data base, NWCODES.DBF, was created to store the valid inventory categories, state abbreviations, and area codes, together with a description of each code. Maintaining the codes in a data base is most appropriate when there are many codes, the descriptions are lengthy, or you wish to use the file to compile statistics, as in the NWOSTATS.PRG program written in Chapter 18. With the codes stored in a data base, you could write a program similar to the Customer File Update and Inquiry program to allow the users to update, delete, or add to the list of codes. This section illustrates a method for storing the codes and descriptions in a memory variable, and introduces some character string manipulation techniques for extracting a particular code, description, or both. Using a memory variable is best when there are few enough codes, with short enough descriptions, to allow you to fit all of them into one variable.

MPCATEGORY consists of a series of the six-character codes, each surrounded by a pair of slashes, and each followed by the corresponding 15-character description. If MPCATEGORY contained the same codes and descriptions entered into the NWCODES.DBF file in Chapter 20, it would look like this:

```
/ACCESS/Accessories    /COVER /Dust covers    /DISK  /Disks
/FORMS /Paper forms    /PRTWHL/Print wheels   /RIBBON/Printer ribbons
/STOR  /Storage boxes  /
```

The methods employed to manipulate this variable merit careful study—the same techniques can be used to validate codes (for example, in an Inventory File update program) or to display or print the description corresponding to a particular code. To find out whether a variable called MCATEGORY contains one of the category codes, it is sufficient to determine whether it appears anywhere within MPCATEGORY. Just as in MPSTATEABB, slash separators are used in MPCATEGORY to ensure that you can unambiguously find a code even if the same sequence of characters happens to occur within one of the descriptions. MCATEGORY could thus be validated with the following test:

```
if ("/" + MCATEGORY + "/") $ MPCATEGORY
```

MPCATEGORY may also be viewed as a translation table, in which the codes and descriptions are stored in fixed positions relative to each other: each description begins eight characters to the right of the slash that precedes the corresponding code. Using a combination of the SUBSTR (substring) and AT (substring search) functions, you can search for any code in the table and extract the matching description. For example, to translate "COVER" to "Dust covers" you would search for "/COVER /" in MPCATEGORY; the matching description is the substring of MPCATEGORY that begins eight characters to the right of the code and is 15 characters long.

The search is carried out with the AT function, which takes two character strings as input and yields as its result a number that expresses the location of the beginning of the first string within the second. For example, AT ("/COVER /", MPCATEGORY) evaluates to 24, because the character string "/COVER /" is found within MPCATEGORY, beginning at the twenty-fourth character. The name of this function suggests an easy (if not quite grammatical) way to read the expression: "Where is "/" + MCATEGORY + "/" *at* in MPCATEGORY?" Counting the characters can be confusing, even if you understand the principle, so you might want to keep a printed copy of the contents of MPCATEGORY handy for reference.

The following commands display the description corresponding to the code stored in the variable MCATEGORY:

```
if ("/" + MCATEGORY + "/") $ MPCATEGORY
   @ 10,10 say;
     substr(MPCATEGORY, at("/" + MCATEGORY + "/", MPCATEGORY) + 8, 15)
endif
```

Note that it is important to test for the existence of a code before attempting to display the description. If the AT function fails to find the specified string, it assumes a value of 0. In the previous example, if

MCATEGORY is not found in MPCATEGORY, the SUBSTR expression therefore yields the 15-character substring of MPCATEGORY that begins at the eighth character—"/Accessories ".

This property of the AT function provides another way to test for the existence of one string in another. For example, the expression

```
if at("/" + MCATEGORY + "/", MPCATEGORY) > 0
```

is equivalent to

```
if ("/" + MCATEGORY + "/") $ MPCATEGORY
```

In order to allow the user to change, delete, or add codes and descriptions, the NWSETUP1.PRG program must first break up MPCATEGORY into its component parts. In the case of the state abbreviations, it is easy for the operator to enter the two-letter abbreviations, separated by slashes, into the variable MPSTATEABB. For the inventory categories, however, editing MPCATEGORY directly would be very confusing to a user who does not understand why the variable is structured the way it is. Also, the consequences of accidentally inserting or deleting spaces are much more serious. Since the substring functions that extract the codes and descriptions assume that each component of MPCATEGORY is a constant length, the descriptions can only be read correctly if the proper spacing is preserved.

It is easy to calculate in advance how many category codes will fit in MPCATEGORY: each takes up 6 spaces for the code, 2 for the surrounding slashes, and 15 for the description, for a total of 23 characters. Thus, MPCATEGORY can accommodate 11 codes (23 * 11 = 253). The NWSETUP1.PRG separates the components of MPCATEGORY into a series of temporary variables for the codes (called MCODE1, MCODE2, through CODE11), and a corresponding set of variables (MDESCRIP1, MDESCRIP2, through MDESCRIP11) for the descriptions. Since there are only 11 sets, you could determine in advance where each one begins and create these variables with a series of explicit STORE commands. Here are the first four:

```
store substr(MPCATEGORY,  2,  6) to MCODE1
store substr(MPCATEGORY,  9, 15) to MDESCRIP1
store substr(MPCATEGORY, 25,  6) to MCODE2
store substr(MPCATEGORY, 32, 15) to MDESCRIP2
```

This is easy to read and understand, and it executes very fast; but if you had 20 shorter codes and descriptions, you might not want to type 40 STORE commands, all of which would have to be changed if you later lengthened or shortened the codes or descriptions.

A more general method is to use a DO WHILE loop that executes 11 times, extracting one code and description on each pass. Before entering the loop, the program increases the length of MPCATEGORY to 254 characters, just as was done for MPSTATEABB, the state abbreviation variable:

```
set console off
store MPCATEGORY + space(254) to MPCATEGORY
set console on
```

The numeric variable, MCOUNT, counts the 11 passes through the loop. Each time through, the program must create a variable with a name consisting of the character string "MCODE" plus the number stored in MCOUNT, and create a similar variable that has a name beginning with "MDESCRIP". Thus, MCODE1 and MDESCRIP1 would be created on the first pass, followed by MCODE2 and MDESCRIP2 on the second pass, and so on. This can be done by combining the character string "MCODE" or "MDESCRIP" with a macro expression containing the number. You cannot use the expression MCODE&MCOUNT for this purpose, because the variable whose value is substituted for the macro expression must be a character variable. The program therefore creates a character string version of MCOUNT by means of the STR and LTRIM functions:

```
store ltrim(str(MCOUNT, 2)) to MCOUNTC
```

The LTRIM function, which removes *leading* spaces from a character string (just as TRIM deletes trailing spaces), is necessary because numbers are always right-justified within the space allotted to a numeric variable. The expression STR(MCOUNT,2) would thus yield variable names containing spaces (which are not permitted in the dBASE III PLUS language) for all of the values of MCOUNT less than 10—"MCODE 8", for example.

The next problem is calculating the offset of each code from the beginning of the field. Think about the starting positions: MCODE1 begins at character 2, MCODE2 begins at character 25, and so on. Because each combination of code plus description takes up 23 characters, each begins 23 characters beyond the start of the previous code. It may help to visualize an imaginary reference point immediately to the left of the entire string, and call this character 0. The first code begins 2 characters beyond this reference point (position 1 is occupied by the slash), the second begins at the reference point plus 23 plus 2 (28 * 1 + 2), the third at the reference point plus 46 plus 2 (23 * 2 + 2), and so on. This concept is illustrated in Figure 21-5. To calculate the starting point for each code, the program must therefore subtract 1 from MCOUNT, multiply the result by 23, and add 2:

```
substr(MPCATEGORY, (MCOUNT - 1) * 23 + 2, 6)
```

The description begins seven characters beyond the beginning of the code, or offsets a total of nine characters from the starting position of each set:

```
substr(MPCATEGORY, (MCOUNT - 1) * 23 + 9, 15)
```

These are the expressions used in the DO WHILE loop in NWSET-UP1.PRG to create the variables for each code (MCODE&MCOUNTC) and description (MDESCRIP&MCOUNTC). To present and collect the variables on the screen, the program displays a line number and then the two memory variables MCODE&MCOUNTC and MDESCRIP& MCOUNTC. With the line number in the @ ... SAY ... GET commands expressed as MCOUNT + 7, the first set of variables is displayed on line 8, the second on line 9, and so on, with the last set on line 18. If you had more variables than would fit on one screen, you could split them into two groups. Using the full-screen edit commands, the operator can change codes, add codes (if not all are in use), or blank out a code with CTRL-Y. After all of the codes have been entered, another DO WHILE loop constructs the string MPCATEGORY by adding together all of the nonblank category codes and matching descriptions. Because MPCATEGORY was initialized as a null string immediately before this loop, it is not necessary to TRIM the resulting variable. Finally, all of the PUBLIC variables are saved on disk.

If you had a few more codes, or each were slightly longer, you could gain some space by using two variables, one for the codes (perhaps called MPINVCODES) and one for the descriptions (MPINVDESC). Using this scheme for the same codes that made up MPCATEGORY, MPINVCODES would look like this:

```
/ACCESS/COVER /DISK  /FORMS /PRTWHL/RIBBON/STOR  /
```

In this application, it is never necessary to search for a specific charac-

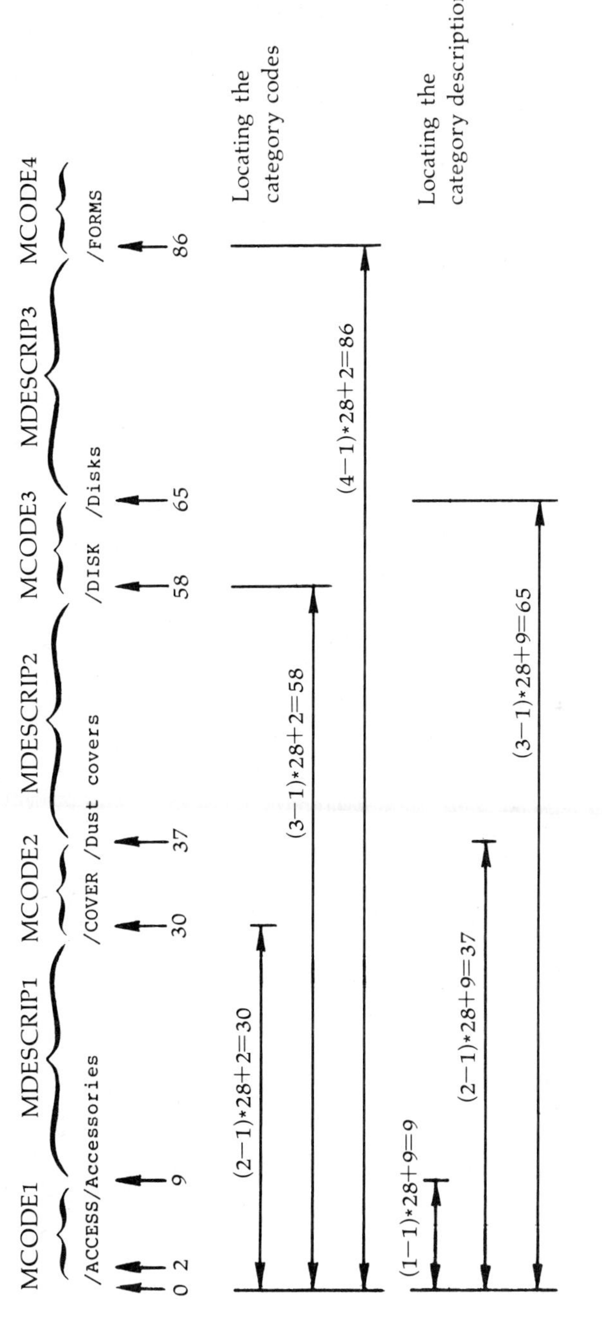

Figure 21-5. Locating the inventory categories and descriptions

ter string in MPINVDESC, so no slashes are required within this variable, which would have the following value:

```
Accessories    Dust covers    Disks          Paper forms    Print wheels
Printer ribbonsStorage boxes
```

To create the temporary memory variables used in NWSETUP1.PRG, you could use the following:

```
store substr(MPINVCODES, (MCOUNT - 1) *  7 + 2,  6) to MCODE&MCOUNTC
store substr(MPINVDESC,  (MCOUNT - 1) * 15 + 1, 15) to MDESCRIP&MCOUNTC
```

To search for a specific value for a variable called MCODE in MPINVCODES, you could use this expression:

```
at("/" + MCODE + "/", MPINVCODES)
```

The results of the search could be stored in another memory variable or used directly in the SUBSTR expression that extracts the matching description from MPINVDESC:

```
substr(MPINVDESC, int(at("/" + MCODE + "/", MPINVCODES) / 7) * 15 + 1, 15)
```

This expression essentially derives the same value from the location of MCODE in MPINVCODES that was stored explicitly in MCOUNT in the previous example. Recall that the INT function takes the integer portion of an expression; so for the first code, located at character 2 in MPINVCODES, INT(2 / 7) yields 0; for the second, located at character 9, INT(9 / 7) is 1, and so on. The matching descriptions are found at positions (0 * 15) + 1, or 0, (1 * 15) + 1, or 16, and so on.

This technique allows you to use memory variables for more codes and descriptions than you can accommodate in a single variable. With more than about 15 codes, however, it makes more sense to store them in a file like NWCODES.DBF.

22

USING PROCEDURE FILES

The programs in the last three chapters have increased the power, flexibility, and user-friendliness of the National Widgets sample system. In the process of writing these programs, standard routines were developed for carrying out such common operations as asking the user a question and validating the answer or centering a page heading on a report. Clearly, whenever the same set of commands occurs in several places within one program, or when the same routine is required by many of the programs that make up an application, it would be preferable to avoid repeating the same command lines many times.

For a simple process like centering a report title (which can be accomplished with a single @ ... SAY command), repeating the centering calculation several times within a program may not seem like a serious problem. Consider, on the other hand, the implications of allowing the user to enter selection criteria not just for printing one-up mailing labels, but for all of the mailing functions and some of the statistical reports in a system. Obviously, it would be much more efficient to place the steps required to specify the criteria in a separate program rather than to add this lengthy routine to many of the existing programs in the system. The main reasons for separating commonly used routines from the main program are as follows:

- Removing a large functional module streamlines the main program, making it easier to read and understand.

- Once the separate modules have been tested, any program that calls them will contain fewer potential sites for errors and will therefore be easier to debug.
- If you modify or add to one of the common routines, the change need only be made in one place.
- The common routines may be used, often with only minor changes, in more than one data base application.

On the other hand, each time a program is called with a DO command, it must be loaded into memory from the disk. Even on a hard disk, this takes a noticeable amount of time. Placing a frequently used set of commands in a separate, stand-alone program is therefore most appropriate when the routine must be called only once (or a few times) during each run of the main program. For example, most of the options in the menus and submenus in the National Widgets system simply call other programs. Even if the called programs are quite short, this organization turns the menu programs into clear, concise functional descriptions of the tasks carried out by the system, uncluttered with the details of how the operations are actually carried out. The time required to load the appropriate program into memory after the operator selects an option is usually not long enough to be objectionable. Similarly, extracting a large, unwieldy routine like the TEXT ... ENDTEXT structure that draws the customer input screen used by NWCUPD3.PRG into a separate program (NWCSCRN.PRG) does not slow down the update program significantly, since this routine is called infrequently (at the beginning of the program and after editing memo fields with the NWCUST5.FMT format file).

If a set of steps must be repeated many times in the same program, however, placing it in a separate disk file is less ideal. Sometimes, the delay caused by multiple disk accesses is acceptable. For example, even if a report-printing program calls a separate program to print the heading on each page, the program will still execute faster than the printer can print. However, if you used a separate program to repeatedly display or collect fields on the screen, the overall degradation in performance would be much more noticeable—and more annoying—to the users. You can solve this problem and, at the same time, improve your productivity as a programmer, by combining commonly used routines into a single procedure file, rather than placing each one in a separate program.

INTRODUCING PROCEDURE FILES

A *procedure file* is a dBASE III PLUS program that may contain the equivalent of up to 32 separate programs. You open a procedure file with

SET PROCEDURE TO *procedure file name*

Procedure files, like any other dBASE III PLUS programs, are assumed to have the extension .PRG unless you explicitly specify a different extension in the SET PROCEDURE command. Once the procedure file is open, dBASE III PLUS can access any of the component procedures more quickly than it can search for a separate program on the disk; if the file is small, it may be loaded into memory in its entirety, after which up to 32 essentially separate routines are available without pausing for an additional disk access.

Each procedure must begin with a PROCEDURE statement that identifies it by name:

PROCEDURE *procedure name*

A procedure name may be up to eight characters long and may contain an embedded underscore (_). Except for the PROCEDURE statement, each procedure in the file is exactly the same as any other dBASE III PLUS program. Like a stand-alone program, a procedure is called with a DO command:

DO *procedure name* WITH *parameter list*

A procedure may call any other program or procedure. When a RETURN command is encountered in the currently running procedure, control returns to the calling program or procedure. Like other dBASE III PLUS programs, procedures may accept input in the form of parameters, in which case the PARAMETERS statement must be the first executable (noncomment) line in the procedure. If there is a program on the disk with the same name as a procedure in the procedure file that is currently open, a DO command that uses this name will execute the procedure rather than the program. Although this precedence may be exactly what you want in a given situation, it is best to avoid duplicating names, because this can be very confusing to other programmers who must read or modify your system.

Also, the recommended convention for naming all of the *programs* in a system with a common prefix, so they may be copied easily or listed with a single command, is not as well suited to naming procedures. Since all of the procedures are contained in one disk file, there is no particular advantage to giving the procedure names a common prefix. In fact, there is a disadvantage: many procedures are general enough to be used in more than one dBASE III PLUS application, so a procedure that prints a report heading would be better named HEADING than NWHEAD if it might later be used outside of the National Widgets system. Omitting the standard system prefix from the procedure names also makes it clear when you read a program whether a particular DO command calls another program or a procedure.

If your application requires fewer than 32 procedures, you can include all of them in a single procedure file and open this file in the system's Main Menu program when you issue the SET commands that customize the working environment. If you need more than 32 procedures, you must divide them among several procedure files. You may have only one procedure file open at a time, but you can open and close the files at will; each SET PROCEDURE command closes the current procedure file before opening the new one. In an application that requires more than one procedure file, you might want to organize the procedures along the same functional lines as the menus, so that each procedure file is opened and closed as few times as possible.

A procedure file may also be closed without opening another (if, for example, you would otherwise have too many files open):

```
SET PROCEDURE TO
```

or

```
CLOSE PROCEDURE
```

When an application requires only one procedure file, it is best to name this file with the standard system prefix, followed by PROC or PROCED to identify it as a procedure file when you list the disk directory. With more than one procedure file, you should choose a more descriptive name for each. Like any other dBASE III PLUS program, a procedure file should begin with a few comment lines that identify the name, purpose, author, and last modification date. It is also a good idea to include at the beginning of the file a set of comment lines identifying the procedures by name, listing them either in the order they appear in the file or by function, briefly describing the purpose of each, and perhaps listing the parameters. You may also want to begin each individual procedure—or at least the longer or more complex ones—with the same set of comment lines used for dBASE III PLUS programs. (In the examples in this chapter, these comments will be omitted from the shorter procedures for the sake of clarity.) Separating the procedures with a line of asterisks (or a line of dashes beginning with an asterisk to identify it as a comment) also makes it easier to pick out the beginning and end of each procedure.

When you begin to use procedure files, you can search through your existing dBASE III PLUS systems for separate programs or sections of programs that may be converted to procedures. Some of these routines may be incorporated without modification into your growing procedure file. With the dBASE III PLUS MODIFY COMMAND editor, you can use CTRL-KR to read the contents of any file into the file you are editing; many text editors and word processors allow you much more flexibility to include parts of one file into another. Be careful if you have been using MODIFY COMMAND as your only program editor: it is all too easy to create a procedure file that exceeds this editor's 5000-character limit.

In many cases, changing an existing routine slightly allows you to make it more general so that it may be called in similar contexts by different programs. In order to do this, you will usually have to provide input to the procedure from the calling program in the form of memory variables, most often as parameters. For example, Chapter 18 presented a program to print the page heading on the Customer Reference List. To turn this routine into a procedure that could print a heading on *any* report, the commands that print the Customer Reference List page title and column titles must be removed and replaced with commands that can print any titles. The text of the titles would then be passed to the procedure as literal character strings or memory variables. This and other typical applications for procedures will be illustrated with examples drawn from the National Widgets system, using sections of programs already described in earlier chapters, together with some completely new procedures. You will find the final version of the National Widgets procedure file listed in Appendix E.

CREATING THE NATIONAL WIDGETS PROCEDURE FILE

Some of the common operations carried out by programs in the National Widgets system could be extracted and turned into procedures with very little modification beyond adding a PROCEDURE statement and, in most cases, assigning a new name. The NWCSCRN.PRG program that draws the Customer File inquiry and update screen could thus become a procedure called CUSTSCRN. The routine that determines whether it is necessary to reindex the Customer File by ZIP code and the Order History File by CATEGORY before a mailing could be removed from the NWCLABL6.PRG program written in Chapter 21 and converted to a procedure called ZIPINDEX. Similarly, the portion of NWCLABL6.PRG that allows the user to specify selection criteria for mailings or reports based on the Customer File could become a procedure called CUSTSEL.

You might also consider placing these routines in separate programs rather than procedures. As procedures, ZIPINDEX and CUSTSEL would each be called only once for a label or report run, and CUSTSCRN would be called infrequently—once at the beginning of the Customer Update and Inquiry program, and thereafter only when the user updated a memo field. Including routines like these in a procedure file is convenient for the original programmer and for other programmers who may need to modify your system, since it keeps all of a system's common routines in one place. However, if you are approaching the limit of 32 procedures, it would be preferable to remove procedures like these and run them as separate programs rather than to add a second procedure file to the system.

To run ZIPINDEX and CUSTSEL either as separate programs or as procedures, one small but very important change must be made: the memory variables created to store the ending ZIP code (MZIPEND) and the components of the selection criteria (MCOND2, ME, MI1, MI2, MD1, and MD2) must be declared PUBLIC. This must be done to make these variables available to the calling program, for use in the LABEL FORM or REPORT FORM command that specifies the criteria. Unlike MZIPEND, the value of MZIPBEGIN is not needed in the calling program; it is used only within the ZIPINDEX procedure to position the Customer File to the correct record before beginning to print.

Similarly, if CUSTSEL were run as a separate program or procedure, MCOND1 would not need to be made PUBLIC, because the SET FILTER command is also located in CUSTSEL. However, MCOND2 and all of the individual variables that make up the selection conditions would have to be declared PUBLIC, because there is no way to determine in advance whether a given condition may end up in MCOND1 (which is local to the procedure) or MCOND2 (which must be returned to the calling program). ME, MI1, MI2, MD1, and MD2 could also be passed as parameters to the CUSTSEL procedure, but by declaring them PUBLIC instead, you can avoid having to initialize a set of corresponding variables in the calling program. If you were close to the limit of 256 active memory variables, you might want to RELEASE these variables after the labels have been printed. Variables that have been declared PUBLIC cannot be erased from memory with RELEASE ALL or any of its variations (RELEASE ALL EXCEPT or RELEASE ALL LIKE), so you must name each variable explicitly in the RELEASE command:

```
RELEASE MZIPEND, MCOND2, ME, MI1, MI2, MD1, MD2
```

With the reindexing steps and the routine for entering the selection criteria removed, the label-printing program would be reduced to only seven lines:

```
use NWCUST

do ZIPINDEX
do CUSTSEL

label form NWCUST1 to print while ZIP <= MZIPEND &MCOND2
set filter to
release MCOND2, ME, MI1, MI2, MD1, MD2

return
```

These few commands hardly merit a whole program; they might just as well be placed directly in the Customer Information Menu. In fact, since the same procedures (reindexing and entering selection criteria) would be called by the other label-printing program already present in the system (NWCLABL4.PRG), you could use one CASE to handle both kinds of labels. Within this CASE, the Customer File could be opened, the two procedures called, and an IF loop used to select the appropriate command to produce either one-up or four-up labels. If your application had more than two menu options that shared this common structure, you could substitute a DO CASE structure for the IF loop. This portion of the Customer Information Menu is listed in Figure 22-1.

Although the CUSTSEL procedure could be extracted almost unchanged from the NWCLABL1.PRG program written in Chapter 21,

```
case MSELECT = 20 .or. MSELECT = 21
   use NWCUST
   do ZIPINDEX
   do CUSTSEL
   if MSELECT = 20
      label form NWCUST1 to print while ZIP<=MZIPEND &MCOND2
   else
      label form NWCUST4 to print while ZIP<=MZIPEND &MCOND2
   endif
   set filter to
   release MZIPEND, MCOND2, ME, MI1, MI2, MD1, MD2
```

Figure 22-1. Calling the ZIP INDEX and CUSTSEL procedures from the Customer Information Menu

one important structural alteration would greatly reduce its size and improve its efficiency, especially if your version contained more than the five criteria included in this example. All of the IF structures that build up the variables MCOND1 and MCOND2 based on the user's selections are very similar and could form yet another procedure, which would be called once by CUSTSEL for each of the variables entered by the user. This procedure will be presented at the end of this chapter.

A Procedure to Display a Status Message On the Screen: MONITOR

Whenever a program performs a potentially lengthy operation, such as indexing a data base or processing a file sequentially to compile statistics, it should display some kind of status message that allows users to monitor the program's progress. Programs like NWCSTAT2.PRG (which compiles statistics on National Widgets' customers based on the type of computer equipment they own) and NWOSTATS.PRG (which compiles statistics from the Order History File) display a status message that describes briefly the operation being performed, together with a running count of the number of records processed. With a minor change in the wording of the descriptive message to make it more general, the task of displaying the fixed portion of this message could be handled by a procedure. Here is the procedure, which is called MONITOR:

```
procedure MONITOR

clear
@ 10,10 say "Compiling Statistics -- Please Do Not Interrupt"
@ 12,10 say "Working on Record              of " + str(reccount(),5)

return
```

To call this procedure from another program or procedure, you would use

```
do MONITOR
```

The task of displaying each record number in the space provided for this purpose in the text of the status message can be accomplished as before, with a single @ ... SAY command within the DO WHILE .NOT. EOF( ) loop that processes all of the records in the file.

Procedures That Require Input From the Calling Program: SAYDATE and CENTER

Using the MONITOR procedure is very straightforward—it always does exactly the same thing, no matter which program calls it, so it does not require any input from the calling program. A more common use of procedures is to perform essentially the same operation to produce different results, depending on the input. The programs written in Chapters 15 through 21 contain numerous examples of relatively short program segments that are repeated, with minor variations, throughout the system. To a large extent, the effective use of procedures depends on the art of recognizing, isolating, and generalizing these program modules.

Printing or displaying dates is an example of a commonly used program segment that requires specific and changing input for each particular use. Most of the printed formats in the National Widgets sample application use the same combination of dBASE III PLUS date conversion functions to print dates in the form July 31, 1987, rather than 07/31/87. Both the date and its position on the page may vary. Most of the reports print the current date, expressed as the DATE( ) function, at the upper left corner of the page, while the program that prints statements places the aging date (entered by the operator into the memory variable MAGEDATE) in the middle of line 25. A general-purpose procedure to print a date in the standard format therefore requires three inputs from the calling program: the date to be printed, and the row and column coordinates to use in the @ ... SAY command. These "inputs" are passed to the SAYDATE procedure as parameters.

Here is the procedure:

```
procedure SAYDATE

parameters MLINE, MCOLUMN, MDATE

@ MLINE, MCOLUMN say cmonth(MDATE) + str(day(MDATE), 3) + ", " + ;
                     str(year(MDATE), 4)
return
```

This procedure might be called from the statement-printing program with the following:

```
do SAYDATE with 25, 52, MAGEDATE
```

You could also use this procedure to print a date field in a columnar report. In this example, the column number is known to the calling program, but the row will change with each call as records are printed on successive lines on the page. A typical call of this type might look like this:

```
do SAYDATE with MLINE, 20, LASTORDER
```

Although this routine was designed with printed reports in mind, it may also be used to display a date in the preferred format on the screen. Nowhere in the procedure is the output device specified, and the date is printed rather than displayed on the console only because the calling program has already routed the output of all @ ... SAY commands to the printer with SET DEVICE TO PRINT. You could use the same procedure to display the current date in the upper right-hand corner of the screen with

```
do SAYDATE with 1, 60, date()
```

A similar strategy might be used to generalize another operation used in many of the National Widgets system programs: centering a line of text on the screen or printed page. Like SAYDATE, this procedure requires three inputs: the field or memory variable to be centered, the row coordinate for the @ ... SAY command, and the overall page (or screen) width that enables the routine to calculate the column coordinate. This is the procedure:

```
procedure CENTER

parameters MLINE, MWIDTH, MTEXT

@ MLINE, (MWIDTH - len(trim(MTEXT))) / 2 say trim(MTEXT)

return
```

The statement-printing program might be rewritten so that it will use a series of calls to this procedure to print the return address at the top of the page:

```
do CENTER with 5, 85, MPCOMPANY
do CENTER with 6, 85, MPADDRESS1
do CENTER with 7, 85, MPADDRESS2
do CENTER with 8, 85, MPADDRESS3
```

Both the SAYDATE and CENTER procedures carry out their functions with essentially a single program statement: the @ ... SAY command. It might seem that there is little to be gained by placing either of these commands in a separate procedure. The call to the procedure occupies about the same amount of space in the main program as the original command, and it could not possibly execute faster, since dBASE III PLUS must process the call and perform the parameter substitutions. Nevertheless, there are three main advantages to using a procedure. If you have named your procedures strategically, it will be abundantly clear to anyone reading the DO command exactly what operation is being performed. Using the standard procedure for a particular function also helps to ensure consistency among programs written by the same person at different times or by several people working together on the same system. Most importantly, using the procedure greatly facilitates the process of changing and refining a developing system. If, for example, you decided to change the date display format from July 31, 1987, to 31 July 1987, only one small part of one program — the procedure file — would have to be changed.

A Procedure to Display a Message On the Screen: MESSAGE

In the Customer File update program written in Chapter 20, line 23 is used to display a variety of error messages for the operator and to confirm that certain commands, like deleting or recovering a customer record, have been carried out as directed. In each case, the program does the same thing:

- Clears line 23
- Displays a message on line 23
- Waits until a key is pressed
- Returns to the top of the loop.

The only *necessary* variable is the message text, but a procedure to display these messages could be made even more general by using parameters for the row and column coordinates. Since the specified line is CLEARed before the message is displayed, the procedure is restricted to displaying text on an otherwise unoccupied line on the screen.

Here is the MESSAGE procedure:

```
procedure MESSAGE

parameters MLINE, MCOLUMN, MMESSAGE

set color to W+, W+

@ MLINE, 0
@ MLINE, MCOLUMN say MMESSAGE
wait ""

set color to W, W+

return
```

This procedure clears the specified line, displays the memory variable MMESSAGE (which contains the message text) at the indicated line and column coordinates, and then pauses until a key is pressed. Two SET COLOR commands were added, so that the message appears in the brighter intensity, after which the display is returned to the normal colors.

The most straightforward way to pass the message text to the procedure is in the form of a character string constant. For example, if the

Customer File is not positioned at a valid record when the CHANGE, DELETE, RECOVER, or MEMO option is selected, an error message must be displayed. The sections of the NWCUPD3.PRG program that carry out these tests might be rewritten as follows to call the MESSAGE procedure:

```
if eof() .or. bof()
   do MESSAGE with 23, 15, "You must SEARCH first -- Press any key to continue"
   loop
endif
```

While this structure is more concise than the original IF loop, the same message text is still repeated four times in the program—once in each of the four options that must display the message. When a program uses the same or similar messages in many different places, it makes sense to store the individual messages or message components in memory variables. For example, the NWCUPD3.PRG program might initialize the following series of message variables when the program is first invoked (before the DO WHILE loop):

```
store " -- Press any key to continue"                    to MPRESSKEY
store "You must SEARCH first"                            to MSEARCH
store "This is the first name"                           to MFIRST
store "This is the last name"                            to MLAST
store " not found"                                       to MNOTFOUND
store "Balance is not 0.00"                              to MNOTZERO
store "There are current transactions"                   to MTRANSACT
store " has been deleted"                                to MDELETE
store " has been recovered"                              to MRECOVER
store " is already on file"                              to MONFILE
store 'Please correct the fields marked with a "*" '     to MCORRECT
```

In fact, if the same set of messages were used in more than one program, you might consider storing the messages in a series of PUBLIC memory variables to make them available throughout the system. With this set of memory variables containing the message texts, the "You must SEARCH first ..." warning could be displayed with the following call to the MESSAGE procedure:

```
if eof() .or. bof()
   do MESSAGE with 23, 15, MSEARCH + MPRESSKEY
   loop
endif
```

If the user tried to search for a nonexistent customer, the program could display the appropriate error message by combining three components: the specified account number, the "not found" message, and the "Press any key ..." message:

```
if eof()
   do MESSAGE with 23, 15, trim(MACCOUNT) + MNOTFOUND + MPRESSKEY
   loop
endif
```

The ease with which a programmer can build, maintain, and modify dBASE III PLUS systems that use procedures for frequently accessed routines becomes clear when you consider the almost casual way that the SET COLOR commands were added to the MESSAGE procedure. Think about the implications of the decision to display all such messages in the brighter intensity or, on a color monitor, in a different color. Without the separate procedure, SET COLOR commands would have to be added before and after the display of each message in each program in the entire system—a task formidable enough to discourage you from making the improvement at all.

Procedures to Ask Questions And Validate Answers: ASK1 and ASK2

Many of the programs written so far ask the user to answer a yes-or-no question like "Do you need to reindex the Customer File by ZIP?" or "Are these selections OK?" All of these questions can be handled by a procedure much like the MESSAGE procedure described in the previous section, except that the new procedure, ASK1, must not only accept input from the calling program (the prompt message text and the row and column coordinates for displaying the prompt) but also pass information (the answer to the question) back to the calling program. The ASK1 procedure looks like this:

```
procedure ASK1

parameters MLINE, MCOLUMN, MQUESTION, MANSWER

@ MLINE, 0

store .F. to MANSWER
@ MLINE, MCOLUMN say MQUESTION get MANSWER picture "Y"
read

return
```

When this procedure is called, the row and column coordinates and the text of the prompt message could be passed either as constants (numeric for the row and column, character for the message) or as memory variables. The answer to the question is passed back to the calling program in the variable MANSWER. Remember that the corresponding variable in the calling program must be initialized prior to the call to ASK1. If a program must ask several different yes-or-no questions and preserve the answers to all of them, you must use a separate variable for the answer to each question. If the answer is acted on immediately, after which the value of the variable is no longer important, you can initialize at the beginning of the program a single memory variable, perhaps called MANSWER to match the corresponding variable in the procedure, and use it in each call to ASK1.

Because the ASK1 procedure initializes the local variable MANSWER right before the DO WHILE loop that collects the user's response to the question, you need not be concerned about what value is passed to the procedure. If you prefer to vary the default answer presented to the user, the initialization of MANSWER should be omitted from the ASK1 procedure, and the initial value passed as a parameter. With ASK1 written this way, the NWCUPD3.PRG program could use this procedure to request confirmation from the user before deleting a customer record with the following:

```
store .F. to MCONFIRM
do ASK1 with 23, 10, "Are you sure you want to delete this customer? (Y/N)",;
            MCONFIRM
```

As an alternative, you could store the text of the question in a memory variable and call the procedure this way:

```
store .F. to MCONFIRM
store "Are you sure you want to delete this customer? (Y/N)" to MASKDELETE
do ASK1 with 23, 10, MASKDELETE, MCONFIRM
```

The same technique could easily be extended to ask questions for which there are more than two possible answers by passing the list of permissible responses to the procedure, along with the text of the question. A new procedure, ASK2, which illustrates this concept, might look like this:

```
procedure ASK2

parameters MLINE, MCOLUMN, MQUESTION, MCHOICES, MANSWER
```

```
@ MLINE, 0

store " " to MANSWER
do while .not. MANSWER $ MCHOICES
   @ MLINE, MCOLUMN say MQUESTION get MANSWER picture "!"
   read
enddo

return
```

Using this procedure, the NWCUPD3.PRG program could request confirmation to delete a customer record with one of the following:

```
do ASK2 with 23, 10, "Are you sure you want to delete this customer? (Y/N)",;
            "YN", MANSWER
```

or

```
do ASK2 with 23, 10, MASKDELETE, "YN", MANSWER
```

A Procedure to Search a Data Base for a Record: ASK3

Many of the programs written for the National Widgets system open a data base with an index and then search the index for a record specified by the user. In the programs that printed the Customer Reference List (NWCREF2.PRG) and customer statements (NWSTPRT.PRG), the operator was asked to identify the customer by account number, and the invoice-printing program (NWINVPRT.PRG) searched the Transaction File invoice number index for a specified invoice number. In each of these programs, essentially the same statements were repeated twice: once to enter the starting customer or invoice number, and again, if the operator had elected to print customers or invoices one at a time, to specify the single record to be printed on each pass through the DO WHILE loop.

In pseudocode, here is what a general-purpose procedure to carry out this task must do:

```
initialize a memory variable to contain the user's input

set up an "endless" loop:
   display a prompt message
   collect the user's entry into the memory variable
   if the variable was left blank,
```

```
        exit the program
    endif
    seek the variable in the index
    if the variable is found,
        exit from this loop
    otherwise,
        display an error message
        wait until a key is pressed
        erase the error message
    endif
end of loop
```

The procedure, ASK3, is listed in Figure 22-2.

The procedure assumes that the prompt message can always be displayed on line 12 and the error message on lines 20 and 21; if this is not the case, these coordinates must be supplied to the procedure as additional parameters. The prompt message is passed to the procedure as the

```
procedure ASK3

parameters MPROMPT, MKEY, MPICTURE, MERRORMSG

do while .T.

   @ 12,10 say MPROMPT get MKEY picture MPICTURE
   read
   if MKEY = " "
      exit
   endif
   seek trim(MKEY)
   if found()
      exit
   else
      @ 20,10 say trim(MKEY) + " " + MERRORMSG
      @ 21,10 say "Press any key to try again"
      wait ""
      @ 20,10
      @ 21,10
   endif

enddo

return
```

Figure 22-2. A procedure to search a data base for a record

parameter MPROMPT, and the field to be collected as MKEY. This rather generic name is intended to reflect the purpose of the variable: it represents an index key that will be used as the object of a SEEK command. The PICTURE used to format the user's input (the parameter MPICTURE) must also be obtained from the calling program, since it varies with the length of MKEY and the type of data the user will enter. The first line of the error message, which informs the user that the specified record could not be found, becomes the variable MERRORMSG. The second line of the error message is also phrased in general terms, as "Press any key to try again" (rather than "Press any key to reenter the invoice number" or "Press any key to reenter the customer"), so that it can fit any context.

The ASK3 procedure presents the prompt message and collects the user's entry into the variable MKEY, using the specified PICTURE to format the input. If MKEY is left blank, the program EXITs the loop and RETURNs to the calling program. In the programs from which these procedures were derived, leaving the index key (for example, the customer account number or invoice number) blank caused the program to return to the Customer Information Menu. There is no way, however, to jump directly from the ASK3 procedure to the Customer Information Menu. Neither the RETURN command nor the RETURN TO MASTER command provides a solution; RETURN always returns control to the program that called a procedure, and RETURN TO MASTER would exit not to the Customer Information Menu but to the highest level program in the system (in this case, the Main Menu program).

Even if there were a way to transfer control directly from ASK3 to the Customer Information Menu, it might not be the best thing to do. For example, if you had just printed an invoice or a statement, an EJECT would be needed to force the last page out of the printer. Placing this command in the procedure, however, would render it unsuitable for use by a program (such as NWCORD1.PRG) that produced no printed output. It is therefore left up to the calling program to decide what actions to take if ASK3 returns a blank value through the parameter MKEY. What to do if the SEEK succeeds in finding a record also depends on the context in which the procedure is called. The statement-printing program requires only a SET DEVICE TO PRINT command to route the output of @ ... SAY ... GET commands to the printer, whereas the program that prints the Customer Reference List must also ask for a starting page number the first time it calls this procedure. Because of the many possible variations, all of these steps are best handled outside of the ASK3 procedure.

In the statement-printing program, the IF loop that asks for the starting customer account number if statements are not being printed one at a time could call ASK3 this way:

```
if .not. MONE

   store ACCOUNT to MACCOUNT
   do ASK3 with "Enter first customer to print", MACCOUNT, "@!",;
                "has no current transactions"
   if MACCOUNT = " "
      return
   endif

endif
```

Within the DO WHILE loop, if statements were printed one at a time, you could ask for the next customer to print with the following:

```
if MONE

   store ACCOUNT to MACCOUNT
   set device to screen
   do ASK3 with "Enter customer to print", MACCOUNT, "@!",;
                "has no current transactions"
   if MACCOUNT = " "
      eject
      return
   else
      set device to print
   endif

endif
```

A Procedure Allowing the User To Interrupt a Report or Label Run: STOPRPT

The programs that print labels allow the user to specify the starting and ending ZIP codes. This allows the user to select customers in a geographic area as defined by the range of ZIP codes; it allows a label run to be resumed from the approximate point of interruption after a paper jam or if the operator cancels the print job to perform some other more urgent task; and it also provides a better way for the user to interrupt a print run than by simply pressing the ESC key.

When the user presses ESC while dBASE III PLUS is printing using the built-in report or label generators, the program displays the message "*** INTERRUPTED ***" on the screen and returns to command level (the dot prompt). As described in Chapter 14, when a dBASE III PLUS program is interrupted with ESC, the user is given three choices: Cancel, Ignore, or Suspend. A new operator who is not familiar with using dBASE III PLUS at the dot prompt may find this message confusing, and even a more experienced user who knows enough to respond C (for "cancel") may have trouble remembering what to do next. No matter how the user arrives at the dot prompt, a safe recovery may involve typing quite a few commands—to close any open data bases, reverse some of the SET commands issued from the menu or report-printing programs, and restart the system. In particular, if a user forgets the SET DEVICE TO SCREEN command, then running any program, including the Main Menu, that uses @ ... SAY ... GET to collect input will cause the prompt message to be printed repeatedly on the printer.

One minimal approach to this problem is to simply instruct the users to QUIT and restart the application whenever they interrupt a print run with ESC. A better solution is to use the ON ESCAPE or ON KEY command to detect the user's keystroke and respond appropriately. The general form of these commands is

ON ESCAPE *command*

and

ON KEY *command*

These commands may be issued, singly or together, at any point in an application; they remain in effect until cancelled with ON ESCAPE or ON KEY. As you might expect, if both ON ESCAPE and ON KEY are active, pressing the ESC key runs the command specified in the ON ESCAPE command, rather than the one in the ON KEY command. Although the *command* may be any valid dBASE III PLUS command, the most flexible way to use this error trap is to execute a DO command that calls another program or procedure.

Ideally, the procedure should ask the user whether to continue printing or stop and return to the menu. Optionally, you may also want to save some information that identifies the last record printed in a memory variable, to serve as the default for the first record to be printed the next time the program is run. For a report printed by a program, it is not necessary to allow the user to interrupt if records (for example, customers) are being printed one at a time. You could set up the test with the following command placed just before the DO WHILE loop that prints the data:

```
if .not. MONE
   store .F. to MSTOP
   on KEY do STOPRPT
endif
```

The simplest way to write the STOPRPT procedure looks like this:

```
procedure STOPRPT

do ASK1 with 23, 10, "Do you want to stop printing? (Y/N)", MSTOP

if MSTOP
   store recno() to MPRECORD
   store MPAGE   to MPPAGE
   save all like MP* to NWMEMORY
endif

return
```

If the user has pressed a key accidentally or has paused the program only to adjust the paper in the printer, answering N to the question "Do you want to stop printing?" causes dBASE III PLUS to return to the calling program and continue printing. If the user chooses to stop printing, the record number of the current record and the current page number are saved in PUBLIC memory variables for use in the next print run. It is up to the report-printing program to decide how to use these variables; in this example, the program could position the data base with GOTO MPRECORD before asking the user which record to print first, and initialize the page number variable MPAGE with MPPAGE rather than a numeric constant. If the report runs to completion, the report-printing program should reset the variables to standard values. For MPPAGE, this value should be 1; for MPRECORD, you might choose 0. The GOTO command that positions the record pointer should only be executed if MPRECORD is not 0; if it is, the data base should remain positioned at the first record (or first indexed record). This command must therefore be conditional:

```
if MPRECORD > 0
   goto MPRECORD
endif
```

Note also that the calling program must test the value of MSTOP on each pass through the DO WHILE loop that prints the records, and if MSTOP is .T., execute the necessary commands to finish printing—including EJECTing the page from the printer and rerouting the output of @ ... SAY commands to the screen with SET DEVICE TO SCREEN.

Safely interrupting a printout produced by a REPORT FORM or LABEL FORM command is slightly different. dBASE III PLUS checks the keyboard buffer to see whether a key has been pressed *between* commands, whereas to allow the user to exit in the middle of a report or label run, your program must detect a key pressed *during* execution of the REPORT or LABEL command. To do this, you must use ON ESCAPE rather than ON KEY, since dBASE III PLUS does continue to monitor the keyboard to test for the ESC character while running commands as well as in between. Note that this technique will not work if the ESC key is disabled with SET ESCAPE OFF. The ON ESCAPE command that activates STOPRPT when the user presses ESC is

```
on escape do STOPRPT
```

In order to allow the operator to resume printing after pressing a key to interrupt, the REPORT or LABEL command must be placed in a DO WHILE loop that causes this command to be repeated as long as MSTOP is .F. This is necessary so that when the STOPRPT procedure returns control to the calling program, execution does not simply resume with the command following the REPORT or LABEL command. The portion of NWCLABL6.PRG that prints the labels could be modified as follows to use this procedure:

```
store .F. to MSTOP
do while .not. MSTOP
   label form NWCUST1 to print while ZIP<=MZIPEND &MCOND2
enddo
```

Since the record pointer is not repositioned by any of the commands in the STOPRPT procedure or by the DO WHILE loop in the calling program, you can interrupt and resume printing as many times as necessary. You could also do considerably more complicated processing in the STOPRPT procedure. In particular, if this procedure is called by custom report-printing programs, it could save the memory variables that contain totals or other statistics being accumulated by the report.

Procedures to Print Report Headings: RPTHEAD and DASHES

In Chapter 18, separate programs were used to print the page header, page footer, and transaction column headings on the Customer Reference List, so that any of these routines could be called from several different places in the NWCREF2.PRG program. Turning these programs (NWCHEAD.PRG, NWCFOOT.PRG, and NWTHEAD.PRG) into procedures could be done simply by placing them in the NWPROC.PRG procedure file and adding a PROCEDURE statement at the beginning of each routine. In a data base system that prints only a few reports, the same page footer might be used on all of them, and it would be easy enough to write a separate procedure for each report heading. However, most applications produce enough printed listings to merit general-purpose procedures to print page headers and footers. In order to write these procedures, you must standardize the form that the headers and footers will take. In most cases, this is actually an advantage; like data entry screens, the reports will seem less intimidating to the users if the same type of information always appears in the same place on the page. The page headers for all of the National Widgets system reports designed so far conform to the following rules:

- Print the date at the left edge of line 1
- Print the page number at the right edge of line 1
- Print the company name centered on line 3
- Print the report title centered on line 4
- Print the column titles on line 7
- Underline the column titles with dashes on line 8
- Print the first line of data on line 10.

The guidelines you adopt for the standard heading format should accommodate the maximum number of lines of page and column titles you anticipate using anywhere in the system. If fewer titles are needed for a particular report, the unused lines may be left blank, since extra space within a page heading is generally not considered objectionable. Rather than simply conforming to the National Widgets system's current standards, the new procedure will accommodate a two-line report title and two lines of column titles. In order to simplify the process of underlining the column titles, the procedure will print one continuous row of dashes instead of underlining each portion of the titles individually. The headings printed by the general-purpose procedure will follow this revised set of rules:

- Print the date at the left edge of line 1
- Print the page number at the right edge of line 1
- Print the company name centered on line 3
- Print the first line of the report title centered on line 4
- Print the second line of the report title centered on line 5
- Print the first line of the column titles on line 8
- Print the second line of the column titles on line 9
- Underline the column titles with a row of dashes on line 10
- Print the first line of data on line 12.

The procedure that prints the report heading looks like this:

```
procedure RPTHEAD

parameters MWIDTH, MTITLE1, MTITLE2, MCOLTITLE1, MCOLTITLE2

do SAYDATE with 1, 0, date()

if .not. MONE
   @  1, MWIDTH - 8 say "PAGE " + str(MPAGE,3)
endif

do CENTER with 3, MWIDTH, upper(MPCOMPANY)
do CENTER with 4, MWIDTH, MTITLE1
do CENTER with 5, MWIDTH, MTITLE2

@  8, 0 say MCOLTITLE1
@  9, 0 say MCOLTITLE2
@ 10, 0 say left(MPSDASH, MWIDTH)

store MPAGE + 1 to MPAGE
store 12        to MLINE

return
```

Three of the items printed in the heading are always available to the procedure: the current date may be expressed as the DATE( ) function, the company name is stored in the PUBLIC memory variable MPCOM-

PANY, and the page number variable created in the report program may be printed and updated by the procedure, as long as it is named MPAGE in the calling program. (Recall that if the values of any variables created in a program are changed by a procedure called by this program, the new values are always passed back to the calling program.) If there were any reason to deviate from the standard names MPAGE and MLINE for the page and line number variables, these items should also be parameters. The variable MONE, which has the value .T. if the program is printing forms (customers, invoices, or statements) one at a time, is also available to the procedure as long as it exists in the calling program. Since the RPTHEAD procedure must test the value of this variable to determine whether or not to print a page number, every program that calls RPTHEAD must create this variable and assign it a value, even if some of these reports will never print "one at a time."

The two lines of report titles and column titles are passed to the procedure as parameters, so that they may be specified either as literal character strings or as memory variables. The procedure also needs the page width in order to right-justify the page number and center the report titles. In the National Widgets sample application, all of the reports begin at the left edge of the paper (column 0), but if necessary you could also pass the left margin to the procedure as a parameter and use this variable in the @ ... SAY commands that print the column titles.

Two of the tasks the RPTHEAD procedure must perform are already handled by procedures presented earlier in this chapter: printing the date in the proper format and centering the company name and page titles. In the National Widgets system, all of the page titles are printed in uppercase. The company name is therefore printed as "upper(MPCOMPANY)" to ensure that regardless of how it was entered into the memory variable file, it always matches the page titles created in the calling program. All of the line numbers are constants, in accordance with the list of report heading guidelines presented earlier. The page number is printed beginning eight characters in from the right edge of the page because it is always exactly eight characters long: five for the text "PAGE " and three for the page number. If the page width is 80, the word "PAGE" therefore begins at column 72, with the last digit of the page number printed in column 79, the last column on the page. (Since the numbering of the column coordinates begins with 0, an 80-column report will use columns 0 through 79.)

The two lines of column titles are printed with @ ... SAY commands. To print the row of continuous dashes on line 10, the procedure assumes the presence of a PUBLIC memory variable called MPSDASH (for single dashes) consisting of 254 hyphens. The creation of this variable and the corresponding variable MPDDASH (double dashes, containing 254 equal signs) will be discussed shortly. The underlining for the column titles consists of a substring of one of these variables of a length equal to the width of the report, MWIDTH. (Note that although the word "substring" is used to describe this partial string, it is clearer and more concise to use the LEFT function rather than the SUBSTR function to print it.) Finally, the procedure increments the page number and sets the line counter to 12 to print the first line of data.

To use this procedure to print the page heading for the Customer Reference List designed in Chapter 18, you could use the following:

```
store "CUSTOMER REFERENCE LIST" to MTITLE1
store "ACCOUNT ID   ADDRESS                                       " +;
      "CONTACT / PHONE / EQUIP      ORDER DATES                   " +;
      "YEAR-TO-DATE   .        TOTAL" to MCOLTITLE2

do RPTHEAD with 132, MTITLE1, "", "", MCOLTITLE2
```

There is no need to create memory variables for the unused title lines, which may be passed to the procedure as null character strings. In this example, the *second* page title was omitted, so that the company name and address and the first (and only) page title are printed on consecutive lines. If you prefer to skip a line between the company name and the title, you could instead leave the first page title line blank. For the column titles, the *first* column title line was left blank to avoid printing a blank line between the column titles and the row of dashes. You might want to try writing a similar procedure to produce a set of column titles in the middle of a report page, like the transaction detail column headings in the Customer Reference List, and one to print a standard page footer.

The MPSDASH and MPDDASH variables are created using the following procedure:

```
procedure DASHES

public MPSDASH, MPDDASH

store "-" to MPSDASH
store "=" to MPDDASH

store 1 to MCOUNT

set console off
```

```
do while MCOUNT <= 8
   store MPSDASH + MPSDASH to MPSDASH
   store MPDDASH + MPDDASH to MPDDASH
   store MCOUNT  + 1       to MCOUNT
enddo

set console on

return
```

This procedure needs no input. MPSDASH is initialized as a single hyphen and MPDDASH as an equals sign; the length of each variable is doubled eight times within a DO WHILE loop. Theoretically, this results in a length of 256 characters (2 to the eighth power), but dBASE III PLUS truncates the variables to the maximum permissible length of 254 characters. The procedure uses SET CONSOLE OFF so that the error message, "***Execution error on + : Concatenated string too large," is not visible to the user.

The DASHES procedure can be run once, at the same time that the other PUBLIC memory variables in the system are initialized for the first time. The best way to use this procedure is to call it either from the Main Menu program or from a setup program that initializes the systemwide PUBLIC memory variables. Since this procedure is run very infrequently (perhaps only once, when the application is installed for the first time), it could also be made a separate program rather than a procedure. In your own applications, if you run short of space for memory variables, you can call the procedure that creates the variables immediately before printing a report and RELEASE them afterward instead of allowing them to be saved in the memory file containing the systemwide options. They must be declared PUBLIC, however, so that they are available to the report-printing program after the DASHES procedure terminates.

A Procedure to Specify Selection Criteria: CRITERIA

An examination of the NWCLABL6.PRG program written in Chapter 21 reveals that the process of building up the variables MCOND1 and MCOND2, which store the user's selection criteria, is carried out by a series of essentially identical tests. For example, here is the section of the program that processes MI1, the variable that stores the lower limit for the TOTINV field:

```
if MI1 > 0
    if len(MCOND1 + "TOTINV>=MI1.and.") <= 240
       store MCOND1 + "TOTINV>=MI1.and." to MCOND1
    else
       if len(MCOND2 + "TOTINV>=MI1.and.") <= 201
          store MCOND2 + "TOTINV>=MI1.and." to MCOND2
       else
          @ 22,20 say "Too many selection criteria were entered"
          @ 23,20 say "Press any key to reenter the condition"
          wait ""
          loop
       endif
    endif
 endif
```

For each memory variable presented to the user as a potential component of the selection criteria, the program must test whether the variable has changed from its initial value. If so, MCOND1 is checked to determine whether it can accommodate the new condition. If MCOND1 is too long, MCOND2 is tested similarly. This process could be efficiently dealt with by a sequence of calls to a separate procedure called CRITERIA, which looks like this:

```
procedure CRITERIA

parameters MCHANGED, MCONDITION

if &MCHANGED
   if len(MCOND1 + MCONDITION) <= 240
      store MCOND1 + MCONDITION to MCOND1
   else
      if len(MCOND2 + MCONDITION <= 201
         store MCOND2 + MCONDITION to MCOND2
      else
         store .T. to MTOOMANY
      endif
   endif
endif
```

Two parameters must be passed to CRITERIA: MCHANGED, which stores the condition that tests whether the initial value presented by the SELECT procedure was changed by the user; and MCONDITION, which contains the phrase to be added onto the previous value of MCOND1 or MCOND2. The following call to CRITERIA could then be used to test the value of MI1:

```
do CRITERIA with "MI1 > 0", "TOTINV>=MI1.and."
```

In NWCLABL6.PRG, the selection by inventory category deviates slightly from the pattern used for all of the other selection criteria—the program links the Customer File and the Order History File with SET RELATION only if MC has changed from its initial blank value. In order to make this test consistent with the others, the SET RELATION command could be moved outside the IF loop that tests the value of MC, or it could be placed within a separate IF structure controlled by the original condition, as follows:

```
if MC <> " "
   set relation to MC + ACCOUNT into NWORDHST
endif
do CRITERIA with 'MC <> " "', "NWORDHST->ACCOUNT<>' '.and."
```

This structure results in slightly faster processing if MC is left blank, since dBASE III PLUS does not have to reposition the Order History File as the record pointer moves through the Customer File.

The logical memory variable MTOOMANY, which must be initialized with a value of .F. on each pass through the DO WHILE loop in the calling program or procedure, acquires a value of .T. in the CRITERIA procedure if too many criteria were entered in MCOND1 and MCOND2. After all the calls to CRITERIA, the value of this variable may be tested as follows:

```
if MTOOMANY
   @ 22,20 say "Too many selection criteria were entered"
   @ 23,20 say "Press any key to reenter the conditions"
   wait ""
   loop
endif
```

If MTOOMANY is .T., an error message is displayed and the user is given another chance to enter the selection criteria. The NWCLABL6.PRG program allows for selections by type of equipment, total invoices, last invoice date, and product category. Using the CRITERIA procedure, adding another selection test to this program would increase its length by only one line—another call to CRITERIA—rather than the 14 lines required using the original program structure.

The procedures described in this chapter illustrate the kinds of operations used in most data base applications that are well suited to running as procedures. During the early development stages of a system, it can be more expedient to place the common routines not in procedures, but in separate programs. This way, when you are testing and debugging each routine, making the inevitable changes involves editing a much smaller file. When each module has been tested and debugged, you can incorporate it into your system's growing procedure file.

In order to edit a procedure file without exiting from dBASE III PLUS, the file must be closed first with SET PROCEDURE TO and reopened after you have made the necessary changes. The dBASE III PLUS MODIFY COMMAND editor will not allow you to edit an open procedure file; you will get a "File is already open" error message if you try. If you use an external word processor or editor, or a memory-resident editor like SideKick, be careful to close the procedure file first and reopen it after each editing session. Recall that your editor will load the procedure file into memory from the disk and save it on disk when you issue the appropriate "save" command, but dBASE III PLUS will still have a copy of the old version of the procedure file in memory. This outdated version of the procedure is the one that will be executed until the next time the entire procedure file is loaded into memory with a new SET PROCEDURE command.

Although the use of procedure files is never *necessary*, it will help you optimize not only one particular data base system, but also subsequent dBASE III PLUS applications you may develop. If you are writing your first dBASE III PLUS system, you can place routines that you know will be called from many programs into a procedure file right from the start. Unless you are an experienced programmer, however, you may not always be able to identify all of these routines until you have written many of the programs in the system. Often, the easiest way to build up a procedure file is to extract sections of existing programs and modify them to form general-purpose procedures. As you write more dBASE III PLUS programs, you will gradually amass a library of standard procedures that may be used with little or no modification in any new system you write. The remaining chapters in this book will add a number of new procedures to the National Widgets procedure file, which is listed in its entirety in Appendix E.

23

PROVIDING ON-LINE HELP AND ACCESS TO DOS

This book has stressed the importance of building a "friendly" and helpful user interface into every dBASE III PLUS program you write, so that people who are not familiar with dBASE III PLUS command syntax can learn and use your applications as easily as possible. The specific techniques used in the programs written so far include the following:

- Phrasing menu option descriptions and report titles in the terminology of the users' business or profession.
- Using longer and more descriptive prompts than the data base field names on data entry and inquiry screens.
- Using PICTUREs, FUNCTIONs, RANGEs, and validation tests to ensure consistency without requiring the operator to remember too many data entry rules.
- Providing default values for frequently repeated fields.
- Displaying a descriptive prompt and, if necessary, additional instructions when a program requests input from the operator (for example, "Enter customer to print, or press <RETURN> to quit").
- Reminding the user to turn on the printer before beginning to print a report.

- Listing the permissible choices when a program asks a question for which there are only a few acceptable answers (for example, "Do you want to print customers one at a time? (Y/N)").
- Displaying clear and descriptive error messages when incorrect data is entered.
- Requiring confirmation from the user before executing potentially destructive commands like deleting a record or zeroing a field throughout a data base.
- Displaying the long descriptions corresponding to short code fields to help the operator confirm that the correct data has been entered (for example, displaying the state name and area code on the Customer File update screen).
- Displaying extra information to help flag unreasonable entries and to allow the exercising of human judgment (for example, in the order entry program, presenting a customer's EQUIPMENT field for comparison with the inventory items ordered).

All of these features are easy to incorporate into any dBASE III PLUS application. Providing help in these small ways can have a tremendous cumulative effect on how long it takes to train new operators and how comfortable nontechnical users feel when working with the computer. As useful as built-in help can be, however, the amount of information you can provide this way is necessarily limited. With only a 24-line by 80-column screen at your disposal, there is not enough room to display minutely detailed instructions on how to operate the programs, and even if there were, it would not always be desirable to do so. In general, extensive help messages should be presented only on demand, so that a novice user has access to enough on-line information to use the application effectively after a short learning period, and more experienced operators can move quickly through the system without being hampered or distracted by a constant barrage of instructions.

This chapter describes two types of on-line help you can include in your dBASE III PLUS applications. The first consists of providing access to operating system commands from within your programs. The second places some of the information contained in the printed documentation on-line in the form of help screens. Chapter 26 discusses the printed documentation that you should provide with your dBASE III PLUS applications. Even in a commercial software package, on-line documentation is not a substitute for a printed user manual, especially for providing an overview of the application, detailing the processing cycle, and outlining the strategy for using the programs. When you help the users start up the system for the first time, you should point out the importance of reading the printed documentation *before* running the application and continuing to consult the manual for more detailed information later on. Of course, they will often fail to follow your advice. (Did you read the dBASE III PLUS manual from cover to cover before beginning to experiment with the software?) The help screens you provide should be designed to supplement, not replace, the printed documentation, and they need not be as detailed or as comprehensive as the user manual. On-line help provides a fast, easy, and convenient way for the users to review the purpose or function of a particular menu option, report, command choice, or data base field with a minimal interruption in their work.

Supplying on-line documentation in the form of informational screens is the most common variety of help system you will encounter. Another important but frequently overlooked way to make an application more user-friendly is to add a selection of operating system commands to your system's menus. By taking advantage of dBASE III PLUS's ability to run any DOS command or external program, you can enable operators who are unfamiliar with MS-DOS command syntax to carry out certain crucial "housekeeping" tasks, such as backing up the data base or checking remaining disk space. At the same time, you can provide more experienced users with a convenient way to execute DOS commands or other programs without having to QUIT and then reload dBASE III PLUS many times in the course of a work session.

ACCESSING DOS COMMANDS AND PROGRAMS FROM THE APPLICATION MENUS

The introduction to dBASE III PLUS programming in Chapter 7 stated that you may use a word processor without exiting from dBASE III PLUS, provided that you have enough RAM in your computer. In fact, you can use the RUN command to execute *any* DOS command, .BAT file, .COM file, or .EXE file from the dot prompt or from within a dBASE III PLUS program. The syntax of the RUN command is

RUN *DOS command or program name*

or

! *DOS command or program name*

dBASE III PLUS provides approximate equivalents for the MS-DOS DIR, RENAME, ERASE, and COPY commands, but if you are already familiar with the DOS commands, you will often find them more convenient. The dBASE III PLUS RENAME, ERASE, and COPY commands do not permit you to use the ? and * characters recognized as "wildcard" symbols by MS-DOS, so you cannot use a single command to operate on a group of files with similar names.

By default, the dBASE III PLUS DIR command lists only data base files, including the number of records, date of last update, and file size. You can, however, list any group of files by including the extension explicitly. For example, you could use the dBASE III PLUS DIR command to list all of the dBASE III PLUS programs on drive B: with the following:

```
DIR B:*.PRG
```

You could display the same set of files with the MS-DOS DIR command:

```
RUN DIR B:*.PRG
```

The difference is that the dBASE III PLUS DIR command lists the file names four across, without the file sizes or date and time of last update, much like the five-column display that results from including the /W (wide) option in the DOS command (DIR B:* .PRG/W). Figure 23-1 illustrates the difference between the two commands.

In order to RUN any external command or program from the dot prompt or from within your application, you will need additional RAM beyond the minimum 256K required to run dBASE III PLUS. You must have enough RAM to load into memory both COMMAND.COM and the program you wish to run, along with dBASE III PLUS. For the intrinsic (built-in) DOS commands (such as DIR, ERASE, RENAME, and COPY) or small utility programs like FORMAT.COM or CHKDSK.COM, 320K to 384K is generally sufficient. To run a larger application like a word

```
. DIR B:*.PRG

NWCMENU2.PRG        NWOPT2.PRG          NWPROC.PRG          NWHELP.PRG
NWCUPD3.PRG         NWMENU2.PRG         NWHELP1.PRG         NWHELP2.PRG
NWRESTOR.PRG        NWBACKUP.PRG        NWRUNDOS.PRG

  67039 bytes in    11 files.
  62464 bytes remaining on drive.


. RUN DIR B:*.PRG

 Volume in drive B has no label
 Directory of  B:\

NWCMENU2 PRG      3078   7-15-86   7:41p
NWOPT2   PRG      4214   9-01-86   7:29a
NWPROC   PRG     12179   9-02-86   9:01p
NWHELP   PRG     13255   9-12-86   6:14a
NWCUPD3  PRG      8007   9-12-86   9:25p
NWMENU2  PRG      4444   9-12-86   4:18p
NWHELP1  PRG     17941   9-15-86  11:03p
NWHELP2  PRG       879   9-15-86   3:09a
NWRESTOR PRG       811   9-12-86  10:44a
NWBACKUP PRG      1837   9-13-86   5:03a
NWRUNDOS PRG       394   9-12-86  10:55a
       11 File(s)     62464 bytes free
```

Figure 23-1. The difference between the dBASE III PLUS and MS-DOS DIR commands

processor or a spreadsheet, you may need 512K or even 640K.

Remember that both COMMAND.COM and the application you wish to run must be available to dBASE III PLUS when you issue the RUN command. If you are working on floppy disks, you may not have room for COMMAND.COM and the external program on your dBASE III PLUS program disk. Before you execute a RUN command from the dot prompt, you must insert the disk containing the necessary files into the default drive, and when you RUN other software from a dBASE III PLUS program, your program should prompt the operator to insert the proper disk into the drive before carrying out the command.

If you have a hard disk system, dBASE III PLUS and your application may reside in one subdirectory, and the other programs you wish to access in other subdirectories. Depending on the ability of an external program to recognize the DOS subdirectory structure, you may be able to RUN the software by using the DOS PATH command to establish a default search path for files not found in the current subdirectory. In general, you can run any program that consists of a single .COM or .EXE file this way. With software that uses overlay files, the PATH command only enables DOS to find the main .COM or .EXE file.

Unless the program allows you to specify the path to search for the overlays, you must either copy the entire package into your dBASE III PLUS subdirectory or execute the program from a batch file. For example, if your copy of dBASE III PLUS resides in a subdirectory called DBPLUS and you wish to access WordStar, which is stored in the WORDPROC subdirectory, you could create the following batch file:

```
CD \WORDPROC
WS
CD \DBPLUS
```

This batch file might be named WORDPROC.BAT and stored either in the DBPLUS subdirectory or a DOS or UTILITY subdirectory used for all of your batch files and DOS utility programs. To invoke the batch file and run WordStar from within dBASE III PLUS, you would type

```
RUN WORDPROC
```

By default, MS-DOS searches for COMMAND.COM on the disk from which the operating system was initially booted. With all IBM hardware and many other hard disk-based compatible systems, this is the hard disk itself (usually drive C:), and COMMAND.COM is already present in the root directory. If you boot your system from a floppy disk in drive A:, MS-DOS continues to search for COMMAND.COM on drive A:, even if this file is also present on the hard disk. You will probably want to copy COMMAND.COM from the boot disk onto the hard disk and change the default location of this file with the MS-DOS SET COMSPEC command. In that way you can avoid having to keep track of which floppy is in the drive, and in addition, COMMAND.COM will be loaded into memory much faster from the hard disk. To instruct the operating system to look for COMMAND.COM in a subdirectory called DOS on drive C:, you would use the following command, either at the MS-DOS prompt or in the AUTOEXEC.BAT file:

```
SET COMSPEC = C:\DOS\COMMAND.COM
```

For the advanced user working at command level, the ability to issue

DOS commands from the dot prompt is mostly a convenience. In a dBASE III PLUS program, the RUN command has far greater potential: it allows you to provide access to DOS commands in a menu-driven environment with a user interface that is consistent with the rest of your application. How many DOS commands should be built into a system depends largely on the expertise and needs of the users. At the very least, you should provide options for backing up the data bases and restoring the files from the backup disks in the event of a system crash. Placing the backup option in the Main Menu decreases the likelihood that this important task will be neglected, partly because running it from the menu is easy enough for anyone to do. Also, seeing the option on the menu serves as a daily reminder to the operators, especially if the display includes the date the system was last backed up.

If you wish to add only a few DOS commands to an application, you can easily place them all in the Main Menu (as will be shown for the National Widgets system). To provide a more comprehensive set of command options, you could instead create a separate Utility Menu. This menu could be called from the Main Menu, or it could serve as a menu-driven, front-end program that insulates the user completely from DOS. If you choose this approach, you can start up the program each time the computer is booted by placing the appropriate command in the AUTOEXEC.BAT file. The menu of DOS commands will thus become the user's first entry point into the system, and the users can select your application's Main Menu as one of the options from this menu.

For the convenience of the more advanced users of your application, you might also want to provide the flexibility to enter and run *any* DOS command or program from one of the menus. You can do this by storing the user's command in a memory variable and invoking it as a macro. A simplified command sequence would look like this:

```
store space(40) to MCOMMAND
@ 10,10 say "Enter any DOS command" get MCOMMAND
read
run &MCOMMAND
```

In the National Widgets system, commands will be added to the Main Menu to allow the users to back up the data bases, restore the data from the backups, and execute any other DOS command using the macro technique just described. The new version of the Main Menu program, NWMENU2.PRG, is listed in Figure 23-2. In order to accommodate the additional options, the menu screen has been rearranged slightly, with

```
* NWMENU2.PRG
* SECOND VERSION OF MAIN MENU PROGRAM FOR ACCOUNTS RECEIVABLE SYSTEM
* WRITTEN BY:  M.LISKIN       04/11/86

clear all
set talk off
set status off
set safety off
set deleted on

set default to c
set bell off
set confirm off
set delimiters on
set delimiters to "[]"
set intensity on
set color to W, W+

store 0 to MSELECT

do NWSETUP1

clear
@  6,10 to 12,70 double
@  8,27 say "  National Widgets, Inc."
@ 10,27 say "Accounts Receivable System"

@ 15,24 say "Today is " + cdow(date()) + ", " + cmonth(date()) + " " + ;
        str(day(date()),2) + ", " + str(year(date()),4)
@ 16,0
wait "                         Press any key to display the Main Menu"

do while .T.

   clear
   text

             National Widgets, Inc.  -  Accounts Receivable System

                                 Main Menu


                    ( 1) - Customer Information Menu
                    ( 2) - Order Processing Menu
                    ( 3) - Financial Transaction Menu
                    (10) - Reindex All Data Bases
                    (11) - Customize System-Wide Options
                    (12) - Back Up Data to Floppy Disks  (Last Done         )
                    (13) - Restore Data from Floppy Disks
                    (14) - Run DOS Commands or Programs

                    (77) - Get Help

                    (88) - Exit to dBASE III PLUS Command Level
                    (99) - Exit to MS-DOS Operating System
   endtext

   @  1, 0 to 24,79 double
```

Figure 23-2. The new Main Menu program

```
   @  3, 1 to  3,78
   @  5, 1 to  5,78
   @ 22, 1 to 22,78
   @ 13,68 say MPBACKUP
   store Ø to MSELECT
   @ 23,27 say "Please enter your selection  " get MSELECT picture "99"
   read

   do case

      case MSELECT = 1
         do NWCMENU1

      case MSELECT = 2
         do NWOMENU

      case MSELECT = 3
         do NWTMENU

      case MSELECT = 1Ø
         do NWREIND2

      case MSELECT = 11
         do NWSETUP1

      case MSELECT = 12
         do NWBACKUP

      case MSELECT = 13
         do NWRESTOR

      case MSELECT = 14
         do NWRUNDOS

      case MSELECT = 77
         do NWHELP1 with "NWMENU", 77

      case MSELECT = 88
         clear
         set talk on
         set status on
         set safety on
         set deleted off
         cancel

      case MSELECT = 99
         clear
         quit

      otherwise
         @ 23,1Ø say "Not a valid selection -- Press any key to try again"
         wait ""

   endcase

enddo          [ .T. ]

return
```

Figure 23-2. The new Main Menu program (*continued*)

some of the blank lines removed and the related options grouped together and renumbered. Notice that a HELP command has also been added to the menu as option 77. (Two ways of writing the NWHELP.PRG program called by this version of the menu will be presented later in this chapter.) All three of the DOS command options were implemented as separate programs, although in their simplest forms they could be carried out with only a few commands placed directly in the CASEs in NWMENU2.PRG. Separate programs were used instead, to facilitate the addition of amenities such as an on-screen explanation of each program's purpose and, for the backup program, a calculation of the number of disks required to back up all of the data base files.

Programs to Back Up the Data Bases And Restore the Files From the Backup

The backup program was added to the National Widgets Main Menu as option 12. Next to the option description on the menu screen, the date the system was last backed up is displayed to remind the users not to allow too much time to elapse between backups. This date, stored in the memory variable MPBACKUP, will be updated each time the backup program is run. It may be declared PUBLIC and created initially, along with the other systemwide options, in the NWSETUP1.PRG program written in Chapter 21. When the system is first installed, it is reasonable to assume that the data bases have not yet been backed up, and to give MPBACKUP a blank initial value as follows:

```
store ctod(" ") to MPBACKUP
```

To help ensure that the user does not start this procedure without enough formatted floppy disks to complete it, the backup program must calculate the combined size of all of the data base files in the system and inform the operator how many disks will be required. As described in Chapter 2, in the estimate of the total disk space required by an application, the size of a dBASE III PLUS data base is approximately equal to the number of records in the file multiplied by the record length. Both of these numbers can be obtained through dBASE III PLUS functions: the number of records in a file can be expressed as the RECCOUNT( ) function, and the record length as RECSIZE( ).

A data base is actually a little larger than the number obtained by multiplying RECCOUNT( ) by RECSIZE( ). Recall that dBASE III PLUS stores a description of the structure of the file at the beginning of the .DBF file. This header consists of 32 bytes of information describing each field in the data base, as well as a constant portion 34 bytes long, which contains the date of last update, record size, number of records in the file, and other information used internally by dBASE III PLUS. You could thus calculate the exact size of the header as 34 + (32 * the number of fields in the file).

For the purpose of the backup program, you can simply assume that each of the data base files has a header no larger than 1000 bytes—or 2000 bytes if your application uses several files with many fields. If you do decide to carry out a more precise calculation that takes into account the exact size of the file header, you can use the FIELD( ) function to determine the number of fields in a data base. A procedure called FILESIZE that computes the size of a data base, including the header, is listed in Figure 23-3.

This procedure calculates the size of the data base in use in the current work area (which must be opened by the calling program) and returns this value to the calling program through the parameter MFILESIZE. Note that the file size stored in MFILESIZE may be used for any purpose. You could, for example, call the FILESIZE procedure before copying a data base to another subdirectory on the hard disk in order to determine whether enough disk space was available for the copy by comparing MFILESIZE with the value of the DISKSPACE( ) function.

The procedure begins by initializing the memory variable MHEADER with the size of the fixed portion of the file header, 34 bytes. Another memory variable, MFIELD, is initialized with a value of 1. This variable is used in the DO WHILE loop to count up to 128, the maximum number of fields in a dBASE III PLUS data base. The actual number of fields in the file is determined by testing the value of the expression FIELD(MFIELD), which returns the name of the data base field identified by number as MFIELD. For example, in the National Widgets Customer File, if MFIELD has the value 2, FIELD(MFIELD) will evaluate to a character string containing the name of field number 2 in the data base, or "COMPANY". If the field does not exist, the FIELD function returns a null string. The FILESIZE procedure therefore tests the length of the expression FIELD(MFIELD); if it is 0, there are no more fields in the structure, and

```
procedure FILESIZE

parameters MFILESIZE

store 1  to MFIELD
store 34 to MHEADER

do while MFIELD <= 128
   if len(field(MFIELD)) = 0
      exit
   else
      store MHEADER + 32 to MHEADER
   endif
   store MFIELD + 1 to MFIELD
enddo

store MHEADER + (reccount() * recsize()) + 1000 to MFILESIZE

return
```

Figure 23-3. A procedure to calculate the size of a data base file

the procedure uses EXIT to escape from the DO WHILE loop without taking the time to count all the way to 128. If the length of the field name is not 0, the value of MHEADER (the size of the header) is increased by 32. When the DO WHILE loop terminates, MHEADER contains the size of the file header.

Because of the way that MS-DOS keeps track of the sizes and locations of your disk files, the actual size of a data base may be somewhat larger than the exact size required by dBASE III PLUS. The FILESIZE procedure therefore calculates the size of the file by multiplying RECCOUNT( ) by RECSIZE( ) and adding to the result the size of the header (MHEADER) plus an extra 1000 bytes.

Estimating the size of the .DBT file that contains the text of the memo fields in files like the National Widgets Customer File presents a potentially more serious problem. There is no way to determine directly the size of a file in bytes, so the backup program will assume, as in the file size estimate in Chapter 2, that approximately half of the customer records contain entries in the memo field and that they will average less than 512 bytes in length (the minimum space allocated to a memo field if any text at all is filled in). Because of the way that memo fields are updated, the memo file may actually be quite a bit larger. When a memo field is edited, the old value is not deleted from the .DBT file or overwritten by the new text. Instead, it is marked as obsolete, and the new text is added to the end of the .DBT file. If memo fields are edited repeatedly, the .DBT file may grow very large. The only way to compact it is to COPY the data base and delete the original file, since the COPY command processes only current memo field entries, just as it ignores deleted records. Depending on what you know about an application and the users, you may want to add to the system a program to periodically COPY each file that contains memo fields, or you might just use a larger estimate in the backup program.

Finally, the backup program must account for the memory variable file, NWMEMORY.MEM; a conservative estimate of 3000 bytes should suffice for most applications.

The backup program, NWBACKUP.PRG, is listed in Figure 23-4. The variable MBYTES, which accumulates the combined size of all of the data bases in the system, is initialized with a value of 3000, the estimated size of NWMEMORY.MEM. For each data base, the program calls the FILESIZE procedure to calculate the total file size, and adds this number into the value of MBYTES. For the Customer File the estimated size of the .DBT file is also included in the computation. Finally, MBYTES is divided by 360,000 (the approximate capacity of a DOS 2 disk) to arrive at the total number of floppies required for the backup. This calculation yields a fractional number of disks, but it would only confuse the user to be informed that, for example, 4.38 disks are needed. The program therefore uses the INT function to take the *integer portion* of the result of the calculation—that is, to drop the fraction—and then add 1 to this number. If MBYTES / 360000 equals 4.38, the INT function yields 4, and adding 1 gives the desired total of 5 disks.

To discourage the operator from simply giving up if not enough disks are available, the program explains that the best thing to do is exit to the menu and use the "Run DOS Commands" option to format more floppies. The program even tells the user exactly what command to type, so that no part of the backup procedure requires any knowledge of DOS commands. If you wished, you could also give the user the option to run the FORMAT program directly from NWBACKUP.PRG. The program assumes that BACKUP.COM is present in the dBASE III PLUS subdirectory or can be accessed via an existing PATH command and that the floppy drive is called A:, as is the case in most IBM and IBM-compatible hard disk systems.

Next the program asks if the operator is ready to back up the system. If the answer is Y (yes), three RUN BACKUP commands are used to back

```
* NWBACKUP.PRG
* PROGRAM TO BACK UP ALL DATA BASES AND MEMORY VARIABLES TO FLOPPY DISKS
* WRITTEN BY:  M.LISKIN       05/23/86


clear
@  5,10 say "Calculating file sizes -- Please do not interrupt"

store 3000 to MBYTES
store 0    to MFILESIZE

use NWCUST
do FILESIZE with MFILESIZE
store MBYTES + MFILESIZE + 0.5 * 512 * reccount() to MBYTES

use NWINVENT
do FILESIZE with MFILESIZE
store MBYTES + MFILESIZE to MBYTES

use NWORDER
do FILESIZE with MFILESIZE
store MBYTES + MFILESIZE to MBYTES

use NWTXN
do FILESIZE with MFILESIZE
store MBYTES + MFILESIZE to MBYTES

use NWORDHST
do FILESIZE with MFILESIZE
store MBYTES + MFILESIZE to MBYTES

use NWTXNHST
do FILESIZE with MFILESIZE
store MBYTES + MFILESIZE to MBYTES

use NWOSTATS
do FILESIZE with MFILESIZE
store MBYTES + MFILESIZE to MBYTES

use NWCODES
do FILESIZE with MFILESIZE
store MBYTES + MFILESIZE to MBYTES

use

store int(MBYTES / 360000) + 1 to MDISKS

@  8,10 say "You will need " + str(MDISKS,3) + " blank, formatted disk(s)"
text

          If you do not have enough blank disks available, you
          should answer "N" (for "no") to the question, "Are you
          ready to back up the data bases?"

          You can format disks without exiting from dBASE III by
          choosing Main Menu Option 14 - Run DOS Commands or
          Programs.  The DOS command for formatting disks is:

              FORMAT A:

endtext
```

Figure 23-4. A program to back up the data bases

```
store .F. to MCONFIRM
do ASK1 with 21, 10, "Are you ready to back up the data bases? (Y/N)";
            MCONFIRM

if MCONFIRM
   run BACKUP NW*.MEM A:
   run BACKUP NW*.DBF A:/A
   run BACKUP NW*.DBT A:/A
   store date() to MPBACKUP
   save all like MP* to NWMEMORY
   wait "Backup complete -- Press any key to return to the menu"
endif

return
```

Figure 23-4. A program to back up the data bases (*continued*)

up the files. Notice that the NW prefix is included in all of the RUN BACKUP commands, in case there are other data bases or memory variable files in the same subdirectory on the hard disk. (*Note:* The use of the /A option in the second and third commands instructs DOS to *add* the new set of files to the same backup disks rather than start a new set.) When the backup is complete, the current date, DATE( ), is stored in the MPBACKUP variable used to display on the Main Menu screen the date the system was last backed up. Finally, a message is displayed for the operator, and a WAIT command pauses the program until a key is pressed, after which you return to the menu.

Main Menu option 13 calls the NWRESTOR.PRG program, listed in Figure 23-5, to recopy the data bases onto the hard disk from the backup floppies. This program is short and simple, but it is very important to include it in the system's menu, to enable any operator to recover easily from a disk crash. The program first issues a warning message that explains the purpose of the program and reminds the operator that the data from the floppies will overwrite the files on the hard disk. Confirmation is required before beginning the file restoration, to make sure the user understands the consequences of this potentially destructive command and to provide a chance to back out if the option was selected by mistake.

In most applications it is not necessary to spend extra time and disks to back up the index files, since they can always be rebuilt from scratch. In fact, an option has already been provided (Main Menu option 10) for this purpose. After the NWRESTOR.PRG program copies the data back onto

```
* NWRESTOR.PRG
* PROGRAM TO RESTORE DATA TO HARD DISK FROM BACKUP FLOPPIES
* WRITTEN BY:  M.LISKIN        05/23/86

clear
text
                            *** CAUTION ***

          This program restores the data bases from backup floppy disks,
          and then rebuilds all of the indexes for these files.

          If you run this program, the data bases on the hard disk will be
          overwritten by the files on the backup disks.

endtext

store .F. to MCONFIRM
do ASK1 with 15, 10, "Are you sure you want to restore the data bases? (Y/N)";
             MCONFIRM

if MCONFIRM
   run RESTORE A: C:
   do NWREIND2
   wait "File restoration complete -- Press any key to return to the menu"
endif

return
```

Figure 23-5. A program to restore the data bases from the backup disks

the hard disk, it automatically invokes the reindexing program so that the user does not have to remember this step. Figure 23-6 lists NWREIND2.PRG, a new version of the NWREIND1.PRG program originally written in Chapter 7. This program remains substantially the same, except for the more esthetic and informative status messages and the addition of the commands required to rebuild the indexes for the two new data bases, NWCODES.DBF and NWOSTATS.DBF, that did not yet exist when NWREIND1.PRG was written.

A Program to Run User-Specified DOS Commands

Figure 23-7 lists a program, NWRUNDOS.PRG, that allows the operator to access any MS-DOS commands or external programs from within a dBASE III PLUS application. This program is called from the National

```
* NWREIND2.PRG
* PROGRAM TO REINDEX ALL NATIONAL WIDGETS SYSTEM DATA BASES
* WRITTEN BY:    M.LISKIN          5/23/86


set talk on

use NWCUST
clear
@ 10, 5 say "Rebuilding Customer File Indexes -- Please do not interrupt"
@ 12, 5 say "This file currently contains " + str(reccount(),5) + " records"
index on ACCOUNT to NWCACCT
index on ZIP to NWCZIP

use NWINVENT
clear
@ 10, 5 say "Rebuilding Inventory File Index -- Please do not interrupt"
@ 12, 5 say "This file currently contains " + str(reccount(),5) + " records"
index on CATEGORY + PARTNUMBER to NWICATPT

use NWTXN
clear
@ 10, 5 say "Rebuilding Transaction File Indexes -- Please do not interrupt"
@ 12, 5 say "This file currently contains " + str(reccount(),5) + " records"
index on ACCOUNT + INVOICE to NWTACCT
index on INVOICE to NWTINVC

use NWORDER
clear
@ 10, 5 say "Rebuilding Order File Indexes -- Please do not interrupt"
@ 12, 5 say "This file currently contains " + str(reccount(),5) + " records"
index on ACCOUNT + INVOICE to NWOACCT
index on INVOICE to NWOINVC

use NWTXNHST
clear
@ 10, 5 say;
  "Rebuilding Transaction History File Indexes -- Please do not interrupt"
@ 12, 5 say "This file currently contains " + str(reccount(),5) + " records"
index on ACCOUNT + INVOICE to NWTHACCT
index on INVOICE to NWTHINVC

use NWORDHST
clear
@ 10, 5 say;
  "Rebuilding Order History File Indexes -- Please do not interrupt"
@ 12, 5 say "This file currently contains " + str(reccount(),5) + " records"
index on ACCOUNT + INVOICE to NWOHACCT
index on INVOICE to NWOHINVC

use NWCODES
clear
@ 10, 5 say "Rebuilding Code File Index -- Please do not interrupt"
@ 12, 5 say "This file currently contains " + str(reccount(),5) + " records"
index on CODETYPE + CODE to NWCODES

use NWOSTATS
clear
@ 10, 5 say;
  "Rebuilding Order Statistics File Index -- Please do not interrupt"
@ 12, 5 say "This file currently contains " + str(reccount(),5) + " records"
index on CATEGORY to NWOSTATS

use
set talk off

return
```

Figure 23-6. A program to reindex all of the data bases

```
* NWRUNDOS.PRG
* PROGRAM TO RUN USER-SPECIFIED DOS COMMANDS OR PROGRAMS
* WRITTEN BY:  M.LISKIN        09/05/85


clear
do while .T.

   clear
   store space(75) to MCOMMAND
   @ 10,10 say "Enter DOS command, or press <RETURN> to return to the menu"
   @ 12, 1 get MCOMMAND
   read

   if MCOMMAND = " "
      exit
   else
      run &MCOMMAND
      wait
   endif

enddo

return
```

Figure 23-7. A program to run a user-specified DOS command or program

Widgets system Main Menu as option 14. The NWRUNDOS.PRG program assumes that the user might want to execute more than one DOS command before returning to the menu, so it sets up an "endless" loop with DO WHILE .T. Within this loop the program clears the screen and initializes the memory variable MCOMMAND, which is used to collect the operator's DOS command line. If the user leaves this field blank, an EXIT command exits from the DO WHILE loop; since there are no other program statements following the ENDDO, the RETURN command returns control to the Main Menu program. If a DOS command is entered, it is executed with RUN &MCOMMAND, followed by a WAIT to pause the program long enough to allow the operator to read or print the screen. When a key is pressed, the program returns to the top of the loop to ask for another command.

The NWRUNDOS.PRG program makes no attempt to test or validate the user's DOS command line, since it is conceivable that almost any command or program might be run this way. Giving the user this much freedom does not entail any more serious risks to the data base than would allowing the user to access the same commands from the dot prompt or at the DOS level. While it is certainly possible to enter a destructive command like ERASE *.DBF, it is unlikely that an ordinary typographical or syntactical error will damage the integrity of the data bases. Entering a wrong command line will in most cases simply result in the standard MS-DOS error message "Bad command or filename." In the worst case, if typing an incorrect command or running a faulty program causes the system to "hang up," it is safe to reboot or turn off the computer, since the CLOSE DATABASES command in each of the system's menu programs ensures that no data base files are left open.

CREATING AN ON-LINE HELP SYSTEM

This section describes two ways to add an extensive on-line help system to a dBASE III PLUS application. The goal is to allow the user to ask for help at various points while running the programs and in response to display a screen (or series of screens) of text describing the purpose of a program or command option or providing more detailed instructions for carrying out a complex procedure. You may have used commercial software packages that designate a key, usually one of the ten function keys, as an instant help key. By pressing this key, you can obtain context-sensitive help, an explanation of the specific command or command option you were using at the moment you requested help.

Implementing an instant help key in a dBASE III PLUS program is complicated by the fact that dBASE III PLUS reacts differently to interruptions when waiting for full-screen input from its response while a program is running. The method described in Chapter 21 for allowing the operator to interrupt a report or label run could easily be adapted to display a help screen when the "interrupt" key is pressed. However, the user would much more frequently want to ask for help when dBASE III PLUS is processing one or more @ ... SAY ... GET commands, and in this situation, a single keystroke cannot be detected. With any pending GETs, pressing the various full-screen edit keys moves the cursor or activates the READ command, while pressing any other key (including any of the special function keys) on the keyboard simply enters data into the field at the current cursor position. You cannot use ON ESCAPE to branch to a help procedure, because pressing ESC is one of the full-screen edit commands—it bypasses the remaining GETs and activates the READ.

Consider what you would have to do to provide instantaneous context-sensitive help at any point in a file update and inquiry program like the NWCUPD3.PRG program that maintains the National Widgets Customer File. Suppose, for example, that you wanted to display a help message describing the particular field the operator is about to enter or edit. The only way to do this is to assign a special code that could be entered into any field in order to request the help screen. To simplify the entry of this code, you could even assign it to one of the ten function keys. Because data collected with an @ ... SAY ... GET command is available to a program only after a subsequent READ, you would have to follow *each* GET command with a READ, in order to determine if the designated help code had been entered into the field, and display the appropriate help screen. But by doing this, you would completely defeat the dBASE III PLUS full-screen edit capability that makes data entry so friendly and forgiving. (This is the same dilemma faced in Chapter 20 with validating data fields at the time of entry.)

A reasonable compromise is to provide in each of your application's menus a HELP option that allows the operator to ask for an explanation of any of the other menu selections. This option can be called by number, like any other menu option. In the NWMENU2.PRG program, the help program is invoked by choosing 77 from the menu. In file update and inquiry programs, there are two ways of implementing the HELP option. One is to add an option that is selected by typing a single letter (H), just like any of the other command options (such as SEARCH, NEXT, and ADD). With this system, to request help in the middle of entering a record, the user would have to exit from the full-screen edit mode with ESC, CTRL-W, or CTRL-END, and then choose the H option. As an alternative, you could use the READKEY( ) function, which detects which key the user pressed to exit from the full-screen edit process, and designate one of these keys as a HELP key. This way, the user could press the HELP key at any moment to ask for assistance instead of having to complete the entry and then ask for help. In either case, the help screen might include an explanation of the command options or a description of the type of data to be entered into each of the fields in the data base.

Displaying the Help Messages With TEXT ... ENDTEXT

Option 77 in the National Widgets Main Menu program calls a help program named NWHELP1.PRG. In an application that requires relatively few help messages, this help program could simply use a series of TEXT

. . . ENDTEXT structures to display the text of the help screens. If you have already written the system documentation, some of these help screens can be extracted directly from the user manual; if not, you can create the help text first and later incorporate this material into your printed manual. Although you could write a separate help program for each menu or program, the National Widgets system uses a more general approach in which a single help program may be called from anywhere in the application. A version of this program, NWHELP1.PRG, that includes help screens for each of the Main Menu options, two of the Customer Information Menu options, and the Customer Update and Inquiry program, is listed in Figure 23-8.

To determine which help screen to display, the NWHELP1.PRG program uses two memory variables, MPROGRAM and MOPTION, which receive their initial values as parameters from the calling program. MPROGRAM contains the name of the calling program, and MOPTION specifies the option within the calling program for which help has been or will be requested. The MOPTION variable gives you the flexibility to display more than one help screen for any program in the system and to allow either the programmer or the user to specify the screen.

When the help program has been called from the Main Menu, the user should be able to request information on more than one menu option before exiting the help system. A common reason for asking for help is uncertainty about which of two similar programs or reports to use in a particular context; in this situation the ability to view several help screens one after the other is preferable to returning to the menu after reading each explanation. The NWHELP1.PRG program therefore sets up a DO WHILE .T. loop, within which the user is asked, if appropriate, which help screen to display. It is easy to determine whether or not NWHELP1.PRG was called from a menu: if it has been, the character string "MENU" is contained in (is a substring of) the parameter MPROGRAM. You can test for this using the $ operator:

```
if "MENU" $ MPROGRAM
```

If NWHELP1.PRG was called from a menu, the variable MOPTION, which is used to collect the operator's choice of help screens, is reinitialized with a value of 0. This ensures that even the first time through the loop, the value passed from the menu program to MOPTION is disregarded. As in many of the other programs in the system, leaving this field blank (that is, 0) is the way the operator signals the desire to exit the help program and return to the menu.

```
* NWHELP1.PRG
* PROGRAM TO DISPLAY HELP SCREENS DESCRIBING MENU OPTIONS
* WRITTEN BY:  M.LISKIN       09/05/85

parameters MPROGRAM, MOPTION

do while .T.

   clear

   if "MENU" $ MPROGRAM
      store 0 to MOPTION
      @ 10,10 say "Which menu option do you need help with? " get MOPTION;
                  picture "99"
      @ 11,10 say "(or Press <RETURN> to Quit)"
      read
      if MOPTION = 0
         exit
      endif
   endif
   clear

DO CASE

CASE MPROGRAM + str(MOPTION,2) = "NWMENU 1"
TEXT
Main Menu Option 1 - Customer Information Menu
----------------------------------------------

Choose this option to enter the Customer Information Menu.  This menu
contains options which allow you to enter, update, display, and print
customer information.  From this menu, you will be able to:

     Add New Customers
     Inquire, Edit, Delete, Recall Customers
     Print Customer Reference List
     Print Rolodex Cards
     Print Customer Equipment Profile
     Print Mailing Labels 1-Up or 4-Up
     Copy the Customer File to Word Processor Format
     Zero Year-to-Date Totals
     Archive and Delete Inactive Customers

ENDTEXT

CASE MPROGRAM + str(MOPTION,2) = "NWMENU 2"
TEXT
Main Menu Option 2 - Order Processing Menu
------------------------------------------

Choose this option to enter the Order Processing Menu.  This menu contains
options which allow you to enter, update, display, and print order data.
You may also print invoices, create invoice transactions, and post the
invoice data to the customer records. From this menu, you will be able to:

     Enter New Orders
     Print Current Order List by Invoice Number
     Print Order Reference List by Invoice Number
     Print Order Reference List by Customer
     Print Orders for Warehouse
     Print Invoices
     Post Invoice Data to Customer File
     Purge and Reinitialize the Order History File

ENDTEXT
```

Figure 23-8. Displaying help messages with TEXT ... ENDTEXT

```
CASE MPROGRAM + str(MOPTION,2) = "NWMENU 3"
TEXT
Main Menu Option 3 - Financial Transaction Menu
-----------------------------------------------

Choose this option to enter the Financial Transaction Menu.  This menu
contains options which allow you to enter, update, display, and print
invoice and payment data, and customer statements.  From this menu, you
will be able to:

     Enter Invoice Transactions
     Enter Payment Transactions
     Print Current Transaction List
     Print Transaction History List
     Print Invoice Register
     Print Cash Receipts Listing
     Print Aging Report
     Print Order Summary by Category
     Print Order Summary by Type of Equipment
     Print Accounting Summary
     Print Statements
     Update Transaction History File
     Purge and Reinitialize Transaction History File

ENDTEXT


CASE MPROGRAM + str(MOPTION,2) = "NWMENU10"
TEXT
Main Menu Option 10 - Reindex all Data Bases
----------------------------------------------------

Choose this option to reconstruct all of the index files for all of the
data bases in the system.

This option can help you recover from disasters such as damage to the
data bases caused by a hardware or software crash, a power failure, or
an operator turning off or rebooting the system with one or more files
open.  You should run this option if the system is ever turned off or
rebooted for any reason with any dBASE III program in the system running
(i.e., one of the menus is NOT on the screen).  You should also run this
option if you ever see either of these two dBASE III error messages:

     Record out of range
     End of file encountered

Both of these messages indicate that one of the indexes associated with a data
base does not match the data contained in the file.

ENDTEXT


CASE MPROGRAM + str(MOPTION,2) = "NWMENU11"
TEXT
Main Menu Option 11 - Customize System-Wide Options
---------------------------------------------------

Choose this option to customize the system for your hardware, and for
your company.  You will be able to change the following:

     Your company name and address (for printing a return address
       on letters, invoices, and statements
     The valid two-letter state abbreviations
     The default state, area code, and sales tax rate for new customers
     The default left margin for letters
```

Figure 23-8. Displaying help messages with TEXT ... ENDTEXT (*continued*)

```
     The next available invoice number
     Up to 11 inventory category codes and descriptions

ENDTEXT


CASE MPROGRAM + str(MOPTION,2) = "NWMENU12"
TEXT
Main Menu Option 12 - Back Up Data to Floppy Disks
--------------------------------------------------

Choose this option to back up the data base files and memory variables
to floppy disks.  The files should be backed up after any data entry
session which results in significant changes to the files or changes
which would be difficult to reconstruct.
To run this option, you must have at least 384K of memory in your
computer, and COMMAND.COM must be present in the current subdirectory
or on a floppy disk in drive A:.  The program BACKUP.COM (supplied on
your DOS system disk) must be available, either in the current
subdirectory, or in any subdirectory, provided that you have used the
DOS PATH command to allow DOS to access files in the directory in
which BACKUP.COM resides.

You must also have ready enough blank, formatted disks to accommodate
your data bases.  The program calculates the number of disks which
will be required and allows you to exit if you do Not have enough
disks.  To format disks, you can either exit to DOS, or choose Option
14 - Run DOS Commands or Programs.  The DOS command for formatting
disks is:   FORMAT A:

ENDTEXT


CASE MPROGRAM + str(MOPTION,2) = "NWMENU13"
TEXT
Main Menu Option 13 - Restore Data from Floppy Disks
----------------------------------------------------

Choose this option to restore the data base files and memory
variables from the backup floppy disks.  This option should be run if
the data on the hard disk is damaged by a hardware or software
failure, or if you have made a serious data entry error which would be
difficult to correct.

To run this option, you must have at least 384K of memory in your
computer, and COMMAND.COM must be present in the current subdirectory
or on a floppy disk in drive A:.  RESTORE.COM must be available either
be in the current subdirectory, or in any subdirectory, provided that
you have used the DOS PATH command to allow DOS to access files in the
directory in which RESTORE.COM resides.

If you run this program, the data bases on the hard disk will be
overwritten by the files from the backup disks.

After restoring the files from the backup disks, all indexes are
automatically rebuilt.

ENDTEXT


CASE MPROGRAM + str(MOPTION,2) = "NWMENU14"
TEXT
```

Figure 23-8. Displaying help messages with TEXT ... ENDTEXT *(continued)*

```
Main Menu Option 14 - Run DOS Commands or Programs
--------------------------------------------------

Choose this option to run any MS-DOS command or external program
without exiting from dBASE III.

To run this option, you must have enough memory in your computer in
addition to the 256K required by dBASE III to load COMMAND.COM and the
external program into RAM together with dBASE III. COMMAND.COM must be
present in the current subdirectory or on a floppy disk in drive A:,
and the program you wish to run must be in the current subdirectory,
or it may be in any subdirectory, provided that you have used the DOS
PATH command to allow DOS to access files in the directory in which it
resides.

ENDTEXT


CASE MPROGRAM + str(MOPTION,2) = "NWMENU88"
TEXT

Main Menu Option 88 - Exit to dBASE III Command Level
-----------------------------------------------------

Choose this option to exit from the menu system, but remain in dBASE III
to work at command level (at the dot prompt).

To exit from dBASE III to the operating system, you can type "QUIT" at
the dot prompt.

ENDTEXT


CASE MPROGRAM + str(MOPTION,2) = "NWMENU99"
TEXT

Main Menu Option 99 - Exit to MS-DOS Operating System
-----------------------------------------------------

Choose this option to exit from the menu system and from dBASE III, and
return to the operating system.

ENDTEXT


CASE MPROGRAM + str(MOPTION,2) = "NWCMENU 1"
TEXT
Customer Menu Option 1 - Customer File Update and Inquiry
---------------------------------------------------------

Choose this option to enter new customers into the system, search for
existing customers by Account Number, edit existing customer records, mark
customers for deletion from the system, and recall customers previously
marked for deletion.  A customer must be present in the Customer File
before you can enter orders or print invoices for the customer.

This program will not allow you to change information which is normally
updated by entering invoice or payment transactions (the year-to-date and
overall dollar totals, and the last order date).

This program will not allow you to delete a customer with a non-zero
balance, or one with transaction activity in the current month.  This is
```

Figure 23-8. Displaying help messages with TEXT ... ENDTEXT *(continued)*

```
the only program in the system which allows you to view "deleted" customer
records, so that you may use the RECOVER option to recover a customer
which was deleted by mistake.

ENDTEXT

wait "Press any key for more information ..."
clear

TEXT
This program gives you the following commands:

     (S)earch    - Search for an existing customer by Account Number
     (C)hange    - Change the data for the customer displayed on the screen
     (N)ext      - Page forward to the next customer in alphabetical order
                   by Account Number
     (P)revious  - Page backward to the previous customer in alphabetical
                   order by Account Number
     (D)elete    - Mark the customer displayed on the screen for deletion
     (R)ecover   - Recover ("undelete") the customer displayed on the
                   screen
     (A)dd       - Add a new customer to the file
     (H)elp      - Display a help screen describing the customer fields
     (M)emo      - Display the COMMENTS field for the customer

ENDTEXT

CASE MPROGRAM + str(MOPTION,2) = "NWCMENU10"
TEXT
Print Customer Reference List
-----------------------------

Choose this option to print a Customer Reference List which contains
all of the information on file about the customer, together with all
of the customer's financial transaction history.

You may print customers one at a time, or you may print the entire
Customer File in alphabetical order by account number.  If you choose
to print the entire file,you may specify the first customer to print
by account number.

The report is printed on 14" x 11" continuous paper.  If you choose to
print single customers, each customer begins on a new page.

If you need to interrupt the report, press the <ESC> key.  When the
message "*** INTERRUPTED ***" appears on the screen, type "QUIT" at
the dot prompt to exit to DOS.  Then, re-enter dBASE III by typing
"DBASE NWMENU".

ENDTEXT


CASE MPROGRAM + str(MOPTION,2) = "NWCUPD3 1"
TEXT
Customer File Update and Inquiry
--------------------------------

This program gives you the following commands:

     (S)earch    - Search for an existing customer by Account Number
     (C)hange    - Change the data for the customer displayed on the screen
     (N)ext      - Page forward to the next customer in alphabetical order
                   by Account Number
     (P)revious  - Page backward to the previous customer in alphabetical
                   order by Account Number
```

Figure 23-8. Displaying help messages with TEXT ... ENDTEXT (*continued*)

```
     (D)elete    - Mark the customer displayed on the screen for deletion
     (R)ecover   - Recover ("undelete") the customer displayed on the
                   screen
     (A)dd       - Add a new customer to the file
     (H)elp      - Display a help screen describing the customer fields
     (M)emo      - Display the COMMENTS field for the customer

ENDTEXT

wait "Press any key for more information ..."
clear

TEXT
The Customer File Fields:

PROMPT              LENGTH      EXPLANATION
---------------------------------------------------------------
Acct Code             10        A unique code used to identify the
                                  customer and alphabetize customer
                                  lists.  Use part of company name
                                  on an individual's last name.
Company               30        Company name, if any.
Address (2 fields)    25        Two lines for the street address.
City                  20        City.
State                  2        Postal state abbreviation.  Auto-
                                  matically capitalized.
Zip                    5        Zip code.
Contact               25        Name of person to contact regarding
                                  orders.
Telephone          3 + 8        Area code and telephone number.
Equipment             25        Type of computer equipment.
Sales Tax Rate         5        Sales tax rate, as a percent.  Must
                                  be between 0.00 and 10.00

ENDTEXT

wait "Press any key for more information ..."
clear

TEXT
The Customer File Fields (cont.):

PROMPT              LENGTH      EXPLANATION
---------------------------------------------------------------

The following may not be edited through this program.  They are
updated automatically when you post transactions and payments.

Y-T-D Invoices        12        Year-to-date dollar invoice total.
Y-T-D Payments        12        Year-to-date dollar payment total.
Total Invoices        12        Cumulative total invoices.
Total Payments        12        Cumulative total payments.
First Order Date       8        Date of customer's first order.
Last Order Date        8        Date of customer's most recent order.
Balance               12        Balance currently owed.

ENDTEXT

OTHERWISE
   @ 10,10 say "Not a valid option -- Press any key to try again"
   wait ""
   loop

ENDCASE
```

Figure 23-8. Displaying help messages with TEXT ... ENDTEXT (*continued*)

```
      wait
      if .not. "MENU" $ MPROGRAM
         return
      endif

   enddo

   return
```

Figure 23-8. Displaying help messages with TEXT ... ENDTEXT (*continued*)

If NWHELP1.PRG is called from any of the individual programs in the system, the precise help screen to display is already known to the calling program: the decision has been made by the programmer based on where in the program help was requested. For example, to add a HELP option to the Customer Update and Inquiry program, you could change the option prompt line to

```
(S)earch (C)hange (N)ext (P)rev (D)el (R)ecover (A)dd (M)emo (H)elp e(X)it
```

The design of the program allows you to make your help messages somewhat context-sensitive. If a program made multiple calls to NWHELP1.PRG, you could invoke the various help screens by assigning different values to the parameter MOPTION. If there is only one help screen, MOPTION could simply be set to 1. In NWCUPD3.PRG the CASE that calls NWHELP1.PRG would therefore look like this:

```
case MOPTION = "H"
   do NWHELP1 with "NWCUPD3", 1
   do NWCSCRN
```

Note that when the help program terminates and control returns to NWCUPD3.PRG, the input screen must be redrawn, just as it is after editing the memo field COMMENTS with the NWCUST5.FMT format file.

Whether the value of MOPTION was passed by the calling program or entered by the user, the screen is cleared and a DO CASE structure is used to select the right help message based on the combination of MPROGRAM and MOPTION. For example, the test for the Main Menu option 2 help screen would look like this:

```
case MPROGRAM + str(MOPTION, 2) = "NWMENU 2"
```

Instead of converting MOPTION to a character string and concatenating it with MPROGRAM, you could also test the two parts of the condition separately:

```
case MPROGRAM = "NWMENU" .and. str(MOPTION, 2) = 2
```

The text of the help screens is displayed using TEXT ... ENDTEXT structures. Because the enclosed text is displayed beginning at the cursor position and continuing to the end without pause, you must make sure that each block of text actually fits on one screen. In NWHELP1.PRG, the longer help messages are divided into two screens—and therefore two TEXT ... ENDTEXT structures—separated by a WAIT command to pause the program so that the operator can read the information and, if desired, print the screen with SHIFT-PRTSC. The message in the WAIT command is phrased to suggest that more information will follow.

If the operator enters an option other than one of the legitimate menu choices, the OTHERWISE clause displays an error message and returns to the top of the loop to ask for MOPTION again. After all of the help text has been displayed, another WAIT command pauses the program long enough to allow the user to read (and perhaps print) the screen. Next, the program again tests to see if the NWHELP1.PRG program was called from a menu. If it was not, the program RETURNs immediately to the calling program; if it was, the main DO WHILE .T. loop is executed again.

Notice that NWHELP1.PRG deviates from the standard capitalization and indentation conventions used throughout the other programs in the National Widgets system. dBASE III PLUS displays the text in a TEXT ... ENDTEXT structure on the screen exactly as it appears in the program: if the entire structure is indented five spaces, the block of text will also be indented five spaces on the screen. To use the full width of the screen, the TEXT ... ENDTEXT structures must therefore begin at the left margin. Because the program does not make use of the indentation normally used to clarify the loop structure, and because the text blocks contain primarily lowercase characters, the CASE, TEXT, and ENDTEXT statements in this program are capitalized to make them stand out from the rest of the program.

This program structure is best suited to an application that contains relatively few help screens that do not change very often. With just the 11 CASEs used in NWHELP1.PRG, the program is already almost 18,000 bytes long. If you ask for help with one of the last few options listed, it takes a noticeable amount of time for dBASE III PLUS to find the right CASE and display the message—and the program presented in Figure 23-8 accounts for only a small fraction of the on-line help the National Widgets system could and should provide. When there are numerous help messages, which must be called from many of the programs in a system, a better strategy is to create a data base to contain the help text.

Displaying Help Messages Stored in a Data Base File

The other viable way to construct the help system is to create a data base that uses a memo field for the text of the help messages. The structure for the help file for the National Widgets system, NWHELP.DBF, is listed in Figure 23-9, together with the index keys. The PROGRAM and OPTION fields correspond to the memory variables MPROGRAM and MOPTION used in the NWHELP1.PRG program. MPROGRAM stores the name of the program to which the help message pertains. If PROGRAM is a menu, the OPTION field contains the menu option number described by the help text. For help messages called by other programs in the system, the OPTION field may be used to differentiate among several screens requested from the same program.

None of the methods you can use to display the memo field HELPMSG allow you to pause the display automatically after filling up one screen with text, so the text of the longer help messages must be divided into two or more records. The SCREEN field is used to number the screens so that they may be displayed consecutively. The key expression for the index file NWHELP.NDX is composed of the fields required to identify the help message text to be displayed (PROGRAM + str(OPTION,2)), and to present the screens in the right order if there is more than one (str(SCREEN,2)). The contents of the NWHELP.DBF file are listed in Figure 23-10. The HELPMSG fields from these records, which are not included in the listing, contain the same text used in the TEXT ... ENDTEXT structures in NWHELP1.PRG.

```
. USE NWHELP INDEX NWHELP

. LIST STRUCTURE TO PRINT

Structure for database: C:NWHELP.dbf
Number of data records:       17
Date of last update   : 05/26/86
Field  Field Name  Type       Width    Dec
    1  PROGRAM     Character      8
    2  OPTION      Numeric        2
    3  SCREEN      Numeric        2
    4  HELPMSG     Memo          10
** Total **                      23



. DISPLAY STATUS TO PRINT

Currently Selected Database:
Select area:  1, Database in Use: C:NWHELP.dbf   Alias:
NWHELP
    Master index file:  C:NWHELP.ndx  Key:
PROGRAM+str(OPTION,2)+str(SCREEN,2)
           Memo file:   C:NWHELP.dbt
          Lock:

File search path:
Default disk drive: C:
Print destination:  PRN:
Margin =     0
Current work area =    1

Press any key to continue...

*** INTERRUPTED ***
```

Figure 23-9. The structure of the help file

The general strategy for using this file is to SEEK the desired combination of PROGRAM and OPTION and then display the HELPMSG field from each of the remaining records that describe this program. After each screen, the program should give the user the option to exit from the help system or display the next screen. Recall that by default, memo field text is displayed using a column width of 50 characters. Since the dBASE III PLUS memo field editor forms the text you type into paragraphs by wrapping the lines at column 67, the help program should use SET

```
. USE NWHELP INDEX NWHELP

. LIST

Record#  PROGRAM   OPTION SCREEN HELPMSG
      1  NWCMENU        1      1 Memo
      2  NWCMENU        1      2 Memo
      3  NWCMENU       10      1 Memo
      4  NWCUPD4        1      1 Memo
      5  NWCUPD4        2      1 Memo
      6  NWCUPD4        2      2 Memo
      7  NWMENU         1      1 Memo
      8  NWMENU         2      1 Memo
      9  NWMENU         3      1 Memo
     10  NWMENU        10      1 Memo
     11  NWMENU        10      2 Memo
     12  NWMENU        11      1 Memo
     13  NWMENU        12      1 Memo
     14  NWMENU        13      1 Memo
     15  NWMENU        14      1 Memo
     16  NWMENU        88      1 Memo
     17  NWMENU        99      1 Memo
```

Figure 23-10. The help file data

MEMOWIDTH to increase the display width for memo fields to at least 67 characters, so that your help message is presented to the user exactly the way you entered it into the record.

The program in Figure 23-11, NWHELP2.PRG, illustrates this method of displaying the help messages. The basic structure of this program is very similar to NWHELP1.PRG. The name of the calling program is passed to NWHELP2.PRG as the parameter MPROGRAM. Since the help file is indexed on more than one field, you must be careful to specify the first portion of the index key—the name of the calling program—in full (eight characters, using trailing blanks if necessary) to match the length of the MPROGRAM field. This is in contrast to NWHELP1.PRG, in which the memory variable MPROGRAM acquired both its length and its value from the calling program, with the conditions in the CASE statements adjusted accordingly.

The program opens the help file and sets up an "endless" loop with DO WHILE .T. Within the DO WHILE loop, if NWHELP2.PRG was called from a menu, the program asks the user which help message to display and uses SEEK to find the record with the specified combination of MPROGRAM and MOPTION. If no matching record is found in the help

```
* NWHELP2.PRG
* PROGRAM TO PROVIDE ON-LINE HELP MESSAGES USING A DATA FILE FOR HELP TEXT
* WRITTEN BY:  M.LISKIN        09/05/85

parameters MPROGRAM, MOPTION

use NWHELP index NWHELP
set memowidth to 75

do while .T.

   clear

   if "MENU" $ MPROGRAM
      store 0 to MOPTION
      @ 10,10 say "Which menu option do you need help with? " get MOPTION;
                picture "99"
      read
      if MOPTION = 0
         exit
      endif
      seek MPROGRAM + str(MOPTION,2)
      if .not. found()
         @ 22,10 say "Not a valid option -- Press any key to try again"
         wait ""
         @ 22,0
         loop
      endif
   else
      seek MPROGRAM + str(MOPTION,2)
   endif

   do while PROGRAM + str(OPTION,2) = MPROGRAM + str(MOPTION,2)
      clear
      ? HELPMSG
      skip
      if PROGRAM + str(OPTION,2) = MPROGRAM + str(MOPTION,2)
         wait "Press X to exit from HELP, " +;
              "or any other key for more information... " to MCONTINUE
         if upper(MCONTINUE) = "X"
            exit
         endif
      else
         wait
      endif
   enddo

   if .not. "MENU" $ MPROGRAM
      exit
   endif

enddo

use

return
```

Figure 23-11. Displaying help messages stored in a data base

file, the program displays an error message and gives the operator another chance to enter the option correctly. If the program was not called from a menu, the program executes the SEEK command with no subsequent error test, based on the assumption that the programmer has entered all of the requisite help screens into NWHELP.DBF. In either case, once the appropriate record is found, a DO WHILE loop is set up to clear the screen, display the HELPMSG field from the current record, SKIP to the next record in the file, and pause with a WAIT command. This loop executes as long as the PROGRAM and OPTION fields match the corresponding memory variables MPROGRAM and MOPTION.

In order to allow the user to exit from the help system without viewing all of the screens, the WAIT command is placed after the SKIP. This way, the program can check to see if there is another help file record with the same combination of PROGRAM and OPTION fields. If so, the user is instructed to press X to exit or any other key to display the next help screen. The key pressed in response to the WAIT command is saved in the variable MCONTINUE and converted to uppercase with the UPPER function for the subsequent test. When the SKIP command advances the help file to a record that describes a different program or option (whether or not there was more than one such record), a plain WAIT command is used to pause the program. Just as in NWHELP1.PRG, the program returns to the calling program after displaying all of the help text if NWHELP2.PRG was not called from a menu. If NWHELP2.PRG *was* called from a menu, the program returns to the top of the DO WHILE loop to ask for another option.

If NWHELP2.PRG is called from a menu, no data base files will be open. If it is called by one of the other programs in the system, there is no way for the help program to identify which data base files are already open and in which work areas. It is therefore the responsibility of the calling program to SELECT an unused work area before calling NWHELP2.PRG (so that opening the help file does not close any other data base required by the calling program) and to SELECT the appropriate work area again afterward.

Using the help file actually requires opening three files: NWHELP.DBF, NWHELP.DBT (which contains the text of the memo fields), and NWHELP.NDX. If this puts you over the limit of 15 open disk files, the calling program must close one of the other data base files and reopen it after returning from the help system. If this is necessary, it is best to select the work area containing the smallest data base, preferably one that is only read (not changed) in the calling program. This way, closing the file is as fast as possible (since no new data must be written to the disk) and reopening it is also fast (because the file is small). For example, if you had to close one of the three files used by the Customer Update and Inquiry program, the best choice would be the code file, NWCODES.DBF, which is open in work area 2.

Notice that you do not have to close the NWCODES.DBF file before calling NWHELP2.PRG, because with work area 2 selected, the file in this work area will be closed automatically by dBASE III PLUS when it opens NWHELP.DBF. For the same reason, it is not necessary to close the help file, because it will be closed when the calling program regains control and reopens NWCODES.DBF. It is somewhat inefficient to open NWHELP.DBF each time the help program is called, although this option will be used relatively infrequently, and most often by an inexperienced operator who is not working at top speed. If you are sure that your application will never run up against the 15-file limit, you could open the help file once in the Main Menu program in a work area you do not otherwise use (perhaps in work area 9 or 10) and leave it open throughout each work session. Doing this, however, would require that you remove the CLOSE DATABASES commands from the menu programs and close the files open in the other work areas individually when each program terminates.

Figure 23-12 lists NWCUPD4, a new version of the Customer Update and Inquiry program that makes use of NWHELP2.PRG. This program employs both of the strategies for calling the help program described in the introduction to this section. The option prompt line includes a new HELP option, accessed by typing the letter H, and a matching CASE was added to the DO CASE structure that processes the user's selection. This case SELECTs work area 10 and calls the help program with a value of 1 for the MOPTION parameter. When the help file returns control to NWCUPD4.PRG, the program uses SELECT NWCUST to switch back to the work area containing the Customer File. At this point, the screen mask, which was erased by the help program, is redrawn with a call to NWCSCRN, just as in the MEMO option that uses NWCUST5.FMT to edit the COMMENTS field. The data entered into the help file record accessed by this call to NWHELP2.PRG contains information on the command line options.

The help screens describing the fields in the data base are accessed by pressing F1 while entering or editing a customer record. Using the READKEY( ) function, you can determine which key the user has pressed to exit from any full-screen editing mode, including a screen drawn with @ ... SAY ... GET commands followed by a READ to collect the data.

```
* NWCUPD4.PRG
* PROGRAM TO INQUIRE, EDIT, ADD, AND DELETE CUSTOMERS
*   WITH ON-LINE HELP
* WRITTEN BY:  M.LISKIN       05/23/86

select 1
use NWTXN   index NWTACCT

select 2
use NWCODES index NWCODES

select 3
use NWCUST  index NWCACCT, NWCZIP
set relation to ACCOUNT into NWTXN
skip -1

set deleted off

store " " to MCITY

do NWCSCRN

do while .T.

   @ 23, 0
   store " " to MOPTION
   @ 23, 0 say "(S)earch (C)hange (N)ext (P)rev (D)el " +;
               "(R)ecover (A)dd (M)emo (H)elp e(X)it" get MOPTION picture "!"
   read

   do case

      case MOPTION = "X"
         set deleted on
         return

      case MOPTION = "H"
         select 10
         do NWHELP2 with "NWCUPD4 ", 1
         select NWCUST
         do NWCSCRN

      case MOPTION = "S"
         store "          " to MACCOUNT
         @ 23, 0
         @ 23,10 say "Enter the account number to search for";
                 get MACCOUNT picture "@!"
         read

         if MACCOUNT = " "
            loop
         endif
         seek trim(MACCOUNT)
         if .not. found()
            @ 23, 0
            @ 23,15 say trim(MACCOUNT) +;
                    " not found -- Press any key to continue"
            wait ""
            loop
         endif
```

Figure 23-12. A Customer Update program that uses NWHELP2.PRG to display help messages

```
case MOPTION = "C"
   if eof() .or. bof()
      @ 23, 0
      @ 23,15 say "You must SEARCH first -- Press any key to continue"
      wait ""
      loop
   endif

case MOPTION = "N"
   if .not. eof()
      skip
   endif
   if eof()
      @ 23, 0
      @ 23,15 say "This is the last name -- Press any key to continue"
      wait ""
      loop
   endif

case MOPTION = "P"
   if .not. bof()
      skip -1
   endif
   if bof()
      @ 23, 0
      @ 23,15 say "This is the first name -- Press any key to continue"
      wait ""
      loop
   endif

case MOPTION = "D"
   if eof() .or. bof()
      @ 23, 0
      @ 23,15 say "You must SEARCH first -- Press any key to continue"
      wait ""
      loop
   endif
   if BALANCE <> 0.00
      @ 23, 0
      @ 23,15 say "Balance is not 0.00 -- Press any key to continue"
      wait ""
      loop
   endif

   select NWTXN
   if found()
      @ 23, 0
      @ 23, 5 say;
        "There are current transactions -- Press any key to continue"
      wait ""
      select NWCUST
      loop
   else
      select NWCUST
   endif

   store .F. to MCONFIRM
   @ 23, 0
   @ 23,10 say "Are you sure you want to delete this customer? (Y/N)";
           get MCONFIRM picture "Y"
```

Figure 23-12. A Customer Update program that uses NWHELP2.PRG to display help messages (*continued*)

```
      read

      if MCONFIRM
         delete
         set color to W+, W+
         @  3,65 say "* DELETED *"
         set color to W, W+
         @ 23, Ø
         @ 23,15 say trim(ACCOUNT) +;
                     " has been deleted -- Press any key to continue"
         wait ""
      endif
      loop

   case MOPTION = "R"
      if eof() .or. bof()
         @ 23, Ø
         @ 23,15 say "You must SEARCH first -- Press any key to continue"
         wait ""
         loop
      endif

      recall
      @  3,65 say "           "
      @ 23, Ø
      @ 23,15 say trim(ACCOUNT) +;
                  " has been recovered -- Press any key to continue"
      wait ""
      loop


   case MOPTION = "A"
      store "         " to MACCOUNT
      @ 23, Ø
      @ 23,1Ø say "Enter the account number for the new entry";
              get MACCOUNT picture "@!"
      read
      if MACCOUNT = " "
         loop
      endif
      seek MACCOUNT
      if found()
         @ 23, Ø
         @ 23,1Ø say trim(MACCOUNT) +;
                     " is already on file -- Press any key to continue"
         wait ""
         loop
      else
         append blank
         replace ACCOUNT with MACCOUNT, STATE with MPSTATE,;
                 CITY with MCITY, AREACODE with MPAREACODE,;
                 TAXRATE with MPTAXRATE
      endif

   case MOPTION = "M"
      if eof() .or. bof()
         @ 23, Ø
         @ 23,15 say "You must SEARCH first -- Press any key to continue"
         wait ""
         loop
      endif
```

Figure 23-12. A Customer Update program that uses NWHELP2.PRG to display help messages (*continued*)

```
          set format to NWCUST5
          edit
          set format to
          do NWCSCRN

       otherwise
          loop

   endcase

   do CUSTGET1

   do while .T.

      store .T. to MVALID

      do CUSTGET2

      if MOPTION $ "CA"
         read
         if readkey() = 36 .or. readkey() = 292
            select 10
            do NWHELP2 with "NWCUPD4 ", 2
            select NWCUST
            do NWCSCRN
            do CUSTGET1
            loop
         endif
      else
         clear gets
      endif

      set color to W+, W+

      if ACCOUNT = " "
         delete
         @ 3,65 say "* DELETED *"
         exit
      endif

      if COMPANY = " " .and. CONTACT = " "
         store .F. to MVALID
         @  5, 1 say "*"
         @ 10, 1 say "*"
      else
         @  5, 1 say " "
         @ 10, 1 say " "
      endif

      if ADDRESS1 = " "
         store .F. to MVALID
         @  6, 1 say "*"
      else
         @  6, 1 say " "
      endif

      if CITY = " "
         store .F. to MVALID
         @  8, 1 say "*"
      else
         @  8, 1 say " "
      endif
```

Figure 23-12. A Customer Update program that uses NWHELP2.PRG to display help messages (*continued*)

```
      if STATE = "  "
         store .F. to MVALID
         @  8,43 say "*"
         @  9,51 say space(20)
      else
         select NWCODES
         seek "S" + NWCUST->STATE
         if found()
            @  8,43 say " "
            @  9,51 say DESCRIP
         else
            @  8,43 say "*"
            @  9,51 say space(20)
         endif
         select NWCUST
      endif

      if len(trim(ZIP)) < 5
         store .F. to MVALID
         @  8,57 say "*"
      else
         @  8,57 say " "
      endif

      if AREACODE = "  "
         @ 10,43 say " "
         @ 11,55 say space(20)
      else
         select NWCODES
         seek "A" + NWCUST->AREACODE
         if found()
            @ 10,43 say " "
            @ 11,55 say DESCRIP
         else
            store .F. to MVALID
            @ 10,43 say "*"
            @ 11,55 say space(20)
         endif
         select NWCUST
      endif

      if STATE = "  " .or. (STATE <> "CA" .and. TAXRATE > 0) .or.;
         (STATE = "CA" .and. TAXRATE <> 6.00 .and. TAXRATE <> 6.50)
         store .F. to MVALID
         @ 12,43 say "*"
      else
         @ 12,43 say " "
      endif

      if MVALID
         exit
      else
         @ 23, 0
         @ 23,15 say 'Please correct the fields marked with a "*" '
         if .not. MOPTION $ "CA"
            store "C" to MOPTION
         endif
      endif

   enddo                        [ not validated ]
```

Figure 23-12. A Customer Update program that uses NWHELP2.PRG to display help messages (*continued*)

```
      set color to W, W+

      if MOPTION = "A"
         store CITY to MCITY
      endif

   enddo

   return
```

Figure 23-12. A Customer Update program that uses NWHELP2.PRG to display help messages (*continued*)

This function also allows you to detect whether or not any data was changed, although NWCUPD4.PRG does not need to make this distinction. The keys that may be detected with READKEY( ) and the values assumed by this function for each key are listed in Table 23-1.

When NWCHELP2.PRG is called from the command option line, the program automatically redisplays the record that was on the screen prior to the request for help, because the commands to display the data are located after the DO CASE structure that processes the help call. When data is being edited on the screen, however, the fields have already been displayed (and some may have been changed by the user) when the screen is cleared to display the help text. When the help program returns control to NWCUPD4.PRG, this program must therefore not only redraw the input field mask, but also redisplay the fields themselves. The most efficient way to accomplish this is to extract the commands that display the data into separate programs or procedures. In NWCUPD4.PRG, there are two groups of fields—those that may not be changed by the operator and are therefore displayed once, before the validation loop, and those that may be edited, which are displayed, collected, and validated within a DO WHILE .T. loop. These commands have been removed from the main program and placed in two procedures, named CUSTGET1 and CUSTGET2, respectively. They are listed in Figures 23-13 and 23-14.

Just as in NWCUPD3.PRG, the new update program performs the READ command only if the operator has chosen the CHANGE or ADD option. After the READ, the value of READKEY( ) is tested to determine whether or not F1 was pressed. If so, the help program is called with a value of 2 for the option, to select the set of help file records that describe the Customer File fields. This choice of values for MOPTION assumes

Table 23-1. READKEY( ) Values for Command Keys Used to Exit a Full-Screen Edit Session

Command Key(s)	READKEY( ) (no data changed)	READKEY( ) (data changed)
CTRL-S or CTRL-H or BACKSPACE or LEFT ARROW	0	256
CTRL-D or RIGHT ARROW	1	257
CTRL-A or HOME	2	258
CTRL-F or END	3	259
CTRL-E or UP ARROW	4	260
CTRL-X or DOWN ARROW	5	261
CTRL-R or PGUP	6	262
CTRL-C or PGDN	7	263
CTRL-Z or CTRL-LEFT ARROW	8	264
CTRL-B or CTRL-RIGHT ARROW	9	265
CTRL-U	10	266
CTRL-N	11	267
CTRL-Q or ESC	12	268
CTRL-W or CTRL-END	14	270
CTRL-M	15	271
RETURN	16	272
CTRL-HOME	33	289
CTRL-PGUP	34	290
CTRL-PGDN	35	291
F1	36	292

that if help is requested from the main command prompt, the user may be confused about how to use the various options, whereas requesting help while editing a record reflects the need for more information about how to fill in the data. In your own programs, you may want to use a similar method for assigning OPTION numbers to the help screens, depending on the context in which you anticipate they will be used.

When the help program returns control to NWCUPD4.PRG, the screen is reconstructed by calling the NWCSCRN program and the CUSTGET1 and CUSTGET2 procedures. Note that the GETS were placed in procedures rather than separate programs, since they are used *every time*

```
procedure CUSTGET1

if deleted()
   set color to W+, W+
   @ 3,65 say "* DELETED *"
   set color to W, W+
else
   @ 3,65 say "           "
endif

@  3,13 get ACCOUNT
@ 14,18 get YTDINV picture "9,999,999.99"
@ 15,18 get YTDPMT picture "9,999,999.99"
@ 17,18 get TOTINV picture "9,999,999.99"
@ 17,62 get FIRSTORDER
@ 18,18 get YTDPMT picture "9,999,999.99"
@ 18,62 get LASTORDER
@ 20,18 get BALANCE picture "@( 9,999,999.99"
clear gets

if dtoc(LASTORDER) <> "  "
   store date() - LASTORDER to MDAYS
   @ 20,45 say "LAST ORDER WAS " + str(MDAYS,4) + " DAYS AGO"
else
   @ 20,45 say space(28)
endif

return
```

Figure 23-13. A procedure to display the Customer File fields that may not be edited

```
procedure CUSTGET2

set color to W, W+

@  5,13 get COMPANY
@  6,13 get ADDRESS1
@  7,13 get ADDRESS2
@  8,13 get CITY
@  8,51 get STATE picture "@!"
@  8,63 get ZIP picture "99999"
@ 10,13 get CONTACT
@ 10,55 get AREACODE picture "999"
@ 10,63 get TELEPHONE picture "999-9999"
@ 12,13 get EQUIPMENT
@ 12,63 get TAXRATE range 0, 10

return
```

Figure 23-14. A procedure to display the Customer File fields that may be edited

a record is displayed, whereas NWCSCRN is called relatively infrequently—only when the memo field COMMENTS is edited or the help program is invoked. Of course, if you have room in your procedure file, there is no reason not to make NWCSCRN a procedure as well. Also note that the program returns to the top of the validation loop and thereby repeats the call to CUSTGET2, rather than calling this procedure explicitly and continuing with the validation tests. This decision was based on the way the help system is likely to be used—the operator may want to "bail out" and ask for help midway through a new entry, leaving most of the fields incomplete. It therefore makes more sense to go back to the top of the loop and ask for the fields again, instead of carrying out all of the validation tests and presenting the operator with numerous error messages.

This chapter presented two ways to structure a help program, and several different ways of calling this program to display the help text. In any given application, you may want to use various combinations of these techniques to make your help messages available to the users under different conditions, and to make the help system as context-sensitive as possible within the limitations imposed by dBASE III PLUS.

24

WRITING HARDWARE-INDEPENDENT PROGRAMS

The programs in Part IV have addressed two primary goals: to add power and flexibility for the users of a dBASE III PLUS system, and at the same time to improve the productivity of the programmer. With the introduction of procedure files, these two goals converged. Using procedures that accept input from the calling program in the form of parameters facilitates the development of a standard library of routines that can be called from many places in a dBASE III PLUS system and incorporated virtually unchanged into many of the applications you write.

With the kinds of procedures written so far, you can reap substantial benefits from the very first application in which they are used, although the gains in programming efficiency increase with each usage. This chapter describes procedures and functions you can use to make a dBASE III PLUS application more independent of the hardware and operating system environment in which it is used. The procedures introduced in this chapter allow you to construct a system that can be modified easily to meet the needs of more than one organization. They employ the same modular design principles developed throughout Part IV to enable you to use components developed for one system in an entirely different dBASE III application with a minimum of changes. These tools are truly useful only when they are incorporated into an application that may be run on more than one kind of computer, or when they are used in many different data base systems designed for diverse system configurations.

dBASE III PLUS provides another set of tools you can use to make your programs more hardware-independent: a selection of functions that enable a program to determine many characteristics of the hardware and operating system environment under which it is running. These functions may be used to write programs that test their environment and take different actions depending on the results. For example, the OS function returns a character string containing the name of the operating system currently running. You can use this function to choose which of several operating system-specific utility programs or external applications to access with a RUN command. The VERSION function allows you to determine which version of dBASE III PLUS is running, so you can selectively implement new features without rendering a program incompatible with earlier versions of the software. (As of this writing, there are no such features.)

CUSTOMIZING THE FUNCTION KEYS

The Customer File Update and Inquiry programs written so far display a command option menu at the bottom of the screen and invite the user to make a selection by typing the first letter of the desired option. Another way to structure this (or indeed, any command menu) is to customize the programmable function keys so they may be used to enter commands. Most IBM and IBM-compatible computers have ten function keys, one of which (usually called F1) is reserved by dBASE III PLUS as the HELP key and cannot be reprogrammed. However, the newer IBM keyboards have 12 function keys, some compatibles have more (and some fewer), and not every computer uses the designations F1 through F10 (or F12) to identify the keys.

To use function keys for the Customer File Update and Inquiry program command options, at least ten keys are required, one for each of the program's options: SEARCH, CHANGE, NEXT, PREVIOUS, DELETE, RECOVER, ADD, MEMO, HELP, and EXIT. Recall that when a function key is pressed, the character string assigned to the key is transmitted to the dBASE III PLUS command parser just as if the same characters were typed by the user. If you assign to each function key the single letter normally used to select one of the options, the user can issue a command either by pressing a function key or by typing a letter, according to his or her personal preference. The easiest way to make the assignments is to use a series of explicit STORE commands for function keys 2 through 10 (the HELP key, F1, which cannot be reassigned, must be handled differently):

```
set function  2 to "S"
set function  3 to "N"
set function  4 to "P"
set function  5 to "D"
set function  6 to "R"
set function  7 to "A"
set function  8 to "C"
set function  9 to "M"
set function 10 to "X"
```

You can make your program more independent of the specific hardware configuration by using the FKMAX and FKLABEL functions in the routines that reassign the function key meanings. FKMAX( ) evaluates to the number of *programmable* function keys on the terminal; thus, this number will be one fewer than the actual number of function keys on the IBM PC and any other keyboard that does not have a separate HELP key. The FKLABEL function accepts a number as input and returns a character string containing the name of the corresponding function key. For example, on a keyboard with ten function keys and with F1 serving as the HELP key, FKLABEL(3) will yield the character string "F4".

Figure 24-1 lists the FXNKEYS procedure, which tests for the presence of at least ten function keys and constructs the Customer File Update and Inquiry program option prompt lines accordingly. In order to accommodate longer key names, the original option prompt line was divided into two new ones, which will be displayed on lines 22 and 23 by the Customer File Update and Inquiry program. If FKMAX( ) is less than 9, function keys cannot be used for the command options, and the procedure assigns a variation of the standard option prompt in the two memory variables MOPTLINE1 and MOPTLINE2. If enough function keys are available, a DO WHILE loop is used to construct these variables based on the names of the keys and the prompt strings to be displayed on the screen.

The methods used to build these strings are similar to the techniques used in the NWSETUP1.PRG program to manipulate the memory variables that stored the inventory category codes and descriptions. The MKEYDEFS variable holds the single letters to be assigned to the function keys; the option prompt line descriptions are stored in the variable MDESCRIPS. On each pass through the DO WHILE loop, the function key to be reassigned can be expressed in the SET FUNCTION command as

```
procedure FXNKEYS

if FKMAX() < 9
   store "(S)earch     (C)hange     (N)ext     (P)revious     (D)elete ";
      to MOPTLINE1
   store "(R)ecover    (A)dd        (M)emo     (H)elp         e(X)it";
      to MOPTLINE2
   return
endif


store "Search     Next      Previous  Delete     " +;
      "Recover    Add       Change    Memo       eXit       " to MDESCRIPS

store fklabel(1) + "=Help      " to MOPTLINE1

store "SNPDRACMX" to MKEYDEFS
store ""          to MOPTLINE2
store 1           to MCOUNT

do while MCOUNT <= 9

   set function fklabel(MCOUNT) to substr(MKEYDEFS, MCOUNT, 1)

   if MCOUNT <= 4
      store MOPTLINE1 + fklabel(MCOUNT) + "=" +;
            substr(MDESCRIPS, (MCOUNT - 1) * 10 + 1, 10) to MOPTLINE1
   else
      store MOPTLINE2 + fklabel(MCOUNT) + "=" +;
            substr(MDESCRIPS, (MCOUNT - 1) * 10 + 1, 10) to MOPTLINE2
   endif

   store MCOUNT + 1 to MCOUNT

enddo

return
```

Figure 24-1. A procedure to customize the programmable function keys

FKLABEL(MCOUNT), so your program does not have to know the names of the keys. The actual value to be assigned to the key is a substring of the MKEYDEFS variable consisting of a single character, whose position in MKEYDEFS is the value of MCOUNT. The variable that holds the key descriptions, MDESCRIPS, is read in groups of ten characters to select the description corresponding to each command option.

Running this procedure on an IBM PC or on most clones results in the following value for MOPTLINE1:

```
F2=Help      F2=Search    F3=Next      F4=Previous  F5=Delete
```

MOPTLINE2 will look like this:

```
F6=Recover    F7=Add        F8=Change     F9=Memo       F10=eXit
```

These variables can then be displayed on lines 22 and 23 by the update and inquiry program to produce the following prompt:

```
F2=Help       F2=Search     F3=Next       F4=Previous   F5=Delete
F6=Recover    F7=Add        F8=Change     F9=Memo       F10=eXit
```

Since the length of the variables depends on the length of the function key names, you might want to use the CENTER procedure to display them rather than specifying the column coordinate explicitly in an @ ... SAY command. Remember also that if you modify an existing update and inquiry program, then whenever the previous version of the program cleared line 23 for an error message, line 22 must be cleared as well.

Since the program has no way to determine whether the user has pressed a function key or typed a single letter option, it is not necessary to change the @ ... GET command that collects the selection and stores it in the variable MOPTION. Of the ten CASEs that process the options, only one must be changed—the one that handles the HELP option. Although you cannot reassign the meaning of the HELP key, you can use the READKEY function to determine whether this key was used to exit from any full-screen edit process, including the READ command used to activate one or more (in this case one) @ ... SAY ... GET commands. The HELP case may be modified as follows:

```
case readkey() = 36 .or. readkey() = 292
   select 10
   do NWHELP2 with "NWCUPD4 ", 1
   select NWCUST
   do NWCSCRN
```

One other loose end remains. When the user exits from the program, it is a good idea to reset the function keys to null values unless you intend to assign them new values and use them to select the Main Menu options. (If this were the case, you would instead call another procedure to assign the menu selection numbers or letters to the function keys.) Here is a general-purpose procedure to reset all of the function keys on the keyboard to a RETURN (symbolized by a semicolon), just as when you assign the key values from the dot prompt:

```
procedure NULLFXN
```

```
store 1 to MCOUNT

do while MCOUNT <= FKMAX()
   set function fklabel(MCOUNT) to ";"
   store MCOUNT + 1 to MCOUNT
enddo
```

A PROGRAM TO UPDATE APPLICATION-INDEPENDENT OPTIONS

The remainder of this chapter describes a second setup program that customizes the systemwide options that are usually independent of the nature of the application. These options, which depend on the user's hardware and operating configuration, are stored in memory variables rather than written directly into the programs as literal constants. This makes the application more easily transportable to different computer systems. The second setup program, NWSETUP2.PRG, can often be included virtually unchanged in most of the systems you write, in contrast to NWSETUP1.PRG, which updates variables (like the inventory category codes and descriptions) that are unique to one application or one organization (although an analogous set of variables may be required in many dBASE III PLUS systems).

Some of the systemwide options that are set in NWSETUP2.PRG, such as the type of monitor in use (color/graphics or monochrome) can be determined by the programs using dBASE III PLUS built-in functions. Others, including the disk drive and subdirectory containing the data base files, should clearly be specified by the user. For another group of options, such as the display colors or attributes and printer control codes, the choice is not so clear-cut. Because these options store aspects of the system that are visible to the operators, they should ideally be customizable without programming, but presenting them for modification may greatly complicate the program or require technical expertise that many users do not possess. Finally, there are options that may assume different values in different applications, but once the choice is made, the consequences are so pervasive that these decisions *must* be made by the programmer.

The complete setup program is listed in Figure 24-2. The program first allows the user to enter some of the options and then proceeds to the choices that are best made by the programmer. Although some of the choices made by the programmer are written explicitly into the code, it is still expedient to use procedures to establish the values of the programmer-specified systemwide options. Modifying a standard skeleton procedure is still easier, faster, and less prone to careless error than writing the program statements from scratch for each application.

```
* NWSETUP2.PRG
* PROGRAM TO UPDATE APPLICATION-INDEPENDENT SYSTEMWIDE OPTIONS
* WRITTEN BY:  M.LISKIN        6/03/86

if .not. file("NWMEMORY.MEM")
   store ""          to MPPATH
   store space(40)   to MPDPATH, MPIPATH, MPOPATH
   store "OFF"       to MPCONFIRM, MPBELL, MPINTENS
endif

clear

do ASKPATH

store iif(MPCONFIRM = "ON", .T., .F.) to MCONFIRM
store iif(MPBELL    = "ON", .T., .F.) to MBELL
store iif(MPINTENS  = "ON", .T., .F.) to MINTENS

@ 15, 0 clear
@ 15, 5 say "Do you want to press <RETURN> after each field entry? (Y/N)";
        get MCONFIRM picture "Y"
@ 16, 5 say "Do you want to use your computer's bell (beeper)?     (Y/N)";
        get MBELL    picture "Y"
@ 17, 5 say "Do you want different colors for data and background? (Y/N)";
        get MPINTENS picture "Y"
read

store iif(MCONFIRM, "ON", "OFF") to MPCONFIRM
store iif(MBELL,    "ON", "OFF") to MPBELL
store iif(MINTENS,  "ON", "OFF") to MPINTENS

@ 20,10 say "Completing system initialization -- Please do not interrupt"
@ 22,10 say "Working on:"

@ 22,25 say "Standard messages  ..."
do STDMSGS

@ 22,25 say "Display characters ..."
do BOXES

@ 22,25 say "Display attributes ..."
do DISPATT

@ 22,25 say "Printer attributes ..."
do PRINTATT

store "american" to MPDATEFORM

return
```

Figure 24-2. A program to establish the application-independent systemwide options

It is assumed that NWSETUP2.PRG is called by NWSETUP1.PRG, either before allowing the user to enter the application-specific variables, or afterward, just before the variables are saved on disk. NWSETUP2.PRG therefore uses the same criterion to determine whether to create its set of PUBLIC variables—it tests for the presence of NWMEMORY.MEM. Note, however, that all of the PUBLIC declarations must be made in NWSETUP1.PRG, before the RESTORE command, in order to ensure that the variables are in fact RESTOREd as PUBLIC, rather than PRIVATE.

Locating the Disk Files That Make Up the Application

The NWSETUP2.PRG program begins by asking the user to specify the full path names, including the disk drive designators and subdirectory names, for the subdirectories containing the files that make up the application. As mentioned in Chapter 11, storing the file path in a PUBLIC memory variable allows the user to move the application to new hardware without having to edit all of the programs and change all of the commands that open disk files. This program will allow the user to specify a different directory path for each type of file in the application (data base, index, report form, and so on), but this may not be necessary in most systems.

It would be a mistake to assume, however, that all of the files reside in the same subdirectory as dBASE III PLUS itself. In a floppy disk system, the user is probably working with dBASE III PLUS in drive A: and the data bases and indexes on a disk in drive B:. To switch applications, you would simply place a different data disk in drive B:. On a hard disk, it is more common to create one subdirectory for the dBASE III PLUS program and a separate subdirectory for each application or set of related files. With either system configuration, many users will create a RAM disk (a portion of RAM that emulates a very fast disk drive) to speed up disk access time. Since the RAM disk is volatile—the contents are lost when the power goes off—it is safest to use it only for unchanging files such as programs, procedure files, report and label forms, and optionally, files like indexes that may be reconstructed from scratch if necessary. The data bases should remain on the floppy or hard disk so they are less vulnerable to power failures, system crashes, or errors made by inexperienced users, who may occasionally turn off the power without remembering to first copy the contents of the RAM disk to a physical disk.

In order to start up the system, dBASE III PLUS must be able to find at least three files—the Main Menu program and the setup programs (in the event that a missing memory variable file causes the menu to call the setup programs). These files are assumed to be in the same subdirectory as the dBASE III PLUS software itself, but they may also be in any other subdirectory made available by the user with a SET DEFAULT or SET PATH command issued from the dot prompt before the Main Menu program was invoked.

The NWSETUP2.PRG program allows the user to enter three separate path names, one for data bases, one for indexes, and a third for the programs and other auxiliary files that make up the application. Collecting the user's selection of the path names is straightforward, but validating the entry is not, since there is no way for your program to easily determine which drives are physically present or what subdirectory structure has been established. One way to carry out the test is to attempt to verify the existence of a file that must be present to run the application. You cannot use the dBASE III PLUS DIR command for this purpose, however, because when a DIR command reports "No files," this is considered to be a normal informational message, not an error condition.

You can, however, use the FILE function to determine whether any file, specified using its full path name, is present on disk. To make the routine completely general, you could create a file—any file—of each type, and include these files in every application you write so you can search for them by name. In this case, the setup program simply tests for the presence of three files known to be necessary to run the National Widgets application: NWCUST.DBF, NWCACCT.NDX, and NWCMENU2.PRG. Even if the users have not yet entered data, these files should be physically present on the disk. To make the routine easy to incorporate into all of your applications, it will be performed by a procedure called ASKPATH, which you can edit if necessary to enter the particular file names to search for in each application. The procedure is listed in Figure 24-3.

This procedure sets up an "endless" loop with DO WHILE .T., within which the variable MVALID is initialized to keep track of the overall status of the validation process. The user is asked to enter the three required path names, collected into three PUBLIC memory variables called MPDPATH, MPIPATH, and MPPPATH, and the entries are validated.

```
procedure ASKPATH

do while .T.

   store .T. to MVALID

   @  2, 5 say "Enter path names for files in this application,"
   @  3, 5 say "including disk drive, for example C:\DBPLUS\ACCOUNTS"
   @  5, 5 say "Data base files              " get MPDPATH picture "@!"
   @  6, 5 say "Index files                  " get MPIPATH picture "@!"
   @  7, 5 say "Programs and all other files" get MPOPATH picture "@!"
   read

   if .not. file("&MPDPATH\NWCUST.DBF")
      @ 10, 5 say "Data base file path not found"
      store .F. to MVALID
   endif

   if .not. file("&MPIPATH\NWCACCT.NDX")
      @ 11, 5 say "Index file path not found"
      store .F. to MVALID
   endif

   if .not. file("&MPOPATH\NWCMENU1.PRG")
      @ 12, 5 say "Program file path not found"
      store .F. to MVALID
   endif

   if MVALID
      exit
   else
      store .T. to MRETRY
      @ 15, 5 say;
        "Indicated paths do not exist -- Do you want to re-enter them? (Y/N)";
        get MRETRY picture "Y"
      read
      if .not. MRETRY
         @ 21, 5 say;
           "Please correct the error and then re-run the setup program"
         @ 22, 5 say "Press any key to continue"
         wait ""
         exit
      endif
   endif

enddo

store trim(MPDPATH) to MPPATH

if trim(MPIPATH) <> trim(MPDPATH)
   store MPPATH + ";" + trim(MPIPATH) to MPPATH
endif

if trim(MPOPATH) <> trim(MPDPATH) .and. trim(MPOPATH) <> trim(MPIPATH)
   store MPPATH + ";" + trim(MPOPATH) to MPPATH
endif

set path to &MPPATH

return
```

Figure 24-3. A procedure to establish file search paths

Although both MS-DOS and dBASE III PLUS allow subdirectory and file names to be entered in any combination of uppercase and lowercase, the user's entries are converted to uppercase for consistency. If any of the test files is not found in the specified subdirectories, an error message is displayed to inform the user. If all the files are found, it is safe to EXIT from the DO WHILE .T. loop and construct the full search path from the user's three entries. Note that each subdirectory name is added into the character string that makes up MPPATH only if it is unique, so as to keep the search path short and speed up file access.

If any of the paths is not found, the procedure still allows the user to exit rather than categorically asking over and over to repeat the entry. The user may simply have forgotten the path name, or if the application is being installed for the first time, he or she may have neglected to copy some of the files into the correct subdirectory. If you wish, you could give the user the option of displaying the disk directory or tree structure (using RUN TREE) or copying the necessary files from a floppy disk, all from within the ASKPATH procedure. In this case, the procedure simply returns to the calling program, leaving it up to the user to correct the problem and rerun the setup program.

The SET PATH command works much like the MS-DOS PATH command established through an entry in the CONFIG.SYS file. Like the operating system, dBASE III PLUS searches first for all files in the current subdirectory. If the specified file is not found, the program searches in turn the subdirectories listed in the SET PATH command. Note, however, that the search path established with the DOS PATH command is *not* recognized by dBASE III PLUS. (It is, however, used to search for commands, programs, or batch files executed with RUN, since in this case the MS-DOS command processor, not dBASE III PLUS, is in control.)

If you elect to permit the user to specify separate path names for different types of files, there is an alternative to storing all of the subdirectories in a single search path. You could instead include the path name variables in all of the commands in your application that open files. For example, with the name of the data base directory stored in a PUBLIC variable called MPDPATH and the indexes located in MPIPATH, you could open a data base this way:

```
use &MPDPATH\NWCUST index &MPIPATH\NWCACCT, &MPIPATH\NWCZIP
```

In all of the commands that use the path name variables, the macro symbol (&) is necessary so that dBASE III PLUS substitutes *the value of the variable MPPATH, MPDPATH, or MPIPATH* into the expression that establishes the search path or constructs the file name. In the above example, if MPDPATH is C:\DBPLUS\ACCOUNTS, &MPDPATH:NWCUST evaluates to C:\DBPLUS\ACCOUNTS\NWCUST. This results in files being opened slightly faster, since dBASE III PLUS does not have to search several subdirectories for the requested files; but if you modify an existing application to use this technique (instead of SET PATH), you must change all of your existing USE and DO commands. This technique is also preferable in any data base system in which new files are created files that should not be located in the dBASE III PLUS subdirectory, since the search path is used only to find existing files, not to create new ones.

Customizing the Data Entry Environment

Next, the setup program allows the user to select the status of the CONFIRM, BELL, and INTENSITY settings. To conform to the syntax of the corresponding SET commands, each of these variables should contain the value "ON" or "OFF". The SET commands could then be written as

```
set confirm   &MPCONFIRM
set bell      &MPBELL
set intensity &MPINTENS
```

It would be a mistake to assume, however, that the user is familiar with the syntax of the SET commands, so the program presents the operator with three yes-or-no questions phrased in less technical terms. For each of the PUBLIC variables, the setup program creates a temporary variable, which is assigned the value .T. if the PUBLIC variable contains the value "ON" or .F. if the value is "OFF".

The assignments are made using the IIF function, based on the existing value at the time the setup program is run, which is either the initial value "OFF" assigned when the variable was first created, or the value entered on a previous run of the setup program. Once the selections have been made, they are translated back to OFF or ON using a similar set of IIF functions.

Procedures to Establish Programmer-Specified System Options

The remainder of the NWSETUP2.PRG program consists of a series of calls to procedures that establish the systemwide options that are best established by the programmer. Many of these options need not be accessible to the users; in fact, there is no reason that the users even need to be aware of the existence of the variables that store the text of commonly displayed messages, the characters used to draw boxes on the screen or lines on a printer, the display colors or monochrome attributes (used in SET COLOR commands), the printer control codes, and the standard date display format (established with SET DATE). To make it easy for the programmer to change any of these options, they may be placed in procedures that can be modified as required for a specific application and called from the setup program.

Some of the procedures, especially those that create a new memory variable by repeatedly adding onto a character variable in a DO WHILE loop, take a noticeable amount of time to run, which can be quite disconcerting to a user who has no idea what the program is doing. The NWSETUP2.PRG therefore displays a message informing the user that the system initialization is being completed, as well as a more specific message prior to running each procedure. Even if the user does not understand exactly what each of these status messages means, the changing display indicates that the system has not crashed and that the program is working as intended.

A Procedure to Create Variables for Standard Messages: STDMSGS

As pointed out in Chapter 22, whenever the same messages are used repeatedly within a program, it is expedient to store the message text in a series of memory variables. This makes the program that uses the messages more concise and allows you to change the text of the messages without having to make the same change many times in one program.

When the same messages are used throughout a data base application, you can store the message text in a series of PUBLIC variables and use them in any program in the system. Here is a procedure that creates variables for the components of many of the standard messages used in the National Widgets system:

```
procedure STDMSGS

store " -- Press any key to continue"                to MPPRESSKEY
store "You must SEARCH first"                        to MPSEARCH
store "This is the first name"                       to MPFIRST
store "This is the last name"                        to MPLAST
store " not found"                                   to MPNOTFOUND
store "Balance is not 0.00"                          to MPNOTZERO
store "There are current transactions"               to MPTRANSACT
store " has been deleted"                            to MPDELETE
store " has been recovered"                          to MPRECOVER
store " is already on file"                          to MPONFILE
store 'Please correct the fields marked with a "*" ' to MPCORRECT
```

Using these variables, the Customer File Update and Inquiry program could display an error message with this kind of command sequence:

```
if eof() .or. bof()
   do MESSAGE with 23, 15, MSEARCH + MPRESSKEY
   loop
endif
```

Procedures to Display Graphics Characters: BOXES and SCRNHEAD

As discussed in Chapter 8, a variation of the @ ... SAY command permits you to draw continuous lines and boxes made up of the single- and double-line graphics characters and the corresponding corner and intersection characters. You may not want to use these characters in your data entry screens, in order to preserve the ability to print the screen with SHIFT-PRTSC on printers other than the IBM Graphics Printer. However, you might like to use graphics characters to improve the appearance of certain screens that would rarely be printed (a menu screen, for example, or a screen used for collecting selection criteria). In this case, or if your organization does have an IBM Graphics Printer, you may not want to limit yourself to the standard single- and double-line graphics characters. For example, you might want to use the larger block characters to construct thicker lines or borders or to place individual characters like arrows or "happy faces" on a screen to highlight certain data items. (Like color, these characters should be used sparingly to avoid creating an overly busy or cluttered screen.)

With the MODIFY COMMAND editor and with many word processors, you can enter any character directly into a dBASE III PLUS program by holding down the ALT key and typing the ASCII code for the character on the numeric keypad (the numbers on the standard typewriter section of the keyboard will not work for this purpose). Thus, you can create a character string that includes these characters in a TEXT ... ENDTEXT structure or within any quoted character string displayed with ? or @ ... SAY. However, repeating this procedure enough times to construct a continuous line all the way across the screen or to draw a border for an input screen can become quite tedious. Also, with many editors, not every character may be entered this way. For example, the graphical representation of the character with the ASCII code 27 is a small left-pointing arrow—a character you might want to use in an input screen. However, this is the code for the ESCAPE character; and typing this character into a program file with MODIFY COMMAND is equivalent to pressing the ESC key, which aborts the editing process rather than entering the character into the file you are editing.

You can display this or any other character using the CHR function, which accepts as input a number representing the decimal ASCII code of a character and returns as output the character itself. Thus, the letter A could be expressed as CHR(65), and the ESCAPE character as CHR(27). The following command would display a small left-pointing arrow at line 10, column 15 on the screen:

```
@ 10,15 say chr(27)
```

Figure 24-4 illustrates a procedure, BOXES, that creates PUBLIC memory variables to draw thick lines and boxes consisting of graphics characters on the screen. The MPULINE and MPLLINE variables contain, respectively, the ASCII characters that produce thick continuous lines in the upper and lower halves of the standard character position. This procedure uses exactly the same method to construct the variables as the DASHES procedure did in Chapter 22, except that the DO WHILE loop is executed only seven times, resulting in a length of 128 rather than 254. Since MPULINE and MPLLINE are used only on the display terminal, they are both shortened to 80 characters using the LEFT function. The BOXES procedure also initializes a variable, MPVERT, that contains the

```
procedure BOXES

public MPLLINE, MPULINE, MPVERT, MPULC, MPLLC, MPURC, MPLRC

store chr(220) to MPLLINE
store chr(223) to MPULINE

store 1 to MCOUNT

do while MCOUNT <= 7
   store MPLLINE + MPLLINE to MPLLINE
   store MPULINE + MPULINE to MPULINE
   store MCOUNT  + 1       to MCOUNT
enddo

store left(MPLLINE, 80) to MPLLINE
store left(MPULINE, 80) to MPULINE

store chr(219) to MPVERT
store chr(219) to MPULC
store chr(219) to MPURC
store chr(219) to MPLLC
store chr(219) to MPLRC

return
```

Figure 24-4. A procedure to create variables that store graphics characters

thick vertical bar character, and four variables containing the characters to be used for the corners of boxes. The latter variables are created mostly for convenience, so that you do not need to remember or look up the ASCII codes for these characters in order to use them in a dBASE III PLUS program to draw boxes on the screen.

The SCRNHEAD procedure uses the characters created by BOXES to display the user's company name, centered, in inverse video within a box on the screen and surrounded by two small arrows:

```
procedure SCRNHEAD

clear
@  1,10 say MPULC + left(MPULINE, 58) + MPURC
@  2,10 say MPVERT
@  2,69 say MPVERT
@  3,10 say MPLLC + left(MPLLINE, 58) + MPLRC

set color to /W, W+
do CENTER with 2, 80, CHR(26) + " " + MPCOMPANY + " " + CHR(27)
set color to W, W+

return
```

This procedure constructs the box with a series of @ . . . SAY commands, using the corner characters, the double vertical bar character, and substrings of the appropriate length of the variables MPULINE and MPLLINE. SET COLOR commands are used to set the background color to inverse video before calling the CENTER procedure to display the company name, and then to return to the usual colors afterward. The arrows are expressed as CHR(26) and CHR(27). Note that if the CENTER procedure did not TRIM the variable MTEXT before displaying it, the bar of inverse video containing MPCOMPANY would extend the full length of the variable (35 characters).

The BOXES procedure is structured so as to make it easy to switch to different graphics characters or to substitute printable characters or even spaces for the graphics characters in an application that must permit the user to print the contents of any screen. Thus, the four corner characters are created with four separate STORE commands, although in this case the same symbol is used for all four corners. If you decided to use plus signs for the corners, dashes or equal signs for the horizontal lines, and the standard vertical bar character instead of the thick graphics character, only the procedure would have to be changed. In fact, if your printer supports continuous-line characters, you could modify the DASHES procedure as well to use these instead of the less attractive dashes and equal signs.

A Procedure to Set the Display Attributes: DISPATT

In the first version of the National Widgets system Main Menu program, the following SET COLOR command was used to establish the foreground and background colors used throughout the system:

```
set color to W, W+
```

To display a message in the brighter intensity, the colors were changed with

```
set color to W+, W+
```

Placing the various options for the display colors or monochrome attributes in a series of PUBLIC memory variables, as done for the disk drive assignments, would greatly facilitate adapting the application to run on different hardware, as well as customizing it for the personal preferences of the users.

In order to allow the users to select the actual colors without knowing the dBASE III PLUS color abbreviations, your setup program would have to present a list of all the possible choices for the foreground and background color combinations. Remember that for the foreground area (data entered by the user), you can specify both the color of the characters and the color of the background; the same is true for the background area (data displayed by dBASE III PLUS). Also, each color may be displayed in either the normal or bright intensity, or even blinking. When you take into account both monochrome and color monitors, this amounts to many options. While it is certainly *possible* to allow the user to choose the colors, it is also reasonable for the programmer to make the selection.

In the National Widgets system, two memory variables are needed: one to activate the brighter colors for highlighting error messages and reminders, and one to return to the standard display. These variables, which will be called MPBRIGHT and MPSTANDARD, could be initialized as follows:

```
store "W+, W+" to MPBRIGHT
store "W,  W+" to MPSTANDARD
```

Your programs could then turn on the brighter intensity display for error messages with

```
set color to &MPBRIGHT
```

To return to the standard colors, you would use

```
set color to &MPSTANDARD
```

You could lend additional flexibility to the system by specifying different display attributes for color and monochrome monitors. It is not even necessary to change a procedure for each installation, because you can use the ISCOLOR function to detect which type of monitor is present. The following procedure sets the standard attributes to use bright underlining for entered data on a monochrome monitor. On color monitors, red letters on a white background are used for the brighter intensity.

```
procedure DISPATT

if iscolor()
   store "R/W, W+" to MPBRIGHT
   store "W,   W+" to MPSTANDARD
else
   store "W+, W+" to MPBRIGHT
   store "W,  U+" to MPSTANDARD
endif

return
```

Applying the same principle to printer control commands gives an application the flexibility to take advantage of the special enhancements available on different printers, all of which use different control code sequences to access these features. Because understanding the printer control sequences is difficult for most inexperienced users, these options are best established by the programmer when an application is first set up; they can be changed by editing the setup procedure if a new printer is purchased.

In a typical application you might define the following set of variables to control the printer:

Variable	Purpose
MPBOLDON	Turn on boldface print.
MPBOLDOFF	Turn off boldface print.
MPENLRGON	Turn on enlarged print.
MPENLRGOFF	Turn off enlarged print.
MPCOMPON	Turn on compressed print (17 characters per inch).
MPCOMPOFF	Turn off compressed print.
MP18LINES	Set page length to 18 lines.
MP66LINES	Set page length to 66 lines.

The values of these variables could be customized to match the particular printer used. For example, for the Epson printer, MP18LINES would be initialized this way:

```
store chr(27) + "C" + chr(18) to MP18LINES
```

This variable could then be used in the NWCCARD2.PRG program, which prints the Customer File data on index or Rolodex cards, like this:

```
@  0, 0 say MP18LINES
```

Similarly, you could boldface the first line of the report title printed by the RPTHEAD procedure with

```
do CENTER with 3, MWIDTH, MPBOLDON + MTITLE1 + MPBOLDOFF
```

Here is the procedure that initializes all of the printer attribute variables for the Epson printer:

```
procedure PRINTATT

store chr(27) + 'E'                to MPBOLDON
store chr(27) + 'F'                to MPBOLDOFF
store chr(27) + 'W' + chr(1)       to MPENLRGON
store chr(27) + 'W' + chr(0)       to MPENLRGOFF
store chr(15)                      to MPCOMPON
store chr(18)                      to MPCMPOFF
store chr(27) + 'C' + chr(18)      to MP18LINES
store chr(27) + 'C' + chr(66)      to MP66LINES

return
```

If you choose the values of your variables strategically, you can make the most of the capabilities of sophisticated dot-matrix or laser printers while still allowing the system to run on less advanced printers with fewer type fonts. For example, many dot-matrix printers have an enlarged typeface that you might want to use for report headings, while most letter-quality printers cannot switch type sizes or styles unless the print element is changed. Almost any printer can boldface, however, so for a letter-quality printer, you could store in the MPENLRGON and MPENLRGOFF variables the same codes assigned to MPBOLDON and MPBOLDOFF. A report heading could always be printed with a distinguishing type style, either boldface or enlarged type, by using

```
do CENTER with 3, MWIDTH, MPENLRGON + MTITLE1 + MPENLRGOFF
```

In a system with more than one printer attached, you may want to give the users the freedom to switch printers at any time without having to change the programs. You can do this with a program or procedure that changes the printer codes to match the user's selection. Figure 24-5 lists a skeleton for this procedure, which might become a Main Menu option.

```
procedure SELECTPR

clear
text

     You may choose any of the following printers:

          (1) - Epson
          (2) - Okidata
          (3) - NEC
endtext

store " " to MPRINTER
do while .not. MPRINTER $ "123"
   @ 10,10 say "Please enter your selection" get MPRINTER picture "9"
   read
enddo

do case
   case MPRINTER = "1"
      * commands to store Epson control codes in PUBLIC variables
   case MPRINTER = "2"
      * commands to store Okidata control codes in PUBLIC variables
   case MPRINTER = "2"
      * commands to store NEC control codes in PUBLIC variables
endcase

save all like MP* to NWMEMORY

return
```

Figure 24-5. A procedure to select among several printers

Establishing the Display Format For Dates

Establishing the display format for dates, which ideally should be under the control of the user, is even more problematic. The default format for displaying and entering dates is month/day/year order (for example, 07/31/87 for July 31, 1987), but you may use the SET DATE command to select any of the following formats:

Type	Format
AMERICAN	MM/DD/YY
ANSI	YY.MM.DD
BRITISH	DD/MM/YY
ITALIAN	DD-MM-YY
FRENCH	DD.MM.YY
GERMAN	DD.MM.YY

Regardless of the display format, you can always compare two dates to determine which one is larger (later), and if you build an index based on a date field, earlier dates will occur earlier in the index. But in order to build a compound index based on the combination of a character field plus a date, the date must be converted to a character string with the DTOC (date-to-character) function before it is concatenated with the character field in the index key expression. In the National Widgets system, for example, you might want to index the Transaction History File by customer account number and invoice date. (*Note:* In this particular system, indexing on ACCOUNT + INVOICE also results in arranging the records in chronological order, but in other applications, you may not have such an easy alternative to using the date field.) You could build the account/date index this way:

```
use NWTXNHST
index on ACCOUNT + dtoc(INVDATE) to NWTHACDT
```

The problem is that once the date is converted to characters, dBASE III PLUS no longer recognizes it as a date. If the dates were entered in month/day/year order, this field would be "alphabetized" like any other character field, beginning with the first character and proceeding from left to right. Thus, any date in January would come before any date in February, just as any name beginning with A alphabetizes before any name beginning with B, regardless of the second letter of the name.

One way to resolve this problem is to use SET DATE ANSI to establish the year.month.day order, which guarantees that when a date is converted to a character variable, the most significant portion of the date (the year) comes first. You may find, however, that the users do not feel comfortable with the ANSI date display format. Although dBASE III PLUS has two FUNCTIONs intended for use in PICTURE clauses for altering the date display format (@E for European format and @D for American), these do not allow you to override the format established with SET DATE.

The alternative is to rearrange the date yourself in order to build the index:

```
index on ACCOUNT + substr(dtoc(INVDATE), 7, 2) + substr(dtoc(INVDATE), 1, 5);
     to NWTHACDT
```

In this expression the first substring function yields the last two characters of the INVDATE field after it is converted to a character string with the DTOC function. If INVDATE were 08/20/87, this substring would equal "87". The second substring function extracts the first five characters, the month and day ("08/20").

If ABC Plumbing had an invoice on August 20, 1987, the index entry would look like this:

```
ABCPLUMB  8708/20
```

Notice that there is no need to include a slash between the year and the month in this expression. In order to build an index that accesses the file in correct chronological order, it is only necessary that the components of the date occur in year/month/day order and that they each occupy a fixed position in the index key expression, so that when comparing two index entries dBASE III PLUS is always comparing a year to another year, a month to a month, and a day to a day. Another way to accomplish this is to use the YEAR, MONTH, and DAY functions to extract the three components of the date and to convert them to character strings with the STR function:

```
index on ACCOUNT + str(year(INVDATE), 2) + str(month(INVDATE), 2) +;
       str(day(INVDATE), 2) to NWTHACDT
```

To SEEK a particular combination of customer account number and invoice date, you must perform the same transformation on the memory variables used as the object of the SEEK. For example, with the index constructed using the SUBSTR function, you could use

```
store "          " to MACCOUNT
store ctod(" ")    to MDATE

@  5,10 say "Enter customer account number" get MACCOUNT picture "@!"
@  6,10 say "Enter invoice date           " get MDATE
read

seek MACCOUNT + substr(dtoc(MDATE), 7, 2) + substr(dtoc(MDATE), 1, 5)
```

If you used the YEAR, MONTH, and DAY functions to build the index, the SEEK command would look like this:

```
seek MACCOUNT + str(year(MDATE), 2) + str(month(MDATE), 2) + str(day(MDATE), 2)
```

The only way to use the ANSI format for internal storage while displaying and entering dates in the more familiar month/day/year order is to use SET DATE commands to switch between ANSI and AMERICAN formats. This is easy for memory variables:

```
store date() to MDATE
set date american
@ 10,10 say "Enter invoice date" get MDATE
read
set date ansi
```

For data base fields, you must SET DATE AMERICAN, collect the data into a memory variable (along with any other fields or variables to be entered by the user), and then return to ANSI format before REPLACE-ing the data base field with the memory variable:

```
store INVDATE to MDATE
set date american
@ 10,10 say "Enter invoice date" get MDATE
read
set date ansi
replace INVDATE with MDATE
```

This allows a date to be entered and validated in the familiar American MM/DD/YY format while being stored internally in ANSI (YY.MM.DD) format. If this command sequence were used frequently, you could incorporate it into a procedure.

Whichever display format you select, you could store it in a PUBLIC memory variable, much like the ones used for the display colors:

```
store "american" to MPDATEFORM
```

The SET DATE command in the previous partial program would then become

```
set date &MPDATEFORM
```

Because the date display format has such far-reaching effects throughout the programs in a system—it determines the structures of the indexes, the syntax of SEEK commands, and the sequence of commands required to enter and edit date fields—it is rarely feasible to allow the users to specify this option. The command to establish the default date display format is therefore included in NWSETUP2.PRG (refer again to Figure 24-2), where it may be changed to suit the requirements of the particular application.

The structure of the NWSETUP2.PRG program is very straightforward: it consists primarily of calls to separate procedures, selected as required for the particular application being developed. In a system with a large procedure file, some of these procedures could be extracted and run as separate programs since they are used infrequently and are somewhat slow in any case. Unlike the SET commands in the Main Menu, which establish the working environment each time the program is run, the options customized through the setup programs need not be changed very often—perhaps only once, when the application is first initialized. If you write systems that run on similar hardware, you will rarely need to edit NWSETUP2.PRG or the procedures it calls; if you do have to make changes for different hardware configurations, the procedures are easily edited to match the needs of the users.

25

NETWORKING AND SECURITY

This chapter introduces the separate but related areas of establishing a password-protected security system to restrict access to a data base and designing multi-user applications for use in a local area network (LAN) environment. The connection between these two subjects is in part historical, because multi-user software has migrated "down" from mainframe computers that support hundreds or even thousands of terminals, to minicomputers with dozens of workstations, and finally to microcomputers. In a mainframe or minicomputer environment, each user may need access to only a small fraction of the available software and data. When *all* of an organization's software and data files, some of which may contain highly sensitive information, reside on a single computer system, it is essential to control access to the system and its various hardware and software resources so that only authorized users can run a program or read a data file. But with a stand-alone microcomputer used exclusively by one individual, that person may require no stronger security measures than simply locking the office door before leaving for the day and storing backup floppy disks in a locked cabinet or safe.

In a network environment where several users may share the same copy of dBASE III PLUS and store files on the same hard disk, it may be necessary to prevent certain users from running some of the programs or from reading or updating sensitive data files. However, networking and security are not inseparable, either in principle or in the way these capabilities are added to a dBASE III PLUS application. A small company or department may own just one single-user microcomputer, but with several different applications coexisting on the same hard disk, a security system may be necessary so that each is accessible only to certain staff members. On the other hand, an organization may have installed a local area network to allow several workstations (perhaps physically separated by the layout of the office) to share relatively expensive peripherals, such as a high-capacity hard disk and a laser printer. Nevertheless, anyone in the office may be permitted to run dBASE III PLUS, access the same applications programs, and even update the same data base files.

Running dBASE III PLUS or any other software in a network environment also involves a different type of security—protecting disk files from the damage that would result from two users updating the same data simultaneously. When one user is performing an operation that involves large-scale updates to a data base, the entire file must be closed to other users. When records are updated one by one, with the full-screen edit commands or an update program like the ones written for the National Widgets Customer File, it is only necessary to ensure that no two users can write to the same record at the same time.

This chapter describes how to tailor a password-protection scheme to the level of security appropriate for your organization. In addition to controlling access to dBASE III PLUS itself and to your dBASE III PLUS programs, techniques will be presented for defining detailed file and field access privilege profiles that determine which whole data bases and individual fields may be viewed, updated, or deleted by any of the application's users. This chapter will also discuss the design and implementation of multi-user dBASE III PLUS applications, and it will present a network version of the file update and inquiry programs written in earlier chapters.

SECURITY

dBASE III PLUS allows you to add a password-protection scheme to a data base application that enforces security at several distinct levels. In order to implement any type of security system, you must use the dBASE III PLUS Administrator, executed via the ACCESS program, rather than the single-user version of dBASE III PLUS, even if you are not running the software on a network. If you have already been running dBASE III PLUS from a hard disk, it must be removed using the UNINSTAL program provided with the software before you install the Administrator and the ACCESS program. On a network, the Administrator must be installed in a shared subdirectory on the file server. Each workstation (including the file server, if this computer is also used as a workstation) must have its own copy of the ACCESS program, which may be stored on a hard disk or executed from a floppy disk.

The security system is created and maintained using the stand-alone PROTECT utility. You can run this program independently or from within dBASE III PLUS with the RUN command (if you have enough memory in your computer). The program uses the same type of pull-down menus and command structure as the ASSIST menus and the CREATE/MODIFY editors used to generate report and label forms and to define VIEWs and query files. PROTECT offers two Main Menu options that invoke pull-down submenus for defining a log-in profile for each user and a file access profile for each data base. The user log-in profile prevents unauthorized personnel from using dBASE III PLUS; coupled with the file access profiles, it also determines whether a given user may access a particular file, and if so, whether the person may add to the file, update or delete records, or merely view the data. By matching up the access privilege schemes defined for the system's users and data base files, you can gain precise control at the field level over what operations each user may perform on each of the files in the application.

Controlling Access To dBASE III PLUS

At the lowest level, a security system may be used solely to control access to the dBASE III PLUS program itself. To implement this type of protection, you select the USERS submenu in the PROTECT program to assign each authorized dBASE III PLUS user a log-in profile consisting of five items (only three of which are required). For every user, you must define a *group name, log-in name,* and *password.* You may also add an optional *account name,* which serves as a longer, more descriptive identification of the user, and an *access level,* which allows for finer control over the user's access to files, fields, and programs.

With a security system in effect, the dBASE III PLUS Administrator displays a log-in screen whenever the program is started up at any workstation, and no one may gain access to dBASE III PLUS without entering a valid combination of group name, log-in name, and password. These three items may be typed in any combination of uppercase and lowercase, and to make it more difficult for anyone to casually discover another user's log-in sequence, the password is not echoed to the terminal. At command level, one user can relinquish control to another without exiting from dBASE III PLUS with the LOGOUT command, which initiates a new log-in sequence so that the new user can enter his or her group name, log-in name, and password. This command should not be used within a dBASE III PLUS program intended for users who are unfamiliar with dBASE III PLUS, because it does not return to the program after logging in the new user, but instead displays the dot prompt.

The *log-in name* is a short code, up to eight characters long, that identifies the individual user. Although it is customary to assign unique log-in names, this is not absolutely necessary, and since the password affords a higher level of security, there is usually no reason to make the log-in names cryptic or difficult to remember. Some common choices for the log-in name are the user's first or last name, initials, or nickname, or an abbreviation derived from the user's job title or description.

Each user is also given a *password,* which may be up to 16 characters long and should always be unique even if the log-in names are not. Whether passwords are assigned by the programmer or manager who maintains the security system or whether they are chosen by the users is a matter of discretion; permitting the users to select their own passwords can reduce the natural feelings of hostility engendered by any security system. In either case, the passwords should be difficult or impossible to guess, a stipulation that rules out most of the choices that first come to mind, including names, nicknames, phone numbers, names of family members, friends, or pets, terms related to the user's job or hobbies, names of favorite songs, or any other words associated in any way with the individual. On the other hand, passwords made up of random sequences of 16 letters and numbers are unnecessarily difficult to remember. One good compromise is to use two or three common but unrelated English words, perhaps separated by punctuation marks, that fill or almost fill the allotted 16 characters; for example, "PLUM-CLOUDY-FERN".

The *group name,* which may be up to eight characters long, is used to classify an organization's staff by application, so that each group of users may be matched up with the set of data base files that compose the application. Once a group name has been assigned to a data base file, only users with a matching group name may access the file. In the National Widgets system, for example, the files in the accounts receivable system might be assigned the group name NWACTREC, while the prospect mailing list files maintained in separate dBASE III PLUS data bases might belong to the MAILLIST group. In order to work with files in two or more groups, a user will need two different log-in profiles. If you do not assign any file access privileges, the group name is used only in the log-in sequence that validates the user's permission to run dBASE III PLUS.

The optional 24-character *account name* may be used to record the user's full name and departmental association or to enter any other information about the user that could be important to the designer or manager of the security system. For example, the account name might be used to distinguish among members of the data processing, accounting, and marketing departments or to note the user's primary area of responsibility in running an application. The account name is not displayed or entered in the log-in sequence; in fact, it may be viewed only from within the PROTECT program, so it should be selected to best serve the needs of the person who maintains the security system.

Finally, you may assign each user an *access level* ranging from 1, the highest and most powerful level, to 8, the lowest level with the fewest privileges. In combination with the file access levels assigned through the FILES submenu of the PROTECT program, a user's access level determines which files are available and what operations the user may perform on each of the fields in each of these files. The access level is also available to your dBASE III PLUS programs in the form of the ACCESS( ) function. If you are implementing a security system only to guard dBASE III PLUS against unauthorized entry, you can retain the default access level of 1 (the highest level) for all users.

The user security profiles entered through PROTECT are stored in a file called DBSYSTEM.DB, which is encrypted to prevent a knowledgeable operator from using the TYPE command or a file inspection utility (like the Norton Utilities or the MS-DOS DEBUG program) to discover the passwords and user names. The encryption is based on the *Administrator password* created the first time the PROTECT program is run; without this password, user profiles cannot be examined or changed.

Controlling Access to Files And Fields Through PROTECT

The FILES submenu in the PROTECT program allows you to define a detailed access profile for a data base file and, optionally, for individual fields within the file. Each data base is given a *group name,* which is matched up with the group names assigned to the system's users to determine who is permitted to open the file for any purpose whatsoever. When you exit from PROTECT, any data base that has been assigned a group name is encrypted, creating a protected copy of the file with a .CRP extension. The unprotected .DBF file may then be removed from the hard disk and the .CRP file renamed so that users working at the dot prompt can open the file in the customary way. Existing programs that open the data base without specifying the extension will then run without modification.

Once encrypted by PROTECT, a data base is maintained in encrypted form so that only authorized users may access the file. Any indexes associated with the data base are encrypted the first time they are opened, and they are maintained thereafter in encrypted form. *No other files are encrypted, including .DBT files.* This means that at the very least, users should be cautioned against entering sensitive information into memo fields; in a system where security is more critical, you might have to forego the relative efficiency of memo fields and substitute long character fields to store notes or comments.

Any data bases not assigned an access profile in PROTECT, along with new data bases defined with CREATE, are not encrypted and may be accessed by all users. The status of the ENCRYPTION option, which is ON by default, determines whether new files generated from protected files by commands such as COPY, SORT, and TOTAL are also encrypted. You can cause these commands to write unencrypted files with

```
SET ENCRYPTION OFF
```

Even with ENCRYPTION OFF, a data base or text file created from an encrypted file will not include fields that the user who issued the command is not permitted to view in the original data base. However, fields that the user can view but not update *are* copied and may be edited in the new, unprotected file. Commands that *always* generate an unprotected file—for example, the options in the COPY command that create text or spreadsheet files—will result in a "File is encrypted" error message unless you first SET ENCRYPTION OFF.

To control access to data base files more closely, you may designate four overall access levels to specify the lowest access level that grants permission to read, update, extend (add), and delete records. (Remember that "lowest" means the *highest* numerical value for the user's access level.) For example, in the National Widgets system, the following access levels will be assigned to the Customer File:

Read privilege level	7
Update privilege level	4
Extend privilege level	4
Delete privilege level	2

According to this scheme, users with access levels 1 to 7 may read (display) data from the file; levels 1 to 4 permit a user to update (edit) records and extend the file (add records); and level 1 or 2 is required to delete records. With these additional controls in effect, any command that might result in a forbidden action returns the "Unauthorized access level" error message. For example, an employee of National Widgets with access level 5 can execute commands like DISPLAY, LIST, and REPORT, but not commands like EDIT, CHANGE, BROWSE, and REPLACE, which can be used to change data or delete records.

By default all four levels are set to 8, but if you encrypt a file and do not define a more detailed access profile, only users with access level 1 will be able to access the data base. This combination of privileges results from retaining the default values for both the user and file access levels. Thus, if you only need to segregate users and files into matching groups without restricting the commands available to any of the users, you can simply assign file group names, leaving all the access levels unchanged from the defaults.

The PROTECT program also allows you to assign field-by-field access privileges for each of the eight overall access levels. Users with the specified access number may be granted one of three privilege levels for each field: FULL, R/O (Read-Only), or NONE. These must be assigned so as to be consistent with the overall access levels specified for the file; for a user who can read but not update a file, it only makes sense to assign the R/O or NONE access privilege for individual fields. If you specify field privileges for any access level, all privileges for lower levels (higher access-level numbers) will default to NONE.

In all of the dBASE III PLUS full-screen commands, such as APPEND, EDIT, and BROWSE, fields not available to the logged-in user are not displayed at all, and fields identified as R/O appear in the background colors, as if they had been displayed with SAY commands rather than GETs. All explicit references to forbidden fields (for example, naming in a REPLACE command a field for which the user has only R/O permission) yield a "Variable not found" error message, even if the field is in full view on the screen. A more serious problem is that referencing the same field in a format file generates the same error message, so you may have to create different versions of your existing format files for use with a protected data base system.

The access profile for a data base file is stored in the .DBF file itself, not in DBSYSTEM.DB. If you need to assign some users in one group high-level access to the files in one application but low-level privileges in another, you can create more than one set of user profiles, stored in different DBSYSTEM.DB files. Each group of users must then invoke dBASE III PLUS from a batch file that first copies the appropriate version of DBSYSTEM.DB to the subdirectory that contains the dBASE III PLUS Administrator software. By strategically combining user and file access profiles, you can establish a very detailed and sophisticated system of access controls that is especially useful when many staff members work at the dot prompt. In contrast, with the single-user version of dBASE III PLUS, it is very difficult to prevent a user who is familiar with working at the dot prompt from reading or changing almost any data created by dBASE III PLUS.

Controlling Access to Programs

Using a security system established with PROTECT, you can control who may use dBASE III PLUS and which users may work with individual data base files, but you cannot automatically restrict access to memory variable files, report and label forms, program and procedure files, or in fact any types of files besides data bases and their associated indexes. Yet in a typical application, it is not unusual to need to limit the programs and menu options available to some of the users. For example, in the National Widgets system, in which the menus are organized along functional lines, you might want to grant separate access privileges to the Customer Information Menu, the Order Processing Menu, and the Financial Transactions Menu. In some systems, almost anyone should be allowed to print reports, but only a few users should be permitted to update the data bases. In other organizations, the opposite is true—the data entry is done by many staff members, but the reports, which compile and summarize confidential financial data, should be run only by the controller or department manager.

Indirectly, a user's file access privileges determine which programs the user may run, since any program that opens data base files will eventually generate an error message if the access profile of the logged-in user prohibits executing any of the commands contained in the program. Thus, a National Widgets shipping clerk permitted to update the Inventory File but not permitted to even read the Customer File could do little with the Customer File Update and Inquiry program—an error message would appear as soon as the program attempted to open the Customer File. Ideally, however, it is better not to allow an operator to even choose any menu option that opens forbidden data bases. In addition, you might want to restrict access to programs like NWSETUP1.PRG and NWSETUP2.PRG, which establish the systemwide options. These programs do not open any data base files and thus are not affected at all by the PROTECT security system.

Of the four fundamental components of a user's log-in profile—the group name, user name, password, and access level—only the access level is available to your dBASE III PLUS programs, in the form of the ACCESS() function. As long as the access level is the primary determinant of a user's privileges, it is easy to control access to individual programs or menu options by testing the value of this function. Here is a procedure that accepts as parameters the name of the program to be run and the lowest access level (the highest number) that still permits a user to run the program:

```
procedure ACCTEST

parameters MACCESS, MPROGRAM

if access() <= MACCESS
   do &MPROGRAM
else
   do MESSAGE with 23, 10, "This option is not available " + MPPRESSKEY
endif

return
```

This procedure receives two inputs from the calling program: the name of the program or procedure to be run, which is stored in the memory variable MPROGRAM, and the lowest access level that should be granted access to the specified program, which is passed to the memory variable MACCESS. The procedure compares the user's access level, expressed as ACCESS( ), to the memory variable MACCESS; if the user passes the test, the program or procedure is executed with DO

&MPROGRAM. Otherwise, the MESSAGE procedure is invoked to display an error message and to pause until the user presses a key, after which control is returned to the menu program. The wording of the error message was chosen so as to be more diplomatic than a more direct and possibly more offensive statement like "You are not authorized to run this program." If this kind of access-level test will be applied to many of the programs and options in the system, the text of the error message should be stored in a PUBLIC memory variable created by the STDMSGS procedure along with the other standard messages used in the application. If this variable were called MPNOTAVAIL, the call to MESSAGE in the ACCTEST procedure would look like this:

```
do MESSAGE with 23, 10, MPNOTAVAIL + MPPRESSKEY
```

In the National Widgets system, three of the Main Menu options will be protected this way. Only users with access levels of 1 or 2 may run the setup programs invoked by option 11, Customize System-Wide Options. An access level of 4 or higher (remember that a higher access level means a lower number) is required to run external programs or DOS commands from within dBASE III PLUS (option 14). Finally, although any user will be permitted—in fact, encouraged—to back up the data bases by using option 12, only users with an access level of 4 or higher will be able to choose option 13 to restore the data bases to the hard disk after a system crash. The rationale is that the restore program should not be accessible to users who may not clearly understand its potential to replace current information with the obsolete data stored on the backup disks if the option is chosen at an inappropriate time.

To implement this protection scheme, you must replace the DO command that runs each of these programs with a call to ACCTEST. For example, the setup option could be accessed through the following call to the ACCTEST procedure:

```
do ACCTEST with 2, NWSETUP1
```

You may also need to control access to menu options that do not call separate programs. For example, you might want to deny some users access to the dot prompt by protecting option 88 (Exit to dBASE III PLUS Command Level), and other command sequences may have been placed directly in the menu programs because they were too short to merit separate programs. The easiest solution to this problem is to extract the command lines into a separate program or procedure, but you could also include the access test in the menu, as follows:

```
if access() <= 4
   clear
   set talk on
   set status on
   set safety on
   set deleted off
   cancel
else
   do MESSAGE with 23, 10, MPNOTAVAIL + MPPRESSKEY
endif
```

Note that in order to prevent a user from working at the dot prompt, you must ensure that the Main Menu program is executed every time dBASE III PLUS is loaded by including a COMMAND line in CONFIG.DB. In the National Widgets system, you could load the Main Menu program (version 3) with this entry in CONFIG.DB:

```
COMMAND = DO NWMENU3
```

Controlling Access to Files And Fields From Programs

With a PROTECT security system in effect, dBASE III PLUS responds with an error message to any attempt to issue a command that would violate the privileges established through the user and file profiles. At command level, the error message is displayed immediately, and the user is offered the usual choices: Cancel, Ignore, or Suspend. In a menu-driven application, users should be shielded from dBASE III PLUS error messages, since they cannot be expected to understand what has caused an error or how to correct it. You can intercept these and other errors with an error-trapping program or procedure activated with the ON ERROR command. The syntax of the ON ERROR command is

ON ERROR DO *program or procedure*

Since the error-handling routine may be called repeatedly from within a single program, it is best to call a procedure rather than a separate program. The procedure can determine exactly which error has occurred by testing the value of the ERROR( ) function. If appropriate, the procedure will display a descriptive message for the user and then take corrective action. The text of the standard dBASE III PLUS error message is available through the MESSAGE( ) function, but you may prefer to substitute your own longer or more colloquial message text. The error-handling routine typically consists of a DO CASE structure that processes the various possible values of the ERROR( ) function to determine what action to take. In theory, this offers the programmer great flexibility in tailoring a program's response to the specific error that has occurred. However, it may not be possible to confine the error-processing mechanism to the error-trapping procedure, since the proper response to a given error may depend heavily on the context of the calling program. Adding password protection to an existing program may therefore require extensive modifications.

A USE command generates the expected "Unauthorized access level" error condition if the user running the program is not permitted any access to the file; the ERROR( ) function will evaluate to 133. If, however, an @ ... SAY ... GET command is used to display a field for which the user's access privilege is R/O or NONE, a "Variable not found" error results and the ERROR( ) function returns the value 12. This is true even if a subsequent CLEAR GETS prevents the user from actually editing the data. Because of this response to a GET command, the general strategy employed in the versions of the Customer File Update and Inquiry program presented so far—displaying fields with GETs, followed by CLEAR GETS to prevent the user from changing the data—is incompatible with the PROTECT security system. Instead, the program will be rewritten to emulate the behavior of dBASE III PLUS in the full-screen edit modes—to display only those fields the user is permitted to read and to collect with GETs only those fields the user may update.

Consider the problem of adding protection at the field level to a program like the National Widgets Customer File Update and Inquiry program. Of the users who are granted any kind of access to the Customer File, one person will be allowed to change *all* of the fields except the account number. Others may view all fields but change only some (there might be more than one such group of users with slightly different access privileges). Still others may view and update only selected fields. For example, suppose that National Widgets wanted to implement the following levels of access:

Program Function Or Option	**Lowest Access Level (Highest Value for ACCESS( ))**
View all fields	7
Change name and address fields	4
Change financial total fields	1
Change account number	No users
SEARCH, NEXT, PREVIOUS, RECALL, HELP	7
CHANGE, ADD, MEMO	4
DELETE	2

Adding this kind of protection system to the National Widgets Customer File Update and Inquiry program requires three basic changes. First, starting up the program with a call to ACCTEST will prevent users who are not even permitted to read the Customer File from entering the program in the first place. Access to the individual options within the program can be controlled in much the same way by testing the value of the ACCESS( ) function. In order to use the CHANGE or ADD options, an access level of 4 or higher is required; to delete records, a user must have an access level of 1 or 2. If an unauthorized user selects one of these options, dBASE III PLUS will generate an "Unauthorized access level" error message, which your error-trapping routine can detect:

```
case error() = 133
   do MESSAGE with 23, 10, MPNOTAVAIL + MPPRESSKEY
```

Note that the MEMO option, intended to allow the user to enter and edit the COMMENTS field, works by opening a format file and invoking the standard dBASE III PLUS EDIT command. If a user with an access level of 3 or 4 tries to delete a record through the format file with CTRL-U, the same error condition will result.

Depending on the exact command sequence used in the update program, it may be preferable to substitute your own access-level test for the automatic checking performed by dBASE III PLUS. Because the error occurs only when the forbidden command is encountered, the user may have to answer several questions before being denied access to the selected option. For example, the DELETE option tests the value of the BALANCE field, checks for the presence of current transactions in the Transaction File, and asks the user for confirmation before issuing the DELETE command that generates the error. If you prefer not to allow the user to progress this far along a dead-end path, you can insert your own access-level test at the beginning of the DELETE sequence:

```
if access() > 2
   do MESSAGE with 23, 10, MPNOTAVAIL + MPPRESSKEY
   loop
endif
```

To handle the "Variable not found" error generated by the GET commands for fields not changeable by the logged-in user, you could use the following in your error-handling procedure:

```
case error() = 12
   return
```

With this error trap, fields that may not be changed by the user are simply not displayed, since the GET command that generates the error is never executed. But because the update program uses a constant screen mask drawn with a TEXT ... ENDTEXT structure, all of the field prompts will be displayed, no matter who runs the program. If you prefer not to remind the users of the existence of fields they cannot edit, you can drop the TEXT ... ENDTEXT structure in favor of a series of @ ... SAY ... GET commands. Those few fields that must always be displayed but must not be changed by any user, such as the ACCOUNT field, could be displayed with SAY rather than GET commands.

Another way to fine-tune access to individual fields is to grant all users FULL access to all fields and then replace the two separate calls to the CUSTGET1 and CUSTGET2 procedures with a single call to a procedure that displays or collects the fields in blocks, as determined by the user's access level. This procedure, CUSTGET3, is listed in Figure 25-1. The procedure first displays the ACCOUNT field, which may not be altered by any user, followed by a CLEAR GETS command to prevent this field from being edited. Next, the fields are displayed in groups, starting with those accessible to the fewest users. After each group of fields, the procedure tests the value of the ACCESS() function and, if the fields may not be edited by this group of users, issues another CLEAR GETS com-

```
procedure CUSTGET3

if deleted()
   set color to &MPBRIGHT
   @ 3,65 say "* DELETED *"
   set color to &MPSTANDARD
else
   @ 3,65 say "           "
endif

@  3,13 get ACCOUNT
clear gets

@ 14,18 get YTDINV picture "9,999,999.99"
@ 15,18 get YTDPMT picture "9,999,999.99"
@ 17,18 get TOTINV picture "9,999,999.99"
@ 17,62 get FIRSTORDER
@ 18,18 get YTDPMT picture "9,999,999.99"
@ 18,62 get LASTORDER
@ 20,18 get BALANCE picture "@( 9,999,999.99"

if dtoc(LASTORDER) <> "  "
   store date() - LASTORDER to MDAYS
   @ 20,45 say "LAST ORDER WAS " + str(MDAYS,4) + " DAYS AGO"
else
   @ 20,45 say space(28)
endif

if access() > 1
   clear gets
endif

@  5,13 get COMPANY
@  6,13 get ADDRESS1
@  7,13 get ADDRESS2
@  8,13 get CITY
@  8,51 get STATE picture "@!"
@  8,63 get ZIP picture "99999"
@ 10,13 get CONTACT
@ 10,55 get AREACODE picture "999"
@ 10,63 get TELEPHONE picture "999-9999"
@ 12,13 get EQUIPMENT
@ 12,63 get TAXRATE range 0, 10

if MOPTION $ "CA"
   read
   if readkey() = 36 .or. readkey() = 292
      select 10
      do NWHELP2 with "NWCUPD4 ", 2
      select NWCUST
      do NWCSCRN
      do CUSTGET3
      loop
   endif
else
   clear gets
endif

return
```

Figure 25-1. A procedure to display and collect the fields accessible to the user

mand. The final test is the same one used in earlier versions of the update program to prevent the execution of the READ command if the user has chosen any option other than CHANGE or ADD. The problem with this approach is that for users with high-level access, the fields are collected in the same "reverse" order in which they are displayed; in the Customer File Update and Inquiry program, this means stepping through all of the financial fields, which would rarely be changed, before the cursor moves into the name and address block.

As an alternative, you can use SAY commands for the fields that may not be edited, as illustrated in the CUSTGET4 procedure listed in Figure 25-2. If necessary, each field could be enclosed in its own IF loop. This would permit the fields to be displayed and collected in the correct order, even if they did not fall neatly into blocks according to access level; however, it would also increase the complexity of the program and slow it down somewhat. Displaying the Read-Only fields with SAYs causes them to appear in the background color rather than the foreground color used for data collected with GETs. If you prefer to present all fields in the same colors instead of imitating the behavior of the dBASE III PLUS full-screen edit commands, you can precede the display commands with a SET

```
procedure CUSTGET4

if deleted()
   set color to &MPBRIGHT
   @ 3,65 say "* DELETED *"
   set color to &MPSTANDARD
else
   @ 3,65 say "           "
endif

@  3,14 say ACCOUNT

if access() <= 4
   @  5,13 get COMPANY
   @  6,13 get ADDRESS1
   @  7,13 get ADDRESS2
   @  8,13 get CITY
   @  8,51 get STATE picture "@!"
   @  8,63 get ZIP picture "99999"
```

Figure 25-2. A procedure to display and collect the fields accessible to the user in correct order

```
    @ 10,13 get CONTACT
    @ 10,55 get AREACODE picture "999"
    @ 10,63 get TELEPHONE picture "999-9999"
    @ 12,13 get EQUIPMENT
    @ 12,63 get TAXRATE range 0, 10
else
    @  5,14 say COMPANY
    @  6,14 say ADDRESS1
    @  7,14 say ADDRESS2
    @  8,14 say CITY
    @  8,52 say STATE
    @  8,64 say ZIP
    @ 10,14 say CONTACT
    @ 10,56 say AREACODE
    @ 10,64 say TELEPHONE
    @ 12,14 say EQUIPMENT
    @ 12,64 say TAXRATE
endif

if access() = 1
    @ 14,18 get YTDINV picture "9,999,999.99"
    @ 15,18 get YTDPMT picture "9,999,999.99"
    @ 17,18 get TOTINV picture "9,999,999.99"
    @ 17,62 get FIRSTORDER
    @ 18,18 get YTDPMT picture "9,999,999.99"
    @ 18,62 get LASTORDER
    @ 20,18 get BALANCE picture "@( 9,999,999.99"
else
    @ 14,19 say YTDINV picture "9,999,999.99"
    @ 15,19 say YTDPMT picture "9,999,999.99"
    @ 17,19 say TOTINV picture "9,999,999.99"
    @ 17,63 say FIRSTORDER
    @ 18,19 say YTDPMT picture "9,999,999.99"
    @ 18,63 say LASTORDER
    @ 20,19 say BALANCE picture "@( 9,999,999.99"
endif

if dtoc(LASTORDER) <> "  "
    store date() - LASTORDER to MDAYS
    @ 20,45 say "LAST ORDER WAS " + str(MDAYS,4) + " DAYS AGO"
else
    @ 20,45 say space(28)
endif

if MOPTION $ "CA"
    read
    if readkey() = 36 .or. readkey() = 292
        select 10
        do NWHELP2 with "NWCUPD4 ", 2
        select NWCUST
        do NWCSCRN
        do CUSTGET3
        loop
    endif
else
    clear gets
endif

return
```

Figure 25-2. A procedure to display and collect the fields accessible to the user in correct order (*continued*)

COLOR command. Also notice that the column coordinates in the SAY commands must be adjusted so that the data does not overwrite the bracket delimiters displayed by the screen mask. A final alternative is to use one procedure to display all of the fields with SAY commands, using a procedure like CUSTSAY (listed in Figure 25-3), and then collect the fields accessible to the user with a separate procedure like CUSTGET5 (shown in Figure 25-4).

When you plan a security system, you can take advantage of the fact that dBASE III PLUS provides more access levels than the two or three required by most applications. With eight levels at your disposal, you

```
procedure CUSTSAY

if deleted()
   set color to &MPBRIGHT
   @ 3,65 say "* DELETED *"
   set color to &MPSTANDARD
else
   @ 3,65 say "              "
endif

@  3,14 say ACCOUNT
@  5,14 say COMPANY
@  6,14 say ADDRESS1
@  7,14 say ADDRESS2
@  8,14 say CITY
@  8,52 say STATE
@  8,64 say ZIP
@ 10,14 say CONTACT
@ 10,56 say AREACODE
@ 10,64 say TELEPHONE
@ 12,14 say EQUIPMENT
@ 12,64 say TAXRATE
@ 14,19 say YTDINV picture "9,999,999.99"
@ 15,19 say YTDPMT picture "9,999,999.99"
@ 17,19 say TOTINV picture "9,999,999.99"
@ 17,63 say FIRSTORDER
@ 18,19 say YTDPMT picture "9,999,999.99"
@ 18,63 say LASTORDER
@ 20,18 say BALANCE picture "@( 9,999,999.99"

if dtoc(LASTORDER) <> "  "
   store date() - LASTORDER to MDAYS
   @ 20,45 say "LAST ORDER WAS " + str(MDAYS,4) + " DAYS AGO"
else
   @ 20,45 say space(28)
endif

return
```

Figure 25-3. A procedure to display the Customer File fields

```
procedure CUSTGET4

if deleted()
   set color to &MPBRIGHT
   @ 3,65 say "* DELETED *"
   set color to &MPSTANDARD
else
   @ 3,65 say "           "
endif

@  3,14 say ACCOUNT
@  5,14 say COMPANY
@  6,14 say ADDRESS1
@  7,14 say ADDRESS2
@  8,14 say CITY
@  8,52 say STATE
@  8,64 say ZIP
@ 10,14 say CONTACT
@ 10,56 say AREACODE
@ 10,64 say TELEPHONE
@ 12,14 say EQUIPMENT
@ 12,64 say TAXRATE
@ 14,19 say YTDINV picture "9,999,999.99"
@ 15,19 say YTDPMT picture "9,999,999.99"
@ 17,19 say TOTINV picture "9,999,999.99"
@ 17,63 say FIRSTORDER
@ 18,19 say YTDPMT picture "9,999,999.99"
@ 18,63 say LASTORDER
@ 20,19 say BALANCE picture "@( 9,999,999.99"

if dtoc(LASTORDER) <> "  "
   store date() - LASTORDER to MDAYS
   @ 20,45 say "LAST ORDER WAS " + str(MDAYS,4) + " DAYS AGO"
else
   @ 20,45 say space(28)
endif


if access() <= 4
   @  5,13 get COMPANY
   @  6,13 get ADDRESS1
   @  7,13 get ADDRESS2
   @  8,13 get CITY
   @  8,51 get STATE picture "@!"
   @  8,63 get ZIP picture "99999"
   @ 10,13 get CONTACT
   @ 10,55 get AREACODE picture "999"
   @ 10,63 get TELEPHONE picture "999-9999"
   @ 12,13 get EQUIPMENT
   @ 12,63 get TAXRATE range 0, 10
endif


if access() = 1
   @ 14,18 get YTDINV picture "9,999,999.99"
   @ 15,18 get YTDPMT picture "9,999,999.99"
   @ 17,18 get TOTINV picture "9,999,999.99"
   @ 17,62 get FIRSTORDER
```

Figure 25-4. A procedure to collect the Customer File fields accessible to the user

```
      @ 18,18 get YTDPMT picture "9,999,999.99"
      @ 18,62 get LASTORDER
      @ 20,18 get BALANCE picture "@( 9,999,999.99"
   endif

   if MOPTION $ "CA"
      read
      if readkey() = 36 .or. readkey() = 292
         select 10
         do NWHELP2 with "NWCUPD4 ", 2
         select NWCUST
         do NWCSCRN
         do CUSTGET3
         loop
      endif
   else
      clear gets
   endif

   return
```

Figure 25-4. A procedure to collect the Customer File fields accessible to the user (*continued*)

could set up many of the tests that determine which users may access the menu and command options so that permission is granted to all users with an access level higher than a given value, and then use several consecutive numbers to allow finer control within a program. For example, access levels 3, 4, and 5 might in general have equal access to the Main Menu options and to the command line options in the update and inquiry programs. You could, however, grant different access privileges to fields in the various data base files based on the precise value of the ACCESS( ) function. This scheme permits you to implement a security system in which one user may have high-level access to one set of data bases and low-level access to another, while another user with a similar access level could have the opposite file privileges.

dBASE III PLUS does not offer functions analogous to ACCESS( ) to enable a program to determine the group name, log-in name, or password of the current user, and although the information is stored in the data base file, you cannot make use of the file and field privilege levels assigned through PROTECT. The file access profile is therefore far more useful in a setting in which many users work with data base files at the dot prompt or through the ASSIST menus. In the course of implementing a similar security system in a menu-driven application like the National

Widgets system, many of the features of the PROTECT security system were duplicated in the new versions of the programs described in this chapter.

Documenting and Protecting The Security System

In most cases, one person in an organization is charged with the primary responsibility for setting up and maintaining the security system. In a small organization, this is often the individual who is the most familiar with using and programming dBASE III PLUS. In larger businesses, it may be someone from the data center or management information systems department who is not personally acquainted with the application's users. While it may be impossible to completely eliminate antagonism between the users of an application and the guardians of the security system, it is to everyone's advantage to foster a spirit of cooperation. Of course, the security system will rapidly be compromised if this cooperative attitude motivates the users or managers to share information that should remain private.

This delicate balance must also be taken into account in documenting the security system and maintaining unprotected copies of encrypted files. It is essential to have a hard copy of the Administrator password, without which there is no way to use the PROTECT program to examine or modify the user and file access profiles, yet it is also important to keep this information out of the hands of the system's users. Similarly, the individual user and file profiles should be documented on paper, not only to make it easier to retrieve a forgotten password but also in the event that the original designer of the security system is unavailable when this information is needed.

dBASE III PLUS provides little or no help in creating this essential documentation. The Administrator password should be written down and stored in a secure location. There is also no standard way to print a hard copy of the user or file profiles established through the PROTECT program. You can, however, produce this documentation by using SHIFT-PRTSC to print an image of each screen as it is completed. If you have a memory-resident desktop utility like SideKick, you can also import the portion of the screen containing the log-in information into a notepad file, which may later be "cleaned up" with SideKick or another editor to yield a less cluttered listing. Obviously, any printed record of the passwords used to protect a data base system from unauthorized access must be stored in a place that is not easily discovered by the users of the system.

Since access to encrypted files depends on the user profiles stored in the DBSYSTEM.DB file, a disk containing a copy of this file should also be filed away in case the original and the backup are damaged in a disk crash. After a data base is encrypted, all unencrypted copies of the file should be removed from the hard disk. However, it may be prudent to periodically create an unencrypted copy of the data, in the event that all existing copies of DBSYSTEM.DB are destroyed. This can be done by a user who has FULL access to all of the fields in a data base with a sequence of commands like the following:

```
USE NWCUST
SET ENCRYPTION OFF
COPY TO NWCUST2
SET ENCRYPTION ON
```

The effectiveness of a security system depends heavily on the cooperation of the individuals involved. In a large organization where the network workstations are located in physically separated locations and users have little or no contact with each other in the course of their jobs, this is generally not a problem. In smaller groups whose members consider themselves friends and view the security system as an additional burden imposed by management, conflicts can arise. A security system can rapidly become worthless if the users share their passwords in order to fill in for each other when someone is busy, sick, or otherwise absent from the office when a deadline approaches.

NETWORK PROGRAMMING

Designing a multi-user data base or adding multi-user capabilities to an existing system introduces many new complications. As long as data is only being read, not written to a file, it is safe to permit access by more than one user. For example, no conflicts would result from printing a Customer Reference List at one workstation in the National Widgets office while another operator uses the NWCORD2.PRG program to display customer and order data on screen. But when several users can access the same data files at the same time, operations involving an entire file—such as a SORT, PACK, or REPLACE command that affects many records—require that a data base be protected against simultaneous attempts to change the contents of the file. If one user were running a PACK command and another user read a record from the disk, changed the contents of one or more fields, and saved the changes, the record might have been moved by the PACK command in the interim; the second user's change would then overwrite an entirely different record.

Updating a data base record by record, using an update program like NWCUPD5.PRG, poses more subtle but equally serious problems. Suppose that two users wanted to open the Customer File at the same time to add, delete, view, and edit records without a special multi-user version of the software. Simply displaying the data is safe, since the file is not changed in any way. Adding records is not so straightforward. When dBASE III PLUS opens a data base, the file header and varying amounts of data are loaded into memory, and the number of records in the file, along with the other information in the file header, is updated on disk only when the file is closed. Imagine what would happen if the first user added records to the file and closed it, while the second user continued to edit and browse through the data base. When the second user finally closed the file, his or her copy of the file header would overwrite the version saved by the first. The record count would no longer reflect the new records added to the data base, and these records, while physically present on the disk, would no longer be accessible. In the event that several users added records simultaneously, some of the new additions might be written over other newly appended records, since each user's copy of the file header would reflect the number of records in the file at the time it was opened at his or her workstation.

Editing or deleting records is generally safe as long as no two users attempt to update the same record simultaneously. Since dBASE III PLUS uses a fixed-length record structure, all changes to a record are rewritten in exactly the same place on disk when the editing process is complete, and the file does not change in size. Problems would arise, however, if two users tried to access the same record at the same time. Each user would begin with the same copy of the data in working memory, and each might make different changes. When the two copies of the record were written to disk, the changes made by the first user to save the record would be overwritten by the copy of the record stored by the second user. The considerations involved in marking records for deletion and recalling deleted records are essentially the same. Deleting a record with CTRL-U in one of the full-screen edit modes or by using the DELETE command at the dot prompt or from within a program does not physically remove the record from the disk—it simply stores the deletion marker (the *) in the first byte of the record. The RECALL command removes this marker and replaces it with a blank space.

These problems exist whether you are updating a data base at command level or from within a dBASE III PLUS program. They are particularly insidious because if the users do not understand the potential problems, they cannot devise procedures to resolve them. In fact, the users may be unaware that not all of their changes have been entered successfully into the data base until long after the damage has been done, by which time it may be very difficult to trace the chain of events that corrupted the data.

Avoiding these potential disasters requires cooperation among the network operating system, the data base management software, and the users. The microcomputer network operating systems supported by dBASE III PLUS provide the means to "lock" an entire file or a single record so that only one user may access the data at one time. These network capabilities are accessed through a set of dBASE III PLUS commands and functions that you may use from the dot prompt and in your programs to protect a data base system from being damaged by multiple simultaneous updates.

Exclusive and Shared Access

dBASE III PLUS permits a file to be opened either for *exclusive* or *shared* use. A file opened for exclusive use, either from the dot prompt or from within a program, may not be accessed by any other users. By default, dBASE III PLUS opens files for exclusive use in any context where it would be dangerous for two users to be able to access the file at the same time; when shared mode is safe, it is the default mode. For example, most commands that operate on data bases open the .DBF file (and the matching .DBT file, if the data base contains memo files) for exclusive use, and index files are assigned the same mode as the associated data base file. Report and label forms are opened in exclusive mode by the CREATE/MODIFY editors, and in shared mode when they are used solely to print data, since printing mailing labels or a report does not alter the label or report form in any way. Although every type of file used by dBASE III PLUS can be opened in shared or exclusive mode, your primary concern when you design a data base application is to guarantee that the data bases are opened and updated safely, since corrupting a data base is a more serious problem that requires far more time and expense to repair than inadvertently damaging a report form.

You can override the default file-opening mode with

```
SET EXCLUSIVE OFF
```

or with

```
SET EXCLUSIVE ON
```

Files opened with EXCLUSIVE OFF are opened in shared mode, and files opened with EXCLUSIVE ON are opened for exclusive use; a file retains the mode in effect at the time it was opened until the file is closed, even if you later change the status of the EXCLUSIVE option. You can also open a data base file for exclusive use, regardless of the status of the EXCLUSIVE option, by including the EXCLUSIVE keyword in the USE command. For example, to open the National Widgets Inventory File in exclusive mode, you would use

```
USE NWINVENT INDEX NWICATPT EXCLUSIVE
```

Commands that rewrite a data base entirely—including INSERT, MODIFY STRUCTURE, PACK, and ZAP—require that a data base be opened for exclusive use. So does REINDEX, since the index file depends on the contents of the data base, and permitting changes to be made to the .DBF file with the index partially constructed would result in an index that no longer matched the data file. When you use these commands in dBASE III PLUS programs, you must make sure that the relevant data base is opened in exclusive mode before you use a command that requires it. If a data base is already open, you can close the file and reopen it with the EXCLUSIVE keyword in the new USE command.

When a file is opened in exclusive mode, no other users are permitted to access the file in any way, and any attempt will result in the "File is in use by another" error message. With several people working independently at command level, this message is sufficient to ensure that users at physically distant workstations do not inadvertently open the same file when doing so would have the potential to damage the data.

Your programs must also handle the two possible error conditions. If a file cannot be opened for exclusive use because it is already being updated by another user, a "File is in use by another" error will result immediately. But even if you succeed in gaining exclusive access to the file and begin execution of a PACK or REINDEX command, you cannot assume that all is well. An attempt by another user to open the file while your command is in progress will generate the same error message. To handle both contingencies, you must provide an error-trapping routine that detects and identifies the error conditions and explains the available options to the operator.

If an error is generated by an attempt to open a data base already opened for exclusive use at another workstation, the simplest approach is to return from the error-trapping routine with RETRY rather than RETURN:

```
case error() = 108
   retry
```

Like RETURN, the RETRY command causes the current program or procedure to terminate and return to the calling program or procedure. The difference is that RETRY causes the calling program to repeat the statement that generated the error rather than proceeding to the next command. However, it is inadvisable to continue to RETRY indefinitely, for two reasons. First, depending on the operation being carried out by the other user, the file may not become available for quite a while. Second, if two users begin running programs that open the same two data bases for exclusive use, but in the opposite order, a type of deadlock, often called a "deadly embrace," can result. Imagine that the first user's program opens NWCUST.DBF, while the second user's program opens NWORDER.DBF. If the first user then tries to open NWORDER.DBF and the second attempts to open NWCUST.DBF, an error-trapping routine that RETRYs indefinitely will hang up the system—since neither user can gain exclusive access to the second file requested.

Instead, the program should RETRY for a specified length of time and then display a message informing the operator that the file is unavailable and offer the advice to "try again later." The error-trapping procedure could include a loop that counts to 100 (or some other number) before executing the RETRY command. If, however, the second attempt to execute the command in the calling program yields the same error, you must prevent the error-handling procedure from counting to 100 and RETRYing the original command indefinitely. The error recovery routine must therefore be able to determine whether it is being called for the first time in a given context, in which case it should return to the calling program with RETRY, or for the second time, which should result in RETURNing and allowing the calling program to inform the user of the error.

Since both RETURN or RETRY reset the value of the ERROR( ) function to 0, you must create another variable to effect this communication between the calling program and the error-trapping procedure. This variable, MRETRY, could be assigned a value of .T. in the calling program and then be reset to .F. by the procedure. The procedure could then test the value of MRETRY to determine whether to exit with RETRY or, if this is the second call, with RETURN. In some applications, you may decide to exit to the Main Menu unequivocally when it is impossible to open a file, but often you will want to give the users other choices. The calling program must therefore be able to determine whether the error condition was successfully overcome with RETRY or whether the first RETRY attempt has failed. A second variable, MERROR, can be used for this purpose; MERROR is initialized as .F. in the calling program and is then reset to .T. if the error-trapping procedure determines that an error has occurred. Here is the CASE that handles this error trap:

```
case error() = 108
   store 1 to MCOUNT
   do while MCOUNT <= 100
      store MCOUNT + 1 to MCOUNT
   enddo
   if MRETRY
      store .F. to MRETRY
      retry
   else
      store .T. to MERROR
      return
   endif
```

Locking Shared Files

To create a true multi-user data base system, you must allow files to be opened for shared use in most of the programs that make up the application. Any time files are opened in shared mode, it is the responsibility of the users and/or programmer to prevent potential conflicts by *locking* either the entire file or individual records whenever necessary. A shared file must be locked to protect against simultaneous access by more than one user whenever a command is executed that affects the entire file. dBASE III PLUS automatically attempts to lock a data base when it encounters a command that obviously requires a file lock; these include APPEND, AVERAGE, BROWSE, COPY, COUNT, DELETE ALL, INDEX, JOIN, RECALL ALL, REPLACE ALL, SORT, SUM, TOTAL, and UPDATE. As soon as the command is completed, the lock is released. Just as when you attempt to open a file for exclusive use, dBASE III PLUS returns an error if the file cannot be locked because it is in use at another workstation; once the file is locked, any other users who try to access the file will receive an error message.

Although this automatic file locking is a convenience for users working at the dot prompt, it is of little benefit to the programmer, since most of the commands that cause dBASE III PLUS to lock an entire file automatically are rarely used in custom programs. If you use procedures or programs to perform essentially the same operations as the aforementioned commands, you must make sure that your programs also lock the data base files they operate on. For example, the NWCSTAT2.PRG program written in Chapter 15 to compile customer statistics based on equipment type performs the equivalent of a series of COUNT, SUM, and AVERAGE commands. In general, the Customer File should be opened for shared use so that several operators may carry out simultaneous inquiries or updates. However, you would not want one user to be able to add or delete records or change the contents of a customer's EQUIPMENT or TOTINV field while the program is accumulating the counts and totals.

You can lock a file explicitly, from the dot prompt or from within a dBASE III PLUS program, with the logical FLOCK ("file lock") function. Unlike all other dBASE III PLUS functions except the corresponding record-locking function, FLOCK( ) has two distinct results. Like all functions, FLOCK( ) *returns a value*—.T. if the file in the currently selected work area can be locked, or .F. if it is already locked by another user. Unlike virtually all other functions, FLOCK( ) also *performs an action*—it attempts to lock the file. Thus, with no other users logged onto the network, the following command sequence locks the Customer File and returns a value of .T.:

```
USE NWCUST INDEX NWCACCT, NWCZIP
? FLOCK()
```

If the Customer File is already in use at another workstation, the FLOCK( ) function evaluates to .F. and the file is not locked by the new user. Even if another user is working with the data base at the instant the FLOCK( ) function is evaluated, there is no way to determine how long the file will remain unavailable: it could be tied up for hours while several indexes required for reports are constructed or the file is updated by a dBASE III PLUS program. On the other hand, the file may become available in a matter of seconds if the other user is making only one quick change to a customer's address. Working at command level, you might just decide to wait and try again in a few minutes, or you might find out who has the file open and ask that person what kind of command or program is being executed and how long it might be expected to run. In order to cope with the same varying possibilities, any program that requests a file lock should not simply evaluate the FLOCK( ) function once—but neither should it keep on trying indefinitely. Just as in the error-trapping procedure described in the previous section, the program should evaluate the FLOCK( ) function repeatedly for some arbitrary period of time before giving up and advising the operator to try again later. You can do this with a simple DO WHILE loop:

```
store 1 to MCOUNT
@ 23, 0
@ 23,15 say "Requesting access to " + trim(DBF()) + " ..."

do while MCOUNT <= 100 .and. .not. flock()
   @ 23,60 say MCOUNT
   store MCOUNT + 1 to MCOUNT
enddo

if .not. flock()
   do MESSAGE with 23, 5, trim(DBF()) +;
                    " not available. Please try later" + MPPRESSKEY
else
   @ 23, 0
endif

return
```

This loop reevaluates the FLOCK( ) function 100 times, which should take about 20 seconds (a little experimenting on your own system under typical network usage conditions will reveal the most appropriate upper limit for MCOUNT). A message is displayed, together with the increasing value of the counter, to reassure the user that the system is in fact working. The DBF( ) function evaluates to a character string containing the name of the data base in the current work area, so the same status message can be used by many of the programs in an application. If the value of FLOCK is still .F. when the DO WHILE loop terminates, the user is informed that the file cannot be locked. If the file is locked successfully, the "Requesting access . . ." message is erased.

In this example, if the file cannot be locked, the program that performs the test simply RETURNs to the calling program. Exactly where to place the loop and what to do if a file cannot be locked after 100 (or 200) attempts depends on the context. Since a similar sequence of commands must be added to many of the programs in an application, it would be desirable to place the commands in a procedure. Displaying the status message and executing the DO WHILE loop could easily become a procedure, with parameters specifying the row and column coordinates for the status display and the maximum number of passes through the loop. However, the decision as to what to do if the file cannot be locked must often be made by the calling program. In a program like NWCSTAT2.PRG, it would not make sense to do anything but exit to the menu that called the program; but unless the program were called from the top-level menu in an application, you cannot use RETURN TO MASTER to jump directly from the procedure to the menu. In a different context (for example, a program that allowed the user to PACK and REINDEX the files in an application one at a time by choosing from a list) you might prefer to allow the operator to select another data base instead of returning immediately to the menu if the first file requested turned out to be unavailable.

The following procedure handles the attempt to lock the file and the display of the error message; if necessary, the calling program must *also* test the value of FLOCK( ) to determine what to do next:

```
procedure FILELOCK

parameters MLINE, MCOLUMN, MTRIES

store 1 to MCOUNT
@ MLINE, 0
@ MLINE, MCOLUMN say "Requesting access to " + trim(DBF()) + " ..."

do while MCOUNT <= MTRIES .and. .not. flock()
   @ MLINE,60 say MCOUNT
   store MCOUNT + 1 to MCOUNT
enddo

if .not. flock()
   do MESSAGE with MLINE, MCOLUMN, trim(DBF()) +;
                   " not available. Please try later" + MPPRESSKEY
else
   @ MLINE, 0
endif

return
```

A typical call to this procedure would look like this:

```
select NWCUST
do FILELOCK with 23, 10, 100

if .not. flock()
   return
endif
```

When you lock a file explicitly with a call to the FLOCK( ) function, you must also remember to unlock the file when the operation that required the lock has finished. A file is unlocked automatically when it is closed, or you can unlock the file while allowing it to remain open with the UNLOCK command. (Note that while files are locked with a *function,* they are unlocked with a *command.*)

Multi-User Update And Inquiry Programs

When you use dBASE III PLUS commands or programs that perform equivalent operations on an entire data base, the necessity to protect the integrity of the data by locking the entire file outweighs the users' inconvenience of sometimes having to wait to access a file. These global operations occur primarily in file maintenance or batch update procedures that are performed relatively infrequently compared to the routine daily updates using programs structured like the Customer File Update and Inquiry program, which access one record at a time. As long as two users are not permitted to access the same record simultaneously, it is safe to open the Customer File for shared use and to allow more than one workstation to run the update and inquiry program.

You can lock individual records in a file with the RLOCK( ) function, also called LOCK( ). This function operates much like FLOCK( )—any call to the function *performs an action* (attempting to lock the current record) and also *returns a value* (.T. if the record is available and the lock is placed successfully, and .F. if it is not). The attempt to lock a record will fail if another user has locked either the same record or the entire file. The function names LOCK( ) and RLOCK( ) may be used interchangeably; the examples in this book will use RLOCK( ) because the "R" serves as an explicit reminder to you or other programmers who may modify your system that it is a *record,* not an entire *file,* that is being locked.

Just as it is unnecessary to lock a file if no changes will be made to its contents, you must lock a record only when the record is being updated. Locking records individually gives users the maximum flexibility to use an application concurrently, because operations that do not alter any data can proceed as if no other users existed. Even most updates can be carried out without conflict, since it is relatively rare that two users would simultaneously attempt to access the same record in the same file.

To add multi-user capability to a program such as the Customer File Update and Inquiry program, we will examine the options one by one to determine what kind of file and record locks are required. The ADD option, which uses APPEND BLANK to add to the data base, requires that the entire Customer File be locked, as noted in the previous section. When the operator selects any of the other options that have the potential to change data—DELETE, RECOVER, CHANGE, or MEMO—the current record must be locked. SEARCH, NEXT, and PREVIOUS do not require a lock, since they only reposition the record pointer and display data from the new current record. These options do require, however, that you test for an error condition, because an attempt to position the record pointer at a record that is locked by another user will result in the "Record is in use by another" error message.

Recall that dBASE III PLUS automatically attempts to lock a file whenever a command that invariably requires a file lock is executed. Thus, it is not strictly necessary to lock the Customer File explicitly when the operator selects the ADD option — the APPEND BLANK command will trigger an automatic lock request from dBASE III PLUS, and your program need only cope with the error generated if the lock fails. However, allowing dBASE III PLUS to lock the Customer File automatically means that the user will be permitted to choose the ADD option and enter an account number for the new customer even if the program subsequently fails to lock the file. This may be exactly what you want, since the file lock in effect at the moment the operator chooses ADD may be released by the time the APPEND BLANK command is encountered. But being allowed to go as far as entering the account code for the new customer could be confusing to a user who does not understand enough about the system to realize that the new record has not actually been added to the data base at this point. In the National Widgets system, the ADD option will call the FILELOCK procedure (described in the previous section) to attempt to lock the file before allowing the user to progress any further in the command sequence. As soon as the new record has been added to the file with APPEND BLANK, the file lock can be released with UNLOCK and the new record locked so that other users may update previously entered records while the fields in the new entry are filled in. Since any call to the RLOCK function locks the current record, the program simply STOREs the value of RLOCK( ) to a memory variable (which is never used for any other purpose).

The DELETE, RECOVER, CHANGE, and MEMO options can use a strategy similar to the one used in the FILELOCK procedure to try to lock the current record for a specified period of time and display an error message if the record is still unavailable:

```
procedure RECLOCK

parameters MLINE, MCOLUMN, MTRIES

store 1 to MCOUNT
@ MLINE, Ø
@ MLINE, MCOLUMN say "Requesting access to " + trim(MACCOUNT) + " ..."
```

```
do while MCOUNT <= MTRIES .and. .not. rlock()
   @ MLINE,60 say MCOUNT
   store MCOUNT + 1 to MCOUNT
enddo

if .not. rlock()
   do MESSAGE with MLINE, MCOLUMN, trim(MACCOUNT) +;
      " not available. Please try later" + MPPRESSKEY
else
   @ MLINE, 0
endif

return
```

The SEARCH, NEXT, and PREVIOUS options do not have to lock the record they access, since they only display data without allowing it to be modified. However, the commands that move the record pointer will generate an error if they position the data base at a record locked by another user. This error can be detected by the error-trapping procedure invoked with ON ERROR. The simplest way to respond is to assume that the locked record will become available shortly and to retry the command that caused the error. The DO CASE structure that tests the value of the ERROR( ) function to determine what action to take could therefore include the following test:

```
case error() = 109
   retry
```

In this example, if a SKIP command generated the error, the RETRY command in the error-handling procedure would cause the calling program to repeat the SKIP. However, just as in the error trap designed to handle the inability to open a file being updated at another workstation, it is inadvisable to RETRY indefinitely, in case the record remained locked by another user for an extended period of time. Instead, the update program should RETRY for a specified length of time and then display a message informing the operator that the requested record is unavailable and offer the advice to "try again later."

Just like the procedure that detects the error resulting from the failure to open a file, the test for a record in use at another workstation counts to 100 and then, if it is the first call, exits to the calling program with RETRY. If this is the second consecutive attempt, the procedure instead RETURNs. The variable, MRETRY, that keeps track of whether this is the first error, should be assigned the value .T. at the beginning of each pass through the main DO WHILE .T. loop in the update program and should be reset to .F. by the procedure. The MERROR variable, which informs the calling program whether the error condition was resolved successfully, is initialized as .F. on each pass through the main DO WHILE .T. loop and is then reset to .T. if the error-trapping procedure determines that an error has occurred. Here is the CASE that handles this error trap:

```
case error() = 109
   store 1 to MCOUNT
   do while MCOUNT <= 100
      store MCOUNT + 1 to MCOUNT
   enddo
   if MRETRY
      store .F. to MRETRY
      retry
   else
      store .T. to MERROR
      return
   endif
```

This procedure is identical to the test for the "File is in use by another" error described previously. If this is the case in your application, the two tests could be combined into one CASE:

```
case error() = 108 .or. error() = 109
   store 1 to MCOUNT
   do while MCOUNT <= 100
      store MCOUNT + 1 to MCOUNT
   enddo
   if MRETRY
      store .F. to MRETRY
      retry
   else
      store .T. to MERROR
      return
   endif
```

Although SKIP and SEEK (as well as other commands that position the record pointer, such as GOTO, LOCATE, and FIND) result in an error condition if they move the record pointer to a locked record, these commands do in fact reposition the pointer. If the users are aware of this fact, it will help them decide what to do next when they are presented with an error message that declares a record unavailable. Obviously, any attempt to update the new record must be postponed until the lock placed at another workstation is released. On the other hand, the operator may have been using the NEXT and PREVIOUS options to browse through the file or trying to find a record based on a partial account number. In these situations, immediately using (or repeating) a NEXT or PREVIOUS command will safely advance the record pointer to another record— which may well be available. You might also consider allowing your error-trapping procedure to RETRY a SKIP or SKIP −1 command, but this may confuse the user by apparently passing over a record that he or she knows is present in the data base.

There is one more detail to be aware of before combining these components into a multi-user update program. With the addition of access controls and file and record locks, the program is doing a great deal of error checking. Despite the use of procedures, retaining exactly the same program structure entails quite a bit of duplication in the DO CASE structure that positions the record pointer. This program can be made more efficient by reorganizing it as illustrated by NWCUPD6.PRG, listed in Figure 25-5. In this version of the program, the user's option is collected as always in the memory variable MOPTION, which is processed with the same basic DO CASE structure. The routines that are common to more than one CASE have been extracted from the DO CASE structure and are processed first with a series of IF loops. The test for the help request is also processed here, partially to speed up the display of the help screen and partially because it is the only test that does not depend on the value of MOPTION. Removing it from the DO CASE structure leaves only related CASEs and makes the program a little easier to read.

The order in which the program carries out the IF tests is important. All of the IF loops are separate, independent tests, and in a given situation, one or more of the conditions in the IF statements may evaluate to .T. In this example, the test for the help request is handled first, followed by the test for the user's access level if the CHANGE, ADD, DELETE, or MEMO option was selected. Because the criteria for granting access to each of these options may be different, the values are stored in a memory variable called MACCLEVELS, which consists of a series of paired values—an option letter followed by a number representing the lowest access level with permission to use the option. The access level for a particular option is extracted with the SUBSTR function; the starting position of the one-character substring is calculated by using the AT function to find the value of MOPTION within MACCLEVELS and then adding 1 to move over one space. The resulting single character is converted to a true number with the VAL function, to match the numeric ACCESS( ) function.

Next, if the user has chosen CHANGE, DELETE, RECALL, or MEMO, the program tests to see if the data base is positioned at a valid record. If not, the "You must SEARCH first" message is displayed. With this test placed after the access-level test, a user who cannot access one of the options common to the two tests—CHANGE, DELETE, and MEMO—will never see an error message implying that corrective action (namely,

```
* NWCUPD6.PRG
* PROGRAM TO INQUIRE, EDIT, ADD, AND DELETE CUSTOMERS
*   WITH ON-LINE HELP
* WRITTEN BY:  M.LISKIN       05/23/86

store .T. to MRETRY
store .F. to MERROR

select 1
use NWTXN   index NWTACCT

select 2
use NWCODES index NWCODES

select 3
use NWCUST index NWCACCT, NWCZIP

if MERROR
   clear
   do MESSAGE with 10, 5, trim(DBF()) + " not available. Please try later";
                 + MPPRESSKEY
   return
endif

set relation to ACCOUNT into NWTXN
skip -1

set deleted off

store " "        to MCITY
store "C4A4D2M4" to MACCLEVELS

do NWCSCRN

set function  2 to "S"
set function  3 to "N"
set function  4 to "P"
set function  5 to "D"
set function  6 to "R"
set function  7 to "A"
set function  8 to "C"
set function  9 to "M"
set function 10 to "X"

do while .T.

   unlock

   store .T. to MRETRY
   store .F. to MERROR

   @ 22, 0 clear to 24,79
   store " " to MOPTION
   @ 22, 5 say;
         "<F1>=Help    <F3>=Next      <F5>=Delete   <F7>=Add      <F9>=Memo"
   @ 23, 5 say;
         "<F2>=Search  <F4>=Previous  <F6>=Recover  <F8>=Change  <F10>=eXit"
   @ 23,75 get MOPTION picture "!"
   read
```

Figure 25-5. A multi-user update and inquiry program

```
if readkey() = 36 .or. readkey() = 292
   select 10
   do NWHELP2 with "NWCUPD4 ", 1
   select NWCUST
   do NWCSCRN
endif

if MOPTION $ "CADM"
   if access() > val(substr(MACCLEVELS, at(MOPTION, MACCLEVELS) + 1, 1))
      do MESSAGE with 23, 10, MPNOTAVAIL + MPPRESSKEY
      loop
   endif
endif

if MOPTION $ "CDRM" .and. (eof() .or. bof())
   do MESSAGE with 23, 15, MPSEARCH + MPPRESSKEY
   loop
endif

if MOPTION = "A"
   do FILELOCK with 23, 5, 100
   if .not. flock()
      loop
   endif
endif

if MOPTION $ "CDRM"
   do RECLOCK with 23, 5, 100
   if .not. rlock()
      loop
   endif
endif

if MOPTION $ "SA"
   store "          " to MACCOUNT
   @ 23, 0
   @ 23,10 say "Enter the customer account number";
           get MACCOUNT picture "@!"
   read
   if MACCOUNT = " "
      loop
   endif
   seek trim(MACCOUNT)
endif

do case

   case MOPTION = "X"
      set function  2 to ";"
      set function  3 to ";"
      set function  4 to ";"
      set function  5 to ";"
      set function  6 to ";"
      set function  7 to ";"
      set function  8 to ";"
      set function  9 to ";"
      set function 10 to ";"
      set deleted on
      return
```

Figure 25-5. A multi-user update and inquiry program (*continued*)

```
case MOPTION = "S"
   if .not. found() .and. .not. MERROR
      do MESSAGE with 23, 15, trim(MACCOUNT) + MPNOTFOUND + MPPRESSKEY
      loop
   endif

case MOPTION = "C"

case MOPTION = "N"
   if .not. eof()
      skip
   endif
   if eof() .and. .not. MERROR
      do MESSAGE with 23, 15, MPLAST + MPPRESSKEY
      loop
   endif

case MOPTION = "P"
   if .not. bof()
      skip -1
   endif
   if bof() .and. .not. MERROR
      do MESSAGE with 23, 15, MPFIRST + MPPRESSKEY
      loop
   endif

case MOPTION = "D"

   if BALANCE <> 0.00
      do MESSAGE with 23, 15, MPNOTZERO + MPPRESSKEY
      loop
   endif

   select NWTXN
   if found()
      do MESSAGE with 23, 15, MPTRANSACT + MPPRESSKEY
      select NWCUST
      loop
   else
      select NWCUST
   endif

   store .F. to MCONFIRM
   do ASK1 with 23, 10,;
      "Are you sure you want to delete this customer? (Y/N)", MCONFIRM

   if MCONFIRM
      delete
      set color to &MPBRIGHT
      @  3,65 say "* DELETED *"
      set color to &MPSTANDARD
      do MESSAGE with 23, 15, trim(ACCOUNT) + MPDELETE + MPPRESSKEY
   endif
   loop

case MOPTION = "R"
   recall
   @  3,65 say "           "
   do MESSAGE with 23, 15, trim(ACCOUNT) + MPRECOVER + MPPRESSKEY
   loop
```

Figure 25-5. A multi-user update and inquiry program (*continued*)

```
    case MOPTION = "A"
       if found()
          do MESSAGE with 23, 10, trim(MACCOUNT) + MPONFILE + MPPRESSKEY
          loop
       else
          append blank
          replace ACCOUNT with MACCOUNT, STATE with MPSTATE,;
                  CITY with MCITY, AREACODE with MPAREACODE,;
                  TAXRATE with MPTAXRATE
          unlock
          store rlock() to MTEMP
       endif

    case MOPTION = "M"

       set format to NWCUST5
       edit
       set format to
       do NWCSCRN

    otherwise
       loop

 endcase

 if MERROR
    do MESSAGE with MLINE, MCOLUMN, "Record not available. Please try later";
                   + MPPRESSKEY
    loop
 endif

 do CUSTSAY
 if .not. MOPTION $ "CA"
    loop
 endif

 do while .T.

    store .T. to MVALID

    do CUSTGET5

    set color to &MPBRIGHT

    if ACCOUNT = " "
       delete
       @ 3,65 say "* DELETED *"
       exit
    endif

    if COMPANY = " " .and. CONTACT = " "
       store .F. to MVALID
       @  5, 1 say "*"
       @ 10, 1 say "*"
    else
       @  5, 1 say " "
       @ 10, 1 say " "
    endif
```

Figure 25-5. A multi-user update and inquiry program (*continued*)

```
if ADDRESS1 = " "
   store .F. to MVALID
   @  6, 1 say "*"
else
   @  6, 1 say " "
endif

if CITY = " "
   store .F. to MVALID
   @  8, 1 say "*"
else
   @  8, 1 say " "
endif

if STATE = " "
   store .F. to MVALID
   @  8,43 say "*"
   @  9,51 say space(20)
else
   select NWCODES
   seek "S" + NWCUST->STATE
   if found()
      @  8,43 say " "
      @  9,51 say DESCRIP
   else
      @  8,43 say "*"
      @  9,51 say space(20)
   endif
   select NWCUST
endif

if len(trim(ZIP)) < 5
   store .F. to MVALID
   @  8,57 say "*"
else
   @  8,57 say " "
endif

if AREACODE = " "
   @ 10,43 say " "
   @ 11,55 say space(20)
else
   select NWCODES
   seek "A" + NWCUST->AREACODE
   if found()
      @ 10,43 say " "
      @ 11,55 say DESCRIP
   else
      store .F. to MVALID
      @ 10,43 say "*"
      @ 11,55 say space(20)
   endif
   select NWCUST
endif

if STATE = "  " .or. (STATE <> "CA" .and. TAXRATE > 0) .or.;
   (STATE = "CA" .and. TAXRATE <> 6.00 .and. TAXRATE <> 6.50)
   store .F. to MVALID
   @ 12,43 say "*"
else
   @ 12,43 say " "
endif
```

Figure 25-5. A multi-user update and inquiry program (*continued*)

```
        if MVALID
           exit
        else
           @ 23,15 say MPCORRECT
        endif

     enddo                          [ not validated ]

     set color to &MPSTANDARD

     if MOPTION = "A"
        store CITY to MCITY
     endif

  enddo

  return
```

Figure 25-5. A multi-user update and inquiry program (*continued*)

searching first) is possible when in fact the user will always be denied access to the requested option.

Finally, the program attempts to lock the file (for the ADD option) or record (if CHANGE, DELETE, RECALL, or MEMO was selected). In this example, there is a moderate amount of overlapping among the conditions in the IF loops that test the value of MOPTION. Even if two sets of steps must be executed for the same set of options, however, two IF loops are used, which makes the program structure clearer and facilitates such later modifications as the addition of new options or changes in the access permission scheme.

It is often the case that the options requiring record locking are the same ones protected by a security system, since they correspond to the dBASE III PLUS commands that change data. However, this connection should not be taken for granted. You might, for example, add an option to the Customer File Inquiry and Update program to display a customer's financial transactions. This is easily accomplished with a program or procedure similar in structure to the NWCORD2.PRG program written in Chapter 16, which displayed order line items. This option, which only displays data, does not require that the Transaction File be locked, but you might choose to permit access only to users with a high access level, since it contains potentially sensitive financial data.

The DO CASE structure in NWCUPD6.PRG thus contains only those commands that are unique to each value of MOPTION. For the

CHANGE option there are no such commands, but the CASE MOPTION = "C" statement ensures that a value of "C" is not rejected by the OTHERWISE clause. After the ENDCASE statement, the value of MERROR is tested to determine whether an error condition has resulted from attempting to position the record pointer to a record locked by another user; if so, the program displays an error message and returns to the top of the DO WHILE loop to request another option.

NWCUPD6.PRG displays all of the fields in the current record with SAY commands, using the CUSTSAY procedure described earlier in this chapter. Unlike earlier versions of the update program, NWCUPD6.PRG does not validate data unless the operator has used the CHANGE or ADD option. Since not all of the users who may view the file have permission to change data, it is no longer safe to assume that erroneous data detected by the validation loop could actually be corrected by the operator running the program. The LOOP command therefore bypasses the validation steps unless MOPTION is "C" or "A". Within the validation loop, the fields that may be edited are redisplayed and collected with GET commands by the CUSTGET5 procedure. If a record has been explicitly locked with RLOCK( ), it must also be released by your program, using the UNLOCK command, to ensure that other users can view and edit the record. UNLOCK can release a lock on either a file or a single record; with more than one lock in effect, UNLOCK releases the lock most recently placed in effect. The UNLOCK command in NWCUPD6.PRG is placed at the top of the main DO WHILE loop. Since each pass through this loop displays or updates a single record, only one record at a time is ever locked by this program except when a new record is added with APPEND BLANK.

User Coordination And Cooperation

Successfully operating an application in a multi-user environment requires a high level of cooperation among the users of the system as well as the dBASE III PLUS programs. Your programs should handle some of the potential conflicts: they should prevent two users from concurrently carrying out operations that have the potential to damage the data base, and they should display clear and informative error messages whenever access to a command or program is denied for any reason. Nevertheless, the degree of cooperation and communication among the users will determine how satisfied (or frustrated) the users are with the performance and flexibility of the application.

This concept is not entirely new or unique to network systems. In an office with only one computer, the users may find themselves competing for time on the machine and debating about whose data processing needs are more urgent at any particular moment. Some of these problems are alleviated with a network, because more than one operator can access not only the computer, but also the same data files. For this reason, it may come as a surprise to users unfamiliar with network programming that they cannot count on being able to access precisely the files they want at any given moment—those files may have been opened for exclusive use at another workstation.

Furthermore, all of the users should be made aware of which operations will restrict or inconvenience the other users on the network. In a LAN environment, it is just as important to run time-consuming processes that lock entire files at times when other users are not impatiently waiting to use the same files. The users must also realize that if more than one person is carrying out a disk-intensive process, such as indexing a data base or reading a file to print a report, it will slow down the performance of the network in general, even for workstations not running dBASE III PLUS. Some amount of scheduling may be necessary so that these operations will be run at times when they inconvenience other users the least. All of this requires both an attitude of cooperation and a depth of understanding of network programming considerations that many people, even if they are familiar with the use of microcomputers in general, may not possess. It is essential that this information be communicated to the users, in nontechnical terms that they can readily comprehend, both in person, by the system designer or manager, and in the printed documentation that accompanies the application.

26

DOCUMENTING THE SYSTEM

If you have experience with more than one or two commercial software packages, you know that the quality of the documentation can make an enormous difference in how easy it is to learn to use a new program. This is no less true of your own dBASE III PLUS systems. If you are an outside consultant developing a unique application for an organization, the users deserve (and will undoubtedly demand) documentation comparable in scope, if not in appearance, to the manuals they would receive with an off-the-shelf package.

Often, when you design a program for use within your own company, it can be tempting to neglect or skimp on written documentation, since you know that you will be available to answer questions in person and train new staff members. This is a mistake, for a number of reasons. Being able to find and understand instructions in a printed manual will help the users feel more independent, more capable, and more in control of the software and, therefore, the computer. If there is a high turnover in personnel, you will spend less time training new users and answering the same questions over and over. Moreover, you cannot always be available at a moment's notice, and if you leave the company, change jobs, or are transferred to another department where your job description does not include supporting your earlier dBASE III PLUS programs, someone else will have to assume this responsibility. A clearly written manual will make these transitions easier for the users.

Documentation is important not only for the average user of a dBASE III PLUS application, who may know or care little about dBASE III PLUS and would be equally satisfied with a custom program written in COBOL, but also for the expert users and other programmers who may someday have to add to or modify your system. Although you may view the application as complete when you have satisfied all of the requirements outlined in the original specifications, it is a rare system that does not continue to grow and evolve as the users refine their needs and expectations.

Even if you anticipate that you will have sole responsibility for maintaining the system in the foreseeable future, you should be conscientious in preparing the printed programmers' documentation. During the period when you are working intensively on a new system and even the smallest details are fresh in your mind, you may find it hard to imagine that someday you may not remember all of the program names, field lengths, and index keys, much less the algorithms you developed for carrying out complex calculations. When you return six months later to design a new report or write a program to compile a new set of statistics, you may be amazed at how unfamiliar your own programs seem. Good documentation is even more important if your work must later be modified by other programmers. Without a clear outline, printed program listings, and cross-reference charts, making even the simplest changes in someone else's dBASE III PLUS programs can become a major undertaking.

DOCUMENTATION FOR THE USER

The documentation you provide for the users of your dBASE III PLUS applications should be complete enough to allow a novice computer user to start up the system for the first time and perform all of the daily processing operations. In order to achieve this goal, you may have to include in your manual some information that is available from other sources, but which you cannot be sure the users will find or comprehend. For example, it would be out of the question to include in your documentation a complete discussion of MS-DOS commands or a tutorial on the use of dBASE III PLUS at command level. After all, these areas are complex enough to have been the subjects of many entire books. However, it should be possible for the users to start up your application without understanding the operating system manual or looking for and studying another book on DOS. You should therefore include specific instructions for formatting blank disks and making a working copy of both dBASE III

PLUS and your programs on floppies or a hard disk. Also, although the users will not have to know much, if anything, about dBASE III PLUS command syntax, they do need to know the full-screen editing commands in order to update the data bases. Although this information may be found in the dBASE III PLUS manual, it should also be presented in your own manual.

The documentation should include the following elements:

- A description of the steps required to make a working copy of your application.
- A description of the steps required to make a working copy of the dBASE III PLUS program.
- A brief description of the system's purpose, overall design, and the hardware required to run it.
- An introduction to the use of the computer keyboard, the data entry process, and the full-screen editing keys.
- Instructions for starting up the application each day.
- Instructions and a suggested schedule for backing up the data base and restoring the system from the backups if necessary.
- The initial data entry sequence required to establish all of the data base files.
- A brief explanation of the purpose and function of each of the menu options.
- Pictures of the input screens for all of the data bases, with typical data filled in.
- An explanation of the type, length, and purpose of the data to be entered into each field.
- A sample page illustrating each printed format (such as reports, labels, and invoices) produced by the system, keyed to the menu option that produces it.
- A description of the processing cycle or calendar, with a list of procedures to be run weekly, monthly, annually, and so forth.
- A description of the password protection system and how to gain access to the various functional modules, if your application includes a security system.
- For a multi-user application, a discussion of the ways in which the

users must coordinate their activities to optimize network performance and user productivity.

- Instructions for recovering from both minor interruptions (like the paper jamming in the middle of a report) and major disasters (like a hard disk crash).

In a multi-user system that utilizes passwords to restrict access to certain fields, files, or menu options, this information should be included in all appropriate sections of the manual. For example, a description of the fields in a data base should include comments to identify fields that are not accessible to every user, so that contradictions between the manual and the users' direct experience with the program do not arouse distrust, and so that it is clear why certain fields cannot be modified with the "standard" dBASE III PLUS editing commands.

Startup Materials and Instructions

The materials you deliver to the users should include a floppy disk (or set of disks) containing a complete copy of all of the files required to run your application. These disks should be treated exactly like the distribution disks provided with any commercial software package. They should be write-protected as a reminder that they are not to be used to run the application, but only to make a working copy. The distribution disks should include

- All of the programs (.PRG files).
- All of the data bases (.DBF and .DBT files) and matching indexes (.NDX files). The data bases should be empty, except for any code files you have already initialized in order to test the system.
- All CATALOG files (.CAT files) used to keep track of the files that make up the application.
- All format files (.FMT files) used to enter or print data.
- All VIEW files (.VUE files) used to establish the relationships among a set of data base files.
- All report and label forms (.FRM and .LBL files).
- All query files (.QRY files) used to store FILTER conditions.

- All memory variable files (.MEM files), including a preliminary set of the systemwide options in the main memory file used by the application.

The documentation should include detailed instructions for making a backup copy of your distribution disks and a working copy of the application either on floppy disks or a hard disk. It is a mistake to assume that the users know any of the required DOS commands (FORMAT, MKDIR, and COPY). The startup instructions should also include the steps required to install the dBASE III PLUS program on the hard disk, since you should not assume that the users will read or understand the instructions in the dBASE III PLUS manual. When you write an application for use in one organization, you usually do not need to account for the range of computers and peripherals that the designers of a commercial package must cope with; in most cases, you know the exact hardware and operating system configuration. If your system currently runs on floppy disks, however, you might want to include instructions for a hard disk installation, since this kind of hardware upgrade is fairly common.

Figure 26-1 illustrates this portion of the National Widgets system documentation. This application is too big to run on floppy disks, so the manual only includes instructions for installing and running the programs on a hard disk. Currently, National Widgets owns an IBM XT, in which the floppy drive is labeled A: and the hard disk C:, but the manual points out how to modify the installation procedure for hard disks that are not addressed as drive C:. This documentation example is written for a single-user system with no password security. If the application were running on a network, or might in the future, you should also include a section describing how to install both dBASE III PLUS and the National Widgets files on the network, and how to log onto the system.

Figure 26-2 illustrates the portion of the National Widgets system manual that gives a brief narrative description of the application, introduces the use of the keyboard in general and its use with dBASE III PLUS in particular, and describes the commands required to start up and shut down the application every day. All the background information that is absolutely required for running your application can usually be summarized in only a few pages. The information in this section is drawn from several sources—the IBM hardware manuals, the MS-DOS documentation, and the dBASE III PLUS manual—all of which may prove long and difficult reading for the average novice user. Notice that the manual includes a reminder that the data files should be backed up after each data

National Widgets, Inc.
Accounts Receivable System

Installing the Software

Before you can begin to use the Accounts Receivable System, you must copy the contents of the distribution disk onto your hard disk. You must also install dBASE III onto the hard disk, if this has not already been done. These instructions assume that you are using dBASE III PLUS version 1.00 and that your floppy disk is called "Drive A:" and that your hard disk is "Drive C:". If this is not the case, you must substitute the correct disk drive names for those in the steps which follow. Remember that you must press **<RETURN>** after typing each of the commands.

To install the single-user version of dBASE III PLUS onto the hard disk:

1. Turn on the computer if it is not already on, with the door on the floppy drive open, to boot (load) the MS-DOS operating system from the hard disk.

2. If you already have a copy of the MS-DOS configuration file (CONFIG.SYS) in the root directory of the disk from which you boot your computer, add the following two lines to this file:

   ```
   FILES = 20
   BUFFERS = 15
   ```

   The FILES command is necessary to allow dBASE III PLUS to open more than the eight disk files permitted by default by MS-DOS. The BUFFERS command is intended to optimize performance on most hard disks.

   You can edit CONFIG.SYS, or create it if it does not already exist, with any editor or word processor that can create an ordinary ASCII text file. You can also use the COPY command to create or recreate the file. At the DOS prompt, type:

   ```
   COPY CON: CONFIG.SYS
   ```

   After typing all of the desired command lines, press **<F6>** to save the file. You must reboot DOS to see the effects of any changes you have made to CONFIG.SYS.

3. Create a subdirectory (with a name like "DBASE III" or "DBPLUS") for the dBASE III program by typing, at the DOS prompt:

   ```
   MKDIR DBPLUS
   ```

4. Switch to the newly created subdirectory by typing:

   ```
   CHDIR DBPLUS
   ```

- Page 1 -

Figure 26-1. The installation section of the National Widgets user manual

National Widgets, Inc.
Accounts Receivable System

5. Place the dBASE III PLUS System Disk 1 in the floppy drive, and switch to the floppy disk to run the dBASE III PLUS installation program by typing:

   A:

6. Run the installation program by typing:

   INSTALL C:

   Because dBASE III PLUS may only be installed once, the program will ask you to confirm that you wish to continue the installation. When you do this, the program will copy the dBASE III PLUS programs from System Disk 1 onto the hard disk, prompt you to insert System Disk 2, and copy the files from this disk onto the hard disk as well. The program will then display a message informing you that the installation was completed successfully.

7. Remember that if you ever need to reformat the hard disk, you must first "uninstall" dBASE III PLUS. You can do this by placing System Disk 1 in drive A: and typing:

   UNINSTAL C:

8. Put away the original dBASE III PLUS program disks in a safe place. You will no longer need them to run the Accounts Receivable System.

- Page 2 -

Figure 26-1. The installation section of the National Widgets user manual (*continued*)

National Widgets, Inc.
Accounts Receivable System

To install the Accouunts Receivable System onto the hard disk:

1. Turn on the computer if it is not already on, with the door on the floppy drive open, to boot (load) the MS-DOS operating system from the hard disk.

2. You can put the Accounts Receivable system files in the same subdirectory as dBASE III PLUS, or you can create a separate subdirectory for the application. Switch to the subdirectory you wish to use for the files (these examples assume you will use the dBASE III PLUS directory) by typing:

   ```
   CHDIR DBPLUS
   ```

3. Make sure that the Accounts Receivable distribution disk is write-protected (that is, the notch on the side of the disk jacket is covered with a piece of tape). Place the disk into the floppy drive, and copy all of the files onto the hard disk by typing:

   ```
   COPY A:*.*
   ```

4. The application requires access to the MS-DOS command processor, COMMAND.COM, and several DOS utility programs. You can make COMMAND.COM available to DOS with the SET COMSPEC command. For example, with COMMAND.COM located in a subdirectory called UTILITY, you could add this command to your AUTOEXEC.BAT file:

   ```
   SET COMSPEC=C:\UTILITY\COMMAND.COM
   ```

   You can make any programs or batch files accessible to DOS by specifying the directory search path with the PATH command. With the DOS utility programs also located in C:\UTILITY, you could add this command to AUTOEXEC.BAT:

   ```
   PATH C:\UTILITY
   ```

   Place your DOS system disk, or a copy of this disk, into the floppy drive. Switch to the directory that will contain COMMAND.COM, and copy this file from the DOS disk with this command:

   ```
   COPY A:COMMAND.COM
   ```

   Switch to the directory that will contain the DOS utilities, and copy the BACKUP.COM, RESTORE.COM, FORMAT.COM, and CHKDSK.COM utility programs into this directory by typing these four commands:

   ```
   COPY A:BACKUP.COM
   COPY A:RESTORE.COM
   COPY A:FORMAT.COM
   COPY A:CHKDSK.COM
   ```

- Page 3 -

Figure 26-1. The installation section of the National Widgets user manual (*continued*)

If you are not sure where to locate these files, place them in the same directory as dBASE III PLUS.

5. Format a disk to use for the backup copy of the Accounts Receivable distribution disk by placing a blank disk (or one which contains data you no longer need) into drive A: and typing:

    FORMAT A:

   When the disk has been formatted, DOS will ask if you wish to format another. You may format additional disks if you wish, and when you are finished, answer "N" to the question to return to the operating system prompt.

   Copy the National Widgets Accounts Receivable files onto the blank disk by typing:

    COPY NW*.* A:

6. Put away the original Accounts Receivable Disk in a safe place. You are now ready to use the program.

Figure 26-1. The installation section of the National Widgets user manual (*continued*)

National Widgets, Inc.
Accounts Receivable System

Introduction to the Accounts Receivable System

The Accounts Receivable System is a set of programs written in the dBASE III PLUS programming language for National Widgets, Inc. Using this system, you will be able to keep track of customer information, produce mailings to customers, enter and print orders and invoices, enter financial transactions, print customer statements, and print a variety of statistical and financial summaries based on the order, invoice, and payment data.

Most of the work you will do with the system will not require any knowledge of dBASE III PLUS command syntax. However, the keyboard commands used by dBASE III PLUS to enter and edit data on the screen will be used throughout the system, and the following general information about the IBM keyboard, dBASE III PLUS, and the Accounts Receivable System data entry programs should be helpful.

1. The IBM keyboard is similar to a typewriter keyboard, with a few important differences. The letters, numbers, and symbols are in the standard office typewriter positions. The numbers on the numeric keypad are identical to those on the main keyboard and may be used interchangeably. The **<NUMLOCK>** key acts like a **<SHIFT LOCK>** key for the numeric keypad, and serves to switch these keys between entering numbers and functioning as cursor movement keys. The four directional arrow keys are used with dBASE III PLUS, and the **<INS>** and **<DEL>** keys perform their usual functions of inserting and deleting characters.

2. The **<CAPS LOCK>** key, unlike **<SHIFT LOCK>** on a typewriter, shifts only the letter keys, not the numbers or other symbol keys. It is therefore useful for typing a mixture of upper case letters and numbers.

3. Remember that the programs will not consider **O** (capital "o") to be the same as **Ø** (zero), or **l** (lower case "L") to be the same as **1** (one). Also, because the space bar generates a real character, namely a blank space, it may not be used to move across the screen the way it is used to move across the paper on a typewriter.

4. The **<CONTROL>** key is used, like the **<SHIFT>** key, by holding it down while pressing another key at the same time. It generates non-printable, non-displayable characters. Because you would never enter such characters as part of your data, they are used by the system as commands. The **<ALT>** key is not used with dBASE III PLUS.

- Page 5 -

Figure 26-2. The introduction to the National Widgets user manual

National Widgets, Inc.
Accounts Receivable System

Some commands that are useful for moving around on the screen while entering and editing data are listed below, and described in more detail in the dBASE III PLUS manual:

Editing the Data in one Record (i.e., on one screen):

Command Key(s)	Function
CTRL-E or UP ARROW	Move to the previous field
CTRL-X or DOWN ARROW or RETURN	Move to the next field
CTRL-S or LEFT ARROW	Move one character to the left
CTRL-D or RIGHT ARROW	Move one character to the right
CTRL-A or HOME	Move one word to the left
CTRL-F or END	Move one word to the right
CTRL-G or DEL	Delete the character at the cursor position
BACKSPACE	Delete the character to the left of the cursor position
CTRL-T	Delete characters from the cursor position to the end of the word
CTRL-Y	Delete characters from the cursor position to the end of the field
CTRL-V or INS	Turn insert mode on or off
CTRL-Q or ESC	Exit from the screen without saving the changes
CTRL-W or CTRL-PGUP or CTRL-END	Save the entire screen

5. The Accounts Receivable system uses the programmable function keys **<F1>** through **<F12>** for some commands. **<F1>** is always the HELP key. It is used to call up a help screen describing your options in the program you are running. The meanings of the other function keys are different for different programs in the system. When these keys are used, their meanings are displayed on the bottom two lines on the screen.

6. You may send an exact image of the screen to the printer by pressing **<SHIFT>** **<PRTSC>** (holding the **<SHIFT>** key down and pressing **<PRTSCR>** at the same time). This is a good way to get a quick printout of a few records without printing an entire report. If you use this command to print a screen containing graphics characters (for example, continuous borders), these characters may not print correctly.

7. When you are entering data, each field, or item of data to be filled in on the screen, has a maximum allowable length, indicated on the screen by a pair of square brackets ("[" and "]"). If you type fewer characters than the maximum, you must press **<RETURN>** or use one of the standard editing commands to move to the next (or previous) data item. However, if you fill the field completely, the program will advance the cursor to the next field automatically.

- Page 6 -

Figure 26-2. The introduction to the National Widgets user manual (*continued*)

National Widgets, Inc.
Accounts Receivable System

8. Some programs in the system may display data on the screen before you have made an entry. Whenever a program displays data within a field, that data will be carried over to your current entry unless you change it. You need only type the changes you wish to make, using the editing functions listed above. When editing a number, typing a new value erases the entire previous entry, whereas in an alphanumeric field (a field where any letters or numbers are allowed, such as a name or address), all characters except the ones you change or delete will be retained.

9. In most cases, the programs format numbers for you, supplying two decimal places for dollar amounts. To enter 12.00, for instance, you need only type "12" (and press **<RETURN>**, since you have not completely filled the field), and the two zeroes and decimal point will be filled in. To enter 12.50, you might type "12.5" or "12.50".

10. Dates are entered and displayed in month/day/year order. When you enter dates, the slashes are supplied automatically, and the cursor will skip over them to speed up your entry. To enter March 10, 1987 into a date field, you need only type "031087". You will not be permitted to enter an "impossible" date like "02/31/87" into any date field. If you do this, the program displays the error message "Invalid date. Press SPACE" at the top of the screen and not permit you to advance to the next field until you have corrected the error.

11. The programs also check certain other entries for validity. You will not be allowed to enter alphabetic characters into a field, such as a zip code, where numbers are required. The programs automatically capitalize where they know capital letters are needed, for example, when you are choosing a command option or entering a state abbreviation or customer account number. However, in places where you might need to enter any combination of upper and lower case letters and numbers, such as an address, you must enter exactly the characters you intend.

    In situations where your response must be one of several possible choices, such as selecting command options from a menu, the system may display an error message if you choose an invalid option. In other cases, usually when you must choose one of a very few possibilities, it simply will not accept any entry other than one of the valid selections, and the cursor will not advance beyond the item's input area on the screen until you have chosen one of these. In these situations, the available choices are clearly indicated on the screen.

    When the data entered into a field must be tested more extensively for validity, such as making sure that a state abbreviation is one of the 50 valid postal abbreviations, the program will allow you to fill in the data entry screen completely and then test all of the fields at the same time. Any errors will be indicated by placing a highlighted asterisk ("*") next to the incorrect item, and you must correct all of the errors before you can go on to the next entry.

- Page 7 -

Figure 26-2. The introduction to the National Widgets user manual (*continued*)

National Widgets, Inc.
Accounts Receivable System

12. You should never interrupt any of the programs by resetting or by turning off the computer in the middle of entering data. If a program is not terminated "normally", i.e., by your issuing the appropriate command to quit, some data may be lost and the integrity of the files may be damaged. If this should ever happen, due to operator error, hardware failure, or a power failure, you should immediately recover all the data files from the most recent floppy disk backups and re-enter whatever data had been entered since that most recent backup copy was made.

13. Whenever it is safe to interrupt the system, for example, while it is printing a report or mailing labels, you use the **<ESC>** key for this purpose. When you press **<ESC>**, the program will display a message asking whether you really want to exit, and if you say yes, it will return to the Main Menu. When it is not safe to interrupt, the <ESC> key will be ignored. In general, printing functions and programs that accumulate statistics may safely be interrupted. When you are running a data entry program, you should always complete the entry you are making and then exit to the menu using one of the standard command options.

- Page 8 -

Starting and Shutting Down the Program

1. If the computer is not already on, turn on the power switches on the computer and the printer, with the door of the floppy drive open. The system will perform a memory test which may take up to a minute; when it is ready, the system will "boot", or load the MS-DOS operating system into memory from the hard disk drive.

2. Switch to the dBASE III PLUS subdirectory by typing:

   CHDIR DBPLUS

3. Type "DBASE NWMENU" and press **<RETURN>** to start up the Accounts Receivable System. The very first time you start up the program, you will be asked to fill in some basic information about your company and your computer system, including your company name, the disk drives to be used for data and index files, and the default (standard) values used for a customer's state and area code. This setup program is described in more detail in the next section.

Figure 26-2. The introduction to the National Widgets user manual (*continued*)

National Widgets, Inc.
Accounts Receivable System

Every time you run the application, the program will display the following signon screen:

```
 ________________________________________________________
|  ____________________________________________________  |
| |                                                    | |
| |              National Widgets, Inc.                | |
| |                                                    | |
| |            Accounts Receivable System              | |
| |                                                    | |
| |____________________________________________________| |
|________________________________________________________|

          Today is Thursday, September 3, 1987

         Press any key to display the Main Menu
```

4. The date displayed will be the current DOS system date. If your system has a built-in clock/calendar, DOS will automatically read the date and time when the system is first booted. If your system does not have a clock, the date will be whatever date you typed in when you first booted the system. You should be careful to enter the date correctly every time you start up the computer.

- Page 9 -

If you notice that the date displayed is January 1, 1980, this means that you did not enter the current date when you booted the system, and you should exit from the menu and from dBASE III PLUS. You may either reboot or use the dos DATE command to set the date. For example, you could set the date to September 3, 1987 by typing, at the DOS prompt:

```
DATE 10/03/87
```

5. Press any key on the keyboard (the space bar is handy), and the system will display the Accounts Receivable System Main Menu.

6. Before you exit from the Main Menu when you have finished working for the day, back up the data bases by choosing Option 12 (described in more detail in the following section). It is important to back up the data bases every time you have entered enough information that you would not want to have to re-enter it in the event of a system crash.

7. Exit from the Main Menu with Option 88 (to continue working in dBASE III PLUS at command level) or Option 99 (to return to the operating system). Make sure to exit from the Accounts Receivable System before you turn off the computer at the end of the day.

- Page 10 -

Figure 26-2. The introduction to the National Widgets user manual (*continued*)

entry session. Because this is a step that is frequently overlooked when an office is busy and the staff is harried, you should take every opportunity to educate the users about the importance of taking this essential procedure very seriously.

A clear outline of the initial data entry sequence is vital for ensuring the accuracy of the information in the data bases. The manual should list not only the information that must be entered into the computer, but also, if possible, specific instructions for gathering this data from the present manual system. As explained in Chapter 4, some important decisions must be made regarding the starting point for accumulating year-to-date or overall totals, as well as the amount of detailed history to be maintained by the system. The documentation should include instructions for initializing the data bases with varying amounts of historical data and describe the implications of choosing each of the alternatives presented.

The system overview should explain which information must be present before other data may be entered. For example, it may seem self-evident to you that the system should not permit an order to be entered unless the customer is already in the Customer File and all of the ordered items have been entered into the Inventory File. However, the reasons behind this restrictive data entry sequence may not be obvious to a clerk accustomed to working with a manual system, in which an invoice may be typed for a new customer, based on the customer's order form, whether or not a ledger card has yet been made up for the customer. In fact, the ledger card would almost certainly *not* exist at the time the order is typed, since the decision as to whether the company will become a regular customer would generally be made later. Similarly, if a new inventory item had not yet appeared on the latest price list or inventory status report, the clerk would just call the warehouse to find out the price rather than reject the order, as the dBASE III PLUS order entry program does.

Daily Processing

For reference during the daily use of your application, the documentation should include an outline of all of the menu options, with a brief description of the purpose and operation of each. The level of detail appropriate for this outline is very similar to the amount of information provided in the help screens displayed by the programs in Chapter 23. In fact, if you have already written an on-line help system, you can avoid retyping much of this material by incorporating the help text into your documentation file.

If you have used TEXT ... ENDTEXT structures to display the help screens, the text is already available in pure ASCII format, and you can simply read a copy of the help program (or programs) into the word processing document containing the appropriate section of the user manual. If the help text is stored in a data base, you can use a LIST command, coupled with an ALTERNATE file, to capture the memo fields in a text file. You can do this from the dot prompt with the following sequence of commands:

```
USE NWHELP INDEX NWHELP
SET MEMOWIDTH TO 78
SET ALTERNATE TO HELPMSGS
SET ALTERNATE ON
LIST HELPMSG OFF
CLOSE ALTERNATE
USE
```

This command sequence lists the contents of the memo field HELPMSG to the screen and to the ALTERNATE file HELPMSGS.TXT, which you may then edit with your word processor to begin creating the manual or which you may import into an existing documentation file.

In many cases, if the menus and programs are well designed, you will not need to provide more specific instructions for many of the menu options. A common flaw in software documentation is to describe in minute detail the steps required for making selections from a menu or filling out a data entry form, both of which might be easy enough to require little or no explanation. At the same time, the kind of information that is harder to deduce, like how often a program should be run or what kind of printed output it produces, is frequently omitted. It is crucial to provide clear explanations of the operations that must be carried out in a certain order to preserve the integrity of the data bases and, especially in a networked environment, to describe how the users must coordinate their manual and computer procedures to avoid conflicts and maximize efficiency.

The description of each menu option should include

- A brief description of the purpose and operation of the program.
- The differences between the option and any other similar menu selections.
- Other procedures that must be run before or after running the option.
- The data bases affected, if this is not obvious from the option prompt displayed on the menu.

- A brief description of any printed output produced.
- The size and type of paper required for a report—for example, continuous form or single sheets of letterhead.
- The order in which records are printed on a report and the selection criteria to be used, including both internal selections and those specified by the user.
- Whether it is safe to interrupt a lengthy procedure without damaging the data bases; if so, when and how to stop the program, the actions the program will take when it is interrupted, and a description of how to resume execution later.

Although it may seem repetitive, all of this information should be included in the section describing each menu option. When you write the documentation, keep in mind how a manual is typically used. Users rarely read the manual from front to back, and even if they do, they will probably do so only once. After that, the manual will be consulted for quick reminders of which option to choose to carry out a particular task. If you have written in the introductory narrative that "all reports are printed on 8 1/2-by-11-inch continuous-form paper unless otherwise noted," this may easily escape the reader's notice the first time through, and later it may be hard to find when the user is searching for instructions on how to print one particular report. Despite the redundancy, it would be better to include the statement "This report is printed on 8 1/2-by-11-inch continuous-form paper" in the description of every menu option that produces such a report.

For the same reason it is important to explain fully the implications of interrupting each potentially long-running program either intentionally or inadvertently. If your program uses an ON ESCAPE routine to allow the user to interrupt long-running reports or calculations, the operation of this procedure should be fully explained. The documentation should also include a description of the implications of canceling each process before it has run to completion. For example, any report program that simply reads the data base files without adding records or updating fields can safely be stopped and resumed later on from the point of interruption. A program like NWOSTATS.PRG, which accumulates order statistics by storing the totals in the NWOSTATS.DBF file, may also be interrupted at any point, since each run zeroes out the Summary File and accumulates a fresh set of totals. The user should be informed, however, that this lengthy process must be repeated from scratch each time. On the other hand, if a power failure occurs in the middle of posting transactions, you may be able to restore the integrity of the data base only by recopying the files from the backup disks, because it may not be possible to determine easily which transactions have already been posted or to resume posting where the program left off.

For each data entry program, your manual should include a picture of the data entry screen, filled in with a typical record, together with a list of all of the fields that are displayed or entered. If you have used TEXT ... ENDTEXT structures to draw the screens, as in NWCSCRN.PRG, you can easily read into your documentation file the program that draws the input form, remove the TEXT and ENDTEXT commands and comment lines, and then type in data from a typical record for purposes of illustration. If you have a RAM-resident utility program like SideKick that enables you to "import" a portion of the screen display into a notepad file, you can also run any program in the system and capture an exact image of the screen with data filled in.

In a separate listing you should provide the following information for each field:

- The field length.
- The field type, in terms the user will understand or that have been clearly defined in the introduction to this section of the manual.
- A brief description of the information to be entered into each field.
- An explanation of why certain fields may not be changed through the data entry program.
- An explanation of why certain fields may not be viewed or changed by all operators, if access is restricted by password protection.
- The implications of changing fields used in other files or programs.
- A list of allowable values or a description of the type of data permitted in any fields that are restricted or formatted by a PICTURE, FUNCTION, or RANGE clause.
- A description of the validation tests applied to the field.
- In a system with password protection, which users may read or update the field.

To complement the startup instructions, your documentation should contain a broad overview of the time cycles that are fundamental to the proper functioning of the system. You should clearly explain

- Which procedures should be performed daily, weekly, monthly, and annually (or at any other specified interval).
- Which procedures must be run before others will work.
- Which procedures or reports may no longer be run after a particular option has been completed (for example, which reports may not be printed after end-of-month processing).
- Which procedures may be run on demand, with a suggested time schedule based on your own experience.
- When and how to make a backup copy of the data base for archival storage (for example, immediately prior to performing end-of-month processing).

DOCUMENTATION FOR THE PROGRAMMER

Throughout this book, a set of standard notational and typographical conventions has been used to document a dBASE III PLUS system *internally* and thus make it easier for you and other programmers to read and understand. These guidelines include

- Assigning all file, field, and memory variable names so they describe their contents as much as possible.
- Using the same names for corresponding fields in related data bases.
- Using common prefixes to identify groups of related files and memory variables and to distinguish memory variables from data base fields.
- Conforming to the standard dBASE III PLUS file extensions.
- Using uppercase and lowercase to distinguish variable names from constants and dBASE III PLUS command and function names.
- Spelling out all dBASE III PLUS command verbs in full.
- Inserting blank spaces within command lines and blank lines between groups of commands to improve readability and identify functional modules.
- Indenting the commands within IF, DO WHILE, and DO CASE structures to make it easier to identify each in a series of nested loops.

- Using comments in the closing loop statements (ENDIF, ENDDO, and ENDCASE) to further clarify the structure of complex programs.
- Using comments to explain complicated command sequences.

This kind of internal documentation, while important, is not sufficient. Accompanying the printed manual that makes it easier for users to learn and operate your application should be a separate set of documentation, for your own use or that of other programmers, to make the system easier to read, understand, modify, and expand. The user manual is intended to be read once from cover to cover and then consulted occasionally for reference. You programmers' manual should be organized so that a new programmer learning about your system can read it from start to finish to understand the structure of the application, and then later find information on one particular function that must be changed or enhanced. Whether or not you use formal flowcharts for this purpose, you should provide enough cross-reference lists that a programmer can easily find every file in the system that must be changed if a field is added to one of the data bases or quickly determine which programs, report forms, data bases, and indexes will be affected by a user's request that a new column be added to a report.

The programmers' documentation can assume that the reader has already studied the user manual and worked with the application, so for the most part, you need not duplicate any information provided elsewhere. The manual should provide enough information for a programmer to recreate the application from scratch (although this should never be necessary) or, more realistically, understand it completely without using the computer. This manual should include

- File structures and index key listings.
- A listing of the contents of all CATALOG files.
- A list of the systemwide PUBLIC memory variables.
- Descriptions of all label and report forms.
- Listings of all format files, programs, and procedure files.
- Cross-references relating the system's programs, report forms, format files, data base files, and indexes.

Throughout this book, file structures and index keys have been documented on paper by opening the data base with all of the associated indexes and using LIST STRUCTURE TO PRINT and DISPLAY STATUS TO PRINT. While this informal listing is fine for inclusion in your system notebook as you develop an application, for the final documentation you may prefer to route the output to an ALTERNATE file, so that you may format the listing or add headings and page numbers to match the rest of the manual. It is also helpful to annotate the structure listing with additional information, such as the PICTURE, FUNCTION, or RANGE most commonly used in the @ ... SAY ... GET commands that display or collect the field, whether the field may be altered by the user, and a brief description of the purpose of the field. Figure 26-3 illustrates an annotated listing for the National Widgets Customer File produced by an ALTERNATE file created in this way.

A list of the PUBLIC memory variables used for the systemwide options can also be saved in a text file and printed as illustrated in Figure 26-4 for the National Widgets system. If the PUBLIC variables include graphics characters and you do not have an IBM Graphics Printer (or a highly compatible dot-matrix printer), you may want to eliminate these variables from the listing or convert them to similar printable characters, with appropriate comments explaining the situation.

Documenting the report and label forms is less straightforward. dBASE III PLUS provides no way to list the report specifications in a standard format, and you cannot simply TYPE out an .LBL or .FRM file, since these are not pure ASCII text files. One way to document the printed formats is to use MODIFY REPORT or MODIFY LABEL to edit the form, and use SHIFT-PRTSC to print the image of the screens that display the report column or label line contents. Alternatively, you could use a utility like SideKick to capture the screen images in a disk file. Apart from the fact that graphics characters are used in the screens, this method is adequate only for very simple reports and labels, because the expressions to be printed are collected in small windows on the screen, with the contents scrolling to allow a long entry in a relatively narrow space. Instead, you may have to settle for a report sample with handwritten annotations, like the one in Figure 26-5, which documents the one-across labels printed from the National Widgets Customer File.

The programmers' manual should of course include complete program and format file listings, arranged in a sequence that makes it easy to trace the logic and flow of control through the system. The best way to order the listings is to match the structure of the menu system. In the National

```
Structure for database : C:NWCUST.dbf
Number of data records :       25
Date of last update    : 08/31/85

Field  Field name  Type       Width    Dec     Picture/Range   Edit?   Description
    1  ACCOUNT     Character     10            "@!"              N     A unique identifier for the customer used to
                                                                         retrieve individual customers and list the
                                                                         data base in alphabetical order.  The account
                                                                         code should consist of part of the customer's
                                                                         company name, or last name for an individual
    2  COMPANY     Character     30                              Y     Company name.
    3  ADDRESS1    Character     25                              Y     First line of the street address.
    4  ADDRESS2    Character     25                              Y     Second line of the street address.
    5  CITY        Character     20                              Y     City.
    6  STATE       Character      2            "!!"              Y     State abbreviation.
    7  ZIP         Character      5            "99999"           Y     Zip code.
    8  AREACODE    Character      3            "999"             Y     Telephone area code
    9  TELEPHONE   Character      8            "999-9999"        Y     Telephone number.
   10  CONTACT     Character     25                              Y     Person to contact regarding orders.
   11  EQUIPMENT   Character     25                              Y     Type of computer equipment owned.
   12  TAXRATE     Numeric        5      2     Range 0 - 10      Y     Sales tax rate, as a percent.
   13  FIRSTORDER  Date           8                              N     First order date.
   14  LASTORDER   Date           8                              N     Most recent order date.
   15  YTDINV      Numeric       10      2                       N     Year-to-date invoice total.
   16  YTDPMT      Numeric       10      2                       N     Year-to-date payment total.
   17  TOTINV      Numeric       10      2                       N     Overall invoice total.
   18  TOTPMT      Numeric       10      2                       N     Overall payment total.
   19  BALANCE     Numeric       10      2                       N     Current balance due.
   20  COMMENTS    Memo          10                              Y     Comments or notes on the customer.
** Total **                     260

Currently selected database:
Select area:  1, Database in Use: C:NWCUST.dbf   Alias: NWCUST
    Master index file:  C:NWCACCT.ndx  Key: ACCOUNT
           Index file:  C:NWCZIP.ndx  Key - ZIP
           Memo File:   C:NWCUST.dbt
```

Figure 26-3. The annotated Customer File structure listing

Widgets documentation, for example, you might begin the sequence like this:

NWMENU2.PRG	(The Main Menu)
NWPROC.PRG	(The Procedure File)
NWCMENU2.PRG	(The Customer Information Menu)
NWCUPD5.PRG	(Customer Information Menu option 1)
NWCSCRN.PRG	(The program that draws the screen for Customer Menu option 1)
NWCUST4.FMT	(The format file that edits the COMMENTS field)
NWCREF2.PRG	(Customer Information Menu option 10)
NWCCARD2.PRG	(Customer Information Menu option 11)

To further aid in locating a particular program, you should provide a list of the program names and a one-line description of each, in the order in which the listings are arranged, as a table of contents for the program listing section of the manual. In a growing and evolving system, you may not want to number the pages consecutively, since you may need to insert additional listings or replace a particular program listing with a newer (and possibly longer or shorter) version, but the order will help you or another programmer locate a particular listing quickly. You might also choose to preserve a printed copy of each major revision of a program, to enable you to reconstruct the logic that motivated the changes and maintain a balanced historical perspective on development of the program. In some cases, the users will change their minds so many times about a program or report that you will want to extract a portion of a previous version to use in a new revision.

The most valuable tool you can provide for another programmer is an effective set of cross-reference tables. The table of contents for the program listings provides a guide to the way the programs and reports are called within the menu hierarchy. You might also create an alphabetical listing of program names (or perhaps all of the file names in the system) and their descriptions, so that any file in the system may easily and quickly be identified. This listing for the National Widgets system is illustrated in Figure 26-6. Another useful cross-reference tool is an outline of all of the programs in the system, arranged in a way that corresponds to the layout of the menus and that includes all of the other programs, procedures, report forms, data base files, and indexes called by each menu option. This listing, illustrated for the National Widgets Main Menu and Customer Information Menu in Figure 24-7, is especially valuable for

```
Variable        Type Current Value                                  Description

MPCOMPANY    pub  C  "National Widgets, Inc.                    "   Company name, for printing return address.
MPADDRESS1   pub  C  "943 Parker Street                         "   Street address, first line
MPADDRESS2   pub  C  "Berkeley, CA  94710                       "   Street address, second line
MPADDRESS3   pub  C  "                                          "   Street address, third line
MPSTATEABB   pub  C  "AL/AK/AZ/AR/CA/CZ/CO/CT/DE/DC/FL/GA/GU       Postal state abbreviations, used to
                     /HI/ID/IL/IN/IA/KS/KY/LA/ME/MD/MA/MI/MN         validate customer STATE field
                     /MS/MO/MT/NE/NV/NH/NJ/NM/NY/NC/ND/OH/OK
                     /OR/PA/PR/RI/SC/SD/TN/TX/UT/VT/VA/VI/WA
                     /WV/WI/WY/"
MPCATEGORY   pub  C  "/ACCESS/Accessories    /COVER /Dust           Inventory categorie and descriptions
                     covers    /DISK  /Disks          /FORMS
                     /Paper forms    /PRTWHL/Print wheels
                     /RIBBON/Printer ribbons/STOR  /storage
                     boxes"
MPSTATE      pub  C  "CA"                                           Default state for new customers
MPAREACODE   pub  C  "415"                                          Default area code for new customers
MPINVOICE    pub  N       10402  (     10402.00000000)              Next available invoice number
MPLMARGIN    pub  N          10  (        10.00000000)              Default left margin for letters to customers
MPTAXRATE    pub  N          6.50  (          6.50000000)           Default sales tax rate for new customers
MPBACKUP     pub  D  06/01/86                                       Date of last backup
MPPATH       pub  C  "C:\DBPLUS"                                    Path for files in application
MPDPATH      pub  C  "C:\DBPLUS                                     Path for data base files
                     "
MPIPATH      pub  C  "C:\DBPLUS                                     Path for index files
                     "
MPOPATH      pub  C  "C:\DBPLUS                                     Path for other files (programs, etc.)
                     "
MPCONFIRM    pub  C  "OFF"                                          Status of CONFIRM option
MPBELL       pub  C  "OFF"                                          Status of BELL option
MPINTENS     pub  C  "OFF"                                          Status of INTENSITY option
MPPRESSKEY   pub  C  " -- Press any key to continue"                Standard messages displayed by system
MPSEARCH     pub  C  "You must SEARCH first"
MPFIRST      pub  C  "This is the first name"
```

```
MPLAST       pub  C  "This is the last name"
MPNOTFOUND   pub  C  " not found"
MPNOTZERO    pub  C  "Balance is not 0.00"
MPTRANSACT   pub  C  "There are current transactions"
MPDELETE     pub  C  " has been deleted"
MPRECOVER    pub  C  " has been recovered"
MPONFILE     pub  C  " is already on file"
MPCORRECT    pub  C  "Please correct the fields marked with
                     a "*" "
MPNOTAVAIL   pub  C  "This option is rot available"
MPLLINE      pub  C  "--------------------------------------    Graphics character for upper line
                     --------------------------------------      of screen box
                     ---"
MPULINE      pub  C  "______________________________________    Graphics character for lower line
                     ______________________________________      of screen box
                     ___"
MPVERT       pub  C  "|"                                         Vertical bar character
MPULC        pub  C  "+"                                         Upper left corner character
MPLLC        pub  C  "+"                                         Lower left corner character
MPURC        pub  C  "+"                                         Upper right corner character
MPLRC        pub  C  "+"                                         Lower right corner character
MPBRIGHT     pub  C  "R+, W+"                                    Colors for highlighting messages
MPSTANDARD   pub  C  "W,  W+"                                    Standard display colors
MPBOLDON     pub  C  " E"                                        Turn on bold print
MPBOLDOFF    pub  C  " F"                                        Turn off bold print
MPENLRGON    pub  C  " W "                                       Turn on enlarged print
MPENLRGOFF   pub  C  " W"                                        Turn off enlarged print
MPCOMPON     pub  C  " "                                         Turn on compressed print
MPCMPOFF     pub  C  " "                                         Turn off compressed print
MP18LINES    pub  C  " C "                                       Set printer for 18 lines per page
MP66LINES    pub  C  " CB"                                       Set printer for 66 lines per page
MPDATEFORM   pub  C  "american"                                  Standard date display format
   50 variables defined,     1115 bytes used
  206 variables available,   4785 bytes available
```

Figure 26-4. The annotated memory variable listing

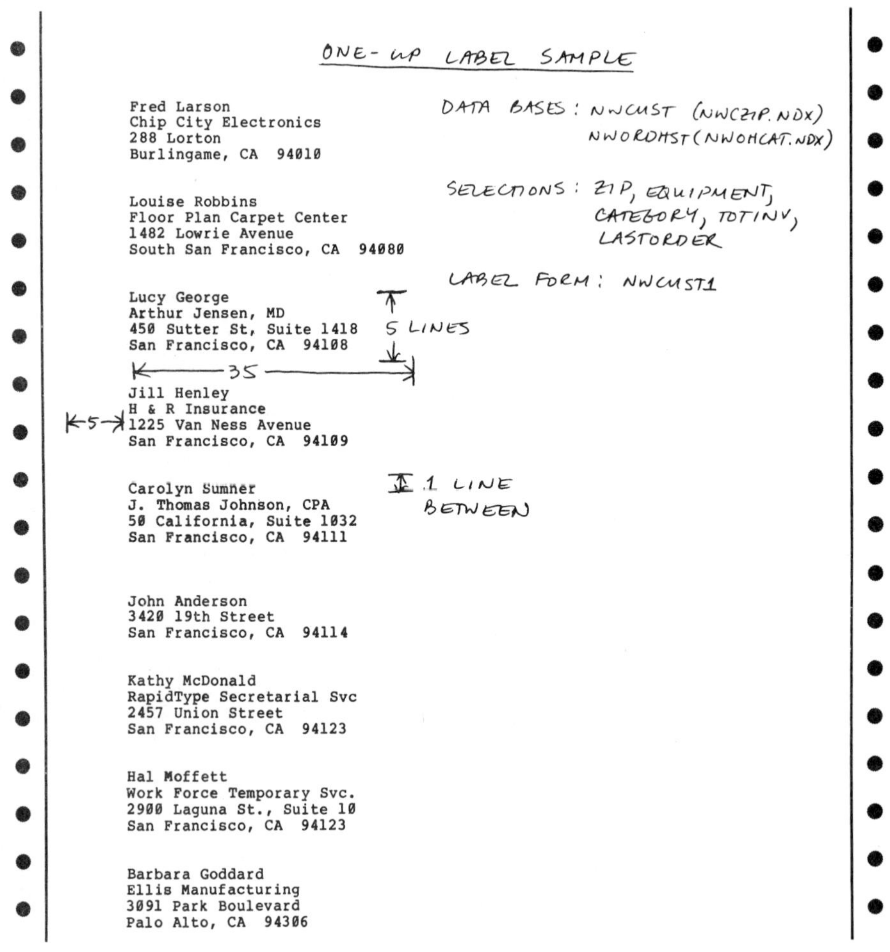

Figure 26-5. The annotated one-across label sample

able for locating all of the files affected by a requested change in one of the menu options and, read from right to left, for finding all of the programs that must be changed if, for example, a data base structure is modified.

```
The National Widgets System Files

NW       CAT        Catalog of all files

NWCODES  DBF        State, area code, and inventory category codes
NWCUST   DBF        Customers
NWHELP   DBF        Help messages
NWINVENT DBF        Inventory items
NWORDER  DBF        Current orders
NWORDHST DBF        Order history
NWOSTATS DBF        Order statistics (for order statistics report)
NWTXN    DBF        Current financial transactions
NWTXNHST DBF        Transaction history

NWCUST   DBT        Memo text for Customer File
NWHELP   DBT        Memo text for Help Message File

NWCUST5  FMT        Edits Customer File memo field

NWINVREG FRM        Prints Invoice Register
NWOSTATS FRM        Prints Order Statistics Report
NWTXNSUM FRM        Prints Transaction Summary Report

NWCUST1  LBL        Prints 1-up mailing labels for customers
NWCUST4  LBL        Prints 4-up mailing labels for customers

NWMEMORY MEM        Public memory variables for system-wide options

NWCACCT  NDX        Customer File by account number
NWCODES  NDX        Code File by code
NWCZIP   NDX        Customer File by ZIP code
NWHELP   NDX        Help Message File by program/option/screen
NWICATPT NDX        Inventory File by category/part number
NWOACCT  NDX        Order File by account number/invoice number
NWOHACCT NDX        Order History File by account number/invoice number
NWOHINVC NDX        Order History File by invoice number
NWOINVC  NDX        Order File by invoice number
NWOSTATS NDX        Order Statistics File by category
NWTACCT  NDX        Transaction File by account number/invoice number
NWTHACCT NDX        Transaction History File by account number/invoice number
NWTHINVC NDX        Transaction History File by invoice number
NWTINVC  NDX        Transaction File by invoice number

NWBACKUP PRG        Backs up data bases to floppy disks
NWCCARD  PRG        Prints Rolodex cards from Customer File
NWCDELET PRG        Deletes customers with no activity for 1 year
NWCMENU2 PRG        Customer Information Menu, Version 2
NWCORD2  PRG        Displays a customer and all orders
NWCREF2  PRG        Prints Customer Reference List
NWCSCRN  PRG        Draws input screen for Customer File
NWCUPD6  PRG        Customer File update and inquiry
NWCVALID PRG        Validates Customer File records
NWHELP1  PRG        Displays on-line help messages using TEXT ... ENDTEXT
NWHELP2  PRG        Displays on-line help messages using Help File
NWINVPRT PRG        Prints invoices
NWINVREG PRG        Prints Invoice Register
NWMENU3  PRG        Main Menu, Version 3
NWSETUP1 PRG        Customizes application-specific system-wide options
NWSETUP2 PRG        Customizes programmer-specified system-wide options
NWOREFA2 PRG        Prints Order Reference List by customer account number
NWOREFI2 PRG        Prints Order Reference List by invoice number
NWOSTATS PRG        Compiles order statistics by inventory category
NWPROC   PRG        Procedure file for system
NWREIND2 PRG        Packs and reindexes all data bases
NWRESTOR PRG        Restores data bases from backup disks
NWRUNDOS PRG        Runs any DOS command or program
NWSTPRT  PRG        Prints statements
NWTHEAD  PRG        Prints transaction detail column headings on Customer
                       Reference List
NWTMENU  PRG        Financial Transaction Menu
NWTPOST  PRG        Posts invoice and payment transactions to Customer File
```

Figure 26-6. The National Widgets alphabetical file list

Main Menu Cross-Reference (NWMENU3.PRG)

Option	Description	Programs	Data Bases
-	Customize System Options (if NWMEMORY.MEM not found)	NWSETUP1.PRG NWSETUP2.PRG	
-	Procedure File for all programs	NWPROC.PRG	
-	On-Line Help System (called by all programs)	NWHELP2.PRG	NWHELP INDEX NWHELP
(1)	Customer Information Menu	NWCMENU2.PRG	
(2)	Order Processing Menu	NWOMENU.PRG	
(3)	Financial Transaction Menu	NWTMENU.PRG	
(10)	Reindex All Data Bases	NWREIND2.PRG	All data bases and indexes
(11)	Customize System-Wide Options	NWSETUP1.PRG NWSETUP2.PRG	
(12)	Back Up Data to Floppy Disks	NWBACKUP.PRG	
(13)	Restore Data from Floppy Disks	NWRESTOR.PRG NWREIND2.PRG	All data bases and indexes
(14)	Run DOS Commands or Programs	NWRUNDOS.PRG	
(77)	Get Help	NWHELP2.PRG	NWHELP2 INDEX NWHELP2
(88)	Exit to dBASE III Command Level		
(99)	Exit to MS-DOS Operating System		

```
Customer Menu Cross-Reference (NWCMENU.PRG)

Option  Description                            Programs      Procedures  Reports     Data Bases
------  -------------------------------------  ------------  ----------  ---------   ----------------------------------
 ( 1)   Customer File Update and Inquiry       NWCUPD6.PRG   MESSAGE                 NWCUST  INDEX NWCACCT, NWCZIP
                                                             ASK1                    NWCODES INDEX NWCODES
                                               NWCSCRN.PRG   CUSTGET3                NWTXN   INDEX NWTACCT
                                               NWCUST5.FMT

 (1Ø)   Print Customer Reference List          NWCREF2.PRG   ASK3                    NWCUST INDEX NWCACCT
                                                             RPTHEAD                 NWTXN  INDEX NWTACCT
                                                             CENTER
                                                             DASHES

 (11)   Print Rolodex Cards                    NWCCARD2.PRG                          NWCUST INDEX NWCACCT

 (12)   Customer Equipment Profile             NWCSTATS.PRG                          NWCUST


 (2Ø)   Print Mailing Labels 1-Up                            ZIPINDEX    NWCUST1.LBL NWCUST INDEX NWCZIP
                                                             CUSTSEL
 (21)   Print Mailing Labels 4-Up                            ZIPINDEX    NWCUST4.LBL NWCUST INDEX NWCZIP
                                                             CUSTSEL
 (22)   Copy to Word Processor Format          NWCCOPY.PRG                           NWCUST INDEX NWCZIP

 (3Ø)   Zero Year-to-Date Totals               NWCZERO.PRG                           NWCUST

 (31)   Archive and Delete Inactive Customers  NWCDELET.PRG                          NWCUST
                                                                                     NWOLDCST
                                                                                     NWCUST INDEX NWCACCT, NWCZIP

 (99)   Return to Main Menu
```

Figure 26-7. The National Widgets menu cross-reference list

APPENDIXES

Appendixes A through G are a reference guide to dBASE III PLUS. Appendix A describes the command syntax notation used in Appendixes B, C, and D, which differs somewhat from the typographical conventions used in the rest of this book in order to conform to the dBASE III PLUS manuals. Appendix B is a concise summary of all of the dBASE III PLUS commands, and Appendix C lists all of the dBASE III PLUS functions. Appendix D reviews the use of the CONFIG.DB file and lists the options that may be set through CONFIG.DB. These appendixes are intended to augment, not replace, the dBASE III PLUS documentation, and to provide some of the kinds of usage tips not found in the manuals. You should consult the reference sections of the dBASE III PLUS documentation for additional details on commands and functions and for a complete listing of all of the full-screen editing keys.

Appendix E lists the complete procedure file developed for the National Widgets system. Many of these procedures may be extracted unchanged for use in your programs, while others will require varying amounts of modification to adapt them to the unique requirements of your own dBASE III PLUS applications.

Appendix F lists the dBASE III PLUS error messages, both in alphabetical order and in numerical order according to the values returned by the ERROR( ) function in each case. The numerical cross-reference listing may be useful in making sure that your error-trapping procedures are as complete as possible. Appendix G lists the currently known "anomalies" in dBASE III PLUS version 1.0 and ways to circumvent the problems they cause. Some of these problems may be corrected in later releases of the software.

A

COMMAND SYNTAX NOTATION

Appendixes B, C, and D provide a concise summary of dBASE III PLUS commands and functions and the options that may be set in the CONFIG.DB file. These appendixes will use the same standard notation as the dBASE III PLUS manual.

UPPERCASE is used for all dBASE III PLUS keywords (words that are recognized by dBASE III PLUS as part of its command vocabulary). These include command verbs; function names; words like FOR, WHILE, and TO, which introduce command clauses; and command options like OFF or DELIMITED. In your work at command level and in dBASE III PLUS programs, you may type the keywords in any combination of uppercase and lowercase. Command words (but *not* function names) may be abbreviated, provided that the portion of the command word you type is at least four characters long; if you include more than four characters, they must all be correct. For example, DELIMITED may be abbreviated to DELI or DELIM, but not DELIT.

Optional portions of a command are enclosed in square brackets ([ ]). When you use these options, remember not to type the brackets.

Two options are separated by a slash (/) if one or the other, but not both, may be used in a command. Many of the SET options have two allowable values (in most cases, ON or OFF); the default status of these options is printed in uppercase, with the alternate value in lowercase. For example, the command to turn the terminal's beeper on or off is written as SET BELL ON/off.

Substitutions are printed in *lowercase italics* and enclosed in angle brackets (<>). When you use these commands, remember not to type the brackets themselves or the exact words between the brackets; instead, you should make the appropriate substitution. For example, the command that creates a new data base is listed as CREATE <*file name*>. To use this command to create the National Widgets Customer File, you would type CREATE NWCUST.

The following terms are used to describe the substitution items:

alias: An optional alternate name for a data base, which may be up to ten characters long and may contain an embedded underscore (_). The alias is specified in the USE command that opens the file; if you do not assign an alias, dBASE III PLUS assigns the file name as the alias. Some commands require that you use the alias rather than the file name if the two are different.

alias->field: A field in a data base open in a work area other than the currently selected work area.

character string: Any sequence of characters, enclosed in single quotes ('), double quotes ("), or square brackets ([ ]).

column: A horizontal screen or printer column coordinate. Columns are numbered from left to right, beginning with 0.

condition: A logical expression with the value .T. or .F.

current: Used to describe the disk drive and subdirectory from which dBASE III PLUS was loaded, the selected work area, the data base file open in the selected work area, or the record at which the dBASE III PLUS record pointer is positioned in this data base.

drive: A disk drive designator (A, B, C, and so on), followed by a colon (:) if it forms part of a file name.

exp: Any syntactically valid dBASE III PLUS expression composed of data base fields, memory variables, functions, and/or constants, combined with arithmetic, character, and/or logical operators. Expressions and constants of the same data type may be used interchangeably in dBASE III PLUS commands and functions. The choice of which to use in the syntax summaries is based on the most common usage.

expC: An expression that evaluates to a character string.

expD: An expression that evaluates to a date.

expL: An expression that evaluates to a logical value (.T. or .F.).

expN: An expression that evaluates to a number.

field: The name of a field in the data base open in the currently selected work area.

file name: A valid MS-DOS file name. You must include the disk drive if the file does not reside on the default drive. The full path name is required if the file is not in the current subdirectory, unless you have used a SET PATH command to specify a search path for files not in the current subdirectory. Any command that manipulates a particular type of file (for example, USE, which opens a data base file, or SAVE TO, which creates a memory variable file) assumes the standard dBASE III PLUS extension unless you override it by explicitly typing the extension. The standard file extensions are

CAT	Catalog data base file
DBF	Data base file
DBT	Data base text file (contains memo field text)
FMT	Format file
FRM	Report form file
LBL	Label form file
MEM	Memory variable file
NDX	Index file
PRG	Program or procedure file
QRY	Query file
SCR	Screen image file
TXT	Text file
VUE	View file

Commands that may operate on any type of disk file (for example, ERASE or RENAME) must always include the extension.

key or *key expression:* The expression used as the basis for indexing or sorting a data base file.

list: One or more items of the same type (fields, files, expressions, indexes, and so on) separated by commas.

memvar: Memory variable.

n: A number.

path: A DOS path name (the path through the subdirectory structure from the current subdirectory to the specified file) followed by a backslash (\).

row: A screen or printer row (vertical) coordinate. Rows are numbered from top to bottom, beginning with 0.

scope: The range of records in a data base to be acted upon by a command. The valid scopes are

ALL	The entire file
NEXT <*expN*>	A number of records equal to the value of *expN*, beginning with the current record
RECORD <*expN*>	A single record; its record number is the value of *expN*
REST	All of the records from the current record (including the current record) to the end of the file

In interpreting the *scope*, dBASE III PLUS takes into consideration any factors that affect the sequence or the range of records to be processed, including indexes, FILTERs, and the status of the DELETED option. For example, with a FILTER in effect and DELETED ON, ALL means all the records that are not marked for deletion and that satisfy the condition in the SET FILTER command. If the data base is opened with one or more indexes, NEXT 10 means the next ten records found in the first index file named in the USE command, and REST specifies the records from the current record to the end of the index.

skeleton: A pattern of letters and wildcard symbols that a file or variable name must match. The two wildcard characters are ?, which stands for any one character, and *, which substitutes for any combination of characters.

variable: Either a memory variable or a data base field.

In most cases, dBASE III PLUS command clauses and options may be used in any combination and typed in almost any order. The order used in the command summary in Appendix B was chosen so that the commands would read as much like English sentences as possible.

B

dBASE III PLUS COMMAND SYNTAX SUMMARY

This appendix contains a brief summary of dBASE III PLUS commands in alphabetical order. This listing is intended to be a reference for looking up the exact syntax of a command or for confirming which options are available. It does not provide a complete explanation of the commands for novice dBASE III PLUS users, nor does it include comprehensive descriptions of how to use full-screen commands like APPEND or menu-driven commands like CREATE REPORT. You will find detailed instructions for using these commands in the "Using dBASE III PLUS" section of the manual, as well as a list of commands grouped by function and a complete list of the full-screen editing commands. You might also want to refer to the *Quick Reference Guide* provided with the dBASE III PLUS manual for a very concise command summary.

Commands such as LIST, COUNT, and UPDATE, which process entire data base files, are useful at the dot prompt but are often too inefficient or inflexible to use in a dBASE III PLUS program. For such commands this appendix includes a short program that exactly simulates the behavior of the built-in command. There may be more than one way to write such a program, and in most cases, you will not want to use the model programs exactly as they are presented in this appendix. Instead, they should be viewed as prototypes for carrying out a particular type of operation; the techniques can be adapted and expanded for incorporation into your own dBASE III PLUS programs.

?/?? [<*exp list*>]

Displays (if you have SET CONSOLE ON) or prints (if you have SET PRINT ON) the expressions in *exp list*, each pair separated by a single space. ? first issues a carriage return and a line feed and thus displays or prints the expressions on the next available line. ?? displays the listed expressions beginning at the current cursor position (on the screen) or the current print head position. When no expressions are listed, ? displays or prints a blank line.

@ <*row*>,<*column*> [[SAY <*exp*> [PICTURE <*picture*>]
  [FUNCTION <*function*>]]
  [GET <*variable*> [PICTURE <*picture*>]
  [FUNCTION <*function*>][RANGE <*exp*>,<*exp*>]]]

@ <*row*>,<*column*> [CLEAR]

@ <*row1*>,<*column1*> [CLEAR] TO @ <*row2*>,<*column2*> [DOUBLE]

Row and *column* may be any valid numeric expressions representing screen or printer coordinates. For the screen, *row* must be between 0 and 24 (or 23 for a 24-line terminal), and *column* must be between 0 and 79. For the printer, both *row* and *column* may range from 0 to 255, provided that lower limits are not imposed by the printer itself. *Function* may be any valid function; and *picture* may be any valid function, template, or combination of the two used to format data output by a SAY clause or to format or validate data collected by a GET clause (see the summary in Tables 8-2 and 8-3). The two *exps* in the RANGE clause may be any valid numeric or date expressions (depending on the type of data being collected).

If a SAY clause is included, the specified expression is displayed on the screen with the *standard* display attributes (if you have SET DEVICE TO SCREEN) or printed (if you have SET DEVICE TO PRINT) at the designated row and column coordinates. Data may be placed on the screen in any order, but printing must proceed from left to right on each line and from top to bottom on each page.

If a GET clause is included, the specified expression is displayed on the screen with the *enhanced* display attributes (if you have SET DEVICE TO SCREEN). If you have SET DEVICE TO PRINT, GET commands are ignored.

@ ... SAY ... GET commands may be combined into a format file, which can be invoked with SET FORMAT TO <*format file name*> and used to draw a custom screen for use with the full-screen APPEND, EDIT,

INSERT, and CHANGE commands. READ commands may be inserted at any point to create a multi-page input screen. In a dBASE III PLUS program, one or more GET commands *must* be followed by a READ in order to allow the user to edit the values of these variables. Using CLEAR or CLEAR GETS instead prevents the data from being altered.

If a RANGE clause is included, it specifies the permissible range of values for a numeric or date field. The user may press RETURN to leave any existing value unchanged; but if a new value is entered, the cursor will not advance beyond this variable unless the value is within the allowable range.

Memo fields may be accessed with @ ... SAY ... GET only if the command is part of a format file used with APPEND or EDIT (not activated by a READ).

@ <*row*>,<*column*> erases the specified row, beginning with the specified column.

@ <*row*>,<*column*> CLEAR erases a rectangular area of the screen; the *row* and *column* coordinates specify the upper-left corner of the area.

@ <*row1*>,<*column1*> TO <*row2*>,<*column2*> draws a continuous single-line box on the screen, or a double-line box if the keyword DOUBLE is included. The two sets of row and column coordinates specify the upper-left and lower-right corners of the box. If the two row coordinates are the same, a horizontal line is produced; if the two column coordinates are identical, a vertical line results.

@ <*row1*>,<*column1*> CLEAR TO <*row2*>,<*column2*> erases the specified rectangular region on the screen.

ACCEPT [<*expC*>] TO <*memvar*>

Collects input from the user and creates the character string memory variable *memvar* to store the input. If *expC* is included, it is displayed as a prompt. If the user presses RETURN without typing anything else, *memvar* will be a null string of length zero.

APPEND [BLANK]
APPEND FROM <*file name*> [FOR <*condition*>] [TYPE DELIMITED [WITH <*delimiter*>/BLANK]/SDF/DIF/SYLK/WKS]

APPEND adds new records to the current data base, using the standard dBASE III PLUS full-screen edit commands. Pressing PGUP allows you to edit existing records; however, these records are displayed in sequential order even if the data base was opened with an index.

APPEND BLANK, most often used in a program, adds a blank record to the current data base and positions the record pointer to the new record without invoking the full-screen edit mode. The fields are usually filled in with REPLACE or GET commands.

APPEND FROM adds records from the named file to the current data base. If a *condition* is specified, it must refer only to fields that are common to both data bases. Unless you have SET DELETED ON, records that have been marked for deletion are APPENDed and are not marked as deleted in the file receiving the data. Data is transferred between two .DBF files by matching up identically named fields. Long character fields are truncated to fit, but numeric fields that are too long to fit are replaced by asterisks.

If the SDF ("System Data Format") option is specified, the file from which records are APPENDed is assumed to be a fixed-length text file with a carriage return at the end of each record and with field widths that match those in the dBASE III PLUS file structure. If the SDF record is too long, the data at the end will be lost; and if it is too short, the fields in the new records that have no counterparts in the SDF file will remain blank.

If the DELIMITED option is specified, the file from which records are APPENDed is assumed to be a text file in which the fields are separated by commas and there is a carriage return at the end of each record. If character fields in the text file are surrounded with any delimiters other than double quotes, the delimiter must be specified in the WITH clause. If DELIMITED WITH BLANK is selected, the fields are assumed to be separated by single spaces.

If the DELIMITED file has too many fields, the ones that do not fit are lost; if there are too few, the fields in the new records that have no counterparts in the DELIMITED file will remain blank.

When dBASE III PLUS APPENDs data from DIF ("Data Interchange Format"), SYLK (Multiplan "Symbolic Link"), and WKS (Lotus Worksheet) files, rows in the spreadsheet become records in the data base, each column supplying data for a field. It is up to you to ensure that the spreadsheet matches the data base structure.

In all variations of the APPEND command, any indexes opened together with the data base are updated to account for the new records.

ASSIST

Invokes a menu-driven mode of operation for dBASE III PLUS.

AVERAGE [<*scope*>] [<*expN list*>] [FOR <*condition*>] [WHILE <*condition*>] [TO <*memvar list*>]

Calculates the average value of each expression in the list for the range of records defined by the *scope* and *conditions*. If no expressions are listed, all numeric fields in the current data base are AVERAGEd. If no *scope* is specified, ALL is assumed. If you have SET TALK ON, the averages are displayed on the screen; and if you have SET HEADING ON, the expressions AVERAGEd are displayed above the results. If a list of memory variables is included, the named numeric variables are created to store the averages.

Example:

```
USE NWCUST
AVERAGE YTDINV, TOTINV FOR CITY = "San Francisco" TO MYTDAVG, MTOTAVG
```

Equivalent program:

```
use NWCUST
store 0.00 to MYTD, MTOT
store 0    to MCOUNT

do while .not. eof()
   if CITY = "San Francisco"
      store MYTD    + YTDINV to MYTD
      store MTOT    + TOTINV to MTOT
      store MCOUNT  + 1      to MCOUNT
   endif
   skip
enddo

store MYTD / MCOUNT to MYTDAVG
store MTOT / MCOUNT to MTOTAVG
? MYTDAVG, MTOTAVG
```

BROWSE [FIELDS <*field list*>] [LOCK <*expN*>] [FREEZE <*field*>] [WIDTH <*expN*>] [NOFOLLOW] [NOMENU] [NOAPPEND]

Enters a full-screen edit mode in which records are displayed on the screen one record per line and fields are aligned in columns. The first record displayed is the current record. You may not display or edit memo fields with BROWSE. Any data displayed on the screen may be edited, records may be deleted or recalled with CTRL-U, and new records may be added (just as in EDIT) by positioning the record pointer to the last record and then pressing PGDN.

If the FIELDS clause is included, only the named fields are displayed, in the specified order. If the LOCK clause is included, *expN* specifies the number of fields remaining fixed on the left side of the screen. If the FREEZE option is included, editing is restricted to the specified field, although you may still pan the display left or right to view the entire record. If the WIDTH option is included, *expN* specifies the maximum display width for any field; within this width, the full contents of the field scrolls as the field is edited. This option is intended to make it easier to view and update records in a data base with many long character fields.

The NOFOLLOW option controls the position of the record pointer after the key field is changed in a data base opened with an index. Normally the record pointer remains positioned at the same record after you change the index key field, and the screen is redrawn with this record at the top. Since the record has moved in the index, this results in a different set of records occupying the screen from the set originally displayed when BROWSE was entered. NOFOLLOW causes the record pointer to be repositioned to the record originally displayed below the one you have changed, so that the screen display remains constant except for the disappearance of the altered record.

The NOAPPEND option prevents records from being added to a data base from within BROWSE.

LOCK and FREEZE may also be set from the BROWSE option menu invoked by pressing CTRL-HOME, which also contains commands to GOTO the TOP or BOTTOM of the file or to a particular record number or to carry out a SEEK command if the file was opened with an index. This menu is not accessible if the NOMENU option is included in the BROWSE command.

CALL <*module name*> [WITH <*expC*>]

Executes a binary program file loaded into memory with the LOAD command. The value of *expC* is passed to the program as a parameter. LOAD and CALL should be used only for subroutines written expressly to be executed this way; .COM or .EXE files (including most commercial software) should be invoked with the RUN command instead.

CANCEL

Causes dBASE III PLUS to exit immediately from the currently running program, close all open program files (but not a procedure file, if one is open), and return to the dot prompt.

CHANGE [<*scope*>] [FIELDS <*field list*>] [FOR <*condition*>]
  [WHILE <*condition*>]

Enters a full-screen mode to edit the specified fields in the range of records defined by the *scope* and *conditions*. If no *scope* is specified, ALL is assumed. CHANGE is identical to EDIT.

CLEAR
CLEAR ALL/FIELDS/GETS/MEMORY/TYPEAHEAD

CLEAR erases the screen, leaving the cursor positioned in the upper-left corner, and CLEARs all pending GETs.

CLEAR ALL closes all data base files, indexes, format files, and CATALOG files in all of the ten work areas, selects work area 1, and releases all memory variables.

CLEAR FIELDS cancels a field list established with SET FIELDS TO <*field list*>, and turns off the field list as if you had typed SET FIELDS OFF.

CLEAR GETS cancels all pending GETs, preventing the user from editing any variables that have not yet been collected by a READ. You may not issue more GET commands than specified by the GETS option in CONFIG.DB (128 if you have not changed the default) between CLEAR GETS, CLEAR, and READ commands.

CLEAR MEMORY releases all memory variables, both PUBLIC and PRIVATE.

CLEAR TYPEAHEAD deletes all characters in the typeahead buffer.

CLOSE ALL/ALTERNATE/DATABASES/FORMAT/INDEX/PROCEDURE

Closes all files of the specified type.

CLOSE ALTERNATE (exactly like SET ALTERNATE [TO]) closes the current alternate file.

CLOSE DATABASES closes all data bases, indexes, and format files in all ten work areas, except a CATALOG file open in work area 10.

CLOSE FORMAT (exactly like SET FORMAT [TO]) closes the format file in the current work area.

CLOSE INDEX (exactly like SET INDEX [TO]) closes all index files in the current work area.

CLOSE PROCEDURE (exactly like SET PROCEDURE [TO]) closes the current procedure file.

CONTINUE

Searches the current data base, starting with the current record, for the next record that satisfies the condition in the most recent LOCATE command, and leaves the data base positioned at the matching record. If you have SET TALK ON, the record number is displayed. If no matching record is found within the *scope* specified in the LOCATE command, an "End of locate scope" message is displayed.

COPY TO <*file name*> [<*scope*>] [FIELDS <*field list*>] [FOR <*condition*>]
[WHILE <*condition*>] [TYPE DELIMITED
[WITH <*delimiter*>/BLANK]/SDF/DIF/SYLK/WKS]
COPY FILE <*file 1*> TO <*file 2*>
COPY STRUCTURE TO <*file name*> [FIELDS <*field list*>]
COPY TO <*filename*> STRUCTURE EXTENDED

Copies the range of records from the current data base defined by the *scope* and *condition* to a new file. This file is created by the COPY command or deleted and re-created if it already exists. Records that have been marked for deletion are COPYed unless you have SET DELETED ON. If no *scope* is specified, ALL is assumed. If a *field list* is included, only the named fields are COPYed, in the specified order; otherwise, the new file has the same structure as the original.

If the SDF option is specified, instead of a DBF file, COPY creates a text file consisting of fixed-length records with a carriage return at the end of each record.

If the DELIMITED option is specified, COPY creates a text file in which the fields are separated by commas, with a carriage return at the end of each record. If a *delimiter* is included, the specified punctuation mark is used to surround character fields instead of the default double quotes. If DELIMITED WITH BLANK is selected, the fields are separated by single spaces and no punctuation surrounds character fields.

When dBASE III PLUS COPYs data to DIF ("Data Interchange Format"), SYLK (Multiplan "Symbolic Link"), and WKS (Lotus Worksheet) files, records in the data base become rows in the spreadsheet, with each field supplying data for one column and the field names entered into the spreadsheet as column titles.

COPY STRUCTURE creates an empty data base file containing the fields listed in the *field list* in the specified order or all of the fields in the current file if no *field list* is given.

The STRUCTURE EXTENDED option creates a structure-extended file that describes the structure of the current file instead of creating a data base with the same structure as that of the current file. The *structure-extended file* is a data base that has one record for each field in the structure of the current file. Its four fields, named FIELD_NAME, FIELD_TYPE, FIELD_LEN, and FIELD_DEC, contain the names, types, and lengths of the fields, as well as the number of decimal places in them. This file may be edited with MODIFY STRUCTURE and used to create a new data base with the CREATE FROM command.

COPY file <*file 1*> TO <*file 2*> creates a copy of *file 1* under the name *file 2*. Any disk file may be copied with this command.

COUNT [<*scope*>] [FOR <*condition*>] [WHILE <*condition*>] [TO <*memvar*>]

Counts the number of records in the current data base in the range defined by the *scope* and *condition*. If no *scope* is specified, ALL is assumed. If you have SET TALK ON, the count is displayed on the screen. If a memory variable is included, the named numeric variable is created to store the count.

Example:

```
USE NWCUST
COUNT FOR CITY = "San Francisco" TO MCOUNT
```

Equivalent program:

```
use NWCUST
store 0 to MCOUNT

do while .not. eof()
   if CITY = "San Francisco"
      store MCOUNT  + 1 to MCOUNT
   endif
   skip
enddo

? MCOUNT
```

CREATE <*file name*>
CREATE <*file name*> FROM <*structure-extended file*>

Creates a new data base file. If you do not specify the *file name,* you will be prompted to enter it. CREATE enters a full-screen mode in which you can define names, types, and lengths of fields, and for numeric fields, the number of decimal places for up to 128 fields, totaling up to 4000 bytes.

If you include the FROM option, the structure of the new file is determined by the contents of the *structure-extended file.* This file is a data base that has one record for each field in the structure it describes. Its four fields, named FIELD_NAME, FIELD_TYPE, FIELD_LEN, and FIELD_DEC, contain the names, types, and lengths of the fields, and the number of decimal places for numeric fields. The file is usually generated with the COPY command using the STRUCTURE EXTENDED option, but it may be created with CREATE, provided that you adhere to the four standard field names that allow dBASE III PLUS to recognize the data base as a structure-extended file.

CREATE LABEL <*label file name*>

Creates a new label form or edits an existing form in a menu-driven environment. If you do not specify the *file name*, you will be prompted to enter it. If you do not have a data base open in the selected work area, you will also be prompted for the data base name. This command is identical to MODIFY LABEL.

To specify the size and shape of the labels, you first select one of the five predefined formats. If necessary, you may then change the label width (1-120 characters), label height (1-16 lines), left margin (0-250 characters), labels across the page (1-15), lines between labels (0-16 lines), and spaces between labels (0-120 characters) if you are printing more than one across.

For each line on the label you may specify as the contents any valid dBASE III PLUS expression up to 60 characters long. If more than one data base is open, you may print fields from any open file by referring to all fields in unselected work areas as <*alias*>—><*field name*>. However, only fields from the current work area may be displayed and selected from the field list accessed with F10 unless you have specified the fields to be accessed with a SET FIELDS command or opened a VIEW that includes a field list.

CREATE QUERY <*query file name*>

Creates a new query file or edits an existing file in a menu-driven environment. If you do not specify the *file name,* you will be prompted to enter it. If you do not have a data base open in the selected work area, you will also be prompted for the data base name. This command is identical to MODIFY QUERY.

You may enter up to seven separate conditions linked with the logical operators .AND., .OR., and .NOT. and grouped ("nested") with parentheses. When more than one data base is open, you may include fields from any open file in your conditions only if you have specified with a SET FIELDS command the fields to be accessed or opened a VIEW that includes a field list.

The selection criteria stored in the query file are placed in effect with SET FILTER TO FILE <*query file name*>.

CREATE REPORT <*report file name*>

Creates a new report form or edits an existing form in a menu-driven environment. If you do not specify the *file name*, you will be prompted to enter it. If you do not have a data base open in the selected work area, you will also be prompted for the data base name. This command is identical to MODIFY REPORT.

To specify the overall page layout for the report, you may enter up to four page-title lines of up to 60 characters each, the page width (1-500 characters), left and right margins, and lines per page (1-500). You can choose to double space the report, to issue a form feed command to the printer before and/or after printing the report, and whether to print the report "plain" (without page numbers, date, and page titles).

You may print one or two levels of subtotals, as well as the text to be placed at the beginning of each group of records as a group or subgroup heading. It is your responsibility to ensure that the data base is sorted or indexed on the same combination of fields that determine the subtotal breaks. You can choose to print a summary-only report that includes no detail records, only the subtotals and grand totals.

For each column on the report, you may specify any valid dBASE III PLUS expression up to 254 characters long as the contents. If more than one data base is open, you may print fields from any open file by referring to all fields in unselected work areas as <*alias*>—><*field name*>. However, only fields from the current work area may be displayed and selected from the field list accessed with F10 unless you have specified the fields to be accessed with a SET FIELDS command or opened a VIEW that includes a field list.

For each column, you may also specify up to four lines of column titles, the width of the column, and for numeric fields, the number of decimal places and whether or not to accumulate totals and subtotals for the column.

CREATE SCREEN <*screen file name*>

Creates a new screen form or edits an existing form in a menu-driven environment. If you do not specify the *file name,* you will be prompted to enter it. You can select one or more data base files to provide the fields displayed or collected on the screen, or you can create a data base at the same time you draw the screen image. This command is identical to MODIFY SCREEN.

To define the screen image, type background text directly on the screen "blackboard" and define the locations where fields are displayed or collected. For each field you may also specify a PICTURE, FUNCTION, or RANGE to format and/or validate the data. Boxes and lines consisting of the single- and double-lined graphics characters may also be included on a screen.

The screen image is saved in two ways—in an .SCR file that stores the screen specifications for subsequent editing, and in a standard format file that is invoked with SET FORMAT TO <*format file name*>.

CREATE VIEW <*view file name*> [FROM ENVIRONMENT]

Creates a new view file or edits an existing file in a menu-driven environment. If you do not specify the *file name*, you will be prompted to enter it. This command is identical to MODIFY VIEW.

To define the view, you first select one or more data bases, each of which may be opened with one or more indexes. You may also define how the files are linked with SET RELATION, specify the list of fields that may be accessed, and optionally, specify a format file and filter condition.

If the FROM ENVIRONMENT clause is included, the view is created based on the files and indexes currently open and the relations, field list, format file, and filter condition currently in effect.

The set of files and relationships among them stored in the view file are placed in effect with SET VIEW TO <*view file name*>.

DELETE [<*scope*>] [FOR <*condition*>] [WHILE <*condition*>]

Marks for deletion the records in the current data base in the range defined by the *scope* and *condition*. If no *scope* is specified, only the current record is DELETEd. Records marked for deletion in this way are physically removed from the file and the space they occupy released only when you PACK the data base. You may SET DELETED ON to cause dBASE III PLUS to ignore deleted records except when they are explicitly accessed by record number. If you have SET DELETED OFF, deleted records are identified by an asterisk (*) next to the record number in LIST or DISPLAY commands and by the "Del" indicator on line 0 in any of the full-screen edit modes. Records thus marked for deletion may be recovered with the RECALL command until the file is PACKed.

DELETE FILE <*file name*>

This command is identical to ERASE.

DIR [<*drive*>:] [<*path*> \] [<*skeleton*>] [TO PRINT]

Displays a directory of the specified files. If no *drive*, *path*, or file name *skeleton* is specified, only data base files are listed, and the display includes for each file the number of records, date of last update, and file size. If a *drive*, *path*, or file name *skeleton* is included, files are displayed four across, much like the listing produced by the MS-DOS DIR command with the /W (wide) option. Even with a SET PATH command in effect, only files from the current subdirectory will be displayed if no *path* is specified.

DISPLAY [<*scope*>] [<*exp list*>] [FOR <*condition*>] [WHILE <*condition*>] [TO PRINT] [OFF]

Displays the specified expressions for the range of records defined by the *scope* and *condition* in the current data base. If no *scope* is specified, only the current record is displayed, and with no *exp list*, all fields are included. The display pauses every 20 lines to allow you to read the screen; pressing any key will display the next group of 20 lines. If you have SET HEADING ON, the field names, memory variable names, or algebraic expressions in *exp list* are displayed as column titles in the same mixture of uppercase and lowercase used in the DISPLAY command. The contents of memo fields are displayed only if the field names are explicitly included in *exp list*. TO

PRINT causes the screen display to be echoed to the printer. OFF suppresses the display of the record numbers. The DISPLAY command is similar to LIST, except that LIST assumes a default *scope* of ALL and does not pause every 20 lines.

Example:

```
USE NWCUST INDEX NWCACCT
DISPLAY NEXT 100 ACCOUNT, COMPANY, DATE() - LASTORDER FOR YTDINV > 0
```

Equivalent program:

```
use NWCUST
store 0 to MCOUNT, MDISPLAYED
? "   Record# ACCOUNT    COMPANY                         DATE() - LASTORDER"

do while MCOUNT <= 100 .and. .not. eof()
   if YTDINV > 0
      ? recno(), ACCOUNT, COMPANY, DATE() - LASTORDER
      store MDISPLAYED + 1 TO MDISPLAYED
   endif
   if MDISPLAYED = 20
      wait
      store 0 to MDISPLAYED
   endif
   store MCOUNT  + 1 to MCOUNT
   skip
enddo
```

DISPLAY FILES [LIKE <*skeleton*>] [TO PRINT]

This command is identical to DIR, except that the optional TO PRINT phrase causes the screen display to be echoed to the printer.

DISPLAY HISTORY [LAST <*expN*>] [TO PRINT]

Displays a list of the commands in history, normally 20 unless you have increased this number with a SET HISTORY command. TO PRINT causes the screen display to be echoed to the printer. If the LAST clause is included, *expN* specifies the number of commands displayed, which is taken from the bottom of the list. The display pauses every 16 lines to allow you to read the screen; pressing any key will display the next group of 16 lines.

DISPLAY MEMORY [TO PRINT]

Displays all active memory variables. The display pauses when the screen is full; pressing any key will display the next screenful of variables. TO

PRINT causes the screen display to be echoed to the printer. For each variable the display includes the name, status (PUBLIC or PRIVATE), data type, stored value, the program that created the variable, and for numeric variables, display value (which may include fewer decimal places than the stored value). At the end of the display, dBASE III PLUS summarizes the number of variables defined, the number of bytes occupied by these variables, the number of remaining variables (256 minus the number already defined), and the number of bytes remaining (the value of MVARSIZ, which is 6000 bytes unless you have increased it with an entry in CONFIG.DB, minus the number already used). This command is similar to LIST MEMORY, except for the pause after filling the screen.

DISPLAY STATUS [TO PRINT]

Displays the current status of the working environment, with a pause between screens to allow you to read the display. TO PRINT causes the screen display to be echoed to the printer.

For each currently active work area, dBASE III PLUS displays the open data base, all indexes (including key expressions), the file alias, the name of the .DBT file if the data base contains memo fields, the name of any open format file, the FILTER condition if one is in effect, and any RELATION used to link the file to another data base. In a network environment, the display also includes any file locks currently in effect and a list of any records currently locked.

The display also includes the file search path, default disk drive, selected printer port, left margin for printouts, the currently selected work area, the status of most of the options controlled by SET commands, and the function key assignments. This command is similar to LIST STATUS, except for the pauses between screens.

DISPLAY STRUCTURE [TO PRINT]

Displays the structure of the current data base file. The display pauses after every 16 fields; pressing any key displays the next 16 fields. TO PRINT causes the screen display to be echoed to the printer. For each field the display includes the name, data type, length, and for numeric fields, number of decimal places. If a field list is in effect, the fields specified in the SET FIELDS commands are marked with a >. dBASE III PLUS also displays the number of records in the file, the date of last update, and the total record length (the sum of the field lengths plus the one character used for the deletion marker). This command is similar to LIST STRUCTURE, except for the pause every 16 fields.

DISPLAY USERS

In a network environment, displays a list of the network workstation names of the users currently logged onto dBASE III PLUS, with the currently logged user marked with a >.

DO <*program name*> [WITH <*parameter list*>]

Runs the specified dBASE III PLUS program or, if a procedure file is open, calls the named procedure. If there is a procedure in the open procedure file with the same name as a program, the procedure will be executed rather than the program. When the called program or procedure terminates, control returns to the line in the calling program that follows the DO command or to the dot prompt if the DO command was executed from command level.

If a *parameter list* is included, the listed expressions are passed to the called program, which must contain a PARAMETERS command with the same number of parameters. The correspondence between the parameters in the DO command in the calling program and the PARAMETERS command in the called program or procedure is established by the order in which they are listed. The parameters may include any valid dBASE III PLUS expressions, but if fields are passed as parameters, the file alias must be specified, even for fields in the currently selected work area. All changes made to the values of any parameters specified as memory variables in the calling program are passed back to the calling program.

DO CASE ... ENDCASE

This program structure selects one out of a number of possibilities. The general form of this structure is

```
DO CASE
    CASE <condition 1>
        <program statements>
    [CASE <condition 2>
        <program statements>]
    [CASE <condition 3>
```

```
        <program statements>]
    [<more cases>]
    [OTHERWISE
        <program statements>]
ENDCASE
```

Any number of statements may be included in a CASE. dBASE III PLUS assumes that only one of the *conditions* in the CASE statements is true. If more than one condition is true, only the statements following the first one will be executed. If the optional OTHERWISE clause is included, it must follow all of the other CASES; if present, the statements following OTHERWISE are executed if none of the conditions in the preceding CASE statements is true. If none of the conditions is true and no OTHERWISE clause is included, no action is taken.

DO WHILE ... ENDDO

This program structure repeats execution of a group of program statements as long as a specified condition remains true. The general form of this structure is

```
DO WHILE <condition>
    <program statements>
ENDDO
```

If the *condition* is never true, the statements within the loop are not executed even once; if the condition never becomes false, the loop will run forever. dBASE III PLUS checks the condition only once on each pass through the loop, so if the condition becomes false midway through, the remaining statements are still executed unless you exit the loop with EXIT or return to the DO WHILE statement with LOOP to force dBASE III PLUS to reevaluate the condition immediately. If the *condition* contains a macro, it is evaluated only once, on the first pass through the loop, so you cannot use a macro if the value of the variable expanded as a macro is changed within the loop.

EDIT [<*scope*>] [FIELDS <*field list*>] [FOR <*condition*>] [WHILE <*condition*>]

Enters a full-screen mode to edit the specified fields in the range of records defined by the *scope* and *conditions*. If no *scope* is specified, ALL is assumed. EDIT is identical to CHANGE.

EJECT

Ejects the paper in the printer to the top of the next page.

ERASE <*file name*>

Erases the specified file from the disk. Any disk file may be ERASEd with this command, so the extension (and path, if the file is not in the current subdirectory) must be included. Only one file at a time may be ERASEd, and you may not ERASE any file that is currently open.

EXIT

Causes dBASE III PLUS to EXIT immediately from the currently running DO WHILE loop and resume execution with the first command following the ENDDO statement.

EXPORT TO <*file name*> TYPE PFS

Exports data to a PFS file from the data base open in the currently selected work area. If a format file is open, it is used to define the PFS screen layout; if not, the standard dBASE III PLUS data entry form is used.

FIND <*character string*>/<*n*>

Searches for the specified record on the first index named in the USE command that opened the current data base. For an index based on a character string, a literal character string need not be enclosed in quotation marks unless it includes leading blank spaces. You may search on less than the full index key value, but the portion you specify must begin at the start of the field. If the character string is stored in a memory variable, the variable name must be preceded by the macro symbol (&) so that dBASE III PLUS searches for the value of the variable rather than the characters that make up its name. If the index is based on a numeric field, you must specify the key value as a numeric constant, not by storing it to a memory variable. FIND works like SEEK, but SEEK can accept any expression as its object.

If the search succeeds, the data base is positioned at the first record whose index key matches the specified string. Even if you have SET TALK ON, no message is displayed. EOF( ) is .F. and the FOUND( ) function has the value .T. If the search fails to FIND a matching record, dBASE III PLUS displays the message "No Find," positions the data base at the end-of-file, and sets the EOF( ) function to .T. and FOUND( ) to .F.

GO/GOTO <*expN*>/BOTTOM/TOP

Positions the current data base to the specified record. GOTO BOTTOM positions the data base to the last record in the file or, with an index open, to the last record in indexed order. GOTO TOP positions the data base to the first record in the file or, with an index open, to the first record in indexed order. If you have used SET DELETED ON or SET FILTER to limit the range of records being processed, GO TOP and GO BOTTOM will position the data base to the first or last record that satisfies all of the specified conditions; however, you may still GOTO any record by number.

HELP [<*keyword*>]

Displays a screen of help text summarizing the syntax and usage of the specified keyword. HELP with no keyword invokes a menu-driven help system.

IF ... ELSE ... ENDIF

A program structure that chooses between two alternatives. The general form of this structure is

```
IF <condition>
   <program statements>
[ELSE
   <program statements>]
ENDIF
```

If the *condition* is true, the statements following IF (which may include another IF loop) are executed. If the condition is false and the optional ELSE is included, the statements between ELSE and ENDIF are executed. With no ELSE clause, no action is taken.

IMPORT FROM <*file name*> TYPE PFS

Imports data from a PFS file and creates a data base file, a format file that matches the PFS screen layout, and a view file to enable you to open the data base and format file together with a SET VIEW command.

INDEX ON <*key expression*> TO <*index file name*> [UNIQUE]

Builds an index for the current data base based on the specified *key expression*. If the *key expression* or *file name* is omitted, you will be prompted to enter it. The expression that specifies the key may be up to 100 characters long. When the INDEX command is completed, it leaves the new index open (and closes any other indexes that were open previously with the current data base) with the record pointer positioned at the end-of-file and the EOF( ) function set to true.

An index may be based on a single character, numeric, or date field, resulting in alphabetical, ascending numeric, and ascending calendar date order, respectively. If the key expression consists of more than one field, it must be a character expression. If date fields are included, they may be converted to characters with the DTOC function; numeric fields may be converted to characters with the STR function.

If the UNIQUE keyword is included, only the first record in a group that share the same value for the *key expression* is included in the index. Thereafter, whenever the file is opened with this index, it will appear to contain unique index keys.

INPUT [<*expC*>] TO <*memvar*>

Collects input from the user and creates the memory variable *memvar* to store the input. If *expC* is included, it is displayed as a prompt. The data type of the memory variable is determined by the data type of the user's entry, which may be any valid dBASE III PLUS expression. If a syntactically incorrect expression is entered, an error message is displayed and the prompt is repeated. If the user presses RETURN or types only blank spaces, dBASE III PLUS repeats the prompt.

INSERT [BLANK] [BEFORE]

INSERT adds a new record to the current data base, using the standard dBASE III PLUS full-screen edit commands to fill in the data. If BEFORE is included in the command, the record is inserted before the current record; otherwise, the new record is inserted after the current record. In either case, all of the subsequent records are moved down to make room for the new entry, which can be very slow in a large data base. If you have SET CARRY ON, the fields normally take their default values from the current record or from the previous record if you have specified the BEFORE option. An alternative is to use an index to access the file in the desired order and allow new records to be APPENDed to the end of the file. This is what happens if INSERT is used with an index open.

INSERT BLANK, most often used in a program, adds a blank record to the current data base and positions the record pointer to the new record without invoking the full-screen edit mode. The fields are usually filled in with REPLACE or GET commands.

JOIN WITH <*alias*> TO <*file name*> FOR <*condition*> [FIELDS <*field list*>]

Creates a new data base file by matching up the current data base and a second file, which is open in another work area and is specified by its *alias*. The matching is done record by record, and the new data base will contain a record corresponding to each pair of records from the two files that satisfies the *condition*. If a *field list* is included, it is used to define the structure of the new file; otherwise, this file contains all of the fields from the current file plus as many fields from the second as permitted by the 128-field limit, except for memo fields, which may not be included in the file created by a JOIN. No field names will be duplicated even if both files contain fields of the same name.

Because dBASE III PLUS reads through the entire second file for each record in the current file, this command can be very time-consuming. If the two files share a common key field, it is much more efficient to CREATE the new file and fill in the records with a short program.

Example:

```
SELECT 1
USE NWORDER
SELECT 2
USE NWCUST
JOIN WITH NWORDER TO NWCSTORD FOR ACCOUNT = NWORDER->ACCOUNT;
  FIELDS ACCOUNT, COMPANY, NWORDER->CATEGORY, NWORDER->PARTNUMBER,;
  NWORDER->QUANTITY
```

Equivalent program:

```
* This program assumes that NWCSTORD.DBF exists, and contains the
* fields ACCOUNT, COMPANY, CATEGORY, PARTNUMBER, and QUANTITY
```

```
select 1
use NWCSTORD
select 2
use NWCUST index NWCACCT
select 3
use NWORDER
set relation to ACCOUNT into NWCUST

do while .not. eof()
   select NWCUST
   if .not. eof()
      select NWCSTORD
      append blank
      replace ACCOUNT with NWCUST->ACCOUNT, COMPANY with;
         NWCUST->COMPANY, CATEGORY with NWORDER->CATEGORY,;
         PARTNUMBER with NWORDER->PARTNUMBER, QUANTITY with;
         NWORDER->QUANTITY
   endif
   select NWORDER
   skip
enddo
```

LABEL FORM <*label format file*> [<*scope*>] [FOR <*condition*>] [WHILE <*condition*>] [TO PRINT] [TO FILE <*file name*>] [SAMPLE]

Prints labels from the current data base, using the specified label format file, for the range of records defined by the *scope* and *conditions*. If no *scope* is specified, ALL is assumed. If the label form references fields from more than one data base, you must make sure that all of the necessary data base and index files are opened and that the files are linked as required with SET RELATION.

TO PRINT causes the labels to be printed as well as displayed on the screen. TO FILE causes an exact image of the printed labels to be stored in the named disk file. SAMPLE causes dBASE III PLUS to print rows of asterisks that occupy the same amount of space as a label to enable you to align the label stock in the printer. After each sample is printed, you are given the choice to print more samples or to begin printing the real labels.

LIST [<*scope*>] [<*exp list*>] [FOR <*condition*>] [WHILE <*condition*>] [TO PRINT] [OFF]

Displays the specified expressions for the range of records in the current data base defined by the *scope* and *conditions*. If no *scope* is specified, ALL is assumed; with no *exp list*, all fields are included. If you have SET HEADING ON, the field names, memory variable names, or algebraic expressions in *exp list* are displayed as column titles, in the same mixture of uppercase and lowercase used in the LIST command. The contents of memo fields are displayed only if the field names are explicitly included in *exp list*. TO PRINT causes the screen display to be echoed to the printer.

OFF suppresses the display of the record numbers. The LIST command is similar to DISPLAY, except that DISPLAY assumes a default *scope* of one record and pauses the display every 20 lines.

Example:

```
USE NWCUST INDEX NWCACCT
LIST NEXT 100 ACCOUNT, COMPANY, DATE() - LASTORDER FOR YTDINV > 0
```

Equivalent program:

```
use NWCUST
store 0 to MCOUNT
? "   Record# ACCOUNT    COMPANY                   DATE() - LASTORDER"

do while MCOUNT <= 100 .and. .not. eof()
   if YTDINV > 0
      ? recno(), ACCOUNT, COMPANY, DATE() - LASTORDER
   endif
   store MCOUNT  + 1 to MCOUNT
   skip
enddo
```

LIST FILES [LIKE <*skeleton*>]

This command is identical to DISPLAY FILES, except that the display does not pause when the screen is full, making the LIST version better for printing the listing.

LIST HISTORY [LAST <*expN*>] [TO PRINT]

This command is identical to DISPLAY HISTORY, except that the display does not pause when the screen is full, making the LIST version better for printing the listing.

LIST MEMORY [TO PRINT]

This command is identical to DISPLAY MEMORY, except that the display does not pause when the screen is full, making the LIST version better for printing the listing.

LIST STATUS [TO PRINT]

This command is identical to DISPLAY STATUS, except that the display does not pause when the screen is full, making the LIST version better for printing the listing.

LIST STRUCTURE [TO PRINT]

This command is identical to DISPLAY STRUCTURE, except that the display does not pause when the screen is full, making the LIST version better for printing the listing.

LOAD <*binary file name*>

Loads a binary file into memory for execution with CALL. Five modules may be LOADed into memory at once. LOAD and CALL should be used only for subroutines written expressly to be executed this way; .COM or .EXE files (including most commercial software) should be invoked with the RUN command instead.

LOCATE [<*scope*>] [FOR <*condition*>] [WHILE <*condition*>]

Searches the range of records in the current data base defined by the *scope* for the first record that matches the specified *conditions*. If no *scope* is specified, ALL is assumed. If a matching record is found, the data base is left positioned at this record; if you have SET TALK ON, the record number is displayed. The CONTINUE command may be used to search for additional records that satisfy the same *conditions*. If no matching record is found within the range of records defined by the specified *scope* and WHILE clause, an "End of locate scope" message is displayed, and the FOUND( ) function assumes the value .F.

LOGOUT

In a data base with a PROTECT security system, closes all open files, exits from the currently running program, and presents a new log-in screen, exactly as if you had QUIT and reentered dBASE III PLUS.

LOOP

Causes dBASE III PLUS to bypass the remaining steps in a DO WHILE loop and return immediately to the DO WHILE statement to reevaluate the condition.

MODIFY COMMAND [<*file name*>]
MODIFY FILE [<*file name*>]

Invokes the dBASE III PLUS editor to create or edit a text file, usually a dBASE III PLUS program or format file. If you do not specify the *file name*, you will be prompted to enter it. If the file already exists, it is loaded into the editor; if not, a new file is created. The MODIFY COMMAND editor can handle a file up to 5000 characters long. You can use the TEDIT option in CONFIG.DB (TEDIT = <*program name*>) to substitute another editor or word processor for the dBASE III PLUS editor so that the external program is invoked by MODIFY COMMAND.

The MODIFY FILE variant does not assume that the file to be created or edited is a program file, so you must always specify the extension.

MODIFY LABEL <*label file name*>

This command is identical to CREATE LABEL.

MODIFY QUERY <*label file name*>

This command is identical to CREATE QUERY.

MODIFY REPORT <*report file name*>

This command is identical to CREATE REPORT.

MODIFY SCREEN <*label file name*>

This command is identical to CREATE SCREEN.

MODIFY STRUCTURE <*file name*>

Changes the structure of the current data base file and adjusts the data records to match the new structure. dBASE III PLUS creates a temporary copy of the file structure, to which you make your changes; the data is then appended from the original file, and this file is renamed with a BAK (backup) extension.

The same rules that govern the APPEND FROM <*file name*> command apply to transferring the data from this backup file to the new structure. You may change field lengths, add or delete fields, or change the data type of a field without losing data (provided that the contents of the field are consistent with the new type). If a character field is shortened, the contents will be truncated to fit; numeric data too long for the new field length is replaced with asterisks. If a field is deleted, the data will be lost; and if a field is added, it will be blank in all of the records. You may also change field names if you do not also add or delete fields or change field lengths or types. Any indexes created for the old file will no longer match the new one and must be rebuilt after the structure is modified.

The APPEND step can be time-consuming in a large file, and it requires an amount of disk space equal to the final size of the new file. To speed up the process, or if you do not have enough space on one disk, you can substitute the equivalent sequence of commands (all disk drive designators are shown explicitly in this example for clarity):

```
RENAME A:NWCUST.DBF TO A:NWCSTOLD.DBF
RENAME A:NWCUST.DBT TO A:NWCSTOLD.DBT
USE A:NWCSTOLD
COPY STRUCTURE TO B:NWCUST
USE B:NWCUST
MODIFY STRUCTURE
APPEND FROM A:NWCSTOLD
```

MODIFY VIEW <*label file name*>

This command is identical to CREATE VIEW.

NOTE/*

Identifies a statement as a comment (nonexecutable) line in a dBASE III PLUS program. You can also include a comment on the same line as a program statement by preceding the comment with &&.

ON ERROR/ESCAPE/KEY <*command*>

Specifies a command to be executed under one of three conditions: when a dBASE III PLUS error occurs, when the ESC key is pressed, or when any key is pressed. The *command* may be any valid dBASE III PLUS command; but most commonly, you would want to invoke another program or procedure rather than execute a single command. This procedure could take corrective action in response to an error or process the user's request to interrupt the currently running program. The three ON commands may be used in any combination; with both ON ESCAPE and ON KEY in effect, pressing ESC invokes the ON ESCAPE routine rather than the ON KEY routine.

ON ESCAPE has no effect if you have also disabled the ESC key with SET ESCAPE OFF. In order to permit an ON KEY procedure to execute correctly, you must include a command to clear the key pressed by the user from the typeahead buffer. You can do this with the INKEY( ) function or the READ or CLEAR TYPEAHEAD command.

Example:

```
procedure STOPLIST

clear typeahead

clear
store .T. to MQUIT
@ 10,10 say "Do you want to return to the menu? (Y/N)" get MQUIT picture "Y"
read
if MQUIT
   return to master
else
   return
endif
```

PACK

Permanently removes from the current data base all records previously marked for deletion and rebuilds any indexes opened with the data base in the USE command. After a file is PACKed, there is no way to recover the deleted records. PACK reclaims the disk space formerly occupied by the deleted records, but the new size and number of records are updated on the disk (and therefore reported correctly by the DIR command) only after the file is closed.

PARAMETERS <*exp list*>

Creates local memory variables corresponding to the values passed to a program or procedure in a DO command. If present, the PARAMETERS command must be the first executable (non-comment) line in the program or procedure. The correspondence between the parameters in the DO command in the calling program and the PARAMETERS command in the called program or procedure is established by the order in which they are listed. The parameters may be any valid dBASE III PLUS expressions; but if fields are passed as parameters, the file alias must be specified, even for fields in the currently selected work area. All changes made to the values of any parameters specified as memory variables in the calling program are passed back to the calling program.

PRIVATE [ALL [LIKE <*skeleton*>]] / [<*memvar list*>]

Declares the specified memory variables private to the program that created them, so that local variables may be given the same names as

PUBLIC variables or variables in a program higher in a chain of programs that call one another. The PUBLIC or higher-level variables are thus hidden from the current program and any programs it calls until the program terminates.

PROCEDURE <*procedure name*>

Used to identify the individual procedures in a procedure file. A procedure name may be up to eight characters long. Each procedure must begin with a PROCEDURE command and should end with a RETURN.

PUBLIC <*memvar list*>

Makes all of the memory variables in the *memvar list* available to all programs in a system. A variable must be declared PUBLIC before it is initialized. Within a program PUBLIC variables may be erased from memory by naming them explicitly in a RELEASE command or by using CLEAR MEMORY or CLEAR ALL, but not RELEASE ALL.

QUIT

Closes all open disk files and exits from dBASE III PLUS to the operating system.

READ [SAVE]

Allows editing of the variables displayed by all of the @ ... SAY ... GET commands issued since the last READ, CLEAR GETS, or CLEAR command. The cursor is positioned initially at the first variable, and all of the variables may be edited with the standard full-screen cursor movement and editing commands.

If the SAVE option is included, the READ command does not also CLEAR the GETs, so that a subsequent READ command may collect the same set of fields again. You must be sure that you do not allow too many GETs between READ commands. By default dBASE III PLUS permits 128 GETs between READs, but you can increase this to 1023 with an entry in CONFIG.DB.

RECALL [<*scope*>] [FOR <*condition*>] [WHILE <*condition*>]

Recovers ("undeletes") all of the records marked for deletion in the current data base in the range of records defined by the *scope* and *conditions*. If no *scope* is specified, only the current record is RECALLed.

REINDEX

Rebuilds all of the index files opened with the current data base in the USE command, based on the original key expression(s) stored in the index file(s). If the original index was created with UNIQUE ON or with the UNIQUE keyword specified in the INDEX command, the new index file will also have this attribute. If an index file has been damaged, dBASE III PLUS may not be able to read the key expression, and you must use the INDEX command instead.

RELEASE [ALL [LIKE/EXCEPT <*skeleton*>]] / [<*memvar list*>]
RELEASE MODULE

Erases from memory the specified variables and frees the space for defining additional variables. When used in a program, RELEASE ALL erases only the variables created within the program.

RELEASE MODULE unloads a binary file placed in memory by the LOAD command.

RENAME <*old file name*> TO <*new file name*>

Renames the specified file. Since you may use this command to rename any disk file, the file extension (or full path name, if the file is not in the current subdirectory) must be specified. If you RENAME a .DBF file that contains memo fields, you must also remember to RENAME the corresponding .DBT file. Only one file at a time may be renamed, and you may not rename any file that is currently open.

REPLACE [<*scope*>] <*field*> WITH <*exp*> [,<*field2*> WITH <*exp2*> . . .]
[FOR <*condition*>] [WHILE <*condition*>]

Substitutes the results of evaluating the specified expressions for the current values of the specified fields, for the range of records in the current data base defined by the *scope* and *conditions*. If no *scope* is specified, only fields in the current record are REPLACEd.

If you REPLACE the values of the key fields in a data base opened with one or more indexes, the indexes are automatically updated. This also means that the index entry for the record is immediately moved to its new location in the index, and the "next" record will not be the same one as before the REPLACE; this type of REPLACEment should therefore not be performed on an indexed file. If you must process the file in indexed order, a short program may be used instead of the REPLACE command.

Examples:

```
* THIS PROGRAM IS EQUIVALENT TO THE COMMAND:
*   REPLACE NEXT 10 ZIP WITH " "

use NWCUST index NWCZIP
seek "94"

store 1 to MCOUNT
do while MCOUNT <= 10 .and. found()
   replace ZIP with " "
   seek "94"
   store MCOUNT + 1 to MCOUNT
enddo

return
```

```
* THIS PROGRAM IS EQUIVALENT TO THE COMMAND:
*   REPLACE ACCOUNT WITH MACCOUNT2 WHILE ACCOUNT = MACCOUNT1

parameters MACCOUNT1, MACCOUNT2

use NWORDER index NWOACCT
seek MACCOUNT1

store 1 to MCOUNT
do while found()
   replace MACCOUNT1 with MACCOUNT2
   seek MACCOUNT1
   store MCOUNT + 1 to MCOUNT
enddo

return
```

REPORT FORM <*report form file*> [<*scope*>] [FOR <*condition*>] [WHILE <*condition*>] [NOEJECT] [PLAIN] [SUMMARY] [HEADING <*expC*>] [TO PRINT] [TO FILE <*file name*>]

Prints a report, using the specified report form file, for the range of records from the current data base defined by the *scope* and *conditions*. If no *scope* is specified, ALL is assumed. If the label form references fields from more than one data base, you must make sure that all of the necessary data base and index files are opened and that the files are linked as required with SET RELATION.

TO PRINT causes the report to be printed as well as displayed on the screen. TO FILE causes an exact image of the printed report to be stored in the named disk file. The HEADING clause may be used to specify an optional extra heading line to be printed on the first line of each page, centered above the page title. The NOEJECT, PLAIN, and SUMMARY keywords may be used to override the values for these parameters, which were specified when the report was created. NOEJECT suppresses the page eject that is sent to the printer before it begins the report. PLAIN causes the report to be printed without page numbers and date, and with the page title and column headings printed only once, on the first page of the report. SUMMARY prints a report that includes only subtotals, sub-subtotals, and totals, with no detail records.

RESTORE FROM <*file name*> [ADDITIVE]

Loads the variables in the specified memory file into memory. Without the ADDITIVE option, any existing variables are first RELEASEd. If the command was issued from within a program, the newly loaded variables become PRIVATE; if it was typed from the dot prompt, they will be PUBLIC. If the ADDITIVE option is included, the variables in the memory file are *added* to the ones currently in memory. With the ADDITIVE option, variables stored as PUBLIC become PUBLIC again, provided that you declare them PUBLIC prior to the RESTORE command.

RESUME

Continues to execute a program previously interrupted with the ESC key and suspended (rather than canceled). Execution resumes with the command following the last one executed when the ESC key was pressed.

RETRY

Returns control from the currently running program to the calling program. Execution resumes with the command that caused the second program to be called. This command is often used in a network environment to attempt to lock a file or a record being accessed by another user. It is also used in error-handling procedures to allow the user to correct the error condition, after which the program retries the operation that caused the error.

Example:

```
clear

do case
   case error() = 1
      ? "File is missing"
      ? "Please check to make sure the right disk is in the drive"
   case error() = 41
      ? "The memo text file for this data base is missing"
      ? "Please check to make sure the right disk is in the drive"
    case error() = 114
      ? "The index file is damaged"
      ? "Please wait while file is reindexed"
      set talk on
      reindex
      set talk off
endcase

store .T. to MRETRY
@ 10,10 say "Do you want to try again? (Y/N)" get MRETRY picture "Y"
read

if MRETRY
   retry
else
   return to master
endif
```

RETURN

Causes dBASE III PLUS to exit from the current program or procedure and return control to the calling program or procedure or to the dot prompt if the program was invoked from the dot prompt. Execution resumes with the command following the one that caused the second program to be called. RETURN TO MASTER jumps to the highest-level dBASE III PLUS program (the user's first entry point into the system) instead of to the calling program. A RETURN command may occur anywhere within a program. If there is no RETURN command, a program terminates after the last statement is executed; thus, it is unnecessary (although it is good practice) to place a RETURN at the end of every program.

RUN <*command*>
!<*command*>

Executes the specified MS-DOS command, batch file, or program. This command requires that COMMAND.COM be available on the disk from which the system was booted (usually the root directory of the floppy disk in drive A: or the hard disk) or in any subdirectory identified to DOS with the SET COMSPEC command. You must have enough additional memory in your computer (beyond the 256K required by dBASE III

PLUS) to load COMMAND.COM and the external program into RAM along with dBASE III PLUS. If you have made entries in the CONFIG.DB file that increase the size of the dBASE III PLUS memory buffers, you will need enough memory to accommodate these buffers. (Also note that MAXMEM should be increased through CONFIG.DB to ensure that the buffers are not overwritten by the external program executed with the RUN command.)

SAVE TO <*file name*> [ALL LIKE/EXCEPT <*skeleton*>]

Saves the specified memory variables on disk in the named memory variable file. If you do not include the ALL LIKE or ALL EXCEPT clause, all memory variables are SAVEd.

SEEK <*exp*>

Searches the index named first in the USE command that opened the current data base for the specified expression. You may search on less than the full index key value, but the portion you specify must begin at the start of the field. If the search succeeds, the data base is positioned at the first record whose index key matches the specified string, and the FOUND( ) function has the value .T. If the search fails to find a matching record, dBASE III PLUS displays the message "No Find," positions the data base at the end-of-file, and sets the EOF( ) function to .T. and FOUND( ) to .F. SEEK is similar to FIND, except that FIND can accept only a single numeric or character string constant as its object, whereas SEEK can accept any valid expression.

SELECT <*work area/alias*>

Switches to the specified work area. A work area may always be selected by number (1-10) or by letter (A-J); and any work area in which a data base file is open may also be selected by the file's alias. When you SELECT a work area, any data bases open in other work areas remain positioned exactly where they were. Fields from these files may be specified for display or for use in calculations by using the notation <*alias*> -><*field name*>.

SET

Invokes a menu-driven, full-screen mode for viewing and changing many of the SET options. The options are described individually. Note that the default values of options with two or more alternate values are indicated in uppercase.

SET ALTERNATE TO [<*file name*>]
SET ALTERNATE on/OFF

SET ALTERNATE TO <*file name*> opens the specified text file. Once the file is open, SET ALTERNATE ON causes all sequential output (all text except that displayed by the full-screen commands) sent to the console to be echoed to the text file. SET ALTERNATE OFF suspends recording of the work session in the ALTERNATE file. You may SET ALTERNATE ON and OFF as many times as necessary. To close the text file, use CLOSE ALTERNATE or SET ALTERNATE TO after the last SET ALTERNATE OFF command.

SET BELL ON/off

Determines whether or not dBASE III PLUS sounds the computer's bell (usually a beeper) when the user's entry completely fills a field or when a data entry error is made (for example, typing an invalid date or entering characters into a numeric field).

SET CARRY on/OFF

Determines whether or not the data entered into each new record APPENDed to a data base is used as the default field values for the next record entered. The status of the CARRY option affects only records added with full-screen commands like APPEND or INSERT; even if you SET CARRY ON, all of the fields in a record added with APPEND BLANK or INSERT BLANK remain blank.

SET CATALOG TO [<*catalog file name*>]
SET CATALOG on/OFF

SET CATALOG TO <*catalog file name*> opens the specified catalog data base in work area 10, or creates it if it does not exist. A CATALOG is a normal dBASE III PLUS data base file with the extension .CAT instead of .DBF, which may be displayed and updated from the dot prompt as long as you do not change the structure. The CATALOG records all files used in an application and their associations. With a CATALOG open, the file lists displayed by the ASSIST menus include only files in the CATALOG. A catalog query clause—substituting a "?" where dBASE III PLUS expects a file name—may be used in any command issued from the dot prompt to call up a list of available files of the correct type. For file types that can only be used in conjunction with a data base, such as index or format files, the catalog query clause displays only the files associated with the data base in use in the current work area.

Normally, when a CATALOG is open, all files created are added to the CATALOG. If you have SET TITLE ON, you will be prompted for an 80-character title for the file, which is displayed along with the file name in response to a catalog query clause. You can temporarily disable this update process with SET CATALOG OFF and reactivate it with SET CATALOG ON.

SET CENTURY on/OFF

Determines whether dates are displayed and entered with four-digit years. With CENTURY OFF, the century is assumed to be 1900 and the year is always displayed as two digits; nevertheless, if a calculation creates a value for a date field in another century, the century is stored and used in subsequent calculations. With CENTURY ON, all dates are displayed and entered with four-digit years.

SET COLOR TO [<*standard foreground/standard background*>]
[, <*enhanced foreground/enhanced background*>] [, <*border*>]
SET COLOR on/off

SET COLOR TO determines the colors or monochrome display attributes used for information displayed by dBASE III PLUS (the *standard* display), data entered by the user (the *enhanced* display), and the *border* (the area of the screen outside the 24-line-by-80-column area used by dBASE III PLUS). The attributes are entered by using the codes listed in Table 8-1. If any of the values are omitted, the defaults are used: white letters on a black background for the standard area, black letters on a white background for the enhanced area, and black for the border.

SET COLOR ON/OFF selects between color and monochrome displays if both are present in the system. The default value is the monitor in use when dBASE III PLUS was loaded.

SET CONFIRM on/OFF

Determines whether the operator must confirm each field or memory variable entry by pressing RETURN. If you SET CONFIRM ON, the cursor does not advance automatically to the next item when a field or memory variable is filled completely—the user must press RETURN.

SET CONSOLE ON/off

Determines whether sequential output (not full-screen displays) appears on the console (the screen). SET CONSOLE OFF may be used to prevent data printed by REPORT, LABEL, or ? commands from also appearing on the screen. Even if you SET CONSOLE OFF, input may be entered by the operator, although it is not echoed to the screen, and all dBASE III PLUS error messages are displayed. This command may be used only from within a program.

SET DATE AMERICAN/ansi/british/italian/french/german

Establishes the display and storage format for date fields and memory variables. No matter which display format is in effect, dBASE III PLUS can carry out date arithmetic and date comparisons, and it can SORT or INDEX on a single date field in correct chronological order. (See Chapter 23 for a more complete discussion of the problems associated with indexing by date.) These are the formats:

AMERICAN	MM/DD/YY
ANSI	YY.MM.DD
BRITISH	DD/MM/YY
ITALIAN	DD-MM-YY
FRENCH	DD.MM.YY
GERMAN	DD.MM.YY

SET DEBUG on/OFF

Determines whether the command lines echoed by SET ECHO ON are displayed on the screen or printed on the printer. If you SET DEBUG ON, the output of the ECHO option is routed to the printer so that formatted screens are not disrupted by the echoed program lines.

SET DECIMALS TO <*expN*>

Determines the number of decimal places displayed when an expression involving division or the SQRT, LOG, or EXP function is evaluated. The default is 2, and you may specify any value between 0 and 15. If you also SET FIXED ON, the SET DECIMALS option controls the display of all numeric variables and calculations, not just those involving division, SQRT, LOG, or EXP. In calculations involving multiplication, the result has a number of decimal places equal to the sum of the number of decimal places in the two quantities multiplied. Otherwise, the number of decimal places is the same as in the quantity with the most decimal places.

SET DEFAULT TO <*drive*>

Establishes the default disk drive to be used by dBASE III PLUS to read and write all disk files unless a different drive is explicitly included with the file name.

SET DELETED on/OFF

Determines whether dBASE III PLUS processes records that have been marked for deletion. If you SET DELETED ON, deleted records are ignored in all commands, except when the record number is specified explicitly (for example, in an explicit GOTO command or in a command with a *scope* of a single record). If SET DELETED ON is issued with a file already open, it does not automatically reposition the record pointer to the first non-deleted record; you should use GOTO TOP for this purpose.

SET DELIMITERS TO [<*delimiter(s)*>] [DEFAULT]
SET DELIMITERS on/OFF

SET DELIMITERS ON/OFF determines whether fields displayed by GET commands are surrounded by delimiters. SET DELIMITERS TO <*delimiters*> designates the actual delimiter character(s) to be used. You may specify either one or two delimiter characters (enclosed in quotes). If you specify one character, it will be used as both the beginning and ending delimiter; if you specify two, the first is used as the beginning delimiter and the second as the ending delimiter. If you SET DELIMITERS ON without assigning delimiters, a colon (:) is used. The DEFAULT option restores this default delimiter after a previous SET DELIMITERS TO command.

SET DEVICE TO printer/SCREEN

Determines whether the output of @ ... SAY commands is routed to the printer or to the screen. When you have SET DEVICE TO PRINT, all GET commands are ignored.

SET DOHISTORY on/OFF

Determines whether commands executed from dBASE III PLUS programs are recorded in history, along with the commands you type from the dot prompt. This option is most often used as a debugging aid, to enable you to retrace execution of a program after a test run. If you SET DOHISTORY ON, you will usually want to increase the number of commands retained in history (from the default 20) with SET HISTORY TO.

SET ECHO on/OFF

Determines whether command lines are echoed to the screen as they are executed. All commands are echoed, including those typed at the dot prompt, but this option is most frequently used to trace the execution of a program for debugging purposes. If you also SET DEBUG ON, the echoed command lines are routed to the printer instead of the screen so that formatted display screens are not disrupted.

SET ENCRYPTION ON/off

In a data base with a PROTECT security system in effect, determines whether new files created by copying existing data bases (with commands such as COPY or SORT) are encrypted. The status of this option does not affect files created with the CREATE command; these must be encrypted through the PROTECT program. The structure of an encrypted file cannot be changed with MODIFY STRUCTURE. To do this, you can SET ENCRYPTION OFF, COPY the file, modify the copy, and then use PROTECT to encrypt the new file and assign access privileges. ENCRYPTION must be OFF in order to COPY or EXPORT a data base file to one of the external formats supported by dBASE III PLUS—DELIMITED, SDF, DIF, SYLK, WKS, and PFS.

SET ESCAPE ON/off

Determines whether dBASE III PLUS responds when the user presses the ESC key. If you SET ESCAPE OFF, a dBASE III PLUS command or program can be interrupted only by rebooting or turning off the computer.

SET EXACT on/OFF

Determines whether character strings are compared using the full length of both strings. If you SET EXACT OFF, dBASE III PLUS examines only the number of characters in the string on the right of the equal sign if this string is shorter. If you SET EXACT ON, the two strings are considered equal only if they are the same length and have the same value.

SET EXCLUSIVE ON/off

In a network environment, determines whether files are opened in exclusive or shared mode. The file open mode is determined by the status of the EXCLUSIVE option at the time a file is opened, even if you subsequently reset the EXCLUSIVE option. Any file opened with EXCLUSIVE OFF can only be accessed by one user at a time. If a file is opened in shared mode, a file or record locking system should be implemented to prevent damage caused by multiple simultaneous updates. A file may also be opened for exclusive use by including the EXCLUSIVE keyword in the USE command.

SET FIELDS TO [<*field list*>/ALL]
SET FIELDS on/OFF

SET FIELDS TO *field list* specifies the fields from one or more open data bases that are accessible from the dot prompt or to your programs. SET FIELDS ON activates the field list defined with SET FIELDS commands, and SET FIELDS OFF temporarily disables the field list. Regardless of the order in which the fields are named in the SET FIELDS command, they are LISTed or displayed for full-screen editing in the order they occur in the file structure(s).

Successive SET FIELDS commands add to the field list, so you are not limited by the 254-character command length limit. However, the ALL option sets the field list to all fields from the data base in the current work area only. To access all fields from the current data base, together with selected fields from other work areas, the SET FIELDS TO ALL command must therefore precede the other SET FIELDS commands. To access fields from more than one file, the files must share a common key field and they must be linked with SET RELATION; usually this means that for each record in the currently selected data base, there is only one matching record in the file accessed through the RELATION.

Even with a field list in effect, APPEND and INSERT add records only to the file in the currently selected work area, and the INDEX, LOCATE, SET FILTER, and SET RELATION commands may access any fields in all work areas. As in any other context where files are linked with SET RELATION, changing the key field in one file does not automatically update the matching record(s) in the file accessed through the RELATION. All fields remain accessible in open files that are not named in a SET FIELDS command or related to a file affected by the field list.

SET FILTER TO [<*condition*>]/[FILE <*query file name*>]

Establishes a condition used to determine which records in the current data base are processed by all dBASE III PLUS commands. With a FILTER in effect, records that do not pass the condition in the filter are ignored, except when the record number is specified explicitly (for example, in an explicit GOTO command, or with a *scope* of a single record). SET FILTER TO FILE reads a condition previously stored in a query file constructed with CREATE QUERY.

All commands that position the data base act relative to the FILTER, so, for example, SKIP positions the file to the next record that passes the test. The SET FILTER command itself does not reposition the record pointer, even if the current record does not pass the FILTER *condition*; this command should therefore always be followed by a command, such as GOTO TOP, which ensures that the file is positioned to the first record that matches the *condition*. Each work area may have a separate FILTER in effect. A FILTER may also reference fields in any work area, but this usually makes sense only if the files are linked with SET RELATION. SET FILTER TO, with no *condition*, cancels any FILTER in effect. If a FILTER depends on fields in more than one file, you must be sure to cancel the FILTER if any of the files involved are closed.

SET FIXED on/OFF

Determines whether dBASE III PLUS displays all numeric expressions with a fixed number of decimal places. If you SET FIXED ON, the SET DECIMALS option determines the number of decimals displayed for all numeric variables; otherwise, SET DECIMALS affects only the results of calculations involving division, SQRT, LOG, or EXP.

SET FORMAT TO [<*format file name*>]

Opens a format file for the current data base that draws a formatted data entry screen for the full-screen APPEND, EDIT, CHANGE, and INSERT commands. SET FORMAT TO, with no file name, or CLOSE FORMAT closes any format file open in the current work area.

SET FUNCTION <*exp*> TO <*expC*>

Assigns a new meaning to one of the programmable function keys. On most IBM and compatible computers, there are 10 or 12 function keys, referred to by the numbers 2 through 10 or 12 (or numeric expressions that evaluate to these values) or the names F2 through F10 or F12 (or the equivalent character string expressions). On computers with named function keys, *exp* must be a character rather than a numeric expression.

You may not reassign the value of the HELP key, usually function key F1, which is reserved for invoking the dBASE III PLUS menu-driven help system. Each of the other function keys may be assigned any arbitrary sequence of up to 30 characters. In this string a RETURN may be symbolized by a semicolon (;).

SET HEADING ON/off

Determines whether dBASE III PLUS displays column headings in LIST, DISPLAY, SUM, COUNT, and AVERAGE commands. If you SET HEADING ON, the field names, variable names, or expressions are displayed as column headings, in the same mixture of uppercase and lowercase used in the command. The width of each column of data on the screen is the width of the quantity displayed or the column heading, whichever is greater.

SET HELP ON/off

Determines whether dBASE III PLUS displays the message "Do you want some help? (Y/N)" when a syntax error is made in a command typed at the dot prompt.

SET HISTORY TO <*expN*>
SET HISTORY ON/off

SET HISTORY determines the number of commands that are retained in history. SET HISTORY OFF temporarily disables the history feature, and SET HISTORY ON turns it back on. With large values of *expN*, the extra memory used to store these commands should be protected by increasing MAXMEM with an entry in CONFIG.DB, so that the command history is not overwritten when you issue a RUN command. The default is 20, and you may specify any value between 0 and 16,000.

SET INDEX TO [<*index file list*>]

Opens the specified index file(s) together with the current data base. You may open up to seven indexes for each data base, all of which will be updated to reflect all new entries and changes made to the key fields. The index named first in the *index file list* is the *master index* that determines the order in which records are displayed or printed; this is the only index that may be used to retrieve records with FIND or SEEK. The SET INDEX command positions the data base to the record that matches the first index entry. SET INDEX TO, with no list of index files, or CLOSE INDEX closes all indexes in the current work area.

SET INTENSITY ON/off

Determines whether the *standard* display colors or monochrome attributes used for data displayed by dBASE III PLUS are the same as the *enhanced* display colors used for data entered by the user. SET INTENSITY OFF eliminates the difference between these two areas and uses the same colors for the *enhanced* area as those SET for the *standard* area.

SET MARGIN TO <*expN*>

Establishes the left margin used for all printed output, including reports and the output of LIST TO PRINT and DISPLAY TO PRINT commands. The default is 0. For reports and labels, this value is added to the value specified in the report or label form.

SET MEMOWIDTH TO <*expN*>

Determines the display width for memo fields in LIST, DISPLAY, and ? commands. The default is 50.

SET MENUS on/OFF

Determines whether a help menu listing the full-screen cursor movement and editing commands is displayed by default in the full-screen commands. Even if you SET MENUS OFF, you may still toggle the help screen display on or off at any time by pressing F1.

SET MESSAGE TO [<*expC*>]

Defines a character string up to 79 characters long that is displayed on line 24 of the screen. The message is only displayed if you have also SET STATUS ON, but it is replaced by the standard dBASE III PLUS messages in menu-driven commands such as ASSIST or any of the full-screen CREATE/MODIFY editors.

SET ODOMETER TO [<*expN*>]

Determines how frequently dBASE III PLUS updates the display of the number of records processed by such commands as APPEND, COPY, and COUNT. The display is updated every *expN* records; higher values for ODOMETER will result in slightly faster command execution. The default is 1.

SET ORDER TO [<*expN*>]

Determines which of the indexes opened with the data base in the current work area will function as the master index (the one that controls the order in which records are processed and the one used for FIND and SEEK commands). The *expN* evaluates to a number that corresponds to the position of the index in the index file list in the USE command that opened the data base. SET INDEX TO 0 causes dBASE III PLUS to process the file in sequential order, as if no indexes were open. SET ORDER is a faster way to switch indexes than SET INDEX, since no files are actually opened or closed.

SET PATH TO [<*path name list*>]

Establishes the search path to be used by dBASE III PLUS to open disk files not found in the current subdirectory. APPEND FROM, the CREATE/MODIFY editors, DO, LABEL, REPORT, RESTORE, SET PROCEDURE, TYPE, and USE all use the search path. Certain commands that create files also search the specified path for files of the same name if you have SET SAFETY ON. These include COPY, CREATE, INDEX, JOIN, SAVE, and SORT. However, the resulting files, together with all other new files you create, are written into the current subdirectory if you do not specify the full path name.

Regardless of the PATH, DIR (with no path name included), DELETE FILE, ERASE, RENAME, and SET ALTERNATE TO act only on files in the current subdirectory unless the full path name is specified. SET PATH TO behaves much like the MS-DOS PATH command and specifies the path names the same way. It is *not* equivalent to the MS-DOS CHDIR (change directory) command (the way SET DEFAULT TO <*drive*> effectively switches the logged-in disk drive). SET PATH TO, with no path names listed, cancels any previously established search path.

SET PRINT on/OFF

Determines whether sequential output (all text except that displayed by the full-screen commands) sent to the console is also echoed to the printer.

SET PRINTER TO [<*DOS device name*>]
SET PRINTER TO [\\SPOOLER/<*computer name*>\<*printer name*>=
<*DOS device name*>]

SET PRINTER TO *DOS device name* selects the local printer, specified by the DOS name of the output port (for example, LPT1: or COM1:), to be used for printed output. The default is LPT1:. This command is equivalent to the MS-DOS MODE command for redirecting printer output, which may be used instead, either before you enter dBASE III PLUS or with a RUN command. If output is redirected to a serial printer, the baud rate and other communications parameters must first be set with a MODE command.

In a network environment, SET PRINTER TO *computer name**printer name*=*DOS device name* routes output to a network printer via the network print spooler. This printer is identified by the network computer and printer names in an IBM network, or as SPOOLER in a Novell network.

SET PRINTER TO redirects printed output to the default printer assigned at the operating system level. In a network environment, it also empties the print spooling file.

SET PROCEDURE TO [<*procedure file name*>]

Opens the specified procedure file, which may contain up to 32 separate procedures. SET PROCEDURE TO, with no procedure file name listed, or CLOSE PROCEDURE closes the current procedure file.

SET RELATION TO [<*key expression*>/RECNO( )/<*expN*> INTO <*alias*>]

Establishes a relationship between the currently open data base and a data base open in another work area, which is specified by its *alias.* Only one RELATION may be SET from any given work area, but multiple RELATIONS may be SET into the same work area from two or more other data bases. The files may be linked by record number or based on a common field or fields.

To link two files by record number, you must open the second file with no index. If the RECNO( ) option is included, or no TO clause is specified, the two files are linked so that the record pointer in the second file is always positioned to the same record number as the first file. If a numeric expression is specified in a TO clause, moving the record pointer in the first file automatically positions the second file to the record number specified by *expN*.

To link two files by a common key, the field(s) in the *key expression* must be present in both files, and the second file must be indexed by this expression. With the RELATION in effect, moving the record pointer in the first file automatically positions the second file to the record with the matching key field value(s), exactly as if you had executed a FIND or SEEK command.

In either case, if dBASE III PLUS fails to find a matching record, the second file is positioned at the end-of-file, the EOF( ) function is .T., and

FOUND( ) is .F. in the second work area. SET RELATION TO, with no RELATION specified, cancels the RELATION SET from the current work area.

SET SAFETY ON/off

Determines whether dBASE III PLUS displays a warning message and requests confirmation from the operator before executing any command (such as COPY, INDEX, or SORT) that would overwrite an existing disk file. SAFETY is SET OFF in most menu-driven dBASE III PLUS applications, since the programmer should determine in advance when a file may safely be overwritten.

SET SCOREBOARD ON/off

Determines whether or not dBASE III PLUS displays status indicators (Del and Ins) and error messages (when invalid data such as an impossible date or input that does not fall within the RANGE specified in an @... SAY...GET command is entered). If you have SET STATUS ON, status indicators are included in the status bar displayed on line 22 and error messages appear on line 0; with STATUS OFF, all the scoreboard information is displayed on line 0. If you SET SCOREBOARD OFF the error messages are not displayed, but dBASE III PLUS still refuses to allow the cursor to advance beyond a field that contains invalid data until the entry is corrected.

SET STATUS ON/off

Determines whether dBASE III PLUS uses the last three lines on the screen for a status display. The *status bar* on line 22 displays the current disk drive, the current data base if one is open, the current record or command, and the current status of the INS, DEL, NUMLOCK and CAPS-LOCK keys. In a network environment, the status bar also informs you whether the current file was opened for exclusive or Read-Only use, and whether the current file or record is locked. Line 23 is used for a *navigation line* describing how to choose among available command options, and line 24 contains a message (which you may customize with SET MESSAGE) describing your options. Even if you have SET STATUS OFF, the status display is always present in the menu-driven commands such as ASSIST and the CREATE/MODIFY editors. You may use a format file with STA-

TUS ON, as long as it does not use lines 22 through 24.

SET STEP on/OFF

Determines whether dBASE III PLUS operates in single-step mode. If you SET STEP ON, dBASE III PLUS pauses after executing each program line. Pressing ESC cancels the program, pressing S suspends execution, and pressing the space bar causes the next command to be executed. SET STEP ON is usually used, together with SET TALK ON and SET ECHO ON (which displays each command line as it is executed), to debug dBASE III PLUS programs.

SET TALK ON/off

Determines whether dBASE III PLUS displays the results of the actions taken in response to your commands—for example, the values STOREd to memory variables, the record number of the new current record after a SKIP or LOCATE command, and the status messages that inform you of the progress of commands that process entire data bases (such as INDEX, DELETE, COPY, COUNT, and REPLACE). Usually you would want to SET TALK ON for working at command level, so dBASE III PLUS provides the most information at all times. In a menu-driven application, you would usually SET TALK OFF so that the messages do not confuse the users or disrupt formatted screens; you may SET TALK ON as necessary to allow the user to monitor the progress of potentially long-running commands.

SET TITLE ON/off

Determines whether dBASE III PLUS prompts you for a title or description of each new file created when a CATALOG is open. If you SET TITLE OFF, files are still added to the CATALOG, but the TITLE field is left blank.

SET TYPEAHEAD TO <*expN*>

Specifies the size of the typeahead buffer. The default is 20, and you may specify any value between 0 (which disables the typeahead buffer) and 32,000. The buffer is also disabled if you SET ESCAPE OFF. If you SET TYPEAHEAD TO 0, commands and functions that depend on the typeahead buffer (ON KEY and INKEY( )) will no longer work.

SET UNIQUE on/OFF

Determines whether an index can contain duplicate key entries. If you SET UNIQUE ON and then index a file, the index will contain only one entry for any given key value. This option may be used to determine if the data base itself contains any duplicate key values (by checking to see if the number of records indexed equals the number of records in the file) or to prepare a list of all of the possible key values (by COPYing all or some of the fields with the index open). Since such an index may not contain pointers to all of the records, it should *not* be used to access the data base for adding new records or editing existing data.

SET VIEW TO <*view file name*>

Opens all the files specified in the *view file*, including data bases, indexes, and the optional format file if one is included in the view, and selects the work area specified when the view was defined. If the view includes RELATIONs, a FILTER condition, or a field list, these are also placed in effect.

SKIP [<*expN*>]

Moves the record pointer forward (if *expN* is positive) or backward (if *expN* is negative) the specified number of records, or if *expN* is omitted, SKIP moves forward one record. If an index is open, dBASE III PLUS moves forward or backward in the index *expN* entries and then repositions the record pointer to the corresponding record. If you have SET DELETED ON or if you have SET a FILTER, only records that pass these selection criteria are counted. If you SKIP past the last record in a file, the data base is positioned at a blank record (which is *not* actually added to the file), and the EOF( ) function is set to .T. If you SKIP backward past the first record in the file, the record pointer remains positioned at the first record in the file and the BOF( ) function is set to .T.

SORT TO <*new file name*> ON <*field1*> [/A]/[/D] [/C] [, <*field2*> [/A]/[/D] ...] [<*scope*>] [FOR <*condition*>] [WHILE <*condition*>]

Creates a new data base file containing the range of records from the current data base defined by the *scope* and *conditions*. You may SORT on up to ten fields. The first field determines the major sort order, within which records are sorted according to the second field, and so on. The sort order is specified by three optional parameters: /A (or the keyword ASCENDING) specifies ascending (low-to-high) order (the default), /D (or DE-

SCENDING) specifies descending (high-to-low) order, and /C specifies *case-independence,* in which the uppercase and lowercase versions of a letter are considered to be equivalent. (Normally, the sort order parallels the way the ASCII character codes are assigned, and all of the uppercase letters precede all of the lowercase letters.) If you combine the A or D options with the C option, only one slash is required, for example, /AC. You may SORT on any combination of numeric, character, and date fields (not logical or memo fields), but the sort keys must be whole fields, not expressions. If you must create a file sorted on a more complex expression, you can build an index based on the desired expression and then COPY the file with the index open.

STORE <*exp*> to <*memvar list*>
<*memvar*>=<*exp*>

STORE creates the named variable(s) and assigns them the initial value and data type specified by the *expression*. Using the equal sign syntax, only one memory variable at a time may be created.

SUM [<*scope*>] [<*expN list*>] [FOR <*condition*>] [WHILE <*condition*>] [TO <*memvar list*>]

Calculates the sum for each expression in the list for the range of records defined by the *scope* and *conditions*. If no expressions are listed, all numeric fields in the current data base are SUMmed. If no scope is specified, ALL is assumed. If you have SET TALK ON, the sums are displayed on the screen, and if you have SET HEADING ON, the expressions SUMmed are displayed above the results. If a list of memory variables is included, the named numeric variables are created to store the sums.

Example:

```
USE NWCUST
SUM YTDINV, TOTINV FOR CITY = "San Francisco" TO MYTDSUM, MTOTSUM
```

Equivalent program:

```
use NWCUST
store 0.00 to MYTDSUM, MTOTSUM

do while .not. eof()
   if CITY = "San Francisco"
      store MYTDSUM + YTDINV to MYTDSUM
      store MTOTSUM + TOTINV to MTOTSUM
   endif
   skip
enddo
? MYTDSUM, MTOTSUM
```

SUSPEND

Temporarily suspends execution of a program and returns control to the dot prompt without closing any files or RELEASEing memory variables. This is equivalent to choosing the SUSPEND option after pressing ESC to interrupt the currently running program. SUSPEND is used primarily for debugging purposes, to pause a program at a specific point. While the program is suspended, you can type any commands at the dot prompt and then use the RESUME command to continue from the point of interruption or the CANCEL command to cancel the program and return to the dot prompt.

TEXT ... ENDTEXT

A program structure used to display or print a block of text. The text between TEXT and ENDTEXT is displayed (if you have SET CONSOLE ON) or printed (if you have SET PRINT ON) without processing or interpretation by dBASE III PLUS.

TOTAL ON <*key field*> TO <*file name*> [<*scope*>] [FIELDS <*field list*>] [FOR <*condition*>] [WHILE <*condition*>]

Creates a new data base containing summarized data for the specified numeric fields in the current data base for the range of records defined by the *scope* and *conditions*. If no *field list* is included, all numeric fields are TOTALed. The new file has the same structure as the current data base, except that memo fields are not included. Each record in the new file contains totals for a group of records in the current file with the same value in the *key field*. The current file must be either sorted or indexed on the *key field*, and the numeric fields must be large enough to accommodate the totals. After completing the command, you may use MODIFY STRUCTURE to delete non-numeric fields from the new file that do not contain meaningful information (such as dates or names, which will contain the contents of the first record in each total group). You can accomplish the same objective with a short program if you first CREATE the total file. If you use this alternative, the structure of the total file need not exactly match the file that generates the totals.

Example:

```
USE NWORDER INDEX NWOINVC
TOTAL ON INVOICE TO NWORDSUM
```

Equivalent program:

```
* This program assumes that NWORDSUM.DBF exists, contains the
* fields INVOICE, PRICE, SUBTOTAL, DISCOUNT, INVAMOUNT, and is
* indexed on INVOICE

select 1
use NWORDSUM index NWOSINVC
select 2
use NWORDER
set relation to INVOICE into NWORDSUM

do while .not. eof()
   select NWORDSUM
   if eof()
      append blank
      replace INVOICE with NWORDER->INVOICE
   endif
   replace PRICE with PRICE + NWORDER->PRICE, SUBTOTAL with;
           SUBTOTAL + NWORDER->SUBTOTAL, DISCOUNT with DISCOUNT +;
           NWORDER->DISCOUNT, INVAMOUNT with INVAMOUNT +;
           NWORDER->INVAMOUNT
   select NWORDER
   skip
enddo
```

TYPE <*file name*> [TO PRINT]

Displays the contents of the specified file on the screen. TO PRINT causes the file to be printed as well as displayed on the screen.

UNLOCK [ALL]

In a network environment, releases the most recent lock placed on the file in the currently selected work area. This may be a file lock placed in effect by a call to the FLOCK( ) function, or a record lock effected by a call to the LOCK( ) or RLOCK( ) function. If the ALL keyword is included, all locks in all work areas are released.

UPDATE ON <*key field*> FROM <*alias*> REPLACE <*field1*> WITH <*exp1*> [, <*field2*> WITH <*exp2*> ...] [RANDOM]

Updates the current data base based on information contained in a second data base file, which is open in another work area and is specified by its *alias*. Records are matched up based on the *key field*, which must be common to both files. The current file must be either sorted or indexed on the common key field. If the second file is not also sorted or indexed on this field, the RANDOM keyword must be included in the command, and the current file must be indexed, *not* sorted on the common key (this is the most efficient way to use the UPDATE command), so that dBASE III

PLUS may use an internal SEEK to find the right record to UPDATE. For each record in the second file, the designated *fields* in the matching record in the current file are replaced with the specified *expressions*, which may reference any fields from both files.

Example:

```
SELECT 1
USE NWTXN
SELECT 2
USE NWCUST INDEX NWCACCT
UPDATE ON ACCOUNT FROM NWTXN RANDOM REPLACE YTDINV WITH YTDINV +;
   NWTXN->INVAMOUNT, TOTINV WITH TOTINV + NWTXN->INVAMOUNT,;
   BALANCE WITH BALANCE + NWTXN->INVAMOUNT
```

Equivalent program:

```
select 1
use NWCUST index NWCACCT
select 2
use NWTXN
set relation to ACCOUNT into NWCUST

do while .not. eof()
   select NWCUST
   if .not. eof()
      replace YTDINV with YTDINV + NWTXN->INVAMOUNT, TOTINV with;
              TOTINV + NWTXN->INVAMOUNT,BALANCE with BALANCE +;
              NWTXN->INVAMOUNT
   endif
   select NWTXN
   skip
enddo
```

USE [<*file name*>] [INDEX <*index file list*>] [ALIAS <*alias*>] [EXCLUSIVE]

Opens the specified data base in the currently selected work area, together with up to seven indexes, if any are named. If you do not specify an alias, dBASE III PLUS automatically assigns the file name as the alias. If an alias is specified, it must be used in place of the file name in the standard <*alias*>–><*field name*> notation for referring to fields in work areas other than the currently selected area.

If no indexes are listed, the USE command leaves the data base positioned at the first record. If one or more indexes are opened with the file, the data base is positioned to the record corresponding to the first entry in the first index named (the master index).

In a network environment, if the keyword EXCLUSIVE is included, the file is opened for exclusive rather than shared use, and only one work station at a time may access the file. This is equivalent to issuing the SET

EXCLUSIVE ON command prior to opening the file. A file must be opened for exclusive use in order to use commands that affect the entire data base, including INSERT, MODIFY STRUCTURE, PACK, REINDEX, and ZAP.

USE, with no file name, closes the data base and all associated index and format files in the current work area.

WAIT [<*expC*>] [TO <*memvar*>]

Pauses execution of the current program until a key is pressed. If *expC* is included, it is displayed as a prompt; otherwise, dBASE III PLUS displays its default prompt "Press any key to continue...." If a TO clause is included, a character memory variable with the specified name is created to store the operator's keystroke. If the operator presses RETURN, *memvar* will become a null string of length zero.

ZAP

Empties the current data base of all records. This command is equivalent to DELETE ALL, followed by PACK. ZAP operates much faster because it does not actually process all of the records, but instead moves the end-of-file marker and resets the record count to 0. Any indexes opened with the data base in the USE command are adjusted to match the new empty file.

C

dBASE III PLUS FUNCTIONS

All dBASE III PLUS functions are expressed as the name of the function followed by the function's input(s) (also referred to as "arguments") in parentheses. Even if the function requires no explicit input, parentheses are used to distinguish the function from a field or memory variable with the same name. A function is considered to have the data type of the output it produces, and it may be used anywhere that an expression of that type is permitted. The examples in this appendix are drawn from the National Widgets data base files.

&<character variable>

Substitute the *value* of the named variable for the variable name. The macro can be used to provide variable input in contexts in which dBASE III PLUS expects a field name or condition. The macro *must* be used in certain commands, like FIND, in which dBASE III PLUS automatically interprets the following word literally, to cause the program to use the *contents* of the variable, instead of the name.

Examples:

```
. STORE "FOR 'IBM' $ UPPER(EQUIPMENT)" TO MCONDITION
. LIST &MCONDITION


. STORE NWTXN->ACCOUNT TO MACCOUNT
. FIND &MACCOUNT
```

ABS(<*number*>)

Input: Numeric expression
Output: Number

Evaluates to the absolute value of the numeric expression. The absolute value of a negative number is the positive number with the same magnitude; the absolute value of a positive number is identical to the number itself.

ACCESS( )

Input: None
Output: Number

Evaluates to the access level of the last user to log in, in a multi-user system. In a single-user system, the function always evaluates to 0. This function may be used to control access to a program or menu option, or to allow a single option to call two or more different programs, depending on the user who requests the option.

ASC(<*character string*>)

Input: Character string expression
Output: Number

Evaluates to the decimal ASCII code of the first character in the character string expression.

Examples:

```
. ? ASC("ABCPLUMB")
  65
. ? ACCOUNT
ABCPLUMB
. ? ASC(ACCOUNT)
  65
```

AT(<*character string 1*>, <*character string 2*>)

Input: Character string expression, character string expression
Output: Number

Evaluates to the starting position of character string 1 in character string 2, or 0 if the first string is not found anywhere within the second.

Example:

```
. ? ACCOUNT
ABCPLUMB
. ? AT("PLUMB", ACCOUNT)
   4
```

BOF( )

Input: None
Output: Logical value

Evaluates to .T. when you attempt to move the record pointer backward past the beginning-of-file by executing a SKIP −*n* command. If the data base is opened without any indexes, the beginning-of-file is the first record. With an index open, it is the record corresponding to the first index entry. After the SKIP −*n* command, the data base remains positioned at the first record. dBASE III PLUS keeps track of the value of the BOF( ) function in each work area, but a work area must be selected to display or test this value.

CDOW(<*expD*>)

Input: Date expression
Output: Character string

Evaluates to a character string containing the name of the day of the week corresponding to the specified date.

Examples:

```
. ? LASTORDER
05/28/87
. ? CDOW(LASTORDER)
Thursday
. ? CDOW(LASTORDER + 30)
Saturday
```

CHR(<*number*>)

Input: Numeric expression
Output: Character

Evaluates to a character string consisting of the single character specified by the decimal ASCII code represented by the numeric expression.

Example:

```
. ? CHR(65)
A
```

CMONTH(<*date*>)

Input: Date expression
Output: Character string

Evaluates to a character string containing the name of the month corresponding to the specified date.

Example:

```
. ? LASTORDER
05/28/87
. ? CMONTH(LASTORDER)
May
```

COL( )

Input: None
Output: Number

Evaluates to a number representing the current cursor column (horizontal) position on the screen. This function may be used to display data immediately following the last item displayed or a fixed number of columns away from the last item, without reference to the absolute cursor position. This is especially useful for preventing gaps in a line of data when the items displayed are variable in length or when a field or memory variable is displayed conditionally.

Examples:

```
@ 2,10     say "Today is "
@ 2,col() say cdow(date())
@ 2,col() say ", "
@ 2,col() say cmonth(date())
@ 2,col() say day(date()) picture "999"

@ 10,10 say "Telephone Number:"
if AREACODE <> " "
   @ 10,col() + 1 say "(" + AREACODE + ")"
endif
@ 10,col() + 1 say TELEPHONE
```

CTOD(<*character expression*>)

Input: Character expression
Output: Date

Evaluates to a true date matching the character string representation of the date supplied as input. This function is the only way to express a date constant in dBASE III PLUS. It must be used anywhere a constant date is required, for example, to initialize a date memory variable, REPLACE a date field with a constant value, or compare a date variable with a constant date.

Examples:

```
. STORE CTOD("  ") TO MDATE

. REPLACE LASTORDER WITH CTOD("09/01/87")

. LIST FOR LASTORDER <= CTOD("12/31/86")
```

DATE( )

Input: None
Output: Date

The current system date as obtained from the operating system.

DAY(<*date*>)

Input: Date expression
Output: Number

Evaluates to a number representing the day of the month in the specified date.

Example:

```
. ? LASTORDER
05/28/87
. ? DAY(LASTORDER)
 28
```

DBF( )

Input: None
Output: Character string

Evaluates to a character string consisting of the full name (or path name, if the file is not in the current subdirectory) of the data base open in the current work area, or a null string if no data base is open.

Example:

```
. USE NWCUST INDEX NWCACCT, NWCZIP
. ? DBF()
C:NWCUST.dbf
```

DELETED( )

Input: None
Output: Logical value

Evaluates to .T. if the current record is marked for deletion, or .F. if it is not.

DISKSPACE( )

Input: None
Output: Number

Evaluates to the number of bytes of free space remaining on the disk in the currently logged drive. This function may be used to test whether enough space remains before beginning a SORT or COPY command. To determine the disk space remaining on a drive other than the current drive, you may reset the default drive with the SET DEFAULT command.

Example:

```
use NWINVENT
set default to A:

if diskspace() > recsize * reccount() + 1000
   copy to A:NWINVENT
else
   ? "There is not enough space on drive A:"
endif

set default to C:
```

DOW(<*date*>)

Input: Date expression
Output: Number

Evaluates to a number representing the day of the week in the specified date.

Example:

```
. ? LASTORDER
05/28/87
. ? DOW(LASTORDER)
 5
```

DTOC(<*date*>)

Input: Date expression
Output: Character string

Evaluates to a character string representation of the date expression supplied as input. This function is often used to convert a date to a character string so that it may be concatenated with another character string for display or printing or for use in an index key expression.

Examples:

```
. ? "Last order date: " + DTOC(LASTORDER)
Last order date: 05/25/87

. USE NWTXN
. INDEX ON ACCOUNT + DTOC(LASTORDER) TO NWTACCDT
```

EOF( )

Input: None
Output: Logical value

Evaluates to .T. when you attempt to move the record pointer past the end-of-file by executing a SKIP *n* command. If the data base is open without any indexes, the end-of-file is the last record. With an index it is the record corresponding to the last index entry. After the SKIP *n* command, the data base is not positioned at any valid record; the RECNO( ) function evaluates to a number one greater than the number of records in the file, and all fields have blank values. EOF( ) is also set to .T. if a FIND or SEEK command fails to find the specified record or if a data base accessed through a SET RELATION command has no record that matches the key expression on which the RELATION is based. dBASE III PLUS keeps track of the value of the EOF( ) function in each work area, but a work area must be selected to display or test this value.

```
seek MACCOUNT
if eof()
   ? "Not found"
else
   ? COMPANY
endif
```

ERROR( )

Input: None
Output: Number

Evaluates to a number corresponding to the error that has just occurred. This function always returns 0 unless an error trapping routine has been established with the ON ERROR command. The ERROR( ) function may be used to detect and respond to certain recoverable error conditions, such as a missing file, or, in a network environment, an attempt to lock a record currently being modified by another user.

Example:

```
do case
   case error() = 1
      ? "File is missing"
      ? "Please check to make sure the right disk is in the drive"
   case error() = 41
      ? "The memo text file for this data base is missing"
      ? "Please check to make sure the right disk is in the drive"
   case error() = 114
      ? "The index file is damaged"
      ? "Please REINDEX and then try this operation again"
endcase
```

EXP(<*number*>)

Input: Numeric expression
Output: Number

Evaluates to the result of raising *e* (the base for natural logarithms) to the power specified by the numeric expression.

FIELD(<*number*>)

Input: Numeric expression
Output: Character string

Evaluates to a character string containing the name of the field specified by number in the data base open in the current work area, or a null string if there is no corresponding field in the current data base. This function may be used to determine the number of fields in a data base or to handle a series of fields as an array.

Example:

```
* This program reads records from NWTXN.DBF and posts the invoice totals
*   to a summary file named NWTSUMM.DBF, which is indexed on PARTNUMBER
* NWTSUMM.DBF is assumed to have 12 fields, one for each month of the year,
*   named JANUARY, FEBRUARY, etc.
* JANUARY is the first field, FEBRUARY the second, and so on
```

```
select 1
use NWTSUMM index NWTSPART

select 2
use NWTXN
set relation to PARTNUMBER into NWTSUMM

do while .not. eof()

   select NWTSUMM

   if .not. eof()
      store FIELD(month(NWTXN->INVDATE)) to MFIELD
      replace &MFIELD with &MFIELD + NWTXN->INVAMOUNT
   endif

   select NWTXN
   skip

enddo

return
```

FILE(<*file name*>)

Input: Character expression
Output: Logical value

Evaluates to .T. if the specified file is present on the disk. If the file name is a literal character string (not a memory variable), it must be enclosed in quotation marks. This function may be used to test for the existence of a file before the user attempts to open it, so that the program may take the appropriate corrective action (creating the file or informing the user) if the file is missing.

FKLABEL(<*number*>)

Input: Numeric expression
Output: Character string

Evaluates to a character string containing the name of the programmable function key specified by number. On keyboards that do not have a separate HELP key, the first function key (usually labeled F1) is reserved for this function; on these keyboards, FKLABEL(1) returns the name of the second function key, that is, the first one that may be reassigned. This function may be used to change the meanings of the function keys without having to know their names.

Examples:

```
. ? FKLABEL(1)
F2

set function FKLABEL(4) to "use NWINVENT index NWICATPT;"
```

FKMAX( )

Input: None
Output: Number

Evaluates to the number of programmable function keys on the terminal. On keyboards that do not have a separate HELP key, FKMAX( ) evaluates to a number one less than the actual number of keys. This function may be used to test for the existence of certain function keys before attempting to reassign their meanings.

Example:

```
if FKMAX() >= 11
   set function 10 to "clear; display;"
   set function 11 to "display status;"
endif
```

FLOCK( )

Input: None
Output: Logical value

Evaluates to .T. if it is possible to lock the file open in the currently selected work area, or .F. if the attempt fails because the file is already locked by another user. This function simultaneously tests the status and attempts to lock the file. Once locked, the file may be unlocked with the UNLOCK command, by closing the file, or by exiting from dBASE III PLUS. This function is generally used for operations that involve an entire file or update many records.

FOUND( )

Input: None
Output: Logical value

Evaluates to .T. when a FIND, SEEK, LOCATE, or CONTINUE command positions the record pointer at a valid record in the data base in the current work area, or when the record pointer is repositioned automatically to a valid record in a data base in another work area linked to the current file with SET RELATION. In general, when EOF( ) is .T., FOUND( ) is .F. dBASE III PLUS keeps track of the value of the FOUND( ) function in each work area, but a work area must be selected to display or test this value.

GETENV(<*character string*>)

Input: Character string expression
Output: Character string

Evaluates to a character string containing the operating system environment parameter specified as input, or a null string if the parameter has not been set.

Examples:

```
. ? GETENV("PROMPT")
$P$G

STORE "PATH" TO MFILEPATH
. ? GETENV(FILEPATH)
C:\;C:\UTILITY

. STORE GETENV("PATH") TO MPATH
. SET PATH TO &MPATH
```

IIF(<*condition*>, <*expression 1*>, <*expression 2*>)

Input: Logical expression, expression, expression
Output: Same data type as expressions 1 and 2

Evaluates to expression 1 if the condition is .T., or expression 2 if the condition is .F. The two expressions may be of any data type, but they must be of the same data type. This function is most useful for displaying fields conditionally at the dot prompt and printing fields conditionally in reports and labels, where you cannot use the equivalent IF ... ELSE ... ENDIF structure.

Example:

```
. ? BALANCE
    256.83
. ? IIF(BALANCE <= 0, "Credit Balance", "Balance Due")
Balance Due
```

Equivalent program:

```
if BALANCE <= 0
   ? "Credit Balance"
else
   ? "Balance Due"
endif
```

INKEY( )

Input: None
Output: Number

Evaluates to a number corresponding to the key pressed by the operator, or the first key in the keyboard buffer if there is more than one. Unlike the WAIT command, the INKEY( ) function does not pause the currently running program. Since the function returns a value of 0 unless a key is pressed at the instant it is evaluated, it is generally used within a DO WHILE loop that monitors the keyboard and registers the user's keypress.

Example:

```
use NWCUST

store Ø to MX

clear
? "Press any key to interrupt this listing"
?
do while MX = Ø .and. .not. eof()
   ? ACCOUNT, COMPANY, TELEPHONE
   store inkey() to MX
   skip
enddo
```

INT(<*number*>)

Input: Numeric expression
Output: Number

Evaluates to the integer portion of the number represented by the numeric expression (the result of dropping any fractional portion). To round off a number to the nearest integer, use the ROUND function instead.

Example:

```
. ? BALANCE
    143.17
. ? INT(BALANCE)
       143
```

ISALPHA(<*character string*>)

Input: Character string expression
Output: Logical value

Evaluates to .T. if the first character of the expression providing the input is a letter of the alphabet.

Examples:

```
. ? ISALPHA("ABC Plumbing")
.T.
. ? ADDRESS1
1850 University Avenue
. ? ISALPHA(ADDRESS1)
.F.
```

ISCOLOR( )

Input: None
Output: Logical value

Evaluates to .T. if the system is using a color/graphics monitor, or .F. if the display is a monochrome screen. This function may be used to detect which type of monitor is present and set the display attributes accordingly. The color selections should be made with caution, however, since not every color/graphics system can actually display colors. For example, the COMPAQ display returns a .T. value.

Example:

```
if iscolor()
   set color to W, W+
else
   set color to W, U+
endif
```

ISLOWER(<*character string*>)

Input: Character string expression
Output: Logical value

Evaluates to .T. if the first character of the expression providing the input is a lowercase letter of the alphabet.

Examples:

```
. ? ISLOWER("ABC Plumbing")
.F.
. ? ADDRESS1
1850 University Avenue
. ? ISLOWER(ADDRESS1)
.F.
```

ISUPPER(<*character string*>)

Input: Character string expression
Output: Logical value

Evaluates to .T. if the first character of the expression providing the input is an uppercase letter of the alphabet.

Examples:

```
. ? ISUPPER("ABC Plumbing")
.T.
. ? ADDRESS1
1850 University Avenue
. ? ISUPPER(ADDRESS1)
.F.
```

LEFT(<*character string*>, <*length*>)

Input: Character string expression, numeric expression
Output: Character string

Evaluates to a substring (part of a string) of the character string represented by the character string expression. The substring begins with the first (leftmost) character, and the length is specified by the numeric expression. If the requested length exceeds the length of the original character string, the substring consists of the full string.

Example:

```
. ? COMPANY
ABC Plumbing
. ? LEFT(COMPANY, 9)
ABC Plumb
```

LEN(<*character string*>)

Input: Character string expression
Output: Number

Evaluates to the length of the character string represented by the character string expression. The length of a data base field is always the full field width. The TRIM function may be used to eliminate trailing blanks.

Examples:

```
. ? TRIM(COMPANY)
ABC Plumbing
. ? LEN("ABC Plumbing")
        12
. ? LEN(TRIM(COMPANY))
        12
```

LOCK( ) or RLOCK( )

Input: None
Output: Logical value

Evaluates to .T. if it is possible to lock the current record in the data base open in the current work area, or .F. if the record is already locked by another user. This function simultaneously tests the status and attempts to lock the record. Once locked, the record may be unlocked with the UNLOCK command. This function is generally used for operations that involve updating records one at a time, so that multiple users may access the same file at the same time.

LOG(<*number*>)

Input: Numeric expression
Output: Number

Evaluates to the natural (base *e*) logarithm of the number represented by the numeric expression.

LOWER(<*character string*>)

Input: Character string expression
Output: Character string

Evaluates to the result of converting the character string represented by the character string expression to all lowercase. This function may be used to convert a character string entered in various mixtures of uppercase and lowercase to a consistent format for comparison to another variable or constant.

Example:

```
. ? EQUIPMENT
Kaypro 10, Brother
. ? "kaypro" $ EQUIPMENT
.F.
. ? "kaypro" $ lower(EQUIPMENT)
.T.
```

LTRIM(<*character string*>)

Input: Character string expression
Output: Character string

Evaluates to a character string consisting of the result of evaluating the specified character string expression, with all leading blanks removed. This function is useful for removing leading blanks created when a numeric expression is converted to a character string with the STR function.

Example:

```
store 1 to MCOUNT

do while MCOUNT <= 15
   store ltrim(str(MCOUNT,2)) to MCOUNTC
   store "     "              to MCODE&MCOUNTC

   @ MCOUNT, 10 say "Enter code " + MCOUNTC get MCODE&MCOUNTC picture "@!"
   read

   store MCOUNT + 1 to MCOUNT
enddo
```

LUPDATE( )

Input: None
Output: Date

Evaluates to the date on which the data base in the current work area was last updated by adding, changing, or deleting data.

MAX(<*numeric expression*>, <*numeric expression*>)

Input: Numeric expression, numeric expression
Output: Number

Evaluates to the number represented by the greater of the two numeric expressions. This function is useful for displaying fields conditionally at the dot prompt and printing fields conditionally in reports and labels, where you cannot use an IF ... ELSE ... ENDIF structure to select the greater value.

Example:

```
. REPLACE ALL SERVICECHG WITH MAX(BALANCE * .05, 5.00)
```

MESSAGE( )

Input: None
Output: Character string

Evaluates to a character string containing the error message normally displayed by dBASE III PLUS in response to the error that has just occurred. This function always returns 0 unless an error trapping routine has been established with the ON ERROR command.

MIN(<*numeric expression*>, <*numeric expression*>)

Input: Numeric expression, numeric expression
Output: Number

Evaluates to the number represented by the smaller of the two numeric expressions. This function is useful for displaying fields conditionally at the dot prompt and printing fields conditionally in reports and labels, where you cannot use an IF ... ELSE ... ENDIF structure to select the greater value.

Example:

```
. REPLACE ALL DISCOUNT WITH MIN(PRICE * .15, 10.00)
```

MOD(<*numeric expression*>, <*numeric expression*>)

Input: Numeric expression, numeric expression
Output: Number

Evaluates to the remainder that results from dividing the first numeric expression by the second.

Example:

```
store date() - LASTORDER to MTIME
store int(MTIME / 365)   to MYEARS
store mod(MTIME / 365)   to MDAYS

? "Last order was " + str(MYEARS, 2) + " years and " + str(MDAYS, 3) + " ago"
```

MONTH(<*date*>)

Input: Date expression
Output: Number

Evaluates to a number representing the month in the specified date.

Example:

```
. ? LASTORDER
05/28/87
. ? MONTH(LASTORDER)
  5
```

NDX(<*numeric expression*>)

Input: Numeric expression
Output: Character string

Evaluates to a character string consisting of the full name (or path name, if the file is not in the current subdirectory) of the index file whose position in the index file list specified in the USE command that opened the data base in the current work area corresponds to the value of the numeric expression. NDX evaluates to a null string if no such index is open.

Example:

```
. USE NWCUST INDEX NWCACCT, NWCZIP
. ? NDX(2)
C:NWCACCT.ndx
. ? NDX(3)

.
```

OS( )

Input: None
Output: Character string

Evaluates to a character string containing the name of the operating system currently running. This function may be used to determine which operating system is active before you use the RUN command to run an external command or program specific to a particular operating system.

PCOL( )

Input: None
Output: Number

Evaluates to a number representing the current print head column position. This function may be used to print data immediately following the last item printed or a fixed number of columns to the right of the last item, without reference to the absolute print head position. This is especially useful for preventing gaps in a line of data when the items printed are variable in length or when a field or memory variable is printed conditionally.

Examples:

```
@ 10,10 say "Telephone Number:"
if AREACODE <> " "
   @ 10,pcol() + 1 say "(" + AREACODE + ")"
endif
```

```
@ 10,pcol() + 1 say TELEPHONE

@ 55,10 say "Thank you for your"
if INVAMOUNT > 100
   @ 55,pcol() + 1 say "large"
endif
@ 55,pcol() + 1 say "order."
```

PROW( )

Input: None
Output: Number

Evaluates to a number representing the current print head row position. This function may be used to print data on the next available row (line) on the page or a fixed number of rows below this row, without reference to the absolute print head position. This is especially useful for preventing gaps in a block of lines of data when some of the items are printed conditionally.

Example:

```
@ 2,10 say COMPANY
if CONTACT <> " "
   @ prow() + 1,10 say CONTACT
endif
@ prow() + 1,10 say ADDRESS1
if ADDRESS2 <> " "
   @ prow() + 1,10 say ADDRESS2
endif
@ prow() + 1,10 say trim(CITY) + ", " + STATE + "  " + ZIP
```

READKEY( )

Input: None
Output: Number

Evaluates to a number corresponding to the key pressed by the operator to exit from any full-screen edit mode, including a series of @ ... SAY ... GET commands followed by a READ. Each key can generate two possible values, depending on whether or not data was changed during the full-screen edit process.

Example:

```
if readkey() = 36 .or. readkey() = 292
   do NWHELP2 with "NWCUPD4 ", 2
endif
```

RECCOUNT( )

Input: None
Output: Number

Evaluates to the number of records in the data base open in the currently selected work area.

Example:

```
@ 10,10 say "Working on record           of " + str(reccount(),5)
```

RECNO( )

Input: None
Output: Number

Evaluates to the record number of the record at which the record pointer is positioned in the data base in the currently selected work area. If the data base is positioned past the end-of-file, RECNO( ) evaluates to one greater than the number of records in the file. This means that if the data base is empty, RECNO( ) has the value 1.

RECSIZE( )

Input: None
Output: Number

Evaluates to the record length of the data base in the currently selected work area. This function may be combined with the RECCOUNT( ) function to calculate the approximate size of a data base (not including the space occupied by the file header).

Example:

```
store recsize() * reccount() to MFILESIZE
```

REPLICATE(<*character string*>, <*number*>)

Input: Character string expression, numeric expression
Output: Character string

Evaluates to a character string consisting of the character string specified as input, repeated a number of times equal to the value of the numeric expression.

Example:

```
@ 1,10 say COMPANY
@ 2,10 say replicate("-", len(trim(COMPANY)))
```

RIGHT(<*character string*>, <*length*>)

Input: Character string expression, numeric expression
Output: Character string

Evaluates to a substring (part of a string) of the character string represented by the character string expression. The length of the substring is specified by the numeric expression, and the substring consists of the rightmost portion of the original string. If the requested length exceeds the length of the original character string, the substring consists of the full string.

Example:

```
. ? COMPANY
ABC Plumbing
. ? RIGHT(trim(COMPANY), 8)
Plumbing
```

RLOCK( ) or LOCK( )

Input: None
Output: Logical value

RLOCK( ) is identical to LOCK( ). See description under LOCK( ).

ROUND(<*number*>, <*decimals*>)

Input: Numeric expression, numeric expression
Output: Number

Evaluates to the result of rounding off the number represented by the first numeric expression to the number of decimal places specified by the second. If *decimals* is a negative number, the specified number of digits to the *left* of the decimal point are rounded off.

Example:

```
. ? BALANCE
    143.57
. ? ROUND(BALANCE, 1)
     143.50
. ? ROUND(BALANCE, 0)
     143.00
. ? ROUND(BALANCE, -2)
     100.00
```

ROW( )

Input: None
Output: Number

Evaluates to a number representing the current cursor row position on the screen. This function may be used to display data on the next available row (line) on the screen or a fixed number of rows away from this row, without reference to the absolute cursor position. This is especially useful for preventing gaps in a block of lines of data when some of the items are displayed conditionally.

Example:

```
@ 2,10 say COMPANY
if CONTACT <> " "
   @ row() + 1,10 say CONTACT
endif
@ row() + 1,10 say ADDRESS1
if ADDRESS2 <> " "
   @ row() + 1,10 say ADDRESS2
endif
@ row() + 1,10 say trim(CITY) + ", " + STATE + "  " + ZIP
```

RTRIM(<*character string*>)

Input: Character string expression
Output: Character string

Evaluates to a character string consisting of the result of evaluating the specified character string expression, with all trailing blanks removed. This function, which is identical to TRIM, is provided for parity with the LTRIM function.

SPACE(<*number*>)

Input: Numeric expression
Output: Character string

Evaluates to a character string consisting of the number of blank spaces specified by the numeric expression. This function is often used to initialize a blank character memory variable so that you do not have to count spaces.

SQRT(<*number*>)

Input: Numeric expression

Output: Number

Evaluates to the square root of the number represented by the numeric expression.

STR(<*number*> [,<*length*>] [,<*decimals*>]

Input: Numeric expression, numeric expression, numeric expression
Output: Character string

Evaluates to a character string representation of the number specified by the first numeric expression. The length of the string is specified by the second expression, and the number of decimal places by the third. If the length is omitted, it is assumed to be 10. If you do not specify the number of decimal places, 0 is assumed. This function may be used to convert a number to a character string so that it may be concatenated with another character string to be displayed, printed, or used in an index key expression.

Example:

```
. ? "Balance: " + STR(BALANCE,10,2)
Balance:       143.57

. USE NWTXN
. INDEX ON ACCOUNT + STR(INVAMOUNT,10,2) TO NWTACCIN
```

STUFF(<*character string 1*>, <*starting position*>, <*length*>, <*character string 2*>)

Input: Character string expression, numeric expression, numeric expression, character string
Output: Character string

Evaluates to a character string consisting of the string represented by character string 1, with the number of characters specified by the length starting at the indicated starting position removed and replaced by character string 2. If the length is 0, no characters are removed before the substitution is made; and if character string 2 is a null string, no replacement is made.

Example:

```
. ? EQUIPMENT
IBM PC, NEC7710
. ? STUFF(EQUIPMENT, AT("PC", EQUIPMENT), 2, "Personal Computer")
IBM Personal Computer, NEC7710
```

SUBSTR(<*character string*>, <*starting position*> [,<*length*>])

Input: Character string expression, numeric expression, numeric expression

Output: Character string

Evaluates to the substring (part of a string) of the specified character string that begins at the position represented by the first numeric expression. If a second numeric expression is included, it specifies the length of the substring. If the length is omitted, the substring begins at the designated starting position and includes all of the remaining characters in the character string expression.

Example:

```
. ? COMPANY
ABC Plumbing
. ? SUBSTR(COMPANY,5,4)
Plum
. ? SUBSTR(COMPANY,5)
Plumbing
```

TIME( )

Input: None

Output: Character string

Evaluates to a character string representation of the current system time.

TRANSFORM(<*expression*>, <*picture*>)

Input: Expression, character string expression

Output: Same data type as expression

Evaluates to the result of formatting the expression with the specified PICTURE. This function may be used to format fields displayed from the dot prompt and to print formatted data in reports and labels, where you cannot use the equivalent @ ... SAY command. The data type of the output is the same as the data type of the original expression; however, you cannot accumulate column totals and subtotals in a report printed by the built-in report generator for any numeric fields formatted with this function.

Examples:

```
. ? COMPANY
ABC Plumbing
. ? TRANSFORM(COMPANY, "@!")
ABC PLUMBING
```

```
. ? BALANCE
   143.57
. ? TRANSFORM(BALANCE, "@CX 9,999,999.99")
     143.57 CR
```

TRIM(<*character string*>)

Input: Character string expression
Output: Character string

Evaluates to a character string consisting of the result of evaluating the specified character string expression, with all trailing blanks removed. This function is identical to RTRIM.

TYPE(<*expression*>)

Input: Any expression
Output: Character

Evaluates to a single character representing the data type of the specified expression, for a character (C), numeric (N), logical (L), or memo (M) expression (date type expressions are not permitted as input). If a variable does not exist or if the expression is not syntactically correct, the function will evaluate to U (undefined). To use this function to test for the existence of a variable, the variable name supplied as input must be enclosed in quotation marks. If the variable name is not enclosed in quotation marks, the *contents* of the variable are evaluated, not the variable itself. This function may be used to validate an expression entered by the user (for example, in response to an INPUT command or a request for a field name).

Examples:

```
. ? TYPE("COMPANY")
C
. STORE "BALANCE > Ø" TO MEXPRESS
. ? TYPE(MEXPRESS)
L
```

UPPER(<*character string*>)

Input: Character string expression
Output: Character string

Evaluates to the result of converting the specified character string expression to all uppercase. This function may be used to convert a character string entered in various mixtures of uppercase and lowercase to a consistent format for comparison to another variable or constant.

Example:

```
. ? EQUIPMENT
Kaypro 10, Brother
. ? "KAYPRO" $ EQUIPMENT
.F.
. ? "KAYPRO" $ upper(EQUIPMENT)
.T.
```

VAL(<*character string*>)

Input: Character string expression
Output: Number

Evaluates to a true number matching the character string representation of the number supplied as input.

VERSION( )

Input: None
Output: Character string

Evaluates to a character string containing the name of the version of dBASE III PLUS that is running. This function may be used to test the version of dBASE III PLUS before you issue a command or use a function not present in an older version.

YEAR(<*date*>)

Input: Date expression
Output: Number

Evaluates to a number representing the year in the specified date.

Example:

```
. ? LASTORDER
05/28/87
. ? YEAR(LASTORDER)
 1985
```

D

THE CONFIG.DB FILE

The CONFIG.DB file may be used to customize the status of the dBASE III PLUS working environment to suit your personal preferences. CONFIG.DB is an ordinary text file consisting of one or more command lines, each of which controls one option. If this file is present in the subdirectory from which you load dBASE III PLUS, or a subdirectory specified in a DOS PATH command, the settings it contains are automatically placed in effect when you start up the program.

Most of the options you can specify in CONFIG.DB may also be established with SET commands either from the dot prompt or from a dBASE III PLUS program. The eight options that may *not* be SET from the dot prompt govern the use of external word processors and the allocation of RAM for memory buffers, which must be known to dBASE III PLUS when the program is first loaded. These options are marked with an asterisk (*) and explained in this appendix. There are also some SET commands that have no CONFIG.DB equivalents. These include all of the commands that require a data base to be open, such as SET FIELDS and SET FILTER, as well as several others: SET DATE, SET DOHISTORY, SET FIXED, SET MESSAGE, SET PRINTER, and SET TITLE.

The syntax used in CONFIG.DB is different from the syntax of the corresponding SET options. The general format for a CONFIG.DB entry is

<option> = *<value>*

instead of

SET <*option*> <*value*>

or

SET <*option*> TO <*value*>

If the <*value*> is a character string, it must not be surrounded by delimiters. For example, to assign the command LIST ACCOUNT, COMPANY to function key 5, you would type, at command level

```
SET FUNCTION 5 TO "LIST ACCOUNT, COMPANY;"
```

The corresponding CONFIG.DB entry is

```
F5 = LIST ACCOUNT, COMPANY;
```

The syntax for the CONFIG.DB entries that have SET equivalents is listed here without further explanation, except for several minor differences that are noted below the commands. See Appendix B for a more complete explanation of all of the SET commands. As in the descriptions of the SET options in Appendix B, the default values of options with two or more alternate values (for example, ON or OFF) are indicated in uppercase.

ALTERNATE = <*file name*>

This command is equivalent to the two SET commands

SET ALTERNATE TO <*file name*>
SET ALTERNATE ON

BELL = ON/off

* BUCKET = <*number*>

This option specifies the amount of memory (expressed in kilobytes) reserved by dBASE III PLUS for PICTURE, FUNCTION, and RANGE clauses in @ ... SAY ... GET commands. The default is 2, and you may specify any number between 1 and 31. This number should be increased if you experience inexplicable problems with @ ... SAY ... GET commands.

CARRY = on/OFF

CATALOG = <*filename*>

CENTURY = on/OFF

COLOR = <*standard foreground/standard background*>, <*enhanced foreground/ enhanced background*>, <*border*>

* COMMAND = <*command*>

The specified command is run automatically when dBASE III PLUS is first loaded. The default CONFIG.DB file provided with dBASE III PLUS contains the line COMMAND = ASSIST so that the program starts up in ASSIST mode. This option may be used to start up the program that serves as the user's first entry point into an application (usually, the Main Menu program). If the user invokes a different command file when loading dBASE III PLUS by typing DBASE <*program name*>, it will override the CONFIG.DB entry.

CONFIRM = on/OFF

CONSOLE = ON/off

DEBUG = on/OFF

DECIMALS = <*number*>

DEFAULT = <*disk drive*>

DELETED = on/OFF

DELIMITERS = <*delimiter character(s)*>

DELIMITERS = on/OFF

DEVICE = SCREEN/print

ECHO = on/OFF

ESCAPE = ON/off

EXACT = on/OFF

F<*number*> = <*character string*>

FIXED = on/OFF

* GETS = <*number*>

This option determines the number of GETs that may be collected between READ, CLEAR GETS, or CLEAR commands. The default is 128, and you may specify any number between 35 and 1023.

HEADINGS = ON/off

HELP = ON/off

HISTORY = <*number*>

INTENSITY = ON/off

MARGIN = <*number*>

* MAXMEM = <*number*>

This option determines the amount of memory (expressed in kilobytes) that is not released by dBASE III PLUS to an external application executed with a RUN command. The default value is 256, and you may specify any number between 200 and 720. If you have increased the amount of memory used by dBASE III PLUS by increasing the values of MVARSIZ, GETS, or BUCKET, MAXMEM should be raised so that these necessary memory buffers are not overwritten when external programs or commands are executed.

MEMOWIDTH = <*number*>

MENUS = ON/off

* MVARSIZ = <*number*>

This option specifies the amount of memory (expressed in kilobytes) reserved by dBASE III PLUS for memory variables. The default is 6, and you may specify any number between 1 and 31.

PATH = <*path name list*>

PRINT = on/OFF

PRINTER = <*DOS device name*>

* PROMPT = <*character string*>

This option changes the dBASE III PLUS command prompt from the standard dot (.) to the specified character string.

SAFETY = ON/off

SCOREBOARD = ON/off

STATUS = ON/off

STEP = on/OFF

TALK = ON/off

* TEDIT = <*file name*>

This option specifies an external text editor or word processing program to be substituted for the standard dBASE III PLUS MODIFY COMMAND editor. The file name should be entered exactly as you would type it at the MS-DOS prompt to invoke the editor (it must not include an extension).

TYPEAHEAD = <*number*>

UNIQUE = on/OFF

VIEW = <*file name*>

* WP = <*file name*>

This option specifies an external text editor or word processing program to be substituted for the standard dBASE III PLUS memo field editor. The file name should be entered exactly as you would type it at the MS-DOS prompt to invoke the editor (it must not include an extension).

E

THE COMPLETE NATIONAL WIDGETS PROCEDURE FILE

```
* NWPROC.PRG
* PROCEDURE FILE FOR NATIONAL WIDGETS SYSTEM
* WRITTEN BY:  M.LISKIN       08/20/85

* PROCEDURE     PURPOSE
* ---------     ---------------------------------------------------------------
* MONITOR       Display a status message to monitor a program's progress
* SAYDATE       Display or print a date in the form "July 31, 1985"
                     Parameters: MLINE, MCOLUMN, MDATE
* CENTER        Display or print a centered line of text
                     Parameters:  MLINE, MWIDTH, MTEXT
* MESSAGE       Display a highlighted message on the screen
                     Parameters:  MLINE, MCOLUMN, MMESSAGE
* ASK1          Ask a yes-or-no question
                     Parameters:  MLINE, MCOLUMN, MQUESTION, MANSWER
* ASK2          Ask a question with a finite number of possible responses
                     Parameters:  MLINE, MCOLUMN, MQUESTION, MCHOICES, MANSWER
* ASK3          Ask for a record by key and search the index for the record
                     Parameters:  MPROMPT, MKEY, MPICTURE, MERRORMSG
* STOPRPT       Stop or continue a print run interrupted by the user
* RPTHEAD       Print a report page heading
                     Parameters:  MWIDTH, MTITLE1, MTITLE2, MCOLTITLE1,
                                  MCOLTITLE2
* FILESIZE      Calculate the size of a data base file
                       Parameters:  MFILESIZE
* ASKPATH       Ask for subdirectory paths for data bases, indexes, other files
* DASHES        Create public variables containing single and double dashes
* BOXES         Create public variables containing graphics characters
* STDMSGS       Create public variables containing standard messages
* DISPATT       Create public variables containing display attributes
* PRINTATT      Create public variables containing printer attributes
* SCRNHEAD      Display company name on the screen using graphics characters
* ZIPINDEX      Determine whether the Customer File must be reindexed,
*                  and ask for the range of zip codes for a mailing
* CUSTSEL       Ask for selection criteria for a mailing
* CRITERIA      Add one criterion to MCOND1 or MCOND2
                       Parameters: MCHANGED, MCONDITION
* ACCTEST       Test user's access level before running a program
                       Parameters: MACCESS, MPROGRAM
```

```
* CUSTGET1      Display customer fields that cannot be edited by the user
* CUSTGET2      Display and collect customer fields that can be edited
* CUSTGET3      Display and/or collect fields based on the user's access level
* CUSTGET4      Display and/or collect fields based on the user's access level
* CUSTSAY       Display all customer fields
* CUSTGET5      Collect customer fields that can be edited by the user
* FILELOCK      Try to lock a data base file
                     Parameters: MLINE, MCOLUMN, MTRIES
* RECLOCK       Try to lock a record
                     Parameters: MLINE, MCOLUMN, MTRIES
* ERRTRAP       Detect and respond to error conditions

******************************************************************************

procedure MONITOR

clear
@ 10,10 say "Compiling Statistics -- Please Do Not Interrupt
@ 12,10 say "Working on Record           of " + str(reccount(),5

return

******************************************************************************

procedure SAYDATE

parameters MLINE, MCOLUMN, MDATE

@ MLINE, MCOLUMN say cmonth(MDATE) + str(day(MDATE), 3) + ", " + ;
                     str(year(MDATE), 4)
return

******************************************************************************

procedure CENTER

parameters MLINE, MWIDTH, MTEXT

@ MLINE, (MWIDTH - len(trim(MTEXT))) / 2 say trim(MTEXT)

return

******************************************************************************

procedure MESSAGE

parameters MLINE, MCOLUMN, MMESSAGE

set color to &MPBRIGHT

@ MLINE, 0
@ MLINE, MCOLUMN say MMESSAGE
wait ""

set color to &MPSTANDARD

return

******************************************************************************

procedure ASK1

parameters MLINE, MCOLUMN, MQUESTION, MANSWER

@ MLINE, 0
```

```
store .F. to MANSWER
@ MLINE, MCOLUMN say MQUESTION get MANSWER picture "Y"
read

return

*******************************************************************************

procedure ASK2

parameters MLINE, MCOLUMN, MQUESTION, MCHOICES, MANSWER

@ MLINE, 0

store " " to MANSWER
do while .not. MANSWER $ MCHOICES
   @ MLINE, MCOLUMN say MQUESTION get MANSWER picture "!"
   read
enddo

return

*******************************************************************************

procedure ASK3

parameters MPROMPT, MKEY, MPICTURE, MERRORMSG

do while .T.

   @ 12,10 say MPROMPT get MKEY picture MPICTURE
   read
   if MKEY = " "
      exit
   endif
   seek trim(MKEY)
   if found()
      exit
   else
      @ 20,10 say trim(MKEY) + " " + MERRORMSG
      @ 21,10 say "Press any key to try again"
      wait ""
      @ 20,10
      @ 21,10
   endif

enddo

return
*******************************************************************************


procedure STOPRPT

do ASK1 with 23, 10, "Do you want to stop printing? (Y/N)", MSTOP

if MSTOP
   store recno() to MPRECORD
   store MPAGE   to MPPAGE
   save all like MP* to NWMEMORY
endif

return

*******************************************************************************
```

```
procedure RPTHEAD

parameters MWIDTH, MTITLE1, MTITLE2, MCOLTITLE1, MCOLTITLE2

do SAYDATE with 1, 0, date()

if .not. MONE
   @  1,MWIDTH - 8 say "PAGE " + str(MPAGE,3)
endif

do CENTER with 3, MWIDTH, upper(MPCOMPANY)
do CENTER with 4, MWIDTH, MTITLE1
do CENTER with 5, MWIDTH, MTITLE2

@  8, 0 say MCOLTITLE1
@  9, 0 say MCOLTITLE2
@ 10, 0 say left(MPSDASH, MWIDTH)

store MPAGE + 1 to MPAGE
store 12        to MLINE

return

********************************************************************************

procedure FILESIZE

parameters MFILESIZE

store 1  to MFIELD
store 34 to MHEADER

do while MFIELD <= 128
   if len(field(MFIELD)) = 0
      exit
   else
      store MHEADER + 32 to MHEADER
   endif
   store MFIELD + 1 to MFIELD
enddo

store MHEADER + (reccount() * recsize()) + 1000 to MFILESIZE

return

********************************************************************************


procedure ASKPATH

do while .T.

   store .T. to MVALID

   @  2, 5 say "Enter path names for files in this application,"
   @  3, 5 say "including disk drive, for example C:\DBPLUS\ACCOUNTS"
   @  5, 5 say "Data base files               " get MPDPATH picture "@!"
   @  6, 5 say "Index files                   " get MPIPATH picture "@!"
   @  7, 5 say "Programs and all other files" get MPOPATH picture "@!"
   read

   if .not. file("&MPDPATH\NWCUST.DBF")
      @ 10, 5 say "Data base file path not found"
      store .F. to MVALID
   endif

   if .not. file("&MPIPATH\NWCACCT.NDX")
      @ 11, 5 say "Index file path not found"
      store .F. to MVALID
   endif
```

```
   if .not. file("&MPOPATH\NWCMENU1.PRG")
      @ 12, 5 say "Program file path not found"
      store .F. to MVALID
   endif

   if MVALID
      exit
   else
      store .T. to MRETRY
      @ 15, 5 say;
        "Indicated paths do not exist -- Do you want to re-enter them? (Y/N)";
        get MRETRY picture "Y"
      read
      if .not. MRETRY
         @ 21, 5 say;
           "Please correct the error and then re-run the setup program"
         @ 22, 5 say "Press any key to continue"
         wait ""
         exit
      endif
   endif

enddo

store trim(MPDPATH) to MPPATH

if trim(MPIPATH) <> trim(MPDPATH)
   store MPPATH + ";" + trim(MPIPATH) to MPPATH
endif

if trim(MPOPATH) <> trim(MPDPATH) .and. trim(MPOPATH) <> trim(MPIPATH)
   store MPPATH + ";" + trim(MPOPATH) to MPPATH
endif

set path to &MPPATH

return

********************************************************************************

procedure DASHES

public MPSDASH, MPDDASH

store "-" to MPSDASH
store "=" to MPDDASH

store 1 to MCOUNT

set console off

do while MCOUNT <= 8
   store MPSDASH + MPSDASH to MPSDASH
   store MPDDASH + MPDDASH to MPDDASH
   store MCOUNT  + 1       to MCOUNT
enddo

set console on

return

********************************************************************************

procedure BOXES

public MPLLINE, MPULINE, MPVERT, MPULC, MPLLC, MPURC, MPLRC

store chr(220) to MPLLINE
store chr(223) to MPULINE
```

```
store 1 to MCOUNT

do while MCOUNT <= 7
   store MPLLINE + MPLLINE to MPLLINE
   store MPULINE + MPULINE to MPULINE
   store MCOUNT  + 1       to MCOUNT
enddo

store left(MPLLINE, 80) to MPLLINE
store left(MPULINE, 80) to MPULINE

store chr(219) to MPVERT
store chr(219) to MPULC
store chr(219) to MPURC
store chr(219) to MPLLC
store chr(219) to MPLRC

return

********************************************************************************

procedure STDMSGS

public MPPRESSKEY, MPSEARCH, MPFIRST, MPLAST, MPNOTFOUND, MPNOTZERO,;
       MPTRANSACT, MPDELETE, MPRECOVER, MPONFILE, MPCORRECT, MPNOTAVAIL

store " -- Press any key to continue"                to MPPRESSKEY
store "You must SEARCH first"                        to MPSEARCH
store "This is the first name"                       to MPFIRST
store "This is the last name"                        to MPLAST
store " not found"                                   to MPNOTFOUND
store "Balance is not 0.00"                          to MPNOTZERO
store "There are current transactions"               to MPTRANSACT
store " has been deleted"                            to MPDELETE
store " has been recovered"                          to MPRECOVER
store " is already on file"                          to MPONFILE
store 'Please correct the fields marked with a "*" ' to MPCORRECT
store "This option is not available"                 to MPNOTAVAIL

return

********************************************************************************

procedure DISPATT

public MPBRIGHT, MPSTANDARD

if iscolor()
   store "R/W, W+" to MPBRIGHT
   store "W,   W+" to MPSTANDARD
else
   store "W+, W+" to MPBRIGHT
   store "W,  U+" to MPSTANDARD
endif

return

********************************************************************************

procedure PRINTATT

public MPBOLDON, MPBOLDOFF, MPENLRGON, MPENLRGOFF, MPCOMPON, MPCMPOFF,;
       MP18LINES, MP66LINES

store  chr(27) + 'E'             to MPBOLDON
store  chr(27) + 'F'             to MPBOLDOFF
store  chr(27) + 'W' + chr(1)    to MPENLRGON
store  chr(27) + 'W' + chr(0)    to MPENLRGOFF
store  chr(15)                   to MPCOMPON
```

```
store  chr(18)                    to MPCMPOFF
store  chr(27) + 'C' + chr(18)   to MP18LINES
store  chr(27) + 'C' + chr(66)   to MP66LINES

return

********************************************************************************

procedure SCRNHEAD

clear
@  1,10 say MPULC + left(MPULINE, 58) + MPURC
@  2,10 say MPVERT
@  2,69 say MPVERT
@  3,10 say MPLLC + left(MPLLINE, 58) + MPLRC

set color to /W, W+
do CENTER with 2, 80, CHR(26) + " " + MPCOMPANY + " " + CHR(27)
set color to &MPSTANDARD

return

********************************************************************************


* PROCEDURE TO REINDEX CUSTOMER FILE BY ZIP IF NECESSARY
*   AND ENTER BEGINNING AND ENDING ZIP CODES
* FROM PROGRAM NWCLABL6.PRG, WRITTEN BY M.LISKIN   6/18/86

procedure ZIPINDEX

public MZIPEND

select 1
use NWCUST

select 2
use NWORDHST

clear
text
                               *** CAUTION ***

          The Customer File must be reindexed by ZIP CODE if you have
          added new customers or changed any zip codes in the file
          since the last time the file was reindexed.

          The Order History File must be reindexed by CATEGORY if you
          have added new records or changed any category codes in the
          file since the last time the file was reindexed.
endtext

* ASK WHETHER TO REBUILD REQUIRED INDEXES IF THEY ARE ALREADY PRESENT
* IF NOT PRESENT, REBUILD THEM WITHOUT ASKING

store .T. to MREINDEXC, MREINDEXO

if file("NWCZIP.NDX")
   @ 13,10 say "Do you need to reindex the Customer File by ZIP code?";
           get MREINDEXC picture "Y"
   read
endif

if file("NWOHCAT.NDX")
   @ 15,10 say "Do you need to reindex the Order History File by CATEGORY?";
           get MREINDEXO picture "Y"
   read
endif
```

```
* REINDEX CUSTOMER FILE IF NECESSARY OR OPEN EXISTING INDEX IF NOT
select NWCUST
if MREINDEXC
   @ 18,10 say "Reindexing Customer File by ZIP -- Please do not interrupt"
   set talk on
   index on ZIP to NWCZIP
   goto top
   set talk off
else
   set index to NWCZIP
endif

* REINDEX ORDER HISTORY FILE IF NECESSARY OR OPEN EXISTING INDEX IF NOT
select NWORDHST
if MREINDEXO
   @ 21, 5 say;
     "Reindexing Order History File by CATEGORY -- Please do not interrupt"
   set talk on
   index on CATEGORY + ACCOUNT to NWOHCAT
   goto top
   set talk off
else
   set index to NWOHCAT
endif

* ENTER RANGE OF ZIP CODES, VALIDATE STARTING ZIP

select NWCUST
store ZIP       to MZIPBEGIN
store "99999"   to MZIPEND
clear

do while .T.

   @  1,10 say "Enter starting zip code:" get MZIPBEGIN picture "99999"
   @  2,10 say "Enter ending   zip code:" get MZIPEND   picture "99999"
   read

   seek trim(MZIPBEGIN)

   if found()
      exit
   else
      @ 22,10 say "There is no customer with that zip code"
      @ 23,10 say "Press any key to reenter the zip code"
      wait ""
      @ 22,10
      @ 23,10
   endif

enddo

return

*******************************************************************************

* PROCEDURE TO ENTER SELECTION CRITERIA FOR MAILINGS
* FROM PROGRAM NWCLABL6.PRG, WRITTEN BY M.LISKIN   6/18/86

procedure CUSTSEL

select 1
use NWCUST   index NWCZIP

select 2
use NWORDHST index NWOHCAT

public MCOND2, ME, MI1, MI2, MD1, MD2
```

```
* ENTER CUSTOMER SELECTION CRITERIA
store space(25)         to ME
store "      "          to MC
store 0.00              to MI1
store 9999999.99        to MI2
store ctod("01/01/01") to MD1
store ctod("12/31/99") to MD2

do while .T.

   store ""      to MCOND1
   store "for " to MCOND2
   clear

   @  1,10 say "Enter type of equipment for customers in this mailing:"
   @  2,10 say "(or press <RETURN> to include ALL equipment types)"
   @  4,20 get ME picture "@!"

   @  6,10 say "Enter range of overall total invoices to include:"
   @  7,10 say "Minimum" get MI1 picture "9999999.99"
   @  7,40 say "Maximum" get MI2 picture "9999999.99"

   @ 10,10 say "Enter range of last invoice dates to include:"
   @ 11,10 say "Earliest" get MD1
   @ 11,40 say "Latest"   get MD2

   read

   * ENTER PRODUCT CATEGORY, VALIDATE IN ORDER HISTORY FILE
   select NWORDHST

   do while .T.

      @ 14,10 say "Enter product CATEGORY:" get MC picture "@!"
      @ 15,10 say "(or press <RETURN> to include ALL categories)"
      read
      if MC = " "
         exit
      endif

      seek MC

      if found()
         exit
      else
         @ 22,10 say "There are no orders with that category"
         @ 23,10 say "Press any key to reenter the zip code"
         wait ""
         @ 22,10
         @ 23,10
      endif

   enddo

   * CONSTRUCT FILTER CONDITION

   do CRITERIA with 'ME <> " "', "trim(ME)$upper(EQUIPMENT).and."

   do CRITERIA with "MI1 > 0", "TOTINV>=MI1.and."

   do CRITERIA with "MI2 < 9999999.99", "TOTINV<=MI2.and."

   do CRITERIA with 'dtoc(MD1) <> "01/01/01"', "LASTORDER>=MD1.and."

   do CRITERIA with 'dtoc(MD2) <> "12/31/99"', "LASTORDER<=MD2.and."

   set relation to MC + ACCOUNT into NWORDHST
   do CRITERIA with 'MC <> " "', "NWORDHST->ACCOUNT<>' '.and."
```

```
      if MTOOMANY
         @ 22,20 say "Too many selection criteria were entered"
         @ 23,20 say "Press any key to reenter the condition"
         wait ""
         loop
      endif

      if len(MCOND2) < 201
         store space(201 - len(MCOND2)) to MEXTRACOND
         @ 18, 5 say;
           "Enter extra selection conditions, or press <RETURN> to leave blank:"
         @ 19, 5 get MEXTRACOND picture "@S70"
         read
      endif

      if MEXTRACOND <> " "
         if type(MEXTRACOND) <> "L"
            @ 22, 5 say "Your extra selection conditions "+;
                        "are not a valid dBASE III expression"
            @ 23,20 say "Press any key to reenter the conditions"
            wait ""
            loop
         else
            store MCOND2 + "(" + trim(MEXTRACOND) + ")" to MCOND2
         endif
      endif

      store .F. to MOK
      @ 24,20 say "Are these selections OK? (Y/N)" get MOK picture "Y"
      read
      if MOK
         exit
      endif

   enddo

   if len(MCOND1) > 0
      store left(MCOND1, len(MCOND1) - 5) to MCOND1
   endif

   if len(MCOND2) = 4
      store "" to MCOND2
   else
      if MEXTRACOND = " "
         store left(MCOND2, len(MCOND2) - 5) to MCOND2
      endif
   endif

   set filter to &MCOND1
   goto top

   return
   ********************************************************************************

   procedure CRITERIA

   parameters MCHANGED, MCONDITION

   if &MCHANGED
      if len(MCOND1 + MCONDITION) <= 240
         store MCOND1 + MCONDITION to MCOND1
      else
         if len(MCOND2 + MCONDITION <= 203
            store MCOND2 + MCONDITION to MCOND2
         else
            store .T. to MTOOMANY
         endif
      endif
   endif
   ********************************************************************************
```

```
procedure ACCTEST

parameters MACCESS, MPROGRAM

if access() <= MACCESS
   do &MPROGRAM
else
   do MESSAGE with 23, 10, "This option is not available " + MPPRESSKEY
   wait ""
endif

return

*********************************************************************************

procedure CUSTGET1

if deleted()
   set color to W+, W+
   @ 3,65 say "* DELETED *"
   set color to W, W+
else
   @ 3,65 say "           "
endif

@  3,13 get ACCOUNT
@ 14,18 get YTDINV picture "9,999,999.99"
@ 15,18 get YTDPMT picture "9,999,999.99"
@ 17,18 get TOTINV picture "9,999,999.99"
@ 17,62 get FIRSTORDER
@ 18,18 get YTDPMT picture "9,999,999.99"
@ 18,62 get LASTORDER
@ 20,18 get BALANCE picture "@( 9,999,999.99"
clear gets

if dtoc(LASTORDER) <> "  "
   store date() - LASTORDER to MDAYS
   @ 20,45 say "LAST ORDER WAS " + str(MDAYS,4) + " DAYS AGO"
else
   @ 20,45 say space(28)
endif

return

*********************************************************************************

procedure CUSTGET2

set color to W, W+

@  5,13 get COMPANY
@  6,13 get ADDRESS1
@  7,13 get ADDRESS2
@  8,13 get CITY
@  8,51 get STATE picture "@!"
@  8,63 get ZIP picture "99999"
@ 10,13 get CONTACT
@ 10,55 get AREACODE picture "999"
@ 10,63 get TELEPHONE picture "999-9999"
@ 12,13 get EQUIPMENT
@ 12,63 get TAXRATE range 0, 10

return

*********************************************************************************

procedure CUSTGET3

if deleted()
   set color to &MPBRIGHT
   @ 3,65 say "* DELETED *"
   set color to &MPSTANDARD
```

```
else
   @ 3,65 say "             "
endif

@  3,13 get ACCOUNT
clear gets

@ 14,18 get YTDINV picture "9,999,999.99"
@ 15,18 get YTDPMT picture "9,999,999.99"
@ 17,18 get TOTINV picture "9,999,999.99"
@ 17,62 get FIRSTORDER
@ 18,18 get YTDPMT picture "9,999,999.99"
@ 18,62 get LASTORDER
@ 20,18 get BALANCE picture "@( 9,999,999.99"

if dtoc(LASTORDER) <> "  "
   store date() - LASTORDER to MDAYS
   @ 20,45 say "LAST ORDER WAS " + str(MDAYS,4) + " DAYS AGO"
else
   @ 20,45 say space(28)
endif

if access() > 1
   clear gets
endif

@  5,13 get COMPANY
@  6,13 get ADDRESS1
@  7,13 get ADDRESS2
@  8,13 get CITY
@  8,51 get STATE picture "@!"
@  8,63 get ZIP picture "99999"
@ 10,13 get CONTACT
@ 10,55 get AREACODE picture "999"
@ 10,63 get TELEPHONE picture "999-9999"
@ 12,13 get EQUIPMENT
@ 12,63 get TAXRATE range 0, 10

if MOPTION $ "CA"
   read
   if readkey() = 36 .or. readkey() = 292
      select 10
      do NWHELP2 with "NWCUPD4 ", 2
      select NWCUST
      do NWCSCRN
      do CUSTGET3
      loop
   endif
else
   clear gets
endif

return

*******************************************************************************

procedure CUSTGET4

if deleted()
   set color to &MPBRIGHT
   @ 3,65 say "* DELETED *"
   set color to &MPSTANDARD
else
   @ 3,65 say "             "
endif

@  3,14 say ACCOUNT
```

```
if access() <= 4
   @  5,13 get COMPANY
   @  6,13 get ADDRESS1
   @  7,13 get ADDRESS2
   @  8,13 get CITY
   @  8,51 get STATE picture "@!"
   @  8,63 get ZIP picture "99999"
   @ 10,13 get CONTACT
   @ 10,55 get AREACODE picture "999"
   @ 10,63 get TELEPHONE picture "999-9999"
   @ 12,13 get EQUIPMENT
   @ 12,63 get TAXRATE range 0, 10
else
   @  5,14 say COMPANY
   @  6,14 say ADDRESS1
   @  7,14 say ADDRESS2
   @  8,14 say CITY
   @  8,52 say STATE
   @  8,64 say ZIP
   @ 10,14 say CONTACT
   @ 10,56 say AREACODE
   @ 10,64 say TELEPHONE
   @ 12,14 say EQUIPMENT
   @ 12,64 say TAXRATE
endif

if access() = 1
   @ 14,18 get YTDINV picture "9,999,999.99"
   @ 15,18 get YTDPMT picture "9,999,999.99"
   @ 17,18 get TOTINV picture "9,999,999.99"
   @ 17,62 get FIRSTORDER
   @ 18,18 get YTDPMT picture "9,999,999.99"
   @ 18,62 get LASTORDER
   @ 20,18 get BALANCE picture "@( 9,999,999.99"
else
   @ 14,19 say YTDINV picture "9,999,999.99"
   @ 15,19 say YTDPMT picture "9,999,999.99"
   @ 17,19 say TOTINV picture "9,999,999.99"
   @ 17,63 say FIRSTORDER
   @ 18,19 say YTDPMT picture "9,999,999.99"
   @ 18,63 say LASTORDER
   @ 20,19 say BALANCE picture "@( 9,999,999.99"
endif

if dtoc(LASTORDER) <> "  "
   store date() - LASTORDER to MDAYS
   @ 20,45 say "LAST ORDER WAS " + str(MDAYS,4) + " DAYS AGO"
else
   @ 20,45 say space(28)
endif

if MOPTION $ "CA"
   read
   if readkey() = 36 .or. readkey() = 292
      select 10
      do NWHELP2 with "NWCUPD4 ", 2
      select NWCUST
      do NWCSCRN
      do CUSTGET3
      loop
   endif
else
   clear gets
endif

return

*****************************************************************************
```

```
procedure CUSTSAY

if deleted()
   set color to &MPBRIGHT
   @ 3,65 say "* DELETED *"
   set color to &MPSTANDARD
else
   @ 3,65 say "           "
endif

@  3,14 say ACCOUNT
@  5,14 say COMPANY
@  6,14 say ADDRESS1
@  7,14 say ADDRESS2
@  8,14 say CITY
@  8,52 say STATE
@  8,64 say ZIP
@ 10,14 say CONTACT
@ 10,56 say AREACODE
@ 10,64 say TELEPHONE
@ 12,14 say EQUIPMENT
@ 12,64 say TAXRATE
@ 14,19 say YTDINV picture "9,999,999.99"
@ 15,19 say YTDPMT picture "9,999,999.99"
@ 17,19 say TOTINV picture "9,999,999.99"
@ 17,63 say FIRSTORDER
@ 18,19 say YTDPMT picture "9,999,999.99"
@ 18,63 say LASTORDER
@ 20,18 say BALANCE picture "@( 9,999,999.99"

if dtoc(LASTORDER) <> "  "
   store date() - LASTORDER to MDAYS
   @ 20,45 say "LAST ORDER WAS " + str(MDAYS,4) + " DAYS AGO"
else
   @ 20,45 say space(28)
endif

return

*********************************************************************************

procedure CUSTGET5

if deleted()
   set color to &MPBRIGHT
   @ 3,65 say "* DELETED *"
   set color to &MPSTANDARD
else
   @ 3,65 say "           "
endif

@  3,14 say ACCOUNT
@  5,14 say COMPANY
@  6,14 say ADDRESS1
@  7,14 say ADDRESS2
@  8,14 say CITY
@  8,52 say STATE
@  8,64 say ZIP
@ 10,14 say CONTACT
@ 10,56 say AREACODE
@ 10,64 say TELEPHONE
@ 12,14 say EQUIPMENT
@ 12,64 say TAXRATE
@ 14,19 say YTDINV picture "9,999,999.99"
@ 15,19 say YTDPMT picture "9,999,999.99"
@ 17,19 say TOTINV picture "9,999,999.99"
@ 17,63 say FIRSTORDER
@ 18,19 say YTDPMT picture "9,999,999.99"
@ 18,63 say LASTORDER
@ 20,19 say BALANCE picture "@( 9,999,999.99"
```

```
 if dtoc(LASTORDER) <> "  "
    store date() - LASTORDER to MDAYS
    @ 20,45 say "LAST ORDER WAS " + str(MDAYS,4) + " DAYS AGO"
 else
    @ 20,45 say space(28)
 endif

 if access() <= 4
    @  5,13 get COMPANY
    @  6,13 get ADDRESS1
    @  7,13 get ADDRESS2
    @  8,13 get CITY
    @  8,51 get STATE picture "@!"
    @  8,63 get ZIP picture "99999"
    @ 10,13 get CONTACT
    @ 10,55 get AREACODE picture "999"
    @ 10,63 get TELEPHONE picture "999-9999"
    @ 12,13 get EQUIPMENT
    @ 12,63 get TAXRATE range 0, 10
 endif

 if access() = 1
    @ 14,18 get YTDINV picture "9,999,999.99"
    @ 15,18 get YTDPMT picture "9,999,999.99"
    @ 17,18 get TOTINV picture "9,999,999.99"
    @ 17,62 get FIRSTORDER
    @ 18,18 get YTDPMT picture "9,999,999.99"
    @ 18,62 get LASTORDER
    @ 20,18 get BALANCE picture "@( 9,999,999.99"
 endif

 if MOPTION $ "CA"
    read
    if readkey() = 36 .or. readkey() = 292
       select 10
       do NWHELP2 with "NWCUPD4 ", 2
       select NWCUST
       do NWCSCRN
       do CUSTGET3
       loop
    endif
 else
    clear gets
 endif

 return

*******************************************************************************

procedure FILELOCK

parameters MLINE, MCOLUMN, MTRIES

store 1 to MCOUNT
do MESSAGE with MLINE, MCOLUMN, "Requesting access to " + DBF() + " ..."

do while MCOUNT <= MTRIES .and. .not. flock()
   @ MLINE,60 say MCOUNT
   store MCOUNT + 1 to MCOUNT
enddo

if .not. flock()
   do MESSAGE with MLINE, MCOLUMN, DBF() + " not available. Please try later";
      + MPPRESSKEY
   wait ""
endif

return

*******************************************************************************
```

```
procedure RECLOCK

parameters MLINE, MCOLUMN, MTRIES

store 1 to MCOUNT
do MESSAGE with MLINE, MCOLUMN, "Requesting access to " + MACCOUNT + " ..."

do while MCOUNT <= MTRIES .and. .not. rlock()
   @ MLINE,60 say MCOUNT
   store MCOUNT + 1 to MCOUNT
enddo

if .not. rlock()
   do MESSAGE with MLINE, MCOLUMN, MACCOUNT +;
      " not available. Please try later" + MPPRESSKEY
   wait ""
endif

return

********************************************************************************

procedure ERRTRAP

do case

   case error() = 12
      return

   case error() = 108 .or. error() = 109
      store 1 to MCOUNT
      do while MCOUNT <= 100
         store MCOUNT + 1 to MCOUNT
      enddo
      if MRETRY
         store .F. to MRETRY
         retry
      else
         store .T. to MERROR
         return
      endif

   case error() = 133
      do MESSAGE with 23, 10, MPNOTAVAIL + MPPRESSKEY

   otherwise
      do MESSAGE with 23, 10, message() + MPPRESSKEY

endcase

return

********************************************************************************
```

F

ERROR MESSAGES

This appendix lists in alphabetical order the error messages displayed by dBASE III PLUS in response to errors encountered at the dot prompt or from within programs, together with the most common causes of the errors and, where appropriate, suggested remedies. Warning messages, informational messages, and most of the messages displayed in the ASSIST menu and the full-screen editors are not included because, for the most part, these messages are self-explanatory.

If you have activated an error detection mechanism with the ON ERROR command, the text of the error message is available to your program through the MESSAGE( ) function, and the error number is stored in the ERROR( ) function. The error-trapping program or procedure can test the value of this function to determine what action to take in response to the error and what message to display for the user. Many errors generated by commands that cannot be used from the dot prompt or from within a dBASE III PLUS program have no error numbers. For each error that does have an assigned ERROR( ) value, the number is listed in parentheses next to the error message.

At the end of this appendix, there is a cross-reference listing in numerical order of all error messages that return a value for the ERROR( ) function, including those not described in the first section.

A DBF file in view is not in current directory.

A data base file referenced in a VIEW that you have attempted to open with SET VIEW TO or MODIFY VIEW cannot be found either in the current subdirectory or in any of the subdirectories accessed through a SET PATH TO command.

ALIAS name already in use. (24)

The alias specified in a USE command has already been assigned to a data base open in one of the ten work areas. This can occur if you try to assign the same alias name to two different data base files or if you try to open the same file in two work areas. The error may also occur if you assign one of the single letters A through J as a data base file name or alias (these letters are reserved for referring to the ten work areas).

ALIAS not found. (13)

The alias specified in a SELECT command cannot be found, usually because you have forgotten which data base files are open or because you have misspelled the alias.

ALTERNATE could not be opened. (72)

The ALTERNATE file named in an ALTERNATE = *filename* entry in CONFIG.DB could not be opened, because the disk directory was full or because an invalid file name was specified.

Beginning of file encountered. (38)

A SKIP −*n* command was executed with the BOF( ) function already set to .T. This will occur on the second consecutive attempt to SKIP backward beyond the beginning-of-file. (The first SKIP −*n* simply sets the BOF( ) function to .T., leaving the data base positioned at the first, or first indexed, record.)

Cannot erase a file which is open. (89)

An ERASE or DELETE FILE command was issued without first closing the specified file with the appropriate USE or CLOSE command (depending on which type of file you are erasing). CLEAR ALL or CLOSE ALL may be used to close all open files.

Cannot JOIN a file with itself. (139)

The file named in the WITH clause in a JOIN command was the same file that is currently open.

Cannot select requested database. (17)

A SELECT command requested by number a work area higher than 10.

Cannot write to read only file. (111)

An attempt was made to write to a file assigned the "Read-Only" attribute at the operating system level.

CONTINUE without LOCATE. (42)

A CONTINUE command was executed without a prior LOCATE command. CONTINUE is used only to search for the next record that matches the condition specified in a previous LOCATE command.

Cyclic relation. (44)

A SET RELATION command was issued to link the current data base to another data base from which a RELATION affecting the current file was already SET. This may be direct; for example:

```
SELECT 1
USE NWCUST INDEX NWCACCT
SELECT 2
USE NWORDER INDEX NWOACCT
SET RELATION TO ACCOUNT INTO NWCUST
SELECT 1
SET RELATION TO ACCOUNT INTO NWORDER
```

It may also occur in a chain of more than two files. For example:

```
SELECT 1
USE NWORDER INDEX NWOINVC
SELECT 2
USE NWTXN INDEX NWTACCT
SELECT 3
USE NWCUST INDEX NWCACCT

SELECT NWCUST
SET RELATION TO ACCOUNT INTO NWTXN
SELECT NWTXN
SET RELATION TO INVOICE INTO NWORDER
SELECT NWORDER
SET RELATION TO ACCOUNT INTO NWCUST
```

Database is encrypted. (131)

An attempt was made to use a data base file encrypted by the PROTECT utility either from a single-user version of dBASE III PLUS or by an unauthorized user in a multi-user system.

Database is not indexed. (26)

A FIND or SEEK command was issued with no index open for the current data base, or you have attempted to SET RELATION TO a data base opened with no index.

Data Catalog has not been established. (122)

An attempt was made to use a catalog query clause (entering a "?" where dBASE III PLUS expects a file name) to list the available files of a given type, but no CATALOG file was open.

Data type mismatch. (9)

Data types were mixed incorrectly in an algebraic expression or condition, or a data type was used that does not match the type required by the context of the command. This can occur if you attempt to REPLACE a field with data of a different type, if the object of a SEEK does not match the data type of the index key expression, or if you attempt to SORT on a logical or memo field.

.DBT file cannot be opened. (41)

An attempt was made to open a data base file containing memo fields for which the .DBT file was not available. This can occur if you copy or rename a .DBF file with the DOS COPY or REN command or the dBASE III PLUS COPY FILE or RENAME equivalent, and forget to copy or rename the .DBT file.

Directory is full.

A previous command attempted to create a new file on a disk that already has the maximum number of directory entries permitted by the MS-DOS operating system.

Disk full when writing file - <file name>. (56)
Abort, Ignore, or Delete old files (A, I, or D)?

A command attempted to write to a disk that has no space remaining. If you choose A (abort), dBASE III PLUS asks you to confirm your intention to interrupt the command:

** WARNING ** Data will probably be lost. Confirm (Y/N)

If you answer Y, dBASE III PLUS returns to the dot prompt, leaving the output file incomplete. If you answer N, dBASE III PLUS repeats the "Abort, Ignore, or Delete" message.

If you choose I (ignore), dBASE III PLUS will retry the write operation, find the disk still full, and repeat the "Abort, Ignore, or Delete" message.

If you choose D (delete old files), dBASE III PLUS confirms your selection with the message

Delete obsolete files to provide disk space...(Esc to abort)

The program then presents the names of the files on the disk, one by one, and allows you to delete each file or to go on to the next one. dBASE III PLUS resumes the operation in progress when all file names have been displayed or when you press ESC to interrupt. If you are able to delete enough unneeded files to make room for the file being written, the original command that generated the error will complete normally.

DO's nested too deep. (103)

An attempt was made to nest (allow one program to call another) more than the maximum of 20 levels (20 programs) deep.

End of file encountered. (4)

A SKIP command was executed with the EOF( ) function already set to .T. This will occur on the second consecutive attempt to SKIP beyond the end-of-file. (The first SKIP simply sets the EOF( ) function to .T., leaving the data base positioned at an empty record beyond the end-of-file.)

This error can also occur if a data base is opened with an index that does not match the data base (perhaps because it was created with a different number of records in the file), so that a record referenced by the index does not exist in the file. It can also occur under certain conditions if an index file, data base file, or report or label format file is damaged by a disk error.

End-of-file or error on keyboard input. (51)

A file specified in a DOS SET ENVIRONMENT command to replace keyboard input was damaged by a disk error.

Exclusive use on database is required. (110)

In a network environment, an attempt was made to execute a command that requires exclusive use of a data base file, with EXCLUSIVE set OFF.

***** Execution error on + : concatenated string too large. (77)**
***** Execution error on − : concatenated string too large. (76)**

An attempt was made to concatenate two or more character strings with "+" or "−" to create a string longer than 254 characters. The resulting string will contain the first 254 characters of the combination.

***** Execution error on ^ or ** : negative base, fractional exponent. (78)**

An expression contains a negative number raised to a power between 0 and 1. (This is the equivalent of extracting a root, such as a square root, of a negative number, which cannot be done.)

***** Execution error on CHR( ) : Out of range. (57)**

The input provided to a CHR function was less than 0 or greater than 255, the range of ASCII character codes.

***** Execution error on LOG( ) : Zero or negative. (58)**

The input provided to a LOG function was zero or negative. (Since the logarithm of a number is the power to which *e*, the base of natural logarithms, must be raised to yield the number and *e* is a positive number, there can be no zero or negative logarithms.)

***** Execution error on NDX( ) : Invalid index number. (87)**

The input provided to the NDX function (which returns the name of the index file opened in the specified position in the index list in the USE command) was not within the allowable range of 1 to 7.

***** Execution error on REPLICATE( ) : String too large. (88)**

An attempt was made to create a character string longer than 254 characters with the REPLICATE function.

***** Execution error on SPACE( ) : Negative. (60)**
***** Execution error on SPACE( ) : Too large. (59)**

The input provided to the SPACE function to specify the length of the string of blank spaces to be created was not within the allowable range of 1 to 254.

***** Execution error on SQRT( ) : Negative. (61)**

The input provided to a SQRT function was a negative number. (You cannot take the square root of a negative number.)

***** Execution error on STORE( ) : String too large. (79)**

An attempt was made to create a character string memory variable longer than 254 characters with the STORE function.

***** Execution error on STR( ) : Out of range. (63)**

One of the two numeric inputs to the STR function was incorrect. Either the length of the desired character string was less than 0 or greater than 19, or you have specified more decimal places than the length can accommodate.

***** Execution error on STUFF( ) : String too large. (102)**

An attempt was made to create a character string longer than 254 characters by using the STUFF function to substitute a longer string for a portion of the original string.

***** Execution error on SUBSTR( ) : Start point out of range. (62)**

The starting point for the substring specified in a SUBSTR function was greater than the total length of the character string.

^^Expected ON or OFF. (73)

One of the SET options in CONFIG.DB that must be either ON or OFF was given some other value.

Field not found. (48)

A field name that does not exist in the data base structure was specified in the FREEZE option of the BROWSE command.

File already exists. (7)

An attempt was made to RENAME a file with the name of another existing disk file.

File does not exist. (1)

An attempt was made to access a file that cannot be found on the disk, either in the current subdirectory or in any of the subdirectories specified in the search path established with SET PATH.

File is already open. (3)

An attempt was made to open a disk file that was already open or to perform an operation not permitted on an open file. This error can occur if you try to open a file, such as an index or report form file, that is already open in another work area. (Attempting to open a data base file in two work areas yields the "ALIAS name already in use" error message.) The error can also occur if you attempt to COPY, SORT, ERASE, RENAME, TYPE, or edit (with MODIFY COMMAND) an open file, or if you try to SORT a file to itself (specify the current file name to receive the sorted output) or to a file that is open in another work area. This error message is also commonly caused by writing a command file that calls itself with a DO command or by writing a cyclic chain of command files in which one program calls another that is still open.

File is in use by another. (108)

An attempt was made to open a file in a multi-user application, when the file has already been opened for EXCLUSIVE use at another workstation.

File is not accessible. (29)

An illegal character (one of the prohibited punctuation marks +, ", <, >, ?, *, [, or]) was used in a file name, or an attempt was made to open a file with the disk directory already full.

File too large—some data may be lost.

An attempt was made to edit a file or memo field larger than 5000 bytes with the standard dBASE III PLUS editor. If you make this error, you should exit immediately from the editor with ESC to avoid truncating the file.

File was not LOADed. (91)

An attempt was made to place a binary file in memory with the LOAD command, but the file is not available. This error can also occur if a CALL or RELEASE MODULE command references a binary file not found at the specified memory location.

Illegal character data length.—detected on field <*n*>.
Illegal decimal length.—detected on field <*n*>.
Illegal field type.—detected on field <*n*>.
Illegal field name.—detected on field <*n*>.
Illegal numeric data length.—detected on field <*n*>.
Maximum record length exceeded.—detected on field <*n*> (137).

One or more of the records in a structure-extended file contains an illegal field name, length, type, or number of decimal places, or the total record length is greater than 4000 characters. The invalid field is field number *n* in the data base structure described by the structure-extended file and therefore record *n* in this file. Since a structure-extended file is created from an existing data base, this error can occur only if you have edited the resulting file and entered incorrect data into one or more of the records. Any values entered for the length or number of decimals for a date or memo field are ignored, without generating an error.

Improper data type in subtotal expression.
Improper data type in subsubtotal expression.

Either a logical expression or memo field was specified as the basis for accumulating subtotals or sub-subtotals in a report form. The error message appears only when you try to run the report, not when you are creating or editing the form.

Index damaged. REINDEX should be done before using data. (114)

An attempt was made to open an index file that was damaged, usually by interrupting an INDEX or REINDEX command with ESC.

Index expression is too big (220 char maximum). (112)

An attempt was made to build an index based on a key expression longer than 220 characters. Note that it is the expression that specifies the index key, which may be 220 characters long; the combination of fields that make up the key itself may not exceed 100 characters.

Index file does not match database. (19)

The index opened with the data base in a USE command was based on a key expression that contains one or more fields not present in the data base. This can occur if you open an index with the wrong data base, or if you change the field names or types and forget to reconstruct the index afterward.

Index interrupted. Index will be deleted if not completed. (113)
Abort indexing? (Y/N)

An INDEX or REINDEX command was interrupted with ESC. You are given the choice to continue building the index or to abort the process, in which case the partially constructed index file is deleted.

Index is too big (100 char maximum). (23)

The fields that form the index key specified in an INDEX command exceed 100 characters in combined length. Note that the expression that specifies the index key may be 220 characters long.

Insert impossible. (Press SPACE)

An attempt was made to insert a new column into a report form, using CREATE REPORT or MODIFY REPORT, when the report already contained 24 columns.

Insufficient memory. (43)

An attempt was made to load dBASE III PLUS, access an external operating system command or program with a RUN command, or LOAD a binary module without enough RAM available. This error will occur if you have used the TEDIT or WP entries in CONFIG.DB to replace the MODIFY COMMAND editor or the memo field editor with an external editor and you try to access either editor without enough memory. This error may also occur if you specify more consecutive GETs between READ, CLEAR, or CLEAR GETS commands than are allowed (the default is 128), or if you try to RUN an external command that causes you to exceed the limit of 20 open DOS files (which will happen if many files are already open within dBASE III PLUS and you then try to load COMMAND.COM, your external program, and whatever files it requires).

Internal error: CMDSET( ): (66)
Internal error: Illegal opcode. (68)
Internal error: Unknown command code. (65)
Records do not balance (program error).
Too many merge steps.
Unassigned file no. (2)
Unknown SCEDIT( ) return code:

These messages all report errors that theoretically "can't happen." Usually they mean that the dBASE III PLUS program files have been damaged, so you should try recopying the non-copy-protected files from the master disk, or uninstalling and then reinstalling the program on your hard disk. In some cases, these errors may mean that your computer or operating system is not sufficiently compatible with the IBM PC to run dBASE III PLUS.

Internal error: EVAL work area overflow. (67)

An attempt was made to use an expression too complex for dBASE III PLUS to evaluate.

Invalid date. (Press SPACE) (81)

An attempt was made to enter an impossible date, such as 13/44/87, into a date variable. Pressing the space bar gives you another chance to enter the date correctly.

Invalid DIF Character. (118)
Invalid DIF File Header. (115)
Invalid DIF Type Indicator. (117)

An attempt was made to APPEND data from a DIF file that contains an invalid character (such as a non-ASCII character), a corrupted file header, or an invalid data type indicator. These problems can occur if the DIF file is damaged by a disk error or by a problem with the program that produced the DIF file.

Invalid DOS SET option. (99)

An attempt was made to SET a DOS option that does not exist.

Invalid function argument. (11)

One of the expressions entered as an argument (input) to a dBASE III PLUS function is the wrong data type or outside of the allowable range.

Invalid function name. (31)

An attempt was made to use a function name not recognized by dBASE III PLUS. This error can also occur where you expect "Syntax error," if you construct an incorrect expression with variable names and parentheses in such a way that dBASE III interprets the name of a variable as an intended function name (because it is followed by a pair of parentheses with one or more "inputs" in between).

Invalid index number. (106)

An attempt was made to specify an index number in a SET ORDER command that is outside the permissible range of 0 to 7 or higher than the actual number of indexes opened with the data base.

Invalid operator. (107)

An attempt was made to use an operator in a way that is not permitted; for example, with inappropriate data types.

Invalid printer port. (123)

An attempt was made to redirect output to a nonexistent printer port with a SET PRINTER TO command, either in a single-user system or to select a local printer from a network workstation.

Invalid printer redirection. (124)

An attempt was made to redirect output to a nonexistent network printer with a SET PRINTER TO \\ command.

Invalid SYLK File Dimension Bounds. (120)
Invalid SYLK File Format. (121)
Invalid SYLK File Header. (119)

An attempt was made to APPEND data from a SYLK file that contains data that is outside the boundaries of the file, has an unrecognizable data format, or has a corrupted file header. These problems can occur if the SYLK file is damaged by a disk error or by a problem with the program that produced the SYLK file.

^—Keyword not found. (86)

A word not recognized by dBASE III PLUS was used in one of the entries in CONFIG.DB.

Label file invalid. (54)

dBASE III PLUS cannot read the specified label form file, possibly because the disk has been damaged, or because you have named a file in your command that is not a dBASE III PLUS label form file.

Line exceeds maximum of 254 characters. (18)

A command line more than 254 characters long was entered into a program or format file.

Master catalog is empty. (149)

A CATALOG query clause was used in a SET CATALOG TO command (SET CATALOG TO ?) was executed, but the list of valid CATALOG files could not be displayed because the master catalog file, CATALOG.CAT, contained no records.

Maximum path length exceeded. (146)

The file search path in a SET PATH command has exceeded the maximum permissible length of 60 characters.

Maximum record length exceeded. (137)

Using either CREATE or MODIFY STRUCTURE, an attempt was made to add a new field to a data base structure or lengthen an existing field so that the total record length would exceed the maximum permissible length of 4,000 characters.

Maximum record length exceeded.—detected on field <*n*>.

See description of the "Illegal data length" messages.

Memory Variable file is invalid. (55)

dBASE III PLUS cannot read the specified memory variable file, possibly because the disk has been damaged, or because you have named a file in your command that is not a dBASE III PLUS memory variable file.

Mismatched DO WHILE and ENDDO. (96)

An ENDDO line was found in a program with no matching DO WHILE statement.

Network is busy. (148)

In a network system running under the dBASE Administrator, more tasks were initiated than the file server can handle. Under these circumstances, you may also get other seemingly unrelated or unreasonable error messages. If this error occurs, try to close any open data bases before you exit from dBASE III PLUS to minimize the chance that data will be lost.

No database is in USE. Enter file name: (52)

An attempt was made to execute a command that requires an open data base file when no data base is open in the currently selected work area. You may enter the file name and the command will resume, but you may not open an index with the file this way. You can also press ESC to cancel the command, open the data base and index(es) with USE and/or SET INDEX, and then type the original command again.

No fields to process. (47)

An attempt was made to use the SUM or AVERAGE command from the ASSIST menus on a data base with no numeric fields.

No fields were found to copy. (138)

A COPY command was executed with a FIELD list in effect (established with the SET FIELDS TO command) that did not include any fields from the currently selected data base.

No find. (14)

The index key value specified in a FIND or SEEK command was not found in the index. When a FIND or SEEK command fails to find the specified record, the EOF( ) function is set to .T. and FOUND( ) becomes .F.

No PARAMETER statement found. (93)

An attempt was made to pass parameters to a program or procedure that does not contain a PARAMETERS statement.

Not a character expression. (45)
Not a logical expression. (37)
Not a numeric expression. (27)

An attempt was made to use an expression of the wrong data type where the data type *must* be character, logical, or numeric; for example, attempting to SUM a character field or misstating the condition in a FOR or WHILE clause so that it is not a logical expression.

Not a dBASE database. (15)

The file specified in a USE command was not recognized as a dBASE III PLUS data base file, possibly because the disk has been damaged, or because you have named in the command a file that is not a dBASE III PLUS data base file.

Not a valid PFS file. (140)

The file specified in an IMPORT command was not recognized as a PFS data base file, possibly because the disk has been damaged, or because you have named a file in the command that was not created by PFS.

Not a valid QUERY file. (134)

The file specified in a SET FILTER TO FILE command was not recognized as a query file, possibly because the disk has been damaged, or because you have named in the command a file that is not a dBASE III PLUS query file.

Not a valid VIEW file. (127)

The file specified in a SET VIEW TO FILE command was not recognized as a view file, possibly because the disk has been damaged, or because you have named in the command a file that is not a dBASE III PLUS view file.

Not enough disk space for SORT.

The specified disk drive does not have room to accommodate both the temporary file used by the SORT command and the final sorted file. (This amounts to the size of the original file plus the size of the final sorted file.)

Not enough records to SORT.

The file specified in a SORT command does not have at least two records.

**** Not Found ** (82)**

The index key value specified in the FIND option of the BROWSE command was not found in the index. In this case, both the EOF( ) and FOUND( ) functions retain their previous values and the same set of records remains on the screen.

Not readable

A DIR command was used to list the data base files on a disk, and dBASE III PLUS was unable to read one of the files, possibly because the file was damaged by a disk error.

Not suspended. (101)

A RESUME command was issued when no command file was interrupted and suspended.

Numeric overflow (data was lost). (39)

An attempt was made to give a numeric field a value too large for the field to accommodate. When this occurs, dBASE III PLUS may display the field in exponential notation (although it cannot be edited in this form) or may replace the contents of the field with asterisks. This error can occur if you try to REPLACE a field with too large a value, or if you issue a TOTAL command that accumulates totals too large to fit in the field widths in the data base structure.

Operation with Logical field invalid. (90)
Operation with Memo field invalid. (34)

An attempt was made to perform an operation that is not permitted for the specified field type. For example, you cannot INDEX or SORT on a memo or logical field or use the value of a memo field in any expression (for example, testing the value in a FOR or WHILE clause, or attempting to display or collect the field with @ ... SAY ... GET).

Out of memory variable memory. (21)

An attempt was made to create a new memory variable when the existing variables already exceeded the amount of space allocated for memory variables (the default is 6000 bytes, which you may change with the MVARSIZ entry in CONFIG.DB).

Out of memory variable slots. (22)

An attempt was made to create more than a total of 256 memory variables.

^ — Out of range.

Too large a value was specified for one of the options in CONFIG.DB (for example, a number greater than 31 for MVARSIZ, the number of kilobytes of memory allocated for memory variables).

Position is off the screen. (30)

An attempt was made to use a row coordinate outside of the range 0 to 24 or a column coordinate outside of the range 0 to 79 in an @ ... SAY ... GET command, with output routed to the screen. This error commonly occurs if you use or adapt a program or format file that is designed to print a report on paper to display data on the screen.

Printer is either not connected or turned off. (126)

An output port was specified in a SET PRINTER TO command, with no peripheral device assigned to that port.

Printer not ready. (125)

An attempt was made to send output to the printer when the printer is not turned on or is off line. This error may occur if you do not redirect output to the correct port in a system with more than one printer.

Query not valid for this environment. (143)

The query file named in a SET FILTER TO FILE command contained references to fields not present in the data base(s) currently open. Usually, this is because the query file was created for use with a different data base or set of data bases.

Record is in use by another. (109)

In a network environment, an attempt was made to access a record that is currently locked by another user.

Record is not in index. (20)

A record number that is not present in the index file was used in a command (for example, GOTO, or a command with RECORD <*n*> as the scope). This can occur if records were added to a data base without opening the index in the USE command and the index was not rebuilt afterward.

Record is not locked. (130)

In a network environment, an attempt was made to update a record that was not first locked.

Record is out of range. (5)

A record number used in a command (an explicit GOTO or a command with RECORD *n* as the scope) is not present in the data base file. This error can occur when an index does not match the data base file and dBASE III PLUS attempts to position the record pointer at the nonexistent record corresponding to an index entry. These problems are commonly caused by rebooting or turning off the system without closing a data base file (and thereby updating the record count) after new records have been appended.

Record not inserted. (25)

This warning message is displayed if you exit from an INSERT command with ESC or CTRL-Q, and the record is not added to the file.

Records do not balance (program error).

See description of the "Internal error" messages.

Relation record is in use by others. (142)

In a network system, one workstation has opened two files and linked them with SET RELATION, a second workstation has used the RLOCK function to lock a record in the file accessed through the RELATION, and the first workstation has attempted to use a GOTO or SEEK command to position the record pointer in the main data base to the record linked to the locked record.

Report file invalid. (50)

dBASE III PLUS cannot read a report form file, possibly because the disk has been damaged, or because you have specified a file that is not a dBASE III PLUS report form file.

Structure invalid. (33)

An attempt was made to use the CREATE FROM command to create a new data base from an invalid structure-extended file. This can occur if the file was damaged by a disk error or if you have used MODIFY STRUCTURE to change the field names or types in the structure-extended file.

Syntax error. (10)

An expression or part of a command is constructed incorrectly. See Chapter 14 for more detailed information on how to diagnose and correct syntax errors.

Syntax error in contents expression.
Syntax error in field expression.
Syntax error in group expression.
Syntax error in subgroup expression.

One of the expressions used to specify the contents of a line in a label form, a column in a report form, or the field(s) on which to base the subtotal or sub-subtotal breaks in a report is incorrect. Because CREATE LABEL, MODIFY LABEL, CREATE REPORT, and MODIFY REPORT check for syntax errors as you create or edit a report or label form, these errors can only occur if the form was created or modified outside of dBASE III PLUS; if a field name or type was changed in the data base structure so that a formerly correct expression is no longer valid; or if a label or report form is used with a different data base that is missing one of the fields specified in the label form or that has a field with the same name but a different type than the one for which the form was designed.

Table is full. (105)

An attempt was made to place more than five binary modules into memory with the LOAD command.

Too many characters in REPORT.

An attempt was made to define a report form so complex that more than the maximum of 1440 bytes was required to store the form.

Too many files are open. (6)

An attempt was made to open more than the number of files permitted by the operating system. With no FILES entry in CONFIG.SYS, the default number of files is 3; this may be increased to 15 by including the command FILES = 20 in the CONFIG.SYS file present in the root directory of the disk from which the system is booted. The maximum refers to disk files of all types, not just data base files.

Too many indices. (28)

More than the maximum of seven index files were named in a USE or SET INDEX command.

Too many merge steps.

See description of the "Internal error" messages.

Too many sort key fields.

More than the maximum of ten fields were named in a SORT command.

^ — Truncated. (74)

A file name specified in CONFIG.DB (for example, in the TEDIT or WP option) is more than eight characters long. dBASE III PLUS truncates the name to the first eight characters.

Unable to load COMMAND.COM. (92)

An attempt was made to execute an external program or command with RUN or, with a TEDIT or WP entry in CONFIG.DB, to use an external word processor assigned to substitute for the standard dBASE III PLUS editor, but COMMAND.COM was not available. COMMAND.COM must be present in the root directory of the disk used to boot the system or in a subdirectory identified to the operating system with the MS-DOS SET COMSPEC command.

Unable to Lock. (129)

In a network environment, an attempt was made to lock a record using CTRL-O in one of the full-screen edit modes, but the record was already locked by another user.

Unable to Skip. (128)

In a network environment, an attempt was made to SKIP to a record that was locked by another user.

Unassigned file no. (2)

See description of the "Internal error" messages.

Unauthorized access level. (133)

In a dBASE III PLUS system with a PROTECT security system in effect, an attempt was made to access a field or file by a user with an access level for which permission has not been granted to carry out the requested operation on the specified data.

Unauthorized login. (132)

Three consecutive unsuccessful attempts were made to log into dBASE III PLUS with a PROTECT security system in effect.

Unbalanced parentheses. (8)

An expression does not have the same number of left and right parentheses. This error will also occur if you do not specify the same number of Start and End conditions in the Nest option of CREATE/MODIFY QUERY, since this command creates an expression containing parentheses.

Unknown function key. (104)

A function key name or number that does not exist on the keyboard was specified in a SET FUNCTION command.

Unknown SCEDIT( ) return code:

See description of the "Internal error" messages.

*** **Unrecognized command verb. (16)**

The first word in a command line is not one of the verbs recognized by dBASE III PLUS.

Unrecognized phrase/keyword in command. (36)

One of the clauses in a command begins with a word not recognized by dBASE III PLUS. This may occur when you leave out a required keyword (like FIELDS or WITH), so that the following word (often a field name) occurs where dBASE III PLUS expects the keyword that normally introduces the clause.

Unsupported path given. (136)

An attempt was made to specify the subdirectory one level up from the current subdirectory as "..\" in a CREATE command. This notation is permitted in other dBASE III PLUS commands.

Unterminated string. (35)

The ending delimiter for a character string was omitted.

Valid only in programs. (95)

An attempt was made to use a command at the dot prompt that is permitted only in dBASE III PLUS programs, such as SUSPEND, DO CASE, DO WHILE, or any of the other components of the dBASE III PLUS programming structures.

Variable not found. (12)

A command specified a field name not found in the current data base or a memory variable name that is not one of the currently active memory variables.

**** WARNING ** Data will probably be lost. Confirm (Y/N) (70)**

The "Abort" option was selected when a command generated a "Disk full when writing file" error message. See description of the "Disk full" error message.

Wrong number of parameters. (94)

The number of parameters specified in the DO command that called a program or procedure did not match the number specified in the PARAMETERS statement in the called program or procedure.

Error Messages by ERROR( ) Number

1 File does not exist.
2 Unassigned file no.
3 File is already open.
4 End of file encountered.
5 Record is out of range.
6 Too many files are open.
7 File already exists.
8 Unbalanced parentheses.
9 Data type mismatch.
10 Syntax error.
11 Invalid function argument.
12 Variable not found.
13 ALIAS not found.
14 No find.
15 Not a dBASE database.
16 *** Unrecognized command verb.
17 Cannot select requested database.
18 Line exceeds maximum of 254 characters.
19 Index file does not match database.
20 Record is not in index.
21 Out of memory variable memory.
22 Out of memory variable slots.
23 Index is too big (100 char maximum).
24 ALIAS name already in use.
25 Record not inserted.
26 Database is not indexed.
27 Not a numeric expression.
28 Too many indices.
29 File is not accessible.
30 Position is off the screen.
31 Invalid function name.
33 Structure invalid.
34 Operation with Memo field invalid.
35 Unterminated string.
36 Unrecognized phrase/keyword in command.
37 Not a Logical expression.
38 Beginning of file encountered.
39 Numeric overflow (data was lost).
41 .DBT file cannot be opened.

42 CONTINUE without LOCATE.

43 Insufficient memory.

44 Cyclic relation.

45 Not a character expression.

46 Illegal value.

47 No fields to process.

48 Field not found.

50 Report file invalid.

51 End-of-file or error on keyboard input.

52 No database is in USE. Enter file name:

53 There are no files of the type requested on this drive.

54 Label file invalid.

55 Memory Variable file is invalid.

56 Disk full when writing file - <file name>.

57 *** Execution error on CHR( ) : Out of range.

58 *** Execution error on LOG( ) : Zero or negative.

59 *** Execution error on SPACE( ) : Too large.

60 *** Execution error on SPACE( ) : Negative.

61 *** Execution error on SQRT( ) : Negative.

62 *** Execution error on SUBSTR( ) : Start point out of range.

63 *** Execution error on STR( ) : Out of range.

65 Internal error: Unknown command code.

66 Internal error: CMDSET( ):

67 Internal error: EVAL work area overflow.

68 Internal error: Illegal opcode.

70 ** WARNING ** Data will probably be lost. Confirm (Y/N)

72 ALTERNATE could not be opened.

73 ^^Expected ON or OFF.

74 ^—Truncated.

76 *** Execution error on − : concatenated string too large.

77 *** Execution error on + : concatenated string too large.

78 *** Execution error on ^ or ** : negative base, fractional exponent.

79 *** Execution error on STORE( ): String too large.

81 Invalid date. (Press SPACE)

82 ** Not Found **

86 ^—Keyword not found.

87 *** Execution error on NDX( ) : Invalid index number.

88 *** Execution error on REPLICATE( ) : String too large.

89 Cannot erase a file which is open.

90 Operation with Logical field invalid.

91 File was not LOADed.

92 Unable to load COMMAND.COM.
93 No PARAMETER statement found.
94 Wrong number of parameters.
95 Valid only in programs.
96 Mismatched DO WHILE and ENDDO.
99 Invalid DOS SET option.
101 Not suspended.
102 *** Execution error on STUFF( ) : String too large.
103 DO's nested too deep.
104 Unknown function key.
105 Table is full.
106 Invalid index number.
107 Invalid operator.
108 File is in use by another.
109 Record is in use by another.
110 Exclusive use on database is required.
111 Cannot write to read only file.
112 Index expression is too big (220 char maximum).
113 Index interrupted. Index will be deleted if not completed.
114 Index damaged. REINDEX should be done before using data.
115 Invalid DIF File Header.
117 Invalid DIF Type Indicator.
118 Invalid DIF Character.
119 Invalid SYLK File Header.
120 Invalid SYLK File Dimension Bounds.
121 Invalid SYLK File Format.
122 Data Catalog has not been established.
123 Invalid printer port.
124 Invalid printer redirection.
125 Printer not ready.
126 Printer is either not connected or turned off.
127 Not a valid VIEW file.
128 Unable to Skip.
129 Unable to Lock.
130 Record is not locked.
131 Database is encrypted.
132 Unauthorized login.
133 Unauthorized access level.
134 Not a valid QUERY file.
136 Unsupported path given.
137 Maximum record length exceeded—detected on field <*n*>.

138 No fields were found to copy.
139 Cannot JOIN a file with itself.
140 Not a PFS file.
141 Fields list too complicated.
142 Relation record is in use by others.
143 Query not valid for this environment.
146 Maximum path length exceeded.
147 Cannot append in column order.
148 Network server busy.
149 Master catalog is empty.

G

dBASE III PLUS ANOMALIES

The anomalies described in this appendix are present in dBASE III PLUS version 1.00; where noted, they have been corrected in later releases of the software. An up-to-date listing of anomalies and "work-arounds" (ways to avoid or circumvent the problems) may be found in the monthly *TechNotes* publication, available by subscription from Ashton-Tate, and in the Ashton-Tate on-line forum accessed through the CompuServe Information Service.

Ashton-Tate defines the term "anomaly" as any failure of the dBASE III PLUS software to behave as might reasonably be inferred from the documentation. Some examples cited in *TechNotes* include commands or functions that do not ever execute as described in the manual, commands or functions that do not execute as described under certain conditions, and commands or functions which fail at the boundaries of the permissible range of data.

&

A macro followed by a space and left parenthesis will result in the "*** Unrecognized command verb" error message. This occurs most often when the macro is used to store the first portion of a command, which is followed by an algebraic expression, all or part of which is surrounded by parentheses. Placing a period (.) after the name of the macro variable solves this problem.

??

When used to display a memo field from within a program, this command produces the correct display the first time it is used. Subsequent ?? commands result in all lines of the memo field except the first being shifted to the right.

@ ... CLEAR TO

@ ... CLEAR TO cannot be used to clear a portion of a single line on the screen; the command is simply ignored. Instead, you can use @ ... SAY to display a character string consisting of the appropriate number of blank spaces, specified either as an explicit character string or by using the SPACE function. This problem has been corrected in version 1.1.

@ ... SAY ... GET

The @C and @X functions always display CR next to a positive number and DB next to a negative number. In an accounting application that requires a positive number to be identified as a debit, these functions cannot be used; you must instead use an IF or DO CASE structure to test the value of the variable and supply the appropriate suffix.

When an @ ... SAY ... GET command includes a RANGE clause, and data outside of the range is entered, pressing the space bar allows the user to reenter the data but does not clear the error message. This has been corrected in version 1.1.

An @ <*row*>, <*column*> command will always clear the specified line on the screen, even if you have used SET DEVICE TO PRINT to direct output to the printer. This has been corrected in version 1.1.

If a program calls another program that creates a PRIVATE memory variable and displays the variable with an @ ... SAY ... GET command, a READ command in the calling program does not allow input into that variable (the GET is ignored). If an @ ... SAY command was used prior to the READ to display the value of the DATE() (current date) function, and if the PICTURE in the GET command intended to collect the PRIVATE variable happened to constitute valid input into the variable (for example, a "99" PICTURE for a numeric variable), all subsequent PICTURE clauses of this type will also be interpreted literally. The only solution is to exit and reload dBASE III PLUS.

The @(function, which surrounds negative numbers with parentheses, displays the field using its full width within the parentheses, filled out with leading spaces. If the @(function is combined with @B, which left-justifies numeric fields, to form the function @(B, the extra spaces are displayed next to the right parenthesis.

If you use the "Y" picture to collect a logical field in a blank record, the field value will be displayed as "Y" but if the user presses RETURN to accept what appears to be a default value, the field will remain blank (its value will remain undefined) and will be interpreted as containing a value of .F. You can avoid this problem by using a REPLACE command to assign the field a default value prior to the @ ... SAY ... GET command.

If the first character of a PICTURE clause used in an @ ... SAY ... GET command that collects a numeric field or memory variable is a literal character rather than an entered digit, pressing RETURN to leave the existing value unchanged will result in resetting the variable to 0.

If you have SET DELIMITERS ON, issuing an @ ... SAY ... GET command that positions the first character of the variable to be collected in column 79 on the screen may cause the system to hang up, requiring you to reboot or turn off the computer.

If you use @ ... SAY ... GET to position data on row 0 of the screen with SCOREBOARD ON and STATUS OFF, the data will not scroll off the top of the screen as new data is displayed. You can correct the display with CLEAR, @ 0,0, SET STATUS, or SET SCOREBOARD, all of which clear line 0 completely.

When @ ... SAY is used to send control codes to the printer, the characters are counted as part of the line of data, although they are not printed on the page. Column coordinates for the data to be printed must be adjusted to take this spacing error into account.

APPEND

If PGUP is used to switch from APPENDing new records to editing previously entered records, the records are displayed in sequential, not indexed, order, even if an index is open. However, if a key field is edited, the index is updated to reflect the change.

If APPEND FROM is used to add records to a data base from an SDF file that contains ASCII zeroes, all of the data in the fields following the zero in each record will be lost. If the TYPE command is used to display the contents of such a file, no data beyond the zeroes will be displayed.

Attempting to use APPEND FROM to read records from a file that has a name exactly eight characters long and no extension will result in the "File does not exist" error message. To avoid this problem, you can rename the file to add an extension or to shorten the name and then terminate the file name in the APPEND FROM command with two periods.

If CTRL-W or CTRL-END is used to exit from APPEND with the cursor in the first field of a new blank record, a blank record will be written to the file. If you have SET CARRY ON, the new record will be a duplicate of the last record in the file. These keys may safely be used to exit from APPEND with the cursor still in the last record you wish to add to the file. With a blank record displayed on the screen, use RETURN or ESC instead.

In a network system, if one workstation is accessing a record in an indexed file, and another workstation APPENDs a record that becomes the next positional record in the index, a SKIP command executed from the first workstation will cause the EOF() function to evaluate as .T. You can avoid this problem by using GOTO RECNO() to reposition the record pointer in the index (after a DISPLAY or other command to inform the user of the change in key value) before the SKIP command.

In a network system, if two workstations add records to the same file with APPEND or APPEND FROM, the index file will be corrupted. You can avoid this problem by locking the entire file with FLOCK or by using APPEND BLANK and then filling in the data with REPLACE commands.

ASSIST

If you have SET INTENSITY OFF or altered the default display colors with SET COLOR, the only way to determine which option is highlighted in the pull-down menus used by ASSIST and the full-screen CREATE/MODIFY editors is to monitor the option section of the status bar and the explanation displayed on the bottom line of the screen. Depending on the colors selected, you may be able to determine which main menu bar option (SETUP, POSITION, etc.) is selected. These menu-driven commands depend on the dual intensity display but do not automatically SET the necessary display attributes when they are invoked.

It is impossible to specify a condition through the ASSIST menus that contains a character string consisting only of blank spaces. Since character strings are entered without quotes, an attempt to enter one or more blank spaces into a condition such as CITY = " " results in the condition CITY = "", which is always .T.

Editing a record found using the LOCATE command disables the CONTINUE option, which is no longer highlighted on the Position menu, and cannot be selected. You can still type CONTINUE at the dot prompt to find the next record that satisfies the condition in the LOCATE command. This has been corrected in version 1.1.

Executing a LOCATE command with no FOR or WHILE condition positions the record pointer at the top of the file, with no error message, but a subsequent CONTINUE results in the "CONTINUE without LOCATE" error message.

Choosing a disk drive from a list of available drives (for example, in specifying the file to open) makes that drive the default drive.

If you have SET CATALOG OFF, the default extension is assigned to all files created through ASSIST, even if the user specifies a different extension. With a CATALOG open, this problem does not occur.

BROWSE

When records are added to a data base in BROWSE and some of the fields are left blank, using PGDN to advance to the next record results in the apparent disappearance of the previous entry. The new records are in fact added to the file, as you can tell from the number of records displayed in the status bar if you have SET STATUS ON. You can avoid this problem by using the DOWN-ARROW instead of PGDN to complete each new record and go on to the next.

The dBASE III PLUS documentation states that the BROWSE NOMENU option prevents the user from calling up the special option menu by pressing CTRL-HOME, whereas in fact it prevents access to the help menu invoked by pressing F1.

In version 1.1, the following command sequence will cause the computer to hang up, requiring you to reboot or turn the system off:

```
USE <file1>
SELECT 2
USE <file2>
EDIT
CLOSE DATA BASES or CLOSE ALL or CLEAR ALL or USE
USE <file1>
BROWSE
```

The problem only occurs if a record was actually changed during the EDIT.

CALL

Misspelling the WITH keyword in a CALL command will cause the computer to hang up, requiring you to reboot or turn the system off. This has been corrected in version 1.1.

CHR

The CHR function cannot be used to send the character with ASCII code 26 (the DOS end-of-file marker) to a printer. With some printers, you can avoid this problem by sending the character with ASCII code 154 (26 + 128) instead, but not all printers interpret these two codes as being identical.

CONFIG.DB

The following options may not be set from the CONFIG.DB file: DATE, DOHISTORY, FIXED, MESSAGE, ODOMETER, PRINTER, and TITLE. These must be SET from the dot prompt or from within a program.

Attempting to change the data field delimiters with DELIMITERS = *delimiters* does not result in an error message, but the command is ignored, and the standard colons are used as delimiters. This has been corrected in version 1.1.

If you turn off the recording of commands in history with HISTORY = OFF, the command has the desired effect, but the status of this option is displayed as ON if you LIST STATUS or DISPLAY STATUS. Using SET HISTORY OFF from the dot prompt corrects the display.

If you specify a prompt 20 characters long or longer in a PROMPT command, the "^--- truncated" error message results, the prompt is truncated to 20 characters, and memory problems may occur. In version 1.1, the prompt is still truncated to 20 characters, and the error message is still displayed, but no memory corruption occurs.

The MAXMEM command does not in fact affect the amount of memory dBASE III PLUS releases when executing an external program or command with the RUN command. However, an error message will result if a value outside the allowable range of 200 to 720 is specified.

COPY

In a network system, the COPY command unlocks a record locked with the RLOCK function.

CREATE

Although the underscore (_) is the only punctuation mark permitted in a dBASE III PLUS file name, the CREATE command does not test the file name you specify to ensure that it conforms to this rule. If you later use a file name containing a punctuation mark other than an underscore in an <*alias*> → <*field name*> reference, a "Syntax error" message will result.

If you attempt to CREATE a data base file with no extension by specifying the first part of the file name followed by a period, the computer will hang up when you save the structure, requiring you to reboot or turn the system off. You can avoid this problem by typing two periods to terminate the file name.

CREATE/MODIFY SCREEN

If you add a new field to an existing data base while defining a screen format, the field is created as a character field with length 1. When you modify the length or type of several new fields, the entire data base is appended into the new structure after each change, as if you had exited from MODIFY STRUCTURE. This can take a long time in a large file. You can avoid this problem by using MODIFY STRUCTURE to add all of the new fields or by creating a temporary copy of the structure before using CREATE/MODIFY screen.

If you create a data base using CREATE SCREEN, you cannot define a numeric field with a length of 1.

Pressing CTRL-T with the cursor immediately to the left of a special character such as !, ?, or @ will cause the computer to hang up, requiring you to reboot or turn the system off. This has been corrected in version 1.1.

CREATE/MODIFY screen does not provide a command for deleting a line or box once it has been created.

If you SET STATUS ON and create a box that ends in column 79, in row 22 or lower, the box will be split in two at row 22. To avoid this problem, SET STATUS OFF, as you would have to do in any case when using a format file that uses lines 22 through 24, before you CREATE or MODIFY SCREEN.

If you press RETURN to add blank lines, and the cursor moves below the status bar, you must move the cursor back up to make it visible again. In version 1.1, the cursor will not move below the status bar; instead, the screen scrolls up.

CREATE/MODIFY VIEW

You cannot remove a FILTER condition from a view from the CREATE/MODIFY VIEW editor. The only way to delete a FILTER condition from a view is to open the view, cancel the FILTER with SET FILTER TO, and then recreate the view with CREATE VIEW FROM ENVIRONMENT.

You cannot access files from other subdirectories using CREATE VIEW FROM ENVIRONMENT. Attempting to use such a view results in the "ALIAS name already in use" error message.

Dates

Blank dates may not be treated correctly in date comparison operations. A logical expression comparing two dates will yield .F. if one of the dates is blank, as if a blank date is neither earlier nor later than any non-blank date. Also, indexing on a date field results in blank dates falling after all other dates. You can avoid these problems by converting dates to character strings in year/month/day order for all operations involving date comparisons if your files might contain blank dates. (See Chapter 23 for a detailed discussion of date formatting options.)

When a condition used in a FOR or WHILE clause includes a constant date expressed by using the CTOD function, if the input to the CTOD function is not actually a character string representation of a true date, no error message will result, and the expression will be interpreted as a blank date.

DO CASE

If the DO CASE statement is inadvertently omitted, no error message results, but the commands between the first CASE and the ENDCASE are never executed. If the ENDCASE is omitted, the program terminates when the first true CASE is completed.

Exponentiation

Using the ** or ^ operator to square a number with many decimal places may cause the computer to hang up, requiring you to reboot or turn the system off. You can avoid the problem by multiplying the number by itself or using the EXP and LOG functions instead.

EXPORT

In a network system, the EXPORT command unlocks a record locked with the RLOCK function.

FIND

A FIND command with a memory variable, expanded as a macro, as its object, may fail to find a matching record if the command line contains a comment, and if the variable contains only a partial key value. (However, if the key includes a space, and the variable consists of all the characters up to the space, the FIND will succeed.) You can avoid this problem by placing the comment marker (&&) immediately following the name of the variable in the FIND command (with no separating space), although this greatly reduces the readability of the comment. This has been corrected in version 1.1.

FOUND( )

If you use FIND or SEEK to search for a record with a non-unique key with DELETED ON, and the first of the records that share the specified key value is deleted, the correct record will be found, but FOUND( ) will have the value .F. However, EOF( ) will be .F., so you can substitute IF .NOT. EOF( ) for IF FOUND( ) in your test for the outcome of the FIND or SEEK. This has been corrected in version 1.1.

HELP

If the HELP.DBS file is missing, the "Help text not found" error message does not remain on the screen long enough to be read easily. This has been corrected in version 1.1, which prompts you to "Press any key to continue."

INDEX

Indexing on a date field results in blank dates falling after all other dates rather than before. The only way to circumvent this problem is to convert the date to a character string in year/month/day order for use as the index key. (See Chapter 23 for a detailed discussion of date formatting options.)

If you SET CENTURY ON and build an index based on a date field converted to characters with the DTOC function, subsequent attempts to BROWSE, GOTO, or EDIT records will result in a "Record not in index" error message. This has been corrected in version 1.1.

If a data base is ZAPped or PACKed without an index open and records are then added to the file using one of the old index files, no error message is displayed, but the new records may not be accessible. The solution is to rebuild the index or ZAP or PACK with the index open.

An INDEX or REINDEX command in which the combined length of the key expression and the index file path name is longer than 100 characters may result in the "File is not accessible" error message and damage to the index file(s) that are open, especially in a data base with a large number of records. This has been corrected in version 1.1.

In some cases, if the index key expression contains a combination of character fields, numeric fields converted to characters with the STR function, and date fields converted to characters with the DTOC function, the resulting index may be corrupted and will not be updated properly by subsequent editing or REPLACE commands. This has been corrected in version 1.1.

In a network system, if you SET EXCLUSIVE OFF and open a data base with two indexes, one of the indexes may become corrupted. This has been corrected in version 1.1.

In a network system running under PC-NET, attempting to use multiple indexes with a data base containing more than about 7,000 records may cause the computer to hang up, requiring you to reboot or turn the system off. This has been corrected in version 1.1.

INKEY

The INKEY function cannot be used to detect the LEFT-ARROW key. In version 1.0, if you have SET ESCAPE OFF, INKEY evaluates to 19 when the user presses LEFT-ARROW, but with ESCAPE ON, it suspends program execution, just the equivalent cursor movement key CTRL-S. In version 1.1, it suspends execution regardless of the status of the ESCAPE option.

INPUT

If you SET ESCAPE OFF, pressing ESC in response to an INPUT command will cause the computer to hang up, requiring you to reboot or turn the system off. This has been corrected in version 1.1.

INSERT

If CTRL-W or CTRL-END is used to exit from INSERT with the cursor in the first field of a new blank record, a blank record is written to the file. If you have SET CARRY ON, the new record will be a duplicate of the last record in the file. These keys may safely be used to exit from INSERT with the cursor still in the last record you wish to add to the file. When a blank record is displayed on the screen, use RETURN or ESC instead.

If PGDN is used to exit from INSERT, and you have SET CARRY ON, the new record will contain data from the next record instead of the previous record. This has been corrected in version 1.1.

LIST

A LIST or DISPLAY TO PRINT command will not print the last line of data until another line is sent to the printer (either through dBASE III PLUS or by pressing the printer's LINE FEED button. This has been corrected in version 1.1; however, in this version, the extra RETURN sent to the printer is also displayed on the screen, resulting in an extra blank line.

MEMO FIELDS

Memo fields from data bases in a work area other than the current work area cannot be accessed using the standard <*alias*> → <*field name*> notation. The attempt results in an "Unrecognized phrase/keyword in command" error message.

Memo fields cannot be included in a file created by a JOIN command. An attempt to include a memo field in the FIELDS clause results in the "Operation with Memo field invalid" error message.

Attempting to display a memo field together with several other fields will result in incorrect formatting of the memo field if the fields displayed before the memo field are so long that there is not enough room to fit the first line of the memo field on the same line using the memo field display width established with SET MEMOWIDTH.

In a network system, if two workstations edit memo fields from the same data base (but associated with different records), the memo file will be corrupted. You can avoid this problem by opening the data base in EXCLUSIVE mode.

MIN

The MIN( ) function will result in a numeric overflow if either of the two inputs is negative, and they are of different lengths. This has been corrected in version 1.1.

MODIFY REPORT

If an existing report form is edited, editing the expression that specifies the contents of a column whose width was defined as narrower than the contents of the column will cause the column width to revert to the default, and you must reenter the desired width.

Selecting the Contents option and then pressing RETURN again without entering an expression to specify the column contents will add an empty column to the report form. If you do not notice and delete this column, no error message will be displayed, but an attempt to run the report will result in the "Syntax error in field expression" error message.

MODIFY STRUCTURE

In a data base with many fields, changing field types in MODIFY STRUCTURE (or using APPEND FROM to append records from a file in which corresponding fields are of different data types) may cause the system to hang up, return to DOS, or display a seemingly unrelated error message.

In a network system, if the current directory is the root directory, the MODIFY STRUCTURE command will result in the "NET 803: Network path not found" error message, and all of the records will be lost. This has been corrected in version 1.1.

Numeric Accuracy

Numbers created as the result of calculations that are too large for all digits to be displayed are shown in exponential notation. If the data thus displayed was placed in a data base field with REPLACE, you cannot edit the field and retain the value.

ON ERROR

In a network system, if you have SET TALK ON and are using ON ERROR to detect and respond to errors, the command specified in the ON ERROR statement will not be executed if a LOCATE command generates an error (for example, because it attempts to access a record locked by another user). If you SET TALK OFF, the command in the ON ERROR statement is executed in response to the error.

PROTECT

On a network system, running the ACCESS program from a subdirectory other than the one on which the Administrator is located will bypass the log-in screen, because the DBSYSTEM.DB file that stores the password information is always located in the Administrator subdirectory of the file server. A user who enters the program this way will be given an ACCESS() level of 0, but will not be able to access files and fields above his or her file and field access level. To avoid this problem, you can run ACCESS with the default drive set to the drive containing the Administrator, and specify the user's drive in the ACCESS command.

PROTECT sometimes adds end-of-file characters while encrypting a data base file. To avoid this problem, you can COPY the STRUCTURE of the original data base file, encrypt the new empty data base, and then APPEND FROM the original file. This has been corrected in version 1.1.

If you attempt to encrypt a data base file that has already been encrypted, and then confirm your intention to overwrite the existing CRP file, the PROTECT program will reset the file and field access privileges to the defaults, rather than to conform to those in the previously created CRP file.

If the last character of a password is "Y", and the user types "I" instead, the Administrator will accept the password and entry will be granted.

RANGE

If a numeric expression rather than a constant is used to specify the upper or lower boundary in a RANGE clause, problems with numeric accuracy and round-off errors may result in an error message if the user enters a value exactly equal to one of the boundaries of the range. You can avoid this problem by using a slightly different boundary value, or by converting the expression to a string with the STR function and then converting that character string back to a numeric value with the VAL function.

READKEY( )

If you exit from a full-screen edit mode with CTRL-W or CTRL-END, READKEY( ) will have the value 270, even if you have altered one of the variables on the screen (in which case READKEY( ) should have the value 14). If you exit with ESC or CTRL-Q, READKEY() will always have the value 12.

REINDEX

A SET INDEX TO command, followed by REINDEX, may result in the "File is not accessible" error message, or a subsequent GOTO command may result in the "Record is not in index" error message. This has been corrected in version 1.1.

If you SET TALK OFF and REINDEX a large data base, the "File is not accessible" error message may result, and subsequent attempts to open the index may result in the "Index damaged. REINDEX should be done before using data" error message. You may be able to avoid this problem if you SET TALK ON before you REINDEX. This has been corrected in version 1.1.

REPLACE

If a numeric field contains digits after the decimal point, a REPLACE command can assign this field an integer value larger than could be entered into the field in any full-screen edit mode, up to the full field width; that is, numeric digits may overwrite the decimal point and the following digits.

In a network system running under PC-NET, if you open a data base with two indexes that have key expressions of different lengths and SET EXCLUSIVE OFF, a REPLACE command on a non-key field may cause the computer to hang up, requiring you to reboot or turn the system off. This has been corrected in version 1.1.

REPORT FORM

In a report form that prints more than 255 columns of data, the page title will not be printed correctly. If the page width and left margin differ by exactly 256, dBASE III PLUS may skip printing the page title. If the line width is greater than 256, the page title is printed in a narrow column, left-justified on the page.

Printing a report form defined with the Plain Page option from within a DO ... WHILE loop with NOEJECT in the REPORT FORM command will cause the computer to hang up on the second pass through the loop, requiring you to reboot or turn the system off. You can avoid this problem by placing any DISPLAY or LIST command before the REPORT FORM command in the DO ... WHILE loop.

RETRY

If an ON ERROR command invokes a RETRY command, a truncated form of the command line whose execution is repeated may be executed if the command crosses a 512-character boundary, counting characters from the beginning of the program file. You can avoid this problem by inserting spaces in the command file to force the command into the next 512-byte block.

RUN/!

Under the Novell network, using a RUN command to access an external program or operating system command will close all files unless you have used the Novell EOJOFF utility to reconfigure the network software before entering dBASE III PLUS.

In a network system, a RUN command issued from a workstation that has locked a record with the RLOCK () function will unlock the record and permit another user to lock and edit it, although DISPLAY STATUS will still display the record lock. Only one of the users' changes will actually be saved on disk.

SAVE

A syntactically incorrect SAVE command will generate an error message, but fail to close the memory variable file, and a subsequent SAVE command that specifies the same file name will result in the "File is already open" error message. The only way to close the file is to exit from dBASE III PLUS. This has been corrected in version 1.1.

SET CARRY

If the last record in a data base with memo fields contains entries in one or more of these fields, the text will be carried over to new records added to the file with APPEND or INSERT after you have SET CARRY ON.

SET CATALOG

An attempt to open a CATALOG with the maximum number of files already open will delete all CATALOG entries except those that refer to files that were open when the SET CATALOG command was executed.

If you specify a file name twelve characters long or longer in a SET CATALOG command, the computer may hang up, requiring you to reboot or turn the system off. This has been corrected in version 1.1, which truncates the file name to eight characters.

If you SET PATH to the root directory of any drive in the system, and then attempt to create a CATALOG in any directory other than the default directory, the "File is not accessible" error message will result.

SET COLOR

If you have used SET COLOR to change the default display colors, there is no way to determine which option is highlighted in the menus used by ASSIST, BROWSE, or any of the full-screen CREATE/MODIFY editors, except by monitoring the option numbers in the status bar and the descriptions on line 24 of the screen. All of these commands depend on the use of standard inverse video for the foreground color, but do not force it to be turned on.

If you issue a SET COLOR command with SCOREBOARD ON and STATUS OFF, the right half of line 0 (the scoreboard area) will immediately take on the new display colors, and the left half will not even when the display is scrolled. You can correct the display with CLEAR, @ 0,0, SET STATUS, or SET SCOREBOARD, all of which clear line 0 completely.

The SET COLOR TO N, command will result in displaying black characters on a black background, even

SET DATE

There is no CONFIG.DB equivalent for SET DATE.

SET DELETED

SET DELETED does not automatically reposition the record pointer to the next non-deleted record. The current record will therefore be included in the group of records processed, even if it is marked for deletion. This is because only commands that reposition the data base take the DELETED option into account. You can solve this problem by following the SET DELETED command with any command that repositions the data base, such as GOTO TOP or GOTO RECNO( ).

SET DELIMITERS

The CONFIG.DB equivalent, DELIMITERS = *delimiters*, generates no error message but has no effect. This has been corrected in version 1.1.

SET DOHISTORY

There is no CONFIG.DB equivalent for SET DOHISTORY.

If you have SET DOHISTORY ON and SET HISTORY to a large number, executing the same commands many times (about 30,000) may result in a seemingly unrelated error message such as "Illegal opcode" or it may cause the computer to hang up, requiring you to reboot or turn the system off.

SET ESCAPE

If you have SET ESCAPE OFF, dBASE III PLUS also ignores CTRL-S. However, CTRL-NUMLOCK may still be used to pause a long listing.

SET FILTER

SET FILTER does not automatically reposition the record pointer to the next record that matches the specified condition. The current record will therefore be included in the group of records processed, even if it does not satisfy the condition. This is because only commands that reposition the data base take the FILTER into account. You can solve this problem by following the SET FILTER command with any command that repositions the record pointer, such as GOTO TOP or GOTO RECNO( ).

If none of the records in the current data base satisfies the condition in a SET FILTER command, a GOTO BOTTOM command will set both EOF( ) and BOF( ) functions to .T. Cancelling the FILTER does not reset these functions, but GOTO TOP will.

If the condition in a SET FILTER command executed from within a program includes memory variables initialized as PRIVATE in that program, subsequent commands issued from the dot prompt may either ignore the FILTER or, with more complex FILTER conditions, result in the "Internal error: EVAL work area overflow" error message. You can avoid this problem by using PUBLIC variables in the FILTER condition, or by cancelling the FILTER from within the program and reestablishing it at the dot prompt.

In a network system, if you SET EXCLUSIVE OFF, open a data base file without any indexes, SET a FILTER, and EDIT records, moving beyond the last record that satisfies the FILTER condition will cause the computer to hang up, requiring you to reboot or turn the system off. You can avoid this problem by opening the file in EXCLUSIVE mode or with an index.

SET FIXED

There is no CONFIG.DB equivalent for SET FIXED.

SET FORMAT

If you open a format file before you open the data base it refers to, it is impossible to close the format file, except by exiting from dBASE III PLUS. An attempt to edit the format file with MODIFY COMMAND will result in the "File is already open" error message. This has been corrected in version 1.1.

SET FUNCTION

If you assign a string of more than three characters to a function key with SET FUNCTION TO, and then assign a new, longer meaning to the same function key, subsequent ACCEPT and INPUT commands may display a portion of the new function key definition as part of the prompt, and these characters may be incorporated into the variables created by these commands, regardless of the user's input. This has been corrected in version 1.1.

SET INTENSITY

If you have SET INTENSITY OFF, there is no way to determine which option is highlighted in the menus used by ASSIST, BROWSE, or any of the full-screen CREATE/MODIFY editors, except by monitoring the option numbers in the status bar and the descriptions on line 24 of the screen. All of these commands depend on the dual intensity display but do not force it to be turned on.

SET HELP

If you have SET HELP ON, responding Y to the offer of help after an error in any of the SET commands causes dBASE III PLUS to display the help screen describing the full-screen SET command rather than the command that generated the error.

SET HISTORY

If you SET HISTORY to a number greater than 20, DISPLAY HISTORY will result in the "Press any key to continue..." message at irregular intervals, and more often than once per screenful of commands.

SET MEMOWIDTH

The dBASE III PLUS manual states that the lower limit for MEMOWIDTH is eight, whereas it is actually five. However, a display width of fewer than eight characters can only be established with an entry in CONFIG.DB, not by typing a SET MEMOWIDTH command at the dot prompt.

An attempt to SET MEMOWIDTH to a value greater than 255 will result in a width equal to the remainder that results when the specified value is divided by 256 (for example, 10 if you SET MEMOWIDTH TO 266).

SET MESSAGE

There is no CONFIG.DB equivalent for SET MESSAGE.

An attempt to SET MESSAGE to a character string longer than 79 characters does not result in an error message, but only the first 79 characters will be displayed.

SET ODOMETER

There is no CONFIG.DB equivalent for SET ODOMETER.

SET ORDER

SET ORDER does not automatically reposition the record pointer to the index entry in the newly selected index that corresponds to the current record. You must therefore follow the SET ORDER command with a command that repositions the record pointer. If the record pointer is positioned at a valid record, you can use GOTO RECNO( ). If the data base is positioned at the end-of-file, RECNO( ) has a value one greater than the total number of records in the file, and GOTO RECNO( ) would result in a "Record is out of range" error message, so you must use GOTO RECCOUNT( ) instead.

SET PATH

If you have specified a directory search path with SET PATH and SET SAFETY ON, the COPY, CREATE, INDEX, JOIN, SAVE, and SORT commands search the path for files of the same name as the file to be created by the command and request confirmation before executing the command. However, the resulting files, together with all other new files you create, are written into the current subdirectory if you do not specify the full path name, so there is no danger of overwriting the file found through the search path.

If you have SET PATH TO ... (the parent directory of the current subdirectory), MODIFY STRUCTURE will appear to work, but when you save the new structure, the computer will hang up, requiring you to reboot or turn the system off, and all the records in the file will be lost.

SET PRINTER

There is no CONFIG.DB equivalent for SET PRINTER.

In a system with a serial printer, this command—and any subsequent attempts to print—will generate a "Printer not ready" error message, even if the printer is on line and the communications parameters have been set properly. With some combinations of computer and printer, there is no way to solve this problem. In some systems, using the MODE command to initialize the printer and redirect output (rather than the SET PRINTER TO) before entering dBASE III PLUS will solve the problem. In some systems, repeating the MODE commands with RUN from within dBASE III PLUS solves the problem. Sometimes an error-trapping routine that executes a RETRY message will enable the system to print to a serial printer. This has been corrected in version 1.1.

A SET PRINTER TO command that does not name the printer port prevents any output from being sent to the printer. You can correct this problem by typing the correct SET PRINTER TO <DOS device name> command.

SET RELATION

Although in most cases the separate clauses in a dBASE III command may be combined in any order, the TO clause in a SET RELATION command must precede the INTO clause: SET RELATION TO <*key expression*> INTO <*alias*> will work, whereas SET RELATION INTO <*alias*> TO <*key expression*> generates a "Syntax error" message.

When two data bases are linked with SET RELATION, dBASE III PLUS ignores the status of the DELETED option and also any FILTER established in the data base accessed through the RELATION. If you SELECT the file, the equivalent SEEK will fail to find a deleted record or one that does not satisfy the FILTER condition.

If you attempt to cancel a RELATION with SET RELATION, the RELATION is cancelled, but a "Syntax error" message results. This problem can be avoided by using SET RELATION TO instead.

In a network system, if one workstation opens two files and links them with SET RELATION, and a second workstation uses the RLOCK function to lock a record in the file accessed through the RELATION, a LIST, COUNT, LOCATE, or INDEX command executed from the first workstation on the main data base file will stop at the record linked to the locked record. You can avoid this problem by using FLOCK to lock the entire file accessed through the relation, or by making sure the second workstation uses UNLOCK to free a locked record as quickly as possible.

In a network system, if one workstation opens two files and links them with SET RELATION, and a second workstation uses the RLOCK function to lock a record in the file accessed through the RELATION, a GOTO or SEEK command executed from the first workstation that would position the record pointer in the main data base file to the record linked to the locked record results in the "Relation record in use by others" error message, and the record pointer remains where it was before the command was executed. GOTO TOP, GOTO BOTTOM, and SKIP do not yield this error.

In a network system, if a workstation opens two files and links them with SET RELATION, and then uses the RLOCK function to lock a record in the file accessed through the RELATION, a LIST command in the main data base file unlocks the locked record.

SET TITLE

There is no CONFIG.DB equivalent for SET TITLE.

SET TYPEAHEAD

The value specified in a SET TYPEAHEAD is ignored in all of the full-screen edit modes, where the typeahead buffer is always 16 characters.

SET UNIQUE ON

An attempt to build an index for a large data base either with SET UNIQUE ON or by including the UNIQUE keyword in the INDEX command may result in one of several errors: The INDEX command may complete, but yield an index that is not unique or not complete. The computer may hang up, requiring you to reboot or turn the system off, leaving an empty NDX file, a W44 file (a temporary file normally erased when the index is constructed), and a "lost cluster" on the disk, which should be repaired by running CHKDSK and specifying the /F option. Finally, the INDEX command may never complete, but will run until it fills up the disk. If this occurs, interrupt by pressing ESC and erase the NDX and W44 files. These problems have been corrected in version 1.1.

SET VIEW

If you change any of the files included in a VIEW, any attempt to open the VIEW, including the MODIFY VIEW command, will result in an error message. Since you cannot edit the VIEW, it must be deleted and recreated.

SKIP

In a network system, a SKIP command that positions the record pointer to a record locked with the RLOCK() function will not generate the expected "Record is in use by another," and any data displayed subsequently will appear to be blank. Accessing the same record with a GOTO command or a SKIP <*n*> will yield the appropriate error message.

In a network system, a SKIP <*n*> command will not advance the record pointer past a record locked by another user. The data base will be positioned at the locked record and the "Record is in use by another" error message will result. You can avoid this problem by using a different command to advance the record pointer, for example, LIST NEXT 10 instead of SKIP 10 (you can use SET CONSOLE OFF to suppress the screen display).

In a network system, if one workstation is accessing a record in an indexed file that is then locked and edited at another workstation, which changes the key field, a SKIP command executed from the first workstation will move the record pointer to the next positional record in the index (for example, the tenth entry if the edited record was formerly the ninth index entry) rather than the record following it in its new position in the index. You can avoid this problem by using GOTO RECNO() to reposition the record pointer in the index (after a DISPLAY or other command to inform the user of the change in key value) before the SKIP command.

SORT

In version 1.1, if you specify an extension other than DBF for a SORTed file, the new file will nevertheless be given the extension DBF.

In some cases, executing a SORT command from the ASSIST menu will corrupt the data base file. This has been corrected in version 1.1.

In a network system, attempting to SORT a file containing more than about 7,000 records may result in the error message "Records do not balance" (program error), and in "garbage" characters being written to the SORTed file. This has been corrected in version 1.1.

TEXT ... ENDTEXT

If a TEXT ... ENDTEXT structure enclosed in an IF ... ENDIF loop contains a line beginning with "If", and the condition in the IF statement evaluates to .F., dBASE III PLUS may attempt to interpret this as another IF statement, and the remaining program statements may not execute as expected, although no error message is displayed. You can avoid this problem by making sure that no line within a TEXT ... ENDTEXT structure begins with "If".

TOTAL

Attempting to TOTAL in a data base with no numeric fields may result in the dBASE III PLUS "Internal error: EVAL work area overflow" or "Internal error: Illegal opcode" error message, or the DOS "Divide overflow" error message. The computer may hang up, requiring you to reboot or turn the system off. This has been corrected in version 1.1.

If a numeric field contains a numeric overflow, a TOTAL command will result in the "Numeric overflow (data was lost)" error message, even if the problem field is not included in the field list in the TOTAL command.

In a network system, the COPY command unlocks a record locked with the RLOCK function.

TRANSFORM

Using a PICTURE that combines the @B and @(functions in a TRANSFORM function may result in extra characters following the parentheses that surround a negative number. This has been corrected in version 1.1.

Numbers displayed with TRANSFORM are always rounded off to the number of decimal places established with SET DECIMALS, and any additional decimal places included in the PICTURE in the TRANSFORM function are displayed as zeroes. You can avoid this problem by using SET DECIMALS to increase the number of decimal places.

USE

The ".." that symbolizes the subdirectory one level up the tree from the current subdirectory in an MS-DOS path name may not be used in a USE command. Attempting to do so will result in the "ALIAS name already in use" error message.

If you SET ESCAPE OFF and execute a USE ? command from within a program, if the user presses ESC instead of choosing a file from the displayed list, the "Cancel, Ignore, Suspend? (C,I,S)" message is displayed. This has been corrected in version 1.1.

WAIT

If you press ESC in response to a WAIT command issued from a procedure file, the program that called the procedure is not closed even if you choose the Cancel option in response to the "Cancel, Ignore, Suspend? (C,I,S)" message.

ZAP

If the ZAP command is used to empty a file with more than one index open, subsequent attempts to open the file with the same indexes will result in the "Index damaged. REINDEX should be done before using data" error message. This has been corrected in version 1.1.

TRADEMARKS

Apple®	Apple Computer, Inc.
COMPAQ®	COMPAQ Computer Corporation
CP/M®	Digital Research, Inc.
dBASE III PLUS®	Ashton-Tate
DisplayWrite™	International Business Machines Corporation
IBM®	International Business Machines Corporation
Kaypro™	Kaypro Corporation
Lotus®	Lotus Development Corporation
MailMerge®	MicroPro International Corp.
Microsoft®	Microsoft Corp.
MS-DOS™	Microsoft Corp.
MultiMate®	MultiMate International Corporation
Multiplan™	Microsoft Corp.
1-2-3®	Lotus Development Corporation
Osborne®	Osborne Computer Corporation
PeachText™	MSA Software Company
pfs™	Software Publishing Corp.
Rolodex™	Zephyr American Corporation
SideKick®	Borland International
Spotlight®	Lotus Development Corporation
VisiCalc®	VisiCorp
Volkswriter®	Lifetree Software, Inc.
WordPerfect®	WordPerfect Corporation
WordStar®	MicroPro International Corp.
ZIP®	United States Postal Service

INDEX

C

D

E

F

G

H

I

N

Q

R

S

The manuscript for this book was prepared and submitted to Osborne/McGraw-Hill in electronic form. The acquisitions editor for this project was Cynthia Hudson, and the project editor was Fran Haselsteiner.

Text design by Nancy Leahong, using Palantino for both text body and display.

Cover art by Yashi Okita. Cover supplier is Phoenix Color Corp. Text stock, 50 lb. Glatfelter. Book printed and bound by R.R. Donnelley & Sons Company, Crawfordsville, Indiana.

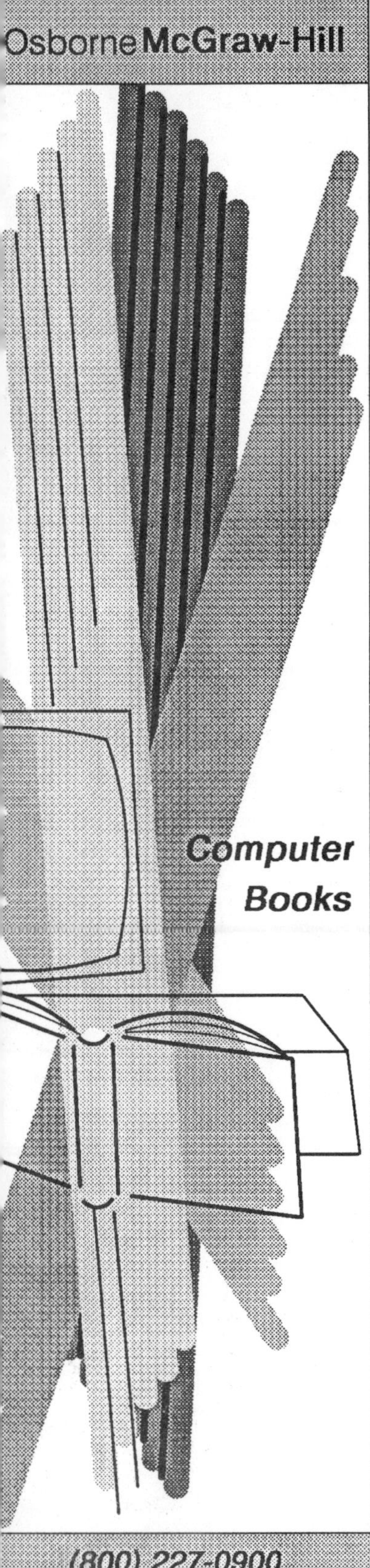

Bookmarker Design — Lance Ravella

Tear off for Bookmark

You're important to us...

We'd like to know what you're interested in, what kinds of books you're looking for, and what you thought about this book in particular.

Please fill out the attached card and mail it in. We'll do our best to keep you informed about Osborne's newest books and special offers.

YES, Send Me a FREE Color Catalog of all Osborne computer books
To Receive Catalog, Fill in Last 4 Digits of ISBN Number from Back of Book (see below bar code) 0-07-881_ _ _ – _

Name: __________________ Title: __________________

Company: __________________

Address: __________________

City: __________________ State: __________ Zip: __________

I'M PARTICULARLY INTERESTED IN THE FOLLOWING *(Check all that apply)*

I use this software
- □ WordPerfect
- □ Microsoft Word
- □ WordStar
- □ Lotus 1-2-3
- □ Quattro
- □ Others __________

I use this operating system
- □ DOS
- □ Windows
- □ UNIX
- □ Macintosh
- □ Others __________

I rate this book:
□ Excellent □ Good □ Poor

I program in
- □ C or C++
- □ Pascal
- □ BASIC
- □ Others __________

I chose this book because
- □ Recognized author's name
- □ Osborne/McGraw-Hill's reputation
- □ Read book review
- □ Read Osborne catalog
- □ Saw advertisement in store
- □ Found/recommended in library
- □ Required textbook
- □ Price
- □ Other __________

Comments __________________

Topics I would like to see covered in future books by Osborne/McGraw-Hill include:

____

IMPORTANT REMINDER
To get your FREE catalog, write in the last 4 digits of the ISBN number printed on the back cover (see below bar code) 0-07-881 _ _ _ – _

Osborne McGraw-Hil
Compute
Book:
(800) 227-0900